While We Slept

*Vladimir Putin, Donald Trump
and the Corruption of American Democracy*

Peter N. Grant Jr.

Dedicated to my mother and father,
without whose support this book would not exist.

CONTENTS

Introduction

The election of Donald Trump was a desired outcome of the Russian campaign targeting the 2016 American presidential election, but not its overall goal. The goal was to discredit the traditions, institutions, and personalities that make up American democracy in the eyes of its own citizens and the world. It succeeded. It succeeded not only by attacking Hillary Clinton, manipulating the media, and poisoning the American public's common information space but also by both clandestinely *and* brazenly supporting the candidacy of Donald Trump, while at the same time implicating the candidate and his campaign in unprecedented levels of corruption and criminality. In this sense, Trump, who expected to benefit from Russia's illegal efforts and whose campaign was riddled with connections to Russian oligarchs, organized crime, and its intelligence services, was as much a target of the Russian effort as its intended beneficiary.

Did Vladimir Putin expect Trump to win? There are good reasons to doubt that he did. Future generations will have a difficult time understanding just how shocking the outcome of the 2016 election was. Even for those who lived through it, after experiencing the intense, day-to-day drama of the Trump administration, it is hard to re-inhabit the naïveté of the pre-Trump era. This is unfortunate, as Trump's election and the people and events that contributed to it can only be made sense of by appreciating just how inconceivable such an outcome was to so many of the most knowledgeable parties involved.

In a complex national election, no one person, action, or

event can be isolated as the sole cause of the outcome. The socio-political, economic, technological, and cultural factors behind Trump's election will be studied for many years. However, no analysis can be comprehensive or complete without reference to the Russian cyber, active measures, and disinformation campaign directed against American democracy, not only because it exerted an unquantifiable influence on the outcome of the election but also because it serves as an indispensable lens through which to study and appreciate the other factors at play.

The significance of 2016 can only be understood with reference to history, both the biographic histories of the individuals who played key parts in the affair, as well as the larger histories of countries and fallen empires. The central protagonists of this story, Vladimir Putin and Donald Trump, were born a world apart and, for most of their lives, seemed to occupy non-overlapping, mutually incomprehensible universes. The following pages establish, beyond any doubt, that there was far more overlap than anybody imagined.

Vladimir Putin was schooled in the world of Russian intelligence. His experience as a young KGB officer in Dresden, watching crowds of protestors destroy the authoritarian system he had sworn to protect, made an indelible impression on the future Russian President. Following the collapse of the Soviet Empire, Putin struck alliances with fellow spies and organized crime as he rose through the ranks of power, first in St. Petersburg and later in Moscow. A core feature of Putin's ascent and later consolidation of power was the manipulation of domestic elections through *kompromat*, propaganda, disinformation, seizure of media, outright violence, and fraud. Variations of these practices were exported abroad, first to Eastern Europe and Central Asia and later to Western Europe and the United States.

To understand Donald Trump, one must understand the milieu in which he rose to national prominence: New York City and Atlantic City in the 1970s and 80s. Both were single-party towns dominated by machine politics, where power lay in the hands of Democratic party bosses who operated a system of patronage and the transactional dispensation of favors. The influence of organized crime was ubiquitous, having infiltrated local government, party politics, city services, the judicial system, organized labor, the construction industry, and, of course, protection rackets and the black markets for illegal goods and services.

Eurasian organized crime serves as a core nexus connecting the corrupt Russian power structure around Putin to Donald Trump and later members of his entourage and campaign. How and why organized crime exploded in the post-Soviet period, the role of specific gangs and gangsters, and the multitude of connections both Putin and Trump share with this netherworld are essential to understand before one delves into the 2016 election itself. Trump's interactions with American organized crime establishes a clear modus operandi that makes his later financial dealings with its Eurasian counterpart as believable as the evidence makes it indisputable.

Throughout this narrative, you'll notice the use of the term Eurasian organized crime rather than "Russian mafia." While Russia is now a sovereign nation, not too long ago, it was part of the vast, multi-ethnic Soviet Empire, which consisted of now independent states throughout Eastern Europe and Central Asia. These states share cultural and historical linkages that find expression in organized crime networks. Eurasian organized crime also infiltrated North America at just the time and place when Donald Trump emerged as a fixture of American life.

A core feature of the post-Soviet era, facilitated by an alliance between Russia's intelligence services and organized crime, is the vast transfer of illicit wealth from the East into the West by means of money laundering. The offshore financial secrecy network and the Western financial industry facilitated this theft. Much of this money found its way into real estate in Western Europe and the United States. Donald Trump engaged in multi-million dollar branding, real estate development, and other business deals with figures close to the apex of the money laundering alliance between Russian intelligence and organized crime. Scandalously, there has been no official inquiry into Trump's financial entanglements with sources from the former Soviet Union. Open-source research into these matters paints a damning picture.

Russia's intelligence services weaponized corruption to suit the purposes of the Kremlin long before it cultivated Donald Trump. These dark arts were central to Putin's ascent to the presidency. Russia used its energy resources to create organized crime-linked oligarchs in Ukraine, who exercised their influence in Kyiv on behalf of the Kremlin and maintained contacts with individuals in Trump's orbit. We will explore how similar processes played out in Austria, Israel, and the United Kingdom and how these developments interlinked with Trump and his associates and later played concerning, often mysterious, roles in the 2016 election.

The events of 2016 played out on a vast geopolitical and strategic scale. The roots of Russia's campaign against the United States began long before Trump became the Republican nominee. Putin's relationships with Bill Clinton, George W. Bush, and Barack Obama, and the foreign policy issues that caused the deterioration of Russian-American relations, are essential to understanding what motivated Putin to take such a risky, potentially reckless course of action in 2016. In particular, Putin's rage at Hillary Clinton and his blaming of her for protests in Russia against his reign set the stage for his act of revenge against the former Secretary of State.

A basic history of Russian intelligence, as well as defining the concepts of *Disinformation* and *Active Measures*, provide critical insight into later Russian operations. The activities of Russian military intelligence, the GRU, in the lead-up to and during the 2016 election are explored in granular detail. The GRU operation unfolded as part of a far-reaching, years-long international cyber and information warfare campaign. Step-by-step, the GRU's cyber operations and hack-and-leak campaign targeting the Democratic National Committee and the Clinton campaign are presented methodically. WikiLeaks and Julian Assange's role in amplifying these operations is also addressed in detail.

Putin's early seizure of Russian television, his paranoia regarding the role of social media in popular revolutions, and how he used an army of internet trolls to attempt to destroy the internet in Russia as a democratic space shed light on the Internet Research Agency's (IRA) propaganda campaign targeting the United States. While the IRA used an army of trolls and well-honed disinformation techniques to denigrate Hillary Clinton and support Trump, its overall mission was broader and more nefarious. It sought to exploit pre-existing fault lines in American society, in particular, working to arouse apathy and distrust among African Americans to suppress their voting numbers to benefit Trump. This effort was mirrored by multiple efforts undertaken by the Trump campaign in his closest supporters.

At the height of the 2016 election, Donald Trump denied having any business dealings in Russia while two of his representatives, Felix Sater and Michael Cohen, both now convicted felons, were negotiating several potential Trump Tower Moscow projects. As the Kremlin easily recognized Trump's lie, it amounted to a counterintelligence nightmare and a form of *kompromat*. A complete picture emerges only when Sater's extraordinary background in organized crime and intelligence circles is understood, along with Cohen's role as Trump's fixer. Between them, Sater and Cohen interacted with figures tied to Eurasian organized crime, individuals at the center of massive Russian money laundering operations, a general from Russian Military Intelligence, and Putin's press secretary.

Trump's campaign chairman, yet another convicted felon, Paul Manafort, has so many connections to Kremlin-backed Russian and Ukrainian oligarchs, Eurasian organized criminals, and Russian intelligence officers that his remarkable life before the 2016 campaign takes up its own chapter. The background of Manafort's Russian paymaster, Oleg Deripaska, with his ties to the Izmaylovskaya criminal organization, the Kremlin, and Republican lobbyists, is described in detail. During the election, Manafort was in regular contact and met twice with Konstantin Kilimnik, described by the Senate Intelligence Committee as a "Russian intelligence officer" who may have been involved in the GRU's hack and leak operation, and provided him with internal Trump campaign data which he delivered to Russian intelligence. Manafort and Kilimnik also met secretly to discuss a mysterious Ukrainian peace plan that would have divided Ukraine along lines favorable to the Kremlin. All the while, Manafort engaged in a series of bizarre and highly suspect real estate transactions, potentially to cover up illegal financial activity.

A little over a month after the GRU began targeting the Clinton campaign, a Trump foreign policy advisor named George Papadopoulos was informed by a Maltese Professor, who had just returned from Moscow and enjoyed longstanding ties to Russia, that the Russians possessed dirt on Hillary Clinton in the form of emails. Papadopoulos shared what he learned with an Australian diplomat and Putin-supporting officials in the Greek government, but told later investigators that he couldn't recall if he had informed anyone on the Trump campaign. The Senate Intelligence Committee didn't find this explanation plausible, and the following pages will show why. Another Trump foreign policy advisor, Carter Page, who spent years living and investing in Moscow and had been cultivated by Russian foreign intelligence, was invited to Moscow during the campaign to speak at a prestigious institution despite being virtually unknown only weeks earlier. Trump delivered his first major foreign policy address at an event coordinated by Jared Kushner and Dmitry Simes of the Center for the National Interest, which for years has been accused of being one of the most pro-Putin think tanks in Washington and had multiple links to the convicted Russian agent Marina Butina.

The June 9th Trump Tower meeting, in which Donald Trump Jr. expected to receive "incriminating" information on Hillary Clinton from the Russian government, was but one part of a Kremlin influence campaign playing out in Moscow, Manhattan courtrooms, and the halls of Congress. It involved the Republican congressman and Trump supporter Dana Rohrabacher, who had been warned by the FBI that he was a target of Russian intelligence and whose long-term associate and friend, Jack Abramoff, had years earlier likely been targeted by the GRU. Aras Agalarov, an Azerbaijani tycoon and Trump business partner with close connections to Putin, Eurasian organized crime, and KGB money laundering operations, set up the meeting. The Russian lawyer who attended the meeting, Natalia Veselnitskaya, enjoyed numerous connections to Russia's government and intelligence services. These facts, along with the shady backgrounds of others in attendance, formed yet another counterintelligence nightmare.

Trump's top donor, Robert Mercer, and his chief ideologue and campaign CEO, Steve Bannon, founded the data analytics firm Cambridge Analytica with a British electioneering and private intelligence firm, SCL Group, which had its own shady connections to the worlds of organized crime and intelligence. Cambridge Analytica had a history of working to suppress black voting in its activities abroad and, mirroring the efforts of the IRA, collaborated with the Trump campaign's internal data operation as it sought to suppress the African American vote. Cambridge Analytica appears to have interacted at times with Russian intelligence and worked with the Trump campaign and the major backers of Brexit. The separation of the UK from the EU was a primary policy goal of the Kremlin, and the so-called "Bad Boys of Brexit" had a litany of connections to Russia, Eurasian organized crime, and Russia's intelligence services. The two most prominent, Nigel Farage and Arron Banks, met with and campaigned on behalf of Trump. Farage knew Julian Assange personally and met privately with Trump and Roger Stone.

Russia's efforts to get Trump elected overlapped with the preferences of the Israeli right and the rulers of the Gulf States. These interests came together at a second Trump Tower meeting where the billionaire Trump supporter Erik Prince, a former Navy SEAL and founder of the infamous mercenary contractor Blackwater, arranged for Donald Trump Jr. to meet with Joel Zamel and George Nader. Zamel founded Psy Group, an Israeli private intelligence firm with suspicious links to Russia in its ownership structure and clientele. George Nader was a pedophile political operative offering the Trump campaign the support of the Gulf Princes. Several firms and individuals from the Israeli private intelligence industry engaged in business relationships with both key Trump supporters and Russians closely connected to Putin and involved in Russian influence campaigns, including the 2016 election.

Michael Flynn, Trump's highest-ranking military supporter and future National Security Advisor, was courted by Russian interests and the Trump campaign almost simultaneously. Before being forced out of government in 2014, an experience that left him feeling betrayed by the Obama administration, Flynn visited the GRU's headquarters outside of Moscow. As a civilian, he was paid tens of thousands of dollars by the Russian propaganda network *RT* and other Russian companies. In 2015, he attended *RT's* 10th anniversary gala and sat directly beside Vladimir Putin. Trump personally tasked Flynn with using his intelligence connections to find Hillary Clinton's 30,000 "missing" emails. The effort brought Flynn into contact with the Republican operatives Barbara and Michael Ledeen, as well as Peter W. Smith, a longtime foe of the Clintons who spent part of 2016 searching the dark web and interacting with alleged Russian hackers who claimed to have the emails, which he wanted to offload to WikiLeaks.

Roger Stone, Donald Trump's oldest political advisor and a decades-long associate of Paul Manafort, was in contact with both Russian military intelligence and WikiLeaks throughout the

2016 election. While publicly parroting the lie that the GRU wasn't behind the online persona Guccifer 2.0, Stone was in private communications with the GRU using Twitter direct messages and, as a close examination of the timeline establishes, may have been in contact with Russian military intelligence over encrypted channels. Stone predicted the leaks of John Podesta's emails before they occurred and was involved with multiple potential WikiLeaks intermediaries throughout the election, which he later illegally attempted to cover up. Throughout all of this, he was in close and repeated communication with Donald Trump, sources in Israel close to Benjamin Netanyahu, Paul Manafort, Steve Bannon, Erik Prince, and multiple other members of the Trump campaign, with whom he undoubtedly discussed his insights into WikiLeaks, among other topics.

Among the complex and byzantine events of 2016, numerous important unanswered questions emerge, which are highlighted in the coming narrative. In large part, this is due to the extensive cover-up and obstruction of justice perpetrated by the Trump administration and its allies. This book only covers the long lead-up to 2016 and the election itself, saving the events of the transition, the Trump presidency, his impeachment over Ukraine, and the 2020 election for future volumes. Due to the density and complexity of the material and length considerations, an editorial choice has been made to save any description of Christopher Steele's activities and the FBI's Crossfire Hurricane investigation for another book. Neither became public knowledge until after the election, and both have severely distorted the lens through which people have viewed the events of 2016.

The information herein is informed by the Special Counsel's Report, several Congressional investigations, thousands of pages of court documents, FBI search warrant affidavits, leaked government documents, personal memoirs, as well as numerous excellent recently published books on these topics. Despite widespread disgust with the media, a comprehensive description of the events of 2016 is impossible without reference to international reporting on these matters. Meticulous footnotes provide readers with the sources for every major factual claim in this book.

Authorities in the Trump administration lied to the American people about what took place during the 2016 election. Government and Congressional inquiries into this all-important matter were obstructed and misrepresented. Government censors redacted much of their findings. The American media's short attention span and short-term financial imperatives prevented a comprehensive description of this epochal betrayal. What follows is a private citizen's humble and doubtless imperfect efforts to portray what happened accurately.

Part I
The Rise of Vladimir Putin and Donald Trump

Chapter 1:
Vladimir Putin, the KGB, and the Rise of the Mafia State

Julian Assange referred to it as *Cablegate*. In the fall of 2010, the largest leak of confidential documents in US history was posted online by the anti-secrecy organization WikiLeaks. 251,287 US diplomatic cables were released, some dating as far back as 1966. US Secretary of State Hillary Clinton denounced the leak in no uncertain terms. "This disclosure is not just an attack on America's foreign policy interests," she stated. "It is an attack on the international community: the alliances and partnerships, the conversations and negotiations that safeguard global security and advance economic prosperity."[1]

In the immediate aftermath of the mass disclosure, American foreign policy was thrown into damage-control mode. Embarrassing revelations had to be dealt with. Delicate relationships needed to be mended. Apologies and explanations were issued to heads of state and influential leaders who were snubbed. In some cases, diplomatic staff were reassigned. But *Cablegate* did more than spill secrets about foreign leaders and countries. The leaks revealed that the men and women of the American diplomatic corps often possessed a subtle and nuanced understanding of the regions in which they were posted and that among them were talented writers with an eye for colorful detail and irony.

10MADRID154_a, as it is labeled on the WikiLeaks database, is one of those quarter million documents leaked online.[2] The cable is designated SECRET, the second highest level of US classification, and NOFORN, meaning providing the information contained within to foreign nationals is strictly forbidden. *10MADRID154_a* reveals that on January 14th, 2010, State Department officials received a "detailed, frank" briefing in Madrid from José "Pepe" Grinda Gonzalez, a Spanish special prosecutor for corruption and organized crime.[3] The cable describes Grinda's comments as "insightful and valuable, given his in-depth knowledge of the Eurasian mafia and his key role in Spain's pioneering efforts to bring Eurasian mafia leaders to justice."

José Grinda was already a legend in anti-organized crime law enforcement circles. His prosecutions led to the conviction and imprisonment of Zakhariy Kalashov, a Georgian crime boss with suspected ties to Russian intelligence who operated out of the Spanish port city of Alicante.[4] In the leaked cable, Kalashov is described as "the most senior mafia figure jailed outside of Russia." Kalashov's arrest was part of a much larger Spanish law enforcement effort, throughout which the symbiosis between Russia's government, intelligence apparatus, and organized crime groups was revealed in vivid, disturbing detail.

In March of 2006, Grinda, a trim, bearded career prosecutor with a dry wit, was assigned to work on Eurasian organized crime-related cases.[5] A year earlier, Spanish authorities conducted three sweeping operations against Eurasian mafia networks operating in the country code-named *Avispa, Troika,* and *Variola.*[6] The operations resulted in the arrest of over 80 Russian crime figures across Spain. Spanish police made use of extensive secret surveillance, recording over 230 wiretaps. Through the conversations they intercepted, they compiled a list of Russian politicians, prosecutors, and military officers communicating with members of organized crime.

Spain's idyllic beaches and affordable real estate had been a draw for Russian organized criminals since the 1990s. Long a destination for British retirees and Germans on holiday, Spain's coastal enclaves experienced a wave of new arrivals from the former Eastern bloc: Russians, Ukrainians, Georgians, and Armenians, among others. A subset among them were members of organized crime groups which were exploding in size and sophistication in the countries of the former Soviet Union. Some were fleeing the rampant gang wars erupting across the streets of Russia in the 90s. Some were ex-KGB or Russian military veterans. Quite a few had emerged from athletic circles in the former USSR, wrestlers, boxers, and weightlifters who had provided the muscle for mafia groups in their home countries and had now struck out abroad.[7]

Grinda and his colleagues noticed a pattern. The infiltration of Russian organized crime into Spain unfolded in distinct phases and revolved around the accumulation of social, political, and financial power. It was the same model organized crime groups had used in Russia, and they were now exporting it abroad. In the first phase, the Russians arrived in Spain flush with money generated by criminal activities conducted elsewhere, making them difficult to prosecute. They would then use that illicit money to buy legitimacy.

"The first thing they try and do after achieving economic profits is to try and legitimize themselves," Grinda said in an interview with *The American Interest.* "In Spain, the people who are most corrupt do two things: First, they buy an incredibly luxurious mansion to show they are there. Second, they buy a soccer team." Grinda further explained how the Russian mafia develops social cachet, "first in their little town, and then [expanding] into creating foundations—charities, legal foundations, medical foundations. And then they will say they are philanthropists. They say that they take care of people."[8]

In the next phase, political power is established by seizing control over the awarding of public contracts. This was less about financial gain and more about establishing relationships with politicians. Mafia-linked contractors bribe Public officials to award public works contracts, and before they know it, they are not only reliant on the mafia to complete high-profile projects but are now compromised by them. "In other words, they are insinuating themselves into the political world. And once there, they can get legislation changed," Grinda explained, describing how the process unfolded in Russia: "We have detected in our investigations that Russian crime organizations, that this power has meant that criminals have been able to make officials purge their criminal records. And the worst is when they actually create their own political parties."

The third and final phase Grinda describes is compromising the financial sector. Using Western law firms and financial experts alongside respected banks and other financial institutions, Eurasian organized crime groups inject and effectively launder billions of dollars into the international financial system. By this point, so entwined are they in the legitimate institutions of national power, the criminal organizations effectively cease looking like mafias at all. More remarkable still, they've now developed potentially compromising relationships with individuals at the highest levels of government and finance.

Spanish authorities were shocked by the high-level Kremlin and Russian intelligence contacts many of the mobsters they were investigating enjoyed. Gennady Petrov, a leading figure in the St. Petersburg-based *Tambovskaya Bratva* criminal organization, was arrested in Mallorca in 2008. Petrov's rise in the St. Petersburg underworld coincided with that of a then little-known deputy mayor named Vladimir Putin. Spanish wiretaps recorded that Petrov was in contact with a deputy Russian prime minister and at least five members of Putin's cabinet.[9] Petrov is also a member of the board of directors of Bank Rossiya, which was described by members of the Obama treasury department in 2014 as "the personal bank for senior officials of the Russian Federation."[10]

Grinda's battle with Russian organized crime and its government patrons, which had won extensive plaudits and praise from the FBI, piqued the interest of US diplomats. So on January 14th, 2010, State Department officials invited Grinda to meet with them in Madrid and speak openly and honestly about his assessment of the threat these groups posed. As the *10MADRID154_a* cable records, he did that and more. Speaking in what he believed was a highly classified briefing at the time, José Grinda told the American diplomats that: "[H]e considers Belarus, Chechnya, and Russia to be virtual "mafia states" and said that Ukraine is going to be one. For each of those countries, he alleged, one cannot differentiate between the activities of the government and OC [Organized Crime] groups."

The cable continues: "Grinda suggested that there are two reasons to worry about the Russian mafia. First, it exercises "tremendous control" over certain strategic sectors of the global economy, such as aluminum… The second reason is the unanswered question regarding the extent to which Russian PM Putin is implicated in the Russian mafia and whether he controls the mafia's actions. Grinda cited a "thesis" by Alexander Litvinenko, the former Russian intelligence official who worked on OC issues before he died in late 2006 in London from poisoning under mysterious circumstances, that the Russian intelligence and security services... control OC in Russia. Grinda stated that he believes this thesis is accurate."

Alexander Litvinenko was a former KGB agent who had worked for a unit dedicated to fighting organized economic crime.[11] He clashed with Putin early in his Presidency and ultimately fled to London. While there, he maintained some questionable allegiances, and some of his claims about Putin have yet to be substantiated. However, when Grinda met with him in London in June 2006, much of what Litvinenko told him corresponded with facts that ongoing Spanish investigations had unearthed.

Litvinenko told Grinda that Russian organized crime was fundamentally entwined with the state, similar to the model Putin established while he was the deputy mayor in St. Petersburg. Furthermore, the Russian security services had largely absorbed various Russian mafia organizations and used them to pursue state purposes.[12] Grinda persuaded Litvinenko to testify as a witness in upcoming legal proceedings in Spain. However, by the end of the year, Litvinenko was dead. He was poisoned with tea laced with the radioactive isotope polonium. Within days, Litvinenko's hair fell out, his body withered, and he succumbed to massive organ failure seventeen days after ingesting the poison.

Over a decade has passed since Grinda's secret briefing with the State Department. Grinda's war against Eurasian organized crime in Spain continues to grind forward. In April of 2019, he was sniffing out a Spanish real estate connection to a €200 billion Russian money laundering scandal currently rocking capitals and national banks from the Baltic states to Scandinavia.[13] For his troubles, Grinda has had three separate contracts placed on his head and now travels everywhere under armed guard. A Spanish lawyer, now deceased, accused Grinda of pedophilia without evidence. Grinda claims his accuser was paid off by a Russian minister, and is suing for defamation.[14]

"These cases are like a long-distance race," Grinda told *ProPublica* in 2017. "We are telling them: not here. We don't want you here." [15]

Vladimir Vladimirovich Putin was born in St. Petersburg on October 7th, 1952. Russia was under the rule of Joseph Stalin, one of the most dreaded dictators of the 20th Century. Comrade Stalin had less than six months left to live. Leningrad, as the great Imperial city was known in Soviet times, still bore the scars from the Great Patriotic War against Nazi Germany, which had ended just seven years earlier. The Siege of Leningrad lasted 872 days and resulted in over a million civilian deaths, making it the longest and bloodiest siege in history. It was a time of suffering, starvation, relentless artillery barrages, and human endurance.

In a 2015 article penned by Putin himself for the publication *Russky Pioner*, the Russian President described his father's activities during the war.[16] Vladimir Spiridonovich Putin was a member of the NKVD, Stalin's infamous secret police and enforcers of his periodic terrors. Putin's father parachuted with 27 comrades behind Nazi lines to sabotage the German advance. However, the small NKVD detachment was betrayed by a group of local Estonians and was set upon by the cold, professional killers of the Wehrmacht.

As Putin tells it, his father split off from the group and was pursued by German soldiers with dogs. He managed to evade capture and almost certain execution by submerging himself into the murky waters of a nearby swamp and breathing through a reed until the Nazis tired of the search and moved on. Of the twenty-eight members of the NKVD demolitions detachment, only four returned to fight another day. Putin's father spent the rest of his life with fragments lodged in his leg, a grim reminder of the horrors of war.

The veracity of this heroic tale will probably always be lost to the fog of war, further obscured by the nationalism and jingoistic propaganda of the Putin era. Given the tenacity of Russian resistance during the Second World War, one is almost inclined to believe it. However, in a way, whether or not these events unfolded precisely as Putin related is beside the point. These were the kinds of stories the young Putin grew up listening to. Perhaps more importantly, these are the stories President Putin chooses to tell the Russian people.

Like his father's wartime escapades, the factual details of Putin's early years are not unknown. Still, they can be difficult to distinguish from the persona Putin the politician carefully constructed for himself upon assuming the mantle of Russian leadership. Unlike most world leaders, Vladimir Putin was plucked from obscurity when Boris Yeltsin selected him in 1999 as his Prime Minister and eventual successor. Thus, he enjoyed the unique advantage of shaping his public image unfettered by an established past.[17]

War damage scarred Leningrad's residential tenement blocks years after the war had ended. The social life of these enclaves was organized around their central courtyards. The courtyard was where a young Putin learned to be a man. In a series of wide-ranging, though carefully crafted, interviews Putin gave upon being introduced to the Russian public and the international community, he presents his younger self as a small and scrappy fighter, a "thug," in his own words.[18] Early friends of Putin and he himself would repeatedly emphasize his youthful willingness to engage in brawls with older, larger men.

Children like Putin were forced to fend for themselves among the varied crowd that populated the courtyards. Education was low on the young Putin's list of priorities, and his early grades were unremarkable. After a few spats with elementary school authorities, Putin eventually found discipline through an embrace of the Soviet martial art Sambo, a mix of Judo and wrestling. By his own account, participation in martial arts benefited Putin, and his grades and behavior improved.[19] However, there was a darker side to the experience. Putin's first martial arts coach, Leonid Usvyatsov, was a criminal recidivist known as Lyonya the Sportsman who was murdered in 1994.[20] He was believed to have ties to the dangerous criminal Vyacheslav Ivankov, whose name will reappear in this story.[21]

One must take the machismo and bravado of Putin's account of his childhood with a grain of salt. Putin's parents doted on their son. Though impoverished by Western standards, his family enjoyed an existence that was materially better off than most Russian families.[22] Some have speculated that the Putins could enjoy the standard of living they did because the elder Putin was on the Russian secret service's active reserve following his stint in the NKVD during the war.

In 1965, a Russian novel changed the course of Putin's life. *The Shield and the Sword* was a thrilling tale of espionage in which the fictional Soviet agent Major Aleksandr Belov infiltrates

Nazi military intelligence. In 1968, the novel was adapted into a popular Russian film that captured Vladimir Putin's 16-year-old imagination.[23] Putin was enthralled, later claiming, "What amazed me most of all was how one man's effort could achieve what whole armies could not. One spy could decide the fate of thousands of people."[24]

From that moment on, Vladimir Putin dreamed of joining the KGB.

A History of the Russian Secret Police and Intelligence Services

The first modern Russian secret police and intelligence service was formed in St. Petersburg in 1881 following the assassination of Tsar Alexander II.[25] The Okhrana was established to combat anarchism, left-wing agitation, and the political terrorism that convulsed Russia in the late 19th century. Distinct from its imperial predecessor, the Third Directorate, the Okhrana expanded its focus beyond anti-Tsarist nobles and aristocrats and developed a system of comprehensive, counterrevolutionary surveillance over broad swaths of society, with a particular focus on students, professors, urban workers, artists, writers and elements of the Russian intelligentsia.[26] Methods it employed included covert operations, the reading of private correspondence, and the use of *agents provocateurs*. By 1883, the Okhrana had opened a branch in Paris to monitor Russian emigres abroad, thus making it an international intelligence operation.

Despite its modern methods, the Okhrana failed at its core mission. In 1917, a revolution in Russia ended 304 years of Romanov rule. December 20th, 1917, six weeks after the Bolshevik revolution, saw the establishment of the Cheka, the earliest officially recognized, direct predecessor to the KGB and, eventually, to the current Russian domestic and foreign secret intelligence agencies: the FSB and the SVR respectively. A separate institution, Russian military intelligence known as the GRU, was established under Stalin in 1942. To this day, individuals affiliated with the Russian secret services are referred to as "Chekists."

The Cheka didn't focus primarily on the collection and analysis of intelligence but instead sought to perfect the dark arts of deception, agitation, propaganda, subversion, repression, and murder to achieve the Communist Party's political ends.[27] To understand the ideology and modus operandi of the Cheka, one can do no better than to read the words of its infamous founder Felix Dzerzhinsky: "We stand for organized terror - this should be frankly admitted. Terror is an absolute necessity during times of revolution. Our aim is to fight against the enemies of the Soviet government and of the new order of life."[28]

During the Russian Revolution and the ensuing Civil War between Communist Red and anti-Communist White forces, Dzerzhinsky and the highest levels of Bolshevik leadership were convinced that a vast Western capitalist conspiracy was orchestrating the forces arrayed against them. While the forces opposing the communist revolutionaries were very real, there was, in fact, no secret international conspiracy against them. International opposition was loud but feckless and ineffective. This conspiratorial, paranoid mindset pervaded the Russian secret services throughout the Cold War and persists to this day.[29]

During the Russian Civil War, the Cheka initiated the "Red Terror." While figures vary, the most reliable place the number of executions at the hands of the Cheka at roughly 100,000, though other estimates range higher.[30] After the Bolsheviks emerged victorious and established themselves as a presence in the global order, the Soviet secret intelligence services underwent a variety of name changes and departmental reorganizations. Upon assuming power, Stalin used the NKVD (a successor agency to the Cheka) to implement a ruthless program of primarily domestic repression but also international espionage activities.

Domestically, the NKVD oversaw a sprawling system of prisons known as gulags that incarcerated millions of Russians. Entire groups of ethnic minorities were forcibly removed from their ancestral homelands at an appalling cost of life. The NKVD also ruthlessly implemented a vast program of extrajudicial execution. Between the years of 1937 and 1938, a period known as the "Great Terror," the NKVD rounded up and imprisoned over 1.5 million people, and an additional 680,000-1,200,000 were summarily shot.[31]

The NKVD was also involved in international, covert activities. Throughout the 1930s, it was behind a string of assassinations of individuals determined to be ideological opponents of Stalin. Most notably, in 1940, Stalin's *bête noire*,

Leon Trotsky, was murdered by an icepick-wielding NKVD assassin while in exile in Mexico City. The NKVD was also highly active in the Spanish Civil War and the Second World War. In the post-war period, it established international Comintern organizations dedicated to spreading communism worldwide.

The death of Stalin in 1953 and the rise of Nikita Khrushchev as the leader of the Soviet Union had far-reaching consequences for the secret intelligence services, which, after a few more name changes, came to be known as the KGB. In 1956, three years after Stalin's death, Khrushchev delivered a famous speech in a secret session of the Soviet Communist Party's 20th Congress. He denounced Stalin and the cult of personality cultivated around him. From that point on, while repression would most certainly exist within the Soviet Union, the era of state-sponsored executions on an industrial scale came to an end.

By the time a desire to join the KGB had taken hold of Putin, it was led by Yuri Andropov. Gaining power in 1967, Andropov was the longest-serving leader in the history of Soviet intelligence. He had an enduring influence on Putin, and his complex legacy was resuscitated during the Putin era by the leaders of the security services to salvage their prestige following the collapse of the USSR. During his tenure as head of the FSB, Putin ordered the restoration of a plaque commemorating Andropov that had been taken down in 1991.[32]

Andropov's worldview was shaped by his experience as the Soviet ambassador in Budapest during the 1956 uprising. From the windows of the embassy, he watched as members of the Soviet-backed Hungarian security services were hanged from lamp posts by angry crowds protesting Soviet domination. Russian tanks suppressed the uprising, but not before the stunning vulnerability of the Communist regime was seared into Andropov's memory. Following this experience, Andropov developed what his staff called a "Hungarian Complex." From then on, whenever a Soviet-backed government seemed threatened by a popular uprising, Andropov advocated the use of military force to protect the regime.

Andropov oversaw a campaign directed against Soviet dissidents and believed the human rights movement in Russia was an imperialist plot to undermine the Communist state.[33] As a result, he expanded the practice of institutionalizing dissidents in

Soviet psychiatric facilities. A notable episode during Andropov's tenure that would have parallels in the Putin era was the assassination of the Bulgarian dissident Georgi Markov on the streets of London in 1978. In the aftermath of the collapse of the USSR, the Russian security establishment believed that Andropov had foreseen the country's economic troubles and sought to address them through limited market mechanisms overseen by the KGB to modernize the Soviet economy. According to this view, it was the rapid democratic and political reforms instituted by the communist reformer Mikhail Gorbachev that had led to the ruin of the state.[34]

In the late 1960s and early 1970s, Andropov, in an attempt to broaden perspectives within the KGB and promote new ways of thinking, embarked upon a recruiting drive to develop a new cohort of officers from differing social groups who possessed better critical thinking skills than previous generations.[35] This new generation included Vladimir Putin and many of the men who would later form his inner circle as President.

Putin in the KGB and the Last Days of East Germany

In an audacious act for a sixteen-year-old boy, Putin took the initiative to visit his regional KGB Directorate. The building, known as the *Bolshoi Dom*, or "Big House," had been the headquarters of Stalin's secret police during the purges. Executions reportedly took place in its basement. An anonymous KGB officer greeted Putin. After expressing his desire to get a job with the KGB, the officer told Putin that they didn't recruit anyone who approached them on their own initiative and that before anyone could join, they had to have either been in the army or attended civilian higher education. Putin inquired which type of higher education the KGB preferred, and the officer, whom Putin suspected just wanted to get rid of him, suggested law. "From that moment on," Putin recalled, "I began to prepare for the law faculty at Leningrad University. And nobody could stop me."[36]

Putin was recruited by the KGB in 1974 during his final year of law school. In his excitement, he told Sergei Roldugin, a talented cellist and one of his best friends. Years later, Roldugin's name was linked to a shell company created by the Panamanian law firm Mossack Fonseca. That shell company is believed to contain some of the illicit fortune Putin amassed as President.[37] Roldugin later recounted his conversation with Putin: "I told him, "I am a cellist. I play the cello. I could never be a surgeon. Still, I'm a good cellist. But what is your profession? I know, you're a spy. I don't know what that means. Who are you? What do you do? And he [Putin] said to me, 'I'm a specialist in human relations.'"[38]

Perhaps unsurprisingly, a great deal of mystery surrounds Putin's intelligence career. Putin officially joined the KGB in 1975, when the Soviet Union was at peace. He spent six months attending KGB officer's school, where he learned basic spy craft. While there, Putin met and befriended Sergei Ivanov, who later became the head of his Presidential administration. According to Ivanov, their teachers included former "Illegals," a term used by Russian intelligence to this day referring to deep cover operatives acting outside of diplomatic cover. "We had very good teachers," Ivanov has said, "Very experienced intelligence operatives. Many of them had worked many years abroad. They included – and I can say this for the first time because those people are no longer with us, although we remember them perfectly – our 'Illegals', who had returned, some of them after 20 years working as an Illegal abroad, and were handing on their experience to us, the younger generation."[39]

After graduating from KGB officer's school, Putin's initial assignment was counterintelligence in St. Petersburg. The work involved trailing foreign visitors and diplomats, most of whom were stationed in Moscow. By the time the twenty-three-year-old Putin joined, the KGB was a bloated bureaucracy responsible for foreign and domestic intelligence. It collected intelligence rather than analyzing it, which was left to the Communist Party. However, most of the voluminous information it collected, newspaper clippings, transcripts of private conversations, and officers' reports, was left unanalyzed.[40] Other agency responsibilities included military counterintelligence, customs and border enforcement, cryptography, monitoring telephone communications, protecting party leadership, and snuffing out illicit free-market activity wherever it could be found.[41]

The primary activity the KGB engaged in at the time was monitoring and harassing Soviet dissidents. While Putin has denied involvement in such activities, he admits to being aware of them.[42] Vladimir Usoltsev, a former KGB colleague of Putin's, claimed that Putin at this time was a member of the Fifth Chief Directorate, the body in charge of monitoring dissidents.[43] His claim has never been proven, nor has it been officially denied.

After six months, Putin was transferred out of counterintelligence and placed into the KGB division responsible for intelligence, the First Chief Directorate. Very little is known about Putin's activities between 1975 and 1983. In 2000, press reports, allegedly based on leaks from German intelligence, suggested that in 1975, Putin was stationed in the West German city of Bonn undercover as a TASS news agency reporter but was subsequently removed in the late 70s for botching an operation. These reports remain unverified.[44]

In 1984, after nine years of service, Putin was promoted to major, and he enrolled in the Andropov Red Banner Institute in Moscow, where he was trained for foreign intelligence work. He studied German in preparation for placement in Germany following graduation. Students at the Institute were provided with codenames, so Putin became Platov. The faculty included luminaries of the "golden age" of Soviet espionage, including Yuri Modlin, who had been a handler of the infamous British double agent Kim Philby.[45]

His instructors studied Putin himself. According to Mikhail Frolov, a retired KGB colonel and instructor at the institute, "At the Red Banner, we didn't just teach the rules of intelligence and counterintelligence. We needed to study our trainees - their professional worth and personal qualities. We had to determine, in the final analysis, whether a trainee was suitable for work in intelligence." Of Putin, Frolov stated, "I remember I wrote about several negative characteristics in his evaluation. It seemed to me that he was somewhat withdrawn and uncommunicative. By the way, that could be considered both a negative and a positive trait. But I recall that I also cited a certain academic tendency among his negative aspects. I don't mean that he was dry. No, he was sharp-witted and always ready with a quip... Vladimir Vladimirovich was assigned to KGB representation in the German Democratic Republic."[46]

Upon graduating, Putin was assigned to East Germany (the German Democratic Republic, or GDR). He, his pregnant wife Lyudmila, and their one-year-old daughter were sent to the industrial city of Dresden. In 1985, Putin, now thirty-three, was provided with a passport and prepared to leave Russia for the first time. Scholars differ in their views on the importance of Putin's assignment. Some suggest Putin's position in Dresden represented a mediocre, low-level assignment in a sleepy city far from the center of the action in Berlin, or more prestigious still, outside of the Eastern bloc in Western Europe or the United States. Others argue that Dresden sat at the center of an important smuggling ring that provided a lifeline to the ailing East German economy and Western technology to the Communist world.[47]

While Dresden may have been a backwater compared to Berlin, the KGB's headquarters in Germany, the GDR itself was on the front lines of the Cold War. It was home to over 380,000 Soviet troops as well as Soviet intermediate-range nuclear missiles. At the time, East Germany and the Soviet Union were drifting in opposite directions. By 1985, Mikhail Gorbachev had risen to power in the USSR and would shortly begin to implement *glasnost* and *perestroika* programs of political and economic reform, respectively. Meanwhile, under the hardline leadership of Erich Honecker, the GDR remained firmly on the path of Communist totalitarianism.

"The work was political intelligence," Putin has said, "obtaining information about political figures and plans of the potential opponent… We were interested in any information about the 'main opponent,' as we called them, and the main opponent was considered NATO." Putin has described his duties as "recruiting sources of information, obtaining information, analyzing it, and sending it to Moscow. I looked for information about political parties, the tendencies inside these parties, their leaders. I examined today's leaders and the possible leaders of tomorrow and the promotion of people to certain posts in parties and the government. It was important to know who was doing what and how, what was going on in foreign ministries of a particular country, how they were constructing their policy on certain issues and in various areas of the world, how our partners would react in disarmament talks. Of course, in order to obtain such information, you need sources. So recruitment of sources, procurement of information, and assessment and analysis were big parts of the job."[48]

As a senior case officer, Putin was stationed in an illegal

intelligence gathering unit known as Directorate S.[49] His KGB office was located across the street from Dresden's local Stasi headquarters. In 2018, Putin's Stasi identification card surfaced in German state archives. The head archivist told the German newspaper *Bild* that the card would have allowed Putin to enter and exit Stasi headquarters without revealing his affiliation with the KGB.[50] Douglas Selvege of the Wilson Center has suggested that Putin likely used the card to easily gain entry to Dresden's Stasi headquarters to discuss "potential targets for recruitment among the local population, foreign students, and visitors to Dresden" with his Stasi comrades.[51]

According to Vladimir Usoltsev, a KGB colleague of Putin's in Dresden, their work consisted of little more than reading about the political situation in local press articles and then summarizing them in an endless series of reports that they would send back to Moscow.[52] Usoltsev also claimed that Putin spent much of his time poring over smuggled Western mail-order catalogs.[53] Putin himself would admit to developing a taste for German beer and gaining 25 pounds.[54] However, the investigative reporter and Putin scholar Catherine Belton has argued that the image of Putin as an unimportant mediocrity may have been constructed to conceal vastly more controversial activities.

In her seminal work *Putin's People*, Catherine Belton notes that the KGB was at the time consorting and aiding various terrorists and terrorist organizations active in Western Europe at the time, including the Red Army Faction (RAF), the Popular Front for the Liberation of Palestine (PFLP), the Palestine Liberation Organization (PLO) and Carlos the Jackal. An RAF source told Belton that members of the group, which was involved in a bombing and assassination campaign in Western Europe, met and took orders from Putin in Dresden precisely because it was far from the eyes of Western intelligence agencies in Berlin.[55] Putin biographer Masha Gessen, on the other hand, spoke with RAF members who claimed that rather than have any connection to terrorism, Putin used them to procure forbidden Western electronic equipment such as a stereo for his personal use.[56] The question of whether or not Vladimir Putin was involved in the planning of terrorist activities remains one of the most sensitive issues in his biography and will come up again. Fiona Hill and Clifford G. Gaddy maintain that it is "virtually inconceivable" that Putin was not involved in a KGB operation in East Germany codenamed Operation LUCH.[57] By the mid-1970s, the KGB Center in Moscow believed it had identified 500,000 individuals in East Germany who were hostile to the socialist system. LUCH was an operation in which the KGB "monitored opinion within the East German population and Party, contacts between East and West Germans, and alleged 'attempts by the USA and FRG [Federal Republic of Germany - West Germany] to harm the building of socialism' in the GDR."[58]

German authorities later became concerned that Operation LUCH was actually an attempt to circumvent the Stasi and recruit agents in the dying days of the GDR to live on after reunification. In 2000, after Putin ascended to power, officials at the *Verfassungsschutz*, the Federal Office for the Protection of the Constitution, investigated the potential role then-President Putin had played in Operation LUCH. Investigators interviewed Putin's Stasi colleagues, some of whom verified the existence of LUCH but were unable to identify the names of any agents or determine Putin's role in the operation.[59]

By the late 1980s, the KGB was focused on stealing Western technology. Not only was the Soviet Union approaching a terminal economic crisis, but it was also dangerously behind in technological development, particularly in micro-processing technology. Intelligence specialists have suggested that Putin may have been engaged in technology theft and espionage activity centered around Robotron. This Dresden-based electronics conglomerate was the Eastern Bloc's largest microchip research center and mainframe computer producer.[60]

Putin's experiences as a KGB agent in Dresden occurred against the backdrop of seismic shifts within the USSR. These historical developments would shatter Soviet hegemony in the GDR and across Eastern Europe. Like Andropov, Putin would watch helplessly as a series of popular uprisings rocked the satellite state in which he was based. Unlike Hungary in 1956 or Prague in 1968, no Soviet tanks would be coming to the rescue in 1989.

While Gorbachev attempted to preserve the Soviet Union through a program of political and economic reform, Erich Honecker struck a hard line in the GDR. From his office in Dresden, Putin could see that Honecker's iron grip was slipping. Protests began to flare slowly but inexorably, and the tide of opposition rose in East Germany. As it was Putin's job to keep his finger on the pulse of political developments in the country, he watched these events first-hand. In addition to studying the nature of the opposition, Putin had a front-row seat as a totalitarian system struggled and failed to reform itself.[61]

In October of 1989, westbound trains rumbled through Dresden carrying East Germans who had claimed political asylum at the West German embassy in Prague. Throngs of Dresdeners attempted to break through the security cordon around the train station, hoping to join their compatriots.[62] By November 9th, the fall of the Berlin Wall had sent shockwaves around the world. Emboldened crowds of citizens gathered across Germany. Putin watched in horror as a crowd of thousands gathered outside the Stasi headquarters across the street from his office. Overwhelmed by the size of the crowd and the rapidity of events, Horst Böhm, the head of the Stasi branch in Dresden who had once awarded Putin a medal, ordered the gates be opened to the protesters. Less than a year later, Böhm took his own life.

In the KGB's Dresden headquarters, pandemonium ensued. Putin and his comrades began shoveling sensitive documents into the furnace. In addition to the papers, everything Putin had been working toward for the past several years was going up in flames before his eyes. "We destroyed everything - all our communications, our lists of contacts, and our agents' networks," Putin recalled of this decisive moment. "I personally burned a huge amount of material. We burned so much that the furnace burst."[63]

As the hour approached midnight, some members of the emboldened crowd turned their attention from Stasi headquarters to the KGB office across the street. Startled, a single security guard dashed up to inform Putin and the four others with him that people were gathering outside. Putin, the officer-in-charge, issued orders to prepare for an assault. He called the Soviet military command in Dresden and described the situation, requesting immediate backup.[64] The response from his military counterpart haunted him for the rest of his life, "We cannot do anything without orders from Moscow. And Moscow is silent."[65]

Abandoned by his superiors, Putin took decisive action. In uniform, he went outside alone and confronted the few dozen protestors. He spoke fluent German and explained that his men were armed and would fire if they entered the compound. The crowd, dazed by the shocking collapse of the Stasi, dispersed.[66] Putin had stood his ground, avoiding the humiliation of having his headquarters ransacked, but the experience was traumatic. "I got the feeling then that the country no longer existed. That it had disappeared. It was clear that the Union was ailing. And it had a terminal disease without a cure - a paralysis of power."[67] Putin later recalled, "I thought the whole thing was inevitable. To be honest, I only regretted that the Soviet Union had lost its position in Europe. I understood that a position built on walls and dividers cannot last. But I wanted something different to rise in its place. And nothing different was proposed. That's what hurt. They just dropped everything and went away."[68]

In 2005, during his annual State of the Nation address to Russia's top leaders, Putin described the collapse of the Soviet Union as one of *the greatest geopolitical disasters of the 20th Century.*[69]

Collapse of the Soviet Union
And the Rise of the Oligarchs and the Mafia State

In 1991, a decisive year in the history of Russia and the development of the contemporary world, the Soviet Empire vanished into the pages of history. The Soviet Union was a political entity distinct from the country now known as the Russian Federation. With a pseudo-federal political structure centered in Moscow, the USSR had ruled over the vast lands and many ethnicities that Russian Tsars had spent centuries conquering. Following victory in the Second World War, Soviet influence extended into the heart of Central Europe. While Russia was the largest republic in the Union, there were 14 others ranging from Eastern Europe to Central Asia. Ethnic Slavic Russians constituted just 51% of the Soviet population.[70] The long-term causes of the USSR's demise include terminal economic decline, the expenditures of a lost arms race, the moral and political bankruptcy of the communist system, ethnic conflict, national independence movements, and re-energized democratic activism. These factors notwithstanding, the collapse and dissolution of the Soviet Union and the oligarchic, corrupt, and authoritarian Russian state that rose from its ashes were not inevitable. The character and decisions of Russia's leaders drove the outcome.

A Siberian politician named Boris Yeltsin emerged as the

unlikely leader of Russia's nascent democracy. Yeltsin was a complex man, capable of bouts of extraordinary energy, industriousness, and bravery. He also was a severe alcoholic prone to depression. Yeltsin likely saved Russia's early experiment in democracy by risking his life and dramatically standing up to a hardline, KGB-led, communist coup attempt. However, later in his career as the President of Russia, as his health and alcohol abuse deteriorated, Yeltsin slipped into insularity and corruption. Russia became overwhelmed by criminality and chaos.

The newly independent Russian Federation faced catastrophic economic problems and severe shortages of all consumer goods. Russia was at a moment of existential crisis. Yeltsin feared a communist resurgence. He was then being advised by a group of young St. Petersburg-based economists consisting, ironically, of ex-Marxists who believed that immediate, radical solutions were the only way forward. At their urging, Yeltsin pushed through a variety of economic reforms, "shock therapy," as it was known, designed to transition the Soviet top-down, centrally planned economy into a private property-based market economy. These reformers differed from those in the Russian intelligentsia interested in political reforms. They were focused on economic reforms to the exclusion of all else.[71]

It is doubtful that Yeltsin fully understood the nature of market economics. Still, he possessed a bold and intuitive leadership style. He favored the dramatic proposals of the young economists from St. Petersburg.[72] Yeltsin was concerned that, given the political and economic instability in Russia, its history of coups and intrigues, and their precarious hold on power, they had little time to enact their ambitious agenda. Driven by fears of Communist resurgence, they drove a stake through the heart of Communism in Russia with blinding speed. However, while they dismembered Communism, they failed to create a replacement system founded upon the rule of law, widespread economic opportunity, and a vibrant civil society.

American political and academic elites participated in the conception and implementation of the shock therapy privatization program. The organization most heavily involved in American economic aid efforts in Russia was the Harvard Institute for International Development (HIID). Lawrence Summers, appointed by Bill Clinton as Under Secretary of the

Treasury and a former Harvard economics professor, was a major supporter of HIID in the administration.[73] Harvard economics professor Jeffrey Sachs, having advised previous countries such as Bolivia and Poland through economic transitions, traveled to Russia and met with and advised the young reformers. While Sachs has vigorously defended his actions in Russia as largely being misunderstood, his support for rapid change at the time was clear. "If you look at how reform has occurred, it has been through the rapid adoption of foreign models," Sachs told *The New York Times* in 1993, "not a slow evolution of modern institutions."[74]

One of the reformers first acts was to end government control over prices. This policy contained a fatal flaw, exploited by organized crime syndicates and a small group of enterprising individuals who came to be known as the oligarchs. Although consumer good prices were liberalized, leading to violent fluctuations, prices for Russia's primary natural resources were kept artificially low and under state control. At the same time, the reformers ended state control over prices, they also eliminated the state monopoly on imports and exports. As a result, well-connected insiders and powerful criminal groups could buy oil, diamonds, timber, and other natural resources at artificially low prices within Russia and then turn around and sell them on the international market for an immense profit.[75] Thus began the full-scale robbery of Russia's abundant natural resource wealth.

After ending central planning of the economy, the radical reformers moved to eliminate the state monopoly on property. They implemented privatization with ruthless efficiency and appeared largely unconcerned with who would end up owning Russia's immense state assets, believing that market mechanisms would eventually sort matters out equitably.[76] This proved a colossal miscalculation, as the oligarchs gained ownership over vast sectors of Russia's strategic resources and economy.

Straddling eleven time zones across Europe and Asia, the countries of the former Soviet Union covered one-sixth of the Earth's landmass. Russia, by far the world's largest country, enjoys immense natural resource wealth, particularly in oil, natural gas, coal, precious metals, and timber. It was at that time, and remains today, a natural resource, commodities-based national economy. With a hasty and chaotic process of privatization underway, the race was on by the bold and the unscrupulous to gain control over the largest transfer of state wealth into private hands in the history of the world.

Many in the new class of oligarchs were well poised to purchase these newly privatized industries because they were flush from establishing banks in the twilight years of the USSR. As part of *perestroika*, in 1988 Gorbachev passed the Law on Cooperatives, which was meant to spur semi-private economic activity ("worker" owned cooperatives as opposed to state-owned) within the Soviet Union. A few savvy operators noticed that the law allowed for establishing financial or credit lines of business, essentially, banks.[77] Many of these banks made fortunes through currency speculation during the period of price liberalization. Russian organized crime infiltrated this proto-banking sector early and on a massive scale, using them to launder vast amounts of illicit money and placing the bankers under protection rackets.[78]

While the control of the Communist Party over the levers of power had led to a certain form of stability, the Soviet Union never genuinely operated under the rule of law. Konstantin Simis, an esteemed Soviet lawyer who defected to the United States in 1977, wrote, "[A]t the root of the general corruption of the Soviet Union lies the totalitarian rule of the Communist party, single-handedly ruling the country. This power is checked neither by law nor by a free press. And the nature of any unrestricted power is such that it inevitably corrupts those who wield it and constantly generates the phenomenon of corruption. So it is that corruption has become the organic and unchangeable essence of the Soviet regime and can be eliminated only by a root-and-branch change in the means of government."[79]

Gorbachev thought he could reform the Soviet Union without destroying it, but failed. Boris Yeltsin effectively banished the Communist Party from government in 1991, and his radical lieutenants did away with the lingering Bolshevik economic legacy in the following months. In the sweep of history, these events of monumental importance unfolded practically overnight. Simis may have been right that a "root-and-branch change in the means of government" may have been a necessary starting point to begin to address corruption in Russia. Still, the Russian experience of the early 1990s vividly demonstrates that simply ending one form of government and social structure is insufficient, that something positive must be put in its place.

What was lacking in Soviet as well as post-Soviet Russia was the rule of law. Capitalism requires well-established and equally applied rules to engender trust among its participants, allowing it to function properly. These rules must be codified in the law, but it is not enough that these laws be written down; there must also be a reliable system of courts and legal processes to protect private property, enforce contracts, and adjudicate disputes.

Fundamentally weakened following the collapse of the Soviet Union, the Russian state under Boris Yeltsin was incapacitated at every level and entirely unable to manage the emergence of capitalism. The Russian court system and organs of law enforcement were not only in a state of chaos but, after decades of Communism, had no practical or intellectual experience in these matters. Despite these challenges, the early Yeltsin era's shock therapy catalyzed unprecedented economic activity over a significant portion of the Earth's natural resource wealth. This led to rivalries and disputes that, one way or another, needed to be resolved. This vacuum was filled by organized crime.

"Russia is the biggest mafia state in the world," Yeltsin admitted in 1994, "the superpower of crime that is devouring the state from top to bottom."[80] The collapse of Communism led to the largest expansion of global organized crime in decades, particularly in the former Soviet Union. On the streets of Russia, this was most vividly embodied by a bloody gang war in the 90s between Slavic gangs on one side and primarily Chechen gangs, among other groups from the Caucuses, on the other.[81] However, in the 1990s, the Eurasian Mafia was involved in more than violent underworld disputes. Organized crime integrated with political and economic elites and absorbed newly unemployed members of the security services. This led to the criminalization of large segments of the Russian government, law enforcement, finance, business, and society.

This criminal underworld has traditionally been known in Russia as the *vor v zakone*, meaning "thieves-in-law," referring to a code of values historically embraced by the Russian criminal class. While elements of *Vor* culture can be traced back to Tsarist times, it was fundamentally shaped by the experience of mass imprisonment in the Stalinist gulags. This prison culture developed its own slang, and inmates sported elaborate tattoos that conveyed information about their experiences and position in the criminal hierarchy. However, after Communism fell and the Russian mafia expanded its influence abroad into ever more sophisticated areas of the global economy and financial system, the old tattooed inmates were replaced by men in suits with high-up business and political connections.

During the late Gorbachev period, organized crime influenced Russia's budding capitalism by establishing protection rackets.[82] The Russian term *krysha*, literally translated as "roof," is the practice of a gang establishing such a racket over a business or group of businesses. During the early phases of privatization, the protection rackets would be used to settle disputes among the nascent class of oligarchs. The symbiosis of crime, business, and politics reached the highest levels of Russia's power structure. The oligarchs' establishment of early banking institutions was partly facilitated by laundered money provided by organized crime. The oligarchs used this capital to purchase large sectors of Russian industry in corrupt insider deals at bargain basement prices. By the mid-90s, the government estimated the black market to comprise 40-50% of the Russian economy.[83]

The most potent Slavic gang to emerge from this time was the Solntsevskaya Bratva, or Solntsevo Brotherhood. Established in Solntsevo, a district southwest of Moscow, the gang was founded by a former waiter and wrestler named Sergei "Mikhas" Mikhailov, who had joined forces with an ex-convict named Viktor "Avera" Averin. During the early years of Russia's corrupt capitalism, the Solntsevskaya exploded in wealth in influence. The syndicate is now truly transnational, with operations across the world. Between 5,000 and 9,000 members are estimated to be organized into twelve semi-autonomous brigades. A leadership council of 12 individuals meets regularly in various locations worldwide.[84]

The Solntsevskaya first made money through prostitution before moving into arms dealing and drugs.[85] Profits from its illegal activities were reinvested into the legal economy, and the group seized control of several banks and over 100 companies. These banks held the gang's common fund, or *obshchak*, used for investments or assisting gang members and their families. Another powerful criminal organization that emerged roughly contemporaneously was the Izmaylovskaya Bratva, headed for a time by a Soviet army veteran named Anton Malevsky, which was involved in the violent privatization of the Russian aluminum industry.[86]

During Yeltsin's first term, seven men became Russia's richest and most powerful oligarchs. They included Boris Berezovsky, Mikhail Khodorkovsky, Mikhail Fridman, Petr Aven, Vladimir Gusinsky, Vladimir Potanin, and Alexander Smolensky. They became known as the *Semibankirschina*, or Seven Bankers, and amassed unparalleled political and economic power over the Russian state. Many were suspected of having been propped up by elements within the Russian security services and had links to the powerful organized crime syndicates proliferating in Russia at the time. However, they soon faced a significant threat. By 1996, Boris Yeltsin was up for reelection and was desperately unpopular in Russia, and it seemed as if the Communists had a good chance of being voted back into power.

The period following the collapse of the USSR was cataclysmic for the Russian population. The economy lost 50% of its value. Russia experienced a demographic collapse, with average lifespans declining precipitously, particularly among Russian men. Alcoholism was rampant. The murder rate skyrocketed as much of the country was convulsed by violent gang wars. Countless women were sold into human trafficking networks and sexual slavery. Yeltsin's battles with the legislative Duma eventually culminated in 1993 with the Russian President ordering the shelling of the parliamentary building using tanks and pushing through the rest of his shock therapy program by Presidential decree.[87] In 1994, Yeltsin also initiated a bloody war in Chechnya against a radical Islamic independence movement that ended in failure.

As the 1996 election approached, the oligarchs of the *Semibankirschina*, who had been ruthlessly competing with one another, realized they had to band together to support the flagging Yeltsin presidency, or the Communists would regain power through popular election. Boris Berezovsky and Vladimir Gusinsky controlled powerful independent television stations and immediately had them churn out programming in support of Yeltsin and attacking the Communists. However, support from the oligarchs would come at a price.

The final phase of the seizure of Russian state assets occurred at this time. The oligarch Vladimir Potanin, who grew up a scion of a well-connected Communist family and was now one of the wealthiest men in Russia, approached an American named Boris Jordan, one of the Credit Suisse First Boston consultants who had overseen the first auction during the voucher privatization period and had recently established his own firm, Renaissance Capital. Potanin described to Jordan an idea that would come to be known as "loans for shares." The basic concept was that powerful oligarchs would provide loans to the Russian government, temporarily benefiting the Yeltsin regime. The government would offer ownership shares of Russia's most valuable state enterprises as collateral. This was the holy grail of privatization, Russia's key strategic natural resources: oil, natural gas, and precious metals. Jordan and his partner Peter Jennings wrote a white paper finalizing the concept for Potanin.[88]

The process that followed was corrupt from the outset. Shares of Russia's most lucrative natural resource wealth were offered as collateral for next to nothing to a select few insiders in a rigged process. It was well-known and expected that the government would never be able to repay the loans. The oligarchs then sold the shares the government "owed" them back to themselves for next to nothing. The Yeltsin government received a brief shot-in-the-arm in the lead-up to the elections, all at the price of placing vast swaths of Russia's geostrategic resources into the hands of a few men. The Russian oligarchic system had reached its apotheosis; these few tycoons now not only owned the most valuable assets in the country but achieved unparalleled influence at the heart of government.

Yeltsin had another powerful ally supporting him during the 1996 election -- the American government. Bill Clinton liked Yeltsin personally, and the American National Security establishment wished to avoid a Communist return to power at all costs. Several American political operatives, some of whom had previously worked on Clinton's campaign, traveled to Moscow and provided campaign advice to Yeltsin's daughter and closest advisor, Tatyana Dyachenko, who passed it on to her father.[89] The Clinton Administration also pressured the International Monetary Fund to provide Russia with $10 billion in the lead-up to the election.[90] This support was offered despite the American government's awareness of corruption in the Yeltsin administration and fraudulent activities around the election.

"They figured out that it was possible to manipulate the process," Thomas Graham, the Chief Political Analyst at the US Embassy in Moscow from 1994-1997, said in an interview with *PBS Frontline*. "They figured out that you could build a fairly formidable electoral machine if you took the control that you had collectively had--particularly over mass media--your support in executive structures, not only in Moscow but more broadly outside the country if you took into account the financial strength you had from these various industries... They figured out that, by using those wisely, you could lead to the result pretty much that you wanted."[91]

When reports of electoral discrepancies and potential voter fraud in the 1996 Russian elections were provided to Michael Meadowcroft, the head of the Organization for Security and Cooperation in Europe's election monitoring team, he claims to have been pressured by the EU and OSCE to disregard such evidence.[92] Thomas Graham admitted that the Clinton Administration was aware of election irregularities. "No Russian now makes any bones that they violated their own laws on finance and use of media and so forth during the elections... But this was a classic case of the ends justifying the means, and we did get the result that we wanted."

As Yeltsin was sworn into his second presidential term in 1996, Russia was in a perilous historical moment. The oligarchs, particularly the Seven Bankers, had seized control of Russia's natural resource wealth using a plan sketched out by Western financial analysts and enjoyed unparalleled influence in the inner circle of the Yeltsin government. Yeltsin was increasingly in poor health and intoxicated. The symbiosis of corrupt government officials, business tycoons, organized crime, and disparate elements of the intelligence and security apparatus was well underway. The future of Russia was anything but clear.

[1] Neuman, Scott. "Clinton: Wikileaks 'Tear At Fabric' of Government," *NPR*. November 29th, 2010

[2] 10MADRID154_a. *Public Library of US Diplomacy - Wikileaks*

[3] Harding, Luke, "WikiLeaks cable: Russian government 'using mafia for its dirty work'," *The Guardian*. December 1st, 2010

[4] Rotella, Sebastian. "A Gangster Place in the Sun: How Spain's Fight Against the Mob Revealed Russian Power Networks," *ProPublica/The Atlantic*. November 10th, 2017

[5] Judah, Ben. "Grinda's War," *The American Interest*. June 12th, 2018

[6] Galeotti, Mark. "Spain versus Russia's kleptocracy," *European Council on Foreign Relations*. May 4th, 2016

[7] Rotella, Sebastian. "A Gangster Place in the Sun: How Spain's Fight Against the Mob

Revealed Russian Power Networks," *ProPublica/The Atlantic*. November 10th, 2017

[8] Judah, Ben. "Grinda's War," *The American Interest*. June 12th, 2018

[9] Rotella, Sebastian. "A Gangster Place in the Sun: How Spain's Fight Against the Mob Revealed Russian Power Networks," *ProPublica/The Atlantic*. November 10th, 2017

[10] "Treasury Sanctions Russian Officials, Members of the Russian Leadership's Inner Circle, And an Entity for Involvement in the Situation in Ukraine," *US Department of the Treasury Press Center*. March 20th, 2014

[11] Holden, Michael. "Litvinenko believed Putin linked to organised crime: ex-KGB spy's widow," *Reuters*. February 2nd, 2015

[12] Rotella, Sebastian. "A Gangster Place in the Sun: How Spain's Fight Against the Mob Revealed Russian Power Networks," *ProPublica/The Atlantic*. November 10th, 2017

[13] Neumann, Jeanette. "Last Stop for Some of Danske Banks Dirty Money: Spanish Real Estate," *Bloomberg*. April 10th, 2019

[14] Judah, Ben. "Grinda's War," *The American Interest*. June 12th, 2018

[15] Rotella, Sebastian. "A Gangster Place in the Sun: How Spain's Fight Against the Mob Revealed Russian Power Networks," *ProPublica/The Atlantic*. November 10th, 2017

[16] Putin, Vladimir. "Жизнь такая простая штука и жестокая." *Russky Pioner*. August 30th, 2015.

[17] Gessen, Masha. *The Man Without A Face: The Unlikely Rise of Vladimir Putin*. New York, NY: RIVERHEAD BOOKS, 2012. Pg. 46

[18] Putin, Vladimir; Gevorkyan, Nataliya; Timakova, Natalya; Kolesnikov, Andrei. *First Person: An Astonishingly Frank Self-Portrait by Russia's President*. New York, NY: PublicAffairs, 2000. Pg. 18

[19] Lee Myers, Steven. *The New Tsar: The Rise and Reign of Vladimir Putin*. New York, NY: Alfred A. Knopf, 2015. Pg. 16

[20] Volchek, Dmitry. "One Russian Blogger's Effort To Unearth The Secrets Of Putin's Rise To Power," *RadioFreeEurope/RadioLiberty*. April 1st, 2020

[21] Unger, Craig. *House of Trump, House of Putin: The Untold Story of Donald Trump and the Russian Mafia*. New York, NY: DUTTON, 2018. Pg. 63

[22] Gessen, Masha. *The Man Without A Face: The Unlikely Rise of Vladimir Putin*. New York, NY: RIVERHEAD BOOKS, 2012. Pg. 47

[23] Lee Myers, Steven. *The New Tsar: The Rise and Reign of Vladimir Putin*. New York, NY: Alfred A. Knopf, 2015. Pg. 17

[24] Putin, Vladimir; Gevorkyan, Nataliya; Timakova, Natalya; Kolesnikov, Andrei. *First Person: An Astonishingly Frank Self-Portrait by Russia's President*. New York, NY: PublicAffairs, 2000. Pg. 22

[25] Fischer, Ben B. "Okhrana: The Paris Operations of the Russian Imperial Police," *History Staff Center for the Study of Intelligence: Central Intelligence Agency*. 1997.

[26] Johnson, Richard J. "Zagranichnaia Agentura: The Tsarist Political Police in Europe," *Journal of Contemporary History Vol. 7, No. 1/2. January-April, 1972. Pg. 221-242*

[27] Sipher, John (Pseudonym - Former CIA Station Chief). "Putin's One Weapon: The 'Intelligence State', *The New York Times*, February 24th, 2019

[28] Waller, J. Michael. *Secret Empire: The KGB in Russia Today*: Boulder, CO: Westview Press, 1994)

[29] Andrew, Christopher; Mitrokhin, Vasili. *The Sword and the Shield: The Mitrokhin Archive and the Secret History of the KGB*. New York, NY: Basic Books. 1999. Pg. 25

[30] Lincoln, W. Bruce. *Red Victory: A History of the Russian Civil War, 1918-1921*. New York, NY: Simon & Schuster. 1989. Pg. 384

[31] Thurston, Robert W. *Life and Terror in Stalin's Russia, 1934-1941*. New Haven and London: Yale University Press, 1998. Pg. 139

[32] Soldatov, Andrei; Borogan, Irina. *The New Nobility: The Restoration of Russia's Security State and the Enduring Legacy of the KGB*. New York, NY: PublicAffairs, 2010. Pg. 91

[33] Andrew, Christopher; Mitrokhin, Vasili. *The Sword and the Shield: The Mitrokhin Archive and the Secret History of the KGB*. New York, NY: Basic Books. 1999. Pg. 5-77

[34] Whitmore, Brian. "Andropov's Ghost," *RadioFreeEurope/RadioLiberty*. February 9th, 2009

[35] Hill, Fiona; Gaddy, Clifford G. "How the 1980s Explain Vladimir Putin," *The Atlantic*. February 14th, 2013

[36] Putin, Vladimir; Gevorkyan, Nataliya; Timakova, Natalya; Kolesnikov, Andrei. *First Person: An Astonishingly Frank Self-Portrait by Russia's President*. New York, NY: PublicAffairs, 2000. Pg. 23

[37] Harding, Luke. "Sergei Roldugin, the cellist who holds the key to tracing Putin's hidden fortune," *The Guardian*. April 3rd, 2016

[38] Putin, Vladimir; Gevorkyan, Nataliya; Timakova, Natalya; Kolesnikov, Andrei. *First Person: An Astonishingly Frank Self-Portrait by Russia's President*. New York, NY: PublicAffairs, 2000. Pg. 44

[39] Parfitt, Tom. "Vladimir Putin's chief of staff muses on their time as young spies," *The Telegraph*. March 5th, 2013

[40] Gessen, Masha. *The Man Without A Face: The Unlikely Rise of Vladimir Putin*. New York, NY: RIVERHEAD BOOKS, 2012. Pg. 60

[41] Lee Myers, Steven. *The New Tsar: The Rise and Reign of Vladimir Putin*. New York, NY: Alfred A. Knopf, 2015. Pg. 23-24

[42] Putin, Vladimir; Gevorkyan, Nataliya; Timakova, Natalya; Kolesnikov, Andrei. *First Person: An Astonishingly Frank Self-Portrait by Russia's President*. New York, NY: PublicAffairs, 2000. Pg. 50

[43] Usoltsev, Vladimir. *Sosluzhivets: Neizvestniye Stranitsi Zhizni Prezidenta*. Moscow: Eksmo, 2004. Pg. 186

[44] Dawisha, Karen. *Putin's Kleptocracy: Who Owns Russia?*. New York, NY: Simon & Schuster, 2014. Pg. 40

[45] Lee Myers, Steven. *The New Tsar: The Rise and Reign of Vladimir Putin*. New York, NY: Alfred A. Knopf, 2015. Pg. 34

[46] Putin, Vladimir; Gevorkyan, Nataliya; Timakova, Natalya; Kolesnikov, Andrei. *First Person: An Astonishingly Frank Self-Portrait by Russia's President*. New York, NY: PublicAffairs, 2000. Pg. 54-55

[47] Belton, Catherine. *Putin's People: How The KGB Took Back Russia And Then Took On The West*. New York, NY: Farrar, Straus and Giroux, 2020. Pg. 27

[48] Putin, Vladimir; Gevorkyan, Nataliya; Timakova, Natalya; Kolesnikov, Andrei. *First Person: An Astonishingly Frank Self-Portrait by Russia's President*. New York, NY: PublicAffairs, 2000. Pg. 69-70

[49] Gessen, Masha. *The Man Without A Face: The Unlikely Rise of Vladimir Putin*. New York, NY: RIVERHEAD BOOKS, 2012. Pg. 64

[50] Roth, Andrew. "Putin's East German identity card found in Stasi archives - report," *The Guardian*. December 11th, 2018

[51] Selvege, Douglas, "Vladimir Putin's Stasi ID: A Press Sensation and It's Historical Reality," *Sources and Methods: A Blog of the History and Public Policy Program, The Wilson Center*. December 17th, 2018.

[52] Usoltsev, Vladimir. *Sosluzhivets: Neizvestniye Stranitsi Zhizni Prezidenta*. Moscow: Eksmo, 2004. Pg. 68

[53] Paterson, Tony. "Putin - the spy who was obsessed with the West," *The Telegraph*. October 26th, 2003

[54] Putin, Vladimir; Gevorkyan, Nataliya; Timakova, Natalya; Kolesnikov, Andrei. *First Person: An Astonishingly Frank Self-Portrait by Russia's President*. New York, NY: PublicAffairs, 2000. Pg. 70-71

[55] Belton, Catherine. *Putin's People: How The KGB Took Back Russia And Then Took On The West*. New York, NY: Farrar, Straus and Giroux, 2020. Pg. 36-45

[56] Gessen, Masha. *The Man Without A Face: The Unlikely Rise of Vladimir Putin*. New York, NY: RIVERHEAD BOOKS, 2012. Pg. 65

[57] Hill, Fiona; Gaddy, Clifford G. "How the 1980s Explain Vladimir Putin," *The*

Atlantic. February 14th, 2013

58 Andrew, Christopher; Mitrokhin, Vasili. *The Sword and the Shield: The Mitrokhin Archive and the Secret History of the KGB*. New York, NY: Basic Books. 1999. Pg. 271

59 Dawisha, Karen. *Putin's Kleptocracy: Who Owns Russia?*. New York, NY: Simon & Schuster, 2014. Pg. 46-47

60 Hoffman, David. "Putin's Career Rooted in Russia's KGB," *The Washington Post*. January 30th, 2000

61 Hill, Fiona; Gaddy, Clifford G. "How the 1980s Explain Vladimir Putin," *The Atlantic*. February 14th, 2013

62 Bowlby, Chris. "Vladimir Putin's formative German years," *BBC News*. March 27th, 2015

63 Putin, Vladimir; Gevorkyan, Nataliya; Timakova, Natalya; Kolesnikov, Andrei. *First Person: An Astonishingly Frank Self-Portrait by Russia's President*. New York, NY: PublicAffairs, 2000. Pg. 76

64 Lee Myers, Steven. *The New Tsar: The Rise and Reign of Vladimir Putin*. New York, NY: Alfred A. Knopf, 2015. Pg. 49

65 Putin, Vladimir; Gevorkyan, Nataliya; Timakova, Natalya; Kolesnikov, Andrei. *First Person: An Astonishingly Frank Self-Portrait by Russia's President*. New York, NY: PublicAffairs, 2000. Pg. 79

66 Lee Myers, Steven. *The New Tsar: The Rise and Reign of Vladimir Putin*. New York, NY: Alfred A. Knopf, 2015. Pg. 51

67 Putin, Vladimir; Gevorkyan, Nataliya; Timakova, Natalya; Kolesnikov, Andrei. *First Person: An Astonishingly Frank Self-Portrait by Russia's President*. New York, NY: PublicAffairs, 2000. Pg. 79

68 Putin, Vladimir; Gevorkyan, Nataliya; Timakova, Natalya; Kolesnikov, Andrei. *First Person: An Astonishingly Frank Self-Portrait by Russia's President*. New York, NY: PublicAffairs, 2000. Pg. 80

69 *Annual Address to the Federal Assembly of the Russian Federation*. April 25th, 2005.

70 Plokhy, Serhii. *The Last Empire: The Final Days of the Soviet Union*. New York, NY: Basic Books, 2014. Pg. xxxi

71 Freeland, Chrystia. *Sale of the Century: Russia's Wild Ride From Communism to Capitalism*. New York, NY: Crown Publishers, 2000. Pg. 27

72 Hoffman, David E. *The Oligarchs: Wealth and Power in the New Russia*. New York, NY: PublicAffairs, 2002. Pg. 178

73 Wedel, Janine R. "The Harvard Boys Do Russia," *The Nation*. May 14th, 1998.

74 Passell, Peter. "Dr. Jeffrey Sachs, Shock Therapist," *The New York Times*. June 27th, 1993.

75 Glenny, Misha. *McMafia: A Journey Through The Global Underworld*. New York, NY: Alfred A. Knopf, 2008. Pg. 56-57

76 Hoffman, David E. *The Oligarchs: Wealth and Power in the New Russia*. New York, NY: PublicAffairs, 2002. Pg. 179

77 Hoffman, David E. *The Oligarchs: Wealth and Power in the New Russia*. New York, NY: PublicAffairs, 2002. Pg. 38-39

78 Galeotti, Mark. *The Vory: Russia's Super Mafia*. New Haven and London: Yale University Press, 2018. Pg. 102

79 Simis, Konstantin. *USSR: The Corrupt Society*. New York, NY: Simon and Schuster, 1982. Pg. 300

80 *Organized Crime in Russia*. Stratfor. August 16th, 2008.

81 Galeotti, Mark. *The Vory: Russia's Super Mafia*. New Haven and London: Yale University Press, 2018. Pg. 160

82 Glenny, Misha. *McMafia: A Journey Through The Global Underworld*. New York, NY: Alfred A. Knopf, 2008. Pg. 55

83 Glenny, Misha. *McMafia: A Journey Through The Global Underworld*. New York, NY: Alfred A. Knopf, 2008. Pg. 61

[84] Varese, Federico. *Mafias on the Move: How Organized Crime Conquers New Territories.* Princeton, NJ: Princeton University Press, 2011. Pg. 65-68

[85] Belton, Catherine. *Putin's People: How The KGB Took Back Russia And Then Took On The West.* New York, NY: Farrar, Straus and Giroux, 2020. Pg. 337

[86] Belton, Catherine. "Rusal: a lingering heat," *The Financial Times.* January 25th, 2010

[87] Hill, Fiona; Gaddy, Clifford G. *Mr. Putin: Operative in the Kremlin.* Washington, DC: BROOKINGS INSTITUTION PRESS, 2013. Pg. 17

[88] Hoffman, David E. *The Oligarchs: Wealth and Power in the New Russia.* New York, NY: PublicAffairs, 2002. Pg. 306-307

[89] Kramer, Michael. "Yanks To The Rescue: The Secret Story Of How American Advisors Helped Yeltsin Win," *Time Magazine.* July 15th, 1996. Pg. 29-37

[90] Shane, Scott. "Russia Isn't the Only One Meddling in Elections, We Do It Too," *The New York Times.* February 17th, 2018.

[91] Thomas Graham Interview Transcript. *PBS Frontline.*

[92] Zaitchick, Alexander; Ames, Mark. "How The West Helped Invent Russia's Election Fraud: OSCE Whistleblower Exposes 1996 Whitewash," *The Exile.* December 9th, 2011.

Chapter 2:
Success At Any Cost:
Trump's Early Years in Manhattan

Meet the Trumps: Friedrich, Frederick, and Donald

Donald Trump moved to Manhattan in 1971 at the age of 25. Despite his ambitions to become the city's premier real estate tycoon, New York City was in a state of decline. America's largest city was lurching towards a fiscal crisis, in the throes of an escalating violent crime wave and riven by racial and ethnic tensions. Certain boroughs, such as the Bronx, were, quite literally, on fire. Where some saw an unfolding urban tragedy, Trump saw an opportunity.

Trump's first apartment was a modest, rent-controlled Upper East Side studio off Third Avenue at 196 East 75th St. In moving to the city and hoping to strike it big, Donald channeled the same restless ambition his grandfather exhibited when he arrived at Ellis Island on October 17th, 1885, as a 16-year-old immigrant from Kallstadt, Germany. Friedrich Trump later opened a restaurant in a rough and tumble section of Seattle, Washington, that likely also served as a low-rent brothel.[1] During the Klondike gold rush, Friedrich closed up shop in Seattle and headed further north to Alaska, where he opened The Arctic Bar and Grill, which offered gold prospectors both hard liquor and "sporting ladies."[2]

Donald's move to Manhattan set him apart from his father, Frederick Trump. Whereas the son dreamed of planting his flag in the world's most glamorous real estate market, the father had earned his fortune by building developments in the outer boroughs for modest, working-class families. After graduating from Wharton's School of Business, Donald joined his father's company and was familiar with its operations. Despite the move to the big city, he commuted from Manhattan each morning to company headquarters on Avenue Z in Brooklyn.

Fred Trump had skipped university and contrived his own shoestring method of financing and flipping houses straight out of high school. By 1926, Fred built and sold nineteen homes in Hollis, Queens.[3] However, the crash of 1929 wiped out the housing market in New York and across the country. With his ambitions temporarily sidelined by the Great Depression, Fred made do operating a supermarket until opportunity in real estate would rear its head again in 1934 with the collapse of the House of Lehrenkrauss.

A German-American firm and family conglomerate established in 1878, the House of Lehrenkrauss had developed a booming business selling "guaranteed" or "certified" mortgages following the conclusion of the First World War. However, events related to the Depression revealed wide-scale fraud within the organization, quickly leading to its demise and the auctioning of its parts. Fred Trump immediately sensed an opportunity. He realized whoever emerged as the owner of the troubled firm's mortgage department would enjoy inside information on homes across Queens and Brooklyn at risk of foreclosure and thus available to be snapped up at bargain prices.

Fred Trump purchased the House of Lehrenkrauss's mortgage department and became one of the most successful developers in Brooklyn for the next three decades. A key element to his success, and the subsequent success of his son in Manhattan, was the deft way Trump built and cultivated access and influential relationships within Brooklyn's Democratic Party establishment. In a one-party town, as New York was at that time, the Democratic borough party bosses determined who could run for elective office or hold positions in municipal government and were all-powerful. With 125,000 more votes than Manhattan's infamous Tammany Hall machine, Brooklyn was a potent force in citywide politics.

Fred Trump established Metropolitan Investors to house his newly acquired mortgage list and opened an office at 66 Court Street in downtown Brooklyn. The same building housed an insurance company owned by the cigar-chomping Democratic

Party boss Irwin Steingut, who provided insurance to the Brooklyn docks, which was being run by the mafia at that time. Trump befriended Steingut and quickly became a donor to the Madison Club, the influential Democratic Club he led. Through the Madison Club, Trump became acquainted with a young accountant named Abe Beame and the clubhouse attorney Abraham "Bunny" Lindenbaum, a future New York City Mayor and Planning Commissioner, respectively. Trump was known to pick up Steingut, Beame, and Lindenbaum in his limousine and treat them to dinner.[4]

Fred Trump became the largest developer in Flatbush and Crown Heights, neighborhoods located in Central Brooklyn that also served as the political base of Steingut's Madison Club. In the same year, Trump completed the purchase of the House of Lehrenkrauss, the administration of Franklin D. Roosevelt established the Federal Housing Administration (FHA) to support the housing market and help spur recovery in the overall economy. Between 1935 and 1942, Fred Trump built over 2,000 single-family homes in Brooklyn using FHA-insured mortgages.[5] The Second World War also provided a boon to Fred Trump's development efforts. After the bombing of Pearl Harbor, his center of operations shifted from Brooklyn to Norfolk, Virginia, the locus of American naval operations across the entire East Coast. The war effort caused a surge in the local workforce, leading to an urgent demand for additional housing. By 1944, Fred completed 1,360 apartment units in Norfolk, which comprised a significant percentage of the total housing built during the war effort.

In little over a decade, Fred Trump emerged from the dark days of the Great Depression and World War Two as a politically connected, multimillionaire, and undisputed real estate powerhouse in Brooklyn. He also became a family man, marrying a 24-year Scottish immigrant, Mary Anne Macleod, in 1936. Fred and Mary proceeded to have five children together. On June 14th, 1946, their fourth child, Donald John Trump, was born. The family eventually settled into a 23-room mansion on Midland Parkway in Jamaica, Queens.

Fred Trump was a workaholic with an authoritarian parenting style. His granddaughter, Ph.D. psychologist Mary Trump, has described him as a "high-functioning sociopath."[6] However, despite his father's disciplinarian tendencies, Donald chronically misbehaved. A neighbor recalled catching a five or six-year-old Donald throwing rocks at her toddler.[7] In *The Art of the Deal*, Trump claims he gave his second-grade music teacher a black eye[8]. Fred Trump sent Donald away to New York Military Academy, hoping the strict regimen of boarding school would straighten him out. Though Trump later claimed he graduated at the top of his class, his grades at NYMA remain unknown as Trump's lawyers demanded that the school seal his records.[9]

Young Donald often shadowed his father as he worked on developments in Brooklyn and Queens. Over the years, Fred accumulated a comprehensive knowledge of nearly every facet of the New York construction and real estate business. Fred Trump imparted an enduring lesson to his son: the importance of publicity and courting the media. Early in his career, Fred floated balloons over Coney Island that carried $50 discounts for his houses. He referred to himself in press releases as "Brooklyn's Largest Builder."[10] Fred offered his opinion on national political and business matters in the newspapers. In 1950, he was named alongside President Eisenhower on a list of the nation's best-dressed men.[11]

After military school, Donald attended Fordham University before transferring into the real estate program at the Wharton School of Business. While there, he displayed the typical brash, egotistical bravura that would become a hallmark throughout the rest of his life. In one instance, a professor of the small real estate class asked the students what drove their decision to study real estate, and Trump replied, "I am going to be the king of New York real estate."[12]

Upon graduating in 1968, Trump was poised to return to the family business and pursue his dream. However, there were two potential stumbling blocks. One was the Vietnam War. While in college, Trump received four draft deferments that kept him out of the war. However, after graduating, he was eligible to be conscripted. On September 17th, Trump underwent an armed forces physical examination and was classified "1-Y", medically unfit to serve unless in the case of a national emergency. It was a dubious diagnosis, given that Trump had played team sports throughout high school. Though no records describe his disqualifying medical condition, Trump has provided conflicting accounts of the medical deferment. He has at times said he had bone spurs in both his heels,[13] and at others, he has claimed that he had bone spurs in one heel but was unable to remember which one.[14] Regardless, his high draft number was never called, making the medical deferment moot.

The second issue was whether his eldest brother, Fred Trump Jr., would take over the family business. According to Trump family biographer Gwenda Blair, while Fred Jr. was social and had a sense of humor, he "did not have the skills or the strategic sense to get what he wanted."[15] Fred Sr. pushed his eldest son relentlessly, and nothing he did lived up to his father's lofty expectations. Friends of Fred Jr. claimed the experience of working with his father made him miserable.[16] Fred Jr. finally gave up on the family business and decided to become a pilot, a vocation his father disdainfully called "a chauffeur in the sky."[17] Donald saw that his brother's abdication left the pathway to leadership of the family company open to him[18]. Fred Jr later married a flight attendant against his father's wishes, but they subsequently divorced. He died of an alcoholism-related heart attack in 1981.

Donald was named company president in 1968, and Fred became chairman. In the six years between joining the company and when he had his first genuine real estate opportunity in 1974, Trump's day-to-day responsibilities primarily consisted of managing up to 22,000 apartments in the outer boroughs, forty-eight privately held corporations, and fifteen family partnerships. By then, Fred Trump had mostly stopped building new developments and focused on managing his existing real estate empire. His young son, on the other hand, was hungry for more.

Trump's move to Manhattan in 1971 marked a new phase in his life. He had learned from his father that one of the most important keys to success is forming relationships with influential and connected people. At 25, he also wanted to be wherever beautiful women congregated. Lucky for him, the watering holes of powerful men and attractive young women all too often overlap. So, upon arriving in Manhattan, Donald Trump joined Le Club.

"It was the sort of place where you were likely to see a wealthy seventy-five-year-old guy walk in with three blondes from Sweden," Trump said of the establishment.[19] Located at 416 East 55th Street, Le Club's stucco exterior was fashionably nondescript, its awning bore no name, and its only identifying feature was a small brass tablet on the door that read "Members

Only." The interior featured billiards, a restaurant upstairs, and a stylishly small dance floor. Le Club's membership roster boasted thirteen princes, thirteen counts, four barons, three princesses, and two dukes.[20] Other celebrity members included Hollywood heavyweights like Al Pacino, Mike Nichols, and George Steinbrenner, owner of the New York Yankees.[21] However, the member who had the most significant impact on Trump's life was Roy Cohn.

Organized Crime and Trump's Mentor and Fixer: Roy Cohn

Organized crime in America is an extension of the free market system and a social phenomenon. Just as important as the criminal syndicates themselves is the corruption in politics, business, organized labor, and law enforcement that enables them to exist. While criminality has existed for as long as there have been laws, organized crime as we know it today emerged in the United States in the period following the Civil War. This era was marked by clashes between the rising class of capitalists known as the Robber Barons and the American labor movement. Both managers and unions hired groups of violent thugs, also known as "goon squads," to either break strikes or attack strikebreakers. This link between the capitalist managerial class, organized labor, and organized crime is critically important. Labor racketeering has, for decades, formed the backbone of organized crime.

In the United States, the ethnic composition of organized crime parallels the history of immigration into the country. At the turn of the 20th Century, most of the "respectable" positions in society were occupied by the white, Anglo-Saxon, Protestant establishment. The first group of large-scale immigrants, the Irish, became a dominant presence in the police forces of many American cities. From 1880 to 1920, the US experienced a vast surge of immigration from Southern and Eastern Europe, primarily immigrants from Italy and Jews leaving the "Pale of Settlement" in the Russian Empire. A minority of individuals from these ethnic groups played an outsized role in the organized crime syndicates that emerged during this period.

In the early 20th Century, the United States prohibited gambling as well as narcotics and alcohol. It was the prohibition of alcohol that first infused vast fortunes into the coffers of the American underworld. A pivotal figure in the history of American organized crime was Arnold Rothstein. The biggest gambler in the United States at the time, Rothstein gained infamy for fixing the 1919 World Series. He also established highly lucrative international illicit trades in alcohol and narcotics. Rothstein enjoyed deep and corrupt connections to Tammany Hall, the Democratic Party organization that ran New York City for decades. After Rothstein was murdered over an outstanding gambling debt, his criminal empire was inherited by his younger protégés, in particular the Sicilian Charlie "Lucky" Luciano and the Russian Jew Meyer Lansky.

Lansky and Luciano were childhood friends, criminal confederates, and pivotal figures in founding the so-called National Crime Syndicate. The National Crime Syndicate consisted of loosely affiliated Italian, Jewish, and Irish gangs from across the nation. After the violence that marked the early period of Prohibition, it was decided the bribe should supplant the bullet. A ruling "Commission" divided territories and arbitrated disputes between a complex and multiethnic network of interlinking but separate crime "families" and syndicates.

New York City was divided into five Mafia families, today known as the Genovese, Gambino, Columbo, Lucchese, and Bonanno Crime Families. The powerful successor to the Capone gang in Chicago became known as The Outfit. Other criminal syndicates operated regionally across the United States in cities such as Buffalo, Philadelphia, Atlantic City, New Orleans, Cleveland, Minneapolis-St. Paul, Los Angeles, and elsewhere.

Lucky Luciano, an important figure in the heroin trade, operated one of the most powerful organized crime families in New York. It was later named the Genovese Crime Family after one of Luciano's lieutenants, Vito Genovese. Meyer Lansky, often referred to as the "financial wizard of organized crime," was the most important and powerful figure in what came to be known as the Gambling Syndicate.

Lansky and his criminal confederates established casinos in South Florida, Las Vegas, Nevada, Havana, Cuba, and elsewhere. In Vegas and Havana, Lansky was trusted by his partners to handle the cash and distribute the illicit casino "skim" through complex hidden ownership structures behind legitimate fronts. Lansky also pioneered complex money laundering schemes, using casinos and banks worldwide in places like the Bahamas and Switzerland. Luciano and Lansky cooperated with

US intelligence during the Second World War and possibly afterward.

It is essential to recognize the interconnected nature of the three core pillars of American organized crime: the sale of narcotics, illicit gambling, and labor racketeering. "Labor racketeering," according to the Department of Labor, "is the infiltration and/or control of a union or employee benefit plan for personal benefit through illegal, violent, or fraudulent means."

The two labor unions most associated with organized crime are the International Brotherhood of the Teamsters (IBT) and the International Longshoreman's Association (ILA). The longtime leader of the Teamsters, Jimmy Hoffa, was deeply connected to the highest levels of organized crime in America. Hoffa and the Teamsters were famously the target of Attorney General Robert Kennedy's war on organized crime. Organized criminals held positions of power and authority within the Teamsters. For example, Anthony "Tony Pro" Provenzano, a *caporegime* in the Genovese Crime Family, was the President of the Teamsters Local 560 in Union City, New Jersey. By controlling the Teamsters, organized crime interests used its enormous pension funds to invest in Las Vegas casinos and large land developments across the West, particularly in Southern California.

Another target of Kennedy's war on organized crime was an attorney named Roy Cohn.

Roy Cohn exploded into the American national consciousness as an infamous player during the Red Scare. With the drawing of the Iron Curtain, the onset of the Cold War, and the discovery of significant Soviet intelligence infiltration of American political, military, and scientific institutions, a sense of fear and, in many cases, near hysteria swept over the United States. As is often the case in such moments, unscrupulous demagogues can seize reasonable fears for their own political purposes.

Cohn was born into the heart of New York's corrupt machine politics. His father, Albert C. Cohn, was a judge and an influential member of the Democratic Party. An essential early relationship in Cohn's life was with the New York-based Pope family. Generoso Pope Sr. was a wealthy, politically influential concrete baron who owned *Il Prospero*, New York's largest Italian language newspaper. Cohn often rode to school with Pope Jr. in his father's limousine.

Pope Sr. was close friends with Frank "the Prime Minister" Costello, the boss of the Luciano crime family (later known as the Genovese family) after Lucky Luciano was deported to Italy. Indeed, Frank Costello was so close to the family that he served as Generoso Pope Jr.'s *actual* godfather.[22] Costello was a legend in his own time, with profound influence over the corrupt New York City political establishment embodied by Tammany Hall.

Pope Sr., through his newspaper, voiced early support for Italian fascism in the 1930s. This brought him into conflict with an anarcho-syndicalist Italian antifascist and exile named Carlo Tresca. Penn State criminologist Alan Block writes that Pope Sr., who had numerous contacts with the mafia beyond Costello, may have been complicit in the murder of Tresca.[23] Tresca's killer, the mafioso Carmine Galante, was later represented by Roy Cohn. Galante became the head of the Bonanno Crime Family and a significant figure in the international heroin trade, overseeing the legendary French Connection.

Generoso Pope Sr. had a significant impact on Cohn's life, introducing him to the corridors of political power. "Gene's father," Cohn stated in an interview, "had more to do with my incipient political career than any other single person."

After a stint working in psychological operations in the CIA, Generoso Pope Jr. founded *The National Enquirer*. Years later, under new ownership, the *Enquirer* was involved in catch-and-kill activities with unflattering stories related to Trump during his 2016 presidential run.

Roy Cohn was a child prodigy. He graduated from Columbia Law School at age 20 and, through his family's political connections, landed a job at the US Attorney's Office in Manhattan. One of his first assignments in the spring of 1949 was to write a legal memo about the US Government employee and accused Soviet agent Alger Hiss.

Hiss was a high-level member of the United States Government who was active in the New Deal, attended the WWII-era Yalta Conference with President Roosevelt, and had a hand in establishing the United Nations. In 1948, a former US Communist Party (CPUSA) member named Whitaker Chambers testified under subpoena before the House Committee on Un-American Activities (HUAC) that Hiss was a spy for the Soviet

Union. In his autobiography, Cohn claims to have been initially skeptical of the charges against Hiss, but that a discussion he had over lunch with three FBI agents assigned to the case not only convinced him of Hiss's guilt but that Communist infiltration was a problem throughout the US government.

According to Soviet records opened up after the end of the Cold War, Hiss indeed was an agent for the GRU, Soviet military intelligence. He had reportedly been recruited upon joining the State Department in 1936. Seventy years later, the GRU engaged in a hack-and-leak operation to benefit Donald Trump during the 2016 American presidential election. Hiss was arrested and convicted of perjury rather than treason, as American authorities did not want to reveal their sources to the Russians.

Cohn truly entered the limelight at the age of 23 during the trial of Julius and Ethel Rosenberg, who were accused of passing nuclear secrets to the Soviet Union. That case again involved Soviet espionage. The US government was shocked by the rapidity with which the Soviet Union developed the atomic bomb, years ahead of American predictions. That, along with the fact that the design for the first Russian bomb was almost identical to America's first atomic weapon design, led to the belief that espionage was the only viable explanation.

In January of 1950, the German refugee, physicist, and member of the British mission in the Manhattan Project, Klaus Fuchs, admitted while under interrogation by Britain's domestic intelligence agency, MI5, to have provided Soviet intelligence with classified documents related to the nuclear program throughout the Second World War. Fuchs, who had been recruited by the GRU in 1941, identified an American laboratory chemist, Harry Gold, as his courier for stolen atomic secrets. Gold was arrested by the FBI, confessed to serving as a Soviet agent, and identified David Greenglass as an additional source at Los Alamos for atomic secrets.

Following his arrest, Greenglass implicated his wife Ruth and his brother-in-law Julius Rosenberg as having recruited him for espionage activities, claiming that Julius had talked Ruth into it. Initially, David did not implicate his sister Ethel Rosenberg as involved in the spy ring. The FBI arrested Julius on July 17th, 1950. Though FBI officials and prosecutors believed that Ethel was only a minor accomplice to her husband Julius' espionage activities, they arrested her a month later as a way to exert leverage over Julius in the hopes that he would betray more Soviet spies operating in the United States. Ten days before the trial, David Greenglass told investigators that Ethel had been present during the meetings where he passed over information to Julius and that she had taken notes.

Roy Cohn wrote the chief prosecutor Irving Saypol's opening and closing statements and influenced the overall strategy of the prosecution.[24] He conducted the questioning of the prosecution's most important cooperating witness. Cohn later boasted that Irving Kaufman, the judge presiding over the trial, owed his position on the bench to Cohn's father, a judge based out of the Bronx. According to Cohn, he had arranged for Judge Kaufman to be assigned to the case through his connections to the district court's clerk's office.[25] Evidence suggests that Cohn engaged in inappropriate *ex parte* communications with Judge Kaufman when he contemplated sentencing.[26] Cohn argued for the death penalty, and that's what the Rosenbergs received.

While in the cases of Alger Hiss and the Rosenbergs, the unearthing of documents, particularly in the former Soviet Union after the end of the Cold War, has led to the scholarly consensus that they were Soviet agents, the vast majority of individuals caught up in what came to be known as the Red Scare were innocent victims and many lives were needlessly destroyed. In the 30s and 40s, Soviet intelligence succeeded in placing high-level operatives in American institutions. However, there was no threat of broad social unrest driven by a Communist fifth column. Unlike much of Europe, the Communist Party was tiny in the United States and exerted relatively little influence over organized labor. The demagoguery, hysteria, and self-serving cynicism of the era found its personification in Wisconsin Senator Joseph McCarthy, which gave rise to the epithet still used in politics today: *McCarthyism*.

Cohn was introduced to McCarthy by George Sokolsky, a radio broadcaster and Hearst newspaper columnist with close ties to the arch-conservative "China Lobby," which supported anti-communist Kuomintang forces in Washington.[27] He started working with McCarthy as his chief counsel on the House Un-American Activities Committee in January 1953. Cohn beat out a young Robert Kennedy for the job, which began a rivalry between the two that lasted for years.

The targets of McCarthy and Cohn's inquiry were wide-ranging and, almost without exception, posed little to no risk of actual Communist subversion. Guilt by association could be established for as simple a matter as representing the ACLU in court. Organizations in their crosshairs included the international public broadcaster Voice of America, the State Department, the Central Intelligence Agency, and the US Army.

McCarthy and Cohn's hunt for hidden Communists inordinately impacted members of the Jewish faith and homosexuals. This was curious indeed, as Roy Cohn was both Jewish and a closeted homosexual.[28] With the enthusiastic support of FBI director J. Edgar Hoover, himself a bachelor who lived with his mother until her death, Cohn and McCarthy's hearings led to the firing of numerous men and women accused of homosexuality from government jobs. The State Department fired over 425 employees over accusations of homosexuality during the final months of the Truman administration in 1953. All of this occurred while Cohn was known to frequent the gay bar scene in Washington, DC.[29]

Although Cohn and J. Edgar Hoover's friendship is well-documented, the nature of their relationship has been the subject of much controversy. One of Cohn and Hoover's mutual friends was a liquor baron named Lewis Rosenstiel. During prohibition, Rosenstiel's company Schenley had been supplied alcohol by Meyer Lansky, a close associate of the Genovese Crime Family. Cohn represented Rosenstiel, and together, they collaborated on forming the American Jewish League Against Communism.

In his controversial biography of J. Edgar Hoover, *Official and Confidential: The Secret Life of J. Edgar Hoover*, author Anthony Summers interviewed one of Rosenstiel's ex-wives, Susan Rosenstiel. She maintained that her husband and Roy Cohn had been in a homosexual relationship and that she had attended parties with Roy Cohn at the Plaza Hotel where J. Edgar Hoover was dressed as a woman. According to Summers, photos of Hoover made their way to Meyer Lansky, who used them for blackmail purposes. Susan Rosenstiel's claims have come under withering criticism, and many professional historians dismiss them outright.

Cohn and McCarthy finally overstepped when they took on the US Army. McCarthy's enemies found the opportunity to pounce when it came to the drafting into the military of G. David

Schine, an unpaid "Chief Consultant" working with McCarthy and Cohn. Schine, the handsome scion of a wealthy New York family, had been hired at Cohn's behest. The two quickly became inseparable, even traveling to Europe together on a quixotic and much-ridiculed trip to search for subversive Communist materials in American overseas libraries. However, as the Korean War was raging on the other side of the world, Schine was drafted into the military. Cohn pulled out all the stops to get Schine out of service, even threatening to "wreck the Army" at one point. In doing so, he sowed the seeds of McCarthy's destruction.

When it became clear that Cohn sought preferential treatment for Schine during wartime, the resulting scandal culminated in the Army-McCarthy Hearings. The hearings ultimately led to McCarthy's downfall and Cohn's banishment from Washington. Cohn was outclassed and out-lawyered by the Chief Counsel of the US Army, Joseph N. Welch, who, in a confrontation with McCarthy, uttered the famous phrase that marked the symbolic end of the McCarthy era, "At long last, have you no sense of decency?"

In 1957, Roy Cohn returned to New York City and became one of the city's most influential power brokers and possibly the most infamous lawyer in the United States. Cohn's second career was a return to his roots, a world that had been embodied for well over a century by Tammany Hall. It was a milieu with which Cohn was intimately familiar. Cohn's father was an influential judge in the Bronx, and young Roy had been fully immersed in the parochial rules and customs of Democratic machine politics in New York City from his early childhood.

In the 1960s, when his bitter rival Bobby Kennedy was Attorney General, Cohn was indicted four times but was acquitted in every case. The cases against Cohn involved mob-linked investments, complex financial crimes, and obstruction of justice charges. They were related to investments Cohn had made alongside elements of the Las Vegas organized crime gambling syndicate.[30] The corrupt Teamsters pension fund's first investment in Nevada was to Sunrise Hospital. Cohn was another investor, alongside Cleveland bootlegger, racketeer, and Vegas casino owner Moe Dalitz. Dalitz was a childhood friend of the Teamster's leader, Jimmy Hoffa. He was also a partner of Meyer Lansky's. Cohn admitted in court that he had met Lansky and Gerardo Catena, the Genovese Crime Family's representative in

New Jersey.[31]

Cohn developed a reputation as a "legal executioner," in other words, one of the most ruthless and hard-hitting attorneys in the United States. His methods were renowned as relentless and often unethical. In the 1970s, he was charged with violating banking laws in Illinois and was again acquitted. In the cases against his clients and himself, Cohn threw the kitchen sink at the prosecution and often won.

To Roy Cohn, any publicity was good publicity. Cohn's contacts within the national media and New York gossip rags were the stuff of legend. By age 13, he was already writing a gossip column for the *Bronx Home News*, the paper read by the power base that elevated his father to a judgeship. He developed a relationship with the famous syndicated Hearst gossip columnist Walter Winchell, who supported Roy during his stint with McCarthy both in print and on the radio.[32] Cohn was childhood friends with Si Newhouse, the owner of the media conglomerate Advance Publications, which included such properties as Condé Nast, publisher of *Vogue*, *Vanity Fair,* and *The New Yorker*. For years, Cohn was the gift to New York gossip columnists who kept giving, even willing to dish on his clients in certain circumstances.

Cohn's connections to organized crime were no secret. He once boasted that he had gotten Irving Saypol, the man who prosecuted the Rosenberg case, his job as US Attorney. However, he admitted that Saypol needed the okay from Frank Costello, the boss of the Genovese crime family, one of the New York Sicilian mafia's infamous Five Families. "In those days, nobody became US Attorney in New York without the O.K. from the mob," Cohn stated. "But Saypol would not have gotten the nod from Costello without me."[33]

Cohn's connections to the FBI, his friendship with J. Edgar Hoover, and his network of judges, prosecutors, and district attorneys made him an ideal lawyer for the mafia. His clients included Genovese boss Anthony "Fat Tony" Salerno, Bonanno boss Carmine "Nino" Galante, and numerous members of the Gambino crime family, including Carmine Fatico, Aniello Dellacroce, Tommy and Joe Gambino, Angelo Ruggiero, and John Gotti.[34] According to Cohn biographer Nicholas von Hoffman, federal anti-organized crime strike force members stated that in the 1970s, members of the Commission, the

American mafia's governing body, held meetings in Cohn's office.[35]

Rooted in Racism:
Donald Trump and Roy Cohn Take On the Justice Department

"I don't like lawyers," was the first thing Donald Trump said to Roy Cohn upon their introduction at Le Club in late 1973. "I think all they do is delay deals, instead of making deals, and every answer they give you is no, and they are always looking to settle instead of fight." Cohn agreed. "I'm just not built that way," Trump continued. "I'd rather fight than fold, because as soon as you fold once, you get a reputation of being a folder."

"Is this just an academic conversation?" Roy asked.

"No, it's not academic at all," Trump replied.[36]

A year earlier, in July of 1972, a black woman approached the Shorehaven Apartments complex managed by Trump and his father and inquired if any units were available. She was told none were and to look elsewhere. Shortly after that, a white woman entered the same building and asked about any vacancies. According to courtroom testimony, she was informed by the same superintendent that she could "immediately rent either one of two available apartments."[37] The superintendent didn't know that both women were "testers" sent by the civil rights organization the Urban League to determine whether discriminatory practices were occurring at the building.

Accusations of racial bias and discrimination against Fred Trump were nothing new. On Memorial Day in 1927, street fights broke out across New York. In the Bronx, a pro-Italian fascist rally descended into violence, and anti-fascists killed two Italian men. In Queens, 1000 robed members of the Ku Klux Klan violently clashed with police. Of the seven individuals arrested, one was 21-year-old Fred Trump for refusing to disperse when ordered to by the police.[38] He was later released without being charged with a crime. During the 2016 campaign, candidate Trump vehemently denied that the Fred Trump in question was his father, but the address listed in the arrest papers revealed that it was.[39]

In 1950, the legendary folk singer Woody Guthrie signed a lease to live in the Beach Haven apartment complex, Fred Trump's first development. Guthrie was disturbed by the racism practiced at the Trump complex.[40] So moved was Guthrie that he went as far as writing a song about the experience entitled "Old Man Trump," which featured the following lyrics: *I suppose that Old Man Trump knows just how/ Much racial hate/ He stirred up in that blood pot of human hearts/ When he drawed that color line/ Here at his Beach Haven family project.*[41]

Complaints about racial discrimination at Trump properties occurred throughout the 1960s. In 1963, a 33-year-old black nurse named Maxine Brown filled out an application to rent a home at Fred Trump's Wilshire Apartment complex in Jamaica, Queens. Years later, the rental agent, Stanley Leibowitz, told the New York Times his boss, Fred Trump, told him to "take the application and put it in a drawer and leave it there." In 1969, at Trump development in Cincinnati, when a white "tester" named Maggie Durham was offered an apartment and attempted to bring in a black family who had just been sent away from the same building hours earlier, the sales agent exploded into a rage.[42]

By the early 1970s, Trump properties were under the microscope by civil rights organizations that noticed a comprehensive pattern of racial discrimination. Finally, the organizations contacted the US government. On the morning of October 15th, 1973, an official from the US Department of Justice contacted Donald Trump at his office. It was a courtesy call to inform him that the DOJ was filing suit against him and his father. A similar suit had been filed earlier against the LeFrak Organization, another powerful New York real estate firm. The suit settled out of court, and the LeFrak organization offered to provide 50 black families with a month rent-free to help desegregate their buildings. Donald Trump, on the other hand, was in no mood to settle.

Though this was Donald's first run-in with government investigators, his father was experienced in these matters. In 1954, Fred Trump was subpoenaed to appear before a Congressional Banking Committee investigating profiteering among FHA developers. Fred had made $4 million by inflating construction cost estimates when applying for FHA loans and pocketing the difference. However, he maintained that nothing he did was illegal and emerged from the scandal uncharged.[43] In 1966, Fred was forced to testify before the New York State Investigations Committee about additional accusations of bilking state construction subsidies by hiding his ownership of an equipment company and charging exorbitant leasing fees.

Though he had to return some of the money, Fred emerged again legally unscathed.[44] Fred Trump was not a man to back down from the government, and his son didn't intend to be either. He just needed to find the right lawyer to fight his cause.

"My view is to tell them to go to hell," Cohn told Trump at Le Club. "[F]ight the thing in court and let them prove that you discriminated."[45]

At a press conference later that year, Cohn announced they were counter-suing the Department of Justice for $100 million. Trump denied any wrongdoing or racial discrimination at his company and accused the government of attempting to force them to rent to welfare recipients. Cohn proceeded with his characteristic bare-knuckle legal tactics, filing a contempt-of-court charge against one of the prosecutors. The judge dismissed both the countersuit and the contempt-of-court charge, and the case was eventually settled, with the Trumps signing an agreement prohibiting them from further discriminatory practices. However, as the agreement contained boilerplate language that by signing the agreement, they weren't admitting guilt, Trump claimed victory.

Trump's Early Manhattan Real Estate Deals
And Proximity to Organized Crime

On June 21st, 1970, railroad giant the Penn Central Transportation Company, the sixth largest corporation in the United States, declared bankruptcy. It was the largest bankruptcy in American history at the time. As part of the reorganization of the ailing industrial behemoth, portions of its vast land holdings were to be sold off. In 1973, Penn Central announced it would sell $1 billion worth of properties across the Northeast corridor. Over a third were located in New York City, comprising some of the most valuable property in the world.[46]

Trump read about the offerings in the paper and wrote a letter to Penn Central expressing his interest that morning. He didn't receive a response for six months. However, the young would-be developer without a single Manhattan property yet to his name had two things going for him. The first was that it was perhaps the most inauspicious moment to sell property in the Manhattan market. Like many of the city's white residents, most major corporations were leaving rather than seeking land. With rising crime rates and an impending fiscal crisis, the number of buyers in Manhattan was at its lowest since the Great Depression.

The second advantage he had was his father's longstanding friendship with the new mayor, Abe Beame. On January 1st, 1974, Abe Beame ascended into Gracie Mansion as the 104th mayor of New York City. He brought his friends from Brooklyn along with him. Stanley Steingut, head of the Democratic Madison Club and recipient of numerous donations from Fred Trump over the years, became speaker of the assembly. Fred had known Beame since he was a young accountant for the Madison Club. If those connections weren't enough, in late 1973, the Trumps had gotten behind and funded the candidacy of a little-known Brooklyn congressman named Hugh Carey, who defeated the Republican incumbent for Governor. It was a high water mark in the history of state politics for the power of the Brooklyn Democratic political machine, and it couldn't have come at a better time for Donald Trump.

"Who the hell is Donald Trump?" was the question Ned Eichler had on his mind when he arrived in New York City. Eichler worked for the Palmieri group, outside agents assigned by the shareholders of Penn Central to sell off its extensive real estate holdings. None of his associates could answer his question.[47] When Eichler met the young developer, he was struck by the intensity of his enthusiasm and the confidence with which he laid out his vision. However, Eichler knew that for anyone to develop anything in New York City, they needed political connections. Donald assured him he had them in spades, but Eichler wanted proof. What kind of proof, Donald asked? Eicher wanted to meet the mayor. Trump smiled, not a problem.

The next day, Ned Eichler was picked up outside his hotel at 1:30 pm sharp by a limo sent by Trump. By 2 pm, Eichler was sitting in the mayor's office with Donald, Fred Trump, City Planning Commissioner John Zuccotti, and Abe Beame, the newly sworn-in mayor of New York City. Donald made a few opening remarks about his high hopes for the deal at the meeting. By the end of the meeting, Beam had his arms around Fred and Donald. "Whatever Donald and Fred want, they have my complete backing," Beame exclaimed.

The Penn Central properties in Manhattan that Trump was initially interested in were the West Side rail yard and site located on 34th St. The former was the largest piece of undeveloped real estate in Manhattan, 93 acres in all. The latter was smaller but busier and in an iconic part of the city. Donald succeeded in impressing Eichler with his vision, relentless enthusiasm, and political clout. By mid-1974, Trump and Eichler were close to finalizing a deal for the properties but faced competing offers. Trump, however, wasn't about to watch this opportunity slip through his fingers.

Amid competing offers that threatened to derail his option, Trump met at the home of David Berger, an attorney representing the interests of Penn Central's shareholders and who was highly influential in determining which bid would ultimately be selected to option the properties in Manhattan. After the meeting, Berger supported Trump's bid, which eventually won the day. It was subsequently discovered that David Berger, in an entirely separate case, had filed a class action lawsuit on behalf of several New York developers against heating oil companies, accusing them of price fixing. Sometime after their meeting, Trump joined the class action suit. As Berger was slated to receive one-third of whatever awards the developers received upon the successful completion of the case, he stood to enjoy significant financial gains. Adding the Trump Organization doubled the number of apartments Berger's clients collectively operated.

The deal's shady and possibly illegal nature caught the attention of Ed Korman, the US attorney in Brooklyn. It had been brought to his attention by a tip received just before the statute of limitations had run out. Korman proceeded to impanel a grand jury. FBI agents interviewed Trump twice, informing him that he was the target of a grand jury investigation. However, given the short timeframe, Korman had just started calling witnesses before the statute of limitations ran out, and the case was abandoned without any charges.[48] This was the second time in the 1970s that Federal authorities, including the FBI had investigated Trump.

While Trump optioned the West Side yards and a site on 34th Street, the first Penn Central property he developed was a top-to-bottom renovation of the old and ailing Commodore Hotel, which stood next to Grand Central Station on 42nd Street. Named after the fabulously wealthy 19th-century shipping and railroad magnate Cornelius "Commodore" Vanderbilt, the once opulent example of Robber Baron chic had fallen on hard times like the city itself. Though the Grand Central section of 42nd Street had not yet been overtaken by pornography palaces like Times Square, the situation was deteriorating. By 1975, the nearby Chrysler Building had defaulted on its mortgage, and the crime rate in Midtown South had risen 18.5% within a year.[49] Once again, where others saw degradation, Trump saw an opportunity.

Closing the deal required Trump to manage a delicate balancing act between the Palmieri sales agents for the hotel, potential financiers, a reputable hotel operator, and the city of New York itself. Throughout the extensive negotiations, Trump employed sheer willpower, force of vision, flattery, media manipulation, family connections, and outright deception. Still, at the end of the day, he got his hotel and his first property in Manhattan. However, the process only really got rolling after a conversation Trump had in 1975 with a midlevel city bureaucrat.

An attorney named Michael Bailkin sat across from Donald Trump in his small office within the bowels of the Lower Manhattan Development Corporation and listened as the developer described his plans for the reinvention of the Commodore Hotel. Trump described his vision to redo the crumbling facade, refurbish the interior, and enlist Hyatt to manage a wholly reimagined hotel that would reverse the seemingly unstoppable slide of midtown itself. Trump went further, saying he could line up financing and get the support of key political players in the city, but he needed to figure out one key detail: how to receive a historic tax abatement from the city. He had tried to push one through the state legislature but failed. Even with the Beame administration behind him, the effort was swallowed up by the fiscal crisis that hit the city like a tidal wave.[50]

Bailkin came up with a novel solution on the spot. He suggested that Trump purchase the property, donate it to the city, and then have the city lease it back to him for 99 years. The city would then be on the hook for the property tax bill and could charge Trump a negotiated rent to cover a previously agreed-upon portion of the tax bill. Trump was thrilled with the idea. Bailkin was transferred from his previous city position and soon ran in and out of City Hall promoting the deal, which was the only significant development deal at perhaps one of the lowest ebbs of the city's financial history.

After additional meetings, the idea was refined so that

instead of Trump donating the hotel to the city, he would donate it to the now largely defunct Urban Development Corporation (UDC). The UDC was created by New York Governor Nelson Rockefeller in 1968 to integrate housing throughout the state. To do so, it was granted extraordinary powers to overrule local ordinances and push through projects without slogging through endless red tape. However, by 1975, the organization had fallen into bankruptcy. Despite this, it retained formidable legal powers which, if placed at the disposal of Donald Trump, had the power to grant him his wish of becoming a Manhattan developer. The irony of having an organization created to integrate housing pad the pockets of a man recently sued by the DOJ for housing discrimination was apparently lost on everyone involved.

Trump encountered resistance from the head of the UDC, critics in city government, and competing hotel operators stunned by what they saw as an unprecedented city giveaway to a young and untested developer, but he deftly navigated these shoals by structuring a deal whereby he would share some profits with the city in a way that allowed him to use creative accounting to limit just how much he shared. Meanwhile, he played the many different sides of the deal off one another by exaggerating the enthusiasm of one party to another, releasing overly optimistic press reports, claiming deals still in negotiation had been completed in his favor, representing documents signed by only himself as done deals, inflating the amount of financing he had secured and generally controlling the information flow among the major players in the deal to keep the project lumbering forward.

However, while the major players now all agreed in principle to move forward on the project, Trump still needed to push the deal through the byzantine maze of New York's multifaceted approval process. To complicate matters, Abraham Beame, fatally weakened by the fiscal crisis, lost his mayoral reelection bid to a charismatic reformer from the Village by the name of Edward Koch. Koch had run on an anti-machine reform platform. Not wanting to leave anything to chance, Trump desperately wanted to have the tax abatement etched in stone before the new mayor, who had campaigned against cronyism and political favoritism, took office. Luckily, Trump knew just the man for the job.

By the mid-1970s, Roy Cohn was more than just an infamous attorney; he was New York City's preeminent power broker and fixer. In the heady days of the transition between the Beame and Koch administrations, Cohn introduced Donald to the outgoing deputy mayor, Stanley Friedman. Known as "Bugsy" ever since growing up in the schoolyards of the Bronx, the cigar-chomping Friedman was a consummate example of a savvy operator in New York machine politics. He had worked his way up to deputy mayor by forging connections and making deposits into the favor bank at the Bronx Democratic clubhouse. Now that Beame was out of office, Friedman needed to find another gig. In his last weeks in office, Cohn offered him a six-figure, cushy job at his law firm and even an office on the fifth floor of his townhouse.

Friedman returned the favor by leading a mad dash in the final weeks of the Beame administration to drag Trump's coveted tax abatement across the finish line. Working at light speed in bureaucratic time, Friedman guided Trump's pet project through nine regulatory agencies. When all was said and done, Trump received a 40-year, $400 million tax abatement, the largest in the city's history. On the final day of the Beame administration, Friedman signed a special permit that allowed Trump to build a hotel restaurant overhanging 42nd Street called the Garden Room.

Cohn wasn't just using Friedman to help Trump. Friedman had long stood in the wings of the Bronx Democratic Party as a potential successor to its then hopelessly corrupt leader, Pat Cunningham. As a child, Cohn sat in on his father's dinner parties with Cunningham's predecessor Ed "Boss" Flynn and Carmine DeSapio, head of the Tammany Hall political machine and ally of mafia chieftain Frank Costello.[51] In 1976, Cunningham was indicted for illegally arranging a judicial nomination, influence peddling and concealing a payment from a bank and prosecutors were just getting started.[52] When Cunningham fell in 1978, Friedman took his place as the leader of the Bronx Democratic Party, a position of immense influence in the city. With the head of the Bronx Democratic Party working in the office next to him, Roy Cohn's influence had seeped into the very marrow of the city.

In addition to Cohn, Fred Trump played an indispensable role in his son's success. Fred attended the first meeting with Mayor Beam and Eichler, providing a reassuring presence for all involved that the real estate veteran was backing the project. He provided the essential guarantee that allowed Donald to take over the Commodore mortgage. To finance the construction, Fred and Hyatt Hotels guaranteed the bank Manufacturers Hanover, which led them to loan out $70 million to get the project underway. When there were construction cost overruns, Fred bailed Donald out with a $35 million unsecured line of credit, a $30 million second mortgage from his old bank Chase, and another loan offered through one of Fred's corporations.[53]

When construction commenced on the Commodore to transform it into the new Grand Hyatt, the subcontractors used for the project were connected to organized crime. Both the concrete contractor and supplier, North Berry and Transit-Mix, respectively, were accused in legal documents of being participants in cartels operated by the mafia. According to the FBI, Cleveland Wrecking, the demolition company, and the first contractor Trump personally selected for the project, was partially owned by an associate of the Scarfo crime family, one of the most violent and notorious gangs operating on the streets of Philadelphia and Atlantic City. According to law enforcement documents, the subcontractor, Wachtel Plumbing, was involved with a mafia-backed shakedown in Atlantic City while it was working on the Hyatt.[54]

Donald took a hands-on approach to overseeing the project, as did his new wife, Ivana Trump. A Czech national born Ivana Zelníčková, she and Trump were married during the Easter of 1977 in a ceremony held at Marble Collegiate Church attended by city luminaries including Roy Cohn and Mayor Beame.[55] Shortly before the wedding, Donald and Ivana sparred over the prenuptial agreement written up by Cohn, who had advised Donald not to marry. Still, matters were temporarily resolved by the time the young couple tied the knot. Donald and Ivana Trump's marriage would develop into one of the most notable, gossiped about, and ultimately infamous of the 1980s.

Nine months after they wed, Ivana gave birth to a son, Donald Jr. He was the first of three children Donald and Ivanka would have together. However, Ivana was far more than a stay-at-home mother. Ivana became heavily involved in Donald's business, regularly visiting the Grand Hyatt construction site. Dressed in designer outfits and heels, she confidently offered her interior design recommendations despite her lack of experience. Donald and Ivana entered the ranks of the New York glitterati and became fixtures of the city's social scene.

Roy Cohn, too, was at the height of his powers. New York's famously liberal social and political establishment let bygones be bygones when it came to Cohn's prominent role in McCarthyism. As Cohn's biographer wrote, "celebrity is its own exculpation."[56] It helped that he was the attorney for the hottest club in 1970s New York, Studio 54, described by Frank Rich in *New York Magazine* as "[t]hat sprawling Valhalla of the disco era, a nexus for boldface names, omnivorous drug consumption, anonymous sex, and managerial larceny."[57]

The epochal club was owned by Cohn clients Steve Rubell and Ian Schrager. Schrager's father, Louis Schrager, had been a Williamsburg-based loan shark and racketeer. According to a New York State Liquor Authority file, the elder Schrager was "a convicted felon who was a known associate of Meyer Lansky and was second only to Herman Siegel in Lansky's loansharking and numbers rackets."[58]

Cohn became a much-coveted gatekeeper to the club and was approached by celebrities, local politicians, and foreign dignitaries for the privilege of gaining entry. By this period, Cohn's intensely promiscuous, secret homosexual life was becoming increasingly brazen, and it wasn't unusual for him to be seen among crowds of young men at the club. Donald and Ivana were regulars.

"What happened at Studio 54 will never, ever happen again," Trump told his biographer Timothy O'Brien. "You didn't have AIDS. You didn't have the problems you do now… I saw things happening there that, to this day, I have never seen again. I would watch supermodels getting screwed, well-known supermodels getting screwed on a bench in the middle of the room. There were seven of them, and each one was getting screwed by a different guy. This was in the middle of the room. Stuff that couldn't happen today because of the problems of death."[59]

Newly married, a regular feature in New York's gossip columns, and riding high off his closing of the Grand Hyatt deal, Trump was about to embark upon a namesake project that would come to define him in the eyes of most Americans to this very day. Though the construction of the Grand Hyatt was less than half done, the young developer had higher ambitions. He wanted to develop a brand-defining residential tower with his name on it.

While Donald Trump has spent decades exaggerating and embellishing his accomplishments and business acumen, it is safe to say that the conception and development of Trump Tower was a career-defining business coup that would propel Trump into the popular imagination as being synonymous with wealth, power, and success. Trump's first inspired insight was the location.

The Bonwit Teller department store was located on the corner of Fifth Avenue and 56th Street, one of the choicest in Manhattan. Just a few blocks from Central Park, the store shared the location with Tiffany's, the famous jewelry store immortalized by Truman Capote's novel *Breakfast at Tiffany's* and the film starring Audrey Hepburn. Unlike others who thought the location was unattainable, Trump was bold enough to make inquiries. In a stroke of luck, the Executive Vice President of the Trump Organization at the time, Louise Sunshine, had a connection inside the department store.[60] Donald reached out and discovered that Bonwit Teller was struggling and was able to swoop down and acquire a six-month lease for $25 million.

Upon acquiring the lease, Trump engaged in another high-wire balancing act among different interests. His financier was interested in the project, but only if he could slash through all the red tape and replace the smaller Art Deco Bonwit Teller building with a vast new residential tower, possibly the tallest in the city to that point. To do so, he needed to gain air rights from the other buildings in the vicinity and special permits and approvals from the city.

Trump succeeded in running the gauntlet of boards and commissions by utilizing his father's and Roy Cohn's political connections, making strategic campaign contributions, glad-handing, and, when necessary, putting up a fight. He eventually won the air rights over the nearby buildings and was granted the required permits and authorizations to begin construction. However, as construction progressed, Trump's relationship with Mayor Koch and his administration deteriorated, leading Koch to push for the rejection of Trump's significant tax abatement. Trump responded by siccing Cohn on the case. They filed a lawsuit and won in court, and the abatement, his second in just a few years, was left untouched.

The inspiration for Trump's new project was Olympic Tower, a nearby 52-story development located on Fifth Avenue across the street from Rockefeller Center. The building was owned by the Greek billionaire Aristotle Onassis. Olympic Tower replaced the department store Best's and was located next door to the jewelry store Cartier. In a model that Trump Tower imitated, it was the first of what became known as mixed-use projects, which incorporated retail, office space, and private residential units. It featured an ample indoor public space decorated with an artificial waterfall. Like Trump, Onassis managed to get the city to award him a significant tax abatement so he could move forward with the project.[61] Trump was friends with one of Olympic Tower's most notable residents, the Saudi billionaire and arms merchant Adnan Khashoggi, and reportedly was so impressed by the size of the living room in his penthouse that he had his decorator clandestinely attempt to find out its exact measurements so he could ensure that the living room for his unit in Trump Tower was larger.[62]

Before construction could begin, the old Bonwit Teller building had to be demolished. When searching for a demolition contractor, Donald opted for Kaszycki & Sons Contractors, the cheapest he could find. William Kaszycki's workers consisted of roughly 200 Polish illegal aliens who Kaszycki's wife recruited.[63] These Poles worked for a mere fraction of union rates, and many were paid even less than the pittance they had originally been promised. After toiling through twelve-to-eighteen-hour days, the workers either slept on the concrete floor of the construction site during the frigid New York winter or as many as eight at a time would pile into an individual motel room. Workers went without hard hats and, worse still, given that they were working in an asbestos-filled environment, were not provided with facemasks or safety goggles. Known as the Polish Brigade, these workers lacked power tools and resorted to demolishing the building with sledgehammers.[64] During the demolition, several Art Deco statues that made up the building's facade were obliterated even though Donald had promised to donate them to the Metropolitan Museum of Art.

Even though the Polish workers were already receiving substandard wages, many were not paid at all. The appalling nature of their work conditions and the fact that many weren't being paid on time or at all led to increasing dissatisfaction and eventually rage onsite. Things finally boiled over when some workers physically threatened to hang Thomas Macari, Trump's representative onsite, off the edge of the building. Following this, Trump hastily contacted Daniel Sullivan, a labor fixer he had worked with on the Grand Hyatt.

A new demolition crew from the Homewreckers Local 95 union was brought on to oversee the project. According to Trump biographer and Pulitzer Prize-winning journalist David Cay Johnston, federal court records subsequently established that the union was under the control of mafia dons who Roy Cohn represented. The demolition proceeded apace, and the corrupt overseers did not raise any issues about the employment of non-union workers or the fact that they were not provided with adequate safety equipment.[65]

The mafia's involvement in a New York City construction project is unsurprising. By the late 1980s, the problem had become so pervasive that Governor Mario Cuomo ordered a full report drawn up by New York State's Organized Crime Task Force. A 239-page report entitled Corruption and Racketeering in the New York City Construction Industry followed, released in December of 1989. The report stated unequivocally that their investigation had "establish[ed] beyond any doubt that corruption and racketeering pervade New York City's construction industry." The report continues: "We use the term "racketeering" to refer to the activities of professional criminals -- those who engage in crime as a business. They may be full-time criminals and members of criminal syndicates, or they may operate as businessmen, union officers, or government officials who systematically use their legitimate positions for illegitimate ends. Racketeers span the gamut from unskilled hustlers to sophisticated leaders of large legitimate or illegitimate organizations. New York City's construction industry has many types of racketeers. By far, the most important are members and associates of New York City's five Cosa Nostra organized crime families. They have been involved in the City's construction industry for decades, utilizing their organizational expertise, underworld networks, and reputation and capacity for violence. Casa Nostra's entrenchment in construction companies and unions makes the industry's "crime problem" all the more serious and the need to address it all the more imperative."[66]

Fred Trump worked with mob-linked individuals during his long career as a developer. While building his Beach Haven development in Brooklyn, he partnered with a brick contractor,

Willie Tomasello, who owned 25% of the project. Tomasello was later identified by the New York State's Organized Crime Task Force as an associate of the Genovese and Gambino Crime families. Tomasello often provided Fred with capital and helped him with union labor disputes.[67] In Tomasello's other ventures, he had worked with individuals associated with the DiBono family and their plastering company, Mario & DiBono. Frank Scalise, a drug runner for the notorious founder of the ruling Commission of New York's Five Families, Charles "Lucky" Luciano, was a hidden partner in Mario & DiBono.[68]

Trump Tower was unusual among contemporary developments in New York at the time in that it was constructed using primarily concrete instead of steel. Indeed, it was the tallest and most expensive private concrete building of its time. By the late 1970s, the unions and contractors that comprised the concrete industry in New York had been infiltrated by organized crime at every level. While other developers at the time, including the powerful LeFrak and Resnick families, were complaining to the FBI about the mafia-dominated concrete cartel, Trump did not seem bothered by the corrupt arrangement.[69]

In 1980, before construction began on Trump Tower, prosecutors subpoenaed Trump regarding his relationship with John Cody, a three-time felon and head of the local Teamsters 282 union. Cody, who had previously worked with Fred Trump, controlled the truckers who made time-sensitive concrete deliveries to construction sites, including Trump Tower, where even the threat of delays could add debilitating expenses to a project.[70] Law enforcement had determined that Cody was a labor racketeer and corrupt associate of the Gambino crime family, with Cody personally paying Carlo Gambino $200,000 per year.[71] The New York Organized Crime Task Force had received a tip that Trump had been the victim of a shakedown in which Cody was to receive a free apartment in the newly constructed tower and, in return, assure labor peace.

"You know how I dealt with him? I told him to go fuck himself all the time," Trump told his biographer Timothy L. O'Brien in 2005, after, O'Brien wryly noted, he was assured that Cody was dead. "If you say it enough, if you say it enough, they go on and go after somebody else. This guy was one psychopathic, crazy bastard… There was something wrong with him mentally. John Cody was real scum."[72]

In response to his subpoena, Trump told prosecutors that he had not been the victim of a shakedown. However, despite his contemporary denials and subsequent bravura, Trump's relationship with Cody was anything but an innocent business relationship. Cody exercised immense power over the project. "My father walked all over him. He did. Any time Trump didn't do what he was told, my father would shut down his job for the day. No deliveries; 400 guys sitting around," Cody's son Michael claimed when asked about his father's relationship with Trump. He described Trump as "a guy who would talk tough, but as soon as you confronted him, he would cry like a little girl. He was all talk, no action."[73]

Cody's influence can be seen in Trump's accommodation of a mysterious Austrian socialite, Verina Hixon. Hixon, believed by some to be Cody's mistress, has maintained that the two were only platonic friends. Though she had no known income, Hixon lived a jet-setting lifestyle among New York's wealthy elite. She initially lived at Olympic Tower, but eventually, six units on the top two floors of Trump Tower worth nearly $10 million were purchased in her name. Donald signed a unique agreement with her that required him to design the units to her specifications. If Trump ever hesitated to fulfill her requests, Cody confronted him personally or sent someone from the union to make sure the brash young developer acquiesced.[74] Cody himself may have intended to live in one of the units. However, in 1984, he was convicted of racketeering and sent to prison. Upon his release, Cody attempted to arrange for his union successor to be assassinated, but the plot failed when the would-be hitman turned out to be an FBI informant.[75] Cody was arrested again for attempted murder and returned to prison. Following Cody's incarceration, Trump engaged in an extended legal battle with Hixon that eventually led to her vacating Trump Tower.[76]

Cody was an associate of Roy Cohn, but he wasn't the only Cohn connection involved with the construction of Trump Tower. At the time, organized crime controlled the concrete industry in New York City through what was known as the Concrete Club.[77] The club consisted of seven companies fronted by seemingly legitimate management but owned by a combination of mafia families, which received a 2% kickback of each contract over $2 million.[78] One of those companies, S & A Concrete, was selected to work on the Trump Tower construction project. The company was fronted by a Cody associate named Ken Auletta, but in reality, it was jointly owned by Anthony "Fat Tony" Salerno and Paul Castellano, the underboss and boss of the Genovese and Gambino crime families, respectively.[79]

Cody, Salerno, and Castellano were all clients of Cohn's. Joe Culek, a chauffeur for Salerno's frontman Edward "Biff" Holloran in the concrete racket, described to a federal prosecutor how he "ran on foot" to Cohn's office and handed him an envelope full of $20,000 cash for Cohn to give to Salerno.[80] Vincent "Fish" Cafaro, a Genovese soldier turned FBI informant,[81] told authorities that he had given Cohn $175,000 cash in what he assumed was used for a payoff to get time taken off Genovese *capo* Mario Gigante's prison sentence.[82] Cafaro told the FBI that Cohn told him three years would cost $250,000.[83] The money was laundered through Cohn's office, and Gigante's sentence was subsequently reduced by two years. A Cohn staffer told investigative journalist Wayne Barrett that Cohn arranged a meeting between Trump and Salerno in his townhouse while S & A Concrete was working on the Trump Tower project.[84] In the summer of 1982, a cement workers' strike paralyzed New York construction except at Trump Tower, where work continued without interruption.[85]

After Olympic Tower, Trump Tower was the second building in New York that allowed for units to be purchased by anonymous Limited Liability Corporations (LLCs) and offshore corporate entities, a practice that lent itself to potential money laundering and abuse. An early buyer was Gino A.G. Bianchini, who was wanted in Italy on criminal charges of illegal currency export.[86] Another early resident, Cuban-born American citizen, and financier Roberto Polo, purchased six Trump Tower apartments using offshore corporations.[87] Polo, who was wanted in three countries and was eventually imprisoned in Italy for embezzlement, was suspected by some to be dealing in money laundering, drug trafficking, and potentially even arms running.[88] Other early criminal residents were Sheldon and Jay Weinberg,[89], a father and son duo who were convicted of masterminding the largest Medicaid fraud in the history of the program up to that point.[90] Investigators working to help the government of Haiti repatriate assets stolen by the exiled dictator Jean-Claude "Baby Doc" Duvalier discovered that in 1983, he had used a

Panamanian shell corporation to purchase a Trump Tower condominium for $1.65 million.[91]

In 1981, Lucchese crime family associate and Cohn-client Robert Hopkins purchased a $2 million 59th and 60th floor duplex at Trump Tower.[92] Cohn put together the deal, arranging for the eye-popping price to raise Trump Tower's early market value during a crucial time in the sales campaign. In fact, at the time of the purchase, the tower's construction had just begun. Hopkins was at the time operating one of the largest illicit gambling operations in New York City, earning up to $500,000 per week through a number-running racket that operated out of over 100 locations.[93] The mafia backer for his criminal operation was Joseph "Joe Beck" DiPalermo, a leading figure in the Lucchese crime family involved in the narcotics trade known by authorities as "the dean of the dope dealers."[94]

The mortgage broker for the deal was yet another individual linked to organized crime, Francis Lamagra. As Hopkins had no legitimate income, Lamagra submitted falsified tax documents to the lending bank by forging the name of an incapacitated accountant. Lamagra attempted the same forgery scam in 1983 for the Bonanno crime family *capo* Louie "Ha Ha" Attanasio but was caught and convicted for conspiring to prepare false tax returns.[95] At the closing, Hopkins arrived with a suitcase carrying $200,000 and proceeded to count the cash on a Trump Tower conference table. Trump was personally present as he did so. After the money was counted to Trump's satisfaction, Lamagra rode in a Trump limo and deposited it in the bank.[96]

Hopkins was arrested while in Trump Tower on charges related to his gambling operation as well as for arranging the murder of a rival mafioso. New York state investigators had tapped the phones to Hopkin's Trump Tower duplex, where they determined he ran his illegal business[97]. Manhattan District Attorney Robert Morgenthau also scrutinized Hopkins for his connection to the Bronx City Planning Commissioner Theodore E. Teah. Teah, a former associate at Cohn's law firm, served as Hopkin's attorney, and his name was on a sales agreement made on behalf of Hopkins that was later used to raise the million-dollar bail for the murder charge. Teah was also a top aide to Cohn partner and head of the Bronx Democratic Party Stanley Friedman, the same Friedman who had pushed through Trump's Grand Hyatt tax abatement in the final days of the Beame administration.[98]

Trump's associations with organized crime extended beyond real estate. In addition to development, Trump pursued a career in licensing his name. He did so for the first time in 1988 when Trump released a line of namesake limousines. The limos were built by Dillinger Coach Works, named for the famed Depression-era gangster. Dillinger Coach Works was owned and operated by John Staluppi and Jack Schwartz. Staluppi, who had been investigated by Long Island's Organized Crime Task Force, the FBI, and Atlantic City's Department of Gaming Enforcement, was a member of the Colombo crime family and was known to have met that family's boss, Carmine "The Snake" Persico, on at least two separate occasions. Jack Schwartz had previously been convicted of extortion.[99] However, before he came to rely on branding as a business model full-time, Donald Trump decided to try out his hand as a casino magnate in Atlantic City

[1] Blair, Gwenda. *The Trumps: Three Generations of Builders and a President.* New York, NY: Simon & Schuster, Inc, 2000. Pg. 50

[2] Johnston, David Cay. *The Making of Donald Trump.* Brooklyn, NY: Melville House Publishing, 2016. Pg. 5

[3] Blair, Gwenda. *The Trumps: Three Generations of Builders and a President.* New York, NY: Simon & Schuster, Inc, 2000. Pg. 121

[4] Barrett, Wayne. *Trump: The Greatest Show On Earth.* New York, NY: Regan Arts, 2016. Pg. 37-39

[5] Blair, Gwenda. *The Trumps: Three Generations of Builders and a President.* New York, NY: Simon & Schuster, Inc, 2000. Pg. 146

[6] Trump, Mary L. *Too Much And Never Enough: How My Family Created The World's Most Dangerous Man.* New York, NY, 2020. Pg. 24

[7] Kranish, Michael; Fisher, Marc. *Trump Revealed: An American Journey of Ambition, Ego, Money, and Power.* New York, NY: Scribner, 2016. Pg. 33

[8] Trump, Donald J.; Schwartz, Tony. *The Art Of The Deal.* New York, NY: Random House Inc, 1987. Pg. 49

[9] Fisher, Marc. "'Grab that record': How Trump's high school transcript was hidden," *The Washington Post.* March 5th, 2019

[10] O'Brien, Timothy L. *TrumpNation: The Art Of Being The Donald.* New York, NY: Warner Business Books, 2005. Pg. 44

[11] Blair, Gwenda. *The Trumps: Three Generations of Builders and a President.* New York, NY: Simon & Schuster, Inc, 2000. Pg. 173

[12] Viser, Matt. "Even in college, Donald Trump was brash," *The Boston Globe.* August 28th, 2015

[13] D'Antonio, Michael. *The Truth About Trump.* New York, NY: Thomas Dunne Books, 2016. Pg. 69

[14] Whitlock, Craig. "Questions linger about Trump's draft deferments during Vietnam War," *The Washington Post.* June 21st, 2015

[15] Blair, Gwenda. *The Trumps: Three Generations of Builders and a President.* New York, NY: Simon & Schuster, Inc, 2000. Pg. 243

[16] Horowitz, Jason. "For Donald Trump, Lessons From a Brother's Suffering," *The*

New York Times. January 2nd, 2006

[17] Kranish, Michael. "Trump pressured his alcoholic brother about his career. Now he says he has regrets," The Washington Post. August 8th, 2019

[18] Blair, Gwenda. *The Trumps: Three Generations of Builders and a President.* New York, NY: Simon & Schuster, Inc, 2000. Pg. 242

[19] Trump, Donald J.; Schwartz, Tony. *The Art Of The Deal.* New York, NY: Random House Inc, 1987. Pg. 65

[20] Andelman, David A. "Le Club, Restaurant of Jet Set, Cited for Health Code Violations," *The New York Times.* July 9th, 1974

[21] Haden-Guest, Anthony. "Donald Trump's Nights Out With Roy Cohn at Le Club," *The Daily Beast.* January 30th, 2016

[22] Delloye, Tate. "The Godfather of Tabloid: How childhood friend of Roy Cohn and son of an influential political fixer with ties to Mussolini left the CIA to start the National Enquirer with a loan from mob boss Frank Costello," *The Daily Mail.* November 20th, 2019

[23] Block, Alan. *Space, Time & Organized Crime.* New Brunswick, NJ. Transaction Publishers. Pg. 150-160

[24] von Hoffman, Nicholas. *Citizen Cohn.* New York, NY: DoubleDay, 1988. Pg. 96

[25] Zion, Sidney. *The Autobiography of Roy Cohn.* New York, NY: Lyle Stewart, Inc, 1988. Pg. 65

[26] Radosh, Ronald; Milton, Joyce. *The Rosenberg File.* New York, NY: Yale University Press, 1997. Pg. 276-277

[27] "The Press: The Man in the Middle," Time Magazine. May 24th, 1954

[28] von Hoffman, Nicholas. *Citizen Cohn.* New York, NY: DoubleDay, 1988. Pg. 108

[29] von Hoffman, Nicholas. *Citizen Cohn.* New York, NY: DoubleDay, 1988. Pg. 132

[30] Turner, Wallace. *Gambler's Money: The New Force in American Life.* New York, NY. Houghton Mifflin. 1965

[31] Bigart, Homer. "US Begins Calling Witnesses in Roy Cohn's Perjury Trial," The New York Times. March 27th, 1964

[32] von Hoffman, Nicholas. *Citizen Cohn.* New York, NY: DoubleDay, 1988. Pg. 76-77

[33] Zion, Sidney. *The Autobiography of Roy Cohn.* New York, NY: Lyle Stewart, Inc, 1988. Pg. 60

[34] Davis, John H. *Mafia Dynasty: The Rise and Fall of the Gambino Crime Family.* New York, NY: HarperCollins Publishers, Inc. 1993. Pg. 161

[35] von Hoffman, Nicholas. *Citizen Cohn.* New York, NY: DoubleDay, 1988. Pg. 415-416

[36] Trump, Donald J.; Schwartz, Tony. *The Art Of The Deal.* New York, NY: Random House Inc, 1987. Pg. 67

[37] Kranish, Michael; O'Harrow Jr., Robert. "Inside the government's racial bias case against Donald Trump's company, and how he fought it," *The Washington Post.* January 23rd, 2016

[38] Bump, Philip. "In 1927, Donald Trump's father was arrested after a Klan riot in Queens," *The Washington Post.* February 29th, 2016

[39] Johnston, David Cay. *The Making of Donald Trump.* Brooklyn, NY: Melville House Publishing, 2016. Pg. 10

[40] Kaplan, Thomas. "Woody Guthrie Wrote of His Contempt for His Landlord, Donald Trump's Father," *The New York Times.* January 25th, 2016

[41] Johnston, David Cay. *The Making of Donald Trump.* Brooklyn, NY: Melville House Publishing, 2016. Pg. 35

[42] Mahler, Jonathan; Eder, Steve. "'No Vacancies' for Blacks: How Donald Trump Got His Start and Was First Accused of Bias," *The New York Times.* August 27th, 2016

[43] D'Antonio, Michael. *The Truth About Trump.* New York, NY: Thomas Dunne Books, 2016. Pg. 15-19

[44] Barrett, Wayne. *Trump: The Greatest Show On Earth.* New York, NY: Regan Arts, 2016. Pg. 64

[45] Trump, Donald J.; Schwartz, Tony. *The Art Of The Deal*. New York, NY: Random House Inc, 1987. Pg. 68

[46] Blair, Gwenda. *The Trumps: Three Generations of Builders and a President*. New York, NY: Simon & Schuster, Inc, 2000. Pg. 255-256

[47] Barrett, Wayne. *Trump: The Greatest Show On Earth*. New York, NY: Regan Arts, 2016. Pg. 86-87

[48] Johnston, David Cay. *The Making of Donald Trump*. Brooklyn, NY: Melville House Publishing, 2016. Pg. 43

[49] D'Antonio, Michael. *The Truth About Trump*. New York, NY: Thomas Dunne Books, 2016. Pg. 100

[50] Barrett, Wayne. *Trump: The Greatest Show On Earth*. New York, NY: Regan Arts, 2016. Pg. 114

[51] Kandell, Jonathan. "Carmine De Sapio, Political Kingmaker and Last Tammany Hall Boss, Dies at 95," *The New York Times*. July 28th, 2004

[52] Martin, Douglas. "Patrick J. Cunningham, 74, Leader of Bronx Dies," *The New York Times*. December 5th, 2002

[53] Blair, Gwenda. *The Trumps: Three Generations of Builders and a President*. New York, NY: Simon & Schuster, Inc, 2000. Pg. 305

[54] Barrett, Wayne. *Trump: The Greatest Show On Earth*. New York, NY: Regan Arts, 2016. Pg. 156

[55] Brenner, Marie. "After The Gold Rush," *Vanity Fair*. September, 1990

[56] von Hoffman, Nicholas. *Citizen Cohn*. New York, NY: DoubleDay, 1988. Pg. 397

[57] Rich, Frank. "The Original Donald Trump," *New York Magazine*. April 30th, 2018

[58] Post, Henry. "Documents Link Studio 54 to Mob," *The Village Voice*. January 15th, 1979

[59] O'Brien, Timothy L. *TrumpNation: The Art Of Being The Donald*. New York, NY: Warner Business Books, 2005. Pg. 53

[60] Barrett, Wayne. *Trump: The Greatest Show On Earth*. New York, NY: Regan Arts, 2016. Pg. 172

[61] Blair, Gwenda. *The Trumps: Three Generations of Builders and a President*. New York, NY: Simon & Schuster, Inc, 2000. Pg. 308-309

[62] Barrett, Wayne. *Trump: The Greatest Show On Earth*. New York, NY: Regan Arts, 2016. Pg. 197

[63] Barrett, Wayne. *Trump: The Greatest Show On Earth*. New York, NY: Regan Arts, 2016. Pg. 181

[64] Johnston, David Cay. *The Making of Donald Trump*. Brooklyn, NY: Melville House Publishing, 2016. Pg. 70

[65] Johnston, David Cay. *The Making of Donald Trump*. Brooklyn, NY: Melville House Publishing, 2016. Pg. 72

[66] *Corruption and Racketeering in the New York City Construction Industry*. Interim Report by the New York State Organized Crime Task Force. Ithaca, NY: ILR Press, 1988. Pg. 13

[67] Johnston, David Cay. *The Making of Donald Trump*. Brooklyn, NY: Melville House Publishing, 2016. Pg. 14

[68] Barrett, Wayne. *Trump: The Greatest Show On Earth*. New York, NY: Regan Arts, 2016. Pg. 49

[69] Johnston, David Cay. *The Making of Donald Trump*. Brooklyn, NY: Melville House Publishing, 2016. Pg. 44

[70] Dickey, Christopher; Daly, Michael. "The Party Girl Who Brought Trump To His Knees," *The Daily Beast*. April 13th, 2017

[71] *Corruption and Racketeering in the New York City Construction Industry*. Interim Report by the New York State Organized Crime Task Force. Ithaca, NY: ILR Press, 1988. Pg. 65

[72] O'Brien, Timothy L. *TrumpNation: The Art Of Being The Donald*. New York, NY: Warner Business Books, 2005. Pg. 70

[73] Dickey, Christopher; Daly, Michael. "The Party Girl Who Brought Trump To His

Knees," *The Daily Beast*. April 13th, 2017

[74] Barrett, Wayne. *Trump: The Greatest Show On Earth*. New York, NY: Regan Arts, 2016. Pg. 186-189

[75] Wolff, Craig. "Ex-Teamster Leader Arrested in Death Plot," *The New York Times*. May 31st, 1991

[76] Dickey, Christopher; Daly, Michael. "The Party Girl Who Brought Trump To His Knees," *The Daily Beast*. April 13th, 2017

[77] Smothers, Ronald. "Jury Is Told Crime Families Control Concrete Business," *The New York Times*. January 15th, 1986

[78] Raab, Selwyn. *Five Families: The Rise, Decline, and Resurgence of America's Most Powerful Mafia Empires*. New York, NY: Thomas Dunne Books, 2016. Pg. 285-290

[79] Barrett, Wayne. *Trump: The Greatest Show On Earth*. New York, NY: Regan Arts, 2016. Pg. 186-189

[80] Rowan, Roy. "The Mafia's Bite of the Big Apple," *FORTUNE Magazine*. June 6th, 1988

[81] Lubasch, Arnold H. "Major Mafia Leader Turns Informer, Secretly Recording Meetings of Mob," *The New York Times*. March 21st, 1987

[82] Raab, Selwyn. *Five Families: The Rise, Decline, and Resurgence of America's Most Powerful Mafia Empires*. New York, NY: Thomas Dunne Books, 2016. Pg. 233

[83] Raab, Selwyn. *Five Families: The Rise, Decline, and Resurgence of America's Most Powerful Mafia Empires*. New York, NY: Thomas Dunne Books, 2016. Pg. 558

[84] Barrett, Wayne. *Trump: The Greatest Show On Earth*. New York, NY: Regan Arts, 2016. Pg. 192

[85] Johnston, David Cay. *The Making of Donald Trump*. Brooklyn, NY: Melville House Publishing, 2016. Pg. 46

[86] Hettena, Seth. *Trump/Russia: A Definitive History*. Brooklyn, NY: Melville House, 2018. Pg. 10

[87] Barrett, Wayne. *Trump: The Greatest Show On Earth*. New York, NY: Regan Arts, 2016. Pg. 193

[88] Dunne, Dominick. "The Fall of Roberto Polo," *Vanity Fair*. October 1998

[89] Barrett, Wayne. *Trump: The Greatest Show On Earth*. New York, NY: Regan Arts, 2016. Pg. 194

[90] Raab, Selwyn. "Family Rises Using Fraud on Medicaid," *The New York Times*. January 9th, 1989

[91] Dorfman, Dan. "On The Trail Of Baby Doc," *New York Magazine*. July 14th, 1986. Pg. 19

[92] Though Trump Tower was marketed at 68 stories, it was in fact only 58 stories. Floor numbers were changed to make the Tower sound taller.

[93] Barrett, Wayne. *Trump: The Greatest Show On Earth*. New York, NY: Regan Arts, 2016. Pg. 195-196

[94] Capeci, Jerry; Robbins, Tom. "Secret mob history of Ray's Pizza," *The New York Post*. September 22nd, 2013

[95] Wakin, Daniel J. "Three Charged in Stock Fraud," *The Associated Press*. December 15th, 1988

[96] Barret, Wayne. "The Case of the Missing Case: How a Trump Probe Died in Rudy's Office," *The Village Voice*. October 12th, 1993

[97] Barrett, Wayne. *Trump: The Greatest Show On Earth*. New York, NY: Regan Arts, 2016. Pg. 195-196

[98] Pileggi, Nicholas. "The Mob and the Machine," *New York Magazine*. May 5th, 1986

[99] Bastone, William. "Trump Limos Were Built With A Hood Ornament," *The Smoking Gun*. September 22nd, 2015

Chapter 3:
Putin's Rise to Power
And the Saga of the Missing KGB Billions

Vladimir Putin returned to Leningrad, which was about to return to its traditional name, St. Petersburg, in early 1990. The Russia he came home to was unrecognizable from the country he had left. Putin was part of an entire generation of spies and intelligence operatives returning from Eastern Bloc and other Soviet missions abroad, dejected and searching for new work or anything that would pay the bills.[1] He returned to his alma mater, Leningrad State University, where he was employed as the assistant to the rector for international affairs. During his last days in Dresden, Putin had met with the head of the KGB's illegal intelligence directorate, Yuri Drozdov, to receive a new assignment.[2] He was transferred to the KGB's active reserve. In the Soviet era, active reserve members were placed in state and civic organizations for monitoring purposes. As the KGB *rezident* at Leningrad State University, Putin kept tabs on the political activities of its students and faculty.[3]

Putin's stint at his old university was short-lived. As the Soviet Union fell apart, St. Petersburg held its first city council election, and a group of democratic activists known as the "informals," who had forged a bond as an early protest movement in the Gorbachev era, were elected. Intellectuals and idealists, the informals had little practical experience governing, and the city they were now tasked with running was on the brink of disaster. The newly empowered but overwhelmed activists turned to Anatoly Sobchak. Sobchak was elected to the Congress of People's Deputies in the elections held under Glasnost.

Sobchak was a sharply dressed law professor with a penchant for public speaking who had advocated for market reforms during the late Soviet period. However, like Gorbachev, he wanted to reform the USSR, not end it.[4] However, the politically ambitious Sobchak would not be the reformer the activists on the city council had hoped for.[5] Sobchak was first elected chairman of the city council and then mayor. Years earlier, he had taught a young law student named Vladimir Putin.

Putin was appointed as Sobchak's advisor on international affairs in May of 1990, a position he held until June of 1991 when he was promoted to head of the Committee for External Relations. In August, in an attempt to save the Soviet Union, the KGB initiated a coup against Gorbachev. The coup failed and set off a series of events that culminated in the dissolution of the Empire in December. While Putin claims to have not supported the coup and even to have submitted a letter of resignation to the KGB, biographers have pointed out that his official story contains too many inconsistencies to be taken seriously. Both Putin and Sobchak spent the days of the coup positioning themselves to survive no matter the outcome.[6]

The Missing KGB Billions and Russian Money Laundering in the West

On Sunday, August 25th, 1991, Nikolay Kruchina's world collapsed around him. Six days earlier, the KGB had launched an attempted coup d'état. It lasted barely four days, after which the coup leader and KGB head Vladimir Kryuchkov and his top lieutenants were arrested. On the 24th, Mikhail Gorbachev stepped down as the general secretary of the Communist Party of the Soviet Union (CPSU) and signed a decree transferring over party property. As the chief-of-staff of the Central Committee, Kruchina oversaw the CPSU's finances, which included billions of dollars within Russia and stashed offshore. On the 25th, the day after Gorbachev had issued his decree transferring party property to the new Russian government, Yeltsin issued a similar proclamation. Later that day, Kruchina met with representatives of the new government in Moscow to discuss the transfer. The meeting did not go well for the shell-shocked apparatchik. That evening, Kruchina returned to his 5th-floor apartment. Sometime after 5 am on the 26th, Kruchina stepped onto his balcony and jumped to his death, taking the secrets of the CPSU's finances with him.[7].

"Plans for the looting of the Soviet State were first discussed in 1984 by specific sectors of the Soviet Politburo, the top officials of the Soviet Government," Richard L. Palmer, CIA Chief of Station in the USSR, testified before Congress. "However, one must keep in mind that this massive effort included many of the highest officials of the Soviet government, several elements of the KGB (now FSB), old and new bankers, industrialists, and, of course, traditional criminals, such as the Russian Mafiya - which already had experience and significant personnel stationed in the West. Their primary goal was to ensure their financial and political status in the future by taking control of the vast funds and resources of the Party and converting them into personal assets that could not be tracked or confiscated by future governments."[8]

The Communist Soviet Union maintained an extensive network of strategically placed state-backed banks and multinational corporations worldwide. These secretive institutions not only funded espionage activities and managed foreign trade, but they also laundered funds that were funneled to communist parties and leftist organizations around the world.[9] Under Andropov, agents in the KGB foreign and economic directorates established ties to black market money movers in anticipation of the collapse of the communist system.[10] For years, the arrangement had been that the CPSU maintained ultimate decision-making powers over the overseas financial network while the KGB was in charge of implementing those decisions. However, by the time Gorbachev began implementing perestroika and glasnost, the KGB took control of the decision-making process, keeping money stashed safely abroad and increasingly siphoning funds out of Russia using the same network.

According to Palmer, in 1986, a secret CPSU planning committee headed by Nikolay Kruchina utilized the services of two KGB First Chief Directorate Officers with experience moving funds overseas. The only written records of these meetings were provided to the head of the KGB, Vladimir Kryuchkov, and Viktor Chebrikov, a Central Committee official in the Politburo. The KGB's Sixth Chief Directorate infiltrated Russia's new cooperatives and banks and established contact with Russia's burgeoning organized crime groups.[11] Between 1986 and

1989, foreign front companies and bank accounts were opened using suitcases full of cash and money appropriated to Soviet diplomatic residencies. After these KGB front companies and accounts were established, official CPSU organizations and party-controlled state enterprises sent their money abroad and stashed it in this secret network. As all this was happening, KGB-established intermediary firms purchased Soviet resources at reduced prices, then sold them abroad at a markup, depositing the profits into the network of shell companies and accounts. As time passed, the scheme became increasingly dependent upon the Eurasian mafia.

On August 23rd, 1990, the deputy general secretary of the CPSU, Vladimir Ivashko, issued a memo entitled "Urgent measures on the organization of commercial and foreign economic activities of the party," in which he called "for the development of an autonomous channel for the obtaining of currency into the party's cash box." The memo further called for the "strict observance of discreet confidentiality" and "the use of anonymous facades to disguise the direct issue of money." By October, the KGB had sent several members of its foreign intelligence unit to coordinate the CPSU's secret international economic activities. This was done based on an agreement between a small group at the highest levels of the KGB and CPSU.

Colonel Leonid Veselovsky of the KGB's First Chief Directorate was transferred to the CPSU's Central Committee Administrative Department. Veselovsky had served as a Field Officer in Portugal in the late 70s and early 80s and had experience with the KGB's clandestine funding operations.[12] Veselovsky outlined his plan in a memo, stating: "The earnings which are accumulated in the Party treasury and are not reflected in the financial reports can be used to purchase the shares of various companies, enterprises, and banks."[13]

With the dissolution of the CPSU, the party's assets fell under the control of the KGB. However, just because the CPSU no longer existed didn't mean its former officials disappeared. Many bureaucrats in the new Russia became inextricably linked to the Eurasian mafia, which was participating in the scam. As Richard Palmer explained, "Organized Crime in Russia is an 'oligarchy' formed by the former officials of the Soviet state and the Russian Mafiya. What makes this group unique is not only the extent of their power, influence, and wealth in Russia, its republics, and increasingly internationally but also that these are two distinctly different groups, sometimes operating independently, sometimes in common. The best estimate is that the criminal Russian Mafiya makes up 10 to 15 percent of Russian Organized Crime, while the remaining 85 to 90 percent are current or former officials of the Soviet party-state."

"Wide-scale infiltration of the Western financial system by Russian organized crime started right on the eve of the collapse of the Soviet Union," Yuri Shvets, a major in the KGB from 1980-90 who defected in 1994, testified before Congress. "The main players were high-ranking officials of the Soviet Communist Party, top KGB leadership, and top bosses of the criminal world. They joined forces by the end of the 1980s on the initiative of the Communist Party, and this unique formation is called today by the Russian people the Russian mafia. The primary objective of this brotherhood was to accumulate maximum personal wealth and build safe havens abroad before Russia plummeted into financial chaos. There was little doubt among them that the collapse was more likely than not in the near future."

Following the failed coup, Leonid Veselovsky fled Russia for Canada, where he linked up with a Soviet-born Lithuanian émigré named Boris Birshtein. Veselovsky claimed to have first met Birshtein in early 1991 while negotiating for the latter to rent a luxurious villa in Moscow that the Central Committee's administrative department controlled. Afterward, Birshtein offered Veselovsky work as a "consultant." Documents suggest that shortly after that, Veselovsky started to direct business towards Birshtein's Zurich-based company, Seabeco AG. Birshtein eventually offered Veselovsky a one-year contract with Seabeco, relocated him to a lakeside villa in Zurich, and provided him with a company-owned Mercedes. Shortly after his association with Veselovsky, Seabeco's fortunes dramatically improved by signing half a dozen profitable contracts with Russian companies. Seabeco went from struggling with its creditors in 1989 to an annual turnaround of over $500 million by 1993.[14] Birshtein was also a business partner of Sergei Mikhailov, head of the Solntsevskaya.[15]

"I have been particularly concerned for some time, Mr. Chairman," James Woolsey, former Director of the CIA, explained to the House Committee on Banking and Financial Services, "at the inter-penetration of Russian organized crime, Russian intelligence and law enforcement, and Russian business. I sometimes illustrate this point with the following hypothetical. If you should chance to strike up a conversation with an articulate English-speaker Russian in, say, the restaurant of one of the luxury hotels along Lake Geneva, and he is wearing a three thousand dollar suit and Gucci loafers, and he tells you he is an executive of a Russian trading company, and he wants to talk to you about a joint venture, he may be what he says he is. He may be a Russian intelligence officer under commercial cover. He may be part of a Russian organized crime group. But the really interesting possibility is that he may be all three and that none of those three institutions have any problem with that arrangement."

While that description fit Boris Birshtein, the man Woolsey mentioned was a suspected KGB asset with links to organized crime named Grigori Loutchansky (AKA Luchansky). According to Woolsey, "During the time that we [the CIA] were working on this issue of organized crime in Russia, Mr. Loutchansky and his company Nordex were a focus of our attention." Loutchansky was released from Latvian prison with the help of the KGB. His multinational trading firm Nordex was set up with former Communist funds and quickly became a multibillion-dollar operation. By 1993, Nordex was given a monopoly over oil imports in Ukraine. Loutchansky had relationships with high-level Russian politicians, the heads of state of Ukraine, Latvia, and Kazakhstan, and important political figures in Israel.[16]

Both Birshtein's Seabeco and Loutchansky's Nordex funded the criminal presidency of Leonid Kuchma in Ukraine, and both were present at a Tel Aviv retreat that included Sergei Mikhailov, the head of the Solntsevskaya Bratva. A Swiss police report published by the Transborder Corruption Archive states that the KGB established the organized crime-linked firms Nordex and Seabeco, which laundered CPSU funds out of Russia. The report further says that Loutchansky was a KGB asset and that Birshtein is an ex-KGB officer who maintains contacts with the Russian and Israeli security services.[17]

While working in the mayor's office, Putin was implicated in several corruption scandals. In the fall of 1991, shortages in Russia had reached a crisis point, and with the onset of winter, there were worries that Russian citizens were at risk of starvation. Russian authorities arranged for natural resources to be traded abroad in exchange for food. Marina Salye, a St. Petersburg city council member, was tasked with traveling to Berlin to arrange for several tons of meat and potatoes to be delivered to St. Petersburg. However, upon her arrival, she was stunned to discover that Vladimir Putin had already arranged contracts for the delivery, and the Germans insisted that the food had been delivered.[18]

The food never arrived in St. Petersburg. In late 1991, Putin had requested permission from Moscow to barter at least $120 million worth of Russian state-owned assets,[19] though Salye claimed that he received over a billion dollars worth of assets.[20] Salye, a prominent voice in the St. Petersburg city council, established a commission to investigate Putin's role in the disappearance of over 90 million Deutschmarks worth of food. Dozens of shoddy contracts were discovered, all of which had been overseen and signed by the legally trained Putin.

The food contracts, a majority of which were prepared incorrectly, making them unenforceable in court, were signed by Putin months before he received official permission. The penalties established for non-delivery ranged from no penalty at all to 1-5%. Commissions for the companies handling the goods ranged from 25-50%.[21] Much of the commission money, awarded to companies with links to Putin and the Mayor's office, simply disappeared. It was further discovered that the contracts used faulty exchange rates to maximize profits. Salye accused Putin of establishing a kickback scheme during a time of near starvation in St. Petersburg that allowed handpicked companies to receive commissions on transactions in which they did not live up to their end of the bargain. Salye believed that the food, originally meant for delivery to St. Petersburg, was instead sent to KGB contacts in Moscow to assist in their preparation for the coup.[22] Felipe Turover, a KGB foreign intelligence agent who worked with Putin in St. Petersburg, told Catherine Belton that the money was pooled into black slush funds, accessible to Putin and his peers in the intelligence services.[23]

In one of Sobchak's earliest decrees, he legalized gambling in St. Petersburg ostensibly to tax the new gaming ventures to pay for social programs. Putin, in addition to his responsibilities in licensing all foreign economic activity in the city, was now a casino mogul. He established a municipal joint-stock company named Neva Chance, which would own 51% of each new casino established in the city. Dozens of city-owned buildings were converted into casinos. However, Neva Chance owned shares in each casino instead of earning profits through rent. The profits were never realized. The casino partners Putin entered into business with were largely composed of ex-KGB officers and members of organized crime outfits.[24] These managers laundered the cash profits of the gambling establishments and then inaccurately reported losses to the city, thus walking away with the profits while the city received nothing.

One of the organizations that participated in the casino scam was St. Petersburg's most powerful organized crime outfit, the Tambovskaya Bratva.[25] The group was founded in the Tambov region by Vladimir Kumarin in 1988. Kumarin was known in St. Petersburg as the *Night Governor*. While the group initially engaged in traditional criminal activities such as drug trafficking, organized theft, and racketeering, following Gorbachev's Law on Cooperatives, it established fronts of newly formed legitimate businesses.[26] Putin and his cronies in the KGB, including the oligarch and billionaire Gennady Timchenko, who attended the Red Banner Academy with Putin, assisted a Tambovskaya associate named Ilya Traber in his violent seizure of St. Petersburg's seaport and its associated businesses.[27]

A Tambovskaya-linked private security company, Baltik-Escort, was established to protect Sobchak and Putin. Founded by Roman Tsepov and Viktor Zolotov, both of whom were involved in the casino scam, the service was not only staffed by multiple members of local criminal groups but served as a liaison between the mayor's office and Vladimir Kumarin as well as Aleksandr Malyshev, the head of the Malyshevskaya criminal organization.[28] Kumarin also profited handsomely from another Putin-licensed company, the Petersburg Fuel Company, which was given exclusive rights to supply fuel to St. Petersburg.[29]

In 2001, *Newsweek* obtained documents that showed Putin sat on the board of a German-Russian firm, the St. Petersburg Real Estate Holding Company (SPAG).[30] A German Federal Intelligence Agency (BND) investigation completed in 1999 reported that SPAG was involved in money laundering activities for the Tambovskaya as well as Colombia's Cali cartel.[31] Vladimir Kumarin was involved in two subsidiaries of SPAG, *Znamenskaya* and *Inform-Future*, both personally licensed by Putin.[32] Kumarin co-owned these subsidiaries with Vladimir Smirnov, who had registered SPAG with Putin in 1992.[33] Smirnov had met Putin in Germany and headed one of the companies Putin had licensed that was involved in the Oil-for-Food scandal.[34] Tens of millions of dollars in city loans were funneled through these subsidiaries to develop properties, some of which sat empty or were never completed. [35]

Upon his return to St. Petersburg in 1990, Putin purchased a dacha on the shores of Lake Komsomolskoye, located north of the city. Six years later, in 1996, he and seven of his closest St. Petersburg-based associates established the Ozero Dacha Consumer Cooperative (Ozero is Russian for "Lake"). The man listed in legal documents as the head of the cooperative was the SPAG-linked Vladimir Smirnov. Another member of the Ozero board was a KGB colleague of Putin's, named Vladimir Yakunin, who became the billionaire head of Russian Railways. Others included Nikolay Shamalov, Yuri Kovalchuk, Viktor Myachin, Sergei and Andrei Fursenko.[36] The group built small mansions next to one another, and security was provided by Rif-Security, which was owned by Smirnov and Tambovskaya head Vladimir Kumarin.[37]

In establishing the Ozero Cooperative and a linked bank account that could be accessed and used by all of its members, Putin could be given money directly and yet avoid the appearance of impropriety as the money was officially being passed through the cooperative. The financial institution used by the Ozero Cooperative is Bank Rossiya. Founded in 1990, the initial largest shareholder of Bank Rossiya was the Communist Party of the Leningrad Oblast, and it may have served as a money laundering vehicle for the KGB.[38] The bank's initial capitalization of 1.5 million rubles was provided by the aforementioned Nikolay Kruchina, the CPSU financial manager, who met his end by leaping out his window.[39]

Following the coup, Bank Rossiya's accounts were briefly closed. However, Putin began working with the bank as early as his first week in office, when he used his position in the mayor's office to funnel city money into the St. Petersburg World Trade Center, a joint venture with Bank Rossiya.[40] Three members of the Ozero Cooperative, Yuri Kovalchuk, Andrei Fursenko, and Vladimir Yakunin, stepped in as early investors.[41] They were shortly followed by two other members of the Ozero Cooperative, Nikolai Shamalov (whose son, Kirill, is married to Putin's daughter) and Andrei Fursenko's brother Sergei. Additional Bank of Rossiya investors included Sergei Kuzmin and Gennady Petrov, the latter of whom was indicted by José Grinda for being a member of the Tambovskaya.[42]

The Ascent to Power: Putin In Moscow

In 1996, Anatoly Sobchak faced a brutal reelection campaign. After years of crime, corruption, and recession, there was widespread disillusionment among voters with both his leadership and democracy itself. To make matters worse, he was under investigation. Yuri Skuratov, the Prosecutor General in Moscow, was looking into corruption in the St. Petersburg mayor's office. In particular, investigators examined the murky privatization of apartments in the city that went to members of Sobchak's family and other officials in the mayor's office, including Putin.[43]

Putin and Sobchak were convinced that the prosecution was politically motivated. Matters went from bad to worse when Sobchak lost the election to one of his deputies and, as a result, lost immunity from criminal prosecution. In addition to Skuratov's investigation of Sobchak, there were several ongoing investigations into Putin by local authorities in St. Petersburg. Under pressure, Putin needed to find a way back into the corridors of power.

After Yeltsin's 1996 reelection, a shuffling of positions in the cabinet led to a power struggle. Putin was invited to Moscow and secured a position in the Presidential Property Management Department. The department, led by Pavel Borodin, a Siberian drinking buddy of Yeltsin's, managed over $600 billion worth of the Kremlin's assets.[44] The position gave Putin access to the inner circle around Yeltsin, known as "The Family." It did not appear to keep Putin particularly busy, and during his time there, he wrote a dissertation on the economics of natural resources, portions of which were plagiarized from an American textbook on the subject.[45]

While in Moscow, Putin maintained his relationships in St. Petersburg. In particular, he displayed loyalty to the much troubled Anatoly Sobchak, which didn't go unnoticed by Yeltsin. Sobchak was faced with being criminally indicted. Several of his subordinates in the mayor's office had already been arrested on bribery charges. Prosecutors attempted to serve him with a summons for an interrogation. When he was finally arrested and interrogated, things became so heated that Sobchak claimed to fall ill and was taken from the interrogation room straight to the hospital. Sobchak's wife claimed that he suffered a heart attack, though few believed her.

Sobchak stayed in the hospital for a month. Prosecutor General Skuratov's patience wore thin, and he arranged for Moscow-based doctors to examine Sobchak to determine if he was fit for interrogation. However, before this could happen, Putin returned to St. Petersburg and had Sobchak transferred to a different hospital under the care of a physician who had once treated Lyudmila Putina. Several days later, Putin chartered a flight that whisked Sobchak and his wife to Finland and eventually to Paris, safely away from the clutches of investigators.

Putin's role in helping Sobchak flee the country was most likely illegal. However, to Boris Yeltsin, it was a remarkable display of loyalty at great personal risk and was worthy of admiration. It is quite possible that this one act did more for Putin's political career than anything else because Yeltsin and those around him would soon grow afraid that they would be prosecuted upon leaving office. Whether legal or not, Putin's loyalty was seen by Yeltsin as his defining quality.

Yeltsin's second and final term in office was even more turbulent and corrupt than his first. The alliance of convenience between the Seven Bankers, who banded together in 1996 during the reelection campaign, failed to last even a year. By 1997, the seven most powerful oligarchs in the country were back at each other's throats, competing to scoop up the few industries left to be privatized[46]. To make matters worse, in 1998, Russia was struck by a terrible financial crisis that led to the devaluation of the ruble and the country's defaulting on its debt.

Under pressure from the Clinton administration, the International Monetary Fund (IMF) poured billions of dollars of loans into the Russian economy in the lead-up to the 1996 election to improve the chances of Yeltsin's reelection. During this period, the Russian Central Bank established through a Paris-based intermediary an obscure offshore shell company known as Financial Management Company Ltd (FIMACO) based in Jersey, a Channel Island tax haven located off the United Kingdom.[47] Between 1993 and 1998, tens of billions of dollars passed through the account. The Central Bank's chairman later admitted this was done to hide money from Russia's creditors. However, others thought it was another scheme to enrich insiders and provide them a way to launder money overseas. Of an $800 million IMF loan supplied to Russia in 1993, $500 million was transferred to FIMACO.[48] The United States Government[49] and the IMF were aware of these off-shore scams as they were happening.[50]

While Putin was at the Presidential Property Management Department (PPMD), a bribery scandal involving Yeltsin and his daughters erupted into an international incident. Pavel Borodin, head of the PPMD, awarded a series of lucrative contracts to repair a palace and several other Kremlin-owned buildings to a Lugano-based Swiss construction company called Mabatex. To win the contracts, Mabatex appeared to bribe officials at the highest levels of the Russian government. In late 1995, it was discovered that Mabatex's founder had transferred $1 million to a Budapest bank account linked to Yeltsin.[51] Mabatex further purchased two yachts for Yeltsin, which were flown by Russian military aircraft from Marseilles to St. Petersburg.[52] Yeltsin, his two daughters, and numerous other Russian officials, including Pavel Borodin, were provided credit cards by Mabatex. It is estimated that the company poured between $10 and $15 million into various credit cards and bank accounts.[53]

The Mabatex scandal was blown open by a whistleblower from the Swiss bank Banco del Gottardo. Or so it seemed until Catherine Belton uncovered that the so-called whistleblower Felipe Turover was a former KGB foreign intelligence officer who had worked with Putin on the Oil-for-Food scandal. The supposed Mabatex scandal was a scheme by the Russian intelligence services to frame and eventually oust Yeltsin, replacing the President of Russia with one of their own.[54]

Turover worked as Banco del Gottardo's debt collector in Russia and provided Swiss Prosecutor General Carla del Ponte with documents and testimony that implicated a largely clueless Yeltsin and his family in the bribery scheme.[55]

Semyon Mogilevich and the Bank of New York Money Laundering Scandal

Another scandal exploded across the headlines when on August 19th, 1999, *The New York Times* reported that billions of dollars had been laundered through the Bank of New York (BNY) by Russian organized crime.[56] The scandal implicated the highest levels of the Russian government, including members of "The Family," and was the largest money laundering operation in US history to that point.[57] Founded in 1784 by a group that included Alexander Hamilton and Aaron Burr, the Bank of New York is one of the oldest financial institutions in the United States.

In Congressional testimony, Thomas A. Renyi, chairman and chief executive officer of BNY, tried to downplay his bank's involvement in Russia.[58] However, BNY had spent the early 90s aggressively courting business in Russia. Responsibility for developing Russian business was given to senior vice president Natasha Gurfinkel Kagalovsky. Kagalovsky successfully wooed Russia's Inkombank to do business with BNY by promising to be "less vigilant." Whereas Inkombank's previous American bank filed Suspicious Activity Reports (SARs) about a number of its accounts, BNY neglected to do so.[59] Natasha's husband, Konstantin Kagalovsky, was a banker and oilman who served as the Russian envoy to the IMF. BNY had at one time or another significant stakes in some of Russia's largest companies, particularly in the energy sector, including Lukoil, Gazprom, and Tatneft.[60]

A key figure in developing relationships between BNY and the Russians was a Swiss banker and BNY shareholder Baruch "Bruce" Rappaport.[61] Rappaport co-owned with BNY the Swiss-based Bank of New York-Inter Maritime Bank (BNY-IMB). From the late 80s, Rappaport had courted Gorbachev and established a series of Soviet joint ventures. By 1992, he had forged relationships between BNY-IMB and 93 Russian banks.[62] Federal investigators flagged millions of dollars of Russian money that flowed through BNY-IMB to BNY as being connected to a $7 billion money laundering operation. Rappaport was alleged to have contacts with the CIA and Mossad and was a personal friend and golfing partner of former CIA director William Casey.[63] He was also involved in moving money related to the Iran-Contra scandal.[64]

In the US and UK, investigators set their sights on a London/New York-based husband and wife duo: Lucy Edwards (born Lyudmila Pritzker) and Peter Berlin, both Russian-born but naturalized US citizens.[65] Edwards was a vice president at BNY working within the Eastern European Division led by Natasha Kagalovsky. Edwards and Berlin later admitted before a Federal Judge to having been involved in a $7 billion money laundering operation involving politically connected banks in Russia.[66] According to Edwards and Berlin, the purpose of the network was to electronically move money between Russia and the United States using BNY's state-of-the-art wire transfer software, Micro/Ca$h-Register.[67] The network serves three main functions. First, it allowed Russians to evade taxes on earnings from legitimate business transactions. Second, it allowed Russians to avoid customs duties on imports. Finally, it allowed Russian organized crime groups to wash their illicit profits.[68]

Investigators believed that the Edwards-Berlin operation was a front masterminded by a Ukrainian mobster named Semyon Mogilevich, who is described in an internal NSA document as "the US government's top Russian organized crime target."[69] Mogilevich secretly controlled Inkombank.[70] The BNY investigation grew out of a British investigation into a company called Arbat International.[71] British investigators believed that Arbat, which had links to Russian business and political elites, had been set up by Mogilevich and was owned by Sergei Mikhailov, head of the Solntsevskaya.[72] The British investigation led to further law enforcement inquiries into illicit activities in the UK, Canada, the United States, Central and Eastern Europe, and Russia itself. One name popped up repeatedly.

Semyon "Seva" Mogilevich was born in Kyiv to a Jewish family in 1946. A chain smoker who weighs over 300 pounds, Mogilevich possesses a comprehensive understanding of global finance and its vulnerabilities. He received the nickname "The Brainy Don" due to this and the fact that he holds an economics degree from the University of Lviv. In the mid-1980s, Mogilevich began scamming Jewish emigres leaving the USSR, offering to buy their possessions in Russia and promising to sell them for better prices on the international market and then send them the profits when they had resettled[73]. Needless to say, their money never arrived.

In the 1980s, Mogilevich set up Arbat International, a petroleum import-export company registered in the British Channel Island tax haven Alderney. 25% of Arbat was owned by Vyacheslav "Yaponchik" Ivankov,[74] a notoriously violent gangster and one of the last tattoo-sporting, old-school members of the traditional Russian *vor v zakone*.[75] As mentioned above, the other owners are Sergei Mikhailov and Viktor Averin. Another Channel Island-based firm, Arigon Ltd., is associated by the FBI as being integral to Mogilevich's criminal activities.[76]

In 1990, Mogilevich moved to Israel and was granted citizenship.[77] Robert I. Friedman, the investigative reporter who first wrote about Mogilevich for *The Village Voice* and was subsequently informed by the FBI that a $100,000 price had been placed on his head, claimed to have been shown a secret Israeli intelligence report about Mogilevich.[78] The report stated that Mogilevich used his Israeli citizenship to travel freely abroad as well as to develop significant political, business, and criminal connections within the country. The report further alleged that Mogilevich owned an Israeli bank with branches in Moscow, Cyprus, and Tel Aviv. Friedman further describes an internal FBI document that claimed Mogilevich was at this time laundering money for both Colombian and Russian organized crime.[79]

In 1991, Mogilevich settled in Budapest and established brothels primarily using German and Russian women in Prague, Budapest, Riga, and Kyiv.[80] Both the Solntsevskaya and Vyacheslav Ivankov were involved in Mogilevich's prostitution empire. Mogilevich used the illicit proceeds to purchase military-grade weaponry destined for the illegal arms market. Other crimes Mogilevich has been accused of include extortion, the narcotics trade, trafficking in nuclear materials, dealing with precious gems, art fraud, and money laundering.[81] The FBI grew so alarmed by Mogilevich's activities that they opened their first-ever office abroad in Budapest in the early months of 2000.[82] The FBI considers Mogilevich one of the most dangerous mobsters in the world, even placing him for a period on their 10 most wanted list.[83]

Mogilevich sits at the nexus of the Russian intelligence services and organized crime and has laundered money for both.[84]

In addition to his connections with the Solntsevskaya and the *vor* Vyacheslav Ivanov, Mogilevich is also an associate of the KGB and criminally linked money launderers Boris Birshtein and Grigori Loutchansky.[85] In 1995, Mogilevich, Mikhailov, Loutchansky and Loutchansky's Ukrainian deputy Vadim Rabinovich attended a summit hosted by Birshtein in Tel Aviv, Israel, to discuss their various possessions and criminal holdings in Ukraine, where they held immense influence which they exercised to benefit of the Kremlin.[86]

The fallout from the BNY affair reached the inner circle of "The Family." The FBI opened an investigation into both Pavel Borodin and Leonid Dyachenko, who was married to Yeltsin's daughter Tatyana.[87] It was discovered that Dyachenko possessed a Cayman Islands bank account containing over $2.7 million linked to BNY.[88] Investigators would not comment on whether Dyachenko had moved any money through Benex. The scandals became so bad that Bill Clinton asked Yeltsin directly about the accusations of bribery against him. Yeltsin categorically denied any involvement and claimed they amounted to nothing but politically inspired attacks.[89]

Putin's Rise to the Presidency
And the September 1999 Apartment Bombings

As these scandals became public and chaos engulfed the Kremlin, Vladimir Putin moved up the ladder of power. After spending less than a year at the Presidential Property Management Department, Putin was made the head of the Main Control Directorate, the body meant to ensure that federal laws, executive orders, and presidential instructions were being properly implemented.[90] While there, he was in charge of the documents related to the Salye Commission. No further investigations were conducted into the scandal from that time forward. This was also the time in which Putin arranged for Anatoly Sobchak to escape to Paris.

Turmoil and a revolving door in the Yeltsin cabinet provided Putin with opportunities impossible at any other time. Fearing for his political future, Yeltsin relieved one of his Prime Ministers and a potential contender in the fast-approaching election, Viktor Chernomyrdin. His replacement, a 35-year-old banker named Sergei Kiriyenko, learned of his appointment the morning it was announced. In the shakeup, Putin was promoted, this time to first deputy director of the presidential administration. He occupied the position for two months.

Yeltsin had grown concerned over the power and independence of the FSB, as it had the power to investigate him and his family. To gain further control over the agency, Yeltsin appointed Putin as its head on July 25th, 1998.[91] Though Putin claimed not to be aware of the appointment until the day it was offered to him, he wasted no time in putting his new position to good use. He immediately offered high-level positions to personal friends from his days in the KGB and St. Petersburg. He then eliminated two internal agencies charged with investigating economic crimes, thus offering significant relief to many of the figures in the Yeltsin administration under scrutiny and his allies in organized crime.[92]

In the wake of the financial crisis that had engulfed the nation, Yeltsin was forced to change Prime Ministers again, this time replacing Kiriyenko with Yevgeny Primakov, the former head of the Foreign Intelligence Service. Though Yeltsin had wanted to return one of his previous Prime Ministers to the job, his relationship with the Russian legislative body, the Duma, had deteriorated so far that he had to settle for Primakov as they refused to ratify anyone else. At the time, Yeltsin was facing potential impeachment inquiries.

Primakov established his independence and determination to strike back against corruption and the oligarchs by authorizing investigations into "The Family" and arguably the most powerful oligarch at the time, Boris Berezovsky.[93] Prosecutor General Yuri Skuratov opened investigations into FIMACO, Berezovsky's defrauding of the airline Aeroflot, and the Mabatex affair. Skuratov was in communication with the Swiss Prosecutor Carla Del Ponte and in early 1999 Swiss law enforcement raided Mabatex headquarters in Lugano while Russian officers raided Aeroflot's offices in Moscow. The noose around "The Family" was tightening.

Yeltsin and his lieutenants believed that Primakov was positioning himself to take over the Presidency in 2000 when the Constitution mandated that Yeltsin leave office. Primakov was busily solidifying his support base in parliament and had entered into a political alliance with the popular but corrupt mayor of Moscow Yuri Luzhkov.[94] After the corruption and economic disasters of recent years, Yeltsin's approval ratings had plunged to single digits. It was widely feared within "The Family" that they would be prosecuted and imprisoned upon Yeltsin leaving office. To make matters worse, Skuratov's investigations were rapidly proceeding.

In early February, a tape emerged that purportedly showed Skuratov at a sauna linked to the Solntsevskaya having sex with two prostitutes.[95] The circumstance gave every appearance of being a honey-trap orchestrated by Russian intelligence.[96] Officials in Yeltsin's administration, who received a copy of the tape before it was publicly released, confronted Skuratov with it in early February 1999, less than a month after his investigations into Yeltsin's inner circle had intensified. Skuratov wrote a letter of resignation and promptly checked himself into the hospital. Yeltsin accepted Skuratov's resignation for the ostensible reason of poor health, but no one believed that explanation.

Skuratov may have submitted his resignation, but he wasn't quite ready to quit yet. According to the Russian constitution, the only authority that could accept the resignation of a Prosecutor General was the Federation Council. The council would have to convene and vote on the matter, and he would be allowed to make a case before them. Putin, in his capacity as head of the FSB, met with Skuratov on several occasions. The first was in Skuratov's hospital room. Putin explained that the "Family" was pleased with his resignation and would be offering him the ambassadorship to Finland as a reward. Skuratov refused the offer and explained that he wanted to continue the work he was doing as Prosecutor General.

Putin spoke with Skuratov again shortly after he had left the hospital. During the call, Putin attempted to sympathize with the prosecutor, bizarrely suggesting that he had heard rumors that a similar tape of himself existed and that it would be best for all concerned if he stepped down from his position.[97] However, when this failed to shake Skuratov's resolve, Putin indicated that he possessed documents that were incriminating regarding Skuratov's apartment in Moscow. Putin also suggested that it was his investigation into Pavel Borodin and Mabatex that was concerning "The Family" the most. Skuratov remained unbowed.

When the Federation Council gathered to vote on the question of his resignation, Skuratov stood before the body in evident good health and claimed that he had been made to resign under duress, though not mentioning anyone in the Yeltsin camp by name. Immediately before the vote, Kremlin sources circulated copies of the tape to members of the Council. Disgusted by the clumsy attempt at blackmail, the Council voted to reject Skuratov's resignation. A few hours later, the tape aired on Russian state television.

The next day Skuratov met Yeltsin face to face in the hospital room where Yeltsin was recovering from one of his many ailments. Putin and Primakov were present. Yeltsin again demanded he resign, suggesting that if he did so the sex tape would stop airing on television. Putin watched the interaction in silence. Cornered, Skuratov again signed the resignation papers. However, he wasn't about to go out without a fight. As he left the hospital, he called the press and made the Mabatex investigation public.[98] Putin again emerged as a key ally. Shortly after the confrontation at the hospital, Putin publicly announced that the FSB had verified the authenticity of the sex tape.

From mid-to-late 1999, events of seismic significance in Russian politics occurred at a blistering and often confusing pace. Regarding the fate of Skuratov, Yeltsin and the Federation Council went back and forth, with Yeltsin forcing his resignation and the Council repeatedly rejecting it. In addition to battling with his own Prosecutor General, Yeltsin dismissed his Prime Minister and perceived rival Yevgeny Primakov, and replaced him with his third Prime Minister in less than a year, Sergei Stepashin. Stepashin lasted less than two months. Days later, Yeltsin barely survived an impeachment vote in the Duma led by the Communist Party.

On August 9th, 1999, Sergei Stepashin was replaced as Prime Minister by Putin. Yeltsin went a step further and publicly named him as his designated successor to the Presidency. Putin's ascent to the loftiest heights of the Russian power structure was aided by a set of strong alliances he had established with members of "The Family" and by the fact that they were in a desperate situation. There was both a parliamentary and presidential election just a few months away. Yeltsin and the oligarchic circle around him were profoundly unpopular. To make matters worse, former Prime Minister Primakov and the mayor of Moscow Yuri Luzhkov were now actively campaigning against Yeltsin and were increasingly favored to win the election.

"I don't like election campaigns," Putin admitted to Yeltsin upon being told he was now the heir apparent. "I really don't. I don't know how to run them, and I don't like them."[99] Yeltsin assured Putin there was already a structure in place to support his candidacy. In addition to positive coverage on state TV, Boris Berezovsky placed the full weight of his independent channel behind supporting Putin and attacking Primakov and Luzhkov.[100] Berezovsky also conceived of a new political party, Unity, which made Putin its standard bearer. However, none of these efforts could guarantee Putin's victory. It was during this time that some of the most mysterious, terrifying, and still currently unexplained events in Russian political history unfolded.

On June 6th, 1999, the Moscow correspondent for the Swedish publication *Svenska Dagbladet* reported that a group within the Russian power structure that was considering, "terror bombings in Moscow which could be blamed on the Chechens."[101] David Satter, the Moscow correspondent for *The Wall Street Journal*, was told by "a Russian political operative who was well connected to the higher levels of Russian power," that there were serious fears within the Kremlin that Yeltsin was going to lose the election and that rumors abounded that Moscow would shortly be the scene of a serious provocation. Satter's source went on to say that if the matter wasn't resolved, "they will blow up half of Moscow."[102]

In June 1999, for reasons never publicized, Russian military forces began to amass on the border of Chechnya, an Islamic, breakaway Russian province that had been the scene of a bloody and inconclusive war in 1994. This was a curious development, as earlier that spring Russian forces were withdrawn from the neighboring province of Dagestan. On August 7th, two days before Putin was made Prime Minister, a Chechen force of Islamic militants under the leadership of Shamil Basaev and an Arab jihadist under the *nom de guerre* Khattab invaded Dagestan. The incursion was fought by local police units and withdrew after two weeks.[103]

The day after the incursion, the Russian investigative weekly *Versiya* published an article claiming French intelligence had tipped them off to a meeting that took place at a villa between Nice and Monaco between Aleksandr Voloshin, head of the Presidential administration, and the Chechen commander Basaev. Further inquiries by the investigative journalist Boris

Kagarlitsky confirmed that such a meeting took place. John B. Dunlop, former acting director of Stanford University's Center for Russian, East European and Eurasian Studies and author of the most extensive investigation into the 1999 bombings, wrote in his book that, "a representative of one of the French intelligence organizations, whose identity is known to me, subsequently confirmed to an experienced Western academic that French intelligence does indeed possess intelligence that roughly coincides with what Boris Kagarlitsky wrote."[104]

According to a senior official in the Ministry of Internal Affairs, had the troops not been withdrawn earlier the Chechens could have easily been repelled. A special-ops commander fighting in Dagestan at the time told *Time Magazine* that Russian forces had Basaev in their sights during his retreat and were poised to engage him but were ordered by Moscow to stand down. "We just watched Basaev's long column of trucks and jeeps withdraw from Dagestan back to Chechnya under cover provided by our own helicopters," The commander told *Time*. "We could have wiped him out then and there, but the bosses in Moscow wanted him alive."[105]

On August 31st, a small bomb exploded at Manezh Square in Moscow, killing one bystander and injuring thirty others. An anonymous individual claiming to represent the Dagestan Liberation Army took credit for the bombing. As car bombs had been a normal means of mob-related assassination in Moscow, most Muscovites shrugged it off. Nikolai Patrushev, a close friend of Putin's who had replaced him as head of the FSB, told a Russian paper, "There is no basis for a more intense regime because of the bomb at Manezh Square."[106]

Following the Chechen withdrawal, the Russian military responded with an indiscriminate bombing campaign of an entirely separate part of Dagestan from where the earlier fighting had been that killed up to 1000 civilians. The bombing raids spurred the Chechens to reinvade Dagestan. At 9:40 pm on September 4th, 1999, the day of the Chechen invasion and less than a month after Putin had been appointed as Yeltsin's successor, an explosion from a truck bomb tore through a five-story apartment building housing Russian soldiers in the Dagestani city of Buynaksk. 64 men were killed instantly and dozens others were buried in the rubble. A few hours later, another bomb-laden truck was discovered and diffused within the city that contained over 6,000 pounds of explosives.

The Buynaksk bombing took place in Dagestan, which was a warzone at the time, and the victims were soldiers. As a result, the initial public reaction in Russia was muted.[107] However, on September 9th, a bomb detonated in the basement of an apartment building at 19 Guryanova Street, located in a working-class neighborhood in Moscow. 100 Russian civilians were either immolated or crushed by debris from the collapsing building, and 690 were injured. That same day, a liberal member of the State Duma, Konstantin Borovoi was provided with a document by rogue members of Russian military intelligence warning of future attacks. Borovoi attempted to provide the information to the Russian security establishment but was rebuffed by the FSB. No additional preventative measures were taken.[108]

At 5 am on September 13th, five days after the Guryanova St. bombing, a 9-story building located at 6 Kashirskoye Highway was detonated, killing 124 of its sleeping residents. Later that morning, with much of Russia in an uproar, the speaker of the State Duma Gennady Seleznev stood and announced that an apartment building had been bombed the night before in the Russian city of Volgodonsk.[109] It was an error, as no bomb had detonated in Volgodonsk, but it was to prove prophetic. Three days later, a truck bomb killed eighteen more Russian civilians when it destroyed the facade of a 9-story apartment building. This time the bombing did take place in Volgodonsk. The coincidence remains unexplained to this day.

Less than a week later, on September 22nd, concerned residents of a building in Ryazan, a working-class suburb of Moscow, called the police after noticing a suspicious group of people entering and exiting the building's basement. When the police arrived 45 minutes later, they were hesitant to enter the basement as it was used as a toilet by local derelicts. However, two officers eventually walked down to inspect. They emerged moments later in a state of alarm shouting that there was a bomb. A call was put to the local bomb squad and the officers immediately evacuated every man, woman, and child from the building except a few invalids who were unable to be moved.[110] Panic spread quickly throughout the entire city and soon residents of other buildings were pouring out into the streets as well.[111]

Yuri Tkachenko, head of the local bomb squad, arrived within minutes. The residents of the building watched nervously as he made his way down into the basement. Tkachenko approached three fifty-pound sacks filled with a white substance, all connected by a timed detonator set to go off at 5:30 am. Tkachenko disarmed the device and used a portable gas analyzer to test the substance within the sacks. They tested positive for hexogen, a Russian-produced military-grade explosive.[112] The sacks were taken from the scene by the FSB at around 1:30 am, but in an oversight, they had left the detonator with the local bomb squad.[113]

On the morning of the 23rd, Russians woke up to the nationwide media reporting that an attempted apartment bombing in the city of Ryazan had been averted by vigilant residents and local authorities. Alexander Sergeev, the head of the Ryazan branch of the FSB, went on television and congratulated the local residents for preventing a terrorist attack.[114] Putin issued a brief statement in which he said, "If the sacks which proved to contain explosives were noticed, then there is a positive side to it." His statement was followed by that of the Chief of the Ministry of Internal Affairs, Vladimir Rushailov, who heaped praise upon the local Ryazan authorities for thwarting an attempted terrorist attack.[115]

Using the eyewitness accounts, local police developed composite sketches of the three suspects. A manhunt ensued, the local airport and railways were cordoned off and roadblocks were erected on all the streets leaving Ryazan. The suspect's car was discovered abandoned in a local parking lot. Shortly thereafter, a Ryazan operator connected a call from a local public phone to Moscow. The voice on the Ryazan end of the line explained that there was no way to get out of town without being detected. The voice from the Moscow end of the line instructed them to, "[s]plit up and each of you make your own way." The operator reported the call to the police, who proceeded to trace the call back to FSB headquarters in Moscow.[116]

On the evening of the 23rd, the three suspects were apprehended. Upon being captured, they produced FSB identification cards.[117] Shocked, local Ryazan authorities were then contacted by FSB headquarters in Moscow and instructed to release the detained bombing suspects.[118] They were released from custody and vanished without ever facing charges or public scrutiny. On the 24th, the head of the FSB and close Putin ally from St. Petersburg, Nikolai Patrushev, made a surprise announcement in which he explained that the incident at Ryazan was an FSB training exercise. The sacks, he further explained, had been filled with sugar. Local residents, police officers, and the Ryazan FSB reacted with incredulity and outrage.[119]

The overall impact of the September terrorist campaign had a frightened and vengeful Russian public baying for blood. On September 23rd, the day after the Ryazan incident, Yeltsin issued an illegal decree authorizing the army to resume operations in Chechnya. The Russian constitution forbids the use of the Russian military against its own territory. Within hours, Russian warplanes began bombing the airport and oil refineries in and around Grozny, the capital of Chechnya. The second Chechen war had begun.

As the planes began their bombing runs, Putin took center stage. From this point on he would be on all the major television stations on a nightly basis. After praising the vigilance of the citizens of Ryazan, mere hours before Patrushev would claim the event was a training exercise, Putin directed his ire toward the alleged Chechen terrorists. Putin's barbed rhetoric, dripping with vulgarity and identifiable gangster slang, proved wildly popular. "We will hunt them down," Putin snarled. "Wherever we find them, we will destroy them. Even if we find them on the toilet. We will rub them out in the outhouse."[120]

By the end of the month, 24 regional governors sent Yeltsin a letter requesting that he step down so that Putin could take his place as President. Yeltsin then ceded full control over the war effort to his heir apparent. On the first day of October, Putin ordered a full ground invasion of Chechnya.[121] 93,000 troops, twice as many as had been used in the 1994 war, poured over the border. The bombing campaign against the civilian center Grozny was total and unrelenting. Putin even secretly traveled to Russian military bases in the region to hand out medals. His conduct proved wildly popular among ordinary Russians.[122]

The September bombings, the renewed Chechen war, and Putin's rapidly rising popularity dramatically changed the political calculus both inside and outside of Russia. Though the largest money laundering scandal in US history had gone public only a month earlier, US policymakers suddenly found their attention turning to the dramatic and violent events unfolding in Russia itself.[123] In the parliamentary elections held on December 19th, 1999, Putin's Unity Party exceeded expectations, vanquishing the party supporting Primakov and Luzhkov. On December 31st, Yeltsin used his annual New Year's Eve address to the nation to make a surprise announcement. Effective immediately, he was stepping down as President of the Russian Federation. Vladimir Putin was now the most powerful man in Russia.

In his first act as President, Putin granted Yeltsin and his family full immunity. With a stroke of a pen, Putin made good on his promise to "The Family." The Skuratov investigations were scrapped, and the man himself was unceremoniously removed from office shortly thereafter. Parliamentary opposition, active during the Yeltsin years, went silent. Though he still had an election to win in a few months, as he was only the "Acting President" until being properly elected, the result appeared to be as predictable as it was inevitable.

Putin didn't bother to run a traditional campaign. He declined to engage in debates or extensive independent interviews but rather allowed the full resources of the Kremlin and the positive coverage of state and friendly-oligarch-owned television stations to campaign for him. Though the war in Chechnya was turning into a bloodbath, Putin restricted access to journalists. News of mass civilian casualties and repeated war crimes dribbled out through the dogged reporting of independent news outlets but reached only a small, uninfluential intelligentsia.[124]

Attempting to curry favor with the new leader of Russia, money poured in from sources both foreign (particularly from Ukraine) and domestic. The organs of state acted aggressively on Putin's behalf. In the lead-up to the election, the Ministry of Internal Affairs' Investigation Committee seized documents that potentially implicated the popular Mayor of Moscow Yuri Luzhkov, and his wife in crimes. Luzhkov declared he wouldn't be running, fell in line behind Putin, and would never show any signs of political independence again.[125]

Two days before the election, NTV, an opposition television station owned by the oligarch Vladimir Gusinsky, aired a town hall debate that allowed the residents of Ryazan to question a representative from the FSB about the mysterious events that had occurred in September. In the intervening months independent media, led by the paper *Novaya Gazeta* among others, had systematically uncovered evidence that riddled official explanations with holes. After suggesting the bombings may have been terrorist acts by the state as opposed to terrorist acts against the state, *Novaya Gazeta* had its website shut down by a cyber attack.[126]

At the NTV town hall, residents of 14/16 Novoselov St. unanimously expressed disbelief that the events of the 23rd of September had been a training exercise. When a person who claimed to be a resident of the building suggested that they did believe the official explanation, they were immediately shouted down by the other residents, who claimed to have never seen them before. It was widely believed the FSB had placed a plant among the residents. The FSB representative on the program was unable to explain why the "sugar" tested positive for the explosive hexogen, or why the local Ryazan FSB was in the dark about the exercise.[127]

The election took place on March 26th, 2000. Despite Putin's newfound popularity, there were still numerous reports of widespread irregularities, particularly in the outer regions of the Federation. Balloting results showed that Putin won in Chechnya by nearly 200,000 votes, an odd outcome considering it was being bombed to rubble under his orders.[128] However, despite significant evidence that election fraud did occur in the Russian 2000 election, nearly every scholar concedes that Putin would have won the election with or without i

---

[1] Lee Myers, Steven. *The New Tsar: The Rise and Reign of Vladimir Putin*. New York, NY: Alfred A. Knopf, 2015. Pg. 55
[2] Gessen, Masha. *The Man Without A Face: The Unlikely Rise of Vladimir Putin*. New York, NY: RIVERHEAD BOOKS, 2012. Pg. 97
[3] Dawisha, Karen. *Putin's Kleptocracy: Who Owns Russia?*. New York, NY: Simon & Schuster, 2014. Pg. 62
[4] Lee Myers, Steven. *The New Tsar: The Rise and Reign of Vladimir Putin*. New York, NY: Alfred A. Knopf, 2015. Pg. 56
[5] Gessen, Masha. *The Man Without A Face: The Unlikely Rise of Vladimir Putin*. New York, NY: RIVERHEAD BOOKS, 2012. Pg. 92
[6] Gessen, Masha. *The Man Without A Face: The Unlikely Rise of Vladimir Putin*. New York, NY: RIVERHEAD BOOKS, 2012. Pg. 118
[7] Plokhy, Serhii. *The Last Empire: The Final Days of the Soviet Union*. New York, NY: Basic Books, 2014. Pg. 150
[8] Statement of Richard L. Palmer, President of Cachet International, Inc. On the Infiltration of the Western Financial Sector By Elements of Russian Organized Crime Before the House Committee on Banking and Financial Services, September 21st, 1999
[9] Goldman, Marshall I. *The Piratization of Russia: Russian Reform Goes Awry*. London, UK: Routledge, 2003. Pg. 157-160
[10] Belton, Catherine. *Putin's People: How The KGB Took Back Russia And Then Took On The West*. New York, NY: Farrar, Straus and Giroux, 2020. Pg. 65-66

[11] Klebnikov, Paul. *Godfather Of The Kremlin: Boris Berezovsky and the Looting of Russia.* New York, NY: Harcourt, Inc. 2000. Pg. 58

[12] Dobbs, Michael; Coll, Steven. "Ex-Communists Are Scrambling For Quick Cash," *The Washington Post.* February 1st, 1993

[13] Klebnikov, Paul. *Godfather Of The Kremlin: Boris Berezovsky and the Looting of Russia.* New York, NY: Harcourt, Inc. 2000. Pg. 59

[14] Dobbs, Michael; Coll, Steven. "Ex-Communists Are Scrambling For Quick Cash," *The Washington Post.* February 1st, 1993

[15] MacKinnon, Mark. "Searching for Boris Birshtein," *The Globe and Mail.* December 29th, 2018

[16] Kerry, John. *The New War: The Web Of Crime That Threatens America's Security.* New York, NY: Simon & Schuster, 1997. Pg. 161-162

[17] "Organized Crime and the Special Services of the Commonwealth of Independent States," *Service for Analysis and Prevention, The Swiss Federal Office Of Police, Strategic Analysis Report [CONFIDENTIAL], Transborder Corruption Archives.* June 2007

[18] Gessen, Masha. *The Man Without A Face: The Unlikely Rise of Vladimir Putin.* New York, NY: RIVERHEAD BOOKS, 2012. Pg. 104-105

[19] Lee Myers, Steven. *The New Tsar: The Rise and Reign of Vladimir Putin.* New York, NY: Alfred A. Knopf, 2015. Pg. 79

[20] Gessen, Masha. *The Man Without A Face: The Unlikely Rise of Vladimir Putin.* New York, NY: RIVERHEAD BOOKS, 2012. Pg. 123

[21] Dawisha, Karen. *Putin's Kleptocracy: Who Owns Russia?.* New York, NY: Simon & Schuster, 2014. Pg. 109

[22] Gessen, Masha. *The Man Without A Face: The Unlikely Rise of Vladimir Putin.* New York, NY: RIVERHEAD BOOKS, 2012. Pg. 118-119

[23] Belton, Catherine. *Putin's People: How The KGB Took Back Russia And Then Took On The West.* New York, NY: Farrar, Straus and Giroux, 2020. Pg. 93

[24] Lee Myers, Steven. *The New Tsar: The Rise and Reign of Vladimir Putin.* New York, NY: Alfred A. Knopf, 2015. Pg. 79

[25] Dawisha, Karen. *Putin's Kleptocracy: Who Owns Russia?.* New York, NY: Simon & Schuster, 2014. Pg. 127

[26] Galeotti, Mark. *The Vory: Russia's Super Mafia.* New Haven and London: Yale University Press, 2018. Pg. 143

[27] Belton, Catherine. *Putin's People: How The KGB Took Back Russia And Then Took On The West.* New York, NY: Farrar, Straus and Giroux, 2020. Pg. 95-101

[28] Dawisha, Karen. *Putin's Kleptocracy: Who Owns Russia?.* New York, NY: Simon & Schuster, 2014. Pg. 127

[29] Lee Myers, Steven. *The New Tsar: The Rise and Reign of Vladimir Putin.* New York, NY: Alfred A. Knopf, 2015. Pg. 85

[30] Hosenball, Mark. "A Stain on Mr. Clean," *Newsweek.* September 2nd, 2001.

[31] Dawisha, Karen. *Putin's Kleptocracy: Who Owns Russia?.* New York, NY: Simon & Schuster, 2014. Pg. 133

[32] Dawisha, Karen. *Putin's Kleptocracy: Who Owns Russia?.* New York, NY: Simon & Schuster, 2014. Pg. 134

[33] Lee Myers, Steven. *The New Tsar: The Rise and Reign of Vladimir Putin.* New York, NY: Alfred A. Knopf, 2015. Pg. 85

[34] Dawisha, Karen. *Putin's Kleptocracy: Who Owns Russia?.* New York, NY: Simon & Schuster, 2014. Pg. 98

[35] Dawisha, Karen. *Putin's Kleptocracy: Who Owns Russia?.* New York, NY: Simon & Schuster, 2014. Pg. 137

[36] Dawisha, Karen. *Putin's Kleptocracy: Who Owns Russia?.* New York, NY: Simon & Schuster, 2014. Pg. 94

[37] Dawisha, Karen. *Putin's Kleptocracy: Who Owns Russia?.* New York, NY: Simon & Schuster, 2014. Pg. 165

[38] Lee Myers, Steven. *The New Tsar: The Rise and Reign of Vladimir Putin*. New York, NY: Alfred A. Knopf, 2015. Pg. 101

[39] Dawisha, Karen. *Putin's Kleptocracy: Who Owns Russia?*. New York, NY: Simon & Schuster, 2014. Pg. 63

[40] Dawisha, Karen. *Putin's Kleptocracy: Who Owns Russia?*. New York, NY: Simon & Schuster, 2014. Pg. 66

[41] Anin, Roman. "Russia: Banking on Influence," *Organized Crime and Corruption Reporting Project (OCCRP)*. June 9th, 2016.

[42] Berwick, Angus. "Spain issues warrants for Russian officials alleged to be linked to crime gang," *Reuters*. May 3rd, 2016.

[43] Gessen, Masha. *The Man Without A Face: The Unlikely Rise of Vladimir Putin*. New York, NY: RIVERHEAD BOOKS, 2012. Pg. 139

[44] Lee Myers, Steven. *The New Tsar: The Rise and Reign of Vladimir Putin*. New York, NY: Alfred A. Knopf, 2015. Pg. 109

[45] Corwin, Julie. "Russia: U.S. Academics Charge Putin With Plagiarizing Thesis," *RadioFreeEurope/RadioLiberty*. March 27th, 2006.

[46] Hoffman, David. "Russia's Clans Go To War," *The Washington Post*. October 26th, 1997.

[47] Bohlen, Celestine. "Secrecy by Kremlin Financial Czars Raises Eyebrows," *The New York Times*. July 30th, 1999.

[48] Dawisha, Karen. *Putin's Kleptocracy: Who Owns Russia?*. New York, NY: Simon & Schuster, 2014. Pg. 188

[49] Sanger, David E. "In House Testimony, Rubin Admits Loans to Russia May Have Been Used 'Improperly'," *The New York Times*. March 19th, 1999

[50] Pirani, Simon; Farrelly, Paul. "IMF knew about Russian aid scam," *The Guardian*. October 17th, 1999

[51] Block, Alan A.; Weaver, Constance A. *All Is Clouded By De$ire: Global Banking, Money Laundering and International Organized Crime*. Westport, CT: Praeger Publishers, 2004. Pg.148

[52] Reeves, Phil; O'Hagan, Simon. "Yeltsin makes his double gin palace while Russia sinks," *The Independent*. December 14th, 1997

[53] LaFraniere, Sharon. "Yeltsin Linked to Bribe Scheme," *The Washington Post*. September 8th, 1999

[54] Belton, Catherine. *Putin's People: How The KGB Took Back Russia And Then Took On The West*. New York, NY: Farrar, Straus and Giroux, 2020. Pg. 118-120

[55] Tagliabue, John; Bohlen, Celestine. "Accusations of Bribery In the Kremlin Mount Up," *The New York Times*. September 9th, 1999

[56] Bonner, Raymond; O'Brien, Timothy L. "Activity At Bank Raises Suspicions of Russian Mob Tie," *The New York Times*. August 19th, 1999

[57] Dawisha, Karen. *Putin's Kleptocracy: Who Owns Russia?*. New York, NY: Simon & Schuster, 2014. Pg. 210

[58] Block, Alan A.; Weaver, Constance A. *All Is Clouded By De$ire: Global Banking, Money Laundering and International Organized Crime*. Westport, CT: Praeger Publishers, 2004. Pg. 7

[59] O'Brien, Timothy L.; Bonner, Raymond. "Bank in Laundering Inquiry Courted Russians Vigorously," *The New York Times*. August 20th, 1999

[60] Block, Alan A.; Weaver, Constance A. *All Is Clouded By De$ire: Global Banking, Money Laundering and International Organized Crime*. Westport, CT: Praeger Publishers, 2004. Pg. 7

[61] O'Brien, Timothy L.; Bonner, Raymond. "Russian Money Laundering Investigation Finds Familiar Swiss Banker in the Middle," *The New York Times*. August 22nd, 1999

[62] Block, Alan A.; Weaver, Constance A. *All Is Clouded By De$ire: Global Banking, Money Laundering and International Organized Crime*. Westport, CT: Praeger Publishers, 2004. Pg. 8

[63] Block, Alan A.; Weaver, Constance A. *All Is Clouded By De$ire: Global Banking, Money Laundering and International Organized Crime*. Westport, CT: Praeger Publishers, 2004. Pg. 27

[64] Walsh, Lawrence E. (Independent Counsel) *Iran-Contra: The Final Report*. New York, NY: Times Books, 1993. Pg. 197

[65] O'Harrow Jr., Robert; LaFraniere, Sharon. "No Open-and-Shut Case," *The Washington Post*. October 3rd, 1999

[66] O'Brien, Timothy L.; Bonner, Raymond. "Banker and Husband Tell Of Role in Laundering Case," *The New York Times*. February 7th, 2000

[67] Block, Alan A.; Weaver, Constance A. *All Is Clouded By De$ire: Global Banking, Money Laundering and International Organized Crime*. Westport, CT: Praeger Publishers, 2004. Pg. 144

[68] O'Brien, Timothy L.; Bonner, Raymond. "Banker and Husband Tell Of Role in Laundering Case," *The New York Times*. February 7th, 2000

[69] "NSA Intelink Blog Boosts Info-Sharing," *Snowden Archive, The Intercept*. June 5th, 2006

[70] Unger, Craig. *House of Putin, House of Trump: The Untold Story of Donald Trump and the Russian Mafia*. New York, NY: Penguin Random House LLC, 2018. Pg. 87

[71] Hirsch, Michael, "The Gangster State," *Newsweek*. September 5th, 1999

[72] Farrelly, Paul. "Elite's underwood links exposed," *The Guardian*. September 5th, 1999

[73] Friedman, Robert I. *Red Mafiya: How The Russian Mob Invaded America*. Boston, New York, London: Little, Brown and Company, 2000. Pg. 241

[74] Block, Alan A.; Weaver, Constance A. *All Is Clouded By De$ire: Global Banking, Money Laundering and International Organized Crime*. Westport, CT: Praeger Publishers, 2004. Pg. 154

[75] Schwirtz, Michael. "For a Departed Mobster, Wreaths and Roses but No Tears," *The New York Times*. October 13th, 2009

[76] OCCRP Archive Research, "Semion Mogilevich Organization: Eurasian Organized Crime," Eurasian Organized Crime, Department of Justice and the Federal Bureau of Investigation, August 1996, Pg. 3

[77] Block, Alan A.; Weaver, Constance A. *All Is Clouded By De$ire: Global Banking, Money Laundering and International Organized Crime*. Westport, CT: Praeger Publishers, 2004. Pg. 154

[78] Harden, Blaine. "Threatened By Mob, Journalist Pushes Back," *The New York Times*. March 5th, 1999

[79] Friedman, Robert I. *Red Mafiya: How The Russian Mob Invaded America*. Boston, New York, London: Little, Brown and Company, 2000. Pg. 241

[80] Block, Alan A.; Weaver, Constance A. *All Is Clouded By De$ire: Global Banking, Money Laundering and International Organized Crime*. Westport, CT: Praeger Publishers, 2004. Pg. 155

[81] OCCRP Archive Research, "Semion Mogilevich Organization: Eurasian Organized Crime," Eurasian Organized Crime, Department of Justice and the Federal Bureau of Investigation, August 1996, Pg. 1

[82] Bonner, Raymond. "F.B.I. Going to Budapest to Hunt Mob," *The New York Times*. February 21st, 2000

[83] Ryan, Jason. "$100,000 Reward for Three Added to FBI Top 10 List," *ABC News*. October 22nd, 2009

[84] Belton, Catherine. *Putin's People: How The KGB Took Back Russia And Then Took On The West*. New York, NY: Farrar, Straus and Giroux, 2020. Pg. 337

[85] Burgis, Tom. *Kleptopia: How Dirty Money Is Conquering The World*. New York, NY: HarperCollins, 2020. Pg. 175-176

[86] Unger, Craig. *House of Putin, House of Trump: The Untold Story of Donald Trump and the Russian Mafia*. New York, NY: Penguin Random House LLC, 2018. Pg. 89

[87] Bonner, Raymond. "Bank Affair and a Yeltsin Son-in-Law," *The New York Times*.

September 21st, 1999

[88] Beckett, Paul; Cloud, David S. "Bank of New York Off-Shore Accounts Tied to Yeltsin Son-in-Law Examined," *The Wall Street Journal.* September 22nd, 1999

[89] Stout, David, "Yeltsin Says Corruption Charges Are Politically Inspired," *The New York Times.* September 9th, 1999

[90] Dawisha, Karen. *Putin's Kleptocracy: Who Owns Russia?*. New York, NY: Simon & Schuster, 2014. Pg. 174

[91] Lee Myers, Steven. *The New Tsar: The Rise and Reign of Vladimir Putin.* New York, NY: Alfred A. Knopf, 2015. Pg. 122-123

[92] Dawisha, Karen. *Putin's Kleptocracy: Who Owns Russia?*. New York, NY: Simon & Schuster, 2014. Pg. 183

[93] Satter, David. *Darkness At Dawn: The Rise of the Russian Criminal State.* New Haven and London: Yale University Press, 2003. Pg. 56

[94] Lee Myers, Steven. *The New Tsar: The Rise and Reign of Vladimir Putin.* New York, NY: Alfred A. Knopf, 2015. Pg. 138

[95] Satter, David. *Darkness At Dawn: The Rise of the Russian Criminal State.* New Haven and London: Yale University Press, 2003. Pg. 57

[96] Lee Myers, Steven. *The New Tsar: The Rise and Reign of Vladimir Putin.* New York, NY: Alfred A. Knopf, 2015. Pg. 135

[97] Lee Myers, Steven. *The New Tsar: The Rise and Reign of Vladimir Putin.* New York, NY: Alfred A. Knopf, 2015. Pg. 139

[98] Lee Myers, Steven. *The New Tsar: The Rise and Reign of Vladimir Putin.* New York, NY: Alfred A. Knopf, 2015. Pg. 140

[99] Lee Myers, Steven. *The New Tsar: The Rise and Reign of Vladimir Putin.* New York, NY: Alfred A. Knopf, 2015. Pg. 150

[100] Gessen, Masha. *The Man Without A Face: The Unlikely Rise of Vladimir Putin.* New York, NY: RIVERHEAD BOOKS, 2012. Pg. 27

[101] Cockburn, Patrick. "Russia 'planned Chechen war before the bombings'" The Independent. January 29th, 2000

[102] Satter, David. *The Less You Know, The Better You Sleep.* New Haven and London: Yale University Press, 2016. Pg. 6

[103] Satter, David. *The Less You Know, The Better You Sleep.* New Haven and London: Yale University Press, 2016. Pg. 3-5

[104] Dunlop, John B. *The Moscow Bombings of September 1999: Examinations of Russian Terrorist Attacks at the Onset of Vladimir Putin's Rule.* Stuttgart, Germany: ibidem-Verlag, 2014. Pg. 66-70

[105] Zarakhovich, Yuri. "Profits of Doom," *Time Magazine.* September 28th, 2003

[106] Knight, Amy. *Orders To Kill: The Putin Regime and Political Murder.* New York, NY: St. Martin's Press, 2017. Pg. 81

[107] Gessen, Masha. *The Man Without A Face: The Unlikely Rise of Vladimir Putin.* New York, NY: RIVERHEAD BOOKS, 2012. Pg. 24

[108] Dunlop, John B. *The Moscow Bombings of September 1999: Examinations of Russian Terrorist Attacks at the Onset of Vladimir Putin's Rule.* Stuttgart, Germany: ibidem-Verlag, 2014. Pg. 85-89

[109] Satter, David. *The Less You Know, The Better You Sleep.* New Haven and London: Yale University Press, 2016. Pg. 8

[110] Satter, David. *The Less You Know, The Better You Sleep.* New Haven and London: Yale University Press, 2016. Pg. 9

[111] Dawisha, Karen. *Putin's Kleptocracy: Who Owns Russia?*. New York, NY: Simon & Schuster, 2014. Pg. 212

[112] Lee Myers, Steven. *The New Tsar: The Rise and Reign of Vladimir Putin.* New York, NY: Alfred A. Knopf, 2015. Pg. 160

[113] Satter, David. *The Less You Know, The Better You Sleep.* New Haven and London: Yale University Press, 2016. Pg. 10

[114] Satter, David. *The Less You Know, The Better You Sleep*. New Haven and London: Yale University Press, 2016. Pg. 11

[115] Knight, Amy. *Orders To Kill: The Putin Regime and Political Murder*. New York, NY: St. Martin's Press, 2017. Pg. 94

[116] Satter, David. *The Less You Know, The Better You Sleep*. New Haven and London: Yale University Press, 2016. Pg. 10

[117] Lee Myers, Steven. *The New Tsar: The Rise and Reign of Vladimir Putin*. New York, NY: Alfred A. Knopf, 2015. Pg. 160

[118] Knight, Amy. *Orders To Kill: The Putin Regime and Political Murder*. New York, NY: St. Martin's Press, 2017. Pg. 94

[119] Dunlop, John B. *The Moscow Bombings of September 1999: Examinations of Russian Terrorist Attacks at the Onset of Vladimir Putin's Rule*. Stuttgart, Germany: ibidem-Verlag, 2014. Pg. 180

[120] Gessen, Masha. *The Man Without A Face: The Unlikely Rise of Vladimir Putin*. New York, NY: RIVERHEAD BOOKS, 2012. Pg. 26-27

[121] Dawisha, Karen. *Putin's Kleptocracy: Who Owns Russia?*. New York, NY: Simon & Schuster, 2014. Pg. 211

[122] Lee Myers, Steven. *The New Tsar: The Rise and Reign of Vladimir Putin*. New York, NY: Alfred A. Knopf, 2015. Pg. 162-164

[123] Dawisha, Karen. *Putin's Kleptocracy: Who Owns Russia?*. New York, NY: Simon & Schuster, 2014. Pg. 210

[124] Lee Myers, Steven. *The New Tsar: The Rise and Reign of Vladimir Putin*. New York, NY: Alfred A. Knopf, 2015. Pg. 162-164

[125] Dawisha, Karen. *Putin's Kleptocracy: Who Owns Russia?*. New York, NY: Simon & Schuster, 2014. Pg. 241

[126] Lee Myers, Steven. *The New Tsar: The Rise and Reign of Vladimir Putin*. New York, NY: Alfred A. Knopf, 2015. Pg. 162-164

[127] Gessen, Masha. *The Man Without A Face: The Unlikely Rise of Vladimir Putin*. New York, NY: RIVERHEAD BOOKS, 2012. Pg. 40

[128] Dawisha, Karen. *Putin's Kleptocracy: Who Owns Russia?*. New York, NY: Simon & Schuster, 2014. Pg. 241

Chapter 4:
Trump's Rise in Atlantic City
and Financial Downfall

Trump in Atlantic City: Casinos, Civic Corruption, and Organized Crime

Donald Trump had dreamed of owning a casino as far back as 1976 when he told reporters about his ambition to build the largest casino in Las Vegas and name it Xanadu. Before he made his move on Atlantic City, Trump lobbied to legalize gambling in New York City. He had designed the Grand Hyatt to accommodate a casino floor. Despite Trump's advocacy, the legal gambling movement in New York slowed to stall, and Trump turned his attention to New Jersey.

Ever since Bugsy Siegel had established the Flamingo Resort and Casino in Las Vegas with money from Meyer Lansky, gambling had primarily been the province of the mafia. However, in 1976, Nevada lost its treasured status as the only state to allow for legal gambling. On the same day Jimmy Carter was elected the 39th President of the United States, voters in New Jersey passed a referendum that allowed for legalized gambling in Atlantic City. Soon after that, developments on Wall Street led to a trend of corporate casino ownership.

In the 1970s and 80s, there was a boom in the high-yield bond market, better known as junk bonds. The man most associated with the junk bond bonanza was a senior executive at the investment bank Drexel Burnham Lambert named Michael Milken, the Junk Bond King. In the 1970s, many once successful blue-chip American companies had fallen on hard times. Milken realized that credit agencies had downgraded many of these corporations to C-grade status, otherwise known as junk. He put together his own high-yield bond department, started taking massive gambles, and raised immense sums of money. Some used the money to become corporate raiders; others invested in casinos.

As David Cay Johnston put it in his book *Temples of Chance*: America Inc. bought out Murder Inc. The first client Milken brought to Drexel was Steve Wynn, owner of the Atlantic City casino, the Golden Nugget. Other mainstream corporations jumped on the 80s junk bond bandwagon to the tune of $5 billion, including Hilton, Holiday Inn, and Ramada.[1] However, in Atlantic City, Donald Trump was destined to become the biggest name on the boardwalk, and while he didn't use Michael Milken to do it, he did rely on the accumulation of vast debt.

Trump's first challenge was finding a suitable casino location in Atlantic City. The city had fallen on hard times, with more people living in Public Housing than anywhere else in America.[2] The casinos were designed to hide this reality, keeping their customers distracted by the flashy lights and attractions littering vast casino floors. The parcel Trump first identified was an ideal location at the center of the boardwalk strip, next to the convention center, and easily accessed by drivers making their way into the city from the local expressway.

Trump's associations with organized crime in Atlantic City began immediately after he stepped out of his limo. This had the potential to pose an enormous problem for him, as New Jersey regulators were meant to deny anyone with links to organized crime a license to own or operate a casino. Trump was determined to lease the parcel for what would become the Trump Plaza Hotel and Casino. Many of the key players in the complex ownership scheme of the site had shady affiliations, none more so than Daniel Sullivan and Kenny Shapiro.

Trump had worked with Daniel Sullivan before to sort out labor issues on the Grand Hyatt and Trump Tower projects. Sullivan had a rap sheet; court records show that he had been arrested on assault charges and had been imprisoned for larceny. He served as a middleman between the mafia and organized labor. In 1966, Sullivan was the last person to see labor lawyer Abraham Bauman alive, presumed murdered, and friends had reported that Sullivan had told them that he knew where Jimmy Hoffa was buried. Sullivan was also an FBI informant.[3]

While Sullivan was working on Trump's Grand Hyatt project, he was overheard by an FBI surveillance team meeting with Theodore Maritas, the corrupt president of the District Council of Carpenters. Maritas, who was under federal investigation, was later indicted for labor racketeering along with a member of the Genovese crime family. Shortly after his arrest, he disappeared. Prosecutors assumed the mob murdered him after he had become a cooperating witness.[4] After FBI agents overheard Sullivan speaking with Maritas, they looked up his file and realized that Sullivan had acted as an FBI informant years earlier.

Special Agent Walter Stowe, an undercover specialist for the FBI, began an ongoing relationship with Sullivan to gain insights into the relationship between organized labor and the mafia. He soon heard about a brash young New York developer trying to open a casino in Atlantic City. Sullivan told Stowe that through a trash hauling business, he owned in Atlantic City, he had met a struggling business owner in possession of a prime piece of boardwalk real estate, which he subsequently purchased. This was the land that Donald Trump wanted to develop for his casino. However, Sullivan didn't own the property outright; he had bought it in a partnership with Kenny Shapiro.

Kenny Shapiro was a Jersey Shore real estate speculator later identified by the New Jersey State Commission of Investigation as a "financier" for the violent Philadelphia mafia syndicate run by Nicodemo "Little Nicky" Scarfo.[5] During his bloodthirsty reign, Scarfo was believed to be involved in over two dozen murders in the 80s alone.[6] The Scarfo crime family infiltrated the 20,000-strong hotel and casino's union and was a force to be reckoned with in the city.[7] Shapiro's office was on the boardwalk, and detectives monitoring it often noted a steady stream of wise guys entering and exiting the premises.

Sometime in April of 1981, Sullivan brought Walter Stowe and Damon Taylor, a supervisor of organized crime investigations at the FBI, to Trump's office. The developer, labor fixer, and two FBI agents had a conversation. An FBI memorandum described the meeting: "The purpose of this meeting was for DONALD TRUMP to express his reservations about building a casino in Atlantic City. TRUMP advised agents that he had read in the press media and had heard from various acquaintances that organized crime elements were known to operate in Atlantic City. TRUMP also expressed at this meeting the reservation that his life and those around him would be subject to microscopic examination. TRUMP advised that he wanted to build a casino in Atlantic City, but he did not wish to tarnish his family's name."[8]

Trump courted the FBI agents, suggesting they send undercover agents to the casino. He invited Agent Stowe to play golf with him at a private Westchester Course and took him out for lunch at the esteemed 21 Club. He even offered Stowe a job with the Trump Organization.[9] However, despite his wining and dining of Agent Stowe, Trump knew perfectly well the kinds of characters he was dealing with. "Some of those guys were tough guys. Shapiro. They were tough guys. In fact, they say that Dan Sullivan was the guy that killed Jimmy Hoffa," Trump told his biographer Timothy L. O'Brien. "They were tough guys and not good guys."[10]

Despite the rumors, Trump leased the property. However, his signature alone wasn't sufficient to push the deal over the finish line. The signature next to his was, unsurprisingly, Fred Trump's. To pay for the lease, Trump relied once again on the line of credit his father had established with Chase Bank. It was the same line of credit that allowed Trump to continue construction on the Grand Hyatt after there had been significant cost overruns.

Trump applied for his first casino license on May 1st, 1981. His decision to lease the property instead of buy it outright was risky. According to New Jersey regulations, for a gambling license to be awarded, all of the owners of a building site needed to be cleared of links to organized crime, not just the individual holding the lease. Therefore, Sullivan and Shapiro were likely to come under scrutiny. Matters were further complicated when Trump agreed to help finance Sullivan's purchase of Circle Industries, a drywall manufacturer. According to the deal, Trump would be a one-third partner in the company. Circle Industries was one of a group of 20 drywall makers known as "The Club." The company was implicated in a racketeering scheme between the carpenters' union and the Genovese crime family.[11] Roy Cohn represented the leaders of the Genovese crime family.

Trump used political connections as he navigated the regulatory bodies. Executive Vice President of the Trump Organization, Louise Sunshine, had worked as a fundraiser for

New York Governor Hugh Carey and had extensive contacts within the administration of New Jersey Governor Brendan Byrne. On the recommendation of media magnate and Roy Cohn friend Si Newhouse, Trump enlisted the services of a new attorney named Nick Ribis.[12] Ribis was personally acquainted with Joe Fusco, the head of the New Jersey Casino Control Commission's (CCC) licensing division. Ribis and Fusco later became business partners.[13]

A conflict existed between New Jersey's promise to enforce casino regulations and the economic imperatives of Atlantic City that Trump exploited with ruthless efficiency. After learning that the casino licensing process took 18 months, Trump invited New Jersey's Attorney General John Degnan and the head of the Division of Gaming Enforcement (DGE) to Nick Ribis' office and threatened to pull out of Atlantic City altogether if the process wasn't expedited. As New York State was still considering whether to legalize gambling, Trump further hinted that he would fully support that effort if he didn't get his way. Degnan, who was about to run for Governor, agreed to speed up the process.[14] After receiving this accommodation, Trump became an opponent of legalized gambling in New York. The measure failed.

Part of the CCC's licensing process included an investigation into Trump's character and integrity. On his licensing application, Trump was asked whether he had ever been the subject of a government investigation. The penalty for incomplete or false answers was the denial of the license. Of course, Trump had been the subject of multiple federal investigations. Though his application has never been made public, there is every indication that Trump intentionally omitted disqualifying facts from it. There appears to have been no mention of the 1979 federal grand jury investigation put together by the United States attorney for Brooklyn Ed Korman into a shady deal Trump struck to obtain an option to buy the West Side Railyards, for which the FBI interviewed Trump. Trump also failed to mention that the FBI questioned him over his relationship with labor racketeer John Cody during the construction of Trump Tower.

The application also inquired whether he had ever been the subject of a civil suit or accused by any government entity of violating a "statute, regulation or code." Of course, Trump had been sued by the Department of Justice for housing discrimination. He lied on the form, stating he had never been investigated. His misrepresentation was shunted into a footnote of the DGE's final report, claiming that Trump had "volunteered information" about the suit before being asked about it during a DGE interview. Without explanation, Scarfo mob associate and co-owner of Trump's leased parcel, Kenny Shapiro, was omitted from the probe and subsequent DGE report. Two weeks after Trump had been awarded the casino license, authorities began 24-hour surveillance over Shapiro's boardwalk office, given the diversity of nefarious criminal contacts he maintained. This is even though Trump's relationship with Shapiro had by then expanded beyond the casino itself and now included negotiations over the purchase of a nearby parking lot.[15]

The DGE looked into Daniel Sullivan but used it as an exercise to discredit him without delving too deeply into his relationship with Trump. Regardless, Trump grew nervous when the DGE started looking into Sullivan, so nervous that he went ahead and told investigators about Sullivan's relationship with the FBI. By doing so, FBI records show that he imperiled a potential FBI undercover operation designed to root out organized crime at his future casino. When contacted by the DGE, Sullivan refused to answer any questions about his relationship with the FBI. No operation was ever conducted at Trump's casino.[16]

After an expedited and incomplete investigation, Trump received his casino license. Ultimately, all he had to do was buy out Sullivan and Shapiro's ownership stake in the parcel, which he did for $8 million. He also pulled out of the Circle Industries deal with Sullivan. Trump's timing was propitious, as Circle Industries was indicted shortly afterward for its involvement in a multimillion-dollar fraud and tax evasion scheme.[17] Trump told the DGE he would have no further personal, social, or business dealings with Sullivan. Nonetheless, he later offered him a job as his chief labor negotiator in 1992. Regarding Kenny Shapiro, Trump also continued to deal with the mafia financier. Shapiro was about to be entangled in a scandal that would reach the highest levels of Atlantic City's municipal leadership.

Atlantic City had just replaced its form of city government, and 47-year-old city commissioner Michael Matthews was running for mayor. During the campaign, Matthews met with Frank Lentino, Frank Gerace, and Al

Daidone, leaders of the Local 54 of the Hotel Workers Union. Matthews later admitted to federal officials that he understood the union leaders to be speaking to him as representatives of the Scarfo crime family.[18] In exchange for $125,000 in campaign contributions, Matthews agreed to use his position in city government to support contractors backed by Scarfo. Daidone, who was later indicted on charges of conspiring to murder a union rival, put Matthews in touch with Kenny Shapiro. In his capacity as financier for the Scarfo mob, Shapiro arranged for $35,000 to be funneled to the Matthews campaign. The cash came from various sources, some of which, according to Sullivan and Shapiro, were made by third parties at Donald Trump's request.

"I understand you're going to be the next mayor of Atlantic City," Matthews recalled Trump telling him during a meeting on December 4th, 1981, during the height of the campaign and the very same month the candidate met with the Scarfo associates. Matthews maintained that Trump "wanted to know if he could donate to my campaign."[19]

It was against state law for casino owners to donate to political campaigns. Sullivan and Shapiro told investigative reporter Wayne Barrett that they spoke with Trump about having his New York subcontractors donate to the Matthews Campaign, with Trump later reimbursing them. Sullivan and Shapiro also claimed that Trump asked Shapiro to make a $10,000 donation to Matthews under the promise that he would be reimbursed. Shapiro made the contribution but claimed that Trump never paid him back. Contributions by entities attached to the Trump casino project accounted for nearly 50% of Matthews' total campaign cash haul.[20]

As the campaign progressed, Matthews, still a sitting city commissioner, advocated for Trump while negotiating zoning and air rights issues with the city. Matthews won the mayor's race by a narrow margin, 359 votes. A year later, Frank Lentino, one of the mafia conspirators funding Matthews' campaign, was recorded discussing the matter with an FBI informant. After a brief stint on the lam in Florida, the story hit the headlines on December 3rd, 1983, and Matthews returned to Atlantic City and was arrested. After Shapiro's grand jury testimony, Trump and others at the Trump Organization were questioned by FBI agents. However, Matthews pleaded guilty during the trial, preventing Shapiro from taking the stand and keeping his grand jury testimony from entering discovery. Ultimately, no charges were filed against Trump.

After securing his casino license and necessary zoning rights, Trump searched for financing and a reputable casino operator. When discussions with "Junk Bond King" Michael Milken failed, Trump entered into negotiations with Harrah's. Harrah's, a Las Vegas institution, had recently been purchased by Holiday Corp, the parent company of the iconic Holiday Inn hotel chain. Though founded by Evangelical Christians, a new generation of management had seen a different kind of light and entered the casino business. The company opened a casino in Atlantic City and wanted to expand its presence on the boardwalk.

Trump didn't tell them that even though construction on his casino was barely off the ground, he had so little money that he relied on his father's credit to keep his Atlantic City project creeping forward.[21] In June of 1982, Trump took Harrah's board members on a tour of his construction site. To make it appear that there was construction taking place, Trump paid a crew of workers to push large mounds of dirt around the previously inactive construction site. His minor deception worked because three weeks later, Harrah's invested $50 million upfront and agreed to secure financing for the construction and, upon its completion, take charge of the day-to-day operations of the casino-hotel. This represented a significant coup for the young dealmaker by nearly every measure.

With the Harrah's windfall in place, Trump purchased a nearby parcel to convert into a parking garage. The location he selected was owned by Salvatore "Salvie" Testa and Frank Narducci Jr. It was a curious ownership arrangement, as Testa, who was known as the "Crowned Prince of the Philadelphia Mob," had murdered Narducci's father by shooting him ten times in the face, neck and chest at point-blank range.[22] Testa and Narducci had apparently buried the hatchet as they were both members of the Scarfo hit squad known as the Young Executioners. Trump purchased the parcel for $1.1 million, a significant markup from the $195,000 that Testa and Narducci had paid. To distance himself from the purchase, Trump routed the payment through an associate and then to a Trump-related entity.[23]

Before his indictment, Mayor Mathews successfully lobbied for Trump to be exempted from several city restrictions related to his new parking lot, including constructing a skyway linking it to his casino. Trump also managed to get the city to approve signs larger than city regulations permitted after the mobbed-up union leader Frank Gerace, who was later indicted alongside Matthews, attended a meeting of the zoning board to make sure one of the union-linked members voted for the exemption.

A corrupt mayor and union leaders were not the only mafia-linked individuals and entities involved in the development of Trump's first casino. During construction, the Trump organization used three subcontractors with links to the Scarfo family. Nicky Scarfo was reported to have visited one of the contractors on the Plaza construction site. Trump brought attorney Paul Victor Viggiano from New York to negotiate with a trade union. Viggiano, who was related to a *capo* in the Genovese crime family, was also an associate of Roy Cohn's partner, Stanley Friedman, in the Bronx Democratic Party. Viggiano partnered with Kenny Shapiro on several Atlantic City real estate deals.[24]

As construction for the then-named Harrah's at Trump Plaza neared completion, Ivana Trump took a significant role in determining the interior design. True to Trump's trademark style, the casino displayed an over-the-top, marble-laden opulence, with columns draped in red cloth and adorned with mirrors. At 39 stories, it was the tallest building in Atlantic City at that point. The official opening took place in May of 1984. However, slot machine malfunctions and false fire alarms dampened the occasion. Harrah's at Trump Plaza significantly underperformed, earning less than half of its projected profits for its first year in operation.[25]

One high roller who dropped big bucks at the Trump Plaza, ultimately more than $11 million, was Robert LiButti, an employee of the Gambino crime family boss and Roy Cohn client, John Gotti. LiButti and his daughter regularly accompanied Trump and his family on helicopter rides to Atlantic City. Trump discussed purchasing a $500,000 racehorse from LiButti but the deal fell through when the horse went lame. The Trump Plaza was later fined $200,000 when New Jersey regulators discovered they were discriminating against black and female craps dealers at LiButti's request. Another $450,000 fine was levied against Trump's casino when it was discovered that it illegally had provided LiButti with $1.6 million in luxury cars.[26] In 1988, Trump and LiButti were filmed sitting next to one another in the front row at WrestleMania.[27] Three years later, LiButti was banned from Atlantic City.

The disappointing first year was just one of many reasons why Trump's relationship with Harrah's had begun to fray. The first, perhaps most characteristic, was that Trump didn't like the name. After much back and forth, he eventually got his way, and Harrah's was dropped for his preferred Trump Plaza Hotel and Casino. However, the name change didn't placate Trump. Displeased with the partnership itself, Trump wanted to own the casino outright. As a result, he dragged his feet on building the garage on the lot he had earlier acquired, hoping to use it to pressure Harrah's into selling its stake. Furthermore, Trump and Harrah's couldn't agree on a business strategy, with Trump wanting to cater to high rollers and Harrah's believing the steady business of slots customers was the recipe for success. However, Trump's acquisition of a competing casino pushed Harrah's over the edge.

The events leading to Trump's purchase of another boardwalk casino began in the Bahamas. In early 1985, a bribery scandal erupted when it was discovered that $431,000 of money from Resorts International, which owned casinos both in the Bahamas and Atlantic City, had found its way into accounts linked to the island's corrupt Prime Minister Lynden O. Pindling. While Resorts denied allegations of bribery, the scandal splashed across the headlines. It fell into the lap of the New Jersey Casino Control Commission right as Resorts gambling license was up for renewal.[28] Despite the pall cast by the scandal, Resorts owner James Crosby had maintained his relationships with influential members of the Commission. As a result, enough voted in favor of Resorts that it maintained its license. While accusations of corruption, insider dealing, and the ensuing media firestorm that erupted was an embarrassment to the state of New Jersey, it proved an even greater problem for Barron Hilton.

Heir to the late Conrad Hilton, Barron sat atop his father's hotel empire. The company was completing the finishing touches on a 60,000-square-foot resort casino situated across the street from Harrah's Marina, the casino owned by Trump's partners at the Plaza. However, unlike Jim Crosby, Barron hadn't adequately massaged his relationships at the CCC. In a shocking turn of events, a newly recondite Commission rediscovered its sense of moral purpose and, two days after the Resorts, voted to deny Hilton's gambling license because of the company's relationship with the prominent Chicago mob attorney Sidney Korshak, whom law enforcement accused of linking legitimate businesses with the underworld. Hilton Hotels reportedly used Korshak to ensure labor peace.[29]

The irony could not have been lost on Trump. A competitor had been vanquished overnight due to his connection to a mobbed-up attorney when Trump's lawyer, Roy Cohn, was perhaps the only mafia lawyer in America who could claim to have been indicted more often than his clients. Having a casino without a gambling license placed Barron Hilton in a difficult position. Trump immediately offered to buy Hilton out but was rebuffed as a slim reed of hope emerged when the CCC voted to hold a rehearing. However, events further afield again intervened to Trump's benefit. This time, it was not in The Bahamas but in Beverly Hills.

By 1985, Michael Milken was at the height of his powers, and the corporate raider era had reached predatory new heights. With a junk bond-fueled fortune at his back, Steve Wynn began circling Hilton Hotels, poised for a hostile takeover. Anxious to keep control of his family company, Barron decided to cut his losses and sell to Trump. Trump christened his new acquisition Trump Castle. Harrah's was enraged that their partner at the Plaza was now opening a competing casino next to Harrah's Marina. After trading lawsuits and public condemnations, Harrah's eventually sold its half of Trump Plaza, and Trump became the sole owner of not one but two casinos on the boardwalk.

Whereas the Trump Plaza took four years from conception to opening day, Trump Castle opened four months after Trump took over from Hilton. Trump was now one of the most prominent players on the boardwalk, but the cost of being king was steep. In a matter of months, Trump saddled himself with enormous debt. The purchase price for Trump Castle was $320 million. Bear Stearns, seeking to emulate Milken and get into the casino game, raised over $352 million of mortgage-backed bonds that allowed Trump to make the purchase. Trump then took out an additional $70 million loan from the bank

Manufacturers Hanover to cover improvements.

Bear Stearns arranged a $250 million bond sale to raise the capital to buy out Harrah's. The acquisition cost him $278 million, which he covered almost entirely with borrowed money. In half a year, Trump had borrowed more than $700 million to fund the Trump Plaza and Trump Castle. It marked an important milestone in Trump's career. He was now operating with an enormous and ever-growing debt load. However, he and the banks were confident the casino business would ultimately pay off.

Trump's takeover of the Plaza and Trump Castle meant he had to face the DGE and CCC again. After Hilton's disastrous relationship with the mob-linked attorney Sidney Korshak, one might think Trump's relationship with Roy Cohn might pose a problem. Particularly since one of Cohn's top clients, Fat Tony Salerno, was not just a player in New York City but also influential in Atlantic City. Salerno, law enforcement officials believed, had sanctioned hits on the men who killed Nicky Scarfo's predecessor. Federal surveillance of Salerno recorded him saying, "I'm the fucking boss, that's who I am. Connecticut is mine; New Jersey is mine."[30]

However, no such problems emerged, and Trump sailed through the licensing process unscathed. His years of courting officials and forging political connections had paid off. Furthermore, Trump could now count another occupant of high office as a valuable ally. In 1982, Republican Thomas Kean defeated Democrat Jim Florio to become the 48th Governor of New Jersey. Kean won the race by 1,797 votes, the narrowest margin of victory in state history. The chief strategist for his campaign was an up-and-coming Republican political strategist and Roy Cohn protégé by the name of Roger J. Stone.

The Trump Whisperer: Enter Roger Stone, Exit Roy Cohn

Roger Stone tells several variations of how he first met Roy Cohn in 1979. Stone is notorious for playing fast and loose with the truth. In recounting his personal history, he has no scruples when highlighting or exaggerating the infamous. Thus, his stories have proven catnip to those reporting on him. Often, they're just too good not to print. However, while this tendency inevitably sows doubt among those who must weigh the veracity of his claims, it also reveals something essential about his character and modus operandi.

In one version of events, Stone first met Roy Cohn at a party held by Sheila Mosler, a socialite and vice chairman of the New York County Republican Committee. In another, Cohn's name came up on a rolodex given to him by Michael Deaver, an advisor to Ronald Reagan. At the time, the 27-year-old Stone was the political director of New York, New Jersey, and Connecticut for the Reagan Campaign. Stone cut a flamboyant character. Unlike most campaign staffers, he was a champion of haute couture and could often be seen in a double-breasted suit sporting a designer watch. Regardless of how initial contact was made, all the stories end up with Roger visiting Roy at his 68th Street townhouse in Manhattan.

"When I got there, Roy was in his bathrobe, eating three strips of bacon burned crisp and both halves of a deviled egg," Stone said. He noticed a heavy-set man sitting next to Cohn.[31]

"Mr. Stone, I want you to meet Tony Salerno," Cohn said, introducing the young Reagan staffer to the underboss of the Genovese crime family.[32]

"So Roy says we're going with Reagan this time," Salerno chimed in. Stone launched into his pitch for the California governor as Cohn and Fat Tony listened intently.

"You know, Tony, everything's fixed." Stone quoted Cohn as saying. "Everything can be handled." Salerno mentioned the Supreme Court. Cohn continued. "Cost a few more dollars."[33]

"He started telling me how he was going to help me set up the Reagan Campaign," Stone said. "[E]verything from union endorsements to office space. He told me to ride down to the courthouse with him. He had a young lawyer with him, and it was clear that Roy knew nothing about the case he was going to argue. But he knew it didn't matter. He used to say, 'Don't tell me the law. Tell me the judge.' Roy knew how the world worked." Cohn had another suggestion for Stone during their first meeting.

"You need to meet Donald and his father," Cohn insisted. "They'd be perfect for this. Let me set up a meeting."

"I went to go see him," Stone recalled, "and Trump said, 'How do you get Reagan to 270 electoral votes?' He was very interested [in the mechanics] - a political junkie. Then he said, 'O.K., we are in. Go see my father.'" Stone traveled to Fred Trump's Avenue Z office in Coney Island. "True to his word, I got $200,000. The checks came in $1,000 denominations, the maximum donation you could give. All of these checks were written to 'Reagan for President.' It was not illegal - it was bundling. Check trading."[34] The Trumps even arranged for Stone to open Reagan's New York City campaign headquarters in a townhouse next to the 21 Club. It was the beginning of a fateful political alliance.

Roger Stone was born in 1952 in Norwalk, Connecticut. He spent much of his childhood in Lewisboro, New York, on the Connecticut border. Half Italian and half Hungarian, Stone's mother wrote for a local newspaper, and his father was a laborer who dug wells for a living. As a child, Stone had supported John F. Kennedy because he was Catholic and "had better hair than Nixon." However, upon receiving a copy of Barry Goldwater's book *The Conscience of a Conservative*, Stone became a staunch Republican at the age of eleven.

Stone developed an early fascination with Richard Nixon and came to believe that he "had been fucked out of the presidency in 1960, thanks to Joe Kennedy and [his] mob friends." Stone penned a letter to Nixon encouraging him to run again. Nixon replied with a thank you note, telling Stone that he had no plans to run again, but he would be in touch if he did.[35]

Stone's first political job was as an aide with the Republican John Davis Lodge, who served as the 79th Governor of Connecticut from 1951–1955. Stone describes Lodge as a "mentor" who appointed the 16-year-old Stone to serve as the Connecticut Chairman of Youth for Nixon. John Lodge's brother, Henry Cabot Lodge, served as an Ambassador to South Vietnam during JFK's administration. Stone claims that in 1979, he asked John Lodge whether he had ever inquired with his brother about who had killed JFK. According to Stone, Lodge told him it was a combination of the CIA, the Mafia, and Lyndon Baines Johnson. Stone's JFK assassination theories are not supported here.

Stone moved to Washington, DC, to attend George Washington University. At a time when the counterculture movement was in full steam, Stone joined the Young Americans for Freedom.[36] During Nixon's 1972 re-election campaign, Stone invited Jeb Magruder, the deputy director of the Committee to Reelect the President (CREEP), to speak before the college's Young Republican Club. "There are a bunch of hippie-type, leftwing, pinko degenerates that attend and harass him, but he handles it okay," Stone recalled of the event.[37] Afterwards, Stone asked Magruder for a job and was hired. He dropped out of college and joined CREEP.

Stone was the assistant to the President of CREEP, Bart Porter, who also ran the organization's dirty tricks operations.[38] During the day, the 19-year-old Stone was a scheduler for Nixon campaign surrogates. "By night, I'm trafficking in the black arts. Nixon's people were obsessed with intelligence." Under orders from Porter, Stone arranged for a spy named Michael McMinoway, operating under the codename Sedan Chair II, to infiltrate the McGovern campaign. Under the pseudonym Jason Rainier, Stone provided donations in the name of the Young Socialist to the campaign of Republican primary challenger Pete McCloskey and then forwarded the receipts to the newspaper. Stone's experiences during the Nixon campaign had an enduring influence on his political ideology and campaign tactics.

After Nixon won reelection in 1972, Stone received a job at the Office of Economic Opportunity, responsible for many programs initiated under Lyndon B. Johnson's War on Poverty. As Stone describes it, Nixon aide H.R. Haldeman's "charge to us was to dismantle, replace, and fire everybody."[39] A year later, Haldeman was embroiled in the raging Watergate scandal and was tried on counts of perjury, conspiracy, and obstruction of justice. Stone had been renting a room from Bart Porter and claimed that Porter was out of town on the evening of the Watergate break-in, so he took urgent phone messages from various individuals associated with the break-in, including G. Gordon Liddy.[40] Nixon became the first and only President to resign to avoid being impeached and removed from office.

A significant Nixon-era influence on Stone was Murray Chotiner, a hugely influential political advisor to Nixon who had been with him since his first campaign for Congress. He pioneered the "dirty tricks" that the Nixon campaign later became famous for. According to historians and biographers, Chotiner served as Nixon's go-between with organized crime and the underworld, including individuals linked to the Meyer Lansky Syndicate like Mickey Cohen, who operated in the part of California that had Nixon's first Congressional district.[41]

"The best part of my job was hand delivering a copy of [the daily news summary] to the small, dark, secret office of

Murray Chotiner," Stone later recalled in his book *Nixon's Secrets*. "Located catty-corner from the White House in a different building from [the Committee to Re-Elect the President]. Murray was not on the directory, and his door didn't even have a number. Chotiner, a portly Jewish attorney from Pittsburgh, had moved West with his brother. They prospered as criminal defense attorneys, mostly for mob guys. Murray and his brother had represented over 221 hoodlums in one year."

"More importantly, he was the first 'political consultant.' Murray Chotiner understood how to communicate systems and the need to push simple and understandable messages, mostly negative, to voters. Chotiner would be present for the duration of Nixon's political career; although at many points hidden in the shadows, he was always only a phone call away."

Following Nixon's fall, Stone got a job in 1973 as a junior staffer for Senator Robert Dole. However, six months after he began, Stone's association with the so-called "Ratfuckers" of the Nixon campaign was revealed during a Congressional hearing, and he was forced to leave Dole's staff. Three years later, Stone served on Ronald Reagan's first unsuccessful attempt to garner the Republican nomination as the campaign's Youth Director. A year later, he formed the National Conservative Political Action Committee with fellow young Republicans Charles Black and Terry Dolan. The Committee pioneered the practice of bundling campaign contributions to circumvent campaign finance limits on individual donations. It served as a precursor to super Political Action Committees (PACs) that would later dominate politics.[42] It was at this time that Stone worked beneath the legendary Republican pollster and negative campaign strategist Arthur Finkelstein, who had an enduring influence on Stone and whose name will pop up several times later in this narrative in events surrounding the 2016 election.[43]

In the spring of 1977, Stone ran to be the chairman of the Young Republicans. A network of influential Republicans between the ages of 18-40, in the days of brokered conventions the Young Republicans was an influential organization. Stone's candidacy was managed by a young Republican operative named Paul Manafort. Manafort convinced Stone's chief rival to run for treasurer instead of president. Stone won after a campaign that Manafort would later describe as "one of the great fuck jobs" after he pulled support for Stone's rival at the last minute.[44]

By the time Stone was elected Chairman of the Young Republicans, he was already working on Reagan's 1980 campaign. His meeting with Roy Cohn in 1979 made quite an impression on the young politico. Years later, when asked who his heroes were, Stone listed Roy Cohn, Richard Nixon, and the Duke of Windsor.[45] After Reagan's election, Cohn and Stone became friends. Cohn even arranged Stone's 30th birthday party at the 21 Club. Stone formed a high-powered Washington lobbying outfit with Charles Black, Paul Manafort, and Lee Atwater called Black, Manafort, Stone & Atwater. Stone brought in one of the firm's earliest clients: Donald Trump. Stone's contacts within the new Reagan administration and Governor Thomas Kean in New Jersey would prove valuable commodities for Trump.

Roger Stone wasn't the only member of the Reagan Campaign that Cohn was connected to. According to notes taken by Cohn's switchboard operator, Reagan's 1980 campaign manager, William Casey, "called Roy almost daily during [Reagan's] 1st election."[46]

Casey was a Wall Street investor and a veteran of America's World War II-era intelligence service, the Office of Strategic Services (O.S.S.). Following the 1980 election, reporters and researchers alleged that Casey cut an "October Surprise" deal with the Iranians, who were holding American diplomatic personnel hostage, to wait until after the election to release them. The allegation received renewed attention after the research of Pulitzer Prize-winning author Kai Bird, who has claimed the validity of the theory is "all but settled."[47]

Nearly four decades later, Stone and another 1980 Reagan campaign alum, Paul Manafort, would be suspected of "colluding" with a foreign adversary to impact a domestic election. Stone addressed the so-called "October Surprise" allegations in a book he co-authored with Saint John Hunt during the 2016 Republican primary attacking Jeb Bush and the Bush family in general. "The Reagan/Bush camp needed to cut a secret deal with the Iranians not to release the hostages before the election," Stone and Hunt write in *Jeb! And The Bush Crime Family: The Inside Story of an American Dynasty*. "As it turned out, the hostages were not released as Carter had promised, and partly as a result of the years-long standoff with the Iranians, Carter lost the election. On January 21st, 1981, the very day that Reagan and Bush were being sworn in, the hostages found themselves on a plane to freedom. Coincidence? The accusations that Reagan and Bush had somehow thwarted the Carter/Iranian deal to free the hostages by election time, thereby winning the election for [Reagan], were rampant. How much of a role did [Bush] play? That's the million-dollar question."

Stone and Hunt continue, "Political researcher Robert Morrow interviewed retired admiral Bobby Ray Inman in 2009 in Austin, Texas. Inman, who was involved in intelligence for over 25 years, told Morrow that he was convinced that the Reagan campaign made a deal with the Iranians not to release the American hostages until after the 1980 general election. Inman said he was completely convinced Reagan campaign chair William Casey was involved in such a deal, but he said he did not think G.H.W. Bush was involved because Casey hated Bush. Inman worked at high levels of the Office of Naval Intelligence and the Defense Intelligence Agency while Bush was CIA director in 1976 and they developed a close working relationship."

"So, as with so many other "facts," we come to our own conclusions. Do we believe that our candidate was honest and would never dream of co-opting a presidential deal for his own gain? No, I say." A curious thing to say, seeing as Stone himself had worked on the campaign.

After the election, Roy Cohn enjoyed access to the Oval Office. He introduced President Reagan to the up-and-coming Australian news magnate Rupert Murdoch. After the meeting, Murdoch joined a CIA-backed propaganda effort to promote Reagan's policies in Latin America.[48] Murdoch-owned Fox News would later be a critical influence in getting Donald Trump elected in 2016.

Donald wasn't the only Trump who benefited from their early relationship with Roger Stone and Roy Cohn. Both Cohn and Stone pulled strings within the Reagan administration to aid with the appointment of Trump's elder sister, Maryann, to a federal judgeship. In 1983, Governor Kean had nominated Maryann for the position. At the time, Stone was still acting as Kean's informal advisor. The nomination was controversial as Maryann had achieved the New Jersey Bar Association's lowest favorable rating. When it appeared that someone else was in line in front of Maryann, Cohn contacted Reagan Attorney General Ed Meese and advocated on her behalf.[49] A few months later, she landed the position.

"Roy can do the impossible," Trump told a Cohn staffer over the phone. Unfortunately for Roy Cohn, perhaps the greatest fixer of his age, there would soon prove to be one challenge he couldn't talk, bribe, threaten, or use his contacts to escape. By the mid-1980s, the AIDS crisis was ravaging the gay community across the United States.

"Should I commit suicide now or later?" is how Cohn responded to his doctor on November 4th, 1984, after receiving the diagnosis that he had AIDS, according to notes kept by a switchboard operator in his office.[50] Cohn never publicly admitted that he had AIDS. Instead, he claimed that he had liver cancer.[51] However, as he grew increasingly ill, Trump pulled away from his lawyer, friend, and mentor by moving his cases to other attorneys without providing Cohn an explanation. When one of Cohn's friends was dying of AIDS, he asked Trump if he could arrange for a hotel room (without mentioning what disease Eldridge was suffering from). Trump did so but sent Cohn the bills, which he refused to pay. Eventually, the hotel asked the dying man to leave as they were worried about their reputation.

"I can't believe he's doing this to me," Roy lamented. "Donald pisses ice water."[52]

Adding insult to injury, the appellate division of New York's Supreme Court charged Cohn with professional misconduct involving dishonesty, fraud, deceit, and misrepresentation. The number of ethical violations had finally caught up with Cohn. In one instance, he had visited a wealthy client in the hospital after he had suffered from a stroke. Cohn claimed that during the visit, the client had made him the trustee to his estate. However, a nurse on duty watched as Cohn guided his dying client's hand to sign a legal document. During the hearing, several people, including Trump, lined up to attest to Cohn's character. However, in the end, it wasn't enough. Cohn was disbarred and died shortly thereafter, on August 2nd, 1986.

Resorts International, the Trump Taj Mahal,
And a Debt-Fueled Spending Binge

By the late 1980s, Trump was a fixture of American life. While his presence in tabloids and gossip columns had introduced him to New Yorkers in the 1970s, he was still largely unknown across the United States. The publication of his ghost-written autobiography *The Art Of The Deal* in 1987 established the enduring legend of Donald Trump. The book was launched at a star-studded party in Trump Tower and would go on to be a bestseller.

The idea that Trump should release an autobiography originated with Si Newhouse, a friend of the late Roy Cohn. Newhouse was the owner of Condé Nast and had noticed an uptick in sales after Trump was featured on the cover of GQ. Newhouse approached Trump about the project, and Donald was interested. The man selected to write the book was a journalist named Tony Schwartz. Though Schwartz came to believe that Trump was a blustering, pathological liar, he did what he was paid to do and produced a flattering portrait.[53] What America read about in 1987 was the heroic rise of America's most famous and successful businessman. In this alternative reality, Trump was a handsome, self-made man who had pulled himself up by his bootstraps to become America's preeminent dealmaker.

The corporate raider was one of the more iconic figures of 1980s Wall Street mythos. Fueled by junk-bond financing, the takeover wars were in full swing, and vast fortunes were being made by individuals like Carl Icahn, who seemed to have the ability to raid corporate America at will. By 1986, Trump wanted in on the action. His goal was to seize control of a public gaming company, ideally one that would allow him to grow his already considerable presence on the Atlantic City boardwalk but also one that would allow him to expand into America's gambling Mecca in Las Vegas.[54] However, the debt-fueled financing that would, for a short time, allow Trump's gambling and real estate empire to rise to Olympian heights would also sow the seeds of his eventual financial downfall.

After discussions with a casino analyst at Michael Milken's bank, Drexel Burnham Lambert, Trump first targeted his recent partner, Holiday Inn. Despite their acrimonious split over the Plaza and Trump's low view of their management, he was attracted to the company's assets, particularly their two Las Vegas casinos. An additional perk to any takeover attempt was that even if a company attempted to thwart it by repurchasing its own shares at a premium, the takeover artist would still profit handsomely from the subsequent rise in stock price. The practice came to be known as greenmail.

Trump financed his purchase of $70 million worth of

shares with a loan from Bear Stearns. To fend off the takeover threat, Holiday assumed $2.4 billion in junk bonds and bank debt from Drexel, the same bank that had goaded Trump into making the takeover attempt in the first place. Trump walked away from the deal, having earned $18.8 million, and Drexel received $95 million in fees and expenses from Holiday Inn.[55] His appetite whetted, Trump next moved on Bally Manufacturing Corp., which operated a competing casino on the boardwalk. Bally bought back Trump's shares in a private transaction at a premium, and Trump walked away yet again with a debt-fueled profit.

Trump's most audacious takeover attempt was of Resorts International, which had opened Atlantic City's first casino following legalization in 1978. On its opening day, lines stretched for blocks, and legend has it that some players preferred to wet their pants rather than lose a seat at the tables.[56] By 1986, Resorts legendary founder Jim Crosby was dead, the company had racked up $700 million in debt, and construction was just getting started on what, upon completion, would be the largest casino in the world, the Taj Mahal. Crosby had been friends with Richard Nixon and his close associate and banker, Charles "Bebe" Rebozo. Congressional Watergate investigators had suspected Resorts International's casino at Paradise Island of being used to launder money that was then routed to Nixon's Committee to Re-Elect the President (CREEP).[57] Following Crosby's death, Resorts' new lead executive, Jack Davis, was hunting for new ownership when Trump appeared on his radar screen.

In its early years, Resorts International had been funded by and employed individuals linked to the Meyer Lansky syndicate.[58] Lansky had relocated his international operations to The Bahamas after the Cuban Revolution forced him out of Havana.[59] Resorts International established casinos in The Bahamas, at the time one of the earliest examples of an offshore banking secrecy jurisdiction. Lansky associates, including Moe Dalitz, who had invested in Sunrise Hospital along with Roy Cohn and the Teamsters Pension Fund, sat on the board of the Bahamian Bank of World Commerce (BWC), which IRS officials believed was used to launder criminal proceeds from the United States offshore to Switzerland.[60]

Castle Bank, which operated in the Bahamas and shared links with Resorts International, was co-owned by a former CIA

Officer named Paul Helliwell, who had served as the paymaster for the Bay of Pigs operation.[61] Clients of Castle included Moe Dalitz and the Pritzker family, who had partnered with Trump on the Grand Hyatt. What Trump learned or understood about Resorts sordid past is unknown but bears further inquiry. Lynden O. Pindling, the leader of The Bahamas, was represented in Washington by Black, Manafort, and Stone.[62]

In March of 1987, Trump purchased $96 million worth of Resorts shares using borrowed money and took control of 88% of shareholder votes.[63] However, even after he wrangled with management and eventually won a highly advantageous casino operating agreement, it wasn't enough for Trump. He wanted to own Resorts outright and was vying to return the public company to private ownership. After the 1987 stock market crash, Resorts shares had dropped to a point where Trump could buy enough to do just that. Regulators, who would have to sign off on such a move, worried about Trump's ability to take on not only the considerable debt held by the company but also the construction costs of the gargantuan Taj Mahal, which were now approaching between $800 million and $1 billion.

Despite the misgivings of several officials, Trump's cache and influence over New Jersey regulators again won the day. However, his plans to buy Resorts outright were derailed when Merv Griffin, a television game show magnate who wanted in on the corporate raiding action, derailed Trump's takeover attempt by making a move himself. After a lengthy public dispute that spilled out into the press, the two ended up negotiating a deal whereby Trump took ownership of the Taj Mahal in Atlantic City, and Griffin took over the rest of the company.

Trump funded his purchase of the Taj Mahal with $675 million in 14% junk bonds, which placed him on the hook for $95 million in annual interest payments for the Taj alone. He then proceeded to take on an additional $125 million in bank loans to allow him to complete the daunting construction project. Leveraged to the hilt, Trump placed an enormous bet on Atlantic City. In 1986, the entire city's gambling revenue was $2.5 billion, which translated into combined returns of only $74 million across every casino.[64] To make matters worse, Trump now owned three casinos on the boardwalk and was at risk of competing against himself.

It was now imperative that Trump complete the

construction of the newly branded Trump Taj Mahal in a timely and cost-effective fashion and manage a seamless rollout. However, the culture among executives at the remarkably small and insular Trump Organization was becoming a liability. Al Glasgow, Trump's casino consultant, described the atmosphere of the Trump Organization at that time to David Cay Johnston as "disorganized crime."[65]

Trump hired an experienced casino hand in the executive Steve Hyde to manage the Trump Plaza in 1986. Still, Hyde found himself butting heads with Ivana Trump, who had taken on a prominent role, despite her lack of experience, managing the Trump Castle. Things became more chaotic when it became an open secret among Trump Organization executives that Trump was carrying on an affair with a young actress and model named Marla Maples. Trump kept the Georgia-born 26-year-old hidden away in a succession of high roller suites held under his bodyguard's name. Trump eventually tired of Ivana's presence in Atlantic City and sent her away to manage the Plaza Hotel, which he had recently purchased in Manhattan. Trump issued an ultimatum to Ivana, "Either you act like my wife and come back to New York and take care of your children, or you run the casino in Atlantic City, and we get divorced[66]."

As the 1980s drew to a close, Trump entered into one of his life's most chaotic and irresponsible phases, capping off the decade with an epic buying spree. At the time, the Plaza Hotel had cost him $409 million, the most money ever paid for a hotel.[67] The man he negotiated with, Thomas Barrack, would later become the billionaire head of his Inaugural Committee and, as of this writing, is under indictment for being an illegal foreign agent of the United Arab Emirates. Trump personally guaranteed $109 million. Trump spent even more money on upgrading the building, which was modeled after a 1907 French chateau. The Plaza's cash flow in 1988 was just over $15 million, and the debt service Trump owed in 1989, his newly purchased prize, was $45 million.

A year later, Trump bought a bankrupt regional airline that he renamed Trump Shuttle for $356 million. Trump, who had no experience running an airline, took out a $380 million loan from Citibank to make the purchase, personally guaranteeing $135 million. The deal closed within days of the Taj buyout. In addition to the 21 depreciating Boeing 727s, Trump also owned the $30 million *Trump Princess*, then the largest in the world that had once belonged to the Saudi arms dealer and figure in the Iran-Contra scandal, Adnan Khashoggi.[68] Roger Stone lobbied successfully to have the harbor of Atlantic City dredged so the yacht could be docked off of the Trump Castle to serve as a high roller's suite.

In 1984, Trump signed a contract with a New Jersey helicopter company to transport high rollers to and from his casinos. The company was co-owned by Joey Weichselbaum, a two-time felon arrested in 1965 for grand theft auto and again in 1979 on charges of embezzlement. Weichselbaum's helicopter company was financially unstable, regularly going bankrupt and reopening under a different name. Regardless, Trump paid the company $100,000 a month for servicing Trump Plaza and $80,000 a month for Trump Castle. Weichselbaum was paid $100,000 monthly and offered a company car and driver.

While his helicopter company serviced Trump's casinos, Weichselbaum was involved in a massive, multi-state cocaine trafficking operation. According to his 1985 federal indictment, Weichselbaum co-owned a used car lot named Bradford Motors, where Columbian drug smugglers would deliver both cocaine and marijuana that would either be distributed on the spot or hidden in vehicles and driven to buyers. The dealership acted as a front for drug dealers who attempted to conceal their illegal transactions through phony car sales. Even though it risked his casino license to associate with criminals, Trump considered using the helicopter company even after Weichselbaum had been indicted. Law enforcement in the Weichselbaum investigation theorized that his role at Trump's casinos may have been more nefarious than simply providing gamblers helicopter rides. According to undercover sources, there was reason to believe that Weichselbaum may have served as a cocaine conduit for high rollers staying at Trump Plaza and Trump Castle.[69] Though Weichselbaum pleaded guilty, he denied that Atlantic City was part of his cocaine distribution network.

Two months after the indictment, Weichselbaum and his brother rented an apartment Trump personally owned at the Trump Plaza condominiums in Manhattan. They each paid $3000 in cash per month for the apartment, which was on the lower end of what would usually be charged. Helicopter services covered the rest. There is every indication that Weichselbaum and Trump maintained a personal relationship. Weichselbaum's parole officer claimed that he had told him of Trump's affair with Marla Maples before it had become public knowledge. Weichselbaum suggested he had cautioned Trump to end things with Maples and even suggested she move into his unit at Trump Plaza condominiums.[70]

Weichselbaum's case was moved from Cincinnati to New Jersey and put before Trump's sister, Maryanne. She recused herself as the presiding judge after making it known that she and her husband had flown on Weichselbaum's company's helicopters. During the trial, Trump sent a letter to the judge describing Weichselbaum as "conscientious, forthright, diligent, and a credit to the community."[71] While others involved in the cocaine ring received up to 20 years, Weichselbaum received three years and was released after 18 months, telling his parole officer he planned on working as a consultant to Trump.

On October 10th, 1989, a helicopter-related catastrophe struck (the helicopter was not operated by Weichselbaum) when one carrying three Trump Organization executives crashed into the trees that separated traffic on the Garden State Parkway.[72] Everyone on board died instantly, including Steve Hyde, Trump's most experienced and trusted hand at operating a casino. As the Taj Mahal was due to open its doors in a matter of months, the timing of the loss could not have been worse. Infighting among upper management, mounting debts, and a deteriorating relationship with his wife increased the volatility of Trump's temper, and he was increasingly taking it out on his staff through explosions and bitter denunciations.

Trump now owed $1.3 billion to junk bond buyers and $1.9 billion to over fifty banks, placing his overall debt at $3.2 billion. Construction on the vast Taj was falling behind schedule and proving far more expensive than initial projections had forecast. It was critically important for Trump that the Taj be completed on schedule by April 2nd as a bond payment was due by May 15th, and Trump needed the cash flow from his new casino to be able to pay it. The Trump organization begged vendors, who had yet to be paid for their services, to press ahead and redouble their efforts to finish the project on time. Though they continued to work, many were later stiffed, with some having to close their doors because of the lost revenue.[73]

When the Taj Mahal finally opened on April 5th, 1990, it was already $108 million over budget, and Trump struggled to meet payroll for his nearly 7,000 employees. Three days earlier, the casino had opened for a disastrous test run in which many of the change dispensers that fueled the Taj's 3,000 slot machines jammed. The casino cage, which served as the on-premises bank, was half the size it needed to be for the gargantuan Taj. Amidst all the chaos, $400,000 was left in a bag used to prop open a door. The official opening fared no better. Few notable celebrities attended the festivities, which were marred by fire alarms. Trump's boardwalk casinos were competing with each other. The American economy was in a recession, and Trump's debt load began squeezing him like a vice. Trump owed 253 subcontractors $69.5 million for the Taj Project alone. It was only a matter of time before the bottom fell out of the Trump empire.

As Trump's professional world unraveled, so did his personal life. His relationship with Ivana crumbled in the face of his open affair with Marla Maples. It was during this period that Ivana claimed in a sworn court deposition that Trump had raped her. She walked back the claim after they had reached a divorce settlement.[74] After entering the eye of the public through his business achievements and the success of *The Art of the Deal*, Trump was now a national tabloid figure, and his divorce from Ivana was one of the most covered scandals of the period.

As Trump's financial position grew more precarious, he engaged in questionable accounting and business practices. In 1989, Jack O'Donnell, the president of Trump Plaza, presented Trump with an accurate 1990 projected operating income of $64 million. Trump exploded as the numbers were not high enough for his liking. O'Donnell, who wrote about the experience in a memoir, was made to go back and produce an over-optimistic, false projected income of $92 million.[75] That inflated number distorted the actual value of Trump's financial portfolio when he was actively seeking loans, which potentially constituted fraud. There was also some discussion at the time of taking the casinos public, and had they done so, the inflated numbers would have constituted a violation of securities law.[76]

Too Big To Fail: The Bankruptcies of Donald Trump

"Donald Trump is driving 100 miles per hour toward a brick wall, and he has no brakes," an agitated banker told Neil Barsky while sitting at a poker table at one of Trump's casinos in May 1990.

"He is meeting with all the banks right now."[77] Barsky, a reporter for *The Wall Street Journal*, followed up with Trump's top lenders: Citibank, Bankers Trust, Chase Manhattan, and Manufacturers Hanover. He learned that Trump's lenders realized they would either have to agree to a massive restructuring of Trump's loans or Donald would have to declare personal bankruptcy. By June 1990, just two months after the Taj opening, Donald Trump was fighting for his financial existence. His yearly interest payments had ballooned to $350 million, far exceeding his cash flow. Trump had attempted to sell or refinance many of the properties and assets he had rapidly accumulated but failed.

As a consequence of the deregulation of the financial industry during the Reagan administration, traditional banks faced competition from savings and loans (S&Ls). They began to seek out revenue through lending to riskier borrowers. Real estate departments within many banks grew in importance and stature. However, by 1989, the Federal Reserve was concerned about how the general economic downturn was impacting the real estate market and had the major American banks review their real estate exposure. Government bank examiners visited Chase Manhattan and discussed the possibility of arranging mergers between banks that were overly leveraged in the cratering real estate market. Specialists at the banks lending to Trump reviewed his files and concluded that he was facing imminent bankruptcy unless something was done to reverse the slide and done quickly.

Trump's debt-fueled spending was enabled by a banking establishment that had bought into the hype of the Trump brand. Trump's fame had led usually cautious financial institutions to disregard traditional lending guidelines and collateral requirements.[78] Major banks in New York City issued loans to Trump and then syndicated them with a broad assortment of international banks from Japan, Germany, France, Canada, and the United Kingdom. This earned Citibank, Trump's largest lender, and others a fortune in syndication fees. It allowed them to reduce their exposure by saddling a host of foreign banks with most of the financing.[79] According to Citibank's lead counsel during their negotiations with Trump, by 1990, Trump owed a combined $4 billion to more than 70 banks, with $800 million personally guaranteed by his assets.[80]

Negotiations between Trump and representatives from the 72 banks that owned pieces of the syndicated loans ensued over 18 months. Nearly one thousand bankers, lawyers, and accountants participated in the process held in Trump Tower and the boardrooms of multiple major financial institutions.[81] Given the sheer size of their exposure to Trump, he had what is referred to as debtor's leverage. The banks had more to lose if Trump went under than if they bailed him out. In other words, Trump was too big to fail.

After an intense back and forth and the courting of hesitant foreign banking institutions, a settlement was eventually reached that provided Trump with an immediate loan of $20 million and a five-year $65 million bailout plan. The interest on nearly half of Trump's bank debt was suspended. Trump was forced to hire a Chief Financial Officer. The man he selected for the job was Stephen F. Bollenbach, a talented negotiator with experience in Atlantic City. The banks imposed a generous monthly allowance of $450,000 for Trump. Though Trump was eventually forced to sell off Trump Shuttle, his yacht, and several other properties, his deal with the bankers fundamentally left him with ownership over his assets.

Trump only stuck to the strict terms of the deal for a short time. His experience with the banks had taught him that they did not want to own or operate hotels or casinos. The realization allowed him to act more freely. By August, Trump defaulted on several loan payments he had agreed to pay and faced little or no reaction from the banks. Nor did the banks complain when he gave Ivana $10 million in his divorce settlement. The banks, likely out of concern for their reputations as opposed to his, joined Trump in stonewalling the House Banking Committee when they announced hearings into the Trump bailout imbroglio. The hearings never took place.[82]

However, Trump still faced trouble with his irate casino bondholders. The Taj Mahal had been financed through $675 million worth of junk bonds with a crushing 14% interest rate. The institutional investors who held roughly half of those junk bonds retained the head of Rothschild's Inc. bankruptcy advisory team, Wilbur Ross. A graduate of Harvard Business School, Ross was widely seen as a bankruptcy expert. After visiting the Taj, Ross determined that the casino would be more valuable if it retained the Trump name. However, there would need to be a prolonged negotiation with the bondholders, and the number one bondholder was the notorious corporate raider, Carl Icahn.

After intensive negotiations between Trump, Ross, Icahn, and the bondholders, a new form of "prepackaged" bankruptcy was agreed upon to reduce Trump's ownership of the Taj to 50.5% but keep him in control of the casino's board. This marked the first of four corporate bankruptcies for Trump. These privately negotiated corporate bankruptcies allowed Trump to narrowly avoid personal bankruptcy even though he was hundreds of millions of dollars underwater.

Despite the negotiated soft landing with the banks and bondholders, Trump was still in desperate financial straits. According to most contemporary outside observers, Trump's reign as America's most famous tycoon had crashed and burned spectacularly in a blizzard of bankruptcy and personal scandal. However, In the dark days of the early 90s, Trump still had a reliable ace up his sleeve: his father, Fred Trump. In December of 1990, a mortgage payment was due on Trump Castle, and it looked to many that Trump might be unable to make the payment. Subsequently, it was discovered that Fred Trump's attorney, Howard Snyder, had visited the castle, purchased $3.5 million in chips, and never cashed out. The action was illegal because regulatory authorities needed to scrutinize loans to casinos. The regulators once again treated Trump with kid gloves, and he escaped with a $65,000 fine.

[1] Johnston, David Cay. *Temples of Chance: How America Inc. Bought Out Murder Inc. to Win Control of the Casino Business*. New York, NY: Doubleday, 1992. Pg. 10
[2] Johnston, David Cay. *Temples of Chance: How America Inc. Bought Out Murder Inc. to Win Control of the Casino Business*. New York, NY: Doubleday, 1992. Pg. 55
[3] O'Harrow Jr., Robert. "Trump's ties to an informant and FBI agent reveal his mode of operation," *The Washington Post*. September 17th, 2017
[4] Raab, Selwyn. *Five Families: The Rise, Decline, and Resurgence of America's Most Powerful Mafia Empires*. New York, NY: Thomas Dunne Books, 2016. Pg. 233
[5] Anastasia, George. *Blood And Honor: Inside the Scarfo Mob - The Mafia's Most Violent Family*. Philadelphia, PA: Camino Books, Inc., 1992. Pg. 166-167
[6] Roberts, Sam. "Nicky Scarfo, Mob Boss Who Plundered Atlantic City in the 80s, Dies at 87," *The New York Times*. January 18th, 2017
[7] Kranish, Michael; Fisher, Marc. *Trump Revealed: An American Journey of Ambition, Ego, Money and Power*. New York, NY: Scribner, 2016. Pg. 126
[8] "Donald Trump: Worried About OC in AC," The Smoking Gun. May 19th, 1997
[9] O'Harrow Jr., Robert. "Trump's ties to an informant and FBI agent reveal his mode of operation," *The Washington Post*. September 17th, 2017
[10] O'Brien, Timothy L. *TrumpNation: The Art Of Being The Donald*. New York, NY: Warner Business Books, 2005. Pg. 118
[11] O'Harrow Jr., Robert. "Trump's ties to an informant and FBI agent reveal his mode of operation," *The Washington Post*. September 17th, 2017
[12] Johnston, David Cay. *The Making of Donald Trump*. Brooklyn, NY: Melville House Publishing, 2016. Pg. 42

[13] Barrett, Wayne. *Trump: The Greatest Show On Earth*. New York, NY: Regan Arts, 2016. Pg. 211-212

[14] Johnston, David Cay. *The Making of Donald Trump*. Brooklyn, NY: Melville House Publishing, 2016. Pg. 42-43

[15] Barrett, Wayne. *Trump: The Greatest Show On Earth*. New York, NY: Regan Arts, 2016. Pg. 219

[16] O'Harrow Jr., Robert. "Trump's ties to an informant and FBI agent reveal his mode of operation," *The Washington Post*. September 17th, 2017

[17] Raab, Selwyn. "Investigators Charge Contractors Formed 'Club' For Tax Fraud," *The New York Times*. July 6th, 1983

[18] Janson, Donald, "Ex-Atlantic City Mayor Said to Confess to Ties to Mobsters," *The New York Times*. April 13th, 1984

[19] Barrett, Wayne. *Trump: The Greatest Show On Earth*. New York, NY: Regan Arts, 2016. Pg. 223

[20] Barrett, Wayne. *Trump: The Greatest Show On Earth*. New York, NY: Regan Arts, 2016. Pg. 224

[21] O'Brien, Timothy L. *TrumpNation: The Art Of Being The Donald*. New York, NY: Warner Business Books, 2005. Pg. 119

[22] Anastasia, George. *Blood And Honor: Inside the Scarfo Mob - The Mafia's Most Violent Family*. Philadelphia, PA: Camino Books, Inc., 1992. Pg. 134

[23] Barrett, Wayne. *Trump: The Greatest Show On Earth*. New York, NY: Regan Arts, 2016. Pg. 232

[24] Barrett, Wayne. *Trump: The Greatest Show On Earth*. New York, NY: Regan Arts, 2016. Pg. 232

[25] D'Antonio, Michael. *The Truth About Trump*. New York, NY: Thomas Dunne Books, 2015. Pg. 162

[26] Isikoff, Michael. "Trump challenged over ties to mob-linked gambler with ugly past," Yahoo News. March 7th, 2016

[27] Isikoff, Michael. "Video shows Trump with mob figure he denied knowing," Yahoo News. November 2nd, 2016

[28] Janson, Donald. "Casino Officials Deny Bribing Bahamanian Leader," *The New York Times*. February 10th, 1985

[29] Johnston, David Cay. *Temples of Chance: How America Inc. Bought Out Murder Inc. to Win Control of the Casino Business*. New York, NY: Doubleday, 1992. Pg. 88

[30] Barrett, Wayne. *Trump: The Greatest Show On Earth*. New York, NY: Regan Arts, 2016. Pg. 244

[31] Toobin, Jeffrey. "The Dirty Trickster," *The New Yorker*. June 2nd, 2008

[32] O'Harrow Jr., Robert; Boburg, Shawn. "The man who showed Donald Trump how to exploit power and instill fear," *The Washington Post*. July 17th, 2016

[33] Labash, Matt. "Roger Stone, Political Animal," *The Washington Examiner*. November 5th, 2007

[34] Brenner, Marie. "How Donald Trump and Roy Cohn's Ruthless Symbiosis Changed America," *Vanity Fair*. August, 2017

[35] Labash, Matt. "Roger Stone, Political Animal," *The Washington Examiner*. November 5th, 2007

[36] Mansfield, Stephanie. "The Rise and Gall of Roger Stone," *The Washington Post*. June 16th, 1986

[37] Labash, Matt. "Roger Stone, Political Animal," *The Washington Examiner*. November 5th, 2007

[38] Toobin, Jeffrey. "The Dirty Trickster," *The New Yorker*. June 2nd, 2008

[39] Labash, Matt. "Roger Stone, Political Animal," *The Washington Examiner*. November 5th, 2007

[40] Roig-Franzia, Manuel. "The Swamp Builders," *The Washington Post*. November 29th, 2018

[41] Summers, Anthony. THE ARROGANCE OF POWER: THE SECRET WORLD OF RICHARD NIXON. Penguin Books. 2001

[42] Roig-Franzia, Manuel. "The Swamp Builders," *The Washington Post*. November 29th, 2018

[43] Johnson, Dennis W. *Democracy for Hire: A History Of American Political Consulting*. New York, NY: Oxford University Press, 2017. Pg. 137

[44] Foer, Franklin. "Paul Manafort, American Hustler," *The Atlantic*. March, 2018

[45] Mansfield, Stephanie. "The Rise and Gall of Roger Stone," *The Washington Post*. June 16th, 1986

[46] Baram, Marcus. "Eavesdropping on Roy Cohn and Donald Trump," The New Yorker. April 1th, 2017

[47] Alter, Jonathan; Sick, Gary; Bird, Kai; Eizenstat, Stuart. "It's All but Settled: The Reagan Campaign Delayed the Release of the Iranian Hostages," *The New Republic*. May 3rd, 2023

[48] Parry, Robert. "How Roy Cohn Helped Rupert Murdoch," Consortium News. January 28th, 2015

[49] Brenner, Marie. "How Donald Trump and Roy Cohn's Ruthless Symbiosis Changed America," *Vanity Fair*. August, 2017

[50] Baram, Marcus. "Eavesdropping on Roy Cohn and Donald Trump," *The New Yorker*. April 14th, 2017

[51] Mahler, Jonathan; Flegenheimer, Matt. "What Donald Trump Learned From Joseph McCarthy's Right Hand Man," *The New York Times*. June 20th, 2016

[52] Barrett, Wayne. *Trump: The Greatest Show On Earth*. New York, NY: Regan Arts, 2016. Pg. 278

[53] Mayer, Jane. "Donald Trump's Ghostwriter Tells All," *The New Yorker*. July 25th, 2016

[54] Barrett, Wayne. *Trump: The Greatest Show On Earth*. New York, NY: Regan Arts, 2016. Pg. 387

[55] Johnston, David Cay. *Temples of Chance: How America Inc. Bought Out Murder Inc. to Win Control of the Casino Business*. New York, NY: Doubleday, 1992. Pg. 97-99

[56] O'Brien, Timothy L. *TrumpNation: The Art Of Being The Donald*. New York, NY: Warner Business Books, 2005. Pg. 116

[57] Hougan, Jim. *Spooks: The Haunting of America*. New York, NY. William Morrow & Co. 1978

[58] Wayne, Leslie. "Resorts International Ups The Ante," *The New York Times*. November 13th, 1983

[59] Madinger, John. *Money Laundering: A Guide for Criminal Investigators (THIRD EDITION)* Boca Raton, FL: CRC Press, 2012. Pg. 11-13

[60] Block, Alan A. *Masters Of Paradise: Organized Crime and the Internal Revenue Service in The Bahamas*. New York, NY: Transaction Pubishers, 1998. Pg. 12 & 51-52

[61] Drinkhall, Jim. "CIA Helped Quash Major, Star-Studded Tax Evasion Case," *The Wall Street Journal*. April 24th, 1980

[62] Isikoff, Michael. "Bush Aides' Lobbying Debated," *The Washington Post*. September 9th, 1988

[63] Johnston, David Cay. *Temples of Chance: How America Inc. Bought Out Murder Inc. to Win Control of the Casino Business*. New York, NY: Doubleday, 1992. Pg. 108

[64] Kranish, Michael; Fisher, Marc. *Trump Revealed: An American Journey of Ambition, Ego, Money and Power*. New York, NY: Scribner, 2016. Pg. 133

[65] Johnston, David Cay. *Temples of Chance: How America Inc. Bought Out Murder Inc. to Win Control of the Casino Business*. New York, NY: Doubleday, 1992. Pg. 108

[66] Brenner, Marie. "After the Goldrush," *Vanity Fair*. September 1990

[67] O'Brien, Timothy L. *TrumpNation: The Art Of Being The Donald*. New York, NY: Warner Business Books, 2005. Pg. 100

[68] Wilson, Peter. "No One Needs a Superyacht, but They Keep Selling Them," *The New York Times*. October 8th, 2019

[69] Hurt III, Harry. *Lost Tycoon: The Many Lives of Donald J. Trump*. Battlebro, VT: Echo Point Books & Media, 1993. Pg. 155

[70] Johnston, David Cay. *The Making of Donald Trump*. Brooklyn, NY: Melville House Publishing, 2016. Pg. 59-63

[71] Barrett, Wayne. *Trump: The Greatest Show On Earth*. New York, NY: Regan Arts, 2016. Pg. 195

[72] Hanley, Robert. "Copter Crash Kills 3 Aides of Trump," *The New York Times*. October 11th, 1989

[73] Reilly, Steve. "Hundreds allege Donald Trump doesn't pay his bills," *USA Today*. June 9th, 2016

[74] Hurt III, Harry. *Lost Tycoon: The Many Lives of Donald J. Trump*. Battlebro, VT: Echo Point Books & Media, 1993. Pg. 55-56

[75] O'Donnell, John R.; Rutherford, James. *Trumped! The Inside Story of the Real Donald Trump - His Cunning Rise and Spectacular Fall*. Hertford, NC: Crossroads Press, 1991. Pg. 177-179

[76] Barrett, Wayne. *Trump: The Greatest Show On Earth*. New York, NY: Regan Arts, 2016. Pg. 432

[77] Barsky, Neil. "Trump, the Bad, Bad Businessman," *The New York Times*. August 5th, 2016

[78] Blair, Gwenda. *The Trumps: Three Generations of Builders and a President*. New York, NY: Simon & Schuster, 2000. Pg. 407

[79] Barrett, Wayne. *Trump: The Greatest Show On Earth*. New York, NY: Regan Arts, 2016. Pg. 427

[80] Flitter, Emily. "Art of the spin: Trump bankers question his portrayal of financial comeback," *Reuters*. July 17th, 2016

[81] Blair, Gwenda. *The Trumps: Three Generations of Builders and a President*. New York, NY: Simon & Schuster, 2000. Pg. 409

[82] Barrett, Wayne. *Trump: The Greatest Show On Earth*. New York, NY: Regan Arts, 2016. Pg. 435

Part II
Convergence

Chapter 5:
Putin Consolidates Power in Russia
And Spreads Corruption Abroad

Putin's First Election and the Consolidation of the 'Vertical of Power'

Yeltsin's resignation on New Year's Eve, 1999, thrust Putin into the glaring lights of international notoriety as the new President of Russia. According to the Russian constitution, he could only hold office on an interim basis until elections were held. To keep "The Family" around Yeltsin safe from prosecution, commanding a strong contingent of allies in the State Duma was also necessary. To this end, Boris Berezovsky conceived of a new political party to rally around Putin called Unity. Berezovsky enlisted the help of two "political technologists," Gleb Pavlovsky and Vladislav Surkov, to bring the party into existence.

Political technologists practice a form of political manipulation developed in the states of the former USSR influenced by the Soviet model of top-down governance and tsarist practices of black propaganda and co-opting the political opposition. By the 21st Century, the practice was influenced by developments in mass media, advertising, and public relations.[1] "[P]olitical technologists," states Professor Andrew Miller, "apply whatever 'technology' they can to the construction of politics as a whole. The manipulation of the media is central to their work but extends beyond this - to the construction of parties, the destruction of others, the framing of general campaign dynamics, and the manipulation of results. If Russia and other post-Soviet states are 'directed democracies', the job of the political technologist is to direct that version of democracy on their

130

employer's behalf."[2]

Vladislav Surkov created Unity in a matter of months, winning a plurality of the vote in the Duma elections.[3] He did so by using state and oligarch-owned media to launch attacks against Putin's rivals and manipulating smaller parties into alliances that benefited Unity. Surkov, a master of postmodern propaganda with artistic pretensions, cut his teeth orchestrating PR and advertising campaigns for Bank Menatep, owned by one of Russia's wealthiest oligarchs, Mikhail Khodorkovsky. After working as the head of PR at Berezovsky's ORT television station, Surkov became Deputy Chief of the Russian Presidential administration.

The campaign team assembled around Putin was led by his associate from St. Petersburg, Dmitri Medvedev. Gleb Pavlovsky was responsible for creating an image of Putin to sell to the Russian people. Pavlovsky was helped by the stark contrast Putin struck with Yeltsin. In the chaos of late 1999, Putin's image as a youthful strongman struck a deep chord in Russian society. Putin also enjoyed the support of the security services, increasingly led by KGB allies from St. Petersburg, who came to be known as the *siloviki*. "The Family" around Yeltsin placed the full support of state media behind Putin. The Kremlin left nothing to chance, and during the election, there were widespread reports of ballot stuffing and irregularities in the regions outside of the main cities.[4] Putin won the election with 52.94% of the vote. Now that his Presidency was official, Putin set about consolidating his power.

In May 2000, the Russian newspaper *Kommersant* received a leaked Kremlin document entitled *Reform of the Administration of the President of the Russian Federation*. The document laid out a strategy by which the Kremlin planned to centralize authority in the Presidential Administration, weaken the Duma, control information flows to the Russian people through state control of media, propaganda, and artificial pro-government protests and gatherings, and establish centralized control over regional governments.[5]

Four days after his inauguration, Putin issued an executive order that served as a basis for the establishment of a "vertical of power," placing the 89 previously independent regional governors of the Russian Federation under the direct supervision of seven superfederal regions led by plenipotentiaries, many of them former KGB, who were appointed by, and answered to, Putin. Instead of allying with liberal parties in the Duma, as many had expected, Unity allied with the Communists. During the election, Surkov oversaw the merging of Unity with its now toothless chief party adversary, which led to the formation of the United Russia party.

Putin placed his closest associates from St. Petersburg into positions of national power. Some of the highest positions were awarded to his colleagues from the FSB and other security services. Former KGB associates of Putin placed into influential positions included Sergei Ivanov, head of the Security Council, Nikolai Patrushev, head of the FSB, and Viktor Cherkesov, who served as Putin's representative to the Northwest region of Russia. The oligarchs worried they were witnessing a power seizure by the feared *siloviki*.

Putin then seized control of independent media. A month after his inauguration, the Russian Prosecutor General's office opened a criminal case against the oligarch Vladimir Gusinsky. Gusinsky's holding company, Media Most, owned the independent television station NTV, which had supported Putin's opponents during the election. Putin saw this as a form of information warfare being waged against him. Gusinsky was arrested and imprisoned in Moscow's Butyrka detention center. He was forced to sell NTV for a fraction of its value, effectively placing it under state control. In return, Gusinsky was allowed to flee the country.[6]

On July 28th, 2000, Russia's wealthiest businessmen were called to the Kremlin. Tensions were high, Putin had become increasingly assertive and even combative with the oligarchs. Except for Berezovsky, who ominously wasn't invited, Russia's top oligarchs sat around a large table in the middle of an ornate Kremlin hall. When Putin arrived, he delivered a crystal clear message: he would allow them to maintain control over the industries they had pilfered from the state during the privatizations of the 1990s, and in return, they would all agree to play by his rules. Chief among them: stay out of politics.

While most of the oligarchs were willing to bend the knee in return for being able to keep their loot, Boris Berezovsky had other ideas. A PhD mathematician, Berezovsky had spent years seizing control of companies and spreading his influence in the corridors of power and believed he could still outmaneuver Putin.

He thought his opportunity to do so arrived with the first major disaster of Putin's term as President. On August 12th, an accident caused the Russian nuclear submarine *Kursk* to sink in the Barents Sea, leading to the death of everyone on board.

Unaware of the severity of the disaster at first, Putin declined to return to Moscow from a vacation in Sochi. Berezovsky took the opportunity to skewer Putin on his television station ORT. Families of the crew members and ordinary Russians directed their fury toward Putin, and Putin, in turn, directed his toward Berezovsky. After being warned by Putin's chief of staff that he should release control of ORT and flee the country, Berezovsky demanded a meeting with Putin himself. Putin agreed and used the opportunity to excoriate Berezovsky, accusing him of hiring prostitutes to play the wives and sisters of the dead submariners for his television broadcasts. Putin then took out a file and began reading accusations of financial misconduct at ORT. At risk of prosecution, Berezovsky fled to London. In a matter of months, Putin had chased Russia's two most prominent media moguls out of the country and had the rest of the country's most powerful oligarchs either seeking favor or looking over their shoulders.

Putin's Seizure of Russia's Geostrategic Resources
And Weaponization of Corruption

Contemporaneous with his efforts to weaken the oligarchs and curb the free press, Putin set about seizing control over Gazprom, Russia's largest corporation and the crown jewel of Russia's vast energy wealth. Russia has the world's largest reserves of natural gas.[7] In June of 2000, Putin removed Viktor Chernomyrdin as chairman of Gazprom's board and replaced him with Dmitri Medvedev. Chernomyrdin was made the ambassador to Ukraine, which was at that time reliant on Gazprom for its energy needs.

Putin's interest in Russia's natural resource wealth dates back to his days in St. Petersburg. He holds a degree from the St. Petersburg Mining Institute, which he was awarded in 1996. Putin met regularly with Vladimir Litvinenko (no relation to the assassinated FSB defector), the school's rector, as well as his close friends Igor Sechin and Vladimir Zubkov, who were studying similar issues related to energy, economics, and natural resource wealth. Following Litvinenko's lead, Putin, Sechin, and Zubkov supported a strategy restoring state control over Russia's oil and gas resources.

As Russia's largest company, Gazprom is used by the Kremlin to advance its geostrategic interests. As far back as the Arab Oil Embargo of 1973, the manipulation of energy supplies has been understood to have financial and political consequences. Central and Eastern Europe have little to no energy resources and rely on natural gas from Russia to keep the lights on. Germany, in particular, has been interested in cheap Russian natural gas to fuel the largest economy in the Eurozone. However, American Presidents dating back to Ronald Reagan have been concerned about the potential adverse consequences of having Europe beholden to Russia for its energy needs.[8]

Gazprom was created out of the old Soviet Ministry of Gas. Viktor Chernomyrdin, who served as its final minister in the dying days of the Soviet Union, changed the ministry's legal status in 1989 to make it an industrial association. Though Gazprom was partially privatized from 1993 to 1994, it maintained all the assets previously held by the state, including production, transportation, distribution, sales, and regulation. Using voucher auctions, Gazprom's management privatized 40% of the company for $100 million, selling a significant portion of Russia's natural resource wealth back to its own managers for a fraction of its value. At its peak market capitalization in 2008, Gazprom was worth $369 billion.[9]

Under Chernomyrdin, Gazprom's CEO was Rem Vyakhirev. Together, Chernomyrdin and Vyakhirev oversaw an orgy of corruption and asset stripping. After Chernomyrdin was relieved of his job as Prime Minister, a position he briefly held under Yeltsin, he and Vyakhirev transferred their assets to their children. Gazprom awarded a $1 billion contract to Stroytransgaz, a pipeline construction company over 50% owned by Gazprom managers and relatives, including Vyakhirev's daughter.[10] During this time, several corrupt intermediary companies were established, including a commodities trading company called ITERA.

ITERA was set up by Igor Makarov, a citizen of Turkmenistan and friend of the country's then President-for-Life Saparmurat Niyazov. Following independence, Turkmenistan sought to sell its natural gas abroad for desperately needed cash.

However, as the regional pipeline infrastructure had been built during the days of the Soviet Union, Makarov needed to negotiate with Gazprom to arrange for the transportation of Turkmen natural gas out of the country. While Gazprom wasn't interested in allowing Turkmen natural gas into Russia to compete with its domestic market, it allowed it to be sold to Ukraine. The gas started pumping in 1994, earning Makarov a handsome profit.[11]

In addition to Makarov, the board of ITERA consisted of Gazprom officials and their relatives. Curiously, ITERA was incorporated in Jacksonville, Florida. Corrupt Gazprom executives used ITERA to strip assets from their own company at outrageously reduced prices. Gazprom sold ITERA a 32% stake in Purgas, a gas-producing subsidiary, for $1,200 when its market value was estimated to be between $200 million and $400 million.

Putin replaced Gazprom's CEO with Alexei Miller, who had worked under him in the St. Petersburg Mayor's Office. Over the years, Putin has steadily replaced members of Gazprom's board with friends and allies. The board's current chairman, Viktor Zubkov, also served under Putin in the St. Petersburg Mayor's office. Board member Dmitri Patrushev is the son of Nikolai Patrushev, former head of the FSB at the time of Putin's election and the apartment bombings, and currently Secretary of the Russian Security Council.

There were hopes that Putin would clean up Gazprom's corrupt practices, but they were quickly dashed. After a brief pause, the asset stripping continued apace by Putin's second term.[12] Rather than end its corrupt practices, Putin's seizure of Gazprom simply changed the beneficiaries. Under Alexei Miller, the company repossessed much of what it had sold to ITERA. The sale of Turkmen gas to Ukraine was then awarded to another corrupt intermediary called Eural Trans Gas, owned by a Ukrainian named Dmytro Firtash, described by the US Justice Department as "an upper-echelon [associate] of Russian organized crime."[13] Euro Trans Gas was later replaced by RosUkrEnergo, 50% of which was owned by Gazprom's Austrian subsidiary Arosgas Holding, and 50% owned by Dmytro Firtash and his partner Ivan Fursin.

According to a *Reuters* special report from 2014, "Gazprom sold more than 20 billion cubic meters of gas well below market prices to Firtash over the past four years - about four times more than the Russian government has publicly acknowledged. The price Firtash paid was so low, *Reuters* calculates, that companies he controlled made more than $3 billion on the arrangement."[14] Bankers close to Putin provided Firtash with $11 billion in lines of credit. Firtash became one of the wealthiest oligarchs in Ukraine and became a major funder of Russian-backed politicians nationwide.

Eural Trans Gas and RosUkrEnergo were fronts for Semyon Mogilevich. The Department of Justice and the FBI have both investigated the matter.[15] In 2006, the head of the Ukrainian Security Service told Global Witness that they were also investigating Mogilevich's involvement.[16] Firtash and Mogilevich shared the same Israeli attorney, Ze'ev Gordon, who was a trustee when Firtash established Eural Trans Gas on December 4th, 2002.[17] A day later, the company was awarded the Turkmenistan-Ukraine gas business from Gazprom.

Firtash acknowledged his ownership stake in Eural Trans Gas and RosUkrEnergo in 2006 after it was discovered that the FBI was investigating a company called Highrock Holding.[18] Firtash was a principal owner of Highrock Holding. Its financial director was a man named Igor Fisherman.[19] Fisherman was indicted alongside Mogilevich by US authorities for his role in a RICO conspiracy.[20] In a classified US diplomatic cable, the acting economic counselor to the US Embassy in Kyiv stated that 34% of Highrock was owned by Agatheas Trading Ltd, whose director was Mogilevich's wife, Galina Telesh.[21] Both Firtash and his minority partner in RosUkrEnergo were described in a 2005 report from the Austrian Federal Criminal Investigation Agency as senior members of the Semyon Mogilevich Organization.[22]

Raiffeisen Investment AG, the investment arm of Raiffeisen Bank of Austria, had concealed Firtash's involvement in RosUkrEnergo.[23] In a leaked State Department cable, diplomat Scott F. Kliner wrote, "US-indicted crime boss Semyon Mogilevich probably uses RZB [Raiffeisen Zentralbank] and its subsidiary Raiffeisen Investment Holding AG (RIAG) as a front to provide legitimacy to the gas company that we suspect he controls, RosUkrEnergo (RUE). RUE makes direct payments of $360,000 annually to each of the two RIAG executives in "consulting fees." We assess that the payments probably are bribes for RIAG to maintain the front for Mogilevich."[24]

In a meeting with William Taylor, the US Ambassador to Ukraine, Firtash acknowledged his ties to Mogilevich, explaining that he needed Mogilevich's permission to enter the natural gas business. Firtash told Taylor that after being awarded the Gazprom contract over ITERA, Igor Makarov summoned him to a dinner that included a former KGB agent, his head of security, Mogilevich, and Sergei Mikhailov, the head of the Solntsevskaya. Firtash credited leaving the meeting alive because of his "good reputation among central Asian leaders."[25]

Putin's experience as Deputy Mayor in St. Petersburg demonstrates his comfort in working with organized criminals, a stance that did not change upon becoming the President of the Russian Federation. Indeed, Putin's utilization of organized crime to further his goals has extended well beyond Russia's borders. A report released by former US Director of National Intelligence Dennis Blair states that there is an "apparent growing nexus in Russian and Eurasian states among government, organized crime, intelligence services, and big business figures."[26]

"[I]nternational organized criminals control significant positions in the global energy and strategic materials markets," former Attorney General Michael Mukasey warned in a speech before the Center for Strategic and International Studies. "So-called 'iron triangles' of corrupt business leaders, corrupt government officials, and organized criminals exert substantial influence over the economies of many countries… One of the most well-known recent examples is the case of Semyon Mogilevich [who]… is said to exert influence over large portions of the natural gas industry in parts of what used to be the Soviet Union[27]."

Putin's relationship with Mogilevich was addressed in a discussion between former Ukrainian President Leonid Kuchma and the then head of the Ukrainian Security Service, Leonid Derkach. The conversation was part of hundreds of hours of recorded discussions leaked by a member of Kuchma's security detail.[28] Transcripts of this recording, as revealed by WikiLeaks, were circulated within the US Government, thus increasing the likelihood of its veracity.[29]

> KUCHMA: *"Have you found Mogilevich?"*
> DERKACH: *"I found him."*
> KUCHMA: *"So, are you two working now?*
> DERKACH: *"We're working. We have another meeting*

tomorrow. He arrives incognito.

Later in the discussion, Derkach revealed a few details about Mogilevich.

> *DERKACH: He's on good terms with Putin. He and Putin have been in contact since Putin was still in Leningrad.[30]*

Russian Energy Politics and the Strategic Spread of Corruption Abroad

The Kremlin uses energy resources and weaponized corruption to pursue its strategic interests abroad. No country has been more impacted by this strategy than Ukraine. The basic political and economic contours of post-Soviet Ukraine developed during the tenure of its second president, Leonid Kuchma. A defining feature of independent Ukraine has been corruption in the natural gas trade, where its most powerful oligarchs have made the bulk of their fortunes. This economic power translated into political influence. The system is simple: Russian natural gas was purchased by intermediaries such as ITERA, ETG, or RUE at artificially low, state-regulated prices and then sold at higher prices, shielded by state-imposed monopolies. The Kremlin selected corrupt Ukrainian beneficiaries such as Dmytro Firtash, a Mogilevich front, who then funded political parties that became corrupted by, and financially beholden to, the Kremlin.

The vast Soviet system of pipelines was designed and constructed by Communist bureaucrats operating in a geographically enormous but politically unified entity. With the collapse of the Soviet Union, these pipelines suddenly found themselves traversing multiple countries with competing and often conflicting interests. Ukraine is strategically located between Russia and the energy-hungry economies of the Eurozone. In 2010, 80% of Russia's natural gas exports to Western Europe flowed through pipelines that crossed Ukrainian territory, representing 56% of Gazprom's total profits.[31]

As mentioned, much of the natural gas that made its way to Ukraine came from Turkmenistan.[32] Intermediaries, such as ITERA, served to enrich corrupt officials in Gazprom, connected insiders in the Turkmen dictatorship, and politically connected oligarchs in Ukraine. Lingering in the shadows was the influence of organized crime, with the name Semyon Mogilevich appearing repeatedly. The chief Ukrainian beneficiary in both ETG and RUE was the mob-linked oligarch and head of the "gas lobby"

Dmytro Firtash, who would become one of the most politically influential figures in Ukraine after being showered with Russian money.

Kuchma's flagrant corruption and criminality were placed in stark relief on November 28th, 2000, with the release of a series of tape recordings of Kuchma's conversations made by Major Mykola Melnychenko, an officer in the Directorate of State Protection.[33] The tapes revealed that Kuchma's intermediaries with organized crime were Ihor Bakay and his business partner Oleksandr Volkov. Bakay was a business partner of Dmytro Firtash and was later wanted by Ukrainian authorities for defrauding the state of $300 million. Bakay fled to Russia, where Putin granted him citizenship for his contributions on "behalf of Russian culture and art."[34]

Volkov, a close aide of Kuchma's, was a representative of the company Seabeco, owned by Boris Birshtein and associated with the first wave of KGB money laundering of CPSU funds. Birshtein's son-in-law later partnered with Donald Trump on Trump Tower Toronto.[35] Kuchma placed Birshtein in charge of a company called Ukraina AG, which was allowed to purchase Ukrainian steel and fertilizer at depressed prices and sell them abroad for a substantial mark-up. Birshtein hired an ex-KGB officer as the company's Vice President, and Belgian prosecutors have traced payments of at least $5 million to members of Kuchma's inner circle.[36]

Seabeco has been accused of funding Kuchma's 1994 Presidential campaign, along with Nordex. Based out of Vienna, Nordex is owned by Grigori Loutchansky. Its Ukrainian representative was, for a time, the oligarch Vadim Rabinovich. A confidential report by the Swiss Federal Office of Police stated the KGB had recruited Loutchansky to set up international business interests in the same way Seabeco had.[37]

Russian energy interests, some with links to organized crime and the security services, have attempted to make inroads into the American political system since at least the late '90s. In August 1997, Republican House Majority Whip Tom DeLay, his wife, and four top aides went on a seven-day, all-expenses-paid trip to Moscow to play golf, meet with church leaders, and speak with Viktor Chernomyrdin, the founder of Gazprom and then Prime Minister of Russia. DeLay gave no advance notice to either the State Department or the American Embassy, which was unusual given his meeting with the Prime Minister.[38]

To avoid running afoul of House ethics rules, Delay claimed a Washington-based non-profit covered the $57,238 cost of the trip. The trip was arranged by the disgraced felon and lobbyist Jack Abramoff and paid for by a Russian oil company with extensive holdings in Gazprom called Naftasib. Using a shell company based in the Bahamas, Naftasib had paid two high-powered Washington lobbying firms $440,000, and as part of their campaign Abramoff had arranged to bring his old friend DeLay to the Russian capital.[39]

During their stay, the Republican entourage was escorted around Moscow by Naftasib executives Marina Nevskaya and Alexander Koulakovsky, along with their machine-gun-toting security guards. After meeting with Chernomyrdin, the Republican Majority Leader enjoyed a "fancy dinner" with Abramoff, Nevskaya, and Koulakovsky. Also in attendance was Ed Buckham, DeLay's former chief-of-staff and organizer of the US Family Network, a public advocacy group with close ties to DeLay that claimed to support "economic growth and prosperity, social improvement, moral fitness, and the general well-being of the United States."[40]

During the dinner, Nevskaya and Koulakovsky expressed an interest in contributing money to DeLay. Koulakovsky asked, "What would happen if the DeLays woke up one morning" and found a luxury car parked in their driveway? The Americans present at dinner claimed that they told their Russian hosts such an act would end up with all of them in jail.

Nine months later, on June 25th, 1998, a single check for $1 million was passed along to the US Family Network via the London-based law firm James & Sarch.[41] According to *The Washington Post*, the money had actually come from Naftasib and was meant to influence DeLay's vote on legislation related to the IMF bailout of Russia. Many House Republicans opposed appropriating any further money to the IMF, decrying it as a bailout. The IMF was hoping to push the Russians to increase taxes on energy companies like Gazprom as a condition for receiving the loan. DeLay came out for the loan and against the tax increases.

Jack Abramoff, who brought DeLay into contact with Naftasib, had worked with Russians since the mid-90s. Between 2001 and 2004, Abramoff was paid $2.1 million by a Dutch shell company named Voor Huisen, which recorded no activity or assets. Several of Abramoff's former partners who had also lobbied for Voor Huisen told *The Boston Globe* that the company was connected to Naftasib.[42] J. Michael Waller, Vice President of the Center for Security Policy and a former colleague of Abramoff's, told *The Globe* that Abramoff approached him to organize the Moscow trip for DeLay. Waller, who refused the offer, said that he had been told by two of Abramoff's colleagues that Abramoff understood that if he performed well for Naftasib, the Russian government would retain him.[43]

"In my estimation, Naftasib and its agents were running what appeared to be an aggressive political intelligence operation against the United States," Waller said in an interview in 2019. "All the indicators were consistent with the pattern of a Russian state-sponsored entity working to corrupt elected American officials, and I had warned people of this possibility and that was my position more than a decade ago and that remains my position today."[44]

Naftasib was a shareholder in Gazprom and listed its largest clients as the Russian Ministry of Defense and the Ministry of Interior. Marina Nevskaya, Vice President of the company, was listed as an instructor at a school for Russian military intelligence officers. 50% of the company was owned by the late Mikhail Khimich, a billionaire who lived part-time in New Zealand and was known to take Nevskaya out on his yacht. Khimich's business partner told local press that Nevskaya was a "colonel-lieutenant in the GRU."[45] There is little public information about Sibneft's other 50% owner, Alexander Koulakovsky, other than a 1994 dispatch from the Russian news agency TASS that claims that he was "arrested by authorities of Hatichoe, Northern Honshu, Japan,... for illegal storage of a handgun and 150 rounds of ammunition."[46]

Case Studies in Corruption: Austria, Israel, and the United Kingdom

Following the end of WWII, Austria was occupied by the Soviet Union for ten years until it pulled out of the country following the promise that it would remain neutral in the Cold War. From that point forward, Austria's capital, Vienna, served as a meeting place where Cold Warriors from the East and West could meet in secrecy and splendor wherever the need arose. In 1968, the first

Western European firm to reach an agreement to directly import Soviet gas was Austria's state-owned energy company OMV.

As a result of this history, OMV is a major, long-term strategic partner of Gazprom.[47] Numerous former Austrian politicians sit on the boards of Gazprom-related subsidiaries. OMV is also closely tied to the conservative ÖVP, the political party of two-time Austrian Chancellor Sebastian Kurz. Under his leadership, Austria supported the construction of the Nord Stream 2 pipeline directly connecting Russia to Central European energy markets, while simultaneously opposing the application of EU market rules on its offshore section.[48]

Following the collapse of the Soviet Union, Russia and Austria maintained their close relations. By the early 90s, Vienna had reprised its role as the meeting place of choice, except this time it wasn't just spies arranging the meetings but international organized criminals. In 1994, a meeting took place at the Vienna Marriott between Russian, Italian, and Colombian crime syndicates to discuss the cooperation in the drug trade and the laundering of profits. The meeting, attended by Solntsevskaya leaders Sergei Mikhailov and Viktor Averin, was an early example of the globalized nature of transnational organized crime. Vienna has also emerged as a money laundering center. Thousands of Austrian companies have been set up to funnel money either to neighboring Switzerland, Liechtenstein, or into the global offshore network.[49] Grigori Loutchansky's Nordex is registered in Vienna.

In 2006, it was revealed that Austria's second largest bank, Raiffeisen, held a 50% interest in RosUkrEnergo on behalf of Dmytro Firtash and Ivan Fursin.[50] Diplomats at the US State Department at the time believed that Raiffeisen was acting as a front for Semyon Mogilevich and that RosUkrEnergo was paying high-level bribes to a Raiffeisen executive.[51] Raiffeisen later partially financed the Trump Tower Toronto deal.[52]

In 2014, in the face of the Maidan Revolution in Ukraine and an indictment and extradition request from the US government, Firtash fled to Vienna, where he currently resides as a fugitive from US justice. Firtash maintains a tightly-knit group of supporters among Austrian officials and society. His lawyer, Dieter Böhmdorfer, was a former Austrian Justice Minister and a member of the far-right Austrian Freedom Party (FPÖ). Firtash's Austrian media advisor, Daniel Kapp, previously served as the press secretary to the former ÖVP party leader Josef Pröll, who runs an investment firm that is part of Raiffeisen Holding.[53]

Putin traveled to Austria for vacations as early as the 1990s and has a personal relationship with several Austrian politicians. He danced with Austria's Foreign Minister Karin Kneissl at her 2018 wedding and gave Thomas Klestil, a former Austrian president, two puppies as a gift. Much as it has done elsewhere, Russia under Putin has courted the Austrian far right, particularly the FPÖ. In 2019, a video emerged of Austrian FPÖ leader and Vice Chancellor Heinz-Christian Strache discussing illegal party donations in return for government contracts with a Russian woman who claimed to be the daughter of Igor Makarov, the President of ITERA.[54] The ensuing scandal led to Strache's resignation and the collapse of the Austrian governing coalition.

In May of 2014, the Russian far-right ideologue Aleksandr Dugin, along with Orthodox Russian oligarch Konstantin Malofeev, hosted a closed-door, invitation-only meeting in Vienna with many luminaries of Europe's far-right movements, including the FPÖ's Heinz-Christian Strache and the French National Front's Marion Maréchal-Le Pen. The purpose of the meeting was to exhibit solidarity with Russia during a time in which it was facing isolation following the annexation of Crimea. In December of 2016, Strache and other FPÖ officials traveled to Moscow, where they signed a 10-year "cooperation agreement" with Putin's political party, United Russia. Before the collapse of the coalition government after the recordings of Strache were released, the FPÖ head of the Austrian Interior authorized a police raid on Austria's own domestic intelligence service after it refused to hand over the name of informants who had infiltrated the country's far-right scene.[55] As Vienna had been the longtime residence of Adolf Hitler, such practices had long been accepted by Austrians.

Another important role Vienna has played was as a transit point for Soviet Jews immigrating to either the United States or Israel. The movement to provide Soviet Jews with the right to leave the country dates back to the 1970s. Within Russia, this consisted of Jewish dissidents and intellectuals who became known as the refuseniks, some of whom gained international notoriety. In the United States, American Jewish activists lobbied for the Jackson-Vanik Amendment, which pushed the Soviets through coercive trade penalties to allow their Jewish residents to leave the country. However, the enormity of what became a mass exodus wasn't felt in Israel until the 1990s and had a major impact on Israeli society and the global reach of Eurasian organized crime.

By the late 1980s, Mikhail Gorbachev needed American loan guarantees to allow him to pursue his reform packages and was preparing to allow Soviet Jews to emigrate *en masse* should they wish. Israeli Prime Minister Yitzhak Shamir became aware of these developments and acted to ensure the majority of those leaving the USSR ended up in Israel. At the time, with the notable exceptions of the Arabs and Palestinians, there was a desire across the political spectrum in Israel to increase the Jewish population. Shimon Peres believed that strengthening the Jewish population would provide Israel with enough confidence to launch peace negotiations with the Palestinians. According to Israeli scholars Lily Galili and Roman Bronfman, Israel's Ashkenazi middle class hoped to counter the increasing "Levantization" of the country through the mass injections of highly educated, white immigrants.[56]

The vast majority of immigrants to Israel from the former Soviet Union were law-abiding citizens. An unintended consequence of the mass relocation of people was the infiltration of Eurasian organized crime into Israel. While Jews consisted of approximately 2.5% of the population of Russia and Ukraine in the period before mass emigration, they were disproportionately represented within the ranks of the oligarchs and organized crime. Antisemitism in the Soviet Union prevented its Jewish residents from ascending the official ladders of power within Soviet institutions.[57] That, coupled with the fact that by outlawing all private commercial activity the Soviet Union criminalized large sectors of its society, led to a situation in which Jews and other minorities such as Ukrainians, Georgians, Chechens, and Uzbeks were over-represented in organized crime.

An early immigrant to Israel from the USSR was Shabtai Kalmanovich. Born in Lithuania, Kalmanovich joined the Red Army after completing university. After the KGB discovered that Kalmanovich's family was attempting to move to Israel, he was recruited as a spy in return for the fast-tracking of his family's emigration papers. Kalmanovich arrived in Israel in 1971 as a full-fledged KBG asset. His handlers instructed Kalmanovich to infiltrate *Nativ*, an Israeli government program that encouraged

Aliyah among Jews behind the Iron Curtain.[58] Kalmanovich advised Prime Minister Golda Meir's Labor government on how to absorb Jews from Communist Eastern Europe and the Soviet Union.[59]

The KGB provided funds for his Israeli investments, and within a few years, Kalmanovich became a wealthy businessman. He used his newfound wealth to establish contacts in Israeli society, including with generals and intelligence officers in the Israeli Defense Force. Kalmanovich befriended IDF Brigadier General Dov Tamari and took him on a trip to Africa as his security consultant.[60] Kalmanovich had significant business interests in Sierra Leone and the South African Bantustan, Bophuthatswana, particularly in the diamond trade.[61] Kalmanovich was a partner in the diamond trade with Marat Balagula,[62] a Brighton Beach, Brooklyn-based mobster whose daughter introduced Michael Cohen, Donald Trump's personal attorney and later a negotiator on the Trump Tower Moscow project, to his wife.

On May 22nd, 1987, Kalmanovich was arrested in London by Scotland Yard on charges related to $2.7 million worth of fraudulent checks in a scheme to defraud Merrill Lynch. The British extradited Kalmanovich to the US to stand trial, but he promptly fled back to Israel after posting bail. However, upon his return to Tel Aviv, Kalmanovich was arrested on charges of being a KGB spy. His numerous trips to East Germany and the Soviet Union had aroused the suspicions of Israeli authorities, who also believed that the Soviets had passed the information Kalmanovich had provided over to the Syrians and hostile Arab countries.

Kalmanovich's early release was heavily lobbied for by Iosif Kobzon. Often referred to as the Russian Sinatra, Kobzon was one of the most famous crooners of the Soviet era. In the post-Soviet era, he became a politician and Duma member. In 1995, the FBI alleged that Kobzon was a high-level member of Eurasian organized crime and operated an organization involved in racketeering, international arms trading, and drug trafficking. In 2003, Swiss authorities froze and confiscated $750,000 worth of Kobzon's assets after alleging it had been laundered by a criminal organization.[63] Kalmanovich was subsequently released after five years for good behavior. At that point, he returned to Russia, where he prospered as a businessman until he was assassinated on November 2nd, 2009, the victim of a professional hit.[64]

In addition to being a Russian intelligence asset, the FBI believed that Kalmanovich was a high-level associate of the Solntsevskaya and the Semyon Mogilevich Organization. In the mid-1990s, an Israeli police sting codenamed Operation Romance identified a senior Interior Ministry official who was receiving bribes from Kalmanovich and Solntsevskaya boss Sergei Mikhailov to issue passports to dozens of members of Eurasian organized crime syndicates.[65]

During the mass Aliyah of hundreds of thousands of Jews out of the former Soviet Union to Israel that took place during the 1990s, dozens of high-level members of Eurasian organized crime syndicates, including members of the Solntsevskaya and Izmaylovskaya, received Israeli passports. Among them were Semyon Mogilevich, Grigori Loutchansky, Vadim Rabinovich, Anton Malevsky, Mikhail Chernoy, and others. Russian oligarchs also received Israeli passports, including Boris Berezovsky, Roman Abramovich, Lev Leviev, and Vladimir Gusinsky. Even gentiles received Israeli passports, most infamously Sergei Mikhailov, who was involved in the bribery scheme with Kalmanovich. After the scheme was unearthed, Mikhailov's citizenship was revoked. Another gentile mafioso who received an Israeli passport was the Uzbek Alimzhan Tokhtakhounov.[66] Counterfeit Russian birth certificates showing a Jewish mother could be purchased in Cyprus for $5,000.[67] Within Israel, sensitivities about the treatment of Russian immigrants and around definitions of Jewishness made these issues fraught with controversy.

There were many reasons that Eurasian organized criminals chose to take advantage of Israel's Right to Return laws. Most obviously, as Jews in Russia, many had been subject to fierce antisemitism, while in Israel they were by and large treated with respect as successful businessmen. Israel also offered a safe harbor from the brutal gang wars that raged across Russia in the early 90s. At a 1995 meeting in Tel Aviv's Panorama Hotel, which was attended by top-level members of Eurasian organized crime, including Sergei Mikhailov, it was agreed that no violence was to take place in Israel to avoid alienating the Israeli government.[68]

According to a leaked FBI Intelligence Section report dated August 1996: "[Semyon] Mogilevich attended a summit meeting of Russian OC [Organized Crime] figures in Tel Aviv, Israel, from October 10-19, 1995. Participants included Sergei Mikhailov, Viktor Averin, Boris Birshtein, Vadim Rabinovich, Leonid Bilunov, and Arnold Tamm. The subjects met in Boris Birshtein's office in the diamond center of Tel Aviv. The subject of the meeting was the sharing of interests in Ukraine. While in Israel, the group traveled around the country, including a visit to a shooting range. The INP [Israeli National Police] obtained telephone coverage of the hotel rooms, detecting telephone calls to Russia, Hungary, and Paris."[69]

Another factor that made Israel appealing was its lack of money laundering laws. Some Jewish immigrants who make their way to Israel come from countries that make it difficult or outright ban taking their assets with them. As a result, the law in Israel is set up to make it easy to move money into the country. Throughout the 1990s, this was taken advantage of by criminal syndicates, and billions of dollars were laundered through the Israeli financial system. Israel is also one of the global centers for the diamond trade, a largely unregulated industry that is prone to money laundering.[70] Through the 1990s, Israeli police estimated that Eurasian gangsters laundered $4 billion through the economy, though estimates range as high as $20 billion.[71] While Israel has made some improvements to its anti-money laundering enforcement, it has been estimated that 20-25% of its economy remains off the books.[72]

The arrival of so many immigrants from the former Soviet Union had profound implications for Israeli electoral politics, particularly because the nature of Israel's parliamentary system often means that minor parties emerge as important elements of governing coalitions and exercise outsized influence. One of the early parties formed to represent the interests of newly arrived immigrants was Yisrael Ba-Aliya, founded by the famous Soviet Refusenik Natan Sharansky.

Sharansky accepted campaign contributions from Grigori Loutchansky despite being warned by members of the US Congress, State Department, and CIA that Loutchansky was tied to organized crime. In an affidavit, Loutchansky claimed that he had given Sharansky $100,000 and that they had met five times in Israel and abroad to discuss "the setting up of a political party to represent the Russian immigrants in Israel."[73] Sharansky introduced Loutchansky to Benjamin Netanyahu before Israel's

1996 elections. The Israeli press reported that Netanyahu received $1.5 million from Loutchansky, a claim Netanyahu has denied.[74]

In 1997, Sharansky admitted receiving $100,000 from the Russian organized criminal Gregory Lerner.[75] Born to a Jewish family in Moscow, Lerner became heavily involved with the Soviet black market in the 1980s. In 1982, he was arrested and spent five years in a labor camp. Upon his release, Lerner met the wife of the high-level Russian mobster Sergey "Sylvester" Timofeev. Lerner and Timofeev became business partners.[76] In 1989, Lerner fled to Vienna after Russian authorities accused him of fleecing a Moscow bank. From there, he immigrated to Israel in 1990. The law caught up with Lerner yet again when Swiss police arrested him on a Russian warrant and extradited him to Moscow. After serving an 18-month sentence, Lerner again returned to Israel.

Lerner operated out of a heavily fortified compound in Ashkelon, Israel, and changed his name to Zvi Ben-Ari. After Sergey Timofeev was killed by a car bomb in Moscow, his widow and child came to live with Lerner in Israel. The FBI recorded Lerner speaking with the feared vor Vyacheslav Ivankov on several occasions and claimed he was one of the only individuals they ever heard speak to Ivankov as an equal. In 1995, Lerner partnered with Russia's Promstroi Bank and founded the Israeli-Russian Finance Company. The Bank of Israel eventually permitted Lerner to handle security transactions with overseas funds controlled by non-residents. Lerner then approached numerous banks in Russia and coaxed them into providing tens of millions of dollars for him to invest in Israel.

A formal investigation into Lerner was only opened in Israel after one of Lerner's former partners filed a complaint against him in Russia. It was discovered that he had been involved in a fraud involving tens of millions of dollars. With the assistance of British and American law enforcement, the Israelis were also able to uncover a wide array of offshore shell companies and accounts held in Panama, Islands throughout the Caribbean, Mauritius, and Luxembourg. Lerner had also established a bank in Cyprus, arguably the number one destination for Russian money laundering worldwide. Money from Russia was filtered through Lerner's vast network of shell companies and then returned to Russia via his bank in Cyprus, which also provided money laundering services to Italian organized crime and Colombian cartels.[77]

Lerner was arrested and entered into a plea bargain with Israeli authorities in which he confessed to having defrauded a Russian bank of $37 million, establishing numerous shell companies for illegal purposes, committing multiple forgeries, having defrauded none other than Semyon Mogilevich, and having attempted to bribe numerous senior Israeli politicians. Lerner had joined the Israeli right-wing Likud Party and had spent a great deal of time developing his relationship with senior Israeli officials.

Lerner had become friends with Sofa Landver, a Soviet-born, politically connected Israeli speech therapist who had taught Shimon Peres Russian. Landver was also the head of the Association for Immigrants from the Soviet Union and a Knesset (Israeli parliament) member of the Labor Party. Landver arranged for Lerner to meet with high-level Labor officials Benjamin Ben-Eliezer and Ehud Barack, who were later warned by law enforcement to keep their distance. Lerner had promised Landver a major contribution to her association but was arrested before it could be made. A witness who had met with Lerner and Landver later told investigating authorities that Lerner had expressed a desire to buy the Bank of Israel.

Following Lerner's arrest, there was outrage within the Russian-Israeli community, who interpreted it as a sign of discrimination by the older guard of Israeli society. In 1998, a large-scale protest fanned by several Russian-language newspapers and Russians in the Knesset took place in Ashkelon. Sofa Landver attended and spoke at the demonstration. Over the course of the investigation, Sofa Landver, Natan Sharansky, and a Soviet-born Israeli politician named Avigdor Lieberman would all be called in for questioning. Lieberman later founded Yisrael Beiteinu, originally a secular nationalist party for Russian-speaking Israelis.

Landver, who later left Labor and joined Yisrael Beiteinu, used her position in the Knesset to lobby for Lerner's parole. He was released from prison in 2003 over the objections of Israel's attorney general. Upon his release, Lerner briefly worked at Global Connections, founded by a former director general of Yisrael Beiteinu and a former advisor to Lieberman. Lerner then became an "advisor" to an energy commodities trading company dealing with oil and gas from the former Soviet Union that he secretly controlled, Pacific Petroleum. Sofa Landver acted as a go-between for Pacific Petroleum and Israel's other energy companies. However, in 2004, Lerner was arrested again for fraudulent activities. Over the course of the investigation, it was discovered that he had sent $1 million from a Swiss bank account to Solntsevskaya head Sergei Mikhailov.[78]

Yisrael Beiteinu later joined a coalition government with Netanyahu's Likud Party, a political merger masterminded by a legendary Republican political consultant named Arthur Finkelstein.[79] Finkelstein mentored numerous individuals intimately associated with the later Trump campaign, including Roger Stone and the pollster Tony Fabrizio.[80] Sofa Landver later served as Minister of Aliyah and Integration. Avigdor Lieberman served as the Israeli Foreign Minister from 2009-2012 and 2013-2015, as well as its Defense Minister from 2016 to 2018, and he is noted for his close relationship with Vladimir Putin.

In 2010, the head of the economic crimes department of the Israeli state prosecutor's office, Avia Alef, was investigating Lieberman for alleged financial improprieties. Over the course of her investigation, Israeli prosecutors came to believe that bank accounts linked to Lieberman had received millions of dollars from five international businessmen: Mikhail Chernoy, Martin Schlaff, Robert Novikovsky, Daniel Gitenstein, and Ben Gertler. In April of 2001, $500,000 was transferred from a company owned by Chernoy to a British Virgin Islands registered company that belonged to Lieberman's driver Igor Shneider.[81]

Mikhail Chernoy (AKA Michael Cherney) is an Uzbek-Israeli businessman who played a vital role in the violent privatization of Russia's aluminum industry in the 1990s. According to Spanish prosecutors, he is a leader of the Izmaylovskaya Bratva criminal organization.[82] He is also believed to have collaborated with the Solntsevskaya and the infamous Uzbek gangster Alimzhan Tokhtakhounov, who later operated a gambling ring out of Trump Tower.[83]

Martin Schlaff is an Austrian-born billionaire. He made his fortune through connections to the East German Government and its secret police force, the Stasi. In 1986, Schlaff met with three Stasi officials in Croatia, where it was agreed that he would build a computer hard disk plant in East Germany. At the time, East Germany was under a Western trade embargo. The

Stasi officers were reportedly impressed with Schlaff and provided him with the codename Landgraf. In 1998, a German Bundestag committee of inquiry looked into the disappearance of funds from East Germany. Over the course of the investigation, the committee confirmed that Schlaff had received tens of millions of marks from the East German Government in return for embargoed goods. The committee found that the safehouse in which Markus Wolf, the head of the Stasi's foreign intelligence service, had sheltered in after the fall of the wall had been paid for by Schlaff. The safe house was located in Dresden, notably where Vladimir Putin was stationed as a young KGB officer.[84]

Robert Novikovsky, also Austrian, co-founded Centrex Europe Energy and Gas AG (CEEGAG), one of three partners with Gazprom in developing the Vienna-based Central European Gas Hub (CEGH). One of Novikovsky's founding partners at CEEGAG is a Swiss lawyer named Hans Baumgartner, who is also a member of the board of directors at RosUkrEnergo.[85] Schlaff and Novikovsky share the same press officer in Vienna and, through a blinding array of shell companies, are linked to Gazprom.[86] Both were also implicated in a bribery case involving former Israeli Prime Minister Ariel Sharon's sons.[87]

"Martin Schlaff and Robert Novikovsky are figures that are connected to Putin. They work on behalf of a Russian company, Gazprom," said former Israeli deputy state prosecutor Yehuda Sheffer. "This case involves connections that go far beyond the focus of the criminal allegations that were investigated. These are people and processes and phenomena that it's not always easy to discover the full truth about."

Avia Alef and her colleagues faced an unprecedented pattern of harassment, including being followed, surveilled by private investigators, attacked in the press, and witness intimidation. Key witnesses changed their testimony and, in some cases, mysteriously died. In December 2012, Israeli Attorney General Yehuda Weinstein closed the Lieberman case against the wishes of his own prosecutors. On May 30th, 2019, Benjamin Netanyahu's son Yair tweeted that his father had appointed Weinstein in 2009 at Lieberman's request on the understanding that he would shut the case against Lieberman. In Weinstein's private practice, he represented Netanyahu and the Izmaylovskaya-linked oligarch Oleg Deripaska.

"[T]here are crossroads in the history of a state where a

person doesn't necessarily have to be corrupt in order to make a decisive contribution to the entrenchment of political corruption," Alef wrote in a Hebrew language book about her experience. "In my personal assessment, in 2012, it was my lot to stand dumbstruck at such a crossroads."[88]

Another country infiltrated by Eurasian organized crime and Russian intelligence is the United Kingdom. The City of London, the heart of Britain's global financial hub, had a close relationship with the Soviet Union as far back as the 1950s. Following the Second World War and the Bretton Woods Conference, the US Dollar was made the world's reserve currency. As the Cold War worsened, the Soviets kept their dollar reserves invested primarily in London to avoid being vulnerable to American political pressure. London became a "Eurodollar" hub; that is, British banks traded in dollars, yet they were not subject to the tight Depression-era American financial regulatory laws. This loophole allowed London to maintain its privileged position in the global financial system and also contributed toward the establishment of the Anglo-American global offshore financial secrecy system.[89]

By 1986, financial liberalization in the UK led to the establishment of numerous unregulated offshore financial centers in the nearby Channel Islands, the Isle of Man, Malta, and Cyprus, and locations further afield located in former British overseas territories in the Caribbean and Pacific, Dubai, Singapore and Hong Kong. These disparate new offshore financial hubs were all former British territories that enjoyed the rule of law, stringent financial secrecy regulation, and the widespread use of anonymous corporate ownership vehicles.[90] As the Soviet Union fell apart, the KGB first used the Anglo-American offshore system to launder Communist Party money abroad and then organized crime and the oligarchic elite eventually used it to stash their ill-gotten gains in the safety and stability of the West.

In 2016, the UK's Office for National Statistics estimated that Russian investors held £25.5 billion in assets in the UK. However, that number is dwarfed by the £68 billion that flowed out of Russia and into Britain's offshore financial satellites between 2006 and 2016. According to a study by Deutsche Bank, which itself has been fined for involvement in Russian money laundering scandals, an additional £67.5 billion in hidden Russian cash might be stashed away in the British financial system.[91] London's white-hot property market became a perennial favorite sink for Russians looking to park money in the West.

While Russia's oligarchs bought up all the choicest properties in London and hobnobbed with the British elite, a campaign of political murder unfolded on the streets of the British capital. An exhaustive, two-year investigation performed by *BuzzFeed News* identified as many as 14 murders on British soil that US intelligence believed to be linked to Russia. In every single case, British law enforcement prematurely cut short the investigations. Most were related to the group that surrounded Boris Berezovsky and the FSB whistleblower Alexander Litvinenko, who was later assassinated after ingesting the radioactive poison.[92]

In 2009, three years after Litvinenko's assassination, the Conservative British Tory Party wished to "normalize" relations with Moscow.[93] The links between the Tories and Russian interests did not go unnoticed by MI5. In 2010, the British domestic intelligence service "vetoed" the appointment of Baroness Pauline Neville-Jones to the cabinet position of National Security Advisor to the Prime Minister in David Cameron's new government because of her links to Dmytro Firtash and Mikhail Chernoy. It was revealed that the Baroness received £20,000 a year from Robert Shetler-Jones, the British-based overseer of Firtash's assets. Furthermore, the Baroness sat on the executive council of the Intelligence Summit, a Washington, DC-based right-wing anti-terrorism conference primarily funded by Chernoy.[94]

As in Austria, Firtash has cultivated a network of wealthy and politically connected members of the British elite to promote his interests in the UK. A key figure in this network is the one-time CEO of Firtash's holding company, Group DF, Robert Shetler-Jones. In 2007, Firtash founded the British Ukrainian Society (BUS) alongside Shetler-Jones and Richard Spring, better known as Lord Risby. Lord Risby became BUS chairman and received payments through a subsidiary of a British Virgin Islands company owned by Shetler-Jones. BUS headquarters is located in the same London office building as another Shetler-Jones-owned company called Scythian Limited.[95] Scythian donated to Baroness Neville-Jones,[96] and to the Tory Party, including £62,500 to the Conservative MP Robert Halfon.[97]

Among the prominent Britons in Firtash's orbit is the Tory Member of Parliament John Whittingdale, who in 2015 was appointed as Secretary of Culture. Whittingdale made numerous all-expenses-paid trips to Vienna, Ukraine, and other locations on behalf of BUS. Whittingdale was also known for his affinity for Eastern European women, and he once dated the daughter of a Soviet military officer.[98] Another is Raymond Asquith, the Earl of Oxford and a member of the House of Lords, who sits on the board of Group DF. Remarkably, Asquith, the former head of MI6's Moscow station, personally drove KGB Colonel and MI6 asset Oleg Gordievsky out of Russia after his superiors became suspicious.[99] In 2005, Firtash invested $1 million in a company set up by Asquith, who, alongside Shetler-Jones, lobbied the US Department of Justice on Firtash's behalf.[100] Before receiving his peerage, Asquith ran a lobbying firm called Asquith & Granovsky alongside Vladimir Granovsky, a consultant for the Kremlin-backed Ukrainian leader Viktor Yanukovych.[101]

On August 21st, 2012, a lobbying group called Conservative Friends of Russia (CFoR) was launched in the home of Russia's Ambassador to Britain, Alexander Yakovenko, during a party attended by over 250 prominent British Tories. A month later, four representatives from CFoR went on a trip to Moscow, where they met with members of Putin's United Russia Party. The visit was arranged by the Russian state cultural agency Rossotrudnichestvo,[102] which the FBI once investigated for its links to Russian intelligence.[103] It was later discovered that the Russian Embassy contact for CFoR, Sergey Nalobin, was the son of a prominent KGB general and that Nalobin was acting under the instructions of the Kremlin to promote links between United Russia and the British Tory party.[104] Nalobin had tweeted pictures of himself with Boris Johnson, who he described as a "good friend."[105]

Cozy relations between Russians and the Tories have continued to the present day. In 2019, it was revealed that the Russian-British citizen Lubov Chernukhin, the wife of a former Russian finance minister, donated £450,000 to the Conservatives, making her the largest female political donor in British history.[106] Chernukhin's husband Vladimir had been elevated by Putin as finance minister before being made the chairman of Vnesheconombank (VEB), a financial institution with close historical ties to the Russian security establishment. Lubov spent over £160,000 at an auction that went towards the Conservative party to play tennis matches with current and former Prime Ministers Boris Johnson and David Cameron.[107] Sergey Nalobin was present at the event where she did so.[108]

British Prime Minister Boris Johnson is friends with a former Russian arms magnate, Alexander Temerko. Since he became a British citizen in 2011, Temerko has donated over £1 million to the Conservative party. In an interview with *Reuters*, Temerko praised the leaders of many of Russia's security agencies, including former FSB head Nikolai Patrushev. Sources informed *Reuters* that Temerko had established relationships with the Russian security services in the 1990s as the head of the Russian state arms company *Russkoye Oruzhie*.[109]

[1] Pomerantsev, Peter. *Nothing Is True And Everything Is Possible: The Surreal Heart Of The New Russia*. New York, NY: PublicAffairs, 2014. Pg. 66

[2] Miller, Andrew. *Virtual Politics: Faking Democracy in the Post-Soviet World*. New Haven and London: Yale University Press, 2005. Pg. 49-50

[3] Dawisha, Karen. *Putin's Kleptocracy: Who Owns Russia?*. New York, NY: Simon & Schuster, 2014. Pg. 206-207

[4] Dawisha, Karen. *Putin's Kleptocracy: Who Owns Russia?*. New York, NY: Simon & Schuster, 2014. Pg. 243-251

[5] Podkopaev, Petr; Dawisha, Karen; Nealy, James (Translators). "The Reform of the Administration of the President of the Russian Federation," *Kommersant*. May 5th, 2000

[6] Hoffman, David E. *The Oligarchs: Wealth and Power in the New Russia*. New York, NY: PublicAffairs, 2002. Pg. 477

[7] Goldman, Marshall I. *Petrostate: Putin, Power and the New Russia*. Oxford, UK: Oxford University Press, 2008. Pg. 139

[8] Goldman, Marshall I. *Petrostate: Putin, Power and the New Russia*. Oxford, UK: Oxford University Press, 2008. Pg. 136-137

[9] Åslund, Anders. *Russia's Crony Capitalism: The Path from Market Economy to Kleptocracy*. New Haven & London: Yale University Press, 2019. Pg. 109

[10] Starobin, Paul; Belton, Catherine. "Gazprom: Russia's Enron?," *Bloomberg Businessweek*. February 17th, 2002

[11] Goldman, Marshall I. *Petrostate: Putin, Power and the New Russia*. Oxford, UK: Oxford University Press, 2008. Pg. 146

[12] Nemtsov, Boris; Milov, Vladimir. "Vladimir Putin: The Bottom Line (Part II - Gazprom)," *Novaya Gazeta*. February, 2008

[13] Winter, Tom. "DOJ: Ex-Manafort Associate Firtash Is Top Tier Comrade of Russian Mobster," *NBC News*. July 26th, 2017

[14] Grey, Stephen; Bergin, Tom; Musaieva, Sevgil; Anin, Roman. "SPECIAL REPORT - Putin's allies channeled billions to Ukraine oligarch," *Reuters*. November 26th, 2014

[15] Goldman, Marshall I. *Petrostate: Putin, Power and the New Russia*. Oxford, UK: Oxford University Press, 2008. Pg. 147

[16] "Funny Business In The Turkmen-Ukraine Gas Trade - A Special Report by Global Witness," *Global Witness*. April 2006

[17] Weiss, Michael. "Married to the Ukrainian Mob," *Foreign Policy*. March 19th, 2014

[18] Goldman, Marshall I. *Petrostate: Putin, Power and the New Russia*. Oxford, UK: Oxford University Press, 2008. Pg. 147

[19] Weiss, Michael. "Married to the Ukrainian Mob," *Foreign Policy*. March 19th, 2014

[20] Superceding Indictment: United States of America v. Semion Mogilevich, Igor

Fisherman, Jacob Bogatin and Anotoly Tsoura

[21] 08KYIV2294_a. UKRAINE: FIRTASH USES CRISIS TO EXPAND INTO BANKING - *Public Library of US Diplomacy - Wikileaks*

[22] Swan, Betsy, "Mueller Reveals New Manafort Link to Organized Crime," *The Daily Beast*. November 2nd, 2017

[23] Goldman, Marshall I. *Petrostate: Putin, Power and the New Russia*. Oxford, UK: Oxford University Press, 2008. Pg. 147

[24] 06VIENNA515_a. USG CONCERNS OVER AUSTRIAN BANKING OPERATIONS - *Public Library of US Diplomacy - Wikileaks*

[25] 08KYIV2414_a. UKRAINE: FIRTASH MAKES HIS CASE TO THE USG. *Public Library of US Diplomacy - Wikileaks*

[26] Simpson, Glenn R. "US Identifies 'Nexus' of Organized Crime," *International Assessment and Strategy Center*. February 10th, 2010

[27] Mukasey, Michael B. "Remarks Prepared for Delivery by Attorney General Michael B. Mukasey on International Organized Crime at the Center for Strategic and International Studies," *Department of Justice*. April 23rd, 2008

[28] Tyler, Patrick E. "New Tapes Appear With Threats by Ukraine's President," *The New York Times*. February 19th, 2001

[29] Dawisha, Karen. *Putin's Kleptocracy: Who Owns Russia?*. New York, NY: Simon & Schuster, 2014. Pg. 329 (Footnote)

[30] Kupchinsky, Roman. "The Strange Ties Between Semion Mogilevich and Vladimir Putin," *Eurasian Daily Monitor Vol. 5, Issue 57*. March 25th, 2009

[31] Balmaceda, Margarita M. *The Politics of Energy Dependency: Ukraine, Belarus, And Lithuania Between Domestic Oligarchs and Russian Pressure*. Toronto, CA: University of Toronto Press, 2013. Pg. 94

[32] Dubien, Arnaud. "The Opacity of Russian-Ukrainian Energy Relations," Institut français des relations internationales. May 2007

[33] Kuzio, Taras. *Ukraine: Democratization, Corruption and the New Russian Imperialism*. Santa Barbara, CA: Praeger Security International, 2015. Pg. 54

[34] Kupchinsky, Roman. "Ukraine: Battle Against Corruption Grinds To A Halt," *RadioFreeEurope/RadioLiberty*. September 26th, 2005

[35] Burgis, Tom. "Tower of secrets: the Russian money behind a Donald Trump skyscraper," *The Financial Times*. July 11th, 2018

[36] MacKinnon, Mark. "Searching for Boris Birshtein," *The Globe and Mail*. December 29th, 2018

[37] "Organized Crime and the Special Services of the Commonwealth of Independent States," *Service for Analysis and Prevention, The Swiss Federal Office Of Police, Strategic Analysis Report [CONFIDENTIAL], Transborder Corruption Archives*. June 2007

[38] Smith, R. Jeffrey; Grimaldi, James V. "A 3rd DeLay Trip Under Scrutiny," *The Washington Post*. April 6th, 2005

[39] Smith, R. Jeffrey; Grimaldi, James V. "A 3rd DeLay Trip Under Scrutiny," *The Washington Post*. April 6th, 2005

[40] Smith, R. Jeffrey. "The DeLay-Abramoff Money Trail," *The Washington Post*. December 31st, 2005

[41] Sherwell, Philip; Harrison, David. "British lawyers linked to $1m payment for favours at US Congress," *The Telegraph*. January 8th, 2006

[42] Kranish, Michael. "Abramoff Ties to Russians Probed," *The Boston Globe*. February 23rd, 2006

[43] Kranish, Michael. "Abramoff Ties to Russians Probed," *The Boston Globe*. February 23rd, 2006

[44] Mason, Cass. "Whatever happened to our 'billionaire' Khimich," *newsroom*. July 12th, 2019

[45] Mason, Cass. "Whatever happened to our 'billionaire' Khimich," *newsroom*. July 12th, 2019

[46] Continetti, Matthew. "Mission to Moscow," *The Weekly Standard*. April 25th, 2005

[47] Weiss, Andrew S. "With Friends Like These: The Kremlin's Far-Right and Populist Connections in Italy and Austria," *Carnegie Endowment for International Peace*. February 27th, 2020

[48] Conley, Healther A.; Ruy, Donatienne; Stefanov, Ruslan; Vladimirov, Martin. "The Kremlin Playbook 2," *Center for Strategic & International Studies (CSIS)*. March 11th, 2019

[49] Robinson, Jeffrey. *The Merger: The Conglomeration of International Organized Crime*. New York, NY: Overlook Press, 2000. Pg. 172-173

[50] Simpson, Glenn R.; Crawford, David. "Investor Is Named in Energy Firm," *The Wall Street Journal*. April 27th, 2006

[51] Rachkevych, Mark. "U.S. official: Austrian bank's ties to RosUkrEnergo suspicious," *The Kyiv Post*. December 3rd, 2010

[52] Burgis, Tom. "Tower of secrets: the Russian money behind a Donald Trump skyscraper," *The Financial Times*. July 11th, 2018

[53] Leschenko, Serhii. "The Firtash Octopus: Agents of Influence in the West," *Eurozine*. September 25th, 2015

[54] Jones, Sam; Hopkins, Valerie. "Russia enjoys warm reception in Austria's corridors of power," *The Financial Times*. May 22nd, 2019

[55] Bennhold, Katrin. "As Far Right Rises, a Battle Over Security Agencies Grows," *The New York Times*. May 7th, 2019

[56] Zur Glozman, Masha. "The Million Russians That Changed Israel to Its Core," *Haaretz*. January 3rd, 2013

[57] Glenny, Misha. *McMafia: A Journey Through The Global Criminal Underworld*. New York, NY: Alfred A. Knopf, 2008. Pg.

[58] Kahana, Ephraim. *Historical Dictionary of Israeli Intelligence*. Lanham, MD: The Scarecrow Press. 2006

[59] Friedman, Robert I. "Did A Mystery Tycoon Double-Cross Israel?" *The Washington Post*. May 8th, 1988

[60] Kahana, Ephraim. *Historical Dictionary of Israeli Intelligence*. Lanham, MD: The Scarecrow Press. 2006

[61] Williams, Phil (Editor). *Russian Organized Crime: The New Threat*. London, UK: Frank Cass Publishers, 1997. Pg. 166

[62] Smillie, Ian. *Blood On The Stone: Greed, Corruption and War in the Global Diamond Trade*. London, UK: ANTHEM PRESS, 2010. Pg. 100-101

[63] "Ioseph Kobzon, dubbed the 'Soviet Sinatra,' dies at 80," *The Los Angeles Times*. August 31st, 2018

[64] Harding, Luke. "Former KGB spy shot dead in Moscow," *The Guardian*. November 3rd, 2009

[65] Friedman, Robert I. *Red Mafiya: How The Russian Mob Invaded America*. Boston, New York, London: Little Brown & Company, 2000. Pg. 277

[66] Melman, Yossi. "Mobster Linked to Olympics Bribe Scandal has Israeli Passport," *Haaretz*. August 2nd, 2002

[67] Robinson, Jeffrey. *The Merger: The Conglomeration of International Organized Crime*. New York, NY: Overlook Press, 2000. Pg. 148

[68] Glenny, Misha. *McMafia: A Journey Through The Global Criminal Underworld*. New York, NY: Alfred A. Knopf, 2008. Pg

[69] "SEMION MOGILEVICH ORGANIZATION, EURASIAN ORGANIZED CRIME," *Department of Justice, Federal Bureau of Investigation*. August, 1996

[70] Orme Jr., William A. "Israel Seen as Paradise for Money Laundering," *The New York Times*. February 21st, 2000

[71] Friedman, Robert I. *Red Mafiya: How The Russian Mob Invaded America*. Boston, New York, London: Little Brown & Company, 2000. Pg. 278

[72] Weinglass, Simona. "Now a member of anti-money-laundering body, has Israel truly cleaned up its act?" *The Times of Israel*. January 13th, 2019

[73] Eldar, Akiva. "Luchansky v. Sharansky," *Haaretz*. March 13th, 2002

[74] Friedman, Robert I. *Red Mafiya: How The Russian Mob Invaded America*. Boston, New York, London: Little Brown & Company, 2000. Pg. 281

[75] Cockburn, Patrick. "Ministers quizzed on links to Russian Mafia," *The Independent*. June 17th, 1997

[76] Weitz, Gidi; Zinshtein. "How a Serial Criminal Got Help From an Israeli Government Minister," *Haaretz*. November 25th, 2011

[77] Robinson, Jeffrey. *The Merger: The Conglomeration of International Organized Crime*. New York, NY: Overlook Press, 2000. Pg. 148

[78] Weitz, Gidi; Zinshtein. "How a Serial Criminal Got Help From an Israeli Government Minister," *Haaretz*. November 25th, 2011

[79] Kraft, Dina. "Understanding the Enigma of Arthur Finkelstein, Unseen Power Broker," *Haaretz*. December 10th, 2012

[80] Shepard, Steven. "GOP campaign guru Arthur Finkelstein dies at 72," *Politico*. August 19th, 2017

[81] Weinglass, Simona. "The one who got away: Ex-prosecutor laments the failure to indict Liberman," *The Times of Israel*. July 10th, 2019

[82] Meers, Jelter. "Prosecutor: UK is Not Fighting Russian Organized Crime at All," *Organized Crime and Corruption Reporting Project*. June 18th, 2018

[83] "Archived Interpol's warrant on Mikhail Cherny, Izmaylovskaya gang," *Transborder Corruption Archive*. May 16th, 2020

[84] Weitz, Gidi. "The Schlaff Saga / Laundered Funds & 'Business' Ties to the Stasi," *Haaretz*. September 7th, 2010

[85] Kupchinsky, Roman. "The Shadowy Side of Gazprom's Expanding Central European Gas Hub," *Eurasia Daily Monitor, Volume 5, Issue 217. The Jamestown Foundation*. November 12th, 2008

[86] Tillack, Hans-Martin. "A tale of Gazoviki, money and greed," *Stern Magazine*. September 13th, 2007

[87] Weitz, Gidi. "State Set to Close Landmark Bribe Case Against Former PM Ariel Sharon," *Haaretz*. April 27th, 2012

[88] Weinglass, Simona. "The one who got away: Ex-prosecutor laments the failure to indict Liberman," *The Times of Israel*. July 10th, 2019

[89] Bullough, Oliver. *Moneyland: The Inside Story of the Crooks and Kleptocrats Who Rule the World*. New York, NY: St. Martin's Press. 2019. Pg. 35-37

[90] Åslund, Anders. *Russia's Crony Capitalism: The Path from Market Economy to Kleptocracy*. New Haven & London: Yale University Press, 2019. Pg. 158-159

[91] Bullough, Oliver. "How Britain let Russia hide its dirty money," *The Guardian*. May 25th, 2018

[92] Blake, Heidi; Warren, Tom; Holmes, Richard; Leopold, Jason; Bradley, Jane; Campbell, Alex. "From Russia With Blood," *BuzzFeed News*. June 15th, 2017

[93] Bryant, Chris. "The Tories rely on Russian money - that's why they ignore Russian meddling," *The Guardian*. November 13th, 2019

[94] Leake, Christopher; Hollingsworth, Mark. "MI5 'vetoed Security Minister over links to Ukraine oligarchs," *The Daily Mail*. August 14th, 2010

[95] Leschenko, Serhii. "The Firtash Octopus: Agents of Influence in the West," *Eurozine*. September 25th, 2015

[96] Leigh, David; Hughes, Solomon. "Oligarch's advisor funds tory," *The Guardian*. October 24th, 2008

[97] Faucon, Benoît; Marson, James. "Ukrainian Billionaire, Wanted by U.S., Builds Ties in Britain," *The Wall Street Journal*. December 2nd, 2014

[98] Jukes, Peter. "WHITTINGDALE: The Dominatrix, the Press, the BBC, And the Russians," *Byline Times*. February 17th, 2020

[99] Thompson, Barney; Pickard, Jim. "Archives 1985 & 1986: Gordievsky defection chilled Anglo-Soviet ties," *The Financial Times*. December 29th, 2014

[100] Faucon, Benoît; Marson, James. "Ukrainian Billionaire, Wanted by U.S., Builds Ties in Britain," *The Wall Street Journal*. December 2nd, 2014

[101] Leschenko, Serhii. "The Firtash Octopus: Agents of Influence in the West," *Eurozine*. September 25th, 2015

[102] Weiss, Michael. "Moscow-on-Thames," *Foreign Policy*. November 23rd, 2012

[103] Horwitz, Sari. "Head of D.C.-based Russian cultural center being investigated as possible spy," *The Washington Post*. October 23rd, 2013

[104] Harding, Luke. "Tory blushes deepen over activities of Conservative Friends of Russia," *The Guardian*. November 30th, 2012

[105] Bienkov, Adam. "Suspected Russian spy pictured with his 'good friend' Boris Johnson," *Business Insider*. February 19th, 2018

[106] Thévoz, Seth; Geoghegan, Peter. "Revealed: Russian donors have stepped up Tory funding," *openDemocracy*. November 5ht, 2019

[107] Sabbagh, Dan; Harding, Luke; Davies, Harry. "Lubov Churnukhin: Tories tennis bidding, record-setting donor," *The Guardian*. February 27th, 2020

[108] Staines, Paul. "A very social spy," *The Spectator*. March 17th, 2018

[109] Belton, Catherine. "In British PM race, a former Russian tycoon quietly wields influence," *Reuters*. July 19th, 2019

Chapter 6:
Donald Trump, Eurasian Organized Crime, And Russian Intelligence

Donald Trump's relationship with Eurasian organized crime and Russia's government and intelligence services stretches back decades. Many of the individuals from the former Soviet Union who did business with Trump, ranging from purchasing units in his buildings to engaging in multi-million dollar branding deals, are alleged to have been involved in KGB money laundering schemes and have links to the Semyon Mogilevich Organization, as well as the Solntsevskaya and Izmaylovskaya criminal syndicates. While some of Trump's business partners were Russian, others came from the former Soviet states of Ukraine, Georgia, Azerbaijan, Uzbekistan, Kazakhstan, and Latvia.

The use of offshore secrecy jurisdictions, opaque corporate ownership structures, and all cash real estate transactions often obscure the provenance of international money flows. However, the weight of decades of circumstantial evidence suggests that Trump must have had some awareness regarding the men he was dealing with. As President of the United States and Commander-in-Chief of the US military, with access to the full scope of the American Intelligence Community, Trump could have easily found out that a disturbing number of the individuals he and his children have done business with are linked to some of the wealthiest and most dangerous criminal organizations on Earth.

Many individuals covered in the chapter are not Russians but are from newly independent countries in Eastern Europe and Central Asia that were once part of the Russian Empire and later the Soviet Union. The Eurasian mafia largely consists of minority groups within the former Soviet Union, including Ukrainians, Georgians, Chechens, Uzbeks, and Jews, among others. Uzbekistan, for example, was a hotbed of organized crime during Soviet times, with local criminals establishing corrupt ties to the Moscow government, including former Soviet Premier Leonid Brezhnev and his son-in-law.[1]

Many of the individuals from the former Soviet Union who immigrated to the United States and ended up in business relationships with Trump, though certainly not all, were Jewish. This was due to a quirk of America's trade and immigration policy with the Soviet Union that led to a subset of its Jewish residents moving to New York City. Antisemitism in the Soviet Union, as well as the outlawing of traditional commercial activities, precluded many Soviet Jews from the conventional ladders of success, driving a distinct minority into the criminal underworld.

Little Odessa and Trump's Introduction to Eurasian Organized Crime

Trump's rise in Manhattan coincided with the birth of "Little Odessa," the largest Russian immigrant enclave in the United States in Brighton Beach, Brooklyn. This was due to the Jackson-Vanik Amendment, a 1974 change in US trade policy that economically coerced the Soviet Union to allow its Jewish residents to immigrate to the United States or Israel. The introduction of economic penalties to punish human rights abuses had profound consequences for the Russian-American relationship and continued to be an essential issue in the 2016 US Presidential election.[2] While the overwhelming majority of new arrivals to the US following the passage of Jackson-Vanik were law-abiding citizens, one of the unintended consequences of the policy was the introduction of Eurasian organized crime into the United States.[3] The KGB used the opportunity to empty its prisons of dangerous criminals, some of whom would become KGB informants after re-establishing themselves in Brooklyn.[4]

Trump came to the attention of Eastern Bloc intelligence agencies shortly thereafter. His 1977 marriage to Czech foreign national Ivana Zelníčková was followed by the Státní bezpečnost (StB), Czechoslovakia's state intelligence service. The StB was known to cooperate with the KGB, though it is unclear whether it shared any information about the Trumps. Czech intelligence started a file on the Trumps soon after they were married as part of their mission to keep tabs on Czech émigrés abroad. Ivana's correspondence with her father, Miloš Zelníčková, was monitored, and he was forced to provide the StB with information regarding his daughter and son-in-law's visits to Czechoslovakia as well as information about Trump's business career.[5]

Trump's earliest known interactions with Eurasian organized crime date back to his first Manhattan real estate project. In 1976, he purchased 200 televisions for the Grand Hyatt from Joy-Lud Electronics, which was known to cater to Soviet diplomats, KGB agents, and Politburo members.[6] Among Joy-Lud's customers were the Soviet Foreign Ministers Andrei Gromyko and Eduard Shevardnadze, the future Russian intelligence chief Yevgeny Primakov, and Kremlin media spokesman Georgy Arbatov.[7] The Manhattan-based Joy Lud was operated by two Jewish Soviet émigrés, a Ukrainian from Odessa named Semyon "Sam" Kislin and a Georgian named Tamir Sapir. For Kislin and Sapir, who would later become billionaires, it began a decades-long relationship with Trump. As late as 2018, Kislin referred to himself in correspondence with the US Embassy in Kyiv as Trump's "advisor."[8]

Former KGB Major Yuri Shvets, who once worked for the Washington, DC *rezidentura*, told Craig Unger that Joy-Lud was a regular destination for Soviet espionage agents based in the United States looking to purchase electronic goods unavailable in the Soviet Union for either their own enjoyment or resale. This parallels Putin's activities in Dresden, where he had members of the Red Brigade purchase Western electronic goods for his own use.[9] Shvets further claimed that in 1972, Kislin had been recruited by a KGB field office in Odessa to establish contacts with Soviet Jews hoping to emigrate from the Soviet Union.[10]

Kislin later became a successful commodities trader through a partnership with the alleged Izmaylovskaya senior leader Mikhail Chernoy. In the 1990s, Mikhail and his brother Lev were involved in the violent privatization of the Russian aluminum industry.[11] Kislin and Chernoy's company, Trans World Commodities, assisted in KGB efforts to launder money out of the former Soviet Union and into the United States.[12] Chernoy acted as a mentor to Oleg Deripaska, a Russian oligarch who later seized control of the Russian aluminum industry and played a vital role in the 2016 US election interference operation.[13]

In 1994, Kislin sponsored a visa for the contract killer and Izmaylovskaya head, Anton Malevsky, to enter the United States. Malevsky was a veteran of the Soviet-Afghan war with connections to the FSB, which supported his efforts in the 1990s to prevent Chechen gangs from overrunning Moscow.[14] A confidential FBI report listed Kislin as a "member/associate" of the mafia organization led by Vyacheslav Ivankov, a notorious Russian *vor* with close ties to Semyon Mogilevich and the Solntsevskaya.[15] Kislin used his newfound wealth to purchase political influence in New York, contributing $46,250 and hosting fundraisers for Rudy Giuliani's 1994 and 1997 mayoral campaigns. In return, Giuliani twice appointed Kislin as a member of New York City's Economic Board of Development.[16] When Giuliani prepared to run for the US Senate seat in New York against Hillary Clinton, Kislin co-chaired a fundraiser that netted the former Mayor of New York $2.1 million.[17]

Tamir Sapir, who immigrated to New York in 1975 from the then-Soviet Republic of Georgia via Israel, sold electronic goods from Joy-Lud Electronics to Soviet officials in exchange for the right to sell commodity goods on the international market. Sapir then used the profits from these lucrative transactions to purchase Manhattan real estate.[18] Sapir was also involved in some of the earliest KGB oil-trading operations between the USSR and the West, which sold domestic oil from the USSR, the price of which was artificially lowered by the state at a massive markup on the international market.[19] Recently declassified documents show that in 1998, the FBI was investigating Sapir for money laundering and extortion and believed that "Sapir is used as a front for Russian organized crime money."[20]

In the early 1980s, Eurasian gangsters working with American organized crime implemented what was known as Daisy Chain Scams, defrauding the State of New York out of nearly a billion dollars in fuel taxes.[21] In late 1984, Trump met personally with David Bogatin, a diminutive but brilliant Soviet army veteran and one of the chief Russian masterminds behind the scam. Bogatin was born on June 2nd, 1945, in Saratov, a Soviet technological center on the Volga River. Conflict with authority and the prison experience had deep roots in Bogatin's family. His grandfather was a Talmudic scholar who was sent to prison in 1937 on religious grounds, where his fellow inmates murdered him within the year. His father was imprisoned in a Siberian gulag for 18 years after an anonymous informant told the authorities that he had defaced a picture of Stalin.

After serving as a Soviet military advisor for three years in North Vietnam, Bogatin returned to Russia, where he worked as a printer. He immigrated to the United States in 1977, working his way up to owning a gas station. From there, Bogatin played the oil spot market, using borrowed money to purchase oil in transit to the United States and then selling upon its arrival at an immense profit as the price of oil in the Northeast was spiking.[22]

In 1982, Bogatin identified the criminal opportunity of a lifetime when New York State changed how it collected gasoline taxes. To simplify the system, a new law shifted the tax collection burden away from gas stations to fuel wholesalers. Bogatin and two associates from the Brighton Beach Russian mafia, Michael Markowitz and Lev Persits, devised a gasoline bootlegging scam by which they shifted the tax money owed through a series of shell corporations, creating a byzantine paper trail, before declaring bankruptcy and pocketing the money for themselves. As the tax on gasoline at the time had reached nearly 30 cents per gallon, the profits were enormous.

Bogatin and his Russian partners approached Colombo crime family *caporegime* Michael Franzese to help them with muscle and to use his connections to obtain certain state licenses. Another Franzese associate, a 400-pound Long Island merchant named Lawrence Iorizzo, had a similar scam running simultaneously. They decided to streamline their efforts. Franzese cut a deal in which the Colombo syndicate would collect 75% of the illicit earnings, and the Russians, who were still relatively new to organized crime in New York City, would receive 25%. IRS officials estimated that the scammers skimmed over a billion dollars in federal taxes.[23]

At the height of the scam, Bogatin faced the same problem Al Capone faced decades earlier: what to do with all the cash? He laundered his ill-gotten gains by purchasing units at Trump Tower. In what would become a definitive business practice over his entire career, Trump engaged in no due diligence whatsoever and asked no questions. As far as he was concerned, cash, dirty or not, was king.

The gas tax scam eventually became a victim of its own

success. The FBI caught wind of it and opened an investigation into the gas bootleggers, code-named Red Daisy Chain. Iorizzo was arrested on separate charges and eventually fingered Bogatin and Markowitz, who were charged in New York and Florida with tax evasion, conspiracy, and fraud. Markowitz was suspected of becoming a government informant and was shot to death in his Rolls-Royce.[24] Franzese cut a deal with the government, quit the mob, and wrote a book about the experience. Iorizzo was brought before the United States Congress and, in sworn testimony before the House Ways and Means Committee, claimed that one of his former partners had been a man named Martin Carey and that Carey had skimmed off millions of dollars through the scam and had donated the money the political campaign of his brother Hugh Carey, then the Governor of New York. His allegations were never investigated.[25]

Before his arrest, Bogatin paid Trump $5.8 million in cash for five luxury condos in his signature new building, Trump Tower. Trump was personally present at the closing of the Bogatin deal.[26] Trump Tower was one of only two buildings in Manhattan at the time that sold units to anonymous shell corporations, making it an ideal money laundering sink.[27] According to the FBI, Bogatin was a member of the Semyon Mogilevich organization.[28] His brother, Jacob Bogatin, was later indicted alongside Mogilevich for stock fraud and money laundering.[29] As recently as 2021, Franzese admitted that he had recently spoken to federal investigators who asked him about Trump's relationship with Bogatin.[30]

David Bogatin claimed to have worked for the CIA in Poland during the mid-1980s.[31] Bogatin's lawyer, Mitchell Rogovin, had served as the former legal counsel for the CIA, including managing a prisoner exchange following the Bay of Pigs disaster, and had also served as chief counsel to the Internal Revenue Service.[32] In an unpublished book seen by the author (it can be found at the Rutgers Law Library), criminologist Alan A. Block reveals that in at least one instance involving a prosecutor from the Eastern District of New York, the CIA pressured him to refrain from charging certain Russian/Israeli gangsters involved in the gasoline scams.

In March of 1986, the newly arrived Soviet Ambassador to the United Nations, Yuri Dubinin, and his daughter Natalia Dubinina paid an unannounced visit to Trump Tower and met with Trump privately in his office. Notably, this was a time when the KGB was redoubling its efforts to make contacts with Western businessmen. Trump was charmed by the ego-stroking Soviet diplomat, who a few weeks later was promoted to be the Soviet ambassador to Washington. Around this time, Trump began making bizarre claims to individuals like Nobel Prize-winning nuclear activist Bernard Lown that he wanted Ronald Reagan to appoint him to be the plenipotentiary ambassador for the United States with Gorbachev and that within one hour of sitting down with the Soviet Premier, he could end the Cold War.[33]

In January 1987, Trump and Dubinin sat next to one another at a luncheon held by Leonard Lauder, heir to the Estée Lauder cosmetics fortune. Later that month, Trump received a letter from Dubinin inviting him on behalf of the KGB-operated Goscomintourist, the Soviet state tourist agency, to visit Moscow and explore the possibility of constructing a hotel.[34] Much of the above version of events comes from an interview with Natalia Dubinina, released a day after Trump's election. Yuri Shvets told Craig Unger that Dubinina was likely a KGB agent and that inconsistencies in her story, including the easily disprovable claim that her father spoke English,[35] and the timing of its release following Trump's surprise election, indicated an attempt to cover up details of early KGB approaches to Trump.[36]

On July 4th, 1987, Donald and Ivana Trump flew to Moscow, where they stayed in the Lenin suite at the National Hotel near Red Square. Their room was almost certainly bugged. During the visit, Trump was taken to see several potential hotel sites. Upon his return, a July 24th, 1987 edition of *Executive Intelligence Review*, the private intelligence publication of the cultish and conspiratorial Lyndon LaRouche Movement, which has itself been suspected of links to Russian intelligence,[37] reported that the Soviets were looking favorably on a Trump presidential bid.[38] On September 1st, 1987, on the advice of Roger Stone, Trump paid $94,801 to run full-page newspaper ads that read: "There's nothing wrong with America's Foreign Defense Policy that a little backbone can't cure."[39] The ads further stated, echoing Kremlin propaganda at the time and Trump's later "America First" mantra, that America "should stop paying to defend countries that can afford to defend themselves." Yuri Shvet's told Catherine Belton and Craig Unger that, by the late 1980s, the KGB considered Trump an asset. He did not claim to have any insight into Trump's mindset.[40]

The Trump Taj Mahal, Shalva Chigirinsky,
And Vyacheslav "Yaponchik" Ivankov

According to Catherine Belton, in November 1990, Trump met Shalva Chigirinsky, a Soviet-born Georgian businessman connected to Eurasian organized crime who also enjoyed high-level links to Soviet foreign and military intelligence. Chigirinsky, at the time wealthy enough to be considered a high roller, met Trump at the Taj Mahal Casino shortly before a string of bankruptcies upended Trump's life and business. Over the course of several nights, Trump showed Chigirinsky around the Taj Mahal, even giving him a tour of the casino's vault. Chigirinsky was an associate of both Sam Kislin and Tamir Sapir and another future oligarch who would become a Trump business partner, an Azerbaijani named Aras Agalarov. According to Belton, Chigirinsky, Kislin, Sapir, and Agalarov were all on the vanguard of a partnership between organized crime and Russian intelligence to move money from the former Soviet Union into the West. Reports in the Russian press claim Chigirinsky is an associate of the Solntsevskaya, and he has admitted that he knows Semyon Mogilevich.

Chigirinsky met Trump through Martin Greenberg, an attorney who wrote Atlantic City's gambling laws and later became the president of the Golden Nugget casino. A year earlier, in 1989, Greenberg and Alfred Luciani, a New Jersey assistant attorney general who also worked on the gambling laws and later became a vice president at the Golden Nugget, met with Chigirinsky in Yalta on the Crimean coast to discuss potential investments which included possibly building a casino in the Soviet Union as well as looking into Russian investment into Atlantic City. Greenberg introduced Chigirinsky to Trump during a visit to the Taj Mahal. Chigirinsky was partnered with Vadim Milshtein, whose father was a veteran of Russian military intelligence. Vadim had also established a "translation agency" that employed a former KGB special forces member and a former Soviet diplomat to the UN.

A year after meeting Chigirinsky, Trump's business empire went belly-up, and he experienced his first of six business bankruptcies. Carl Icahn and Wilbur Ross, who later became President Trump's Secretary of Commerce, oversaw a bankruptcy process that proved remarkably generous to Trump. Martin Greenberg, who introduced Trump to Chigirinsky, represented the bondholders during the restructuring. While it is unknown if Chigirinsky played any part in restructuring Trump's debt, he has admitted that he knew Carl Icahn. Chigirinsky told Catherine Belton that he was never financially involved in the Trump Taj Mahal. However, she noted that he discussed its business in terms that indicated he did have some level of involvement.[41] The Trump Taj Mahal was later fined $10 million by the Financial Crimes Enforcement Network (FinCEN) for violating anti-money laundering laws.[42] Chigirinsky fled Russia in 2009 due to a tax evasion investigation and currently resides in Israel.[43] In 2015, Chigirinsky's 12-year-old daughter accused him of sexual assault.[44]

1991 was an inauspicious year for both the Soviet Union and Donald Trump. While Trump was plunged into the first of his six bankruptcies, the USSR ceased to exist. The collapse of the Soviet Union unleashed a flood of Russian flight capital and émigrés Westward, which would come at an opportune moment for the financially desperate Trump. On March 8th, 1992, one of those new arrivals to New York was the sadistically violent *vor* Vyacheslav Ivankov.

Ivankov was born in Tbilisi, Georgia. In 1980, he was involved in the formation of the Solntsevskaya.[45] Two years later, he was arrested for robbery, possession of firearms, forgery, and drug trafficking and was sentenced to 14 years of hard labor in a Siberian gulag. During his stint in prison, the copiously tattooed Ivankov was officially crowned a *vor y zakone*, or thief-in-law.[46] According to US Court records and classified FBI documents, in 1991, Semyon Mogilevich reportedly paid off a judge to secure Ivankov's early release from prison.[47]

In December 1991, at a gathering of *vor y zakone* at Vedentsovo, outside of Moscow, Ivankov had been chosen to ruthlessly prosecute a war on behalf of the Slavic gangs against increasingly powerful criminals from the Caucuses, in particular from Chechnya.[48] He was later sent to the United States to establish control over the burgeoning Russian criminal enterprises in Brighton Beach, Brooklyn. Ivankov's criminal comrades may also have sent him out of Russia to prevent any violations of the shaky peace that had been established with the Chechens and other gangs from the Caucuses.[49]

Ivankov arrived at JFK airport in New York City on March 8th, 1992, where he was met by an Armenian *vor* who handed him a suitcase containing $1.5 million cash. He hit the ground running and quickly established two "combat brigades" consisting of 250 members, some of whom were special forces veterans from the Soviet war in Afghanistan. The brigades, which were on a $20,000 monthly retainer to extort legitimate businesses and kill Ivankov's enemies, were led by a former member of the KGB.[50] The Russian-American gangsters in Brooklyn had little choice but to fall in line.

In May of 1994, the FBI established C-24, the first squad solely dedicated to fighting Russian organized crime in New York.[51] Ivankov, whom FBI agents had learned about on some of the first and last trips ever made by FBI agents to Russia in the early days of the Yeltsin administration, was target number one. However, the FBI had a problem. They had no idea where Ivankov was. Despite his reputation, he had vanished upon arriving in America.

"At first, all we had was a name," said FBI Agent James Moody. "We were looking around, looking around, looking around, and had to go out and really beat the bushes. And then we found out that he was in a luxury condo in Trump Tower."[52]

Ivankov not only lived in Trump Tower but also enjoyed the perks of being a high roller at the Trump Taj Mahal casino in Atlantic City, which had become the go-to destination for Russian mobsters across the East Coast. Casinos, especially those in tough financial straits like the Taj Mahal, keep close tabs and detailed files on their high rollers to ensure they know everything they need to keep them at the tables. While under FBI surveillance, Ivankov visited the Trump Taj Mahal nineteen times between March and April of 1993, gambling over $250,000 in the space of a month.[53] When the FBI finally arrested Ivankov on June 8th, 1995, for extorting and threatening to murder two Russian bankers, he was found to have two firearms, a lock pick set, a bug detector, an electronic voice changer, and a passport kit not dissimilar to the one's used by the KGB. He was also found with a phone book that contained working phone and fax numbers for the Trump Organization, including a number for the Trump Organization's Trump Tower residence.[54]

1996: Trump's Second Visit to Moscow

In November of 1996, Trump traveled to Moscow with Howard Lorber, CEO of Vector Group, a holding company with tobacco and real estate interests that held a lease on a site near the Kremlin that Trump had his eyes on as the potential location for a Trump Tower Moscow.[55] Ducat Place, as the site was known, was controlled by a Russian cigarette company called Liggett-Ducat, a subsidiary of the Vector Group.[56] Lorber, who Trump has described as his "best friend,"[57] later served on candidate Trump's economic advisory team.[58] Trump told *The New Yorker* in a 1997 profile that Lorber had "major investments in Russia."[59]

With Lorber by his side, Trump met with Moscow's mayor, Yuri Luzhkov. Luzhkov oversaw a vast system of corruption and criminality and was a friend of Vyacheslav Ivankov's.[60] He was also believed to be connected to Mogilevich through Sistema, a business conglomerate that supported Luzhkov's political machine.[61] Luzhkov was also close friends with Shalva Chigirinsky.[62] His wife, Yelena Baturina, was a business partner of Chigirinsky's.[63] Trump and Lorber were accompanied by their mutual friend Bennett LeBow, a tobacco executive who had founded the Vector Group. A year earlier, LeBow attended a Clinton-Gore fundraiser, bringing a Ukrainian businessman with alleged links to organized crime named Vadim Rabinovich as his guest.

Rabinovich once served as the Ukrainian representative of Nordex, the Vienna-based commodities trading firm established by the KGB and believed to be involved in money laundering, drug smuggling, and nuclear proliferation.[64] Nordex was operated by the Latvian spook-turned-mobster Grigori Loutchansky, who himself had met Bill Clinton at a 1993 fundraiser.[65] Loutchansky was sprung from prison in 1993 with the help of the KGB and then used Nordex to launder Communist Party funds into the West.[66] In 1995, Loutchansky and Rabinovich had attended a meeting in Tel Aviv with, among others, Semyon Mogilevich and Sergei Mikhailov, head of the Solntsevskaya, to discuss their holdings in Ukraine.[67]

Several other Americans joined Trump, Lorber, and LeBow during their 1996 trip to Moscow. One was David Geovanis, a Moscow-based American businessman who was the Vector Group's Moscow real estate developer. Geovanis holds a Russian passport and may be a dual Russian-American citizen. Several witnesses testified before the Senate Intelligence Committee that Geovanis possesses potentially compromising information about Trump's relationships with women in Moscow and has suggested that the Russian government is likely aware of this. The Committee further assessed that Geovanis' pattern of conduct with women in Moscow had made him and those around him vulnerable to Russian intelligence *kompromat* operations.[68] Photographs exist of Geovanis standing with scantily clad Russian women in front of a portrait of Joseph Stalin.[69] In Moscow at the time, international businessmen were regularly taken out to nightclubs or parties where prostitutes were present, and Russian intelligence eagerly took advantage of these opportunities.

Leon Black, founder of the multi-billion dollar investment management firm Apollo Global Management, also joined Trump on his 1996 trip to Moscow. Black had worked with Geovanis in the Beverly Hills office of the investment firm Drexel Burnham Lambert, which invented the Junk Bond market and later collapsed after its founder, the "Junk Bond King" Michael Milken, was arrested and convicted of securities and tax violations. Black was Milken's right-hand man at Drexel.[70] LeBow was a major investor with Drexel and often flew its executives on private jets to parties costing millions of dollars.[71] While Trump never worked directly with Drexel, he had used the kind of Junk Bonds they pioneered to fund his debt-fueled purchases in the late 1980s, including pouring $675 million worth of Junk Bonds into the Taj Mahal Casino.[72] Years later, as President, Trump issued an executive pardon to Milken.

In 2021, Leon Black resigned from Apollo Global Management after news leaked that he had maintained a relationship with the wealthy financier and sex offender Jeffrey Epstein long after it had been known that he had been involved in the sexual grooming and rape of multiple underage girls. Black wired Epstein $50 million *after* he was convicted of soliciting prostitution from a teenage girl.[73] Between 2012 and 2017, Black paid Epstein $158 million for "financial services."[74] Trump was also a friend and associate of Epstein's from 1987 until a falling out occurred between them in 2004.[75] As of this writing, a former Russian model is suing Black, alleging that he raped and harassed her. Black admits that the two were in a consensual relationship but claims she is now extorting him.[76]

Geovanis was assigned to show Trump around Moscow during his 1996 visit. Trump was also joined on the trip by Matthew Calamari, his former bodyguard and later Chief Operating Officer at the Trump Organization, a Goldman Sachs executive named Ron Bernstein, and the architect Theodore Liebman. On one of their first evenings in Moscow, the Vector Group threw a party for Trump in "The Library" room at the five-star Baltschug Kempinski Hotel in Moscow, where Trump and his entourage likely stayed the evening.[77] According to a 1996 FBI confidential report, the Baltschug Kempinski was owned by Semyon Mogilevich.[78]

During the party, Trump may have initiated a romantic relationship with a Russian woman, possibly a former Miss Moscow, whose name is redacted from the Senate Counterintelligence report. Trump was married to his second wife, Marla Maples, at the time.[79] As of this writing, Trump has been accused by over 26 women since the 1970s of various sexual abuse charges ranging from harassment to rape.[80] David Geovanis has made suggestive comments to friends about Trump and the unnamed Russian. In communications seen by the Senate Intelligence Committee, Robert Curran, a photographer and close friend of Geovanis, wrote to him in 2017 inquiring about Trump's activities with the unnamed Russian woman that evening, asking, "What exactly happened… Did they hook up or whatever?"

"I saw them again the next day, and they were together, so…" Geovanis replied.[81]

Leon Black told the Senate Intelligence Committee that he "did not recall" Trump engaging in compromising behavior during the trip. He remembered attending a concert with Trump followed by a "discotheque" where they possibly met up with Geovanis, though his memory was hazy. Black also admitted that while they were in Moscow, he and Trump "might have been in a strip club together."

In December 2015, Geovanis attended a holiday party thrown by the former Chief Financial Officer of Rosneft, Peter

O'Brien. Jokes were exchanged among the twenty or so businessmen in attendance, and Geovanis was encouraged to tell a story about his 1996 trip to Moscow with Trump. Some had heard Geovanis tell such stories before. O'Brien later testified that Geovanis spoke of "spending time with [Trump] during that trip, and the mention of Trump being with younger women, including in official meetings, which some people in Russia thought was weird." O'Brien continued, "[Geovanis] told a little bit about how [Trump] had spent time going around to some different meetings in Moscow to talk about potential real estate deals. And the culmination of the story was that [Trump] had a meeting in the Moscow mayor's [Luzhkov] office and he showed up with two beautiful young women on his arm, and people thought that was kind of strange. A, that he was with them, and B, that he hadn't just left them wherever he met them."

"The implication of his story," O'Brien maintained, "was that [Trump] had spent the night with these two women and showed up at this first meeting the next day." O'Brien further explained, "For years in Russia there were a number of Russian government officials or others who were exposed in these strip clubs doing not very nice things that their wives, if they have wives, probably didn't know about. I think most of us appreciated that there was that risk in these types of clubs. So, I think once David told that story, we were all concerned about that."[82]

Geovanis' and Black's connections to Russia deepened in the years that followed the 1996 trip to Moscow. Between 1997 and 2001, Geovanis worked in the Moscow and London offices of Soros Private Equity Partners, the investment fund operated by George Soros. After that, Geovanis worked as a real estate manager for Oleg Deripaska's holding company, Basic Element. After leaving Basic Element, Geovanis joined a real estate investment group closely associated with Arkady Rotenberg, a billionaire Russian oligarch and close personal friend of Putin's. Geovanis claimed that he sometimes plays hockey with veterans of the FSB and the Federal Protection Office (FSO), Russia's equivalent to the Secret Service, and that relationships he maintains are good for business. Following the 2016 election, Geovanis was hired by Bennet LeBow to open a Moscow office for his coal processing company, Somerset International. Somerset's sales materials advertise its relationships with Oleg

Deripaska, Roman Abramovich, Viktor Vekselberg, and Arkady Rotenberg. Geovanis' deputy at the company was a former member of the Russian security services.[83] Neither Geovanis nor LeBow made themselves available to the Senate Intelligence Committee during its investigation.

Leon Black is an associate of Allan Vine, an American investor in Russia known as a "consigliere" to the sanctioned oligarch Suleiman Kerimov. In 2011, Black met privately with Vladimir Putin.[84] That same year, Black was named an advisor to the Russian Direct Investment Fund (RDIF), owned by the Russian state bank Vnesheconombank (VEB).[85] *The New York Times* has described VEB as being "intertwined" with Russian intelligence,[86] and the bank has been used as cover for Russian intelligence officers operating in the United States.[87] Following the invasion of Crimea, Black was quietly removed from the list.[88] Following Trump's 2016 victory, Putin sent the RDIF's CEO Kirill Dmitriev to a secret meeting with the conservative billionaire, Trump supporter, and former Navy SEAL Erik Prince on the Seychelles islands to discuss opening a Trump-Putin back channel.[89] Black's Apollo Global Management loaned Jared Kushner's real estate company $184 million during Trump's presidency, roughly three times the size of the average loan given out by the company's real estate arm.[90]

In 1997, Trump expressed interest in erecting a 311-foot bronze statue of Christopher Columbus by the Russian artist Zurab Tsereteli on the Hudson River. Mayor Luzhkov served on a committee that worked to place Tsereteli's works abroad.[91] Trump had met Tsereteli through Geovanis and Luzhkov during his trip to Moscow the year before.[92] In 1993, Luzhkov had customs fees waived on raw materials supposedly used to construct one of Tsereteli's works, including 600 tons of bronze and, inexplicably, 8,500 tons of soft-grade copper used for electrical wiring. Tsereteli's art projects appear to have been a front for a massive tax and customs evasion scam involving Russian natural resource exports. The man who provided the seed capital to send Tsereteli's statue to America was the KGB and organized crime affiliated Grigori Loutchansky.[93] However, the project never got off the ground.

Later, in 1997, Trump and Howard Lorber met in Trump Tower with Aleksandr I. Lebed, a retired Russian general and presidential hopeful. The meeting was closed to the press. Trump and Lebed discussed a possible Trump Tower Moscow.[94] "I hope I'm not offending you by saying this, but I think you are a litmus testing paper. You are at the end of the edge," Lebed said to Trump. "If Trump goes to Moscow, I think America will follow. So I consider these projects of yours to be very important. And I'd like to help you as best I can in putting your projects into life."[95]

Trump World Tower, Deutsche Bank, and the Trump Sunny Isles Towers

In October 1998, Trump broke ground on Trump World Tower near the United Nations building. A third of the units sold on floors 76-83 were purchased by individuals or LLCs connected to former Soviet states. Sam Kislin issued multi-million dollar mortgages to buyers of Trump World condos, including to Vasily Salygin, who later became an official in the Ukrainian Party of Regions at the time Trump's future campaign chairman, Paul Manafort, advised its leader.[96] An Uzbek diamond dealer named Eduard Nektalov purchased a 79th-floor unit for $1.6 million.[97] At the time, he was being investigated for a money laundering scheme involving diamonds and Columbian drug cartels. He was later murdered on 6th Avenue for cooperating with authorities.[98] Nektalov, a member of the ancient Central Asian Bukharan Jewish community, was the third cousin of the Uzbek-Israeli diamond magnate Lev Leviev, whose interlocking relationships with Putin, Trump, and Jared Kushner will be explored shortly.[99]

Trump World Tower was made possible by $425 million in loans from Deutsche Bank, made at a time when no other bank would touch Trump.[100] Over the next two decades, Deutsche lent Trump upwards of $2 billion.[101] Deutsche has a close relationship with Russia's government-controlled VTB bank, known for its past financing of intelligence agencies and operations. In 2008, VTB's CEO Andrey Kostin hired over 100 Deutsche employees to start a VTB investment bank.[102] Kostin's son had been working at Deutsche since 2000 but later died in a freak motorcycle accident.[103] Deutsche Bank has participated in a variety of multi-billion dollar money laundering operations funneling dirty Russian money into the Western financial system. Using a method known as "Mirror Trading," Deutsche employees whisked $10 billion out of Russia and into the offshore financial system.[104] Deutsche Bank was also involved in a $20 billion money laundering scheme that funneled Russian money through Moldova and into the European financial system.[105] A now-deceased whistleblower named Val Broeksmit, the son of a Deutsche Bank executive who committed suicide, reportedly told the FBI that VTB Bank underwrote Deutsche Bank's loans to Trump.[106] However, this claim has not been substantiated, and questions have been raised as to Broeksmit's credibility.[107]

In the early 2000s, Trump's business model transitioned from owning buildings outright to licensing the Trump brand and receiving sales fees. A confluence of events occurring at the turn of the century made the Trump Organization an appealing money laundering sink. First, news of the multi-billion dollar Bank of New York money laundering scandal, partially masterminded by Semyon Mogilevich, spilled out into the public in 1999.[108] While there was no serious criminal investigation into the matter, it did require that new money laundering avenues be explored and exploited. In addition to this, the passage of the Patriot Act following the September 11th terrorist attacks led to significantly more banking regulations to combat money laundering. However, a loophole allowed real estate to be exempted from these protections, making it a more appealing option for launderers operating out of the former Soviet Union.[109]

In 2001, Trump signed an agreement with developers Michael and Gil Dezer, which led to six buildings bearing Trump's name in Sunny Isles, Florida, which goes by the nickname "Little Russia" due to its high density of Russian residents. *Reuters* found that Russian buyers spent $98.4 million at Trump's six Sunny Isles towers, plus one in Hollywood, FL. However, as up to a third of all units sold were purchased by anonymous shell corporations, that number is likely higher. The exclusive sales agent for three of the Trump-branded towers was an Uzbek immigrant with an office in the Trump International Beach Resort named Elena Baronoff, who first arrived in the US as a Soviet cultural attaché in public diplomacy.[110] Baronoff traveled with the Trump children on a trip to Russia in the winter of 2007-2008,[111] and was allegedly friends with Sergey Lavrov, the Russian Foreign Minister under Putin.[112] She died of cancer in 2015.

Bayrock, Tevfik Arif, and Felix Sater

In the early 2000s, Trump was introduced to a development

company called Bayrock by Tamir Sapir, who, since his early partnership with Sam Kislin, had become a billionaire after investing the money he had earned from trading fertilizer and oil between the US and Soviet Union into New York real estate. Sapir was awarded the oil export contract by Shalva Chigirinsky, who had gained partial ownership of a Moscow oil refinery through his relationship with Mayor Luzhkov. Since their first meeting, Chigirinsky had remained close to Trump's orbit, befriending Sotheby's owner Alfred Taubman, who was later convicted in a price-fixing scheme, and his son-in-law Louis Dubin, who was close to Trump. Chigirinsky hired Louise Sunshine, a former executive vice president at the Trump Organization. He claims that he once almost purchased Mar-a-Lago but was talked out of it by Taubman, who complained about low-flying aircraft. Chigirinsky also socialized with the casino magnate Steve Wynn, a longtime Trump friend and rival.[113] Wynne was later accused by dozens of employees and others of a repeated pattern of sexual assault and harassment.[114]

Bayrock, which partnered with Trump on several aborted projects before collaborating on Trump Tower Soho, was founded by Tevfik Arif. A Kazakh-born ethnic Turk, Arif used to work at the USSR's Commerce and Trade Ministry, which was led at the time by a KGB lieutenant general and was systematically engaged in espionage against the West.[115] According to the Russian press, Arif had been involved with gangsters in the Uzbek capital, Tashkent, specifically Mikhail Cherney and Alimzhan Tokhtakhounov, the latter a high-level associate of Mogilevich and Ivankov.[116] In 1993, Arif served as the Kazakh "agent on the ground" for the Trans World Group, which had attempted to corner the Russian aluminum market in the early 90s and was jointly operated by British-based metals traders the Reuben brothers and Mikhail and his brother Lev Chernoy.[117] In 2001, after a brief stint in Turkey, Arif established the real estate firm Bayrock and hired a man named Felix Sater.

Born in Moscow in 1966, Sater immigrated to Brighton Beach via Israel with his family at the age of seven in the first wave of 70s Jewish émigrés to flee the Soviet Union. His father, Michael Sheferofsky, was a Brooklyn-based Russian mafiosi who ran protection rackets and collaborated with the Genovese crime family.[118] During his childhood, Sater befriended a Ukrainian-American girl named Laura Shusterman, who would later marry

Trump's personal attorney, Michael Cohen.[119] Cohen had met Shusterman through a mutual acquaintance, the daughter of the powerful Brooklyn-based Russian mobster Marat Balagula.[120]

Throughout the 1980s and 90s, Eurasian organized crime in the United States forged alliances with the Italian-American Mafia, including the Five Families in New York. Its tendrils spread into white-collar crime, fuel tax scams, Medicare fraud, infiltration of the diamond market,[121] Wall Street pump-and-dump stock scams, and sophisticated commodity-trading schemes.[122] Sater's father, Sheferofsky, was arrested in 2000 and, in a remarkably similar circumstance to what would later happen to his son, struck a deal with the Brooklyn prosecutor Loretta Lynch. Lynch later served as Barack Obama's Attorney General. Sheferofsky spent six years assisting the FBI with organized crime cases.[123]

While it is undisputed that Sheferofsky was affiliated with the Brighton Beach, Brooklyn-based Russian mafia, there has been much debate over whether he worked for Semyon Mogilevich. The claim that he did so is based upon a Supreme Court petition for a writ of certiorari in Palmer v John Doe 14-676, which described Sheferofsky as "a Mogilevich crime syndicate boss."[124] However, when the journalist Seth Hettena questioned the attorney who authored the writ about the provenance of this information, he learned that it had come from the website Deep Capture.[125] The conspiratorial site was funded by Patrick Byrne, the founder and chief executive of Overstock.com, who at one point was in a romantic relationship with the convicted Russian agent Maria Butina.[126] This admission made Hettena doubt Sater's connection to Mogilevich.

On the other hand, Catherine Belton spoke with two "former Mogilevich associates" who told her that Sheferofsky had been an "enforcer" for Mogilevich's interests in Brighton Beach.[127] British journalist Paul Wood also told Seth Hettena that he had learned from someone within the Mogilevich organization that there was a connection between Sater himself and Mogilevich. A former colleague of Mogilevich, Dietmar Clodo, told the Russian independent publication *The Insider* that Sater was friends with Mogilevich, Sergei Mikhailov, and Vyacheslav Ivankov and even served as shamash (Hebrew for "helper" or "assistant") to Mogilevich when he visited the United States.[128]

After graduating college, Sater's career on Wall Street was

cut short when, on October 1st, 1991, he stabbed a commodities broker in the face with the stem of a margarita glass during a barroom brawl. After leaving prison in 1995, Sater became involved with a $40 million pump-and-dump stock scheme operated by a firm called White Rock that involved four of New York's Five Families. Some of the brokerages involved had been investigated for their connections to the Bank of New York scandal, which involved Mogilevich. The money earned from all this illegal activity was then laundered through New York's Diamond District.

The White Rock scam was interrupted when the FBI came across a storage locker Sater kept that contained a 12-gauge shotgun, two Tec-9 assault pistols, and financial documents showing Sater had set up a sophisticated offshore money laundering operation. However, by the time Federal authorities sought him out, Sater had fled to Russia.[129] According to Sater, he went to Russia as a consultant for AT&T as it negotiated a $100 million deal to rent a transatlantic cable to the US. He claims he met with high-level Russian military intelligence officers in this capacity. In one version of events, Sater was sitting down for dinner with his Russian intelligence contacts when he was noticed by an American defense contractor named Milton Blane, who was impressed enough by Sater's contacts that he recruited him to provide information for US intelligence. Sater claims he leaped at the opportunity.

The information Sater provided the US intelligence community and the FBI was remarkable. Using his Russian intelligence contacts, he accessed a facility that stored a Russian anti-missile system and provided information on it to US intelligence. He helped the CIA track down several stinger anti-aircraft missiles that it had provided to the anti-Soviet mujahideen but had subsequently lost track of. Upon returning to the US to face the consequences of his illegal stock market activities, he provided the FBI with a piece of paper that contained five satellite phone numbers associated with Osama Bin Laden. Following the September 11th terrorist attacks, Sater used connections with Taliban leader Mullah Omar's personal assistant to identify several al Qaeda money launderers. He also posed as a money launderer and, on behalf of the FBI, traveled to Cyprus and Turkey in this capacity to infiltrate two international criminal syndicates.[130]

Sater also provided information to the FBI regarding the American and Eurasian mafia's infiltration of financial and securities markets. Like his father, Sater's case was overseen by Loretta Lynch. His FBI handler, Leo Taddeo, told a judge that Sater played a crucial role in taking down Frank Coppa, a Bonanno family *capo* who worked with other American and Eurasian mobsters to set up a stock pump and dump scam. In 2000, the FBI convicted 19 individuals in connection with the scheme.[131] Around this time, the FBI grew increasingly alarmed by attempts out of Russia to infiltrate the global financial system. During Congressional testimony, head of the FBI's organized crime section, Thomas Fuentes, described the criminals the FBI was most worried about as "a group of individuals who are three or four levels above the street thug level. So while we have Eurasian and Russian organized crime groups involved in street-level racketeering, traditional racketeering acts of loan sharking, gambling, and prostitution, we have another group of international criminals who are generally sitting outside the United States and penetrating the global financial network from afar; and that includes banking, as well as the securities industry... These are the individuals that are the greatest threat, as we see it. They were the most difficult - they are very sophisticated. They are using multinational companies. In some of our cases, we are talking about investigations going on right now in a single case involving a single group in 35 countries."[132]

According to Catherine Belton, Sater's connections in organized crime, including Semyon Mogilevich, who is known to cooperate with Russia's foreign intelligence agency, connected him to Russian military intelligence. For many years, Eurasian organized crime figures in Brighton Beach had agreed to serve as informants to the FBI in return for having charges against them dropped. Mogilevich once offered to provide information to the FBI to avoid being indicted but was turned down on suspicion that he was only doing so to manipulate American authorities to his benefit.[133] Yuri Shvets told Belton that Russian military intelligence likely funneled information through their "asset" Sater to increase his "standing and influence" with the FBI. Inevitably, comparisons have been made to the FBI's infamous experience with their mobster-informant Whitey Bulger, who implicated his FBI handler in crimes and used his relationship with the Feds for his own criminal purposes.

Shvets believes that Sater's information came from an alliance between Mogilevich and Shabtai Kalmanovich, the Soviet-born Lithuanian-Israeli with connections to the Solntsevskaya who was arrested by Israeli officials in 1988 for being a KGB spy.[134] After his release and return to Russia, Kalmanovich and Mogilevich operated a global arms sales and smuggling business that provided weapons to all sides of the civil war in Afghanistan that followed the Soviet pull-out, including the Taliban and their enemies, the Northern Alliance. Mogilevich and Kalmanovich performed tasks for Russian intelligence. A former Mogilevich associate told Belton that the information regarding Bin Laden's phone numbers and the stinger missiles would likely have come from Mogilevich.[135] The assassinated FSB defector Alexander Litvinenko accused Mogilevich of selling weapons to al Qaeda. He claimed the FSB had a relationship with al Qaeda as well as with Islamist rebels in Chechnya, though these claims remain unsubstantiated.[136] Litvinenko was poisoned with radioactive polonium.

Contemporaneous with being an informant for US law enforcement and intelligence, Sater became a managing director at Bayrock, which had an office in Trump Tower. In 2002, he met and began working with Donald Trump. In 2005, Trump signed an agreement that gave Bayrock exclusive rights to represent the Trump Organization in Russia.[137] Sater initially identified the Sacco & Vanzetti pencil factory on Kutuzovsky Prospekt as a potential location for a Trump Tower Moscow. However, the deal fell through after a biography of Trump by Timothy O'Brien alleged that he had massively overinflated his net worth.[138] Despite the setback, Trump trusted Sater enough to have him accompany Ivanka and Trump Jr. on a 2006 trip to Moscow. Sater took the Trump children on a tour of the Kremlin and arranged for Ivanka to sit in Putin's private chair in his Kremlin office.[139]

Rebirth and Reality TV: Donald Trump and The Apprentice

The early 90s were a brutal time for Trump financially and in terms of the carefully honed reputation he had crafted for himself in the late 1970s and throughout the 80s. After the wildly successful publication of 1987's *The Art of Deal*, which portrayed

Trump as a self-made tycoon, a tabloid frenzy over his divorce from Ivana and a series of bankruptcies damaged his image. Behind the scenes, he was faring even worse than most could have imagined. Between 1985 and 1994, Trump's tax returns show that his losses totaled a staggering $1.17 billion.[140]

Trump eventually landed on a novel solution to his problems. If he couldn't live up to being America's greatest businessman in real life, he would do so on "reality" television. In the early 2000s, reality TV swept over American culture like a tsunami. One of the first and most popular reality TV shows was *Survivor*, created by a Brit named Mark Burnett. After a stint in the British military, Burnett struggled to become a television producer in Los Angeles. After reading The Art of the Deal, a seed was planted in Burnett's mind that later would flower into one of the most popular shows of the reality TV era: *The Apprentice*.

In 2003, after having found success with Survivor, Burnett pitched Trump on the idea of having a starring role in his own reality TV show. After only 45 minutes, Trump agreed.[141] *The Apprentice* was billed as "The Ultimate Job Interview," in which contestants competed with one another on various tasks and were ultimately judged by Trump as to who would eventually get a position at the Trump Organization. At the end of each episode, one contestant would be eliminated, with Trump saying the now iconic phrase, "You're Fired."

The show was picked up by *NBC* and championed by producer Jeff Zucker, who later became the president of CNN.[142] While in reality, Trump's business empire had either crumbled or was underwater, on reality TV, Trump was "the latest real estate developer in New York." This statement, proclaimed in Trump's opening monologue on the show, was not true. It didn't matter. Trump also portrayed himself as a comeback artist. "About thirteen years ago, I was in serious trouble. I was billions of dollars in debt. But I fought back, and I won - big league."

The show's first season was a smash success and set the stage for fourteen more seasons with Trump at the helm. Fundamentally, it reintroduced Trump to the American people on a new and popular medium. While Trump had first mastered the New York tabloids and used The Art of the Deal to embody the excesses of the 1980s, he used reality TV to reinvent the Trump brand and flash it across millions of American television screens. Trump's success on reality television exemplified not only his skill at self-promotion but also his remarkable knack for being on the cutting edge of changes in media consumption. This would be repeated later when Trump became a fixture on social media, particularly on Twitter.

The Apprentice also saved Trump financially. Trump earned $197 million directly from the show over sixteen seasons and an additional $230 million in earnings that sprung out of the show. Some of that money came from sponsorship and advertising deals from companies that wanted to take advantage of Trump's renewed fame. Others came from real estate licensing deals, some from partnerships put together by Felix Sater and Tevfik Arif, who had connected with Trump at just the moment when his celebrity status was again on the rise.

[1] Finckenauer, James O.; Waring, Elin J. Russian Mafia in America: Immigration, Culture And Crime. Boston, MA: Northeastern University Press, 1998. Pg. 98-100

[2] Pifer, Steven. "Congress, Russia, and sanctions," The Brookings Institute. January 18th, 2017

[3] Statement of Grant D. Ashley, Assistant Director, Criminal Investigative Division, Federal Bureau of Investigation Before the Subcommittee on European Affairs, Committee on Foreign Relations, United States Senate, Concerning Transnational organized Crime. October 30th, 2003. Pg. 6-7

[4] Friedman, Robert I. Red Mafiya: How The Russian Mob Has Invaded America. New York, NY: Little Brown And Company, 2000. Pg. 12-13

[5] Harding, Luke. "'A very different world' - inside the Czech spying operation on Trump," The Guardian. October 29th, 2018

[6] Melby, Caleb; Geiger, Keri. "Behind Trump's Russia Romance, There's a Tower Full of Oligarchs," Bloomberg. March 16th, 2017

[7] Hettena, Seth. Trump/Russia: A Definitive History. Brooklyn, NY: Melville House Publishing, 2018. Pg. 76-78

[8] Smith, Matt; Williams, Lance. "Russian-American business exec with ties to Trump is drawn into impeachment inquiry," Reveal. October 5th, 2019

[9] Gessen, Masha. The Man Without A Face: The Unlikely Rise Of Vladimir Putin. New York, NY: RIVERHEAD BOOKS, 2012. Pg. 65

[10] Unger, Craig. American Kompromat: How the KGB Cultivated Donald Trump and Related Tales of Sex, Greed, Power and Treachery. New York, NY: Penguin Random House, 2021. Pg. 27-30

[11] Royce, Knut. "FBI TRACKED ALLEGED RUSSIAN MOB TIES OF GIULIANI CAMPAIGN SUPPORTER," The Center for Public Integrity. December 14th, 1999

[12] Belton, Catherine. Putin's People: How The KGB Took Back Rusia And Then Took On The West. New York, NY: Farrar, Straus And Giroux, 2020. Pg. 66-67

[13] Belton, Catherine. "Rusal: A lingering heat," The Financial Times. January 25th, 2010

[14] Volchek, Dmitry. "One Russian Blogger's Effort To Unearth The Secrets Of Putin's Rise To Power," RadioFreeEurope/RadioLiberty. April 1st, 2020

[15] Block, Alan. All Is Clouded By De$ire: Global Banking, Money Laundering, and International Organized Crime. Westport, CT: Praeger Publishers, 2004. Pg. 154

[16] Friedman, Robert I. Red Mafiya: How The Russian Mob Has Invaded America. New York, NY: Little Brown And Company, 2000. Pg. 271

[17] Nemtsova, Anna; Rawnsley, Adam; Dickey, Christopher. "Trump and Giuliani

Connections to Ukraine Corruption Go Back Years," *The Daily Beast*. October 1st, 2019
[18] "The Boomerang Effect," *Forbes*. March 31st, 2006
[19] Belton, Catherine. *Putin's People: How The KGB Took Back Rusia And Then Took On The West*. New York, NY: Farrar, Straus And Giroux, 2020. Pg. 451
[20] "FBI Records: The Vault – Tamir Sapir," https://vault.fbi.gov/tamir-sapir/tamir-sapir-part-01/view
[21] Williams, Phil (Editor). *Russian Organized Crime: The New Threat?* Portland, OR: Frank Cass Publishers, 2000. Block, Alan A. "On the Origins of Fuel Racketeering: The Americans and the Russians in New York," Pg. 156-176
[22] Horrock, Nicholas; Myers, Linnet. "Extradition Target Says His Real Crime Is Success," *The Chicago Tribune*. April 3rd, 1992
[23] Raab, Selwyn. "Mafia-Aided Scheme Evades Millions in Gas Taxes," *The New York Times*. February 6th, 1989
[24] Raab, Selwyn. "Mob-Linked Businessman Killed in Brooklyn," *The New York Times*. May 3rd, 1989
[25] Friedman, Robert I. *Red Mafiya: How The Russian Mob Has Invaded America*. New York, NY: Little, Brown and Company. Pg. 50
[26] Barrett, Wayne. *Trump: The Deals and the Downfall*. New York, NY: HarperCollins, 1992. Pg. 194
[27] Unger, Craig. *House of Putin, House of Trump: The Untold Story of Donald Trump and the Russian Mafia*. New York, NY: Penguin Random House LLC, 2018. Pg. 12-13
[28] Intelligence Section, Organizational Intelligence Unit. "SEMION MOGILEVICH ORGANIZATION: EURASIAN ORGANIZED CRIME," *Department of Justice, Federal Bureau of Investigation*, August 1996. Pg. 10
[29] United States District Court for the District of Pennsylvania. United States of America v. Semion Mogilevich, Igor Fisherman, Jacob Bogatin, Anatoly Tsoura. SUPERSEDING INDICTMENT. Criminal No. 02-157.
[30] Hettena, Seth. "Investigators probed Trump's 40-year-old ties to Russian Mobster," *SETHHETTENA.com*. February 10th, 2021
[31] "Polish bank founder sentenced to prison in New York," *UPI*. May 14th, 1992
[32] Horrock, Nicholas; Myers, Linnet. "Extradition Target Says His Real Crime Is Success," *Chicago Tribune*. April 3rd, 1992
[33] Feinberg, Scott. "Donald Trump Angled for Soviet Posting in 1980s, Says Nobel Prize Winner (Exclusive)," *The Hollywood Reporter*. May 26th, 2017
[34] Harding, Luke. "The Hidden History of Trump's First Trip to Moscow," *Politico Magazine*. November 19th, 2017
[35] Sciolino, Elaine. "MAN IN THE NEWS; NEW RUSSIAN IN CAPITAL: YURI VLADIMIROVICH DUBININ," *The New York Times*. May 21st, 1986
[36] Unger, Craig. *American Kompromat: How the KGB Cultivated Donald Trump and Related Tales of Sex, Greed, Power and Treachery*. New York, NY: Penguin Random House, 2021. Pg. 73-80
[37] Mintz, John. "Some Officials Find Intelligence Network 'Useful,'" *The Washington Post*. January 15th, 1985
[38] Unger, Craig. *House of Putin, House of Trump: The Untold Story of Donald Trump and the Russian Mafia*. New York, NY: Penguin Random House LLC, 2018. Pg. 50-51
[39] D'Antonio, Michael. *The Truth About Trump*. New York, NY: St. Martin's Press, 2015. Pg. 181-182
[40] Unger, Craig. *American Kompromat: How the KGB Cultivated Donald Trump and Related Tales of Sex, Greed, Power and Treachery*. New York, NY: Penguin Random House, 2021. Pg. 94/Belton, Catherin. *Putin's People: How The KGB Took Back Rusia And Then Took On The West*. New York, NY: Farrar, Straus And Giroux, 2020. Pg. 477
[41] Belton, Catherine. *Putin's People: How The KGB Took Back Russia and Then Took On The West*. New York, NY: Farrar, Straus And Giroux, 2020. Pg. 448-454
[42] Hudak, Steve. "FinCEN Fines Trump Taj Mahal Casino Resort $10 Million for

Significant and Long Standing Anti-Money Laundering Violations," *The Financial Crimes Enforcement Network*. March 6th, 2015

[43] "Moscow eyes bigger Sibir stake amid shareholder probe," *Reuters*. July 17th, 2019

[44] Tepfer, Daniel. "Russian billionaire fails to win back daughter in Bridgeport court," ctpost. July 9th, 2019

[45] Galeotti, Mark. *The Vory: Russia's Super Mafia*. New Haven and London: Yale University Press, 2018. Pg. 146

[46] Finckenauer, James O. *Russian Mafia in America: Immigration, Culture and Crime*. Boston, MA: Northeastern University Press, 1998. Pg. 110-111

[47] Block, Alan A.; Weaver, Constance A. *All Is Clouded By Desire: Global Banking, Money Laundering and International Organized Crime*. Westport, CT: Praeger Publishers, 2004. Pg. 150

[48] Handelman, Stephen. *Comrade Criminal: Russia's New Mafiya*. New Haven and London: Yale University Press, 1995. Pg. 260

[49] Galeotti, Mark. *The Vory: Russia's Super Mafia*. New Haven and London: Yale University Press, 2018. Pg. 193-194

[50] Friedman, Robert I. *Red Mafiya: How The Russian Mob Has Invaded America*. Boston, New York, London: Little Brown and Company, 2000. Pg. 132-133

[51] Hettena, Seth. *Trump/Russia: A Definitive History*. Brooklyn, NY: Melville House, 2008. Pg. 35

[52] Friedman, Robert I. *Red Mafiya: How The Russian Mob Has Invaded America*. Boston, New York, London: Little Brown and Company, 2000. Pg. 132

[53] Belton, Catherine. *Putin's People: How The KGB Took Back Rusia And Then Took On The West*. New York, NY: Farrar, Straus And Giroux, 2020. Pg. 454

[54] Hettena, Seth. *Trump/Russia: A Definitive History*. Brooklyn, NY: Melville House, 2008. Pg. 37

[55] Ignatius, David. "A history of Donald Trump's business dealings in Russia," *The Washington Post*. November 2nd, 2017

[56] Rogin, Josh. "Another Trump adviser with deep ties to Russia," *The Washington Post*. August 10th, 2016

[57] Hettena, Seth. *Trump/Russia: A Definitive History*. Brooklyn, NY: Melville House Publishing, 2018. Pg. 42

[58] Tankersley, Jim. "Donald Trump's new team of billionaire advisers could threaten his populist message," *The Washington Post*. August 5th, 2016

[59] Singer, Mark. "Trump Solo," *The New Yorker*. May 12th, 1997

[60] 10MOSCOW317_a. "THE LUZKHOV DILEMMA," *Wikileaks*. February 12th, 2010

[61] Hirsch, Michael. "The Gangster State," *Newsweek*. September 5th, 1999

[62] Stanley, Alessandra. "The Power Broker," *The New York Times*. August 31st, 1997

[63] "Is Russian Businessman Hiding in Israel Connected to Moscow Mayor's Firing?" *Haaretz*. October 1st, 2010

[64] Farris, Anne. "VISA REVOKED, UKRAINIAN STILL ATTENDED EVENT," *The Washington Post*. December 19th, 1997

[65] Woodward, Bob. "WHITE HOUSE GAVE DNC TOP-SECRET INTELLIGENCE," *The Washington Post*. April 8th, 1997

[66] Kerry, John. *The New War: The Web Of Crime That Threatens America's Security*. New York, NY: Simon & Schuster, 1997. Pg. 161-162

[67] Unger, Craig. *House of Putin, House of Trump: The Untold Story of Donald Trump and the Russian Mafia*. New York, NY: Penguin Random House LLC, 2018. Pg. 89

[68] Report of the Select Committee on Intelligence United States Senate On Russian Active Measures Campaigns And Interference in the 2016 US Election Volume 5: Counterintelligence Threats and Vulnerabilities. Pg. 638-642

[69] dos Santo, Nina. "Senate investigators pursue Moscow-based former Trump associate," *CNN*. February 21st, 2019

[70] Saporito, Bill. "King of the Hill," *Time Magazine*. June 24th, 2001

[71] Pearlstein, Steven. "Icon Of An Era," *The Washington Post*. February 14th, 1990

[72] Buettner, Russ; Bagli, Charles V. "How Donald Trump Bankrupted His Atlantic City Casinos, but Still Earned Millions," *The New York Times*. June 11th, 2016

[73] Goldstein, Matthew; Eder, Steve; Enrich, David. "The Billionaire Who Stood by Jeffrey Epstein," *The New York Times*. October 12th, 2020

[74] Goldstein, Matthew; Rosman, Katherine. "Apollo C.E.O. to Step Down After Firm Finds More Payments to Jeffrey Epstein," *The New York Times*. January 25th, 2021

[75] Reinhard, Beth; Helderman, Rosalind S.; Fisher, Marc. "Donald Trump and Jeffrey Epstein partied together. Then an oceanfront Palm Beach mansion came between them." *The Washington Post*. July 31st, 2019

[76] Vandeveld, Mark. "Lawsuit claims ex-Apollo CEO Leon Black sexually assaulted Russian model," *The Financial Times*. June 1st, 2021

[77] Report of the Select Committee on Intelligence United States Senate On Russian Active Measures Campaigns And Interference in the 2016 US Election Volume 5: Counterintelligence Threats and Vulnerabilities. Pg. 648-650

[78] Intelligence Section, Organizational Intelligence Unit. "SEMION MOGILEVICH ORGANIZATION: EURASIAN ORGANIZED CRIME," *Department of Justice, Federal Bureau of Investigation*, August 1996. Pg. 23

[79] Black, Aaron. "Five provocative nuggets from the Senate intel report on Trump and Russia," *The Washington Post*. August 21st, 2020

[80] Relman, Eliza. "The 26 women who have accused Trump of sexual misconduct," *Business Insider*. September 17th, 2020

[81] Report of the Select Committee on Intelligence United States Senate On Russian Active Measures Campaigns And Interference in the 2016 US Election Volume 5: Counterintelligence Threats and Vulnerabilities. Pg. 653 [Footnote 4241]

[82] Report of the Select Committee on Intelligence United States Senate On Russian Active Measures Campaigns And Interference in the 2016 US Election Volume 5: Counterintelligence Threats and Vulnerabilities. Pg. 654-655

[83] Report of the Select Committee on Intelligence United States Senate On Russian Active Measures Campaigns And Interference in the 2016 US Election Volume 5: Counterintelligence Threats and Vulnerabilities. Pg. 642-649

[84] Busvine, Douglas. "Russia's $10 billion fund staffed up, ready for deals," *Reuters*. September 15th, 2011

[85] Clark, Simon. "American Billionaires Vanish From Russian Fund's Website," *The Wall Street Journal*. September 3rd, 2014

[86] Protess, Ben; Kramer, Andrew E.; McIntire, Mike. "Bank at Center of U.S. Inquiry Projects Russian 'Soft Power,'" *The New York Times*.

[87] Pham, Scott; Warren, Tom; Leopold, Jason; Cormier, Anthony; Templon, John; Singer-Vine, Jeremy; Holmes, Richard; Kozyreva, Tanya; Loop, Emma. "The Banker Was A Spy," *BuzzFeed News*. September 22nd, 2020

[88] Simon, Clark. "American Billionaires Vanish From Russian Fund's Website," *The Wall Street Journal*. September 3rd, 2014

[89] Mueller, III, Robert S. *Report On The Investigation Into Russian Interference In The 2016 Presidential Election*. Department of Justice, Washington, DC. March 2019. Pg. 151-155

[90] Drucker, Jesse; Kelly, Kate; Protess, Ben. "Kushner's Family Business Received Loans After White House Meetings," *The New York Times*. February 28th, 2018

[91] Gordon, Michael R. "Russia's New Court Sculptor: Only the Colossal," *The New York Times*. January 25th, 1997

[92] eport of the Select Committee on Intelligence United States Senate On Russian Active Measures Campaigns And Interference in the 2016 US Election Volume 5: Counterintelligence Threats and Vulnerabilities. Pg. 649

[93] Hettena, Seth. *Trump/Russia: A Definitive History*. Brooklyn, NY: Melville House Publishing, 2018. Pg. 50-54

[94] Swarns, Rachel L. "Unlikely Meeting of Minds: Lebed Meets The Donald," *The New York Times*. January 23rd, 1997

[95] Haberman, Maggie. *Confidence Man: The Making of Donald Trump and the Breaking of America*. New York, NY: Penguin Press. 2022. Pg. 134

[96] Melby, Caleb; Geiger, Keri. "Behind Trump's Russia Romance, There's a Tower Full of Oligarchs," *Bloomberg*. March 16th, 2017

[97] Unger, Craig. *House of Putin, House of Trump: The Untold Story of Donald Trump and the Russian Mafia*. New York, NY: Penguin Random House LLC, 2018. Pg. 123-124

[98] Horowitz, Craig. "Iced," *New York Magazine*. November 19th, 2004

[99] Popper, Nathaniel. "Assassination of Diamond Dealer Rocks Tight Bukharan Community," *Forward*. May 28th, 2004

[100] Enrich, David. *Dark Towers: Deutsche Bank, Donald Trump, And An Epic Trail Of Destruction*. New York, NY: HarperCollins, 2020. Pg. 77-78

[101] Enrich, David. "The Money Behind Trump's Money," *The New York Times*. February 4th, 2020

[102] Enrich, David. *Dark Towers: Deutsche Bank, Donald Trump, And An Epic Trail Of Destruction*. New York, NY: HarperCollins, 2020. Pg. 109-110

[103] Corcoran, Jason. "Deutsche Bank's Kostin, Son of VTB's Chief, Dies in Bike Crash," *Bloomberg*. July 4th, 2011

[104] Caesar, Ed. "Deutsche Bank's $10 Billion Scandal," *The New Yorker*. August 22nd, 2016

[105] Down, Aisha Kehoe. "Deutsche Bank: Lawbreaking Likely in Russian Laundromat," *Organized Crime and Corruption Reporting Project (OCCRP)*. April 17th, 2019

[106] Stedman, Scott; Levai, Eric; DeNault, Robert J. "Trump Deutsche Bank Loans Underwritten By Russian State-Owned Bank, Whistleblower Told FBI," *Forensic News*. January 3rd, 2020

[107] Enrich, David. "Me and My Whistle-Blower," *The New York Times*. October 1st, 2019

[108] O'Brien, Timothy L. "Bank Settles U.S. Inquiry Into Money Laundering," *The New York Times*. November 9th, 2005

[109] Hudson, Michael; Stanescu, Ionut; Adler-Bell, Samuel; Rice, Andrew; Williams, Margot; Cabra, Mar; Plattner, Titus; Holcova, Pavla. "America's Own Island Haven: Manhattan," International Consortium of Investigative Journalists (ICIJ). July 3rd, 2014

[110] Layne, Nathan; Parker, Ned; Reiter, Svetlana; Grey, Stephen; McNeill, Ryan. "Russian elite invested nearly $100 million in Trump buildings," *Reuters*. March 17th, 2017

[111] Hettena, Seth. *Trump/Russia: A Definitive History*. Brooklyn, NY: Melville House Publishing, 2018. Pg. 84

[112] Horowitz, Paul. "In Taormina, a Playground for the Jet Set, Trump's Worlds Will Collide," *The New York Times*. May 25th, 2017

[113] Belton, Catherine. *Putin's People: How The KGB Took Back Rusia And Then Took On The West*. New York, NY: Farrar, Straus And Giroux, 2020. Pg. 454-455

[114] Berzon, Alexandra; Kirkham, Chris; Bernstein, Elizabeth; O'Keefe, Kate. "Dozens of People Recount Pattern of Sexual Misconduct by Las Vegas Mogul Steve Wynn," *The Wall Street Journal*. January 27th, 2018

[115] Farnsworth, Clyde H. "K.G.B. Runs Commerce Unit, U.S. Says," *The New York Times*. October 28th, 1987

[116] Hettena, Seth. *Trump/Russia: A Definitive History*. Brooklyn, NY: Melville House Publishing, 2018. Pg. 98

[117] Shaw, Craig; Şentek, Zeynep; Cândea, Ștefan. "World leaders, mobsters, smog and mirrors," *The Black Sea*. December 20th, 2016

[118] Hettena, Seth. *Trump/Russia: A Definitive History*. Brooklyn, NY: Melville House Publishing, 2018. Pg. 89-90

[119] Unger, Craig. *House of Putin, House of Trump: The Untold Story of Donald Trump and the*

Russian Mafia. New York, NY: Penguin Random House LLC, 2018. Pg. 132

[120] Cohen, Michael. *Disloyal: The True Story Of The Former Personal Attorney To President Donald J. Trump*. New York, NY: Skyhorse Publishing, 2020. Pg. 73-74

[121] Lallemand, Alain. "Drugs, diamonds and deadly cargoes," *The International Consortium of Investigative Journalists (ICIJ)*. November 18th, 2002

[122] Belton, Catherine. *Putin's People: How The KGB Took Back Rusia And Then Took On The West*. New York, NY: Farrar, Straus And Giroux, 2020. Pg. 461

[123] Burgis, Tom. *Kleptopia: How Dirty Money Is Conquering The World*. New York, NY: HarperCollins, 2020. Pg. 79

[124] Supreme Court of the United States. Palmer v United States of America No. 14-676. Petition for a Writ of Certiorari. Pg. 13

[125] Hettena, Seth. "Time to Put a Lie about Felix Sater to Rest (Updated)," *SethHettena.com*. July 20th, 2019

[126] Corkery, Michael. "Overstock C.E.O. Takes Aim at 'Deep State' After Romance With Russian Agent," *The New York Times*. August 15th, 2019

[127] Belton, Catherine. *Putin's People: How The KGB Took Back Rusia And Then Took On The West*. New York, NY: Farrar, Straus And Giroux, 2020. Pg. 461

[128] Kirilenko, Anastasia. "Gangster Party candidate: Trump's ties to Russian organized crime," *The Insider*. April 6th, 2018

[129] Hettena, Seth. *Trump/Russia: A Definitive History*. Brooklyn, NY: Melville House Publishing, 2018. Pg. 92-93

[130] Burgis, Tom. *Kleptopia: How Dirty Money Is Conquering The World*. New York, NY: HarperCollins, 2020. Pg. 81-84

[131] Feuer, Alan. "19 Charged in Stock Scheme Tied to Mob," *The New York Times*. March 3rd, 2000

[132] United States Congress House of Representatives. Committee On Commerce, Subcommittee on Finance and Hazardous Material. Organized Crime On Wall Street. September 13th, 2000. Pg. 276

[133] Goldman, Adam; Benner, Katie. "Bruce Ohr Fought Russian Organized Crime. Now He's a Target of Trump." *The New York Times*. August 27th, 208

[134] "Ex-KGB Spy gunned down in Moscow," *BBC News*. November 3rd, 2009

[135] Belton, Catherine. *Putin's People: How The KGB Took Back Rusia And Then Took On The West*. New York, NY: Farrar, Straus And Giroux, 2020. Pg. 463

[136] "Litvinenko Ties Putin to Crime Lord From Beyond Grave," *Organized Crime and Corruption Reporting Project (OCCRP)*. January 27th, 205

[137] Behar, Richard. "Donald Trump And The Felon: Inside His Business Dealings With A Mob-Connected Hustler," *Forbes*. October 24th, 2016

[138] Helderman, Rosalind S.; Hamburger, Tom. "Former Mafia-linked figure describes association with Trump," *The Washington Post*. May 17th, 2016

[139] Apuzzo, Matt; Haberman, Maggie. "Trump Associate Boasted That Moscow Business Deal 'Will Get Donald Elected,'" *The New York Times*. August 28th, 2017

[140] Beuttner, Russ; Craig, Susanne. "Decade in the Red: Trump Tax Figures Show Over $1 Billion in Business Losses," *The New York Times*. May 8th, 2019

[141] O'Brien, Timothy. *Trump Nation: The Art of Being The Donald*. New York, NY: Hachette Book Group, 2005. Pg. 14-15

[142] Smith, Ben. "Jeff Zucker Helped Create Donald Trump. That Show May Be Ending." *The New York Times*. September 20th, 2020

Chapter 7:
Vladimir Putin, Three American Presidents, And the Road to 2016

The deterioration of Russian-American relations to the point that Putin felt embittered and emboldened enough to target the 2016 presidential election unfolded over many years and across successive American administrations of both parties. Bill Clinton and George W. Bush attempted to forge a strong personal relationship with Putin. However, the magnitude of global events and conflicting geostrategic imperatives proved too immense to be overcome.

The impact that the Global War on Terror and policies such as pre-emptive war and regime change had on Putin's strategic calculus cannot be overstated. After a brief period of cooperation following the September 11th attacks, the US invasion of Iraq marked a downturn in the relationship from which it would never fully recover. US-supported "Color Revolutions" that broke out on Russia's periphery struck at the heart of fears and resentments regarding the disintegration of Russian authority that Putin had nursed since his KGB days in Dresden.

By the time Barack Obama took office, it was hoped that the two countries could at least cooperate on vital areas of mutual interest. This was not to be. The Arab Spring and a NATO bombing campaign in Libya again stirred Putin's deepest fears. These fears were realized when Russians poured into the streets of Moscow in 2011 to protest election irregularities. Putin pinned the blame for the protests in Moscow squarely on the American Secretary of State, Hillary Clinton. Putin believed that the United

States diplomatic and intelligence establishment was targeting him personally for regime change. Finally, Western support for the Maidan Revolution in Ukraine and the overthrow of its pro-Kremlin government was the straw that broke the camel's back. These events set the stage for Putin's most daring act yet.

Putin and the American President: Vladimir Meets Bill and George

Towards the end of his last term, Bill Clinton met then-Prime Minister Putin on September 12th, 1999, at the Asia-Pacific Economic Cooperation Forum held in Auckland, New Zealand. It was Putin's second encounter with the American President. Years earlier, Clinton had visited St. Petersburg as Mayor Sobchak's guest. Deputy Mayor Putin made sure that the trip proceeded safely and securely. Though Clinton complained to the secret service that he had been "kept in a goddamn cocoon," the trip took place without incident.

Putin and Clinton's meeting in New Zealand occurred while Russia was in crisis. The question of Yeltsin's successor hung over the Russian political establishment. Three days before the meeting, explosives leveled an apartment building in Moscow. The Second Chechen War, which Putin used to ascend to the Presidency, was underway. Despite these storm clouds, Putin was treated to Clinton's famous charm. A believer in personal diplomacy, Clinton tried to form a bond with Putin. Despite their mostly warm rapport, Putin deflected the concerns Clinton raised. Clinton expressed reservations about the conflict in Chechnya to Putin. Putin listened politely but demurred. The events unfolding in Chechnya were an invasion of Russia, Putin argued, framing the war as part of a global conflict against Islamic terrorism. Back in Moscow, Putin had told American diplomats that Osama Bin Laden had made several trips to Chechnya. While plausible, the American government was unable to verify its accuracy.[1]

Bill Clinton visited Moscow on June 3rd, 2000. After a private dinner of cold boiled boar, baked ham and cabbage, and goose with berry sauce, Clinton and Putin listened to a jazz tribute to Louis Armstrong conducted by a Russian band leader.[2] Putin complained to Clinton that after becoming the President he was having trouble finding Judo sparring partners. They engaged in an ultimately fruitless discussion about missile defense. Putin argued the Anti-Ballistic Missile (ABM) treaty was essential to global stability. While they were able to sign a symbolic joint principals document, the issue remained an open source of contention.

Clinton last met Putin at the Waldorf-Astoria Hotel in New York on September 6th, 2000, where Clinton came to realize that, despite being polite, Putin was running out the clock until the next administration. The American presidential campaign was in full swing, with Vice President Al Gore going head-to-head with Texas Governor George W. Bush. Putin became visibly intrigued when Clinton provided his analysis of the upcoming election. The vote, Clinton explained, was going to be extremely close, and he predicted it would come down to a handful of states, particularly Florida. Clinton's analysis proved prescient, and after a ruling by the Supreme Court, the disputed election of 2000 was won by George W. Bush.

Like Clinton, Bush sought to establish a friendly relationship with Putin. The night before his first trip to Europe as President, which included a meeting with Putin in Slovenia, Bush brought together five outside experts on Russia. Vice President Dick Cheney and National Security Advisor Condoleezza Rice attended the meeting. Rice, the first African-American woman to hold the position, had studied Russian at Moscow State University and served as a Russian policy expert for Bush's father, President George H.W. Bush.

Former US diplomat Tom Graham argued that the greatest task facing Russian-American relations was managing Russia's decline as a world power. Michael McFaul, a professor at Stanford and expert in democratic transitions, suggested that the most important task was to integrate Russia into the liberal democratic order and support its development of democratic institutions. Bush listened attentively and told the gathering that it was essential to have Russia on America's side because one day "we all would be dealing with China's rise."[3]

At their first meeting in Slovenia, Bush was accompanied by Condoleezza Rice, and Putin was joined by Vladimir Rushailo. Bush asked Putin who Rice should contact when it came to sensitive matters, and Putin replied with the name of his old KGB associate Sergei Ivanov, who was then serving as Minister of Defense. Bush, as expected, informed Putin of his intention to get out of the ABM Treaty and that he hoped they could do so mutually. Putin told Bush he was unwilling to do so, but he betrayed no anger or threatened retaliation.

Putin then launched into a verbal assault on Pakistan, explaining that it was supporting Islamic extremists, including the Taliban in Afghanistan and the terrorist organization al Qaeda. In December of 1996, al-Qaeda's second-in-command Ayman al-Zawahiri had been arrested while trying to enter Chechnya and had spent six months in FSB captivity before being released in May of 1997.[4] The extremists, Putin complained, were being funded by Saudi Arabia, and if nothing were done it would lead to a catastrophe. "I was taken aback by Putin's alarm and vehemence and chalked it up to Russian bitterness toward Pakistan for supporting the Afghan mujahideen, who had defeated the Soviet Union in the 1980s," Condoleezza Rice wrote later. "Putin, though, was right: the Taliban and al Qaeda were time bombs that would explode on September 11th, 2001. Pakistan's relationship with the extremists would become one of our gravest problems. Putin never let us forget it, recalling that conversation time and time again."[5]

Bush asked Putin about a story he had read in an intelligence briefing. The born-again Christian Bush had read that Putin's mother had given him a cross that had been blessed in Jerusalem. The story went that when Putin's dacha had burned down, the cross had miraculously survived the fire. Putin dramatically re-enacted the scene when the firefighters presented him with the undamaged cross. It was, Putin said, "as if it were meant to be."

"Vladimir," Bush replied, "that is the story of the cross. Things are meant to be."[6] The story made a big impression on Bush. It is doubtful he knew then that Putin's dacha had been part of the Ozero Cooperative. Not everyone in the meeting was as impressed by the story. Rice later wrote that she never knew what to make of the story and had a difficult time seeing a former supporter of the atheistic Soviet Union as a religious man.

"I looked the man in the eye," Bush said at a press conference later that day after being asked by a reporter whether he trusted Putin. "I found him to be very straightforward and trustworthy. We had a very good dialogue. I was able to get a sense of his soul."

The September 11th, 2001 terrorist attacks were the seminal moment of Bush's Presidency and led to a brief high point in the US-Russian relations. That afternoon in Moscow, Putin was rushed into a conference room by security aides. Images of black smoke pouring from gaping holes in the World Trade Center streamed across a television. Two years earlier, in the wake of the Moscow apartment bombings, Putin warned in the pages of *The New York Times* that Americans could one day face terrorism of a similar kind.[7]

"What can we do to help them?" Putin asked Sergei Ivanov.[8] He attempted to get in touch with Bush, the first world leader to do so, but the American President was unavailable at that moment, being whisked away on Air Force One to a secure location in Louisiana. Ivanov received a call from his counterpart in Washington, Condoleezza Rice, who had just been rushed down to a bunker over fears that the White House was a target. Putin took the receiver.

"Mr. President," Rice said, "the President is not able to take your call right now because he is being moved to another location. I wanted to let you know that American forces are going up on alert."

"We already know, and we have canceled our exercises and brought our alert levels down," Putin replied. A Russian military exercise simulating nuclear war with the US had been scheduled to take place that day. "Is there anything else we can do?" Rice thanked Putin, and amidst the chaos, a brief, hopeful thought crossed her mind: *the Cold War really is over.*[9]

Putin hoped to link the Russian war in Chechnya with America's Global War on Terror. He told Bush he would use his influence in the former Soviet republics of Tajikistan and Kyrgyzstan and provide them with the Kremlin's permission to serve as supply lines for America's invasion of Afghanistan. Russia had a painful history with Afghanistan and no love for the Taliban. Russian generals briefed their counterparts in the American military, sharing their experiences. Material was provided to the Northern Alliance, the Taliban's indigenous military foe.

"My God," Putin shouted in English less than a month later as he entered the Oval Office. "This is beautiful."[10] The night before, Taliban forces had fled the Afghan capital Kabul. The next day, Bush and Putin traveled with their wives to visit Bush's ranch in Crawford, Texas. Putin and his wife stayed in Bush's guest house and ate barbecue. However, no amount of personal bonhomie could change the fundamental dynamics between the two nations. Three weeks after they visited Texas, America withdrew from the ABM Treaty. To Russian eyes, the move destabilized the nuclear balance of power. A year later, Bulgaria, Estonia, Latvia, Lithuania, Romania, Slovakia, and Slovenia were invited to join the NATO alliance. The encroachment of the world's most powerful military alliance was seen in Moscow as another strategic setback.

After what appeared to be a lightning-quick victory in Afghanistan, Bush and the neoconservatives in his administration set their sights on Iraq. Putin joined much of the world in opposing an American invasion. He not only disputed the American claim that the country had weapons of mass destruction, but firmly believed that only a despot the likes of Saddam Hussein could hold the country together. Remove Saddam, Putin believed, and you not only destabilize Iraq but the entire region.

The Iraq War was a milestone in the deterioration of Russia's relations with the West and the United States in particular. As Iraq disintegrated into chaos and civil war, Putin resented the fact that Bush had dismissed his warnings. [11] The war shaped his views of American intentions abroad, leading him to believe that the policy of regime change, whether overt or covert, was a permanent goal of the American political and security establishment.

Events on Russia's periphery threatened to destabilize the relationship further. In November of 2003, massive protests in Tbilisi led to the peaceful ouster of Georgia's last Soviet-era President. The Rose Revolution was the first of the Color Revolutions, which swept through multiple states across the former Soviet Union. Almost exactly a year later, the Orange Revolution in Ukraine led to the collapse of the Kremlin-friendly regime in Kyiv. Like Georgia, events in Ukraine were driven by widespread, popular street demonstrations.

The 2004 Ukrainian election between Viktor Yushchenko and the Kremlin's preferred candidate, Viktor Yanukovych, was rigged through a far-reaching campaign of fraud and falsification involving the corrupt apparatus of the state supporting Yanukovych. Voter rolls were filled with the names of the deceased supporting Yanukovych's Party of Regions. Telephone intercepts revealed that the Yanukovych campaign had tampered with the Ukrainian electoral commission's server to falsify election results on a mass scale. However, in a showing of mass solidarity and indignation, Ukrainians refused to take the theft of an election sitting down. Tens of thousands took to the streets in Kyiv, congregating in the Maidan, the city's central square.

Ukrainians erected tents across Maidan square and demonstrations reached into the hundreds of thousands. Protestors adopted the color orange, the color used by Yushchenko's campaign. All told, one in five Ukrainians participated in the Orange Revolution. While the Ukrainian Central Election Commission initially declared Yanukovych the victor, nearly every major Western government and institution refused to recognize the election results. On November 28th, Yanukovych gave a verbal order to deploy Interior Ministry internal troops to disperse the protestors, but they turned back when the military informed them that they would defend the protestors. Eventually, the parliament voted not to recognize the legitimacy of the Yanukovych government, and on December 3rd, the Ukrainian Constitutional Court invalidated the results of the election and called for another round of voting. On December 26th, a new round of voting took place, and Viktor Yushchenko was elected President.

The Orange Revolution was a stinging defeat for Putin and fundamentally shaped not only his views and actions vis-a-vis Ukraine but towards the West as well. The stunning turnaround should have spelled Viktor Yanukovych's political demise. To help resurrect his career, Yanukovych found a virtuoso turnaround artist, PR genius, and master of the political dark arts all wrapped in one, someone who reimagined his look and feel as a candidate: Paul Manafort, the future chairman of the Trump campaign.

Bush and Putin's interpretation of the events in Georgia and Ukraine could not have been further apart. Following 9/11 and the invasions of Afghanistan and Iraq, Bush spoke in almost messianic terms about spreading freedom and democracy in the world. Putin was horrified by what he saw as chaotic, popular coups secretly guided by the invisible hand of Western intelligence agencies hoping to encircle Russia and eventually dismember the Russian state itself through cleverly manipulated popular uprisings. In this context, Putin viewed Bush's Freedom Agenda as a ploy to promote American interests at Russia's expense.[12]

Though Bush had gone to great lengths to maintain a warm personal relationship with Putin, as he made his way into the medieval Bratislava Castle to meet with Putin he was determined to press him on the state of democracy in Russia. Putin's project to centralize power and muzzle the free press had not gone unnoticed in Washington. Bush, himself an oil man, had friends who knew the Russian oil tycoon Mikhail Khodorkovsky personally and were appalled by his arrest and the hostile state takeover of his company Yukos. Bush brought up these issues during a private meeting with Putin, causing it to degenerate into petty arguments.

"I think Putin is not a democrat anymore," Bush told the Slovenian prime minister a few weeks later. "He's a tsar. I think we've lost him."[13]

Barack Obama, Hillary Clinton,
And the Descent of Russian-American Relations

After a historic campaign, a 47-year-old Democratic Senator from Illinois, Barack Obama, was elected the first African-American President of the United States. The incoming Obama Administration's overall Russia strategy in his first term became known as "the Reset." The chief intellectual architect of the Reset was the Stanford Academic, Russia specialist and democracy activist Michael McFaul. In his new role as senior director for Russian affairs at the White House, McFaul initiated a policy review and began drafting policy papers.

Though aware of Putin's authoritarian tendencies, McFaul supported a policy of "principled engagement." Though the relationship had been damaged by a recent Russian invasion of Georgia, Russian forces had stopped short of occupying the whole country. At the same time, issues such as replacing the Strategic Arms Reduction Treaty (START), dealing with the Iranian nuclear threat, and securing new supply lines into Afghanistan to reduce dependence on Pakistan were important American objectives that required Moscow's cooperation.[14] The official in charge of introducing the Reset policy to Russia was the new Secretary of State.

Hillary Clinton had been widely considered a shoo-in to become the 2008 Democratic presidential nominee and the odds-on favorite to be elected the next President of the United States. However, after a hard-fought primary, she lost in a stunning upset to Obama, whose campaign had painted her as an out-of-touch bastion of the political establishment. Obama asked Clinton to serve as his Secretary of State despite their past rivalry. Though polarizing at home, Clinton regularly topped polls as the world's most respected woman. As Secretary of State, she was the most famous diplomat on the planet.

Hillary took on a more proactive role during her husband's presidency than any other First Lady in American history. Her decision to do so was not welcomed in all corners and began what would become one of the longest and most controversial tenures for a woman in American public life. She accompanied Bill on his first visit to Russia in January of 1994. At the time, Washington was aflame with calls to appoint a special prosecutor to investigate Bill Clinton's conduct. Joined by her daughter Chelsea, Hillary touched down in Moscow after a turbulent descent. Feeling queasy, she vomited on the floor of the limo as they made their way into Russia's capital city.[15] After sprucing herself up at Spaso House, the American Ambassador's residence in Moscow, Hillary left to meet with Boris Yeltsin's wife, Naina.

While Bill and Boris discussed nuclear disarmament and NATO expansion, Hillary and Naina visited a local hospital where Hillary described the healthcare plan they were fighting to get passed through the US Congress to curious Russian physicians. Hillarycare, as it came to be known, never passed into law. That evening, Hillary was seated next to Boris Yeltsin at a lavish state dinner held in the Hall of Facets at St. Vladimir Hall. Yeltsin "kept a running commentary about the food and wine," Hillary recalled, "informing me in all seriousness that red wine protected Russian sailors on nuclear-powered submarines from the ill effects of strontium 90."

The Clintons formed a friendship with the Yeltsin's, visiting one another on numerous occasions in Moscow and Washington. After a four-year Independent Counsel investigation, Bill Clinton was impeached by the House of

Representatives but acquitted in the Senate. The turn of the millennium represented a year of great change for both families. Bill, having served two terms as President, returned to civilian life. Hillary successfully ran for Senate in New York, a move many interpreted as a stepping-stone to the presidency. Yeltsin stepped down as Russian President on New Year's Eve. Hillary's relationship with his successor was decidedly less friendly.

Senator Clinton wasn't afraid to condemn the Putin regime. In 2005, following the assassination of the American journalist Paul Klebnikov in Moscow, she delivered blistering comments about the murder in the Senate. She urged the Bush White House to bring the case up directly with Putin.[16] During the primary contest against Barack Obama, Clinton brought up Putin to highlight Obama's lack of experience. "We're running for the hardest job in the world," Clinton said in a TV interview. "You're not going to get any breaks from Putin."[17]

After two terms in office, the Russian constitution required Putin to step down from the presidency. However, as he had no intention of relinquishing power, he simply swapped places with his Prime Minister Dmitry Medvedev, who had been his subordinate in the St. Petersburg mayor's office and remained the de facto ruler of Russia. During a 2008 Democratic primary debate in Cleveland, Ohio, the moderator asked the candidates for their thoughts on Medvedev. "I can tell you that he's a hand-picked successor, that he is someone who is obviously being installed by Putin, who Putin can control, who has very little independence, the best we know," Hillary answered. "So this is a clever but transparent way for Putin to hold on to power."[18]

While candidates Clinton and Obama voiced skepticism about Medvedev, in government they opted to give him a chance. Medvedev seemed to be making the right noises about reform, but how long a leash Putin would ultimately provide him was a matter of debate in the White House. On March 6th, 2009, Secretary Clinton traveled to Geneva to meet with Russian Foreign Minister Sergei Lavrov, known for his formidable diplomatic skills, refined tastes in whiskey and poetry, and occasional difficulty in getting along with his female counterparts.[19]

Clinton and her team wanted to offer Lavrov a gift that symbolized the reset. *En route* to Geneva, they landed on the idea of a red button on a yellow base with a label that read "reset" in Russian. McFaul was asked how to spell "reset" in Russian.

Unaware of the planned gift to Lavrov, he offered his best guess, *peregruzka*. A minor flap ensued when Clinton presented the "reset button" to Lavrov at a press conference. After inspecting the gift, Lavrov informed the gathering that the Americans had made an error and that the button was labeled *overload* rather than *reset*. The minor gaffe proved prophetic.

Obama's first face-to-face meeting with Putin occurred at the latter's Novo-Ogaryovo dacha on July 7th, 2009. Obama was a popular but untested newcomer to the world stage, while Putin had held the reins of power in Russia, even now as Prime Minister, for nearly a decade. Whereas Putin nursed grievances dating back to his days in the KGB and the fall of the USSR, Obama had spent his early years reconciling his identity as a mixed-race black man in America and seemed preternaturally comfortable in his own skin. Where Putin could be taciturn, aggressive, and sarcastic, "No Drama" Obama was calm, polite, and cerebral.

Obama had enjoyed a fruitful and workmen-like first visit with Medvedev that April in London. Medvedev appeared eager to form a positive relationship with the new American President but was still tough when it came to defending Russian interests. However, on three key foreign policy issues facing the Obama White House, the New START nuclear treaty, accommodating supply lines to Afghanistan, and increasing pressure on the Iranian regime over their nuclear program, the Americans walked away cautiously optimistic that they had a partner who might work with them on the reset. The question remained, would Putin?

Putin and Obama's first meeting was scheduled to last for an hour. Obama opened the meeting by expressing optimism for Russian-American relations. Following the advice of Russia hand Bill Burns, Obama asked for Putin's candid views on what had gone right and wrong between their two countries. Putin launched into a 50-minute uninterrupted diatribe "filled with grievances, raw asides, and acerbic commentary."[20] While Putin claimed he liked George W. Bush personally, he "loathed his administration."

Putin told Obama that after the support he had lent to the United States following the September 11th attacks, including arranging for military supply routes to Afghanistan, he had been disrespected and snubbed. Putin further decried the American military debacle in Iraq and said, in no uncertain terms, that the Bush administration had orchestrated the Color Revolutions, which he deemed a direct threat to Russian security. Putin punctuated each aggrieved story he told the new American President with exact names, dates, and places.

As the meeting's scheduled end approached and Putin's lecture continued unabated, Burns and McFaul worried that Obama might not get a word in edgewise. Their worries were misplaced. The meeting was extended two hours past its scheduled end time, during which Obama delivered a calm but firm message on his proposed reset. Obama argued that it was in neither country's interest to allow their differences to prevent the countries from working together in areas of mutual benefit. Obama further emphasized that he represented a break from the Bush administration and reminded Putin that he had been against the Iraq War.

As the meeting ended, McFaul believed that Putin had made a considerable impression on Obama. Obama realized that it would be a challenge to maintain contact with Putin and yet still show respect to Medvedev, who, technically, as President, was in charge of Russian foreign policy. However, his first meeting with Putin left no doubt in Obama's mind that Putin was still in charge of Russia. Nonetheless, Obama didn't meet with Putin again until after his re-election in 2012. Throughout his presidency, Obama never held an official summit with Putin in Moscow or Washington.

Hillary arrived for her first trip to Moscow as Secretary of State in October and held a reception at Spaso House, where she invited Russian journalists, lawyers, and civil society leaders. Though she privately promised that American diplomats would bring up human rights abuses with their Russian counterparts, there were media reports that the Obama administration would take a more hard-nosed approach and reduce criticism on these matters coming out of Washington.[21] Clinton sought to dispel these rumors during an interview on the independent radio station *Ekho Moskvy*.

"I have no doubt in my mind that democracy is in Russia's best interests," she said in response to a question regarding human rights. "[R]especting human rights, an independent judiciary, a free media are in the interests of building a strong, stable political system that provides a platform for broadly shared prosperity. We will continue to say that and we will continue to support those who also stand for those values."[22]

Hillary's first face-to-face with Putin as Secretary of State occurred at his dacha outside of Moscow on March 19th, 2010. The meeting started inauspiciously; Putin kept Clinton waiting in front of a large ceramic mantelpiece, standing awkwardly in front of an increasingly anxious international press clutch. When Putin finally arrived, he launched into a lecture regarding American sanctions in Iran. After Hillary responded by forcefully defending the American position, Putin promptly dismissed the press from the room.[23] After a contentious back and forth in private about trade and the World Trade Organization, Clinton decided to change the subject and brought up an issue she knew was close to Putin's heart.

"Prime Minister Putin," Hillary interjected, "tell me about what you are doing to save tigers in Siberia." Putin, surprised but pleased by the question, led Hillary to his private office. "He launched into an animated discourse in English on the fate of the tigers in the east, polar bears in the north, and other endangered species. It was fascinating to see the change in his engagement and bearing. He asked me if my husband wanted to go with him in a few weeks to tag polar bears on Franz Josef Land. I told him I'd ask, and that if he couldn't go, I'd check my schedule. Putin raised an eyebrow in response."[24]

The Arab Spring, Protests in Russia, and Putin's Rage at Hillary Clinton

On December 17th, 2010, a twenty-six-year-old named Mohamed Bouazizi set himself on fire to protest the corruption that stifled his home country of Tunisia and much of the Arab world. Bouazizi's dramatic act launched the Arab Spring, a series of national protest movements and insurrections that shook the political foundations of the Middle East to its core and had profound implications for Russian-American relations. In 2011, the American-supported Egyptian regime of Hosni Mubarak was toppled by mass popular protests. In a controversial move that buoyed democratic activists and horrified traditional American allies in the region, Obama came out in support of the protestors and called for Mubarak to step down.

The events in Egypt inspired similar protests in Libya. Muammar Gaddafi, the dictator who had ruled over Libya for nearly four decades, had no intention of leaving peacefully. Gaddafi was poised to crush the rebellion violently and threatened to send his security forces "house by house" to Benghazi, the center of anti-regime activity.[25] The Obama administration feared a massacre. After intense internal debate and pressure from US allies France and Britain, Obama agreed to support the enforcement of a no-fly zone over Libya to prevent a humanitarian disaster. However, he would only do so with a mandate from the UN Security Council. That meant he needed Russia, if not to support, to at least abstain from the vote.

Vice President Joseph R. Biden met with Medvedev in Moscow, pushing him to support a no-fly zone over Libya. Surprisingly, despite opposition from the Russian foreign ministry and other security officials, Medvedev didn't dismiss the idea outright. Whereas many others in the Russian establishment saw the NATO exercise as just another exercise in American military hegemony, Medvedev seemed to find the humanitarian case for intervention persuasive. On March 17th, the Security Council passed United Nations Resolution 1973, which authorized the use of military force to prevent a massacre in Libya.

Putin was apoplectic and criticized Medvedev publicly. Weeks earlier, he had warned that chaos and instability would lead to a rise in violent Islamic extremism. At his next meeting with Obama, Medvedev, under pressure at home with an election looming, expressed his displeasure with the Libyan adventure. At that time, it was unclear to American officials if Putin was planning to run for president again. Medvedev denounced the Americans for claiming to start the war to protect civilians but, in actuality, pursuing regime change. Ben Rhodes, a White House advisor present at the meeting, believed Medvedev was doing so to look tough in front of Russian hardliners. With the possible return of Putin on his mind, Obama told Medvedev that the reset had to be strong enough to outlast their personal relationship.[26]

In September 2011, delegates from United Russia gathered in a party congress. The election was ten weeks away, and it was still unclear who would run for president. Putin and Medvedev strode out to the stage together. After a few tantalizing but noncommittal comments, Putin left the floor to Medvedev. "It is a pleasure to speak here," Medvedev began. "I think it's right that the party congress supports the candidacy of the current prime minister, Vladimir Putin, in the role of the country's president." The congress erupted in applause.[27] Putin was returning to the presidency.

A month later, a NATO airstrike hit a convoy carrying Gaddafi as he fled the rebels. In the aftermath, a wounded and dazed Gaddafi hid in a drainage pipe but was found and dragged out by an angry mob. After being brutalized and tortured, Gaddafi was executed. Putin was horrified by Gaddafi's gruesome fate. "Almost all of Gaddafi's family has been killed, his corpse was shown on all global television channels, it was impossible to watch without disgust," Putin told the media. "The man was all covered in blood, still alive and he was being finished off."

To Putin, Gaddafi's death epitomized the logical conclusion of the Western policies of humanitarian interventionism and regime change: provoke mass unrest, dress up a naked power grab with hypocritical rhetoric about democracy and human rights, and the moment a country's leader exhibits the slightest sign of weakness, swoop in with military force. Haunted by the images of Gaddafi's violent end, Putin, more than ever before, viewed Western-backed protests as not only a force of destabilization in the world but as a threat to his regime.

Despite these fears, Putin failed to recognize the tide of discontent within Russia, which was poised to surface upon announcing his return to the presidency. The oil boom that had coincided with his first two terms had ended by 2011, and with it, the explosive growth rate of the Russian economy that took place throughout 2000-2007. Further, young Russians and the urban intelligentsia, many of whom had come of age in Putin's Russia, were dismayed by the idea of living under potentially two additional terms of his rule.

Another factor Putin failed to consider was the explosive growth of the internet and social media in Russia. By 2011, over 53 million Russians were online, and the internet was still relatively free compared to the state-run television stations.[28] Digital platforms such as LiveJournal, YouTube, Twitter, Facebook, and VKontakte (a Russian version of Facebook) became online meeting grounds for thousands of mostly young anti-Putin Russians who became known as "internet hamsters." Dripping with mockery and disdain, online-savvy youth used the internet as an outlet for years of pent-up frustration.

In an early sign of trouble, Putin attended a mixed-martial arts match in Moscow and was booed by the audience. Though state television edited out the booing, the internet-savvy opposition figure Alexei Navalny quickly distributed the raw footage online.[29] Putin's political party, United Russia, had slid even further in the public's esteem. With parliamentary elections scheduled in December, this posed a serious problem. As the Arab Spring continued to rage, Putin watched as authoritarian leaders were either overthrown or besieged all around him. Determined not to become a victim of the widespread discontent sweeping the globe, Putin left nothing to chance. In the days before the election, Putin launched a blistering pre-emptive attack against Golos, a Russian non-profit civil election monitor and the only election watchdog independent of the Russian Government.[30]

"Representatives of some states are organizing meetings with those who receive money from them, the so-called grant recipients, briefing them on how to 'work' in order to influence the course of the election campaign in our country," Putin said in a televised speech, referencing the fact that the US Agency for International Development (USAID) covered the operating costs of Golos headquarters. Golos also received grants from the National Endowment for Democracy and training from the National Democratic Institute. The EU, Sweden, Norway, and Britain also offered financial support to the non-profit. To Putin, this was nothing short of foreign interference in Russian elections and akin to a betrayal.[31]

On December 4th, 2011, United Russia won the parliamentary elections with 49.32% of the vote, giving it control over the Duma. That day, fourteen Russian independent media and civil society non-profit websites were temporarily shut down by widespread distributed denial of service (DDoS) attacks. Organizations targeted included the radio station *Ekho Moskvy*, the independent newspaper *Kommersant,* and Golos. Golos switched to using a blog on the website LiveJournal, and after LiveJournal came under attack, it switched to using Google Docs to update fraudulent election activities in real time.[32]

Despite the attacks, Golos and Western election observers from the Organization for Security and Cooperation in Europe (OSCE) documented thousands of irregularities, including widespread ballot stuffing and a lack of transparency.[33] However, what truly sets this election apart from those that came before was the prominent role played by the internet and online video services. Golos released an online map of reported irregularities that quickly went viral. Thousands of Russians uploaded amateur videos of fraudulent acts taking place at polling locations, and protestors soon began organizing online.

"Russian voters deserve a full investigation of all credible reports of electoral fraud and manipulation," Hillary Clinton said in a public statement at a conference in Bonn, Germany, the day after the election. "The Russian people, like people everywhere, deserve the right to have their voices heard and their votes counted. And that means they deserve free, fair, transparent elections and leaders who are accountable to them."[34]

By that evening, thousands of protestors had gathered outside Chistye Prudy metro station in Moscow, chanting "Russia without Putin" and "Putin is a thief!" The Kremlin flooded the streets with riot police and troops, leading to some 300 hundred arrests of protestors, but it wasn't enough to squelch the growing popular discontent.[35] Similar to what was occurring in the Arab Spring, protestors were using the internet to communicate and plan gatherings. Soon, online calls were being made to organize nationwide protests on December 10th.[36] It was Putin's nightmare, one he had inherited from Andropov and witnessed firsthand in Dresden with the collapse of the GDR. He was swift to blame Hillary Clinton.

"The first thing that the secretary of state did was say that [the elections] were not honest and not fair, but she had not even yet received the material from the observers," Putin said at a meeting with political allies in which he announced the formation of his presidential campaign. 32,000 people had already signed up for a scheduled protest outside the Kremlin on Facebook. Putin further claimed that hundreds of millions of dollars of foreign money had been spent to influence the Russian election. However, his attacks never strayed too far from Clinton. "She set the tone for some actors in our country and gave them a signal," Putin continued. "They heard the signal and with the support of the US State Department began active work."[37]

Putin's use of the term "active work," also translated as "active measures," refers to the KGB practice of political warfare, suggesting Putin believed that the protests were the product of a Western intelligence operation. On December 9th, the day after Putin's inflammatory comments regarding Clinton, Obama met with Michael McFaul in the Oval Office. McFaul had at one point early in his career worked for the National Democratic Institute in Moscow. Obama questioned McFaul about America's democracy promotion efforts in Russia. McFaul explained that he had promoted increasing funding to Golos and cleared Clinton's statements in Germany. Obama supported McFaul's actions but instructed him to diffuse tensions over the election.[38]

The next day, despite warnings from Russia's chief public health official, Gennady Onishchenko, that protestors risked SARS infection, tens of thousands of protestors flooded the streets of Moscow in the largest demonstration since the fall of the Soviet Union.[39] Chants of "Putin is a thief" and "Russia without Putin" again filled the air. The chaos of the Arab Spring looked as though it had reached Moscow.

Despite the protests, Putin won the election and was poised to begin his 3rd official term as Russia's president. Before returning to his role as prime minister, Dmitri Medvedev signed a law extending the Presidential term from four years to six, thus almost ensuring 12 more years of Putin's rule. However, Putin's return to power was marred by a 20,000-strong protest and the violent police reaction that rocked Bolotnaya Square in Moscow the day before his inauguration.[40] Unmistakable evidence, in Putin's eyes, of American meddling in Russian internal affairs at his expense, for which Hillary Clinton was the chief culprit.

Another low in Russian-American relations occurred early in Obama's second term when he signed the Magnitsky Act into law. The act was attached as an amendment to the repeal of the Jackson-Vanik amendment, a 1974 law that imposed trade penalties on the Soviet Union and other communist countries that denied their citizens the right to emigrate. It was intended to pressure the USSR into providing its Jewish citizens, often referred to as Refuseniks, with the right to emigrate to Israel or the United States. The Magnitsky Act gave the American Government the power to sanction, seize the assets of, and refuse entry to individual Russian officials deemed guilty of human rights abuses.

The Obama administration initially opposed the law, fearing it would complicate the already fraught relationship with Russia.[41] However, it had strong bipartisan support on the hill, passing the Senate 92-4, and was loudly championed by Senator John McCain. The true champion of the Magnitsky Act was the investor-turned-activist Bill Browder, who orchestrated a savvy and emotionally powerful lobbying campaign on Capitol Hill that captured the attention of some of America's most prominent lawmakers. A complex and controversial figure in his own right, Browder emerged as one of the most public, vocal, and effective international opponents of the Putin regime. The act was named for Browder's lawyer, Sergei Magnitsky, who uncovered a large tax fraud being perpetrated by Russian officials cooperating with elements of organized crime and, for his efforts, was incarcerated and allegedly beaten to death in prison.

Eurasianism, Revolution in Ukraine, and the Invasion of Crimea

Yale Professor Timothy Snyder argues that Putin has slowly but firmly fallen under the spell of the early 20th-century Russian religious and political theorizer Ivan Ilyin. "The oligarch-in-chief, Vladimir Putin, chose the fascist philosopher Ivan Ilyin as his guide," Snyder has written. "The fascism of the 1920s and 1930s, Ilyin's era, had three core features: it celebrated will and violence over reason and law; it proposed a leader with a mystical connection to his people; and it characterized globalization as a conspiracy rather than a set of problems."[42]

While Ilyin died in obscurity in Switzerland, Putin organized his reburial in Moscow in 2005. Putin took to quoting Ilyin in speeches and radio commentary. Eurasianist thought in Russia dates back to the 1920s. Its ideology holds that the Mongol conquests severed Russia from the decadent traditions of Europe and created a unique, "pure" civilization with a messianic purpose in the world. In the 1990s, these ideas began to resurface in Russia, particularly those associated with the neo-fascist Russian intellectual Alexander Dugin. According to Snyder, Dugin used the terms "Eurasia" and "Eurasianism" to filter Nazi ideas into a Russian context that focused on the corruption of the West and the evil of the Jews.

Dugin's political ideas were influenced by Jean PÂRVULESCU, a Romanian intellectual he had come to know in Paris. PÂRVULESCU was a conspiracy theorist and heir to the ideas of Julius Evola, an occultist and leading figure in European neo-fascism. PÂRVULESCU explained to Dugin that the world could be divided between the people of the land and the people of the sea, "Eurasianists" and "Atlanticists.." Atlanticist peoples, the British and Americans, are defined by maritime economies that separate them from the "earthy truths" and leave them susceptible to "abstract (Jewish) culture." These were reworkings of Nazi ideas. Dugin later wrote under a pen name that referenced the Nazi war criminal Wolfram Sievers. Upon returning to Russia in 1993, Dugin, whom friends called the "St. Cyril and Methodius of fascism," founded the National Bolshevik Party. Dugin openly called for "fascism, borderless and red," and his followers were known for raising their fists and hailing death.[43]

Dugin's ideas began circulating among high-level Russian officials. In 1999, he became a special advisor to the speaker of the Duma Gennady Seleznev. Dugin's 1997 work *Foundations of Geopolitics: The Geopolitical Future of Russia* is required reading for every Russian military officer above the rank of colonel at the General Staff Academy. In *Foundations*, Dugin writes, "At the global level, for the construction of a planetary New Empire the chief 'scapegoat' will namely be the USA—the undermining of whose power which (up to the complete destruction of its geopolitical constructs) will be realized systematically and uncompromisingly by the participants of the New Empire. The Eurasian Project presupposes in this its relationship of Eurasian expansion in South and Central America to remove its output from under the control of the North (here, the Hispanic factor could be used as a traditional alternative to the Anglo-Saxon) and also to provoke every kind of destabilization and separatism within the borders of the USA (it might be possible to lean on the political forces of the African-American racists). The ancient Roman formula of 'Carthage must be destroyed,' will become the absolute motto of the Eurasian Empire, because it itself will absorb the essence of all geopolitical planetary strategy awakening to its continental mission."[44]

Eurasianist ideas gained credence among Putin's closest advisors and were discussed during late-night meetings. They further found a geopolitical vehicle in a proposed, Russian-led alternative to the European Union (EU), the Eurasian Economic Union (EEU). Putin hoped he could cajole post-Soviet states such as Ukraine to join it, as opposed to the Western-dominated EU. American policy makers in the Obama administration were united in their opposition to the EEU, chief among them was Hillary Clinton. In 2012, Clinton described the EEU as "a move to re-Sovietize the region." She continued, "We know what the goal is and we are trying to figure out effective ways to slow down or prevent it."

The spread of Eurasianist ideas in the upper echelons of Kremlin leadership coincided with an emerging conservatism in the Orthodox Church that Putin encouraged. Following an anti-Putin protest by the Russian female punk group Pussy Riot in an Orthodox church, the Duma passed an anti-blasphemy law in 2013 with the support of Putin.[45] Months later, another law was passed that imposed fines for propagandizing "nontraditional" sexual relationships among minors, nontraditional being a colloquialism for homosexuals.[46] The law was as much a rebuke to the values of the EU as it was a statement of renewed Russian social conservatism.

Putin presented himself as a defender of Orthodox values and the great foe of the EU and the decadent, degenerate values he argued it represented. "In many countries today, moral and ethical norms are being reconsidered; national traditions, differences in nation and culture are being erased," Putin said in his 2013 State of the Nation speech at the Kremlin. "They're now requiring not only the proper acknowledgment of freedom of conscience, political views, and private life but also the mandatory acknowledgment of the equality of good and evil, which are inherently contradictory concepts."[47]

Putin arrived in Ukraine in July 2013, hellbent on preventing its government from signing what was known as the Association Agreement, which would have put Ukraine on a path towards joining the EU. It was a path many in Ukraine, especially in the south and west, wanted to travel down. Three years earlier, Paul Manafort had engineered a stunning political comeback that saw Viktor Yanukovych win the 2010 Ukrainian presidential election. While campaigning against the Association Agreement, Putin appeared with Yanukovych at the Monastery of the Caves, one of the holiest sites in Orthodox Christianity, to commemorate the baptism of Prince Volodymyr, the founder of the medieval state of Kievan Rus, whom both Russia and Ukraine look to as the predecessor to their modern states. Putin spoke at the ceremony, emphasizing the historical linkages and "common destiny" of Russia and Ukraine. "We are all spiritual heirs of what happened here 1,025 years ago."[48]

Putin had let his view on Ukraine slip at a 2008 NATO conference in Bucharest in which Putin referred to the country as an "artificial state."[49] He went on to tell George W. Bush, who was present at the meeting, "Ukraine is not even a state. Part of its territory is in Eastern Europe and the greater part is a gift from us." The gift Putin was referring to was Crimea, which Khrushchev had transferred to the Ukrainian Soviet Socialist Republic in 1954.

Putin attempted to coerce Ukraine into dropping the Association Agreement by launching a trade war. Russia banned the imports of goods built by Roshen, a company owned by Ukraine's pro-EU foreign minister. In August 2013, Russia placed a stranglehold on nearly all commercial activity with Ukraine through draconian enforcement of customs. The next month, Putin's special envoy to Ukraine, Sergei Glazyev, traveled to Yalta in Crimea and issued a chilling warning to Ukraine that signing the Association Agreement would be akin to suicide.[50]

Glazyev served as Putin's advisor on Eurasian integration.[51] He was also a member of the Eurasianist think tank the Izborsk Club, alongside Alexander Dugin and the fascist novelist Alexander Prokhanov. The Izborsk Club's founding manifesto reads: "Today's Russian State, despite the loss of great territories, still carries the mark of empire. The geopolitics of the Eurasian continent once again forcefully gathers spaces that had been lost. This is the legitimation of the 'Eurasian project' initiated by Putin."[52]

In October, Putin met with Yanukovych in the Russian resort city of Sochi, soon to be the site of the Winter Olympics. He had never cared for Yanukovych personally and felt the Ukrainian leader was betraying him by even holding conversations with the Europeans. Throughout the process, Putin warned Yanukovych that the Europeans would never accept him, and that even if he did sign the agreement, he would be overthrown and replaced by his political enemies.[53] However, in Sochi, Putin issued direct threats, some of them aimed at Yanukovych personally. The Ukrainian president left Russia visibly shaken.[54]

A second, secret meeting took place between Putin and Yanukovych at a military airport outside of Moscow on November 9th. It was here Putin broke the back of whatever was left of Yanukovych's resistance. Before the meeting, the plan had been to sign the agreement; this was no longer the case after it ended. On November 21st, 2013, Yanukovych ordered the suspension of negotiations between Ukraine and the EU over the Association Agreement, which most observers had expected to be signed at the upcoming Vilnius Summit. The act sent shockwaves throughout the pro-EU constituencies in Ukrainian society and left EU diplomats dismayed. However, American diplomats in Moscow were unsurprised. Ambassador Michael McFaul assessed that Ukraine ultimately meant more to Russia than it did to the EU.[55]

However, events on the ground in Ukraine itself would upend the calculations of all parties involved. The day Yanukovych announced the death of the Association Agreement, hundreds of pro-EU Ukrainians gathered on Maidan Square in central Kyiv. Over the next few days, they were joined by thousands. These early protests eventually attracted up to 100,000 people. This time, the protestors weren't waving orange but flags sporting the stars of the EU and the Ukrainian national colors of blue and yellow. As the crowds swelled, the political crisis in Kyiv spread to Moscow, Brussels, and Washington. The Maidan Revolution, also known as the Revolution of Dignity, was underway.

The protests were a grassroots movement representing a broad cross-section of Ukrainians who were pro-EU or just disgusted with the prevailing corruption of the Yanukovych regime. Though they started peacefully, signs of impending violence began to emerge. On November 24th, protestors clashed with police outside a government building. At 4:30 am on November 30th, the Berkut riot police violently cleared Maidan Square, beating dozens of protestors and students and badly injuring 79 in the process. The next day, protesters reoccupied the square, and the crisis deepened. Within days, government buildings were being occupied, and protestors were setting up encampments and barricades. As winter descended across Ukraine, there were no signs that the protests were about to let up any time soon.[56]

Yanukovych was paralyzed before the growing protest movement, vainly hoping the cold winds of winter would disperse the crowds and end the crisis. On December 17th, as the situation in Kyiv grew more dire, he met with Putin again in Sochi. Putin sought to shore up Yanukovych's shaky regime by offering $15 billion in loans to Ukraine and reducing the price of Russian gas sold to the country by a third. Putin even issued a public statement that few believed, downplaying the likelihood that Ukraine would join the EEU.[57]

"Obama was wary," former Deputy National Security Advisor Ben Rhodes later wrote. "He didn't see the protests as a chance to transform Ukraine because he was skeptical that such a transformation could take place."[58] The tumult in Ukraine was taking place less than two years after much of North Africa and the Middle East had been convulsed by the Arab Spring. Most of the countries involved had either slipped back into despotism or, in the case of Syria, descended into brutal civil war. Obama's view, and one shared by many in Europe as well, was that the Western powers should strive for a settlement that would keep the gradual integration of Ukraine with Europe on track.

Perhaps the most controversial American official in the events rocking Ukraine was Victoria Nuland, the Assistant Secretary of State for European and Eurasian Affairs. Nuland traveled to Kyiv where, before meeting with Yanukovych, she visited an encampment of protestors. Along with US Ambassador Geoffrey Pyatt, Nuland was filmed passing out sandwiches, pastries, and cookies. The Kremlin propaganda apparatus seized on the footage as evidence that the American Government was behind the protests.[59]

Two months later, an audio recording, believed to have been intercepted by Russian intelligence, was leaked of a conversation between Nuland and Pyatt. The recording was anonymously posted on YouTube under the title "Puppets of Maidan." It captured Nuland and Pyatt discussing the strengths and weaknesses of Ukrainian opposition leaders. It also revealed differences in how the US and EU approached the crisis. The most explosive line came from Nuland, who, in reference to getting the UN involved, said, "So that would be great, I think, to help glue this thing and have the U.N. help glue it, and you know ... fuck the EU."[60]

"I was stunned," Ben Rhodes recalled. "The Russians had almost certainly intercepted the phone call. That was hardly surprising - in these jobs, you have to assume that any number of governments could be listening in if you're not on a secure phone. What was new was the act of releasing the intercepted call and doing it so brazenly, on social media... A Rubicon had been crossed - the Russians no longer stopped at hacking information; now, triggered by the threat of Ukraine sliding out of their sphere of influence, they were willing to hack information and put it into the public domain."[61]

As the protests showed no sign of abating, the Russians finally decided to take decisive action. According to documents discovered by Ukrainian authorities, Putin's chief ideologue, Vladislav Surkov, ordered explosives, specialist weapons, and crowd control equipment to arrive in Kyiv by December 26th. On January 6th, Kyiv-based FSB officers drew up two plans, "Operation Boomerang" and "Operation Wave," designed to wipe out the protests using overwhelming force. The plan called for 10,000 internal troops, 12,000 police, and 2,000 Berkut riot police to seal off Maidan Square while special forces and Ukrainian security service snipers took out key protestors as the surrounding buildings were stormed. However, the full extent of the plan could not be executed as there was pushback among the security forces.[62]

The descent into violence began on February 18th and reached a bloody crescendo on the 20th. Over 100 civilian protesters were killed, many by sniper fire. Ukrainians would later refer to these victims as the Heavenly Hundred, and subsequent government authorities blamed dozens of Russian FSB agents for the civilian deaths, a claim the FSB had vociferously denied.[63] However, 18 riot police were also killed, and there have been numerous reports of gunfire coming from the protestors. Conspiracy theories regarding these pivotal days are widely subscribed to, with many in Russia believing it was a CIA provocation.[64]

Hoping to forestall further bloodshed, European diplomats raced to Kyiv and met with Yanukovych. The discussions, which Russian Foreign Minister Sergei Lavrov denounced, revolved around a compromise in which Ukraine would hold early elections, and the protesters would receive amnesty. Mid-meeting, a panicked Yanukovych broke off negotiations to call Putin. Putin was in Sochi for the Winter Olympics, seething that the $51 billion games he had spent years planning were being sullied and overshadowed by the violence in Kyiv. Yanukovych explained to Putin that he was ordering the withdrawal of the riot police and would be holding new elections. "You will have anarchy," Putin shouted. "There will be chaos in the capital."[65]

Despite Putin's protests, Yanukovych accepted the

European compromise. However, by then, the protesters refused anything other than Yanukovych's ousters. Possibly frightened by reports that protesters were receiving arms shipments from the West, Yanukovych fled the capital for Eastern Ukraine and eventually Crimea. After an emergency meeting that went into the early morning hours of February 23rd, Putin ordered a mission to secretly shepherd Yanukovych to the southern Russian city of Rostov.[66]

Michael McFaul was in Sochi with Bill Burns for the Olympics when they heard that the Yanukovych government had fallen. Both agreed that they could expect a severe reaction from Putin. They attempted to arrange a hasty meeting between Putin and Burns, but the Kremlin refused. "I am guessing [Putin] believed the CIA had again overthrown an anti-American regime," McFaul later mused, "just as he thought they had in Tunisia, Egypt, and Libya in 2011, and tried to do against him in 2011-12. After we allegedly toppled his ally in Ukraine, Putin was done worrying about what we thought of him or how we could cooperate."[67]

Indeed, Putin was done worrying about what the West thought of him. At the same meeting where Yanukovych's rescue operation was greenlit, Putin set another momentous plan in motion. "We ended at about seven in the morning," Putin later described. "When we were parting, I said to my colleagues: we must start working on returning Crimea to Russia."

Reports of mysterious "Little Green Men" entering Crimean territory began circulating four days later. These were Russian soldiers and members of the GRU in unmarked uniforms. It was the beginning of the Russian annexation of Crimea, the first violation of national borders in Europe since the Second World War. Despite overwhelming evidence to the contrary, Russian diplomats and Vladimir Putin himself denied that the invasion was taking place at all. The Russian invasion led to a war that engulfed much of eastern Ukraine and killed thousands. In a referendum not recognized by Kyiv or the international community that took place barely a month later, amidst the presence of heavily armed Russian troops, Russia claimed that 93% of Crimeans voted to secede from Ukraine and join Russia.[68]

The United States and its allies responded by imposing sweeping sanctions on Russian individuals and companies involved with the annexation. While Obama officials believed that their response to Russian aggression in Ukraine was swifter and firmer than Bush's response had been to aggression directed against Georgia, numerous Republican critics on the Hill criticized the administration for what they perceived as a weak response. "Some even praised Putin as a strong leader, someone to be admired," Ben Rhodes later wrote. "Watching this, Obama told me that it represented something of a turning point for a Republican party that had been rooted in opposition to Russia for decades. In Obama's view, the praise for Putin that you could see on Fox News went beyond partisanship, though that was part of it; Putin was a white man standing up for politics rooted in patriarchy, tribe, and religion, the antiglobalist."

Some of these folks," Obama told Rhodes, referring to hard-right elements in the United States, "have more in common with Putin than with me."[69]

While in the KGB, Putin was taught that the United States was the "Main Enemy." From this perspective, US-backed NGOs in Russia or Ukraine weren't there to strengthen civil society, combat corruption, monitor elections, and promote democracy but were Western intelligence fronts fomenting rebellion, revolution, and regime change. The Iraq War, the post-Soviet Color Revolutions, the Arab Spring, the 2011 protests in Moscow, Eurasianist ideology, and the Maidan Revolution all contributed to strengthening Putin's convictions and worldview. So he waited, biding his time, for his opportunity to strike back and wreak his revenge.

---

[1] Talbott, Strobe. *The Russia Hand: A Memoir of Presidential Diplomacy*. New York, NY: Random House, Inc. 2002. Pg. 359-360

[2] Tyler, Patrick E. "Clinton and Putin Meet At Kremlin With Wide Agenda," *The New York Times*. June 4th, 2000

[3] McFaul, Michael. *From Cold War To Hot Peace: An American Ambassador In Putin's Russia*. New York, NY: Houghton Mifflin Harcourt, 2018. Pg. 62-63

[4] "Bin Laden's top lieutenant sought base in Chechnya," *The Times of London*. October 27th, 2002

[5] Rice, Condoleezza. *No Higher Honor: A Memoir of My Years in Washington*. New York, NY: Crown Publishers, 2011. Pg. 62-63

[6] Bush, George W. *Decision Points*. New York, NY: Crown Publishers, 2010. Pg. 196

[7] Putin, Vladimir. "Why We Must Act," *The New York Times*. November 14th, 1999

[8] Lee Myers, Steven. *The New Tsar: The Rise and Reign of Vladimir Putin*. New York, NY: Alfred A. Knopf, 2015. Pg. 203

[9] Rice, Condoleezza. *No Higher Honor: A Memoir of My Years in Washington*. New York, NY: Crown Publishers, 2011. Pg. 74-75

[10] Lee Myers, Steven. *The New Tsar: The Rise and Reign of Vladimir Putin*. New York, NY: Alfred A. Knopf, 2015. Pg. 211

[11] Zygar, Mikhail. *All The Kremlin's Men: Inside The Court Of Vladimir Putin*. New York, NY: PublicAffairs, 2016. Pg. 37

[12] Burns, William J. *The Back Channel: A Memoir of American Diplomacy and the Case for Its Renewal*. New York, NY: Random House, 2019. Pg. 209

[13] Baker, Peter. "The Seduction of George W. Bush," *Foreign Policy*. November 6th, 2013

[14] McFaul, Michael. *From Cold War To Hot Peace: An American Ambassador In Putin's Russia*. New York, NY: Houghton Mifflin Harcourt, 2018. Pg. 87-88

[15] Clinton, Hillary Rodham. *Living History*. New York, NY: Simon & Schuster, 2003. Pg. 217

[16] Knight, Amy. *Orders To Kill: The Putin Regime and Political Murder*. New York, NY: St. Martin's Press, 2017. Pg. 125

[17] Sheehy, Gail. "Hillaryland At War," *Vanity Fair*. June 30th, 2008

[18] "The Democratic Debate in Cleveland," *The New York Times*. February 26th, 2008

[19] McFaul, Michael. *From Cold War To Hot Peace: An American Ambassador In Putin's Russia*. New York, NY: Houghton Mifflin Harcourt, 2018. Pg. 99

[20] Burns, William J. *The Back Channel: A Memoir of American Diplomacy and the Case for Its Renewal*. New York, NY: Random House, 2019. Pg. 277-278

[21] Harding, Luke. "Clinton hails US-Russian cooperation on Iran," *The Guardian*. October 13th, 2009

[22] Clinton, Hillary Rodham. *Hard Choices*. New York, NY: Simon & Schuster, 2014. Pg. 230

[23] Landler, Mark. "Russia, Suspected In Hacking, Has Uneasy History With Hillary Clinton," *The New York Times*. July 28th, 2016

[24] Clinton, Hillary Rodham. *Hard Choices*. New York, NY: Simon & Schuster, 2014. Pg. 242-243

[25] "Libya protests: Defiant Gaddafi refuses to quit," *BBC News*. February 22nd, 2011

[26] Rhodes, Ben. *The World As It Is: A Memoir Of The Obama White House*. New York, NY: Random House, 2018. Pg. 152

[27] Lee Myers, Steven. *The New Tsar: The Rise and Reign of Vladimir Putin*. New York, NY: Alfred A. Knopf, 2015. Pg. 389

[28] Keen, Andrew. "How Russia's Internet 'Hamsters' Outfoxed Putin," *CNN*. December 13th, 2011

[29] Lee Myers, Steven. *The New Tsar: The Rise and Reign of Vladimir Putin*. New York, NY: Alfred A. Knopf, 2015. Pg. 392-393

[30] Osborn, Andrew. "Kremlin accused of silencing Russia's independent election watchdog," *The Telegraph*. December 1st, 2011

[31] Lally, Kathy. "Russia targets US-linked election monitor," *The Washington Post*. November 30th, 2011

[32] Soldatov, Andrei. "Vladimir Putin's Cyber Warriors," *Foreign Affairs*. December 9th, 2011

[33] Schwirtz, Michael; Herszenhorn, David M. "Voters Watch Polls in Russia, and Fraud is What They See," *The New York Times*. December 5th, 2011

[34] "Remarks at the Bonn Conference Center," *US Department of State*. December 5th, 2011

[35] Elder, Miriam. "Russian police and troops clash with protestors in Moscow," *The Guardian*. December 6th, 2011

[36] Balmforth, Tom. "Russian Protestors Mobilize Via Social Networks, As Key Opposition Figures Jailed," *RadioFreeEurope/RadioLiberty*. December 7th, 2011

[37] Herszenhorn, David, M.; Barry, Ellen. "Putin Contends Clinton Incided Unrest Over Vote," *The New York Times*. December 8th, 2011

[38] McFaul, Michael. *From Cold War To Hot Peace: An American Ambassador In Putin's Russia*. New York, NY: Houghton Mifflin Harcourt, 2018. Pg. 245

[39] Elder, Miriam. "Putin faces wave of protests as opposition calls for new Russian

elections," *The Guardian*. December 9th, 2011

[40] Barry, Ellen; Schwirtz, Michael. "Arrests and Violence at Overflowing Rally in Moscow," *The New York Times*. May 6th, 2012

[41] Trindle, Jamila. "The Magnitsky Flip-Flop," *Foreign Policy*. May 15th, 2014

[42] Snyder, Timothy. *The Road To Unfreedom*. New York, NY: Tim Duggan Books, 2018. Pg. 16

[43] Snyder, Timothy. *The Road To Unfreedom*. New York, NY: Tim Duggan Books, 2018. Pg.88- 89

[44] Gilbert, Alan. "The Far-Right Book Every Russian General Reads," *The Daily Beast*. February 26th, 2018

[45] Neuman, Scott. "Russian Parliament Moves Ahead on Anti-Blasphemy Measure," *NPR*. April 10th, 2013

[46] Kramer, Andrew E. "Russia Passes Bill Targeting Some Discussion of Homosexuality," *The New York Times*. June 11th, 2013

[47] Luhn, Alec. "President Vladimir Putin hails Russia's 'defense of traditional values' in his state of the nation speech," *The Independent*. December 12th, 2013

[48] Lee Myers, Steven. *The New Tsar: The Rise and Reign of Vladimir Putin*. New York, NY: Alfred A. Knopf, 2015. Pg. 446

[49] Kuzio, Taras. *Ukraine: Democratization, Corruption and the New Russian Imperialism*. Santa Barbara, CA: Praeger Security International, 2015. Pg. 100

[50] Lee Myers, Steven. *The New Tsar: The Rise and Reign of Vladimir Putin*. New York, NY: Alfred A. Knopf, 2015. Pg. 447

[51] Åslund, Anders. "Ukraine's Choice: European Association Agreement or Eurasion Union," *Peterson Institute for International Economics Policy Brief*. September 2013

[52] Snyder, Timothy. *The Road To Unfreedom*. New York, NY: Tim Duggan Books, 2018. Pg. 92-95

[53] Zygar, Mikhail. *All The Kremlin's Men: Inside The Court Of Vladimir Putin*. New York, NY: PublicAffairs, 2016. Pg. 259

[54] Kuzio, Taras. *Ukraine: Democratization, Corruption and the New Russian Imperialism*. Santa Barbara, CA: Praeger Security International, 2015. Pg. 104

[55] McFaul, Michael. *From Cold War To Hot Peace: An American Ambassador In Putin's Russia*. New York, NY: Houghton, Mifflin, Harcourt, 2018. Pg. 395

[56] Steinzova, Lucie; Oliynyk, Kateryna. "The Sparks of Change: Ukraine' Euromaidan Protests," *RadioFreeEurope/RadioLiberty*. November 21st, 2018

[57] "Putin Pledges Billions, Cheaper Gas To Ukraine," *RadioFreeEurope/RadioLiberty*. December 17th, 2013

[58] Rhodes, Ben. *The World As It Is: A Memoir Of The Obama White House*. New York, NY: Random House, 2018. Pg. 270

[59] Gessen, Keith. "The Quiet Americans Behind the U.S.-Russia Imbroglio," *The New York Times*. May 8th, 2018

[60] Chiacu, Diona; Mohammed, Arshad. "Leaked audio reveals embarrassing U.S. exchange on Ukraine, EU," *Reuters*. February 6th, 2014

[61] Rhodes, Ben. *The World As It Is: A Memoir Of The Obama White House*. New York, NY: Random House, 2018. Pg. 268

[62] Kuzio, Taras. *Ukraine: Democratization, Corruption and the New Russian Imperialism*. Santa Barbara, CA: Praeger Security International, 2015. Pg. 106

[63] Olearchyk, Roman. "Ukraine and Russia exchange terror accusations," *The Financial Times*. April 3rd, 2014

[64] Gatehouse, Gabriel. "The untold story of the Maidan massacre," *BBC News*. February 12th, 2015

[65] Lee Myers, Steven. *The New Tsar: The Rise and Reign of Vladimir Putin*. New York, NY: Alfred A. Knopf, 2015. Pg. 458

[66] "Vladimir Putin describes secret meeting when Russia decided to seize Crimea," *The Guardian*. March 9th, 2015

[67] McFaul, Michael. *From Cold War To Hot Peace: An American Ambassador In Putin's Russia.* New York, NY: Houghton, Mifflin, Harcourt, 2018. Pg. 401

[68] Herszenhorn, David M. "Crimea Votes to Secede From Ukraine as Russian Troops Keep Watch," *The New York Times.* March 16th, 2014

[69] Rhodes, Ben. *The World As It Is: A Memoir Of The Obama White House.* New York, NY: Random House, 2018. Pg. 272

Chapter 8:
Eurasian Organized Crime, Miss Universe Moscow, And Attempts to Meet Putin

Donald Trump Jr. in Moscow and the Trump Tower Soho Project

Out of everyone in the Trump family, no one traveled to Moscow as frequently as Donald Trump Jr. After he toured the Kremlin with Sater and his sister Ivanka, Don Jr. returned to Moscow at least six times. At a 2008 real estate conference in Moscow, he said, "We see a lot of money pouring in from Russia." At another New York real estate conference that year, Don Jr. said, "In terms of high-end product influx into the US, Russians make up a pretty disproportionate cross-section of a lot of our assets."[1]

Meanwhile, Trump continued to pursue licensing and branding agreements instead of owning buildings outright. One notable project was the hotel-condo hybrid project, the Trump Tower Soho, which Trump introduced to great fanfare during an episode of *The Apprentice*. The Trump Organization partnered on the project with Felix Sater and Tevfik Arif's real estate firm Bayrock. While Bayrock licensed Trump's name to promote its developments, financing came from elsewhere. According to its promotional literature, one investor was a billionaire from Kyrgyzstan named Alexander Mashkevich (AKA "Sasha" Machkevitch).

Alongside Patokh Chodiev and Alijan Ibragimov, Mashkevich is part of the so-called "Oligarch Trio" that owns Eurasian Natural Resources Corporation (ENCR), a multibillion-dollar Kazakh metals and energy giant.[2] Mashkevich and Chodiev met in Belgium while working for Seabeco, a company established for KGB money laundering purposes that employed KGB Colonel Leonid Veselovsky, infamous for having set up KGB front companies the world over.[3] Belgian authorities accused the "oligarch trio" of engaging in a $55 million money laundering scheme, but the case was settled.[4] Seabeco's founder, Boris Birshtein, was a business partner of Solntsevskaya boss Sergei Mikhailov and hosted Mikhailov, Semyon Mogilevich, Grigori Loutchansky, Vadim Rabinovich, and others at the 1995 Tel Aviv summit.[5] The "Trio" has done business with the Reuben Brothers and the Izmaylovskaya-connected Chernoy brothers, and Mashkevich is a known associate of Mogilevich.[6]

In 2005, Mashkevich and Tamir Sapir, who knew Trump from his Joy-Lud days, arrived in Antalya, Turkey, on their superyachts for Tevfik Arif's 52nd birthday party. The opulent event was attended by Turkey's future authoritarian President Recep Tayyip Erdoğan.[7] Trump called into the party via videoconference and proposed a birthday toast to his "friend" Arif.[8] Five years later, Mashkevich and Arif were arrested on a yacht off the shore of Turkey for engaging in an orgy that allegedly included underage girls. The charges against them, which included human trafficking, were eventually dropped.[9]

The Trump Organization and Bayrock partnered on the Trump Soho project with the Sapir Organization, and Trump received an 18% equity stake and ongoing management fees. Much of the funding for the project came from the FL Group, an Icelandic investment bank that plowed $50 million into Bayrock in an arrangement midwifed by Sater. Jody Kriss, a former employee of Bayrock who was involved in a lawsuit against Bayrock, claimed that Bayrock was a criminal enterprise and that Sater had told him that the money behind FL was mainly Russian and that the firm was close to Putin.[10] Kriss's suit was settled out of court in 2018.[11]

As of this writing, lawyers for Kazakhstan's largest city, Almaty, and BTA Bank allege that Kazakh billionaire Mukhtar Ablyazov and former Kazakh Energy Minister and ex-mayor of Almaty Viktor Khrapunov, who are related by the marriage of their children, stole hundreds of millions of dollars and laundered it through US real estate purchases, including the Trump Soho. Ablyazov is accused of stealing $440 million from BTA, a bank he used to head, and Khrapunov is accused of embezzling $300 million from Almaty during his tenure as mayor. The lawsuit alleges that Sater assisted Viktor Khrapunov's son Ilya in making a $3 million down payment on three Trump Soho units using the stolen proceeds.[12]

Tamir Sapir and Felix Sater are members of the Brooklyn-headquartered, international Hasidic movement Chabad-Lubavitch. Another Bayrock employee and Sater associate, Daniel Ridloff, is also a member.[13] Sater and Ridloff have been accused of engaging in money laundering activities together, including through Trump properties.[14] In 2014, Chabad of Port Washington named Felix Sater its "man of the year." Though not Jewish, Tevfik Arif is a major donor to Chabad of Port Washington.

In 2007, Trump hosted and attended a wedding at Mar-a-Lago between Sapir's daughter Zina and Rotem Rosen, CEO of the American branch of Africa Israel, a holding company owned by the Uzbek-Israeli diamond magnate and Putin confidant Lev Leviev. Leviev is Chabad's number one global benefactor and was the key figure behind the establishment of the pro-Putin Federation of Jewish Communities of Russia and the elevation of Chabad's Berel Lazar, a vocal Putin supporter, to the position of Chief Rabbi of Russia.[15] As of this writing, Leviev is wanted by Israeli police for questioning related to a diamond smuggling scandal and is believed to be living in Moscow.[16] In May 2008, Trump met with Leviev to discuss potential real estate projects in Moscow. A month later, Trump attended a bris for Zina and Rotem's newborn son, which Leviev had arranged to take place at the gravesite of Rabbi Menachem Mendel Schneerson, Chabad's holiest site. Russian anti-corruption NGOs accuse Leviev of links to the Izmaylovskaya.[17]

Jared Kushner is also a member of Chabad, and the Kushner family has donated generously to the organization over the years.[18] Several of Chabad's top donors are involved in the global diamond trade, through which a great deal of money is laundered, and Kushner has done business with some of the more infamous of them. The Brighton Beach, Brooklyn Russian mafia was involved in the diamond trade as far back as the 1980s when Marat Balagula coordinated with the Lithuanian-Israeli mobster and KGB agent Shabtai Kalmanovich to secure mining interests in Sierra Leone.[19]

In 2015, the Kushner Company purchased several floors

of the old New York Times building in Manhattan from Lev
Leviev's Africa Israel Investments USA.[20] Kushner has also
purchased Manhattan real estate with $50 million in investments
from Raz Steinmetz, whose uncle is the billionaire French-Israeli
diamond magnate Beny Steinmetz.[21] Though not a member of
Chabad, Steinmetz has collaborated with Leviev in the past,[22] and
was recently found guilty by a Swiss court of corrupting foreign
officials and forging documents.[23] Another major Chabad donor,
billionaire, and key figure in the Israeli diamond industry is Dan
Gertler. He was sanctioned after using corrupt political
connections in the Democratic Republic of Congo to secure his
diamond and copper mining interests.[24] Years later, the Trump
administration secretly eased sanctions on Gertler five days
before he left office.[25]

Jared and Ivanka are friends with the Russian oligarch
and Chabad member Roman Abramovich and his wife. Kushner
has met with Abramovich three or four times, and Ivanka has
been friends with Abramovich's wife, Dasha Zhukova, for over a
decade.[26] Abramovich was at one point the top donor to Chabad
in Russia, the second being Oleg Deripaska.[27] Abramovich
recently had his British visa revoked. He tried to move to
Switzerland but was refused entry due to suspected ties to
organized crime.[28] Abramovich ultimately settled in Israel,
becoming its second richest resident.[29]

Trump Tower Toronto, Boris Birshtein, the Solntsevskaya,
And Maison de L'Amitie

In 2007, the Trump Organization broke ground on the Trump
International Hotel and Tower Toronto. Trump's original partner
on the project dropped out after it was revealed that he was a
fugitive wanted on charges of bankruptcy fraud and
embezzlement and was extradited to the US. Taking his place was
the Russian-born billionaire Alexander Yevseyevich Shnaider,
who moved to Canada via Israel. Shnaider made his fortune
through a personal and business relationship with his (now
former) father-in-law and mentor, the aforementioned former
employer of the "Oligarch Trio," Boris Birshtein.[30]

Born in Soviet-occupied Lithuania, Birshtein first
emigrated from the USSR to Israel before settling in Canada in
1982. By the mid-80s, Birshtein and Seabeco were involved in a

Soviet program to establish international business ventures headed by Georgi Arbatov, a KGB asset codenamed Vasili. Seabeco was later engaged in the exfiltration of billions of dollars of Communist Party funds out of Russia after the party was outlawed following a KGB-led coup attempt that Boris Yeltsin accused Birshtein of financing. Following the collapse of the USSR, Birshtein wielded influence in numerous post-Soviet states, including Ukraine, Moldova, and Kyrgyzstan. As mentioned, in 1995, Birshtein hosted a high-level mafia meeting in Tel Aviv to discuss the divvying up of power and influence in Ukraine. One attendee of that meeting, Solntsevskaya head Sergei Mikhailov, confirmed to *The Financial Times* that he had a business relationship with Birshtein, who he described as wielding immense influence in Ukraine. Mikhailov also recalled meeting a young Alexander Shnaider at a restaurant in Belgium, the location of the Seabeco office where Alexander Mashkevich met Patokh Chodiev for the first time. In 1996, Belgian authorities raided Birshtein and Shnaider's houses in Antwerp, and the two relocated back to Toronto.

Shnaider had begun working at Seabeco sometime in his 20s, and within a decade, he became a billionaire after establishing his own company, Midland, with his partner Eduard Shyfrin. The company was launched after Birshtein provided Shnaider with some of his interests in the Ukrainian steel industry. Shnaider used Midland's proceeds from serving as a middleman between the post-Soviet steel industry and international markets to purchase Ukraine's vast Zaporizhstal steel mill in the late 90s, in what competitors have described as a corrupt, insider deal. In 2003, Midland purchased the Red October steel plant in Volgograd, Russia, which supplies the Russian military.

In 2010, Shnaider was informed by his partner Shyfrin that buyers acting on behalf of the Russian government were pressuring them to sell their stake in the Zaporizhstal mill for "politically strategic" reasons and that if they didn't, their interests in Russia would be at risk. The deal was financed by VEB, a sanctioned Russian state-owned bank with a history of serving as a cover for espionage operations. VEB was chaired at the time by Vladimir Putin, who is known to have a relationship with Boris Birshtein. Midland received $850 million on the sale. $50 million went to Rinat Akhmetov, Ukraine's wealthiest oligarch who has connections to organized crime, was a key financial backer of the pro-Russian Party of Regions political party, and was a client of Paul Manafort's.[31] A $100 million "commission" was paid via Cyprus-based shell companies to the arrangers of the deal. Shortly after the Zaporizhstal deal closed, Shnaider plowed $40 million into the Trump Tower Toronto construction project.

The Trump Tower Toronto project was funded to the tune of $310 million by Austria-based Raiffeisen Zentralbank ÖSTERREICH.[32] Raiffeisen has a long history of investing in former Soviet republics. Andrey Kozlov, a deputy of the Russian Central Bank, accused Raiffeisen of laundering money for senior Russian officials and was shot in the head and killed shortly after the accusation was made.[33] Leaked diplomatic cables reveal that American officials believed Semyon Mogilevich used Raiffeisen as a front for his criminal activities.[34] In 2003, Mogilevich was indicted alongside Jacob Bogatin for a $360 million stock fraud involving a fake company, YBM Magnex, listed on the Toronto Stock Exchange.[35]

In 2004, Trump purchased *Maison de L'Amitie*, a 62,000-square-foot, 17-bedroom mansion in Palm Beach for $41 million. Jeffrey Epstein was also interested in buying the mansion, and reportedly, the conflict between him and Trump over it led to their falling out.[36] Four years later, as the Florida real estate market crashed and the US lurched into the subprime mortgage crisis, a family trust established by the billionaire Russian oligarch Dmitry Rybolovlev paid Trump $95 million for the mansion.

Rybolovlev made his fortune during the privatization of the Russian chemical industry, becoming chairman of Uralkali, a potash fertilizer exporter. In 1996, he was charged with murdering a competitor and spent 11 months in jail before the case was dismissed. Rybolovlev is known to be close to Yuri Trutnev, a senior Putin advisor. At the time of the sale, the mansion was in disrepair and suffering from a severe mold problem. Rybolovlev, who reportedly never stepped foot in the mansion, had it torn down and divided into lots that sold separately.[37]

"The oligarchs are just fronts for Putin," Trump told Michael Cohen following the purchase, as Cohen recounts in his memoir *Disloyal*. "He puts them into wealth to invest his money. That's all they are doing - investing Putin's money."

According to Cohen, Trump believed Putin was far and away the wealthiest man in the world, controlling 25% of the Russian economy and companies like Gazprom. Trump further thought that there was a bank in Switzerland with a single customer, Putin, and that he was worth over a trillion dollars. "Putin isn't president of Russia," Cohen recalled Trump telling him, "He's the ruler. He's the dictator. The Tsar. He can do whatever he wants. He's going to be leader for the duration of his life." Cohen claimed that Trump believed that Putin was the buyer of *Maison de L'Amitie*.[38]

Russian Money and Eurasian Organized Crime
At the Trump Ocean Club Panama

In 2005, Trump began working on a development in Panama, one of the world's most infamous money laundering sinks, called the Trump Ocean Club. Roger Khafif, a Miami-based developer who had promoted Trump properties at sales meetings in Russia, pitched the idea of a Panama property during a meeting at Trump Tower. Trump got behind the concept, announced in 2007, and used the project to provide Ivanka with experience in the property business. Khafif's Newland International Properties Corp. financed construction through a bond underwritten by Bear Stearns. They needed to prove they could sell the apartments to sell the bond. The man responsible for these presales was a Brazilian named Alexandre Henrique Ventura Nogueira, who met with Ivanka ten times during the project.[39]

Nogueira had arrived in Panama from Spain, where in 2005, authorities had opened proceedings to fine him for money laundering violations. Nogueira, whose company was called Homes Real Estate, told reporters that 50% of the Trump Ocean Club's sales went to Russians and that some were part of the "Russian mafia." Nogueira's international sales director was a Russian living in Canada named Eleanora Michailova. She later explained that Homes would set up Panamanian shell companies for customers that would then engage Khafif's company, Newland, in pre-sales agreements. This practice concealed the identity of the buyers.[40]

In four of these companies, the man listed as the director was Homes Real Estate's representative in Ukraine, Igor Anopolskiy. In March 2007, Anopolskiy was arrested in Kyiv on charges of human trafficking. Anopolskiy had been a shareholder in a Ukrainian travel agency, whose previous shareholders included Oxana Marchenko, wife of a former Ukrainian presidential chief of staff, Viktor Medvedchuk. Medvedchuk, a vocal opponent of Ukraine's pro-EU, anti-corruption protest movement, is known for his close ties to the Kremlin. Vladimir Putin is the godfather of his and Marchenko's daughter. As of this writing, Ukrainian authorities have charged Medvedchuk with treason for his associations with Russia.[41]

One of Nogueira's most important pre-sales customers was a Columbian con artist and drug money launderer named David Helmut Murcia Guzmán. According to the US Attorney for the Southern District of New York, Guzmán laundered narcotics proceeds through DMG Group, a pyramid scheme that attracted illicit funds from across the world. Two other groups that invested in DMG were the armed rebel group *Fuerzas Armadas Revolucionarias de Colombia* (FARC) and the paramilitary organization *Autodefensas Unidas de Columbia*. The US government classifies both as terrorist organizations. Nogueira purchased ten units at the Trump Ocean Club for Guzmán. Guzmán's lawyer in Panama claims that the units were purchased with cash brought over by Columbian "mules."

Another individual listed as a director of four Panamanian shell companies used to purchase pre-sale units is Alexander Altshoul. A Belorussian residing in Toronto, Altshoul is known for maintaining close relations with Canada's Russian and Eastern European populations. On two separate occasions, his name came up as being involved in real estate fraud during legal proceedings against different parties. Altshoul and Nogueira have acted as foreign representatives of Guzmán's DMG Group. Altshoul brought in family and friends to put deposits down on ten Trump Ocean Club apartments and one hotel unit. One of his investing partners was a Moscow-based relative, Arkady Vodovozov, who in 1998 was jailed for five years in Israel on charges of kidnapping and threats to kill and torture.

In 2008, Trump held a star-studded bash at Mar-a-Lago to celebrate the success of pre-sales at the Trump Ocean Club and to prompt further business. Nogueira was in attendance and was introduced by Trump as "the guy selling Panama." Altshoul also attended alongside another Homes Real Estate partner from the former Soviet Union named Stanislav Kavalenka. Kavalenka, who served as an officer on three Panamanian shell companies that had purchased units, had been accused by Canadian prosecutors four years earlier of economically benefiting from the forced prostitution of Russian women. The charges were withdrawn when the women in question failed to show up to court.

At the Trump Ocean Club's inauguration ceremony in 2011, Trump was photographed standing next to Andrey Bogdanov and Ivan Kazanikov, two Russians who bought at least six units for $4.4 million. Bogdanov had worked at the Russia-based Master-Bank before its license was revoked for failing to observe money laundering laws. Bogdanov is also a director and shareholder in a company called ZAO Makmar alongside Boris Bulochnik, a principal at Master-Bank who was arrested "in absentia" by Russian authorities for having intentionally bankrupted the bank. *Global Witness* was told by a convicted money launderer and former CIA contractor that Bogdanov and Kazanikov operated fronts that laundered money out of the former Soviet Union. Kazanikov has sat on the Trump Ocean Club's "committee of merchants" for over five years. Both purchased their units through Nogueira, who is currently being investigated in Brazil for money laundering and is now a wanted fugitive in Panama.[42]

Trump Organization Developments
And Branding Deals in the Former Soviet Union

The Trump Organization has, on numerous occasions, attempted to build Trump-branded towers in former Soviet states. In 2006, Donald Trump Jr. and Ivanka traveled to Ukraine. They met with government officials to discuss building a hotel and golf course in Kyiv and a hotel and yacht club in Yalta, which is currently part of Russian-occupied Crimea. Felix Sater and Tevfik Arif from Bayrock were involved in exploring some of the early deals. The Trump Organization also engaged Dmitry Buriak, whose company DeVision is one of Ukraine's largest real estate developers. DeVision's parent company, Petrochemical Holding, had a managing director convicted of abuse of power in 2002 for his work with Gazprom. Buriak was investigated by Lithuanian authorities over whether he and another company owned by Petrochemical Holding had been used by Russian intelligence to funnel money to the ruling Lithuanian Labor Party. A recent Lithuanian investigation into political and electoral interference found that Buriak and Petrochemical Holding posed "a threat to the interests of Lithuania." It remains unclear why the Trump Organization's projects in Ukraine never came to fruition.[43]

In September 2010, David Orowitz, senior vice president for acquisitions and development at the Trump Organization, traveled to Riga, the capital of the former Soviet state of Latvia. Orowitz was looking for potential sites for a Trump-branded hotel and entertainment complex. In June 2011, Ivanka Trump held a four-hour meeting at Trump Tower with Igor Krutoy and a Latvian businessman named Viesturs Koziols to discuss the Riga project. Krutoy, a famous composer in Russia, has received official state honors for his music and has served as a celebrity representative for Putin's 2018 re-election campaign. Originally from Ukraine, Krutoy is also close to Rinat Akhmetov. After meeting with Ivanka, Krutoy held a press conference in Riga to tout the potential Trump project. Standing alongside Krutoy to help promote the project was Ainārs Šlesers, a businessman and former Latvian deputy prime minister.

Šlesers also met with Donald and Ivanka Trump in New York, and detailed plans were drawn up and exchanged with the Trump Organization. However, the project hit a snag when Krutoy and Koziols were called in for questioning by the Latvian Corruption Prevention and Combating Bureau, which was investigating Šlesers for having used his public office to influence decisions on property developments that benefitted companies he was a hidden owner of. The inquiry became known as the "Oligarch Affair." Leaked transcripts of secret recordings made during the investigation show that Šlesers told potential investors that he had "an agreement with Trump" and that they were "ready to make the Trump Plaza Riga." Latvian officials requested that the FBI interview Trump. The Trump Organization provided the FBI with written answers, and the inquiry was pursued no further.[44]

In 2012, plans were announced for a $250 million Trump Tower to be built in Batumi, a port city on the Black Sea in the former Soviet Republic of Georgia. Typical of the Trump business model, the Trump Organization provided its brand while financing came from the Silk Road Group, a holding company with an unorthodox corporate structure established in

Georgia shortly after the fall of the Soviet Union. The project was the brainchild of Giorgi Rtskhiladze, a Soviet-born Georgian-American who initially invited Trump's ex-wife Ivana to Georgia to discuss the concept in 2009 before taking the idea to his friend in New York, Michael Cohen, Trump's personal lawyer and a vice president at the Trump Organization.[45]

Cohen entered Trump's orbit after investing in Trump World Tower. As mentioned, in 1994, he married a Ukrainian woman named Laura Shusterman and, through her, became friends with Felix Sater. Cohen's father-in-law, Fima Shusterman, was convicted of a money laundering-related crime in Ukraine in 1993. Fima Shusterman set Cohen up in a partnership with two Soviet-born partners in the taxi business. Fima and his wife later bought three units of Trump World Tower through Cohen, and Federal investigators told Seth Hettena that Fima Shusterman introduced Cohen to Trump. The nature of Trump and Shusterman's relationship is unclear[46]

Cohen's uncle owned the El Caribe Country Club in Brighton Beach, renting space for years to Evsei Agron, Marat Balagula, and Boris Nayfield, leading figures in the Brooklyn-based Russian mafia. As Cohen tells it, he worked in the club as a teenager, and while the gangsters influenced his attitude, he was not a gangster himself.[47] Cohen later owned a stake in the club, only selling it after Trump was elected president. In 1999, Cohen received a $350,000 check from an NHL player named Vladimir Malakhov at a time when the Russian mafia was regularly extorting Russian professional athletes.[48] Though the money was ostensibly related to a Florida apartment deal, Malakhov's agent later testified that the money was meant to go to Vitaly Buslaev, a leader of the Izmaylovskaya.[49]

Cohen traveled with Rtskhiladze to Georgia twice to scope out potential sites. The Trump Organization hoped Batumi would serve as a launchpad for several Trump Towers in the region. Cohen and Rtskhiladze also looked into the development of the Trump Diamond in Astana, Kazakhstan. The pair traveled to Astana, meeting with then-Kazakh Prime Minister Karim Massimov to discuss the project. The Trump Organization went as far as to sign a letter of intent and had the architect John Fotiadis, who also worked on Trump Tower Batumi, design an obelisk-shaped building for the site. The Trump Diamond eventually lost out to another bidder. In 2012 alone, Trump sought to trademark his name in Armenia, Belarus, Iran, Kyrgyzstan, Moldova, Tajikistan, Turkmenistan, Ukraine and Uzbekistan.[50]

Unlike the Trump Diamond, Trump Tower Batumi moved forward. Rtskhiladze formed Silk Road Transatlantic Alliance, a Delaware-incorporated partnership with George Ramishvili, chairman of the Silk Road Group. Ramishvili had made a fortune after the fall of the USSR, transporting oil from former Soviet states to be sold in European markets. The Silk Road Group does business throughout the former Soviet Union and the Persian Gulf in energy, transportation, banking, winemaking, and digital media. In 2005, it was announced that the BTA Bank, the largest financial institution in Kazakhstan, would provide hundreds of millions of dollars in loans to help develop Georgia, including developing hotels in Batumi. All of the loans went to subsidiaries of the Silk Road Group. According to reporting in *The New Yorker*, BTA's then deputy chairman may have been a hidden partner in several subsidiaries. If true, it constituted bank fraud.[51]

Before the Trump Organization engaged with the Silk Road Group to build Trump Tower Batumi with the financing partially provided by BTA Bank. BTA was (and as of this writing still is) involved in complex litigation involving its former chairman, Mukhtar Ablyazov, who stands accused of embezzling a fortune from the bank. However, the case also involves complex regional politics involving the powerful officials in Kazakhstan who may be pursuing the litigation for their own corrupt purposes. Felix Sater is also involved and has been accused by BTA of laundering some portion of hundreds of millions of dollars of embezzled funds through Trump properties.[52] Ablyazov's son-in-law, Ilya Khrapunov, stands accused of laundering funds embezzled by his father through purchases at the Trump Soho. Ablyazov and the Silk Road Group had been past business partners, owning a bank together in Georgia. A lawyer for BTA later accused the Silk Road Group of participating in Ablyazov's embezzlement scheme. A $50 million settlement was eventually reached.

The Trump Organization was legally required to perform due diligence to ensure it wasn't dealing with money linked to criminal activity. Trump visited Georgia in 2012 to promote the project and was paid a $1 million upfront licensing fee. BTA's assets and all of its records, including those involving its dealings with the Silk Road Group, are now held under the authority of Kazakhstan's sovereign wealth fund. The fund is directed by Timur Kulibayev, the son-in-law of the country's former dictator, Nursultan Nazarbayev. In addition to being a majority owner of BTA, Kulibayev also sits on the board of Gazprom. The Trump Organization dropped out of Trump Tower Batumi immediately after Trump was elected.

A month after Trump traveled to Georgia, the Trump Organization announced it was pursuing a project in the post-Soviet state of Azerbaijan. Trump Tower Baku, which never officially opened and partially burned down in 2018, was located in an unglamorous section of the Azerbaijani capital, which makes little sense for a supposedly five-star hotel and residence. The Azerbaijanis working on the project were family members of Ziya Mammadov, a notoriously corrupt billionaire who has served as Transportation Minister of the oil-rich nation on the Caspian since 2002. It is widely believed that Mammadov used his children as fronts and was the silent owner of Baku XXI Century, the company that owned Trump Tower Baku. A network of shell companies linked to Mammadov have reaped immense profits through lucrative contracts approved by the Transportation Ministry.[53]

Ziya Mammadov has a close financial relationship with the Darvishi brothers, members of an Iranian family linked to the Revolutionary Guard. Leaked American diplomatic cables revealed that Kamal Darvishi formerly ran a Revolutionary Guard-controlled business that acquired materials to build ballistic missiles and was sanctioned for aiding Iran's nuclear program. Mammadov ensured that the Darvishis were awarded state contracts, including constructing the Baku-Iranian Astara highway. American diplomats in the region assumed that Mammadov corruptly awarded overpriced construction contracts to Iranian Revolutionary Guard fronts and that he himself was a hidden partner. At the same time, Mammadov was engaging in a series of large-scale construction projects, including Trump Tower Baku, that could have been an excellent way for him to launder the kickbacks he received. The Revolutionary Guard, which was under severe sanctions at the time, could have used the Mammadov-linked shell companies to move money into the international financial system.

The Trump Organization has publicly characterized its involvement in the project as consisting of little more than a simple licensing deal. In fact, they also signed a technical-services agreement in which the Trump Organization agreed to assist in making sure the building was up to Trump design standards.[54] The designer of the hotel and several of the contractors visited Trump Tower in New York in order to secure approval for their various plans. Ivanka Trump visited Baku in 2014, toured the site and was deeply involved in design issues during the construction of the building. Prior to the Trump Organization's involvement, contractors involved in the construction of the tower were paid in large sums of cash and bribery and graft were routine. Like Trump Tower Batumi, the Trump Organization dropped out of Trump Tower Baku after he was elected president.[55]

A Gambling Ring in Trump Tower: the Taiwanchik-Trincher Organization

Between 2011 and 2013, the FBI executed a court-ordered warrant to surveil unit 63A at Trump Tower in New York.[56] One of the premier units in the building, Trump himself had owned it following the completion of the building in 1983. Eleven years later, Trump personally sold the unit to Oleg Boyko (AKA Oleg Boiko), a Russian oligarch and banker close to Boris Yeltsin. According to the Senate Intelligence Committee, Boyko has ties to the Russian government, intelligence services and organized crime and at one point employed David Geovanis.[57] At the time, Boyko owned the National Reserve Bank with Alexander Lebedev, a ten year veteran of the KGB.[58] In 2009, Boyko sold the unit to a US-Israeli dual-citizen named Vadim Trincher for $5 million, which moved through a series of shell companies Trincher had established in Cyprus. The unit was located just a few floors below Trump's penthouse.

Born in Ukraine, Trincher was a childhood math prodigy and professional gambler. He used the money he had won from the world premier Foxwoods Poker Classic to purchase the Trump Tower unit. However, instead of continuing his career in professional poker, Trincher went into business with the notorious *vor* Alimzhan Tokhtakhounov, known by the nickname Taiwanchik, or "Little Taiwanese," due to his Asiatic features.[59] The Taiwanchik-Trincher Organization, as the Department of Justice described it in an 84-page indictment, operated an illegal sports gambling and money laundering racket out of Trump Tower.[60]

Tokhtakhounov is an Uzbek *vory v zakone* closely connected to Sergei Mikhailov and the late Anton Malevsky, the respective leaders of the Solntsevskaya and Izmaylovskaya, as well as with Semyon Mogilevich and the late Vyacheslav Ivankov, who was assassinated in 2009. He was a childhood friend of Mikhail Chernoy, who he grew up with in Tashkent, the Uzbek capital where he also allegedly associated with Bayrock owner Tevfik Arif.[61] In his most famous caper, Tokhtakhounov fixed the figure skating event at the 2002 Winter Olympics in Salt Lake City by paying a bribe to ensure that the Russian duo Elena Berezhnaya and Anton Sikharulidze won gold. A federal jury in Manhattan voted to indict Tokhtakhounov on charges of conspiracy to commit wire fraud, sports bribery, and a violation of the Travel Act. The case was brought by then-US attorney in Manhattan James Comey.[62]

The Taiwanchik-Trincher Organization operated high-stakes online and telephonic sports betting out of Trincher's Trump Tower home. Tokhtakhounov used his status as a *vor* to attract gamblers and adjudicate disputes, occasionally resorting to the threat of violence. Its patrons included powerful Russian and Ukrainian who would bet up to $2 million on a soccer match. Others included an Uzbek mafia boss named Salim Abduvaliyev and an Azerbaijani named Gennady "Roman" Manashirov who was charged with bribing officials at the Russian Interior Ministry. Trincher's son Ilya partnered with Hillel "Helly" Nahmad, the wealthy heir to a Monaco-based, Lebanese-Jewish banking and art-collecting dynasty. Nahmad owned the entire 51st floor of Trump Tower, which he and Ilya Trincher used to host an illegal, high-stakes poker ring. Their patrons included Leonardo DiCaprio, Tobey Maguire, and Alex Rodriguez. According to the indictment, the Trump Tower-based gambling operations were also used to launder over $100 million dollars. One of the principal leaders of the Taiwanchik-Trincher Organization was Anatoly Golubchik, who also owned a condo at the Trump International Beach Resort located in "Little Russia," Sunny Isles Beach, Florida. Golubchik was also the owner of Lytton Ventures, a shell company whose director was listed as Galina Telesh, the ex-wife of Semyon Mogilevich.[63]

Vadim Trincher and his wife used the proceeds of his

crimes to donate thousands of dollars to the Republican National Committee, George W. Bush, John McCain, and Lindsey Graham. A fundraiser the couple had planned to host for Newt Gingrich was only called off after a leak had sprung from the roof of their Trump Tower apartment. Trincher had also attended a celebrity poker tournament alongside Bill Clinton and in 2012 donated between $5,000-10,0000 to the Clinton Foundation. Ilya Trincher knew Marc Lasry, a billionaire poker enthusiast who had employed Chelsea Clinton at his investment fund.[64]

In April 2013 the FBI executed a predawn morning raid on Trincher's Trump Tower Apartment, the culmination of over two years of surveillance. The agent who led the investigation into Tokhtakhounov and the Taiwanchik-Trincher Organization was Mike Gaeta, head of the FBI's Eurasian organized crime unit in New York. Inside they found a trove and jewelry and gold worth millions of dollars and over $2 million in casino chips. While Vadim and Ilya Trincher and Helly Nahmad received prison sentences, Alimzhan Tokhtakhounov remained at large in Russia where he moved around freely. Seven months after the FBI raid on Trump Tower, Tokhtakhounov was spotted standing near Donald Trump in the VIP section of the Miss Universe pageant in Moscow in November of 2013.[65]

Aras and Emin Agalarov, Miss Universe Moscow,
And the Quest to Meet Putin

Trump had purchased the rights to the Miss Universe Organization in 1996, which owned the rights to the Miss USA and Miss Teen USA, and for years had used the pageants as a means to promote his image as an international playboy and to bolster his business interests abroad. Holding the pageant in Moscow was the brainchild of a portly British PR agent named Rob Goldstone and his client Emin Agalarov, the pop star son of Aras Agalarov, an Azerbaijani oligarch and billionaire construction maven. Emin was married to Leyla Aliyeva, daughter of the notoriously corrupt president of Azerbaijan. Aras Agalarov, nicknamed "Putin's Builder," has not only worked on ultra-luxury real estate developments for Russia's oligarch classes, but also is regularly awarded Russian government construction contracts ranging from infrastructure projects to soccer stadiums.

He also has considerable holdings in US real estate.[66]

Aras Agalarov is close friends with Shalva Chigirinsky and is also affiliated with Sam Kislin and Tamir Sapir. He co-owns Europe's largest outdoor market, located on the outskirts of Moscow, with Tevfik Arif. According to Catherine Belton, the KGB allowed Agalarov to move to the United States in 1989 where he set up Crocus International and was used as an agent to funnel money into the West. Yuri Shvets told Belton that Crocus could not have been established without the permission of the KGB.[67] According to the Senate Intelligence Committee, the Agalarovs are closely connected with Russian organized crime and have close relations with individuals involved with "murder, prostitution, weapons trafficking, kidnapping, extortion, narcotics trafficking, money laundering, and other significant criminal enterprises."[68]

Agalarov enjoys close relations with the Russian government, including with Vladimir Putin and his press secretary Dmitry Peskov. Other individuals in the Russian state power structure close to Agalarov are the Prosecutor General Yuri Chaika, 69, and the First Deputy Premier Igor Shuvalov, 70, both of whom have been subjects of Alexei Navalny's anti-corruption exposés. Emin Agalarov is known to be friends with Grigoriy Lepsveridze, a musician sanctioned by the US for his connections to organized crime. He also once employed Artem Klyushin, a bot developer for the Kremlin who has supported Russian malign influence operations. Emin also reportedly performed at Solntsevskaya Bratva head Sergei Mikhailov's 55th birthday party.[69]

Between January and April of 2013, the President of the Miss Universe, Paula Shugart, negotiated with Goldstone and the Agalarovs regarding hosting the pageant in Moscow. The discussions centered around hosting the event at Crocus City Hall, a Moscow-based venue owned by Aras Agalarov. In 2010, it hosted the 60th anniversary of the Russian military intelligence's special missions department. After it was agreed that the show would be privately funded by Agalarov, Shugart took the offer to Trump who happily approved. Aras and Emin Agalarov were then invited to attend the Miss USA pageant in Las Vegas to sign the contract.[70]

Trump first met Rob Goldstone and the Agalarovs on June 15th, 2013, in Las Vegas, where they held a large private dinner in a restaurant at the Palazzo Hotel and Casino.[71] Of the twenty people present at the dinner, Trump was accompanied by Michael Cohen. They were joined by Irakly "Ike" Kaveladze, a Georgian-American vice president of Agalarov's company Crocus International. In 2000, the Government Accountability Office identified a business operated by Kaveladze that had opened up two bank accounts at two separate US banks and was used to move $1.4 billion from individuals in the former Soviet Union and Eastern Europe into the US financial system. The GAO report suggested this was done "for the purpose of money laundering."[72] Kaveladze's top client at the time was Crocus International.

Yuri Shvets told Catherine Belton that Kaveladze was an "illegal" Russian agent sent by the KGB to infiltrate the United States and gain citizenship. After graduating college, Kaveladze was hired as a vice president at Crocus International and his status as a US citizen allowed him to open up US bank accounts.[73] Kaveladze's company, International Business Creations, shared an address with other Agalarov companies and did business with the Commercial Bank of San Francisco,[74] which was partially owned by Boris Avramovich Goldstein, a Latvian linked to the KGB.[75] The Commercial Bank of San Francisco also appears to have participated in the much larger Bank of New York money laundering scandal involving Semyon Mogilevich.

Following dinner at Palazzo, Trump and the entourage attended an adult-themed club at the hotel called "The Act" at the behest of the Agalarovs.[76] The Act was infamous for its lewd and sexualized entertainment, one example of which included a skit that featured college girls urinating on their professor.[77] The next day Trump and the Agalarovs attended the Miss USA pageant, which was being held in Las Vegas at the time, where they announced that the Miss Universe pageant would be held in Moscow that year. Two days later, Trump tweeted: "Do you think Putin will be going to the Miss Universe Pageant in November in Moscow - if so, will he become my new best friend?"[78]

Throughout the planning process of the 2013 Miss Universe Pageant in Moscow, both Donald Trump and Aras Agalarov reached out to Vladimir Putin and high level members of his administration with invitations to attend. On June 21st, 2013, Rob Goldstone sent Emin Agalarov an email with the subject "Putin" in which he wrote, "[Trump] has a personal email [address] for VP [Vladimir Putin]" but that he needed a mailing address. The next day Goldstone emailed Emin a draft of the invitation to Putin with the subject line "Draft of Putin letter for Donald Trump - please show to Aras and let me know before I send to Trump."

"DT wants to send a letter to Putin inviting him to Miss Universe," Trump's longtime personal assistant Rhona Graff wrote to Paula Shugart on June 24th. "I asked Rob G[oldstone] to draft something we could tweak. If you see the letter below, he references a trip to Moscow by DT in advance of the actual pageant. What is he talking about?" The Goldstone letter Graff referred to, written in Trump's voice, stated: "I have always valued your kind offer for me to visit Moscow, and I will be doing so later this year prior to the contest. I want to personally invite you as my guest of honor to the November 9th Miss Universe Pageant, and would also hope to meet privately with you during my stay in Moscow."

"I have no idea," Shugart replied. "I'm finding out now." She discovered that Trump had told the Agalarov's that he would fly to Moscow in advance of the pageant in order to "facilitate a meeting" with Putin. Three days later, June 27th, Goldstone again inquired with Emin as to where Trump's assistant should send the "letter to Putin," to which he replied he was "[o]n it." The next day, Goldstone sent Graff and Shugart the information for "who to forward letter from Mr. Trump to President Putin." It included the contact details for Dmitry Peskov, Putin's personal Press Secretary. Peskov, Goldstone explained, "is in direct daily contact with the President and has been briefed to expect an email and physical letter." Graff then emailed another Trump Organization assistant a file titled "Dear President Putin.docx" and asked her to print it out. The next day she emailed Shugart and Goldstone a copy of the letter signed by Trump.

Later in September of 2013, there were further efforts to arrange a meeting between Trump and Putin. Goldstone wrote to Shugart and Graff on September 12th saying that he was travelling to Moscow and might have an opportunity to meet with "Putin's personal private secretary." Goldstone further suggested that he could use the opportunity to bring up a potential meeting between Trump and Putin during the meeting, and that it was suggested to him that he take a signed copy of the invitation letter with him to the meeting. Paula Shugart assumed that Goldstone was talking about meeting with Dmitry Peskov, and took the possibility of a meeting seriously as she believed that Aras Agalarov enjoyed personal access to Putin.

"'Not a bad idea," Rhona Graff replied to Goldstone. "Let me talk to Mr. Trump about it and I will get back to you asap." The next day, Graff wrote to Goldstone, "He'll sign it in the morning and I'll let you know Paula when someone can come over to pick it up."

"I will have a hand signed letter from Donald Trump to President Putin asking to meet when he is in Moscow Nov 5 to 9th," Goldstone wrote to Emin Agalarov and Ike Kaveladze on the day he received Graff's affirmative reply. "Hopefully we can get this letter to Peskov or some other person next week in Moscow."

"Trumps [sic] letter is with Peskov he will pass on to the president," Emin Agalarov wrote to Goldstone on September 18th.

"According to [Trump's] office," Goldstone wrote to Emin, "he is keen to make himself available at any time to meet President Putin, and if necessary, would fly in earlier on Nov 6th."

By this point, Trump was repeatedly expressing his desire to meet with Putin to various people ranging from Paula Shugart to Emin Agalarov. He also added Alex Sapir and Rotem Rosen to his private guestlist of individuals he wanted to be flown over to join him in Moscow for the pageant.[79] Alex Sapir is the son of Tamir Sapir, the former co-owner of Joy Lud Electronics, who later connected Trump to Felix Sater's and Tevfik Arif's real estate company Bayrock.[80] The Israeli-born Rotem Rosen was Alex Sapir's brother-in-law and then CEO of the Sapir Organization. He was also known as Lev Leviev's "right-hand man" and had served as the CEO of Leviev's Africa Israel Investments USA.[81]

Meanwhile, Trump was engaged in a media charm offensive, lavishing praise on Putin. On September 13th, in the aftermath of an editorial Putin published in *The New York Times* attacking the notion of American exceptionalism, Trump said on Piers Morgan's *CNN* show, "You think of the term as being fine, but all of a sudden you say, what if you're in Germany or Japan or any one of 100 different countries? You're not going to like that term," said Trump. "It's very insulting, and Putin really put it to [Obama] about that."[82] He referred to his invitation to Putin to attend the Miss Universe pageant on Fox and Friends three days later, claiming, "I know he'd like to go." On October 3rd, Putin told interviewer Larry King that Putin had "done a really good job outsmarting our country." On October 17th, Trump told David Letterman that he'd "done a lot of business with the Russians" and described Putin as a "tough guy" before falsely claiming that he had "met him once."[83]

Despite Trump's effusive media campaign and the efforts of those around him, the proposed meeting with the Russian president remained elusive. As the pageant approached, Trump grew ever more obsessed with meeting Putin and urged his employees and contacts in Russia to make it happen. On October 23rd, a little over two weeks before the pageant, Goldstone wrote Emin an email with the subject "Putin Trump meeting?" and asked, "[w]hat is the status on a possible meeting between Trump And Mr. Putin? Trump Office is asking."

"Roman [Grachev] will find out," Emin replied. Grachev was the director of Crocus City Hall and had been the one to transmit the Putin invitation to Dmitry Peskov. Goldstone pinged Emin again a day later, pushing to hear about the potential meeting. On Sunday, October 27th, Grachev's deputy informed Goldstone and the group around Agalarov that Putin would come to a decision regarding a meeting with Trump that Tuesday. Throughout this period, Aras Agalarov himself also pushed for the meeting. At one point, Ike Kaveladze overheard Agalarov discussing the potential meeting with Peskov.

"[W]hen I told the Presidential Administration that Trump was coming, and I told them what kind of event we were hosting, and how it will be seen by many people all over the world, the Presidential Administration responded that Vladimir Putin would like to meet Mr. Trump," Agalarov stated in a later interview. When asked why Putin wanted to meet Trump, Agalarov replied, "I convinced him to. You know the government here often pays visits to exhibitions, and we have a lot of national exhibitions taking place here. And I remember once when Putin was visiting one of the exhibition[s], I told him that we will have Donald Trump here for one of these events and we would have an audience of [many people]... Putin pays attention to events like the Olympic Games, Formula 1, FIFA

World Cup. He is interested in global events, and of course, he was interested in this event. He thought he should meet this person who brought this global event to Russia. That was the main reason."

In October 2013, Putin personally awarded Aras Agalarov Russia's highest civilian medal, the Order of Honor. The day before, Paula Shugart was in Moscow for the ceremony and told Rhona Graff that Aras would bring up the potential Trump meeting with Putin. On the day of the ceremony, Shugart emailed Graff photos of Aras accepting the medal. "This was just sent to me. They were discussing DJT while this was happening. Stay tuned."

"Well, I think if this is a serious and substantial offer to meet Putin, DJT would reconsider his travel plans," Graff replied. "Let's talk when you know more."

"I'll know more in the morning, but it sounds serious," Shugart wrote to Graff. "I told my contact it would be major reshuffling, and it would need to be worth it. Did you give him [Donald Trump] a heads up?"

"Any news on Putin?" Graff asked the following day.

"No," Shugart replied, "but at least I made Emin aware of the situation tonight at the event. We are following up in the AM. He said the meeting is definitely happening, he just isn't sure if Putin wants 7th, 8th or 9th. He was told 7th but hasn't received confirmation on information." Shugart was at this point working on setting up the Trump-Putin meeting daily, and discussed it with Trump nearly every time they spoke with one another. Despite these efforts, the meeting with Putin was never finalized.

On October 31st, ten days before the Miss Universe pageant, the Crocus Group and the Miss Universe Organization hosted a charity auction in Moscow. The Senate Intelligence Committee was able to get its hands on the event's initial invite list, which featured a rogues gallery of Russian government, military, and intelligence officials, members of Eurasian organized crime, and individuals who have participated in malign influence campaigns. Among the names were Russia's former President Dmitry Medvedev, Minister of Defense Sergey Shoigu, former intelligence head and Prime Minister Sergei Stepashin, Putin's chief propagandist Vladislav Surkov, the close Putin aide and the subject of Alexei Navalny's corruption investigations Vladimir Kozhin,[84] the oligarch and Head of Alfa-Bank Petr Aven, the

Azerbaijani CEO of LUKOIL Vagit Alekperov, Oleg Deripaska's (now ex) wife Polina Deripaska (who had been friends with Emin Agalarov for years), one-time KGB general and head of Russian Railways Vladimir Yakunin, the oligarch and key Putin ally Roman Abramovich, the Soviet era military leader Boris Gromov, the CEO of Russia's largest state-owned bank Sberbank Herman Gref and an FSB-linked lawyer named Anatoly Kucherena who only months earlier had represented Edward Snowden upon his arrival in Moscow. While it is unclear who among the invited attended, the list provides a glimpse into the Agalarov's relationships within the Russian power structure.[85]

Trump arrived in Moscow on November 8th and was taken by a Russian police escort to the Ritz Carlton. According to the Senate Intelligence Committee, the hotel has at least one Russian intelligence officer on its staff, the Russian government routinely surveils its rooms and prostitutes are a regular presence.[86] Upon his arrival, Trump briefly met with Miss Universe executives and the Agalarovs. Following the meeting, Keith Schiller, Trump's longtime head of personal security, claims he was approached by a Russian offering to send five women up to Trump's suite that evening. Schiller testified that he turned the man down and didn't take the offer seriously.[87]

Trump then attended an early evening function at the sushi restaurant Nobu, located 15 minutes from the Kremlin and hosted by Aras Agalarov and Sberbank.[88] The event was attended by Sberbank CEO Herman Gref, known for his close relations with Putin. Spanish intercepts indicate that Gref has communicated with members of the St. Petersburg-based and Putin-linked Tambovskaya Bratva, including with one of its leaders, Gennady Petrov.[89] Days after the event, Trump sent a letter of praise to Gref, inviting him to join him for lunch or dinner when he was next in New York.

After Nobu, Trump traveled to Crocus City Hall for the pageant rehearsal. While there, he was given a tour by Emin Agalarov, and at one point during their discussion, Paula Shugart overheard them discussing a potential Trump Tower Moscow. At 10 pm that evening, Trump attended Aras Agalarov's birthday party at Zafferano, a restaurant in Crocus City Hall. The party was also attended by the Miss Universe contestants, Aras Agalarov's friends and family, and numerous members of the Russian elite.

While at the dinner, Trump was photographed with Igor Krutoy. As mentioned, Krutoy had discussions with Trump, Trump Jr., and Ivanka regarding a potential Trump Tower Riga project in Latvia. However, the project was derailed when Krutoy and his partner became involved in a Latvian corruption investigation. Krutoy, a music composer, had written songs for Emin Agalarov and, at one point, owned a neighboring home to Aras Agalarov in New Jersey. He is also a close personal friend of Rinat Akhmetov, a Ukrainian oligarch who was a client of Paul Manafort, Trump's future campaign chairman.[90]

Trump returned to the Ritz somewhere between 1:40 am and 2 am. While he had initially been booked to stay in the Presidential Suite, he was moved to the Carlton Suite. Trump's room bill indicates possible social activity after the birthday party, with a $720 charge from the hotel's rooftop O2 Lounge, $306 charged to the room for shisha (a Middle Eastern water pipe also known as Hookah), and $146 in charges to the in-room bar, the timing of which is unclear. According to Schiller, as he escorted Trump to his room, he told him about the offer of five women he had received earlier that day, and the two laughed at the suggestion. Schiller then claims to have waited outside Trump's room for a few minutes before retiring to bed. The Senate Intelligence Committee noted that Schiller gave conflicting answers about the proposition of sending women up to Trump's room, at one point telling them that he took the offer as a "joke" and then later saying he took it seriously. However, he steadfastly denied any such activities involving Trump and Russian women took place.[91]

The next morning Trump made a brief appearance at a music video shoot for Emin Agalarov in which he had a brief cameo. He then attended a press conference in which he dubiously claimed to have a relationship with Putin and offered him effusive praise. Throughout much of the day, Trump repeatedly asked whether anyone had heard if Putin would be attending the event. Aras Agalarov later told *The Washington Post* that he had promised Trump that he would meet Putin. Eventually, Aras received a phone call from Putin's Press Secretary Dmitri Peskov. After handing the phone to Trump, an apologetic Peskov told Trump that Putin very much wanted to attend but that a traffic jam had delayed a diplomatic event at the Kremlin with the royal family of the Netherlands that Putin was obligated to attend.[92]

While at the pageant, Trump sat next to Aras Agalarov, and behind them sat Artem Klyushin, Emin Agalarov's social media manager, who had also worked on Kremlin influence operations. Senior Putin aide Vladimir Kozhin also attended, along with many other Russian personalities and oligarchs, including Alimzhan Tokhtakhounov.[93] Another guest, the Russian comedian Vladimir Vinokur, was an associate of high-level members of the Solntsevskaya Bratva and attended meetings held by Semyon Mogilevich in Budapest.[94]

Trump only stayed in Moscow for one night, returning to the US to attend the 95th birthday of conservative evangelist Billy Graham. Back in the US, Trump began tweeting about a potential Trump Tower Moscow project done in partnership with the Agalarovs. Shortly thereafter, Aras Agalarov's daughter visited the Miss Universe office in New York and brought with her a small black, *Fedoskino*-style lacquer box that contained a sealed letter from Putin to Trump, the contents of which remain unknown.[95]

Despite the extraordinary depth and number of contacts between Donald Trump and individuals from Russia and former Soviet states, many of them connected to organized crime and the intelligence establishment, it likely only scratches the surface. The Trump Organization has had business operations in at least 20 countries, including Turkey, the Philippines, India, Indonesia, Uruguay, Ireland and Scotland, among others.[96] For years, Trump refused to release his tax returns to the public. While they leaked to *The New York Times*, and eight years of them were released to prosecutors in New York, these still only consist of Trump's representations to the government. As of this writing, Trump remains under an ongoing IRS audit that has lasted for over a decade.[97] His refusal to reveal the identity of all his creditors means that the extent of his foreign financial entanglements remain largely unknown to this day.

Trump's finances are further obscured by the fact that he uses a web of privately held, Delaware registered LLC's and other corporate entities to hold his assets. Delaware LLC's don't need to publish financial statements or disclose the identity of their owner. According to *The Wall Street Journal*, half of the revenue Trump reported in a 2016 federal financial disclosure form came from assets held by 96 LLC's. Trump doesn't just hold his own assets in secretive LLC's, he sells to them. Since the 1980s, 20%

of all Trump condos, more than 1300, have been sold to shell companies in all-cash transactions made without a mortgage or inquiries from lenders. Similar information regarding international condo sales is not publicly available.[98]

In 2014, James Dodson, a golf journalist and co-author of golf legend Arnold Palmer's memoir, was invited to play golf with Trump and some of his family members at the Trump National Golf Club Charlotte. While riding with Eric Trump in a golf cart, Dodson asked who was funding the acquisition of the golf courses, explaining that he knew of no banks that would invest in golf courses following the Great Recession. According to Dodson, Eric replied, "Well, we don't rely on American banks. We have all the funding we need out of Russia."[99]

[1] Crowly, Michael. "Trump Jr.'s love affair with Moscow," *Politico.* July 12th, 2017

[2] Behar, Richard. "Trump And The Oligarch 'Trio,'" *Forbes.* October 24th, 2016

[3] Dawisha, Karen. *Putin's Kleptocracy: Who Owns Russia?* New York, NY: Simon & Schuster, 2014. Pg. 24

[4] MacNamara, William; Pignal, Stanley. "Case against three ENRC oligarchs settled," *The Financial Times.* August 17th, 2011

[5] MacKinnon, Mark. "Searching For Boris Birshtein," *The Globe and Mail.* December 29th, 2018

[6] Burgis, Tom. *Kleptopia: How Dirty Money Is Conquering The World.* New York, NY: HarperCollins, 2020. Pg. 174-175

[7] Hettena, Seth. "Who is Tevfik Arif, Part II," *SethHettena.com.* October 3rd, 2017

[8] Goldstein, David; Hall, Kevin G.; Stone, Peter. "A birthday video call captures a telling moment in Trump's Russia connections," *McClatchy DC Bureau.* April 5th, 2017

[9] Silverman, Gary. "Trump's Russian riddle," *The Financial Times.* August 14th, 2016

[10] O'Brien, Timothy. "Trump, Russia and a Shadowy Business Partnership," *Bloomberg.* June 21st, 2017

[11] Dolmetsch, Chris; Voreacos, Davis. "Trump-Linked Real Estate Firm Settles Suit by Ex-Employee," *Bloomberg.* February 22nd, 2018

[12] Belford, Aubrey; Reitveld, Sander; Paluch, Gabrielle. "Steppe to Soho: How Millions Linked to Kazakhstan Mega-Fraud Case Ended up in Trump Property," *Organized Crime and Corruption Reporting Project (OCCRP).* June 25th, 2018

[13] Schreckinger, Ben. "The Happy-Go-Lucky Jewish Group That Connects Trump and Putin," *Politico.* April 9th, 2017

[14] Pappenfuss, Mary. "Former Trump Associate Felix Sater Must Face Money Laundering Suit," *HuffPost.* December 1st, 2020

[15] Chazan, Guy. "In Russia, a Top Rabbi Uses Kremlin Ties to Gain Power," *The Wall Street Journal.* May 8th, 2007

[16] Megiddo, Gur; Neuman, Efrat. "Police Want to Question 'King of Diamonds' Lev Leviev in Massive Smuggling Case," *Haaretz.* November 5th, 2018

[17] "Letter to Dr. Ernest Strasser, Minister of the Interior, Bundesministerium fur Inneres," *Society Against Terror and Corruption.* January 14th, 2004 (Hosted by the *Trans-Border Corruption Archive*)

[18] Maltz, Judy. "Kushner Foundation Gives $342K to Chabad — Still Surprised About Jared and Ivanka's Synagogue?" *Forward.* January 9th, 2017

[19] Smillie, Ian. *Blood On The Stone: Greed, Corruption and War in the Global Diamond Trade.* New York, NY: Anthem Press, 2010.

[20] Dent, Wendy; Pilkington, Ed; Walker, Shaun. "Jared Kushner sealed real estate deal

with oligarch's firm cited in money-laundering case," *The Guardian*. July 24th, 2017

[21] Drucker, Jesse. "Bribe Cases, a Jared Kushner Partner and Potential Conflicts," *The New York Times*. April 26th, 2017

[22] Coren, Ora. "Leviev, Steinmetz Buy 10 Floors in Diamond Tower," *Haaretz*. August 17th, 2005

[23] Nebehay, Stephanie. "Swiss court finds Israeli businessman Beny Steinmetz guilty of corruption," *Reuters*. January 22nd, 2021

[24] Weitz, Gidi; Blau, Uri; Feldman, Yotan. "Ace of Diamonds," *Haaretz*. July 2nd, 2009

[25] Megiddo, Gur; Melman, Yossi. "Trump Admin Secretly Eased Sanctions on Israeli Mining Tycoon Dan Gertler," *Haaretz*. January 25th, 2021

[26] Baker, Stephanie; Reznik, Irina; Kazakina, Katya. "Billionaire Ally of Putin Socialized With Kushner, Ivanka Trump," *Bloomberg*. August 17th, 2017

[27] Barkat, Amiram. "The Rabbi and the Man in the Kremlin," *Haaretz*. December 31st, 2004

[28] "Roman Abramovich was deemed potential 'security threat' by Swiss police," *BBC News*. September 25th, 2018

[29] Halbfinger, David M. "Roman Abramovich, After Visa Troubles in Britain, Surfaces in Israel," *The New York Times*. May 28th, 2018

[30] Burgis, Tom. "Tower of secrets: the Russian money behind a Donald Trump skyscraper," *The Financial Times*. July 11th, 2018

[31] Lynch, Ian J. "Manafort and His Ukraine Patron: "FinCEN Files" Further Illustrate Gaping Holes in Oversight," *Just Security*. October 5th, 2020

[32] Burgis, Tom. "Tower of secrets: the Russian money behind a Donald Trump skyscraper," *The Financial Times*. July 11th, 2018

[33] Knight, Amy. *Orders To Kill: The Putin Regime And Political Murder*. New York, NY: St. Martin's Press, 2017. Pg. 129

[34] 06VIENNA514_a. "USG CONCERNS OVER AUSTRIAN BANKING OPERATIONS," *Wikileaks*. February 17th, 2006

[35] Howlett, Karen. "YBM officers pocketed millions, U.S. says," *The Globe and Mail*. April 26th, 2003

[36] Reinhard, Beth; Helderman, Rosalind S.; Fisher, Marc. "Donald Trump and Jeffrey Epstein Partied Together. Then an ocean front Palm Beach mansion came between them." *The Washington Post*. July 31st, 2019

[37] Crowley, Michael. "Trump and the oligarch," *Politico Magazine*. July 28th, 2018

[38] Cohen, Michael. *Disloyal: The True Story Of The Former Personal Attorney To President Donald J. Trump*. New York, NY: Skyhorse Publishing, 2020. Pg. 245-250

[39] Parker, Ned; Grey, Stephen; Eschenbacher, Stefanie; Anin, Roman; Brooks, Brad; Murray, Christine. "Ivanka and the fugitive from Panama," *Reuters*.

[40] "NARCO-A-LAGO: MONEY LAUNDERING AT THE TRUMP OCEAN CLUB PANAMA," *global witness*. November 2017

[41] "Ukraine charges Putin ally Medvedchuk with treason," *The Associated Press*. May 11th, 2021

[42] "NARCO-A-LAGO: MONEY LAUNDERING AT THE TRUMP OCEAN CLUB PANAMA," *global witness*. November 2017

[43] Kumar, Anita. "Before his claims of corruption, Trump tried to build a resort in Ukraine," *Politico*. November 4th, 2019

[44] Swaine, Jon. "FBI looked into Trump plans to build a hotel in Latvia with Putin supporter," *The Guardian*. March 29th, 2018

[45] Davidson, Adam. "Trump's Business of Corruption," *The New Yorker*. August 14th, 2017

[46] Hettena, Seth. "A Brief History of Michael Cohen's Criminal Ties," *Rolling Stone*. April 10th, 2018

[47] Cohen, Michael. *Disloyal: The True Story Of The Former Personal Attorney To President Donald J. Trump*. New York, NY: Skyhorse Publishing, 2020. Pg. 61-72

[48] Hettena, Seth. *Trump/Russia: A Definitive History*. Brooklyn, NY: Melville House Publishing, 2018. Pg. 80-81

[49] Felshtinsky, Yuri. "Who is Mr.Cohen? Trump's attorney received $350,000 for the Izmaylovskaya Criminal Group," *Gordon*. April 12th, 2017

[50] Hall, Kevin G.; Weider, Ben. "Trump dreamed of his name on towers across former Soviet Union," *McClatchy DC Bureau*. June 28th, 2017

[51] Davidson, Adam. "Trump's Business of Corruption," *The New Yorker*. August 14th, 2017

[52] Klasfeld, Adam. "Federal Judge Advances Lawsuit Accusing Felix Sater of Laundering Loot Through Trump Properties," *Law & Crime*. November 30th, 2020

[53] Davidson, Adam. "Donald Trump's Worst Deal," *The New Yorker*. March 5th, 2017

[54] Adams, Tom; Aftergut, Dennis. The Trump Organization - A Racketeering Enterprise? MEMORANDUM to Representative Jackie Speier, House of Representatives, California, 14th District. January 9th, 2018. Pg. 12

[55] Davidson, Adam. "Donald Trump's Worst Deal," *The New Yorker*. March 5th, 2017

[56] Ross, Brian; Mosk, Matthew. "Russian mafia boss still at large after FBI wiretap at Trump Tower," *ABC News*. March 21st, 2017

[57] Report of the Select Committee on Intelligence United States Senate On Russian Active Measures Campaigns And Interference in the 2016 US Election Volume 5: Counterintelligence Threats and Vulnerabilities. Pg. 645

[58] Zagoyrodnov, Artem. "Alexander Lebedev: A man who gets what he wants," *Russia Beyond*. July 1st, 2009

[59] Hettena, Seth. *Trump/Russia: A Definitive History*. Brooklyn, NY: Melville House Publishing, 2018. Pg. 114-116

[60] United States District Court of the Southern District of New York. United States of America v. Alimzhan Tokhtakhounov, Vadim Trincher, et al. Sealed Indictment.

[61] Unger, Craig. *House of Putin, House of Trump: The Untold Story of Donald Trump and the Russian Mafia*. New York, NY: Penguin Random House LLC, 2018. Pg. 201-204

[62] Daly, Michael. "Russian Who Fixed the Winter Olympics Had a Link to Trump," *The Daily Beast*. February 7th, 2018

[63] Henry, James S. "The Curious World of Donald Trump's Private Russian Connections," *The American Interest*. December 19th, 2016

[64] Bastone, William. "Trump Tower House Arrest For Racketeer," *The Smoking Gun*. March 22nd, 2017

[65] Corn, David; Levintova, Hannah. "How Did an Alleged Russian Mobster End Up on Trump's Red Carpet?" *Mother Jones*. September 14th, 2016

[66] Corn, David; Isikoff, Michael. *Russian Roulette: The Inside Story Of Putin's War On America And The Election Of Donald Trump*. New York, NY: Hachette Book Group, Inc, 2018. Pg. 1-6

[67] Belton, Catherine. *Putin's People: How The KGB Took Back Rusia And Then Took On The West*. New York, NY: Farrar, Straus And Giroux, 2020. Pg. 456-457

[68] Report of the Select Committee on Intelligence United States Senate On Russian Active Measures Campaigns And Interference in the 2016 US Election Volume 5: Counterintelligence Threats and Vulnerabilities. Pg. 261

[69] Kirilenko, Anastasia. "Gangster Party candidate: Trump's ties to Russian organized crime," *The Insider*. April 6th, 2018

[70] Report of the Select Committee on Intelligence United States Senate On Russian Active Measures Campaigns And Interference in the 2016 US Election Volume 5: Counterintelligence Threats and Vulnerabilities. Pg. 261-272

[71] Cheney, Kyle; Herszenhorn, David. "The would-be president and the oligarch," *Politico*. July 12th, 2017

[72] Report to the Ranking Minority Member, Permanent Subcommittee on Investigations, Committee on Governmental Affairs, United States Senate. SUSPICIOUS BANKING ACTIVITIES Possible Money Laundering by U.S.

Corporations Formed for Russian Entities. United States General Accounting Office. October 2000

[73] Belton, Catherine. *Putin's People: How The KGB Took Back Rusia And Then Took On The West*. New York, NY: Farrar, Straus And Giroux, 2020. Pg. 4557-458

[74] Bonner, Raymond. "Laundering Of Money Seen as 'Easy'," *The New York Times*. November 29th, 2000

[75] Royce, Knut. "San Francisco Bank Linked To Laundering Probe at Bank of New York," *The Center for Public Integrity*. December 9th, 1999

[76] Cohen, Michael. *Disloyal: The True Story Of The Former Personal Attorney To President Donald J. Trump*. New York, NY: Skyhorse Publishing, 2020. Pg. 178-179

[77] Corn, David; Isikoff, Michael. *Russian Roulette: The Inside Story Of Putin's War On America And The Election Of Donald Trump*. New York, NY: Hachette Book Group, Inc, 2018. Pg. 8

[78] Report of the Select Committee on Intelligence United States Senate On Russian Active Measures Campaigns And Interference in the 2016 US Election Volume 5: Counterintelligence Threats and Vulnerabilities. Pg. 275

[79] Report of the Select Committee on Intelligence United States Senate On Russian Active Measures Campaigns And Interference in the 2016 US Election Volume 5: Counterintelligence Threats and Vulnerabilities. Pg. 275-281

[80] "Alex Sapir," *The Real Deal*

[81] "Rotem Rosen," *The Real Deal*

[82] Kaczynski, Andrew. "Donald Trump Praised Putin For Bashing The Term "American Exceptionalism" In 2013," *BuzzFeed News*. August 1st, 2016

[83] Kaczynski, Andrew; Massie, Chris; McDermott, Nathan. "80 times Trump talked about Putin," *CNN*

[84] Krutov, Mark. "Documents Show Firm That Created Security, Communications Systems For Russian Government Also Worked On 'Putin's Palace,'" *RadioFreeEurope/RadioLiberty*. February 3rd, 2021

[85] Report of the Select Committee on Intelligence United States Senate On Russian Active Measures Campaigns And Interference in the 2016 US Election Volume 5: Counterintelligence Threats and Vulnerabilities. Pg. 279-286

[86] Report of the Select Committee on Intelligence United States Senate On Russian Active Measures Campaigns And Interference in the 2016 US Election Volume 5: Counterintelligence Threats and Vulnerabilities. Pg. 639

[87] Dilanian, Ken; Allen, Jonathan. "Trump Bodyguard Keith Schiller Testifies Russian Offered Trump Women, Was Turned Down," *NBC News*. November 9th, 2017

[88] Pismennaya, Evgenia; Kravchenko, Stepan; Baker, Stephanie. "The Day Trump Came to Moscow: Oligarchs, Miss Universe and Nobu," *Bloomberg*. December 21st, 2016

[89] Kirilenko, Anastasia. "Tambovskaya gang calling: How mafia keeps in touch with Putin's entourage (Intercepted conversations)," *The Insider*. November 15th, 2018

[90] Swaine, Jon. "FBI looked into Trump plans to build a hotel in Latvia with Putin supporter," *The Guardian*. March 29th, 2018

[91] Report of the Select Committee on Intelligence United States Senate On Russian Active Measures Campaigns And Interference in the 2016 US Election Volume 5: Counterintelligence Threats and Vulnerabilities. Pg. 292-294

[92] Rucker, Philip. "'The gorilla in the room': Inside Trump's failed efforts to meet Putin in 2013," *The Washington Post*. May 16th, 2018

[93] Corn, David; Levintova, Hannah. "How Did an Alleged Russian Mobster End Up on Trump's Red Carpet?" *Mother Jones*. September 14th, 2016

[94] Kirilenko, Anastasia. "Gangster Party candidate: Trump's ties to Russian organized crime," *The Insider*. April 6th, 2018

[95] Report of the Select Committee on Intelligence United States Senate On Russian Active Measures Campaigns And Interference in the 2016 US Election Volume 5:

Counterintelligence Threats and Vulnerabilities. Pg. 298-301

[96] Massoglia, Anna; Evers-Hillstrom, Karl. "World of Influence: A guide to Trump's foreign business interests," *OpenSecrets.org*. June 4th, 2019

[97] Gordon, Marcy; Wiseman, Paul. "A lesson from Trump taxes: An underfunded IRS is outmatched," *The Associated Press*. September 30th, 2020

[98] Frank, Thomas. "Secret Money: How Trump Made Millions Selling Condos To Unknown Buyers," *BuzzFeed News*. January 12th, 2018

[99] Littlefield, Bill. "A Day (And A Cheeseburger) With President Trump," *WBUR*. May 11th, 2017

Part III
The Campaign of 2016

Chapter 9:
Russian Intelligence and the 2016 Election

In July of 2021, *The Guardian* reported on the existence of a leaked classified Kremlin report entitled "No 32-04 \ vd," written by Vladimir Symonenko, the head of the Kremlin's expert department responsible for providing Putin with analysis and reports. The report addresses the upcoming American presidential election, writing that from the Russian perspective - *perspektivny* - Donald Trump was the "most promising candidate." It further provided a psychological analysis of the candidate, describing him as an "impulsive, mentally unstable, and unbalanced individual who suffers from an inferiority complex." Referring to "certain events" that took place "during non-official visits to Russian Federation territory," it hinted that the Russian state possessed *kompromat* on Trump. "It is acutely necessary," the report reads, "to use all possible force to facilitate his [Trump's] election to the post of US President."[1]

The leaked report pointed out American vulnerabilities, including the "deepening political gulf between left and right," surfacing in the US "media-information" space. It suggested that Russian intelligence could plant "media viruses" into America's political discourse that would take on a life of their own and impact specific populations. Responsibility for collecting and systematizing information and "preparing measures to act on the information environment of the object," an apparent reference to hacking, was given to Sergei Shoigu, the defense minister in charge of Russian military intelligence, the GRU. Russia's Foreign Intelligence Agency, the SVR, under the leadership of Mikhail Fradkov, was tasked with gathering information in a support capacity. The FSB, under Alexander Bortnikov, was in charge of counterintelligence.

Symonenko distributed an executive summary of the report on January 14th, 2016. Two days later, Putin personally signed an order for Alexander Manzhosin to convene a closed session of the Russian National Security Council. On January 22nd, Putin sat at the head of the table in a meeting at the Kremlin that included Shoigu, Fradkov, and Bortnikov. Also present was security council secretary Nikolai Patrushev, former head of the FSB during the time of the September 1999 Apartment bombings. The participants agreed that Trump's election would strategically benefit the Kremlin, both by causing "social turmoil" in the United States while also handicapping the negotiating position of the American President abroad. At that momentous meeting, Putin ordered his intelligence chiefs to execute a multi-agency effort to interfere in the 2016 American election.

Or did he? As of this writing, there is no confirmation that the report "leaked" to *The Guardian* isn't, in fact, an excellent example of Russian disinformation itself.

The Dark Arts: Active Measures and Disinformation

The Russian cyber and disinformation campaign targeting the 2016 presidential election was preceded by similar malicious activities across Eastern and Western Europe and in the United States conducted by many of the same units and individuals involved in the 2016 election. While technological developments exponentially increased their potency, the basic ideas and methodology behind Russian active measures and disinformation practices have been honed over decades. Understanding the fundamental concepts behind these attacks and the actions the attackers took immediately before their assault on America's democracy is essential.

Active measures is a term of art used to describe a form of political warfare conducted first by the Soviets and later by Russia's security and intelligence services. The US Information Agency describes active measures as "a Soviet term that refers to the manipulative use of slogans, arguments, disinformation, and carefully selected true information, which the Soviets used to try and influence the attitudes and actions of foreign publics and governments."[2] Retired KGB Major General and defector Oleg Kalugin has described these "subversion" practices as "the heart and soul" of Russian intelligence. He further states that they are meant to "weaken the West, to drive wedges in the Western community alliances of all sorts, particularly NATO, [and] to sow discord among allies."[3]

Active measures are influence operations designed to confuse and discredit Russia's opponents, chief among them the KGB's self-described "Main Adversary," the United States. Various forms of active measures include the use of forged or fake materials targeting politicians, government officials, the academic community, and the public at large, media manipulation either covertly or through state-funded media, establishing and funding front groups, the use of agents of influence or *agents provocateurs*, incitement of radical elements in foreign publics and at their most extreme, assassinations and political terrorism.

Covert active measures are often done in tandem with overt propaganda campaigns conducted by the Russian government, state-funded media, and witting or unwitting third-party intermediaries. They are the deliberate product of intelligence bureaucracies and are utilized with specific end goals. Soviet active measures campaigns against the United States included attempts to undermine notable politicians and public personages, the FBI, the State Department, and civil rights leaders, among others. The Soviets placed a special emphasis on both exploiting and inciting racial violence and hatred within the US.

Disinformation is central to all forms of active measures. According to legend, the term was coined by Joseph Stalin, who gave it a French-sounding name to suggest that it had Western origins.[4] As distinct from misinformation, the unintentional spread of false information, disinformation is spread intentionally and for a purpose. It can be aimed at the public or select targets through private information channels. Disinformation does not need to be false; it can also consist of weaponized bits of the truth selectively disseminated. To function, liberal democracies rely on citizens enjoying a shared factual, epistemic framework. As such, they are the specific target of, and uniquely vulnerable to, disinformation operations. Counterintuitively, the revelation of disinformation campaigns to their intended targets can *increase* their potency by increasing suspicion towards all forms of public information, which is the end goal of disinformation campaigns.

Russian Espionage, Hacking, and Cyber Warfare in the Lead-Up to 2016

In October of 1996, officials at NASA, the Department of Energy, the National Oceanic and Atmospheric Administration, the Environmental Protection Agency, the US Navy, and the Air Force detected a series of mysterious cyber intrusions into their networks. Later, investigators discovered that vast amounts of data were being stolen from US government and military agencies in an operation they came to call Moonlight Maze 5. After years of investigation, the culprit was determined to be Russian intelligence. A grim milestone had been passed. It was the first known example of state-on-state digital espionage in history.[5]

In March of 1999, the FBI hosted officials from the Russian Ministry of Internal Affairs at a dinner in Washington, DC. During the meal, FBI agents requested assistance from their Russian counterparts to help them find the Moonlight Maze hacking ring they believed to be based in Moscow. Surprisingly, the Russians agreed to help, and just under two weeks later, several American investigators flew to Russia. The investigators were stunned when a general from the Russian Defense Ministry admitted that the Russian Academy of Sciences had committed the hack at the behest of Russian intelligence. After assuring the visiting Americans that such activities would not be tolerated, the general conspicuously vanished the next day, and the investigators were stonewalled for the rest of the trip. Though the Moonlight Maze hacking operations were briefly suspended during the American investigators trip to Moscow, they resumed two months after they returned to the US.[6] State sponsored cyber attacks have continued, in one form or another, almost continuously ever since.

The first decade of the 21st Century saw vast numbers of the global population gain access to the internet and profound changes to the nature of the internet itself. In 2000, roughly 304 million people were online; by the decade's end, that number had swelled to nearly 2 billion.[7] On February 4th, 2004, a little-known Harvard undergraduate named Mark Zuckerberg launched a social media website called "TheFacebook." By 2006, what had become known as Facebook was made available to the general public and quickly became the most widely subscribed to social network on the planet. 2006 also saw the emergence of Twitter, and the purchase of YouTube by Google. The basic contours of the social media landscape were coming into focus. A year later, Apple released the first iPhone, inaugurating a device revolution allowing people to access the internet from the palm of their hands.

2007 was also a landmark year in the history of cyber warfare. In April, authorities in the formerly Soviet-occupied Baltic country Estonia removed and relocated a controversial statue of a World War II-era Red Army soldier from a central square in the capital city of Tallinn. For ethnic Estonians, the statue symbolized the post-war Soviet occupation. However, to Estonia's Russian minority population, the statue represented the Soviet's victory over Nazi Germany, and its removal sparked outrage and protests. Russian state media responded by calling the Estonian government fascist, a strategy later employed in Ukraine.[8] A day after the removal, multiple Estonian websites were brought down by denial-of-service attacks, a simple means of overwhelming a website's server. The targets included the Estonian presidency and parliament, nearly every major government ministry, Estonian political parties, half of the country's major news sites, and its two largest banks, among other institutions.[9]

Three days into the relentless cyber assault, it became clear that the operation was not simply conducted by a haphazard group of pro-Russian independent hacktivists. Powerful cybercriminal organizations such as the misleadingly-named Russian Business Network, a criminal gang based out of St. Petersburg infamous for its online spam and fraud campaigns, were directing botnets of thousands of computers they had seized control of worldwide to contribute to the assault against Estonia's online infrastructure. The tactics the hackers employed also changed, from simply taking Estonian websites offline to defacing them with Nazi imagery, echoing Russian state propaganda.[10]

As most attacks originated out-of-country, Estonia's cyber defenders responded by cutting the entire country off from all foreign web connections. It was a dramatic move, as Estonia was one of the most highly connected countries on the Earth. However, when they eventually restored the connections, the attacks continued and expanded in sophistication. On May 9th, the date Russia celebrates the Soviet victory over Nazi Germany, the attacks reached a crescendo. That day, 58 Estonian websites were taken offline, and one of the country's largest banks, Hansabank, had its services interrupted for 90 minutes.[11]

Given their diffuse nature, attributing precisely who was behind the attacks was a difficult question to answer definitively. Estonian government officials accused the Russian government of orchestrating the attacks.[12] Others believed the attacks represented a hybrid relationship between independent Russian hackers, cybercriminal organizations, and the Russian government. However, when Estonian diplomats approached NATO officials about invoking Article 4, which calls for the leaders of NATO member states to convene to discuss the security threats faced by a fellow member, they were rebuffed. It was the first of many messages sent to the Russians that they could engage in cyber attacks with impunity.

The following year, 2008, Russia refined its offensive cyber capabilities further. In August of that year, war broke out between Russia and Georgia over the breakaway provinces of South Ossetia and Abkhazia. According to NATO analysts, what followed was the first example of Russia utilizing cyber and information warfare to complement conventional military operations.[13] On August 8th, a day after the conventional war began, denial-of-service attacks struck 38 websites. Institutions attacked included the Georgian President's website and those for the country's parliament, supreme court, Ministry of Foreign Affairs, the Georgian National Bank, and the US and UK embassies. Cyber security professionals again traced the use of large, international botnets linked to the cybercriminal Russian Business Network, which both provided tantalizing clues of Russian state involvement and muddied the waters regarding direct attribution.[14]

The Georgian War also had significant repercussions for an institution that would play a central role in 2016: Russia's military spy agency, the Main Intelligence Directorate, known as the GRU. During the Cold War, the GRU was tasked with spreading Soviet influence in the developing world, while its operations in the West mainly consisted of stealing military secrets.[15] The GRU survived the collapse of the Soviet Union intact, unlike the KGB, which was divided into the FSB and SVR, Russia's respective domestic and foreign intelligence agencies.

By the conclusion of the Georgian War, Russian officials were disappointed with how the GRU conducted itself. While the Spetsnaz special forces under GRU command performed admirably, there was a widespread belief that the agency had provided faulty intelligence throughout the campaign. As a result, Medvedev demoted the GRU in name and stripped the organization of some of its responsibilities, including transferring control over the Spetsnaz to a different military agency and dividing many of its intelligence responsibilities between the FSB and SVR.[16] Despite these humiliations, what followed was a period of changing priorities and reform from which the GRU emerged as one of the premier hacking organizations in the world.

The exact reasons for this transformation are not publicly known. In 2011, the GRU's chief, Aleksandr Shlyakhturov, was replaced by Igor Sergun, who ably guided the agency through a period of change and was adept at managing his relationship with Putin.[17] During this period, the GRU also appears to have gone on a recruitment drive, establishing a "science company" in 2013 as part of a larger Russian Defense Ministry effort to recruit top talent from Russia's universities.[18] These developments in the GRU occurred when Russian theories regarding information warfare began to mature.

In February 2013, the chief of staff of the Russian military, General Valery Gerasimov, wrote an article for the publication *Military-Industrial Kurier* entitled "The Value of Science in Prediction."[19] Gerasimov describes the Kremlin's understanding of the events of the Arab Spring and the Color Revolutions as regime changes orchestrated by the CIA.[20] He notes that the 21st Century has seen a blurring of the distinction between war and peace. Wars are rarely officially declared anymore. Advances in information technology allow wars to be waged continuously through information channels. This new form of warfare can be waged "throughout the entire depth of [the enemy's] territory" instead of just the frontlines of traditional conventional wars. In articulating this new version of hybrid information warfare, Gerasimov provides insights that can be applied to Moscow's offensive cyber activities of the recent past. The first major target of this new form of hybrid warfare was Ukraine.

Between 2013 and 2016, Russian intelligence appears to

have used the online hacktivist community *Anonymous* as a means of spreading disinformation intended to discredit opposition figures in Ukraine. During this time, the group *Anonymous Ukraine* published over 100 posts on the website CyberGuerrilla, which included 37 leaks mainly consisting of data stolen from email inboxes. While it is unknown how many of these posts were produced by actual Ukrainians and how many were produced by Russian intelligence, the presence of up to a dozen forgeries indicates professional tradecraft. The careful placement of forgeries among real, stolen information was a practice as old as Russian intelligence itself. Experts believed that the *Anonymous Ukraine* leaks were the product of GRU Unit 74455,[21] initially identified by cybersecurity professionals as "Sandworm."[22]

After large-scale protests in Kyiv swept Viktor Yanukovych from office, Putin responded by invading Eastern Ukraine and illegally annexing Crimea. The Russian invasion was as much psychological warfare as conventional, in that Putin brazenly denied it was happening while it was happening, and many of the Russian soldiers involved did not wear identifying insignia, thus earning them the name "little green men." The GRU's Unit 74455 assisted the invasion by sprinkling Ukrainian social media with forgeries and fake posts promoting Russian propaganda and exaggerating pro-Russian/Ukrainian separatist sentiments. While these posts received little attention, the Russians were honing their methods.

In the months after Yanukovych fled to Moscow, a pro-Russian hacker group calling itself CyberBerkut (in reference to the Berkut special police force that fired upon protestors in Kyiv's Maidan square) began publishing posts online referring to pro-European Ukrainians as fascists and anonymously distributing forged emails supposedly between the Ukrainian military and American State Department suggesting the Ukrainian revolution was planned by the CIA.[23] In March 2014, NATO announced that several of its websites had been targeted by denial-of-service attacks by a "Ukrainian hacker group," CyberBerkut.[24] Britain's National Cyber Security Centre would later expose CyberBerkut as an online front for the GRU.[25]

Among CyberBerkut's methods was the selective leaking of the hacked private communications of Ukrainian opposition leaders, US diplomats, and EU officials. CyberBerkut targeted Ukraine's Central Election Commission three days before the

Ukrainian Presidential election, gaining access to its network, wiping dozens of its computers, and disabling real-time vote display. The hackers proceeded to leak photos of the Election commissioner's passport and that of his wife, as well as his correspondence with Western officials, in an attempt to falsely convey the idea that the West was meddling in Ukraine's upcoming election.[26] After frantically troubleshooting in the days before the election, on election day itself, the Commission's IT administrators discovered that hackers had placed an image on the Commission's website that falsely declared a far-right candidate had won the election. While they prevented it from being publicly displayed, they couldn't stop Russian state television from reporting the falsified result in an apparent attempt to reinforce the GRU's lie. The morning following the election, the Commission was again targeted by cyber attacks which attempted to prevent it from posting the legitimate election results.[27]

While the initial cyber attacks conducted by the GRU in Ukraine were technically simple, consisting of data exfiltration and leaks, manipulating websites, and wiping computers, by the end of 2015, there was unmistakable evidence that their cyber warfare capabilities were expanding beyond information warfare and into the physical destruction typically associated with conventional warfare. On December 23rd, 2015, a highly sophisticated cyber attack took down a power plant in Western Ukraine. It plunged a quarter of a million Ukrainians into darkness for six hours in the dead of winter.[28] Cyber security experts quickly named the culprit Sandworm, which we know today to be GRU Unit 74455.[29]

While much more technically advanced and potentially more devastating than information warfare, the hack against Ukraine's physical energy infrastructure represented the kind of cyberwarfare that the American security establishment felt more comfortable with. After having developed malicious computer worms that physically destroyed their targets, an infamous example being Stuxnet, which targeted and destroyed Iranian centrifuges used to separate nuclear material, American cyber warriors and defenders largely saw the risks posed by cyber war through this lens. Less attention was paid to the potential information, propaganda, and psychological elements of cyber operations.

A year before the Ukrainian blackout, on November 14th, 2014, GRU Officer Ivan Sergeyevich Yermakov performed technical reconnaissance on the US nuclear power developer Westinghouse Electric Company (WEC), researching its employees and their backgrounds in the nuclear industry. Between that time and January of 2015, Yermakov and others in his unit sent spear-phishing emails, which enabled them to steal employee log-in information of individuals involved in advanced nuclear reactor development and new reactor technology.[30] Yermakov's intrusions were eventually discovered by American authorities, who noticed that the malware used in the Ukrainian power grid hack was being used against American targets. The Department of Homeland Security issued an Industrial Control Systems (ICS) Alert warning potential targets of the ongoing sophisticated malware campaign. However, while American authorities were concerned with the security of the country's physical infrastructure, less attention was paid to the information cyber war being waged with increasing frequency and ferocity against institutions across the Western world. Ukraine was only the beginning.

In addition to posing as pro-Russian Ukrainian hackers, the GRU also established a false flag hacktivist group ostensibly linked to the infamous terror organization the Islamic State called the CyberCaliphate.[31] The GRU's use of the Islamic State as a front is indicative of the complex relationship between Russia and the terrorist group. The Russian's ally in Syria was the brutal regime of Bashar al-Assad, which, in theory, would make the Russians the enemy of the Islamic State. However, the existence of the terrorist organization and the fears it aroused, particularly in Europe and the United States, served several Russian propaganda and strategic goals. Firstly, the existence of the Islamic State bolstered Russian arguments that the only alternative in Syria to Sunni jihadists was the Assad regime. Second, by prolonging the Syrian Civil War, the Islamic State exacerbated the refugee crisis that was destabilizing the entire European unification project. Third, the Islamic State's well-publicized murders of US citizens heightened fears and partisan tensions in the United States were used to attack the political fortunes of President Obama and his would-be successor, Hillary Clinton.

The CyberCaliphate's first known attack in the United

States took place against the local news outlet, the *Albuquerque Journal*. On Christmas Eve 2014, the Albuquerque Journal's website was hacked to feature Islamic State-related images with the headline "Christmas Will Never Be Merry Any Longer." A similar attack using identical imagery was conducted on January 6th, 2015, against local Maryland television station *WBOC* 16. Six days later, in the aftermath of the massacre at the satirical French publication *Charlie Hebdo*, the CyberCaliphate struck again, this time seizing control of the US Central Command Twitter profile and posting the message, "AMERICAN SOLDIERS, WE ARE COMING, WATCH YOUR BACK. ISIS."[32] This was the first of seven posts that used publicly available information to create the false impression that US Central Command had been compromised when it was only their Twitter profile.[33]

Ten days after the CentCom stunt, on January 23rd, 2015, GRU hackers compromised the French television station TV5/Monde. The GRU spent months studying vulnerabilities within TV5/Monde's network and implanting sophisticated malware. In the meantime, their malicious activities continued unabated. On January 26th, GRU hackers seized control of Malaysia Airlines' website. They replaced its homepage with a facetious "404 - Plane Not Found" message, a crude reference to the twin aviation disasters suffered by the company the year before, including the missing Flight 370 and Malaysia Airlines Flight 17, which was shot down over Ukraine. The GRU hackers concealed their identities by writing, "Hacked by Lizard Squad, Official CyberCaliphate," beneath a doctored photo of a pipe-smoking lizard sporting a monocle.[34] The same day as the Malaysia Airlines website was defaced, the GRU sent spear-phishing emails to three prominent YouTube personalities who had interviewed President Obama four days earlier at the White House in what is known as an "island-hopping technique," in which attackers focus on companies or individuals who are affiliated, but less secure, than their primary target.[35]

On February 10th, the CyberCaliphate engaged in a frenzy of activity. First, they seized control of Newsweek's Twitter feed and posted documents allegedly leaked from the Defense Cyber Investigations Training Academy along with messages threatening Michelle Obama and her family, writing, "#CyberCaliphate Bloody Valentine's Day #MichelleObama! We are watching you, your girls, and your husband!"[36] At the same time, five US military spouses received threatening messages from the CyberCaliphate in which they were addressed by name and told, "We're much closer than you can even imagine." To round out a busy day, the GRU registered and took live cyb3rc.com and posted a threat against the Pentagon, writing, "We are destroying your national cybersecurity system from inside," adding, "We know everything about you and your relatives, and we're much closer than you can ever imagine." The website posted a mix of public domain and possibly stolen documents from the Department of Defense.[37]

Also in February of 2015, GRU Unit 54777, the GRU's chief practitioners of psychological warfare, sent a dozen US Senators an email from a fictional identity supposedly from a group called "Patriots of Ukraine." By this time, the Russian war in Ukraine's eastern regions was approaching its second year. The message, written in shoddy English, included a petition to "save" Ukraine and accused Ukrainian military officers of selling weapons to terrorists. While the email hardly made a ripple in the Capitol, it was significant insofar as it marked the first known operation directed by the GRU's new psyops unit against US politicians.[38]

In addition to US politicians, primarily from the Democratic party, and US Diplomatic personnel, the group most targeted by the GRU were Russian, Ukrainian, and international journalists. Starting in mid-2014, over 200 journalists were targeted by GRU hackers. In March 2015, an openly gay Russian television broadcaster, Pavel Lobkov, was hacked. Months earlier, Lobkov revealed on live Russian television that he was HIV-positive, at the time a groundbreaking admission to be made in Russia. Shortly after that, Lobkov's private Facebook messages, some of which were sexually explicit, were leaked online. Fifty of the reporters targeted were from *The New York Times*, and another fifty were foreign correspondents based out of Moscow or Russian journalists working in the independent media. Many others worked for independent publications in Ukraine.[39]

On April 8th, nearly two and a half months after their initial incursion into the French broadcaster TV5/Monde, during which time they carefully identified vulnerabilities, the GRU launched a devastating attack that placed Islamic State propaganda on the station's affiliated social media accounts and took down its 11 channels being broadcast to over 50 million people in 200 countries and territories.⁴⁰ France, which had been subjected to Islamic State terrorist attacks, was shaken by the incident. The day after the attack, the GRU, using a false online identity, posted a detailed but subtly misleading technical analysis of the attacks, blaming them on cyber jihadists. While the strange description initially confused French investigators looking into the incident, they eventually recognized it as yet another part of an operation that marked the most devastating cyber attack against televised communications yet seen.⁴¹ The TV5/Monde attack was followed by a similar GRU operation in which they briefly seized control of a UK-based TV station called the Islam Channel.⁴²

The same month as the TV5/Monde attack, officials in the Bundestag, the German parliament, as well as members of German Chancellor Angela Merkel's Bundestag office, were targeted with Spear Phishing emails ostensibly from the United Nations but, in fact, sent by the GRU. Dmitriy Sergeyevich Badin, a then-24-year-old GRU Officer in the elite hacking Unit 26165 conducted the attack.⁴³ Based on Komsomolsky Prospekt in Central Moscow, Unit 26165 was commanded by Viktor Netyksho, a mathematically gifted specialist in probabilistic functions and neural networks. The Unit, also known as the 85th Main Center of the GRU Special Service, specializes in breaking encryption and computer network exploitation.

By early May, GRU malware stole passwords and spread through the network, seizing control of the Bundestag's IT infrastructure, paralyzing its online services, and blocking access to its external website. The paralysis lasted for several days, during which time Badin's team exfiltrated 16 gigabytes of data.⁴⁴ Among the stolen data were the complete inboxes of multiple German parliamentarians. Merkel's office was among those that were breached.

More aggressive than ever, international in scope, and with a rapidly increasing operational pace of activity, Unit 26165 was now ready to embark upon its most daring mission yet: a cyber assault against the 2016 American election. One of their early targets, among others, was the Democratic National Committee. However, at the time they attempted to breach the DNC's server, evidence suggests that Netyksho's hackers were unaware that they had been beaten to the punch. The DNC's network had already been breached by another group of hackers linked to Russia's foreign intelligence service, the SVR.

Russian Foreign Intelligence
and the Infiltration of the Democratic National Committee

In the summer of 2015, hackers from Russia's foreign intelligence service, the SVR, breached the Democratic National Committee's network.[45] This was not unusual. Political organizations and campaigns have long been the target of cyber espionage. In 2008, the US government discovered a cyberespionage campaign against the Obama and McCain campaigns conducted by hacking units connected to China.[46] Like the Chinese before them, the SVR hackers appeared to be engaging in the traditional espionage activity of clandestine information gathering. It would only be later that the GRU would weaponize the stolen information by publicizing it to the wider world. Later analysis by cybersecurity experts would find no evidence that the SVR and GRU hackers were working in tandem or even aware of the other's presence.[47]

The SVR is famous for its human intelligence espionage operations. In 2010, the FBI arrested ten deep-cover SVR agents operating in the United States. These "illegal" agents, referring to the Soviet and later Russian practice of running long-term espionage operations using deep-cover sleeper agents operating outside of official diplomatic cover, used forged documents to present themselves as everyday Americans. The purpose of the operation was multifaceted, including gathering information on nuclear weapons, Congressional politics, CIA leadership, and American foreign policy vis-a-vis Iran.[48]

In 2009, SVR illegal agent Lydia Guryev came close to gaining access to the inner circle of the new American Secretary of State Hillary Clinton. Operating under the false name Cynthia Murphy, Guryev lived with her husband Vladimir Guryev (AKA Richard Murphy) in Montclair, NJ.[49] Under the cover of Cynthia Murphy, Guryev had been a long-term employee of the financial advising firm Morea Financial Services. In February 2009, she sent a covert message to her SVR handlers in Moscow informing them that she had gained access to Alan Patricof, a wealthy New York financier and close confidant and fundraiser for Bill and Hillary Clinton.[50] Moscow Center replied that Patricof was "a very interesting target" and that Guryev should "try to build up little by little relations with him moving beyond just [work]."

Higher-ups at the SVR hoped Patricof could provide "remarks re US foreign policy," as well as "rumors" about the oddly phrased White House internal "kitchen."[51]

What Guryev and the SVR didn't know was that the FBI had been monitoring the illegals since the early 2000s. The Guryev's home was bugged and periodically searched by FBI agents when they were out. By June 2010, the FBI grew concerned about Guryev's attempts to infiltrate Hillary Clinton's inner circle, as well as flight risk issues. On June 27th, the FBI pounced and arrested ten Russian illegals in a case that was complacently treated in the American media as an almost comical throwback to the Cold War.

While the illegals episode showed that the SVR was still heavily involved in its traditional human intelligence activities within the United States, SVR hackers were also engaged in extensive cyber espionage activities. The analysis of SVR malware indicates that the agency has been active since 2008 and began targeting governments in 2010.[52] In one of their earliest known operations, in 2010 SVR hackers targeted a Washington, DC-based private research institute with spear phishing emails containing links to a comedic video entitled "Office Monkeys. If clicked, the user's computer would be compromised by SVR malware.

In the Summer of 2014, the General Intelligence and Security Services of the Netherlands (AIVD) penetrated the computer servers of a hacking group operating out of a university building adjacent to Red Square in Moscow. Remarkably, the Dutch were able to gain access to security camera footage, so they were able to see not only what the Russians were doing online but also exactly who was doing it behind the keyboard. With this information, they later determined that the hacking group, referred to by cyber security professionals by several names, including "Cozy Bear," was, in fact, led by the SVR.[53]

The Dutch watched as the SVR launched a series of ever more aggressive cyber assaults against the United States. In November 2014, SVR hackers targeted the US State Department and gained access to its unclassified network. After quietly being tipped off by the Dutch, FBI, and NSA cyber defenders were able to kick the Russians out. Undeterred, the SVR hackers next attempted to access President Barack Obama's emails. While they could not crack into the carefully guarded servers that controlled

Obama's personal Blackberry, they managed to exfiltrate data from officials who were in contact with Obama and thus see some of the messages the President sent and received.[54] In 2015, SVR hackers launched a cyber assault against the Pentagon's email system and temporarily shut it down.[55]

Sometime in the Summer of 2015, Dutch intelligence warned their American counterparts that the SVR had gained access to the internal servers of the Democratic National Committee (DNC). The information prompted an inept attempt by the FBI to warn DNC officials about the compromise. On August 6th, 2015, FBI Special Agent Adrian Hawkins called the DNC front desk and was transferred to an IT contractor named Yared Tamene. Agent Hawkins explained to Tamene, who wasn't a cybersecurity expert, that there were signs that the DNC had been compromised and provided several IP addresses that he said would help them locate the intrusion. Tamene was unsure during the conversation whether the voice on the other end of the line was really an FBI agent or whether he was a victim of a prank. Agent Hawkins cryptically suggested that Tamene look into malware created by "the Dukes," yet another name used by cyber security professionals referring to the SVR hackers. After the call, a confused Tamene conducted a brief and inadequate search of the DNC's log files but could not detect any malign activity. He informed Andrew Brown, the DNC's chief technology officer, of the odd incident and pursued the matter no further.[56]

Two months passed before the FBI followed up with the DNC, during which time the SVR was burrowed deeper into the DNC's internal servers. Sometime in October, Agent Hawkins left Tamene two voice mails but received no response. When Hawkins finally re-established contact with Tamene in November, months after their initial conversation, he provided him with a DNC IP address that the FBI claimed had been hijacked and was being used by the Russians. However, the FBI's internal deliberations took so long that the Russians had already switched to using another one by the time Agent Hawkins told Tamene to look into the IP address. In December, Agent Hawkins personally traveled the few short blocks between the FBI and DNC respective headquarters, but Tamene wasn't there, so he left a message with a lobby security guard for Tamene to call the FBI. It wasn't until February of 2016, seven months after their initial contact, that Agent Hawkins met with Tamene and two of his DNC colleagues at a restaurant called Joe's Cafe in Sterling, VA.

Tamene realized that Agent Hawkins was indeed a Special Agent with the FBI. Internal DNC documents reveal that Tamene had been unsure whether the calls from Agent Hawkins were legitimate or pranks.[57] While the failure of the FBI and DNC to effectively communicate provided the SVR with months of unfettered access to the DNC's internal servers, this set of hackers appeared to be engaging in traditional espionage. The DNC and FBI were even less prepared for the GRU hackers, who would not only steal information for intelligence purposes but planned to use it in an attempt to sway the American election.

A Tale of Two Campaigns:
The Clinton Email Scandal and Trump's Praise of Putin

Hillary Clinton announced her candidacy on April 12th, 2015. Her bid for the nation's highest office was widely expected by friend and foe alike. As far back as early 2014, Congressional Republicans were preparing an all-out assault on the former First Lady. In a meeting with Roger Ailes, then Republican Speaker of the House John Boehner told the head of *Fox News* that he was shortly going to launch a Congressional Select Committee to investigate the Secretary of State's actions during an attack against an American diplomatic compound in Benghazi, Libya that left four people, including a US Ambassador, dead.

The House Select Committee looking into the Benghazi attacks was established in May 2014 and was led by Republican Congressman Trey Gowdy. It was the sixth House committee to look into the attacks. The Senate Select Committee on Intelligence had identified several mistakes and failures with the American response but pointed out that "there were no efforts by the White House or any other Executive Branch entities to 'cover-up' facts or make alterations for political purposes."[58] Echoing this, the House Intelligence Committee also found that the Obama administration was not guilty of deliberate wrongdoing.[59]

Unmoved by these findings, Gowdy's Committee requested Clinton's emails during her tenure as Secretary of State from the State Department. State Department lawyers discovered that Hillary hadn't been using government servers but instead sent and checked emails from a personal BlackBerry device linked to a private email server in Clinton's home in Chappaqua, NY.[60] The State Department contacted Clinton and other living former Secretaries to request the return of all relevant correspondence. Hillary Clinton's chief of staff, Cheryl Mills, and two lawyers ultimately looked through over sixty thousand emails. Of those, roughly thirty thousand were delivered to the State Department in 12 boxes.[61]

Mills and Clinton's lawyers determined that the other 32,000 emails were unrelated to her work as Secretary of State. In December 2014, Mills instructed a technician working with Platte River Networks, the IT-Support company used by Clinton, to change the email retention policy on Clinton's server to delete emails after 60 days. However, the technician mistakenly failed to make the change. Clinton's use of a private email server became public knowledge on March 2nd, 2015 when *The New York Times* broke the story.[62] Two days later, Gowdy's Special Committee on Benghazi issued a subpoena for Benghazi-related emails. A week after that, Cheryl Mills informed the Platte River Network technician about the request to retain. The technician later told the FBI that sometime between March 25th and 30th, he experienced an "oh shit moment" upon remembering that he had failed to carry out Mills' earlier request to set the personal emails to be deleted after sixty days. Following his realization, the technician used a free utility called BleachBit to delete the emails.[63] This act, which would be misrepresented as "bleaching" or "acid washing" the server, served as the predicate for countless unsubstantiated accusations and conspiracy theories.

The Clinton email scandal, which plagued her campaign throughout the 2016 election, dovetailed with the Russian interference campaign. Congressional Republicans were candid about the goal of their investigations, which was to hobble Clinton politically. "Everybody thought Hillary Clinton was unbeatable, right?" Republican Congressman Mark Meadows told *Fox News* host Sean Hannity. "But we put together a Benghazi Special Committee, a select committee. What are her numbers today? Her numbers are dropping."[64]

Another email-related issue was whether Clinton had sent classified material over her personal email server, which would have violated federal law. On July 6th, 2015, the intelligence agency inspector general Charles McCullough III referred the matter to the FBI. On July 10th, the FBI opened an investigation into the Clinton email matter codenamed "Midyear Exam."[65] The FBI's Clinton email investigation and the behavior of FBI Director James Comey would also amplify the impact of the impending Russian operations.

Hillary Clinton entered the 2016 Presidential race not simply as the presumptive Democratic primary frontrunner, though the Democratic Socialist Senator from Vermont Bernie Sanders would seriously test that proposition, but also as the odds-on favorite to succeed Barack Obama in the Oval Office. When Donald Trump descended the escalator in Trump Tower to announce his candidacy, it was seen in a very different light. While Trump was lavished with the kind of frenzied media attention he had courted since the mid-1970s, most serious observers scoffed at the real estate developer's chances and even questioned whether the entire exercise was anything more than a publicity stunt.

The American political class failed to appreciate the potential power of a Trump candidacy. When he launched his campaign on June 16th, 2016, most political observers perceived Trump's crude racial appeals and controversial antics as disqualifying scandals. They were effective appeals to the Republican base. Trump's weaponization of racial resentment was not new to Republican politics. Political strategists in the Nixon White House articulated what became known as the Southern Strategy, which used African American support for Democrats to stoke the resentment of White voters and drive them toward the Republicans.[66] John McCain's selection of Alaska Governor Sarah Palin as his running mate in 2008, who became a darling of the Republican base, further primed Republican voters for outsider candidates and stoked resentments against the so-called "elite." The emergence of the Tea Party during Obama's first term further paved the way in the Republican electorate for an exotic, outsider candidate. Perhaps most importantly, the American media provided Trump with billions of dollars worth of free media attention.[67]

The Trump candidacy was the logical conclusion of forces that have shaped the Republican Party for decades. However, one critical exception marked him apart from all who came before. Donald Trump's repeated, effusive, and public praise of Vladimir Putin is unique in the history of American presidential politics. In particular, his repeated positive references to the Russian strongman initially seemed bizarre for the would-be standard bearer of a party that had been defined since the 1980s by the legendary Cold Warrior Ronald Reagan.

Trump repeatedly and publicly praised Putin in the lead-up to the 2013 Miss Universe Pageant held in Moscow. This continued into the presidential campaign. Trump paired his praise for Putin with attacks on Obama. On March 21st, 2014, in the aftermath of the Maidan Revolution in Ukraine. Trump tweeted, "I believe Putin will continue to rebuild the Russian Empire. He has zero respect for Obama or the US!" A few weeks later, Trump praised Putin's illegal annexation of Crimea. "Well, he's done an amazing job of taking the mantle," Trump said of Putin during an interview with *Fox Business News*. "And he's taken it away from the President, and you look at what he's doing. And so smart. When you see the riots in a country because they're hurting the Russians, OK, 'We'll go and take it over.' And he really goes step by step, and you have to give him a lot of credit."[68]

"I was over in Moscow two years ago, and I will tell you – you can get along with those people and get along with them well," Trump told *Fox News* host Bill O'Reilly on June 16th, 2015, the day he announced his presidential bid. "You can make deals with those people. Obama can't." Trump's public outreach to Putin continued into the Presidential election. In early July, he told CNN's Anderson Cooper that if he were President, Putin would return the fugitive NSA whistleblower Edward Snowden to the US. "I think I get along with him fine," Trump said of Putin. "I think he would be absolutely fine. He would never keep somebody like Snowden in Russia. He hates Obama. He doesn't respect Obama. Obama doesn't like him either. But he has no respect for Obama. Has a hatred for Obama. And Snowden is living the life. Look if that -- if I'm president, Putin says, hey, boom, you're gone. I guarantee you this."

While Trump lavished praise on Putin throughout the early stages of his campaign, unbeknownst to the American public, Michael Cohen and Felix Sater were negotiating a deal to build a Trump Tower in Moscow. On October 28th, 2015, Trump signed a letter of intent for the project. Thus, his pro-Putin commentary in this period must be seen in the light of a potentially highly lucrative business deal. Trump's praise of Putin was not only a one-way street. On December 17th, 2015, Putin told *ABC News* that Trump was "a very colorful person. Talent, without any doubt." Putin continued, "[H]e is absolutely the leader in the Presidential race. He wants to move to a different level of relations, to more solid, deeper relations with Russia, and how can Russia not welcome that – we welcome that."[69]

"[I]t is always a great honor to be so nicely complimented by a man so highly respected within his own country and beyond," Trump replied to *ABC News*. Two days later, while on the program *Morning Joe*, Trump defended Putin against accusations that he was behind the deaths of opposition reporters. "He's running his country, and at least he's a leader, unlike what we have in this country," Trump told Joe Scarborough. Trump insisted on equating the United States with Russia, "I think our country does plenty of killing also, Joe, so you know. There's a lot of stupidity going on in the world right now, a lot of killing going on, a lot of stupidity."

On February 2nd, 2016, a day after the Republican Primary season began, the Russian neo-fascist Alexandre Dugin wrote a screed online praising Trump. In it, he describes Trump as "tough, rough, says what he thinks, rude, emotional and, apparently, candid." While Dugin didn't think that Trump had a chance to win the election, "as the globalist elites and financial oligarchy control practically everything in the USA," he did mention that Russia wanted "to put trust in Donald Trump." The article ended with Dugin admonishing Americans to "Vote for Trump, and see what will happen."[70]

From Espionage to Active Measures:
Russian Military Intelligence Enters the Fray

On March 10th, 2016, the GRU commenced its cyber assault on the Democratic Party, the Clinton campaign, and American democracy. Under the command of Viktor Netyksho, Unit 26165 was primarily responsible for infiltrating the DNC, the Democratic Congressional Campaign Committee (DCCC), and the personal email accounts of high-level Clinton campaign staffers. However, they would later receive valuable assistance from Unit 74455. Both units were divided into specialized departments, with some focused on developing various kinds of malware while others conducted spear phishing campaigns that gained access to their adversaries.[71] The department responsible for spear phishing and other computer intrusion activities was led by Boris Alekseyevich Antonov, "Head of Department." His "Assistant Head of Department" was the aforementioned Dmitriy Badin, who, in May of 2015, led the successful cyber intrusion into the German Bundestag. Two other GRU officers operating within Antonov's department who would play a major role in the hack were 25-year-old Senior Lieutenant Aleksey Viktorovich Lukashev and 29-year-old Ivan Sergeyevich Yermakov.[72]

Lukashev's specialty was creating emails that resembled official Google security warnings, fooling recipients into giving away their passwords and security information.[73] Starting on March 10th, up to fifty spear phishing emails were sent daily to individuals affiliated with Clinton's current and earlier campaign efforts. One of the first people targeted was a low-level organizer from Clinton's 2008 campaign in Texas.[74] While obsolete email addresses and Clinton campaign cybersecurity procedures initially frustrated the GRU hackers, they persisted.

By March 19th, Lukashev's spear phishing tactics changed, and instead of targeting official campaign email addresses, he focused on breaking into the personal Google email accounts of senior Clinton staffers. Individuals targeted included campaign manager Robby Mook, senior advisor Jake Sullivan, political consultant Philippe Reines, and campaign chairman John Podesta. At 11:28 am Moscow time on the 19th, Lukashev and his team generated a malicious link and embedded it in an email made to look like a Google security alert that was sent to Podesta six minutes later. Upon receipt, Podesta's staff forwarded the mysterious email to the campaign IT help desk. Clinton's IT security responded within minutes, recognizing the threat and suggesting that Podesta change passwords and activate additional security protocols. However, in a critical communication failure, Podesta's staff misinterpreted the advice and clicked the link in the email, springing Lukashev's trap. The staffers entered the new password after being directed to a GRU website designed to look like an official Google page. Russian military intelligence gained access to Podesta's private correspondence. Two days later, Lukashev exfiltrated five gigabytes of data, over 50,000 emails, from Podesta's inbox.

In the following days, numerous other Clinton Campaign staffers were targeted, including communications director

Jennifer Palmieri and Clinton's close aide Huma Abedin.[75] By April 6th, Lukashev created an email address posing as a well-known member of the Clinton campaign by changing the spelling of their name by a single letter and sent spear-phishing emails from the account to over 30 campaign employees. He got an employee of the DCCC to open a document labeled "hillary-clinton-favorable-rating.xlsx," which directed them to a GRU-created website.[76] At that point, Lukashev's colleague Ivan Yermakov began scanning the DCCC's network connections to identify ways to break in.

Six days later, on April 12th, the GRU gained access to the DCCC computer network and installed a customized malware known as X-Agent on at least ten DCCC computers. This X-Agent malware had been developed and customized. It was monitored by 26-year-old Lieutenant Captain Nikolay Yuryevich Kozachek, who worked in Unit 26165's department responsible for developing malware under the command of Lieutenant Colonel Sergey Aleksandrovich Morgachev.[77] X-Agent allowed the GRU hackers to monitor and record all the activities of the infected computers as well as steal passwords. On April 15th, GRU hackers logged onto a DCCC computer and searched the keywords "Hillary," "Cruz," and "Trump" in an attempt to locate the Democrat's opposition research into Trump.

While up to this point, the GRU appeared to be pursuing the kind of digital espionage similar to what their counterparts at the SVR were doing, the first evidence that something very different was afoot emerged on April 12th, the day they gained access to the DCCC network. That day, the GRU paid $37 worth of Bitcoin to a Romanian web hosting company to register the domain name ElectionLeaks.com. While the site never became operational, it is the first evidence that instead of a traditional espionage operation, the GRU was planning to weaponize the information it had stolen to exert an influence on the outcome of the 2016 election.

On April 18th, Lukashev stole the credentials of a DCCC employee with access to the DNC's network. Once inside, the GRU installed X-Agent malware on thirty-three DNC computers. The hackers proceeded to exfiltrate large quantities of data from the DCCC and the DNC using malware called X-Tunnel, which moved documents through encrypted channels. Among the documents stolen by the GRU from the DNC network on April

22nd was the Democrats' opposition research into Trump. Three days later, they stole over 70 gigabytes of data from a single DCCC file server.[78] The GRU hackers even managed to compromise the DNC's telephone system, which enabled them to listen into phone calls and voicemails during a heated primary battle between Hillary Clinton and her progressive challenger, Bernie Sanders. The GRU continued stealing data from Democratic networks until at least May 25th.[79]

On April 19th, a day after the breach of the DNC, Unit 26165 paid in Bitcoin to register DCLeaks.com using the same Romanian web hosting company they had used for ElectionLeaks.com. Throughout May, the GRU worked to ready DCLeaks.com for public consumption. The first tranche of stolen files uploaded to the site before it went live were emails stolen from the former supreme commander of NATO forces, Philip Breedlove, a year earlier. The site went public on June 8th and eventually published thousands of documents stolen from the personal email accounts of individuals affiliated with the Clinton Campaign.

At some point during this timeframe, the GRU's Unit 26165 passed along the contents of John Podesta's email inbox to hackers in Unit 74455, known to cybersecurity experts as "Sandworm," which was commanded by Colonel Aleksandr Vladimirovich Osadchuk.[80] After publishing the DCLeaks.com site, officers from Unit 74455 attempted to make the site appear to be the product of "American Hacktivists." They created a DCLeaks Facebook page and Twitter handle, @dcleaks_, then utilized an array of fake social media avatars to promote the website, much like they had attempted to do in earlier Ukrainian operations. Despite these efforts, the GRU initially failed to attract much attention to the site.

Warning signs began to appear in March that the Democratic Party and the Clinton campaign were the targets of a sophisticated foreign cyber assault. FBI Special Agent Lafayette Garrett emailed the DNC's IT team twice over the month, informing them that DNC staffers had been the targets of spear phishing emails.[81] By late March, FBI agents met with Clinton Campaign lawyer Marc Elias and senior staffers at her campaign headquarters in Brooklyn to warn them that foreign hackers were targeting them with spear phishing emails.[82]

In April, FBI Special Agent Adrian Hawkins again

contacted Yared Tamene and requested computer logs that would assist the FBI in identifying the IP addresses being used to penetrate the DNC's network. Hawkins was contacted by Michael Sussman, a cybersecurity expert and lawyer with the firm Perkins Coie, who represented the DNC. Sussman recommended to DNC higher-ups that they cooperate with the FBI.[83] However, by this point, the GRU was so deeply embedded and had exfiltrated so much data that the damage was done.

On April 20th, DNC Consultant Alexandra Chalupa received a warning from Yahoo that her account was the target of state-sponsored hackers. She took a screenshot of the warning and shared it with her colleagues. Eight days later, DNC IT staff discovered that unauthorized users had compromised their network.[84] At around 4 pm on April 28th, DNC Executive Director Amy Dacey was informed that the DNC's network had been compromised. Dacey contacted Michael Sussmann, who proceeded to enlist the services of CrowdStrike, an elite cyber security firm based out of Silicon Valley. As they didn't want to alert the hackers that they were on to them, the compromise of the DNC's network was kept secret.[85]

On Friday, May 6th, CrowdStrike installed advanced threat detection software onto the DNC network and, within two hours, discovered the existence of two "sophisticated adversaries" lurking within. CrowdStrike would later report that they found no evidence that either foreign actor was aware of the presence of the other as there didn't appear to be any evidence of coordination between the two.[86] What followed was a cat-and-mouse game between CrowdStrike, attempting to remove the intruders, and the GRU, trying to cover its tracks and maintain a hidden presence on the DNC's network.

To be confident that they had removed the hackers from the DNC's network, CrowdStrike proposed a solution requiring the DNC to shut their entire system down and suggested May 20th to carry this out. However, the DNC didn't want to disrupt its system before a candidate secured the nomination. Even though Clinton was leading, her progressive opponent, Bernie Sanders, was a viable challenger at the time. Furthermore, the Democrats were operating under the assumption that the state-sponsored hackers they faced were engaged in traditional espionage activities, not suspecting that the Russians intended to weaponize the stolen data. As a result, they delayed the systems shutdown for weeks, waiting until June. Meanwhile, as the cyber intrusion was being kept secret from most DNC staffers, they continued to behave as if their internal communications and activities were secure.

Meanwhile, GRU hackers reacted to events as they unfolded. On May 31st, Yermakov conducted an open-source investigation into CrowdStrike and attempted to determine how much the cyber security firm knew about the GRU malware programs X-Agent and X-Tunnel. The next day, the GRU used the computer program CCleaner to delete evidence of their presence on the DCCC's server. To an extent, they succeeded. A Linux version of the X-Agent malware remained on the DNC's network until October.[87] Finally, on June 10th, after weeks of prevaricating, the DNC shut down its server. During a meeting with 100 staffers, DNC Chief Operating Officer Lindsey Reynold instructed everyone to hand over their laptops and mobile devices and maintain absolute secrecy.[88] Two days later, after a marathon work session by CrowdStrike, the DNC's system was up and running again.

[1] Harding, Luke; Borger, Julian; Sabbagh, Dan. "Kremlin papers appear to show Putin's plot to put Trump in White House," *The Guardian.* July 15th, 2021
[2] "Soviet Active Measures in the Post-Cold War Era 1988-1991," *A Report Prepared at the Request of the United States House of Representatives Committee on Appropriations by the United States Information Agency,* June 1992
[3] GEN (Ret) Alexander, Keith B. "Disinformation: A Primer in Russian Active Measures and Influence Campaigns," *Prepared Statement Before the United States Senate Select Committee on Intelligence.* March 30th, 2017
[4] Pacepa, Ion Mihai; Rychlak, Ronald J. *Disinformation: Former Spy Chief Reveals Secret Strategies for Undermining Freedom, Attacking Religion, and Promoting Terrorism.* WND Books. Pg. 4-6
[5] Rid, Thomas. *Active Measures: The Secret History of Disinformation and Political Warfare.* New York, NY: Farrar, Straus and Giroux, 2020. Pg. 5
[6] Greenberg, Andy. *Sandworm: A New Era Of Cyberwar And The Hunt For The Kremlin's Most Dangerous Hackers.* New York, NY: Doubleday, 2019. Pg. 74-76
[7] "INTERNET GROWTH STATISTICS," *Internet World Stats: Usage and Population Statistics*
[8] McCauley, Kevin N. *Russian Influence Campaigns Against the West: From the Cold War to Putin.* North Charleston, SC: Createspace Independent Publishing Platform, 2016. Pg. 384
[9] Traynor, Ian. "Russia accused of unleashing cyberwar to disable Estonia," *The Guardian.* May 16th, 2007
[10] Greenberg, Andy. *Sandworm: A New Era Of Cyberwar And The Hunt For The Kremlin's Most Dangerous Hackers.* New York, NY: Doubleday, 2019. Pg. 83
[11] Rid, Thomas. *Active Measures: The Secret History of Disinformation and Political Warfare.* New York, NY: Farrar, Straus and Giroux, 2020. Pg. 334
[12] Lee Myers, Steven. "Cyberattack on Estonia stirs fear of "virtual war," *The New York Times.* May 18th, 2007
[13] McCauley, Kevin N. *Russian Influence Campaigns Against the West: From the Cold War to*

Putin. North Charleston, SC: Createspace Independent Publishing Platform, 2016. Pg. 386

[14] Markoff, John. "Before the Gunfire, Cyberattacks," *The New York Times*. August 12th, 2008

[15] Troianovsky, Anton; Nakashima, Ellen. "How Russia's military intelligence agency became the covert muscle in Putin's duels with the West," *The Washington Post*. December 28th, 2018

[16] Greenberg, Andy. *Sandworm: A New Era Of Cyberwar And The Hunt For The Kremlin's Most Dangerous Hackers*. New York, NY: Doubleday, 2019. Pg. 236

[17] Galeotti, Mark. "We Don't Know What To Call Russian Military Intelligence And That Might Be A Problem," *War on the Rocks*. January 19th, 2016

[18] Troianovsky, Anton; Nakashima, Ellen. "How Russia's military intelligence agency became the covert muscle in Putin's duels with the West," *The Washington Post*. December 28th, 2018

[19] Gerasimov, Valery. "The Value of Science in Prediction," *Military Industrial Kurier*. February 27th, 2013

[20] Galeotti, Mark. "I'm Sorry for Creating the 'Gerasimov Doctrine,'" *Foreign Policy*. March 5th, 2018

[21] Rid, Thomas. *Active Measures: The Secret History of Disinformation and Political Warfare*. New York, NY: Farrar, Straus and Giroux, 2020. Pg. 351-353

[22] Lamoth, Dan. "U.S. joins other nations in accusing Russia of Cyber Attack in Republic of Georgia," *The Washington Post*. February 20th, 2020

[23] Rid, Thomas. *Active Measures: The Secret History of Disinformation and Political Warfare*. New York, NY: Farrar, Straus and Giroux, 2020. Pg. 354-358

[24] "NATO websites targeted in attack claimed by Ukrainian hacker group Cyber Berkut," ABC News. March 15th, 2014

[25] "Reckless campaign of cyber attacks by Russian military intelligence service exposed," *National Cyber Security Centre*. October 3rd, 2018

[26] Rid, Thomas. *Active Measures: The Secret History of Disinformation and Political Warfare*. New York, NY: Farrar, Straus and Giroux, 2020. Pg. 360

[27] Greenberg, Andy. *Sandworm: A New Era Of Cyberwar And The Hunt For The Kremlin's Most Dangerous Hackers*. New York, NY: Doubleday, 2019. Pg. 46-47

[28] Zetter, Kim. "Inside the Cunning, Unprecedented Hack of Ukraine's Power Grid," *Wired*. March 3rd, 2016

[29] Finkle, Jim. "U.S. firm blames Russian 'Sandworm' hackers for Ukraine outage," *Reuters*. January 7th, 2016

[30] United States of America vs. Aleksei Sergeyevich Morenets, et al, Indictment. United States District Court of Pennsylvania. Criminal No. 18-263. October 3rd, 2018

[31] Rid, Thomas. *Active Measures: The Secret History of Disinformation and Political Warfare*. New York, NY: Farrar, Straus and Giroux, 2020. Pg. 366

[32] Javers, Eamon. "These Cyberhackers May Not Be Backed By ISIS," *CNBC*. July 14th, 2015

[33] Fung, Brian; Peterson, Andrea. "The Centcom 'hack' that wasn't," *The Washington Post*. January 12th, 2015

[34] Agence France-Presse. "Malaysia Airlines website hacked by 'Lizard Squad,'" *The Guardian*. January 26th, 2015

[35] "Operation Pawn Storm Ramps Up It's Activities; Targets NATO, White House," *Trend Micro*. April 16th, 2015

[36] Crook, Jordan. "Hacked Newsweek Twitter Account Tweets Threats At Obama Family," *TechCrunch*. February 10th, 2015

[37] Rid, Thomas. *Active Measures: The Secret History of Disinformation and Political Warfare*. New York, NY: Farrar, Straus and Giroux, 2020. Pg. 368

[38] Troianovsky, Anton; Nakashima, Ellen. "How Russia's military intelligence agency became the covert muscle in Putin's duels with the West," *The Washington Post*.

December 28th, 2018

[39] Satter, Raphael; Donn, Jeff; Vasilyeva, Nataliya. "Russian hackers hunted journalists in years-long campaign," *The Associated Press*. December 22nd, 2017

[40] Menn, Joseph; Thomas, Leigh. "France probes Russian lead in TV5Monde hacking: sources," *Reuters*. June 10th, 2015

[41] Rid, Thomas. *Active Measures: The Secret History of Disinformation and Political Warfare*. New York, NY: Farrar, Straus and Giroux, 2020. Pg. 371

[42] Bond, David. "GRU took 'complete control' over UK-based TV station in 2015," *The Financial Times*. October 5th, 2018

[43] Grozev, Christo. "Who Is Dmitry Badin, The GRU Hacker Indicted By Germany Over The Bundestag Hacks?" *Bellingcat*. May 5th, 2020

[44] Bennihold, Katrin. "Merkel Is "Outraged" by Russian Hack but Struggling to Respond," *The New York Times*. May 13th, 2020

[45] Lipton, Eric; Sanger, David E.; Shane, Scott. "The Perfect Weapon: How Russian Cyberpower Invaded the US," *The New York Times*. December 13th, 2016

[46] Isikoff, Michael. "Chinese hacked Obama, McCain campaigns, took internal documents, officials say," *NBC News*. June 10th, 2013

[47] Rid, Thomas. *Active Measures: The Secret History of Disinformation and Political Warfare*. New York, NY: Farrar, Straus and Giroux, 2020. Pg. 385

[48] Shane, Scott; Savage, Charlie. "In Ordinary Lives, U.S. Sees the Work of Russian Agents," *The New York Times*. June 28th, 2010

[49] Patterson, Thom. "The Russian spies living next door," *CNN*. July 19th, 2017

[50] Solomon, John; Spann, Alison. "FBI watched, then acted as Russian spy moved closer to Hillary Clinton," *The Hill*. October 22nd, 2017

[51] Smith, Ben. "Clinton friend was spy's target," *Politico*. June 29th, 2010

[52] Ikeda, Scott. "Cozy bear is back in the spotlight; Notorious Russian hackers caught spying on EU and Eastern European Nations," *CPO Magazine*. October 25th, 2019

[53] Modderkolk, Huib. "Dutch agencies provide crucial intel about Russia's interference in US elections," *de Volkskrant*. January 25th, 2018

[54] Schmidt, Michael S.; Sanger, David E. "Russian Hackers Read Obama's Unclassified Emails, Officials Say," *The New York Times*. April 25th, 2015

[55] Bennetts, Marc. "Cozy Bear hackers linked to Kremlin blamed for decade of cyber-espionage," *The Times of London*. July 16th, 2020

[56] Miller, Greg. *The Apprentice: Trump, Russia and the Subversion of American Democracy*. New York, NY: Custom House, 2018. Pg. 21-22

[57] Lipton, Eric; Sanger, David E.; Shane, Scott. "The Perfect Weapon: How Russian Cyberpower Invaded the US," *The New York Times*. December 13th, 2016

[58] US Senate Select Committee on Intelligence. *REVIEW of THE TERRORIST ATTACKS ON U.S. FACILITIES IN BENGHAZI, LIBYA, SEPTEMBER 11-12, 2012*, January 15th, 2014

[59] Lochhead, Carolyn. "House panel: no administration wrongdoing in Benghazi attack," *The San Francisco Chronicle*. August 1st, 2014

[60] O'Harrow Jr, Robert. "How Clinton's email scandal took root," *The Washington Post*. March 27th, 2016

[61] Stewart, James B. *Deep State: Trump, The FBI, And The Rule of Law*. New York, NY: Penguin Press, 2019. Pg. 34

[62] Schmidt, Michael S. "Hillary Clinton Used Personal Email Account at State Dept., Possibly Breaking Rules," *The New York Times*. March 2nd, 2015

[63] Kiely, Eugene. "The FBI Files on Clinton's Emails," *FactCheck.org*. September 7th, 2016

[64] Bade, Rachel. "McCarthy's Benghazi gift to team Hillary," *Politico*. October 1st, 2015

[65] Stewart, James B. *Deep State: Trump, The FBI, And The Rule of Law*. New York, NY: Penguin Press, 2019. Pg. 38

[66] Boyd, James. "Nixon's Southern strategy 'It's all in the charts,'" *The New York Times*.

May 17th, 1970

[67] Confessore, Nicholas; Yourish, Karen. "$2 Billion Worth of Free Media for Trump," *The New York Times*. March 15th, 2016

[68] Kaczynsky, Andrew; Massie, Chris; McDermott, Nathan. "80 Times Trump talked about Putin," *CNN*

[69] Santucci, John. "Trump Says 'Great Honor' to Get Compliments From 'Highly Respected' Putin," *ABC News*. December 17th, 2015

[70] Dugin, Alexandre. "Russian Geopolitican: Trump Is Real America," *KATEHON*. February 2nd, 2016

[71] Mueller, III, Robert S. *Report On The Investigation Into Russian Interference In The 2016 Presidential Election*. Department of Justice, Washington, DC. March 2019. Pg. 36

[72] USA v. Netyksho, et al. Indictment. United States District Court for the District of Columbia. July 13th, 2018

[73] Rid, Thomas. *Active Measures: The Secret History of Disinformation and Political Warfare*. New York, NY: Farrar, Straus and Giroux, 2020. Pg. 378

[74] Satter, Raphael. "Inside story: How Russians hacked the Democrats' emails," *The Associated Press*. November 4th, 2017

[75] Satter, Raphael. "Inside story: How Russians hacked the Democrats' emails," *The Associated Press*. November 4th, 2017

[76] USA v. Netyksho, et al. Indictment. United States District Court for the District of Columbia. July 13th, 2018. Pg. 7

[77] USA v. Netyksho, et al. Indictment. United States District Court for the District of Columbia. July 13th, 2018. Pg. 4

[78] Mueller, III, Robert S. *Report On The Investigation Into Russian Interference In The 2016 Presidential Election*. Department of Justice, Washington, DC. March 2019. Pg. 40

[79] Rid, Thomas. *Active Measures: The Secret History of Disinformation and Political Warfare*. New York, NY: Farrar, Straus and Giroux, 2020. Pg. 383-384

[80] USA v. Netyksho, et al. Indictment. United States District Court for the District of Columbia. July 13th, 2018. Pg. 5

[81] Miller, Greg. *The Apprentice: Trump, Russia and the Subversion of American Democracy*. New York, NY: Custom House, 2018. Pg. 23

[82] Clinton, Hillary. *What Happened*. New York, NY: Simon & Schuster, Inc. 2017. Pg. 337

[83] Miller, Greg. *The Apprentice: Trump, Russia and the Subversion of American Democracy*. New York, NY: Custom House, 2018. Pg. 23

[84] Rid, Thomas. *Active Measures: The Secret History of Disinformation and Political Warfare*. New York, NY: Farrar, Straus and Giroux, 2020. Pg. 384

[85] Miller, Greg. *The Apprentice: Trump, Russia and the Subversion of American Democracy*. New York, NY: Custom House, 2018. Pg. 43-44

[86] Rid, Thomas. *Active Measures: The Secret History of Disinformation and Political Warfare*. New York, NY: Farrar, Straus and Giroux, 2020. Pg. 385

[87] USA v. Netyksho, et al. Indictment. United States District Court for the District of Columbia. July 13th, 2018. Pg. 12

[88] Satter, Raphael. "Inside story: How Russians hacked the Democrats' emails," *The Associated Press*. November 4th, 2017

Chapter 10:
WikiLeaks, Weaponized Emails,
And the Mad Dash to Election Day

WikiLeaks, Guccifer 2.0, and the Amplification of the Russian Campaign

On the day the DNC network was brought back online, the infamous Australian hacktivist and founder of the anti-secrecy organization WikiLeaks, Julian Assange, injected himself into events in dramatic fashion. Assange was interviewed by the British television station *ITV* from within his sanctuary in the Ecuadorian Embassy in London, where he had been hiding from Western law enforcement since late 2010. "We have upcoming leaks in relation to Hillary Clinton, which are great," Assange claimed, continuing, "WikiLeaks has a very big year ahead."[1]

Assange has described WikiLeaks as "an uncensorable system for untraceable mass document leaking and public analysis," maintained by servers located across the world and hundreds of domain names and mirror sites which make it nearly impossible for its content to be removed from the internet.[2] In Assange's view, governments, institutions and political parties that support "authoritarianism" are "conspiracies" that rely upon secrecy, therefore the revelation of these secrets is a direct assault on these so-called conspiracies. "Consider what would happen," Assange wrote in a 2006 essay entitled *Conspiracy as Governance*, "if one of these parties gave up their mobile phones, fax, and email correspondence—let alone the computer systems which manage their [subscribers], donors, budgets, polling, call centers, and direct mail campaigns. They would immediately fall into an organizational stupor..."[3]

Despite his anarcho-idealist rhetoric, numerous analysts and commentators have noted that Assange's activities through WikiLeaks have disproportionately targeted the United States in ways that have often redounded to the benefit of its authoritarian adversaries, in particular Russia.[4] In November 2010, WikiLeaks released a trove of over 800,000 US State Department cables. Under Assange's direction, WikiLeaks provided the Russian national Israel Shamir with a large cache of cables that contained unredacted information about political dissidents in the Kremlin-backed dictatorship of Belarus. Weeks later, Shamir was seen leaving the Belarusian interior ministry, and shortly after that, the country's authoritarian leader, Aleksandr Lukashenko, ordered a crackdown on his political opponents. The episode was disturbing enough that several formerly sympathetic WikiLeaks activists cut ties with the organization.[5]

In December 2010, Assange was arrested in Britain to face questioning by Swedish law enforcement regarding a rape claim. Assange posted bail and fled to the security of the Ecuadorian Embassy. Shortly after that, Vladimir Putin himself offered words of encouragement to Assange. The day after his arrest, Putin dismissed criticisms of Russia by calling out what he perceived as Western and particularly American hypocrisy. "As far as Democracy goes, it should be a complete democracy. Why, then, did they put Mr. Assange behind bars?" Putin continued, "There is an American saying: He who lives in a glass house shouldn't throw stones."[6]

In January 2011, Russia issued Assange a visa. A year later, the Russian state-backed *RT* gave Assange his own talk show entitled "The World Tomorrow." Assange's first guest was the leader of Hezbollah.[7] In 2013, WikiLeaks played a central role in arranging for NSA whistleblower and leaker Edward Snowden to receive asylum in Moscow. At Assange's suggestion, Snowden traveled to the Russian capital accompanied by the WikiLeaks activist Sarah Harrison.

Before his bombshell announcement regarding the 2016 American election, Assange offered rhetorical support to Putin. Ironically, he did so by criticizing the Panama Papers, a vast leak of documents that revealed the financial schemes of powerful people worldwide, including Putin. Following the release, WikiLeaks tweeted that it was a "Putin attack [that] was produced by OCCRP, which targets Russia & former USSR and was funded by USAID & Soros." The *Organized Crime and Corruption Reporting Project* is a nonprofit funded in part by USAID and the US State Department.

In addition to Assange's suspicious relationship with Putin's Russia, his disdain for Hillary Clinton has been well documented. In November of 2015, Assange wrote to other members of WikiLeaks in a Twitter Group Chat that "[w]e believe that it would be much better for GOP to win... Dems+Media+Liberals woudl [sic] then form a block to reign [sic] in their worst qualities... With Hillary in charge, GOP will be pushing for her worst qualities., dems+media+neoliberals will be mute... She's a bright, well connected, sadistic sociopath."[8]

Shortly after Assange promised to release Hillary-related leaks, the DNC decided to publicize the fact that they had been the victim of a Russian state hacking operation. On June 8th, Michael Sussman and several DNC officials met with *Washington Post* reporter Ellen Nakashima. They provided her information on the hack with the understanding that she would withhold publication until the DNC secured its system.[9] On June 14th, the *Washington Post* published the article, "Russian government hackers penetrated DNC, stole opposition research on Trump."[10] CrowdStrike further published technical details of the Russian operation.

The day the *Post* article went live, a GRU-controlled Twitter account, @dcleaks_, sent WikiLeaks a direct message (DM). "You announced your organization was preparing to publish more [sic] Hillary's emails," referring to Assange's television interview. "We are ready to support you. We have some sensitive information too, in particular her financial documents. Let's do it together. What do you think about publishing our info at the same moment?" The GRU concluded that DCLeaks.com was failing to arouse adequate attention. While there is no evidence Assange responded to this initial outreach, Johns Hopkins Professor Thomas Rid has written that the GRU likely passed the contents of John Podesta's inbox to WikiLeaks anonymously sometime before June 12th.[11] To this day, there remains no official account of how WikiLeaks came into possession of John Podesta's emails.

A day after the *Post's* story, officers from Unit 74455 attempted to discredit it by creating an online persona named Guccifer 2.0 and publishing a WordPress blog that claimed the

DNC had been "hacked by a lone hacker." Guccifer was a portmanteau of "Gucci" and "Lucifer," previously used by Marcel Lazăr Lehel, a Romanian hacker who had pled guilty to computer crimes in May 2016. Lehel also made the unsubstantiated claim to *NBC News* that he had gained access to Clinton's server.[12] He made this claim during a time of feverish speculation and a well-known FBI criminal inquiry into Clinton's use of the server. The GRU's Guccifer 2.0 leaked several items that had been stolen from John Podesta's inbox on its WordPress page, including Democratic opposition research into Trump. Hours before it was published, officers from Unit 74455 had logged into their Moscow-based server and searched for several specific keywords that were included in the language of the post, including "some hundred sheets," "illuminati," and "worldwide known."[13]

The GRU utilized an old Soviet trick, modifying four of the five documents by adding a fake watermark across the pages reading "CONFIDENTIAL" to make them seem more important. However, in doing so, they made an error that assisted online sleuths and subsequent investigators in attributing the leak to Russia. The GRU officer who edited the documents neglected to wipe his metadata left after editing the documents, and it was discovered that the username of the machine behind the edit, written in Russian Cyrillic, was "Feliks Edmundovich," the nickname for the infamous founder of the Soviet Cheka, Feliks Dzerzhinsky.[14]

Before ending the post with, "Fuck the Illuminati and their conspiracies!!!!!!!!! Fuck CrowdStrike!!!!!!!!!," Guccifer 2.0 claimed to have sent "thousands of files and mails" to WikiLeaks. In reality, the GRU had yet to transfer all of its stolen files to WikiLeaks. The GRU may have been using the Guccifer 2.0 persona to signal its intentions to Julian Assange that they wanted to send him files for WikiLeaks to publish. WikiLeaks acknowledged Guccifer 2.0's post, writing in a June 15th tweet, "DNC 'hacker' released 200+ page internal report on Trump, says gave WikiLeaks the all [*sic*] rest."

"Do you have secure communications?" WikiLeaks wrote to Guccifer 2.0 a week later via Twitter DM. "Send any new material here for us to review, and it will have a much higher impact than what you are doing. No other media will release the full material."

On July 6th, WikiLeaks reached out to Guccifer 2.0 via Twitter again. "[I]f you have anything hillary related we want it in the next tweo [*sic*] days prefable [*sic*] because the DNC is approaching," WikiLeaks wrote, referring to the upcoming Democratic National Convention. "She will solidify bernie supporters behind her after."

"ok . . . i see," Guccifer 2.0 replied.

"we think trump has only a 25% chance of winning against hillary," WikiLeaks wrote, "so conflict between bernie and hillary is interesting."[15]

On July 14th, Guccifer 2.0 sent WikiLeaks an email with the subject line "big archive" and an encrypted attachment titled "wk dnc link1.txt.gpg" containing instructions on accessing an online archive of stolen DNC emails. Four days later, WikiLeaks replied that it had gained access to "the 1gb or so archive" of documents and promised to publish them "this week."[16] On July 22nd, three days before Hillary Clinton was set to receive the Democratic nomination in Philadelphia, WikiLeaks released over 20,000 stolen DNC emails. The GRU's clandestine cyber espionage campaign had morphed into political warfare through active measures.

These active measures were not limited to releasing stolen emails but also disseminated weaponized disinformation. On July 10th, four days after WikiLeaks first reached out to Guccifer 2.0 requesting the leaked files, 27-year-old DNC staffer Seth Rich was shot in the back while walking through the Bloomingdale neighborhood in Washington, DC, and died an hour and a half later. While the reasons for his murder remain unknown, local police believed Rich's death was due to a botched robbery. Three days later, the Russian foreign intelligence agency the SVR released a forged intelligence "bulletin" claiming that Rich was on his way to the FBI to provide information on Hillary Clinton and had been assassinated by a Clinton hit squad. Russian television stations, online trolls, Julian Assange, and the right-wing media ecosystem in the US ran with the false story throughout the rest of the election and for years to come after that.[17]

Aftershocks: The Clinton and Trump Campaigns React to the Leaks

The WikiLeaks dump came at a fraught moment for the Clinton Campaign. After defeating Bernie Sanders in a tighter race than anyone expected, the Clinton Campaign wanted to use the Democratic National Convention to unite the party. However, the contents of the DNC emails made that significantly more difficult. Furthermore, the leaks came on the heels of yet another email controversy. Just a few weeks earlier, on July 2nd, Clinton spent three and a half hours answering questions posed by two FBI agents at the J. Edgar Hoover building in Washington, DC.[18] It was the final interview to close out the FBI's criminal investigation into Clinton's handling of classified information in her emails during her tenure as Secretary of State.

While the FBI found that Clinton was not guilty of criminal wrongdoing, its Director, James Comey, feared that the public would view their findings as politically motivated. As a result, he took the extraordinary step of calling a press conference on July 5th without informing the leadership at the Justice Department. Comey also violated the FBI's long-standing tradition of not casting judgment on individuals they do not charge with a crime.

"They do not know what I am about to say," Comey said, opening the press conference by emphasizing that he had not coordinated his remarks with Attorney General Loretta Lynch or anyone else at the Obama Justice Department. "Although we did not find clear evidence that Secretary Clinton or her colleagues intended to violate laws governing the handling of classified information, there is evidence that they were extremely careless in their handling of very sensitive, highly classified information."

Comey's "extremely careless" remark did little to dispel the aura of scandal around Hillary's emails. Later analysis by the *Columbia Journalism Review* revealed that the American media dedicated more coverage to the Clinton email scandal than all of Trump's campaign scandals combined.[19] Clinton's first instinct was to hit back hard against Comey's characterization, but her staffers cautioned her against a confrontational approach. They suggested she move on from a scandal they incorrectly assumed had finally been put to bed.[20]

What the Benghazi investigations and the Director of FBI had succeeded in doing was to turn the term "Clinton emails" into shorthand for "Clinton corruption." Thus, when WikiLeaks leaked the DNC's internal communications, the event was filtered through a media narrative that associated Clinton-related emails with a criminal investigation and was presented to an American public that was primed to associate Clinton's emails with corruption. Little attention was paid to who stole the emails in the first place and the purpose of the leak.

The leaked emails included ones in which DNC chairwoman Debbie Wasserman Schultz, who was meant to be a neutral arbiter in the nominating process, referred to Bernie Sanders's campaign manager Jeff Weaver as a "[d]amn liar" and "an ass."[21] In another, Schultz wrote to a DNC colleague regarding Sanders, "[h]e isn't going to be President." Other examples of anti-Sanders sentiment included calls to question his faith and descriptions of his campaign as "a mess."[22] While private snark and preferentialism are nothing new to political parties, Sanders supporters who believed the DNC had treated them unfairly erupted in anger. The day before the convention, Schultz was forced to step down from her position.

While the Clinton and Sanders Campaigns had been working together since June to smooth over differences, there was still bitterness in the Bernie camp about his treatment in the primary and frustration among Clinton supporters that Sanders seemed unable to get his followers in line.[23] When the convention rolled around, disgruntled Sanders supporters protested outside the venue and scuffled with Philadelphia police.[24] When Clinton was officially nominated, a contingent of hardcore Sanders supporters walked out of the convention hall.[25] While Sanders urged his followers to support Clinton, Assange's prediction to the GRU that the leak would exacerbate inherent tensions within the Democratic party proved prescient. Clinton campaign manager Robby Mook attempted to explain to the press that the leaks were due to Russian hacking and were an attempt to aid Donald Trump, but the story gained little traction.[26]

"Listen, does it even matter who hacked this data?" Vladimir Putin glibly asked about the DNC leaks while being interviewed in Vladivostok. "The important thing is the content that was given to the public." Putin continued, "There's no need to distract the public's attention from the essence of the problem by raising some minor issues related with the search for who did it." When pressed further about Russia's involvement, Putin replied, "I want to tell you again, I don't know anything about it, and on a state level, Russia has never done this."[27]

Deputy campaign manager Rick Gates said the Trump campaign was "very happy about the release."[28] While they may have been happy, they were not surprised. Sometime beginning in April or May, Roger Stone informed Donald Trump personally and several high level members of his campaign that WikiLeaks was preparing to release information that would be damaging to Clinton.[29] While Stone had been fired from his position on the campaign in August of 2015 (he maintains he left on his own accord),[30] Stone remained closely connected with the campaign in an unofficial capacity.

Before the DNC leak, Trump campaign officials held regular "family meetings" with members of the Trump family, and Donald Trump Jr. would frequently inquire about the location of the 30,000 emails "missing" from Clinton's private server. Others interested in locating the emails included Jared Kushner, former head of the Defense Intelligence Agency Michael Flynn, Trump's first campaign chairman Corey Lewandowski and his replacement Paul Manafort, Alabama Senator Jeff Sessions, and Trump campaign policy advisor Sam Clovis.

Roger Stone told Rick Gates that the Clinton-related documents provided to WikiLeaks could have come from the Russians. When Assange announced that WikiLeaks was preparing to release leaks related to Hillary Clinton, Gates later testified that the campaign was elated and considered the leaks a "gift." At the time, the Trump campaign believed that WikiLeaks possessed emails from Clinton's personal server. Paul Manafort told Gates that the Republican National Committee was "energized" by the potential of Clinton-related WikiLeaks dumps and that the RNC was going to "run the WikiLeaks issue to ground." Trump and Kushner were willing to cooperate with the RNC on a WikiLeaks strategy.

When *The Washington Post* reported that the Russians had hacked the DNC, the Trump campaign reacted positively. According to Gates, the responses among those in the campaign ranged from disbelief to feeling that it would benefit the campaign if the information were released. The Trump campaign planned "a press strategy, a communications strategy, and messaging based on the possibility the emails existed." Further conversations were held among Trump campaign staffers "about what the campaign could plan for in the way of emails."[31]

A day after the *Post* story, Paul Ryan and Republican House Majority Leader Kevin McCarthy attended a meeting with

Ukrainian Prime Minister Vladimir Groysman in which Groysman described how the Kremlin funded right-wing, populist candidates across Europe to destabilize democracy. "I'll guarantee you that's what it is," Kevin told Ryan and several other Republican Congressmen after the meeting. "The Russians hacked the DNC and got the opp [opposition] research they had on Trump." McCarthy continued, "There's two people I think Putin pays: Rohrabacher and Trump." Unaware that the interaction was being recorded, several of the gathered lawmakers laughed. "Swear to God," McCarthy added. Ryan interjected. "This is an off-the-record. No leaks, alright? This is how we know we're a real family here."[32]

Trump not only took advantage of the hack and leak operation, he dismissed the idea of any Russian involvement. In a July 25th tweet, Trump wrote, "The new joke in town is that Russia leaked the disastrous D.N.C. emails, which should never have been written (stupid) because Putin likes me."[33] Then, after rejecting the idea that Russia was involved in the leak, Trump encouraged them to become involved. At a news conference on July 27th, Trump said before the entire world, "Russia, if you're listening, I hope you are able to find the 30,000 emails that are missing. I think you will probably be rewarded mightily by our press."

Within five hours of Trump's remarks, the GRU targeted Clinton's personal office. Lieutenant Lukashev of Unit 26165 sent spear phishing emails to 15 email accounts at a domain hosted by a third-party server and used by Clinton's personal office.[34] He then targeted seventy-six email addresses at a domain for the Clinton campaign.[35] Apparently, when Trump spoke, the GRU was listening.

A Threat Comes To Light:
The Obama Administration and US Intelligence Responds

According to *The Wall Street Journal*, in 2015, American intelligence agencies intercepted Russian government officials discussing Trump's "associates" months before he announced his candidacy. The content of some of these conversations included meetings outside of the US between Russian government officials and Trump aides and advisors. There was no mention of who these individuals were or whether they were connected to

Trump's upcoming campaign.[36] By late 2015, British and other European intelligence agencies began passing "quite sensitive" reports to their US counterparts of contacts between Trump advisors and Russian agents.[37]

The first members of the Obama administration to raise an alarm that Russia might interfere in the 2016 election were the Russia hands Victoria Nuland and Celeste Wallander. As early as March and April of 2016, Nuland raised alarms that Putin might attempt to make the US election appear illegitimate as "payback" for US support of the revolution in Ukraine and to delegitimize democratic elections in the eyes of Russian citizens. Despite their fears, Obama's intelligence chiefs remained skeptical.[38] By that point, the SVR and GRU were already burrowed deep within the DNC's networks and had exfiltrated the contents of John Podesta's inbox.

By the spring of 2016, European intelligence agencies were warning their US counterparts that Russian money might be flowing into the 2016 election.[39] However, it wasn't until Guccifer 2.0 started leaking stolen materials on June 15th that the Russian threat to the election "crystallized" in the mind of the Obama administration. From almost the very beginning, Administration officials had technical attribution that the Russians were behind the attacks. The first Situation Room meetings focusing on Russian interference began in July. At that time, the overriding fear in the Obama White House was the potential for Russian hackers to attack America's physical election infrastructure.[40]

Beginning on June 23rd, GRU hackers targeted the Illinois Board of Elections.[41] By exploiting a vulnerability in the State Board of Elections website, the GRU gained access to and extracted data from a database that contained information on millions of registered Illinois voters.[42] Once inside, GRU hackers could delete and alter voter information. However, there is no evidence that they did so.[43] Later that same month, the FBI warned election officials in Arizona that Russian hackers had gained access to their voter registration database.[44] The GRU ultimately targeted election systems in all 50 states.[45]

Arizona authorities took the relevant systems offline between June 28th and July 8th. Four days later, on July 12th, Illinois election IT staff noticed "spikes" in the data flow across the voter registration database server, indicating rapid and repeated queries on the application status page of the Illinois paperless voter registration website. Following this discovery, Illinois officials took the system offline.[46] Later in July, the FBI opened an investigation into the Illinois breach and discovered that the GRU had stolen the records of up to 500,000 Illinois voters, including names, birthdates, home addresses, and partial social security numbers. Certain members of the Obama administration began to believe that the Russians were sending them a message that they could edit the vote tallies if they wished to.[47]

In late July, CIA sources within the Kremlin provided the agency with intelligence that Putin had personally authorized an operation aimed against the 2016 US Presidential election. Two separate CIA sources reported that Putin had articulated that the purpose of the operation was to harm Clinton and help elect Donald Trump. This information led to the Russian operation becoming the overriding concern of CIA Director John Brennan, who sequestered himself in his office for two days to analyze all of the available intelligence. In early August, Brennan contacted White House Chief of Staff Denis McDonough and asked to see President Obama. After speaking with McDonough and Deputy National Security Advisor Avril Haines, Brennan dispatched a courier to deliver an "eyes only" intelligence summary for Obama, McDonough, Haines, and National Security Advisor Susan Rice.

The next day, Brennan arrived at the Oval Office for a noon meeting with Obama, McDonough, Haines, and Rice. The participants were shocked by the information Brennan communicated to them. Obama ordered Brennan to procure more information as quickly as he could and to utilize the full intelligence apparatus of the United States in dealing with the threat. Brennan laid out a plan to brief the appropriate Congressional leaders and establish a multi-agency fusion-cell involving the FBI and NSA to focus on the issue. Brennan emphasized the importance of secrecy to avoid compromising the CIA's sources in the Kremlin. No information related to Russian interference was included in any of the President's Daily Briefs, as even its highly limited circulation was considered too broad.[48]

On August 4th, Brennan had a regularly scheduled call with his counterpart in Russian intelligence, Alexander Bortnikov, head of the FSB. While the call was supposed to be about the Syrian Civil War, Brennan issued a warning. "I told Mr. Bortnikov," Brennan later testified, "that if Russia had such a campaign underway, it would be certain to backfire. I said that all Americans, regardless of political affiliation or whom they might support in the election, cherished their ability to elect their own leaders without outside interference or disruption. I said American voters would be outraged by any Russian attempts to interfere in the election."[49] Bortnikov denied Russia's involvement but told Brennan he would inform Putin of his comments.

Debate raged within the White House regarding how to respond to the situation. In July, Celeste Wallander and Michael Daniel, Special Assistant to the President and Cyber Security Coordinator, brought together an interagency committee to develop potential countermeasure options against Russia. The options considered ranged from additional sanctions, retaliatory leaks and revelations, public and private messages, and cyber disruption operations. Victoria Nuland urged reciprocal measures be deployed that would impose steep costs on Putin personally by leaking embarrassing information on the Russian leader related to his secret wealth. However, Secretary of State John Kerry ordered Nuland to stand down.

By August, US intelligence concluded that the Russians could edit vote tallies.[50] Late in the month, Michael Daniels concluded that the Russians had attempted to penetrate the voting systems of all 50 states.[51] While the intelligence community later assessed that the Russians wouldn't have been able to change enough votes to determine the result of the election, there were serious fears that the Russians could discredit the results in the eyes of the American electorate, particularly among the supporters of the conspiracy infatuated Trump.

Obama feared that if he retaliated against Putin, he might set off an escalatory tit-for-tat that could lead to the very outcome he wished to avoid by provoking the Russians to meddle with the votes. There were also fears that retaliation might threaten to reveal the sources that had provided them with crucial details of the Russian operation. The administration's thinking was shaped by the almost universal expectation that Hillary Clinton would win the election. It is important to emphasize just how implausible a Trump presidency seemed to many at the time, particularly among those in power in Washington, DC. Many thought the response to the Russian activities could be safely handed over to an incoming Clinton administration.

In late July, discussions occurred within the CIA and NSA about potential retaliatory measures that could be deployed against the Russians.[52] Three days after the Democratic Convention, Robert Joyce, the head of Tailored Access Operations (TAO), the National Security Agency's cyber-warfare intelligence-gathering unit, gave a highly unusual interview to *ABC News*. The outlet reported that NSA hackers were likely targeting Russian government-linked hacking teams. Joyce informed *ABC* that the NSA had the technical capabilities and legal authority to "hack back" against adversary groups. "In terms of the foreign intelligence mission, one of the things we have to do is try to understand who did a breach, who is responsible for a breach," Joyce told ABC. "So we will use the NSA's authorities to pursue foreign intelligence to try to get back into that collection, to understand who did it and get the attribution. That's hard work, but that's one of the responsibilities we have."[53]

Unbeknownst to him at the time, Joyce's comments may have inspired one of the more remarkable leaks in the history of the internet. On August 13th, a mysterious hacker group calling themselves the Shadow Brokers after characters from the sci-fi video game Mass Effect used the account @shadowbrokers to tweet a link to the file-sharing site Pastebin. Upon clicking the link, you were greeted with the following message: *!!! Attention government sponsors of cyber warfare and those who profit from it !!! How much you pay for enemies cyber weapons?*

The Shadow Brokers hacked the NSA's Tailored Access Operations unit, also known as the Equation Group, and stole its most secret, dangerous, and coveted hacking tools. After providing a sample of these tools, the Shadow Brokers offered to sell the rest to the highest bidder, writing the following message: *We follow Equation Group traffic. We find Equation Group source range. We hack Equation Group cyber weapons. You see pictures. We give you some Equation Group files, you see. This is good proof, no? You enjoy!!! You break many things. You find many intrusions. You write many words. But not all, we are auction the best files.*

The NSA had been hacked, and whoever was responsible was now threatening to sell its most dangerous cyber weapons to the highest bidder. Given the timing of their appearance and their sophistication, Russian state actors emerged early on as one of the chief suspects behind the Shadow Brokers. On August 16th, the infamous NSA leaker Edward Snowden tweeted, "circumstantial evidence and conventional wisdom indicates Russian responsibility." He further claimed that the leak "is likely a warning that someone can prove responsibility for any attacks that originated from this malware server." Snowden concluded that someone appeared to be "sending a message that an escalation in the attribution game could get messy fast."

The identity behind the Shadow Brokers remains a mystery, with some cyber security experts speculating that the threat had come from a disgruntled individual within the NSA.[54] Regardless of who was behind the hack, a shot had been fired across the NSA's bow at a critical moment when the United States was under sustained cyber assault. Despite this looming threat, NSA Director Admiral Michael Rogers advocated a muscular cyber response to Russian actions but was overruled by the Pentagon. Officials in the White House worried that attacking the Russians might lead to escalation and could indicate to the American public that they were not confident in the integrity of the voting system.[55]

Meanwhile, the decentralized, state-based manner in which America's election infrastructure was organized made a unified national response impossible. Parochial distrust of officials in Washington and hyper-partisanship were also proving implacable. Secretary of Homeland Security Jeh Johnson convened election officials from all fifty states on an August 15th conference call. He floated the idea of designating electoral infrastructure as "critical infrastructure," allowing States to voluntarily opt in for better information sharing and easier access to federal resources. The response was negative, with certain individuals even suggesting it was an attempt at a federal takeover.[56] The Republican secretary of state in Georgia, Brian Kemp, accused Johnson of making a politically calculated move and attempted to persuade his counterparts to refuse help from Washington. Kemp went as far as rejecting the idea that Russia was interfering with the election in the first place[57]

Throughout August and into September, Brennan briefed select individuals in the Congress about the Russian campaign. Due to the sensitivity of the intelligence, he met with lawmakers one at a time. House Minority Leader Nancy Pelosi was briefed on August 11th, followed by the Ranking member of the House Intelligence Committee, Adam Schiff, on the 17th, and the Senate Majority Leader Harry Reid, on the 25th.[58] However, when he briefed several high-level Congressional Republicans, Brennan faced partisan challenges almost immediately. While Paul Ryan took the briefing seriously,[59] Republican House Intelligence Committee member Devin Nunes of California seemed unconcerned and even dismissive.

"You're trying to screw the Republican candidate," Senate Majority Leader Mitch McConnell complained to Brennan during his briefing. Shocked by McConnel's partisan rejection of the CIA's analysis, Brennan grew angry, and the meeting devolved into a shouting match.[60]

A day earlier, on September 5th, Obama confronted Putin at a G20 meeting in Hangzhou, China. With only their interpreters present, Obama told Putin "to cut it out" and warned of "serious consequences" if they did not.[61] After being told by Obama that they knew what the Russians were up to, Putin demanded proof and accused the Americans of meddling in Russia's internal affairs. At a press conference later that day, Obama obliquely referred to the exchange and issued a subtle threat. "We're moving into a new era here where a number of countries have significant capacities," Obama said about developments in cyber warfare. "Frankly, we've got more capacity than anybody, both offensively and defensively."[62]

On September 8th, Lisa Monaco, James Comey, and Jeh Johnson briefed 12 senior Republican and Democratic lawmakers, some of whom, like McConnell and Nunes, had already been briefed by Brennan. The meeting took place in a secure, underground conference room.[63] After providing further details on the Russian interference campaign, they proposed issuing a bipartisan statement to inspire state election officials to utilize the Department of Homeland Security's (DHS) cybersecurity services. While the Democrats were willing, the Republicans in the room refused, arguing that publicizing the information would amplify the impact of the Russian operation.

"You security people should be careful you're not getting used," McConnell protested. Lisa Monaco interpreted the statement as McConnell suggesting that the intelligence about Russia was being exaggerated for political purposes.[64] McConnel went further, casting doubt on the intelligence itself and dismissing the Obama administration's fears as overblown. Finally, McConnel threatened to publicly treat any statement issued on the matter of Russian political interference in the election as a political act. The Obama administration officials left the meeting disturbed by the partisanship they had witnessed.

In the second week of September, Obama invited the four highest-ranking officials in Congress, Nancy Pelosi, Paul Ryan, Harry Reid, and Mitch McConnell, to the Oval Office. Obama requested that they issue a joint statement regarding the threat from Russia and encourage states to take advantage of DHS resources. McConnell refused, stating that elections were a state issue. Exasperated, Obama admonished McConnell that foreign electoral interference shouldn't be a partisan issue, but McConnell was unmoved. After the meeting, Ryan drafted a statement that mentioned Russia by name. McConnell refused to sign and sat on the statement for weeks, insisting that Russia not be named and that it say that the federal government wouldn't be seizing control of state election infrastructure.[65]

Losing patience, California Democrats Diane Feinstein and Adam Schiff released a statement on September 22nd announcing that they had "concluded that Russian intelligence agencies are making a serious and concerted effort to influence the US election" and that the "effort is intended to sow doubt about the security of our election and may well be intended to influence the outcomes of the election."[66] When the joint statement discussed weeks earlier was finally released on September 28th, it did not mention Russia. The statement came and went without attracting much attention in the relentless news maelstrom of the campaign and the politically balkanized media atmosphere.

At some point in September, Jim Comey offered to write an op-ed in which he would mention the Russian involvement in the release of the DNC emails as well as its intrusions into voting infrastructure but was turned down by the White House. However, as independent media reports began referencing Russian hacking operations against the election, the conversation in the White House turned towards considering the release of a public declaration about the Russian campaign. Though Comey had earlier offered to write an op-ed, he cautioned that a public declaration might play into the Russian's hands by raising doubts about the integrity of the election. Jeh Johnson, on the other hand, argued that it would be an unforgivable scandal if, given what they knew, they said nothing and Trump won.[67]

It was decided that Jeh Johnson and James Clapper would issue a joint statement. The document they produced stated that the DNC hack had been ordered by individuals at the highest levels of the Russian government. It also highlighted that state electoral infrastructure had been probed, though it didn't link these activities to Russia.[68] The statement also claimed it would be "extremely difficult" for even nation-state actors to alter the results of the election, which Johnson privately felt was misleading as altering the results of a few important districts in swing states could change the result of an election.[69]

Those aware of the upcoming joint statement expected it to attract significant media attention. The statement was released at 3 pm on October 7th. However, unbeknownst to its author, October 7th was destined to become one of the most infamous days in American political history. The news that the US intelligence community assessed that the Russian government was behind the hacking of the DNC would, remarkably, barely make a ripple.

Access Hollywood, the GRU, WikiLeaks, Porn Stars, and the FBI: A Perfect Storm

When the joint statement was released on October 7th, Trump was involved in preparation for his upcoming debate with Hillary. Senior staffers had just received advance notice that in one hour, approximately 4 pm, *The Washington Post* was going to release what came to be known as the *Access Hollywood* tape, in which Trump was recorded boasting about attempting to seduce a married woman. "I don't even wait," Trump told Bush. "And when you're a star, they let you do it. You can do anything. ... Grab 'em by the pussy. You can do anything."

"This is fatal," Paul Ryan told RNC chairman Reince Priebus in a private phone conversation. "How can you get him out of the race?" Priebus explained to the Speaker of the House that it was impossible; there was no mechanism to strip Trump of the Republican Party nomination. A day later, Trump convened a meeting at Trump Tower to discuss the fallout of the tape. Priebus didn't mince words. "I'll tell you what I'm hearing,"

Priebus replied when asked by Trump what he had been hearing. "Either you'll lose in the biggest landslide in history, or you can get out of the race and let somebody else run who can win."[70]

Despite Priebus's stark assessment, Trump maintained a core group of loyalists, including his children and the former mayor of New York, Rudolph Giuliani. His new campaign chairman was also among those who remained loyal at this critical moment. Steve Bannon replaced Paul Manafort on August 17th after *The New York Times* had run a story about a secret ledger found in Ukraine that listed illicit payments by the ousted Yanukovych government to the Republican political Svengali. Bannon had been recommended to Trump by Rebekah Mercer, the daughter of the libertarian hedge fund billionaire and top Trump donor Robert Mercer.[71]

At 4:32 pm on October 7th, 32 minutes after *The Washington Post* broke the Access Hollywood story, WikiLeaks released 2,050 emails from John Podesta's inbox. It was a surprise capper and only the first of a staggered series of leaks that would last through the election to one of the most infamous days in the history of American politics. However, not everyone was surprised. On September 26th, Roger Stone had told Paul Manafort, no longer employed by the campaign but still involved in an unofficial capacity, that "John Podesta was going to be in the barrel" and that "there were going to be leaks of John Podesta's emails." Another person unsurprised by the Podesta leaks was Donald Trump. On September 29th, Trump had been riding in a limo with Rick Gates on their way to La Guardia airport when he took a call from Roger Stone. After the call concluded, Trump told Gates that "more releases of damaging information would be coming."[72]

WikiLeaks was also in direct contact with Donald Trump Jr. On September 20th, WikiLeaks sent Trump Jr. a Twitter DM, writing: "A PAC run anti-Trump site putintrump.org is about to launch." WikiLeaks continued, "The PAC is a recycled pro-Iraq war PAC. We have guessed the password. It is 'putintrump.' See 'About' for who is behind it. Any comments?"

"Off the record, I don't know what this is, but I'll ask around," Trump Jr. replied.[73]

"Guys, I got a weird Twitter DM from WikiLeaks. See below," Trump Jr. wrote to campaign staffers. "I tried the password, and it works, and the about section they reference contains the next pic in terms of who is behind it. Not sure if this is anything but it seems like it's really WikiLeaks asking me as I follow them and it is a DM. Do you know the people mentioned and what the conspiracy they are looking for could be? These are just screen shots but it's a fully built out page claiming to be a PAC let me know your thoughts and if we want to look into it."[74]

"Hiya, it'd be great if you guys could comment on/push this story," WikiLeaks wrote to Trump Jr. again on October 3rd, attaching a likely fabricated quote from Hillary Clinton claiming to want to "drone" Julian Assange.

"Already did that earlier today," Trump Jr. replied thirty minutes later. "It's amazing what she can get away with."[75]

"I love WikiLeaks!" Trump proclaimed at a rally three days after the Podesta leaks. Two days later, @WikiLeaks sent the following DM to Donald Trump Jr.: "Strongly suggest your dad tweets this link if he mentions us ... there's many great stories the press are missing and we're sure some of your follows [*sic*] will find it. btw we just released Podesta Emails Part 4." Shortly after that, Trump tweeted, "Very little pick-up by the dishonest media of incredible information provided by WikiLeaks. So dishonest! Rigged System!" Two days later, Trump Jr. tweeted the link from his account: "For those who have the time to read about all the corruption and hypocrisy all the @wikileaks emails are right here: wlsearch.tk."[76]

While Trump luxuriated in the WikiLeaks disclosures, Michael Cohen was involved in covert damage control in the wake of the *Access Hollywood* tape. The night after the tape was released, Cohen was informed by Trump's press secretary Hope Hicks that a rumor was circulating of the existence of a tape in which Trump could be seen with prostitutes while he was in Moscow for the 2013 Miss Universe Pageant. Hicks had heard that the celebrity tabloid website *TMZ* might have the tape and wanted Cohen to utilize his relationship with its founder Harvey Levin to learn what he could.[77]

In addition to the potential emergence of the Moscow tape, the *Access Hollywood* scandal dredged up old problems. Stephanie Clifford, a pornographic actress who went by the name of Stormy Daniels, had engaged in an extramarital, sexual affair with Donald Trump after meeting him at a golf tournament in 2006. Following the release of the *Access Hollywood* tape, Trump and his enablers feared that he wouldn't be able to survive another sex scandal politically. Cohen was tasked with making the problem go away.

Unbeknownst to the voting public, Donald Trump had entered into a "catch and kill" alliance with his longtime friend David Pecker, the CEO of American Media Inc (AMI), the parent company of the tabloid *The National Enquirer*. Shortly after he announced his candidacy, Trump and Michael Cohen sat down with Pecker for a meeting in August 2015 in Trump Tower. During the meeting, Pecker offered to buy the rights to and bury potentially embarrassing or unflattering stories about Trump and to do so in coordination with Cohen.[78] In addition to buying and withholding Trump-related matters from the public, *The National Enquirer* also routinely wrote stories attacking Trump's Republican primary opponents and Hillary Clinton.

In late 2015, AMI paid a former Trump World Tower doorman $30,000 to bottle up an as-yet unsubstantiated story that Trump had fathered a love child with a former employee.[79] Shortly after that and at Trump's direction, AMI arranged to pay $150,000 to Karen McDougal, the 1998 Playboy Playmate of the Year who had a 10-month sexual relationship with Trump from 2006-2007, for exclusive rights to the story and then never ran it.[80] However, in the aftermath of the *Access Hollywood* tape, Pecker refused to buy the Stormy Daniels story. Cohen arranged for a $130,000 payment to Clifford using his own money by drawing down a home equity line.[81] Cohen, whom Trump reimbursed, made the payments using a private company, Essential Consultants LLC, and pseudonyms for the various parties.[82]

Cohen's payment to Daniels went through on October 27th, with the election just under two weeks away. Three days later, he received a message from his friend Giorgi Rtskhiladze, whom he and Trump had worked with on a potential Trump Tower Batumi project in the formerly Soviet Republic of Georgia. "Stopped the flow of some tapes from Russia, but not sure if there is anything else. Just so u [*sic*] know…"

"Tapes of what?" Cohen replied.

"Not sure of the content, but the person in Moscow was bragging had [*sic*] tapes from Russia trip." Rtskhiladze was referring to the Moscow tape. "I'm sure it's not a big deal, but there are lots of stupid people."[83] Rtskhiladze later claimed he was referring to a rumor a friend had overheard at a Moscow party.[84] The identity of the "person in Moscow" is not known.

Throughout August, hackers in Unit 74455 carried out cyber espionage operations against VR Systems, an elections software and hardware provider.[85] The operation was led by GRU officer Anatoliy Kovalev, who, back in June, had started researching website domains used by State Boards of Elections, secretaries of state, and other elections-related organizations to search for vulnerabilities.[86] The NSA later assessed that the GRU's attack on VR Systems obtained information on election-related software and hardware and was likely used to launch spear phishing attacks against local government organizations involved in voter registration.[87] Intelligence officials speaking to *The New York Times* in 2017 claimed that two other providers of critical election infrastructure had been breached in addition to VR Systems. The identity of these companies and the exact nature of the breaches remain classified.[88]

VR Systems provided election-related software and hardware solutions for local election officials in Florida, California, Illinois, Indiana, New York, North Carolina, Virginia, and West Virginia. In Florida alone, 62 out of its 67 counties used VR Systems software, including the Democratic stronghold Miami-Dade. VR Systems also serviced 23 out of 100 counties in North Carolina. After the election, it was discovered that VR Systems routinely used remote access software to troubleshoot customer problems from a distance. Election security experts have described the use of remote access software as a critical security lapse because, depending on how a network is configured, it can not only allow outside intruders in but potentially provide them with access to the entire target network.[89]

Government guidelines regarding voter registration systems do not ban the use of remote access software but recommend that tech providers use encrypted virtual private networks (VPN) when they do so. However, if a hacker was inside VR Systems' network when a VPN was established or had obtained a VR Systems employee's VPN credentials, they could have remotely infiltrated the customer's network.[90] This was how Unit 74455 hackers accessed the Ukrainian electric grid only a year earlier.[91] Nor was VR Systems the only election-related company engaged in remote access. After initially denying doing so, Elections Systems and Software, the largest provider of voting machines in the US, later admitted to using remote access software with several customers between 2000 and 2006.[92]

According to the Special Counsel's report, the Russians successfully installed malware on their network after sending spear-phishing emails to VR Systems employees.[93] VR Systems, on the other hand, has maintained that the attempts were unsuccessful. To bolster this claim, they point to an investigation by the private cyber security firm FireEye, which concluded that hackers had not breached the company. However, FireEye's analysis was conducted over a year after the alleged intrusion, ample time for evidence of the hack to be scrubbed by the perpetrators. When the DHS investigated the matter in 2018, over two years after the alleged breach, they found no malware in their system. Questions remain as to whether the FireEye and DHS investigations looked into the full spectrum of ways hackers could have compromised VR Systems and their customers or whether the scope of the inquiry was too limited to be considered comprehensive.[94]

On August 30th, Florida held a state primary election. Before the close of the polls, an election results webpage hosted by VR Systems for the heavily Democratic Broward County prematurely and illegally displayed election results. VR Systems blamed the incident on a "clerical error."[95] Whatever caused the anomaly led to a chain reaction in which other Florida counties could not display their results promptly following the close of the polls. While there is no evidence that any of the results in Florida were tampered with, local election officials have admitted that hackers could have changed election results if a VR Systems employee's credentials had been stolen.[96]

The public statements issued by VR Systems reveal an inconsistent timeline of events related to handling the spear-phishing emails sent by the GRU. In a letter sent to the North Carolina State Board of Elections, VR Systems claimed that the spear-phishing emails had been caught and identified upon receipt before any employees could open them. However, in a subsequent letter to Senator Ron Wyden (D-OR), VR Systems claimed they identified the spear-phishing emails around the same time that they participated in a September 30th conference call between the FBI and Florida election officials to discuss the efforts of foreign hackers to target the state's election infrastructure.[97]

On October 31st, GRU hackers created the email address. They sent spear-phishing emails to over 100 Florida-based VR Systems state election customers containing a malware attachment disguised as a Word document masquerading as a user guide for VR Systems electronic poll book software - devices that contain voter check-in information that has replaced the thick binders of paper used previously. A month earlier, VR Systems sent a legitimate email to North Carolina customers containing a user guide, indicating that the GRU knew how to design their emails to appear like VR Systems' usual correspondence. Officials in Florida's Washington County and another unnamed country seem to have clicked and been infected by the malware.[98]

One VR Systems customer, Durham County in North Carolina, experienced a series of unexplained technical glitches and anomalies in the lead-up to and on election day itself. On November 6th, the Sunday before the election, Durham-based election workers were attempting to load voter data from a county computer onto USB flash drives, which would then be inserted into laptops that poll workers would use to determine voter eligibility. However, the data transfer from the central county computer to the flash drives inexplicably took up to ten times longer than usual. The problems continued into the next day and threatened to disrupt election day. As a result, Durham County officials contacted VR Systems. Even though VR Systems was aware at that time that Russian hackers had targeted them, the company accessed the county computer remotely.[99]

On election day, numerous laptops used by Durham County poll workers to determine voter eligibility crashed, froze, or indicated that individuals had already voted when they hadn't. Several laptops displayed a false warning that voters needed to produce ID when North Carolina law had changed, so that was no longer necessary. The problems got so bad that state officials ordered Durham to switch to using paper records. The process of doing so led to significant delays, and it remains unknown how many of those who experienced the inconvenience left without voting. The events in Durham remain unexplained, and while there is no direct evidence of Russian hackers causing the problems, the possibility cannot be ruled out.

The Clinton campaign struggled to deal with the steady WikiLeaks releases of John Podesta's emails in the month leading up to the election. Clinton staffer Glen Caplin was placed in charge of roughly a dozen other staffers and, working out of an office they called the "room of tears," they poured over the content of the released emails to monitor them for potential items that could embarrass the campaign. While most leaked emails were innocuous, others revealed petty infighting that proved unflattering during campaign season in the harsh glare of October.[100]

Most leaked emails revealed little more than the snark and petty grievances common to all campaigns. In one email, Chelsea Clinton is referred to as a "spoiled brat" by former Clinton Foundation executive Doug Band. Another featured Robby Mook sarcastically referring to New York Mayor Bill De Blasio as a "terrorist." In yet another, the president of the liberal think tank the Center for American Progress, Neera Tanden, refers to Hillary's political instincts as "suboptimal." One email featured Clinton staffer Jennifer Palmieri criticizing Catholic Republicans by describing their faith as "the most socially acceptable politically conservative religion." The Clinton campaign tried unsuccessfully to push the media narrative toward the fact that the emails were stolen by Russia rather than on the relatively innocuous content of the emails themselves. This misplaced media focus, paired with the steady drip way WikiLeaks released the emails, turned them into a significant issue for the campaign as it closed in on election day. However, it would take the director of the FBI to turn the storm into an F-5 hurricane.

On October 28th, 2016, just over a week before the election, James Comey sent a letter to Congress stating that the FBI was reopening the Clinton email criminal inquiry. The letter was leaked to the press, and a media furor erupted, serving as an October Surprise gut punch to the Clinton Campaign. A separate investigation into the disgraced former Democratic lawmaker Anthony Weiner, who was married to Clinton aide Huma Abedin, had inadvertently uncovered emails that were possibly pertinent to the Clinton email investigation. Even though long-standing FBI policy forbids it from influencing the outcome of an election, and despite the fact that DOJ officials warned him that any announcement would violate this policy, Comey decided it was better to disclose rather than conceal the reopening of the investigation.[101]

Two days before the election, Comey sent a second letter to Congress in which he said that, after working "around the clock," the FBI had reached the same conclusion they had in July and that the case was again closed. However, the damage was done. Millions of Americans had already cast early votes. The Clinton campaign learned through focus groups that voters were conflating the DNC and Podesta emails released by WikiLeaks with the "email scandal" that was being so thoroughly flogged by the press.[102] The Trump campaign was excited by this late-stage development, with many Trump aides believing for the first time that he might win the presidency.[103] The respected statistician Nate Silver has stated, "Hillary Clinton would probably be president if FBI Director James Comey had not sent a letter to Congress on Oct. 28."[104]

On November 8th, supporters of both candidates traveled to the polls with bated breath. For many Democrats and within the Washington and coastal elite, a Trump presidency remained unthinkable. Confidence was high that Hillary Clinton would be the next President of the United States. This assessment was shared by Vladimir Putin and the Russians, who, according to the CIA, possessed yet more damaging information on Clinton that they planned to release after election day, along with supposed proof that voter data had been tampered with to bolster Trump's claims that the election was rigged.[105]

In a small election-day gesture to support his father, Donald Trump Jr. retweeted @Ten_GOP, which billed itself as the "Unofficial Twitter account of the Tennessee GOP." The message read, "This vet passed away last month before he could vote for Trump. Here he is in his #MAGA hat.. #voted #ElectionDay." While the message retweeted by candidate Trump's eldest son may have just been one among the over 1 billion election-related tweets generated since August, it contained a dark secret.[106] Unbeknownst to Don Jr or the other Trump campaign aides, including Kellyanne Conway and campaign digital director Brad Parscale, who had also retweeted messages from it, @Ten_GOP was, in fact, the creation of propagandists in St. Petersburg and just one small part of a sweeping Russian disinformation campaign targeting American voters.[107]

---

[1] "Assange on Peston on Sunday: 'More Clinton leaks to come,' *ITV News*. June 12th, 2016

[2] Khatchadourian, Raffi. "No Secrets," *The New Yorker*. May 31st, 2010

[3] Assange, Julian. "Conspiracy as Governance," December 3rd, 2006. Pg. 5

[4] Becker, Jo; Erlanger, Steven; Schmitt, Eric. "How Russia Often Benefits When Julian Assange Reveals the West's Secrets," *The New York Times*. August 31st, 2016

[5] Ball, James. "Why I felt I had to turn my back on Wikileaks," *The Guardian*. September 2nd, 2011

[6] Becker, Jo; Erlanger, Steven; Schmitt, Eric. "How Russia Often Benefits When Julian Assange Reveals the West's Secrets," *The New York Times*. August 31st, 2016

[7] Stanley, Alessandra. "The Prisoner as Talk Show Host," *The New York Times*. April 17th, 2012

[8] Mueller, III, Robert S. *Report On The Investigation Into Russian Interference In The 2016 Presidential Election*. Department of Justice, Washington, DC. March 2019. Pg. 44

[9] Miller, Greg. *The Apprentice: Trump, Russia and the Subversion of American Democracy*. New York, NY: Custom House, 2018. Pg. 50

[10] Nakashima, Ellen. "Russian government hackers penetrated DNC, stole opposition research on Trump," *The Washington Post*. June 14th, 2016

[11] Rid, Thomas. *Active Measures: The Secret History of Disinformation and Political Warfare*. New York, NY: Farrar, Straus and Giroux, 2020. Pg. 386

[12] McFadden, Cynthia; Uehlinger, Tim; Connor, Tracy. "Hacker 'Guccifer': I Got Inside Hillary Clinton's Server," *NBC News*. May 4th, 2016

[13] USA v. Netyksho, et al. Indictment. United States District Court for the District of Columbia. July 13th, 2018. Pg. 15

[14] Rid, Thomas. *Active Measures: The Secret History of Disinformation and Political Warfare*. New York, NY: Farrar, Straus and Giroux, 2020. Pg. 389

[15] Mueller, III, Robert S. *Report On The Investigation Into Russian Interference In The 2016 Presidential Election*. Department of Justice, Washington, DC. March 2019. Pg. 45

[16] USA v. Netyksho, et al. Indictment. United States District Court for the District of Columbia. July 13th, 2018. Pg. 18

[17] Isikoff, Michael. "Exclusive: The true origins of the Seth Rich conspiracy theory. A Yahoo News investigation," *Yahoo News*. July 9th, 2019

[18] Clinton, Hillary. *What Happened*. New York, NY: Simon & Schuster, Inc. 2017. Pg. 309

[19] Watts, Duncan J.; Rothschild, David M. "Don't blame the election on fake news. Blame it on the media." *Columbia Journalism Review*. December 5th, 2017

[20] Clinton, Hillary. *What Happened*. New York, NY: Simon & Schuster, Inc. 2017. Pg. 311

[21] Abramson, Alana; Walshe, Sushannah. "The 4 Most Damaging Emails From The DNC Wikileaks Dump," *ABC News*. July 25th, 2016

[22] Shear, Michael D.; Rosenberg, Michael. "Released Emails Suggest the D.N.C. Derided Sanders Campaign," *The New York Times*. July 22nd, 2016

[23] Allen, Jonathan; Parnes, Amie. *Shattered: Inside Hillary Clinton's Doomed Campaign*. New York, NY: Crown Publishing Group, 2017. Pg. 273

[24] Samuelsohn, Darren. "Protests in Philly spawn skirmishes, arrests and another flag fire," *Politico*. July 28th, 2016

[25] Rhodan, Maya. "Bernie Sanders Supporters Storm Out Of Convention In Protest," *Time Magazine*. July 26th, 2016

[26] Herb, Jeremy. "Mook suggests Russians leaked DNC emails to help Trump," *Politico*. July 24th, 2016

[27] Rudnitsky, Jake; Micklethwait, John; Riley, Michael. "Putin Says DNC Hack Was A Public Service, Russia Didn't Do It," *Bloomberg*. September 1st, 2016

[28] Shimer, David. *Rigged: America, Russia, and One Hundred Years of Covert Electoral Influence*. New York, NY: Alfred A. Knopf, 2020. Pg. 171

[29] *Report of the Select Committee on Intelligence United States Senate on Russian Active Measures Campaigns and Interference in the 2016 U.S. Election Volume Five: Counterintelligence Threats And Vulnerabilities*. Pg. 222

[30] Haberman, Maggie. "Did Roger Stone Jump, or Was He Pushed From Donald Trump's Campaign," *The New York Times*. August 8th, 2015

[31] *Report of the Select Committee on Intelligence United States Senate on Russian Active Measures*

Campaigns and Interference in the 2016 U.S. Election Volume Five: Counterintelligence Threats And Vulnerabilities. Pg. 225-229

[32] Entous, Adam. "House Majority Leader says to colleagues in 2016: 'I think Putin pays' Trump," *The Washington Post.* May 17th, 2017

[33] Lipton, Eric; Sanger, David E.; Shane, Scott. "The Perfect Weapon: How Russian Cyberpower Invaded the US," *The New York Times.* December 13th, 2016

[34] Mueller, III, Robert S. *Report On The Investigation Into Russian Interference In The 2016 Presidential Election.* Department of Justice, Washington, DC. March 2019. Pg. 49

[35] USA v. Netyksho, et al. Indictment. United States District Court for the District of Columbia. July 13th, 2018

[36] Harris, Shane. "Russian Officials Overheard Discussing Trump Associates Before Campaign Began," *The Wall Street Journal.* July 12th, 2017

[37] Isikoff, Michael. "Trump advisors had 'sensitive' contacts with Russian agents for months, Clapper testifies," *Yahoo News.* May 8th, 2017

[38] Shimer, David. *Rigged: America, Russia, and One Hundred Years of Covert Electoral Interference.* New York, NY: Alfred A. Knopf. 2020, Pg. 168

[39] Harris, Shane. "Russian Officials Overheard Discussing Trump Associates Before Campaign Began," *The Wall Street Journal.* July 12th, 2017

[40] Shimer, David. *Rigged: America, Russia, and One Hundred Years of Covert Electoral Interference.* New York, NY: Alfred A. Knopf. 2020, Pg. 169-173

[41] Sweet, Lynn. "Mueller report confirms Russians 'compromised' Illinois State Board of Elections," *Chicago Sun-Times.* April 18th, 2019

[42] Mueller, III, Robert S. *Report On The Investigation Into Russian Interference In The 2016 Presidential Election.* Department of Justice, Washington, DC. March 2019. Pg. 50

[43] *Report of the Senate Select Committee on Intelligence United States Senate on Russian Active Measures Campaigns and Interference in the 2016 U.S. Election Volume One: Russian Efforts Against Election Infrastructure With Additional Views.* Pg. 22

[44] Shimer, David. *Rigged: America, Russia, and One Hundred Years of Covert Electoral Interference.* New York, NY: Alfred A. Knopf. 2020, Pg. 172

[45] Sanger, David E.; Edmondson, Catie. "Russia Targeted Election Systems in All 50 States, Report Finds," *The New York Times.* July 25th, 2019

[46] *Report of the Senate Select Committee on Intelligence United States Senate on Russian Active Measures Campaigns and Interference in the 2016 U.S. Election Volume One: Russian Efforts Against Election Infrastructure With Additional Views.* Pg. 23

[47] Shimer, David. *Rigged: America, Russia, and One Hundred Years of Covert Electoral Interference.* New York, NY: Alfred A. Knopf. 2020, Pg. 173

[48] Miller, Greg. *The Apprentice: Trump, Russia and the Subversion of American Democracy.* New York, NY: Custom House, 2018. Pg. 149-154

[49] Brennan Testimony, House Intelligence Committee, May 23rd, 2017. Pg. 12

[50] Shimer, David. *Rigged: America, Russia, and One Hundred Years of Covert Electoral Interference.* New York, NY: Alfred A. Knopf. 2020, Pg. 174-176

[51] *Report of the Senate Select Committee on Intelligence United States Senate on Russian Active Measures Campaigns and Interference in the 2016 U.S. Election Volume One: Russian Efforts Against Election Infrastructure With Additional Views.* 116th Congress 2nd Session. Pg. 12

[52] Rid, Thomas. *Active Measures: The Secret History of Disinformation and Political Warfare.* New York, NY: Farrar, Straus and Giroux, 2020. Pg. 412

[53] Ferran, Lee. "The NSA Is Likely 'Hacking Back' Russia's Cyber Squads," *ABC News.* July 30th, 2016

[54] Suiche, Matt. "Shadow Brokers: the insider theory," *Medium.* August 17t, 2016

[55] Lipton, Eric; Sanger, David E.; Shane, Scott. "The Perfect Weapon: How Russian Cyberpower Invaded the US," *The New York Times.* December 13th, 2016

[56] Shimer, David. *Rigged: America, Russia, and One Hundred Years of Covert Electoral Interference.* New York, NY: Alfred A. Knopf. 2020, Pg. 183

[57] Miller, Greg. *The Apprentice: Trump, Russia and the Subversion of American Democracy.* New

York, NY: Custom House, 2018. Pg. 159

[58] *Report of the Senate Select Committee on Intelligence United States Senate on Russian Active Measures Campaigns and Interference in the 2016 U.S. Election Volume Three: U.S. Government Response to Russian Activities.* 116th Congress 2nd Session. Pg. 12

[59] Shimer, David. *Rigged: America, Russia, and One Hundred Years of Covert Electoral Interference.* New York, NY: Alfred A. Knopf. 2020, Pg. 187

[60] Miller, Greg. *The Apprentice: Trump, Russia and the Subversion of American Democracy.* New York, NY: Custom House, 2018. Pg. 158

[61] Landler, Mark; Sanger, David E. "Obama Says He Told Putin: 'Cut It Out,' on Hacking," *The New York Times.* December 16th, 2016

[62] Miller, Greg; Nakashima, Ellen; Entous, Adam. "Obama's secret struggle to punish Russia for Putin's election assault," *The Washington Post.* June 23rd, 2017

[63] Miller, Greg. *The Apprentice: Trump, Russia and the Subversion of American Democracy.* New York, NY: Custom House, 2018. Pg. 161-162

[64] *Report of the Senate Select Committee on Intelligence United States Senate on Russian Active Measures Campaigns and Interference in the 2016 U.S. Election Volume Three: U.S. Government Response to Russian Activities.* Pg. 32

[65] Shimer, David. *Rigged: America, Russia, and One Hundred Years of Covert Electoral Interference.* New York, NY: Alfred A. Knopf. 2020, Pg. 188

[66] *Report of the Senate Select Committee on Intelligence United States Senate on Russian Active Measures Campaigns and Interference in the 2016 U.S. Election Volume Three: U.S. Government Response to Russian Activities.* 116th Congress 2nd Session. Pg. 32

[67] Shimer, David. *Rigged: America, Russia, and One Hundred Years of Covert Electoral Interference.* New York, NY: Alfred A. Knopf. 2020, Pg. 192

[68] *Joint Statement from the Office of Homeland Security and the Office of the Director of National Intelligence on Election Security.* DHS Press Office. October 7th, 2016

[69] Shimer, David. *Rigged: America, Russia, and One Hundred Years of Covert Electoral Interference.* New York, NY: Alfred A. Knopf. 2020, Pg. 193

[70] Alberta, Tim. *American Carnage: On The Front Lines Of The Republican Civil War And The Rise Of President Trump.* New York, NY: HarperCollins, 2019. Pg. 368-373

[71] Green, Joshua. *Devil's Bargain: Steve Bannon, Donald Trump, And The Nationalist Uprising.* New York, NY: Penguin Books, 2017. Pg. 199

[72] *Report of the Select Committee on Intelligence United States Senate on Russian Active Measures Campaigns and Interference in the 2016 U.S. Election Volume Five: Counterintelligence Threats And Vulnerabilities.* 116th Congress, 1st Session. Pg. 244

[73] Ioffe, Julia. "The Secret Correspondence Between Donald Trump Jr. and Wikileaks," *The Atlantic.* November 13th, 2017

[74] *Report of the Select Committee on Intelligence United States Senate on Russian Active Measures Campaigns and Interference in the 2016 U.S. Election Volume Five: Counterintelligence Threats And Vulnerabilities.* Pg. 256

[75] Ioffe, Julia. "The Secret Correspondence Between Donald Trump Jr. and Wikileaks," *The Atlantic.* November 13th, 2017

[76] *Report of the Select Committee on Intelligence United States Senate on Russian Active Measures Campaigns and Interference in the 2016 U.S. Election Volume Five: Counterintelligence Threats And Vulnerabilities.* 116th Congress, 1st Session. Pg. 257

[77] Palazzolo, Joe; Rothfeld, Michael. *The Fixers: The Bottom-Feeders, Crooked Lawyers, Gossipmongers, and Porn Stars Who Created the 45th President.* New York, NY: Random House, 2020. Pg. 171

[78] Palazzolo, Joe; Rothfeld, Michael. "The Fall of Donald Trump's Fixers," *The Wall Street Journal.* January 10th, 2020

[79] Palazzolo, Joe; Rothfeld, Michael. *The Fixers: The Bottom-Feeders, Crooked Lawyers, Gossipmongers, and Porn Stars Who Created the 45th President.* New York, NY: Random House, 2020. Pg. 146

[80] Palazzolo, Joe; Rothfeld, Michael; Alpert, Lukas I. "National Enquirer Shielded

Donald Trump From Playboy Model's Affair Allegation," *The Wall Street Journal.* November 4th, 2016

[81] Palazzolo, Joe; Hong, Nicole; Rothfelf, Michael; O'Brien, Rebecca Davis; Balhaus, Rebecca. "Donald Trump Played Central Role in Hush Payoffs to Stormy Daniels and Karen McDougal," *The Wall Street Journal.* November 9th, 2018

[82] Palazzolo, Joe; Rothfeld, Michael. "Trump Lawyer Used Private Company, Pseudonyms to Pay Porn Star 'Stormy Daniels'," *The Wall Street Journal.* January 18th, 2018

[83] Palazzolo, Joe; Rothfeld, Michael. *The Fixers: The Bottom-Feeders, Crooked Lawyers, Gossipmongers, and Porn Stars Who Created the 45th President.* New York, NY: Random House, 2020. Pg. 201-202

[84] Baker, Stephanie; Bedwell, Helena. "Georgian Businessman Offers More Texts With Cohen to Rebut Mueller Footnote," *Bloomberg.* April 24th, 2019

[85] Mueller, III, Robert S. *Report On The Investigation Into Russian Interference In The 2016 Presidential Election.* Department of Justice, Washington, DC. March 2019. Pg. 51

[86] USA v. Netyksho, et al. Indictment. United States District Court for the District of Columbia. July 13th, 2018. Pg. 26

[87] Cole, Matthew; Esposito, Richard; Biddle, Sam; Grim, Ryan. "Top-Secret NSA Report Details Russian Hacking Effort Days Before 2016 Election," *The Intercept.* June 5th, 2017

[88] Perlroth, Nicole; Wines, Michael; Rosenberg, Matthew. "Russian Election Hacking Efforts, Wider Than Previously Known, Draw Little Scrutiny," *The New York Times.* September 1st, 2017

[89] Zetter, Kim. "Software vendor may have opened a gap for hackers in 2016 swing state," *Politico.* June 5th, 2019

[90] Zetter, Kim. "How Close Did Russia Really Come to Hacking the 2016 Election," *Politico Magazine.* December 26th, 2019

[91] Zetter, Kim. "Inside the Cunning, Unprecedented Hack of Ukraine's Power Grid," *Wired.* March 3rd, 2016

[92] Zetter, Kim. "Top Voting Machine Vendor Admits It Installed Remote-Access Software on Systems Sold to States," *MOTHERBOARD.* July 17th, 2018

[93] Mueller, III, Robert S. *Report On The Investigation Into Russian Interference In The 2016 Presidential Election.* Department of Justice, Washington, DC. March 2019. Pg. 51

[94] Zetter, Kim. "How Close Did Russia Really Come to Hacking the 2016 Election," *Politico Magazine.* December 26th, 2019

[95] Rossman, Sean. "Server shutdown confused Leon County online election results," *Tallahassee Democrat.* August 31st, 2016

[96] Zetter, Kim. "How Close Did Russia Really Come to Hacking the 2016 Election," *Politico Magazine.* December 26th, 2019

[97] Letter to Senator Ron Wyden from VR Systems CEO Mindy J. Perkins, May 16th, 2019

[98] USA v. Netyksho, et al. Indictment. United States District Court for the District of Columbia. July 13th, 2018. Pg. 26

[99] Zetter, Kim. "How Close Did Russia Really Come to Hacking the 2016 Election," *Politico Magazine.* December 26th, 2019

[100] Allen, Jonathan; Parnes, Amie. *Shattered: Inside Hillary Clinton's Doomed Campaign.* New York, NY: Broadway Books, 2017. Pg. 344

[101] Perez, Evan; Brown, Pamela. "Comey notified Congress of email probe despite DOJ concerns," *CNN.* October 30th, 2016

[102] Allen, Jonathan; Parnes, Amie. *Shattered: Inside Hillary Clinton's Doomed Campaign.* New York, NY: Broadway Books, 2017. Pg. 348

[103] Alberta, Tim. *American Carnage: On The Front Lines Of The Republican Civil War And The Rise of President Trump.* New York, NY: HarperCollings, 2019. Pg. 389

[104] Silver, Nate. "The Comey Letter Probably Cost Clinton The Election,"

FiveThirtyEight. May 3rd, 2017

[105] Shimer, David. *Rigged: America, Russia, and One Hundred Years of Covert Electoral Interference.* New York, NY: Alfred A. Knopf, 2020. Pg. 199

[106] Levy, Gabrielle. "Twitter wins big in 2016 election," *U.S. News & World Report.* November 8th, 2016

[107] Collins, Ben; Poulsen, Kevin; Ackerman, Spencer; Swan, Betsy. "Trump Campaign Staffers Pushed Russian Propaganda Days Before the Election," *The Daily Beast.* October 18th, 2017

Chapter 11:
Disinformation, Social Media,
And the Internet Research Agency

The Russian Independent Press Reveals the Internet Research Agency

On September 9th, 2013, a St. Petersburg-based correspondent for the Russian independent newspaper *Novaya Gazeta*, Alexandra Garmazhapova, revealed the existence of a "troll factory" seeding the internet with Kremlin-authorized propaganda. Located in Olgino, a historic district in the Lakhta-Olgino Municipal Okrug north of the Gulf of Finland, the "troll factory" operated under the nondescript moniker the Internet Research Agency (IRA).

While it would later become infamous for targeting the United States, in late 2013, the focus of the IRA's propaganda was domestic, praising Vladimir Putin and his ally, Moscow mayor Sergey Sobyanin, while attacking Russia's most prominent opposition politician, Alexei Navalny, who was running against Sobyanin at the time. The IRA's activities were discovered by Russian journalists remarkably quickly; Garmazhapova revealed that the IRA had been registered on the Russian Unified State Register of Legal Entities less than two months earlier, on July 26th, 2013.[1]

The 24-year-old Garmazhapova and fellow journalist Andrei Soshnikov visited the IRA's Olgino office, posing as job applicants. They had likely been alerted of its existence by an August 29th post on the Russian social media site VKontakte by an IRA employee named Natalya Lvova.[2] Lvova described being hired as an "internet operator" on a team whose job it was to post political messages online. Lvova revealed that each team member was responsible for writing 100 online comments daily and was provided with guidance on what to comment on. One day, they might support Sobyanin; the next, they might attack Navalny.

Garmazhapova and Soshnikov were interviewed by a young IRA manager, Alexei Soskovets, who had extensive contacts with the pro-Kremlin youth organization NASHI. Over a year earlier, *The Guardian* had reported on a series of leaked emails that had revealed NASHI's internal deliberations on how to use internet comments to boost Putin and discredit the opposition to him, Navalny in particular.[3] Soskovets explained to the two undercover journalists that while automated bots could be used to post the messages, they were often discovered and banned by Russian search engines, so it was decided to use real people posting, Soskovets said, "according to the vector which we indicate."

Garmazhapova's reporting showed that the IRA's primary focus was Russian domestic politics. However, she did reveal that even at this early stage, the Russian trolls criticized the US on Russian internet forums, somewhat bizarrely, as being overcrowded with skyscrapers and Americans as being "selfish" and "greedy." She also published screenshots of online troll posts dating back to May 2013, suggesting that the activities pre-dated the official registration of the IRA that July. Other screenshots showed how IRA trolls had labeled Navalny, who was in the middle of an ultimately unsuccessful mayoral campaign, as the "Hitler of our time."

Garmazhapova and Soshnikov also revealed that the IRA suffered from bad management and low morale. "You can go crazy," one IRA worker told them. "They told us we have to write four LiveJournal [a Russian social network site] posts a day, write on city forums, and comment in the media. Nobody upstairs reads our posts, I just copy texts from Wikipedia."

A month after Garmazhapova's article appeared, *The Atlantic* published "Russia's Online-Comment Propaganda Army," which reported on the Lvova post. It named the Internet Research Agency, marking the first mention of the organization by a Western publication.[4] However, while the Western press was slow to pick up on the rise of Kremlin-backed trolls, independent Russian journalists covered the phenomenon with prescience and accuracy. On May 21st, 2014, the Russian Journalist Ilya Klishin was the first to report that the Kremlin's trolls were targeting the West.[5] By that time, the IRA had moved its headquarters from Olgino to a drab office located at 55 Savushkina Street, St. Petersburg.[6]

Klishin's reporting, further developed by Andrei Soldatov, revealed that a key figure behind the Kremlin's embrace of internet trolling was the politician and strategist Vyacheslav Volodin. Upon Putin's return to the presidency in 2011, Volodin was promoted to deputy chief of the presidential administration and was placed in charge of dealing with the large-scale anti-Putin protests. As opposition leaders had utilized social media to organize the street demonstrations, Volodin decided to turn the tables and promoted the "systemic manipulation of public opinion through social media."[7]

According to Klishin, the effort was deemed so successful that the Kremlin decided to direct the effort abroad. Russian expats in Germany, Thailand, and India began posting pro-Putin messages online. Klishin further reported the existence of emails leaked by hackers purporting to be members of the group *Anonymous* that detailed the efforts of the "trolling" group targeting the United States. In all likelihood, this group refers to the IRA. Klishin wrote that "organizers of this campaign likely studied the demographic structure of the main social networks in the US, the online behavior of its citizens, relevant hashtags on Twitter, and groups supporting US President Barack Obama." The Russian trolls also conducted research into "audiences, owners, official and actual editorial policies" of the news outlets *The Huffington Post*, *The Blaze* and *Fox News*, analyzing their attitudes towards Russia and Obama.[8]

A few weeks before the Klishin article appeared, *The Guardian* published an editorial about the pro-Russian trolls polluting the comments sections beneath their articles on the crisis in Ukraine.[9] News of the leaked emails made it into a Western publication roughly two weeks after Klishin's article when *BuzzFeed News* published the story "Documents Show How Russia's Troll Army Hit America" on June 2nd, 2014. The article expanded the list of news sites in the Russian trolls' crosshairs to include *Politico* and the far-right *WorldNetDaily*. "Foreign media are currently actively forming a negative image of the Russian Federation in the eyes of the global community," Svetlana Boiko, an IRA team leader, wrote in a strategy document that was released in the leak. "Like any brand formed by popular opinion, Russia has its supporters ('brand advocates') and its opponents. The main problem is that in the foreign internet community, the ratio of supporters and opponents of Russia is about 20/80 respectively."[10]

Around this time, *Novaya Gazeta* scored another scoop when it revealed that the man funding the Internet Research Agency was the late Yevgeny Prigozhin, a billionaire former restaurateur known as "Putin's Chef," who enjoyed numerous state contracts through his catering and other companies with state organs linked to the Russian intelligence and defense establishment. Prigozhin is now infamous for his control over the Wagner mercenary group, his violent activities during the Russian invasion of Ukraine, and his attempted coup against Putin. Born in Leningrad in 1961, Prigozhin is an ex-convict with ties to the organized criminal syndicates that allied with Putin during his critical years as deputy mayor of St. Petersburg.[11] In 1979, 18-year-old Prigozhin was convicted and given a suspended sentence for theft. Two years later, he was convicted of "robbery in an organized group, fraud, involvement of minors in prostitution" and sentenced to twelve years in prison.[12]

Prigozhin was released after serving nine years and started a business selling hot dogs in St. Petersburg. He was invited by an old classmate at a sports boarding school, Boris Spektor, to manage a chain of convenience stores that, following the rationing of communism, were wildly popular.[13] Through his relationship with Spektor, Prigozhin invested in the newly legalized casino business in St. Petersburg. As deputy mayor, Putin was in charge of licensing the new gaming ventures, most of which were operated by former KGB officers with links to organized crime and used to establish "black cash" slush funds.[14]

In 1996, Prigozhin established Concord Catering.[15] He scored his first major success when he opened up several restaurants, including The Customs House, as well as New Island Restaurant on the Vyatka River in St. Petersburg, which became some of the most fashionable dining destinations in town. In addition to being a favorite dining spot for International Monetary Fund officials, New Island was also patronized by St. Petersburg's deputy mayor, Vladimir Putin. While not a chef himself, Prigozhin claimed that Putin respected his story of having worked his way up from being a street vendor. Putin also appreciated that Prigozhin often waited on him, serving and clearing his food.[16]

Prigozhin built an early relationship with Putin's bodyguard during his time as Deputy Mayor, Viktor Zolotov.[17] Zolotov later served as the Head of the National Guard of Russia and is a member of the powerful Russian Security Council. Baltik-Escort, the security firm that Zolotov oversaw and that looked after Putin and Anatoly Sobchak, had been founded by another Putin confidant with suspected ties to organized crime, Roman Tsepov. According to sources interviewed by *Forbes Russia*, Prigozhin was "well known" to Tsepov. Baltik-Escort also provided security services to the St. Petersburg-based Malyshevskaya and Tambovskaya.

In 2001, Putin brought the French head of state Jacques Chirac to dine at Prigozhin's New Island restaurant. A year later, New Island fed both Putin and George W. Bush on the latter's visit to St. Petersburg. Afterward, Bush wrote a letter of thanks to Prigozhin. In 2003, Putin celebrated his birthday at New Island. Being held in Putin's good graces paid off handsomely for Prigozhin. While Prigozhin enjoyed success as a restaurateur, the true source of his wealth came from a series of lucrative state contracts.

Concord Catering was contracted to provide food for St. Petersburg's 300th anniversary and Dmitry Medvedev's inauguration.[18] Prigozhin scored a larger success when he was contracted to provide meals for St. Petersburg's and Moscow's schools.[19] However, his greatest coup came with a massive nearly $3 billion annual contract to provide food, sanitation, and laundry services for the Russian military. The idea to outsource these services came from Anatoly Serdyukov, who Spanish prosecutors discovered was a principal coordinator between Putin's inner circle and the Tambovskaya. After being appointed Minister of Defense by Putin in 2007, Serdyukov outsourced services that the Russian MOD once administered to a firm called Voentorg. A Prigozhin friend and ally, Leonid Teyf, was the firm's first deputy chief and promptly outsourced the multi-billion dollar contract to Concord Catering. Teyf, who maintained a mansion in Raleigh, North Carolina, was arrested by the FBI in late 2018 for a slew of crimes, including money laundering and attempting to arrange the murder of his wife's lover.[20]

Prigozhin returned the favor of the Kremlin's largesse by engaging in covert, often violent acts on its behalf. In one instance, he inserted a female mole from his personal intelligence network into *Novaya Gazeta* to surveil one of Russia's few independent publications.[21] In the fall of 2013, he sent men to violently assault a blogger in Sochi who had published criticisms of Putin online. Individuals working for Prigozhin also organized pro-Russian demonstrations in Ukraine and were involved in the poisoning of an individual connected to Alexei Navalny's Anti-Corruption Foundation.[22] Among other tasks, Prigozhin provided the funding for the Internet Research Agency.

On March 11th, 2015, Andrei Soshnikov published an expose that further blew the lid off the IRA. According to a whistleblower who spoke and provided documents to Soshnikov, the IRA put out false stories that Ukrainian oligarchs were behind the assassination of the prominent opposition leader Boris Nemtsov.[23] In one of the internal documents leaked to Soshnikov, the IRA lays out its propaganda and disinformation strategy directed at the US: "The USA has several internal problems. We single out three: The problem with the mass proliferation of weapons, and the corresponding mass shootings, crimes and incidents (...); American policemen exceeding their authority in a way which has become commonplace. If, twenty years ago, a suspect could count on a preliminary investigation and immunity, now, on being detained, beatings and even killing have become routine business (...); The Obamacare program, which provoked vast problems and discontent among American citizens (...); The problem of the NSA and total surveillance of American citizens by the intelligence services."[24]

Little over a month after Soshnikov published his article, another IRA whistleblower went public. In April 2015, the activist and investigator Lyudmila Savchuk described her experiences working at the troll factory. "We had to write very positive comments about the government. We were given information and told how we should use it — for example, that life is more and more beautiful, and we're living better and better. And if it's about the US, we have to do everything to make the reader conclude that people there live badly and that it's not going well."[25] Savchuk expanded upon her description of the organization in a subsequent interview with *The Washington Post*. "There are departments. Mine is responsible solely for

LiveJournal blogs, and others are for commenting on the media. There's also a group that masquerades as journalists. They operate fake news portals that pretend to be Ukrainian news sites, with names like 'Kharkiv News' or the 'Federal News Agency.' We had video bloggers. Some made themselves look like members of the Russian opposition."[26]

The IRA received its most extensive treatment by the Western media in an article called "The Agency" by Adrian Chen for *The New York Times Magazine* on June 2nd, 2015.[27] It revealed disinformation and propaganda targeting the United States. Social media accounts linked to the IRA promoted a Manhattan art exhibit called "Material Evidence" that featured photos and supposed artifacts from the crises unfolding in Ukraine and Syria that presented the conflicts along the narrative favored by the Kremlin. On September 11th, 2014, dozens of Twitter accounts linked to the IRA sent hundreds of tweets about a non-existent explosion at the Columbiana Chemicals plant located in St. Mary Parish, Louisiana, using the hashtag #ColumbianaChemicals. The IRA tweets tagged American journalists, media outlets, and politicians in an attempt to provide their disinformation traction. More than simply tweeting about the false story, the IRA established a fabricated Louisiana news website covering the false story, along with a YouTube video and a Wikipedia page. A month later, on December 13th, the IRA pushed two false stories in one day, one promoting a false story about an Ebola outbreak in Atlanta and another about the shooting of an unarmed black man in the same city.

However, the reaction of the American intelligence community, law enforcement, and the social media tech companies was to overlook and underplay these revelations entirely. In an interview with David Shimer, Steven Hall, the CIA's Division Chief overseeing Russia, claimed that he felt the IRA was such a poorly kept secret that it wasn't likely to be very influential.[28] Hall later realized that the Russians were being vastly more aggressive in this arena than the CIA had appreciated and didn't care if they were discovered. Being discovered may have been part of the plan all along. What is remarkable is that in the lead-up to the 2016 election, Russian journalists had uncovered ample evidence that the US was being targeted, and apparently, few in the United States were paying attention or alarmed if they were.

"When I began researching the story," Adrian Chen
wrote in *The New Yorker* two days after the first WikiLeaks email
dump, "I assumed that paid trolls worked by relentlessly
spreading their message and thus indoctrinating Russian Internet
users. But, after speaking with Russian journalists and opposition
members, I quickly learned that pro-government trolling
operations were not very effective at pushing a specific pro-
Kremlin message." He continued, "[t]he real effect, the Russian
activists told me, was not to brainwash readers but to overwhelm
social media with a flood of fake content, seeding doubt and
paranoia, and destroying the possibility of using the Internet as a
democratic space."[29]

Project Lakhta:
The Internet Research Agency's Campaign against the United States

The Internet Research Agency, or a predecessor organization
before its registration, appears to have begun making Russian
language posts on Twitter as far back as 2009, with tweets
directed at a domestic audience.[30] By 2013, the IRA started
targeting the United States with disinformation over Twitter. As
its operations against the United States ramped up throughout
2014, the IRA began utilizing other social media platforms in the
following sequence: YouTube, Instagram, and, lastly, Facebook.[31]
        The IRA was part of a broader effort known as Project
Lakhta, the stated goal of which was "to spread distrust towards
candidates for political office and the political system in general"
in the United States.[32] Lakhta was the name of the St. Petersburg
suburb where Prigozhin set up his first troll factory, and he
reportedly maintains a villa in the district as well.[33] The Internet
Research Agency is just one of multiple Russian corporate entities
that were connected to Prigozhin. Given the length and depth of
Putin's relationship with Prigozhin, dating back to his earliest
days as deputy mayor of St. Petersburg, it is inconceivable that
the Russian president isn't aware of the overall aims and methods
of the project. The fact that Prigozhin likely possesses
compromising information on Putin's early partnerships with
organized crime and yet maintains his trust and confidence
indicates the close nature of their relationship.
        The IRA employed hundreds of people and was headed
by a management group, the General Director of which was

Mikhail Bystrov, a former colonel in the Moskovsky District police department in St. Petersburg.[34] A young tech entrepreneur named Mikhail Burchik served as the IRA's Executive Director, the number two position in the leadership hierarchy.[35] The organization is subdivided into various departments, including a graphics department, a data-analysis department, a search engine optimization department, an IT department that maintains its digital infrastructure, and a finance department that budgets and allocates funding for the IRA's various propaganda and disinformation operations.[36] The finance department, led by Elena Khusyaynova, who also manages the finances for the other legal entities involved with Project Lakhta, budgeted $12 million for its activities in 2016.[37]

In April 2014, the IRA established a department focused on the US population, known variously as the "translator project" or the American Department. Less than a month earlier, Barack Obama had ordered sanctions to be applied on Russia as a response to its military incursion into Crimea.[38] The "translator project" was headed by a 27-year-old Azerbaijani entrepreneur named Dzheykhun Aslanov. Nicknamed Jay Z, Aslanov reportedly liked dogs and partying.[39] In 2009, he spent several months in the United States, visiting Boston and New York.[40] Aslanov oversaw many of the operations directed at the 2016 US presidential election. However, while the IRA targeted the 2016 election and attempted to aid the candidacy of Donald Trump and hurt Hillary Clinton, its overall aims were more comprehensive.

"The data now available make it clear that Russian efforts are not directed against one election, one party, or even one country," John Kelly, the CEO of *Graphika* and an expert on the Internet Research Agency, later testified. "We are facing a sustained campaign of organized manipulation, a coordinated attack on the trust we place in our institutions and in our media - both social and traditional. These attacks are sophisticated and complex, and the committee's bi-partisan work to untangle and expose them sets a great example for the country."[41]

According to Kelly, the IRA crafted fictitious online personas to infiltrate targeted communities. They infiltrated both right and left-wing radical communities to amplify the disdain and mistrust between them. The IRA targeted the most divisive political issues in the US. They utilized pop culture references and radical political discourse to influence young minds. They used bots and trolls for inorganic amplification. Lastly, they occasionally executed cyber attacks in conjunction with their information operations.

After the establishment of the "translator project," members of the IRA traveled to the US on a reconnaissance and intelligence fact-finding mission. On June 4th, 2014, IRA operatives Aleksandra Y. Krylova and Anna V. Bogacheva entered the US, claiming they were traveling for personal reasons to receive visas.[42] Krylova had joined the IRA in September of 2013, and by the time of her visit to the US, she occupied the third highest position in the organization, while Bogacheva served as the director of the IRA's data analysis group. They were to be joined by the deputy head of the "translator project," Robert S. Bovda, but his visa application was rejected.[43] Krylova and Bogacheva compiled itineraries and instructions for the trip, bringing cameras, SIM cards, and disposable cell phones. They prepared "evacuation scenarios" in the event that the purpose of their trip became known to US authorities.[44]

Over three weeks, Krylova and Bogacheva visited nine states, including Colorado, Michigan, Nevada, New Mexico, California, New York, Illinois, Louisiana, and Texas. Upon their return, Krylova provided her superior, Mikhail Burchik, with an intelligence report documenting what they had learned over their travels. Later that year, on November 26th, a third, as yet unnamed individual working for the IRA visited Atlanta, Georgia, for four days.[45] Within just a few weeks of their return, the IRA pushed false stories about an Atlanta-based Ebola outbreak and a police shooting of an unarmed black man.

Like corporate digital marketing techniques, the IRA created and managed campaigns, including paid advertisements, across multiple social media platforms, using fictitious personas and imitating activist groups to reach both a broad audience and targeted subgroups. The IRA also created standalone websites and used their social media personas to direct traffic to them. While most of the activity occurred on Twitter, Instagram, Facebook, and YouTube, the IRA was also active on Reddit, Tumblr, Medium, PayPal, LinkedIn, and Pinterest.[46] Only a minority of the content was election-related. The primary focus was on divisive content related to race relations, immigration, far-right movements, gun rights, Islam and immigration, and other controversial issues roiling American society.

On January 7th, 2015, the IRA established its earliest known Instagram account. Throughout the 2016 election and into 2017, IRA Instagram accounts received 187 million engagements, which is the sum of likes and comments received on a post divided by the number of followers. According to Facebook, which owns Instagram, roughly 20 million Instagram users were affected.[47] Not all of the content was politically divisive or election-related. In the case of an account created on January 7th, @army_of_jesus, it started as an Kermit the Frog and later *The Simpsons* meme account in an apparent attempt to build an audience before switching to explicitly political content almost exactly a year later on January 15th, 2016. This model of producing innocuous, community-building content before switching to disinformation and propaganda was used on numerous accounts across multiple platforms.[48]

Three days after establishing their first Instagram account, the IRA made its first post on Facebook on January 10th, 2015. Facebook later estimated that IRA propaganda on its platform reached 126 million people. The IRA made 61,500 Facebook posts across 81 pages, resulting in 77 million engagements. On Twitter, the IRA used 3841 accounts to produce 10.4 million tweets, 6 million of which were original, leading to 73 million engagements. On YouTube, the IRA created 1,100 videos, which they distributed over 17 account channels.

The IRA's election-related content was pro-Trump and anti-Clinton. While a small number of posts from early 2015 supported Rand Paul, from July 2015 onward, the IRA supported Trump.[49] On February 10th, 2016, an internal document outlining what themes would be emphasized moving forward circulated within the IRA. It instructed the trolls to focus on "politics in the USA" and "to use any opportunity to criticize Hillary and the rest (except Trump and Sanders - we support them)."[50] Support for Sanders was seen as a way to harm Clinton and exacerbate ideological fault lines. In addition to supporting Sanders, the IRA used its online personas to support the candidacy of Green Party candidate Jill Stein.[51]

The IRA's activities surged during critical moments in the election campaign. For example, IRA online activity targeting the election surged on days related to the Benghazi investigation, the Iowa Caucus, both the Republican and Democratic Conventions, during primary and then general election debates and in the days leading up to and including election day itself.[52] IRA propagandists also responded to real-world events, such as when Hillary Clinton fell ill at a 2016 9/11 memorial ceremony in New York the trolls began disseminating posts raising questions about Clinton's health. The activity of the IRA's left-leaning fake personas spiked on October 6th, 2017, the day before WikiLeaks released the Podesta emails. This raises questions as to whether the troll factory had inside knowledge regarding the date of the leak.[53]

IRA Targeting of African Americans and Black Lives Matter

While the IRA targeted conservative and right-wing Americans, focusing on issues such as gun rights, immigration, religion, Southern culture, and others, above all else, they chiefly targeted African Americans. In Soviet times, the communist school curriculum taught that the exploitation of black people in the US epitomized the inherent evil of the capitalist system.[54] As far back as 1928, the Comintern drew up a plan and allotted $300,000 towards recruiting Southern blacks in an attempt to create a "separate negro state" in the South. Prominent African Americans were invited to Moscow by the Kremlin.[55]

In addition to using American racism for its own recruitment and propaganda purposes, Soviet intelligence also targeted prominent African Americans. In 1967, the KGB authorized a plan to plant articles in the African press portraying Martin Luther King Jr. as an "Uncle Tom" secretly being paid by the US government to prevent the Civil Rights movement from harming President Lyndon Johnson.[56] King may be the only person in history to be simultaneously targeted by both KGB and FBI disinformation campaigns.

In the 1980s, Soviet intelligence engaged in a global disinformation campaign spreading the falsehood that the US government created AIDS.[57] Many in Africa and even the US still believe this to be true today. In the 1980s, the KGB forged a National Security Council document, giving it the title "Carter's Secret Plan to Keep Black Africans and Black Americans at Odds," then sent it via a cutout to a small African American newspaper based out of San Francisco. A Soviet news agency redistributed the article to Soviet embassies, who took the story worldwide.[58] In the lead-up to the 1984 Los Angeles Olympics, the KGB forged letters from the Ku Klux Klan and sent them to African nations to attempt to dissuade them from attending the games. "The Olympics — for the whites only," the letters read.[59]

In early 2016, researchers at the University of Washington set about studying online conversations around the #BlackLivesMatter movement, unaware of Russian trolling operations. The focus was on "framing contests," in this context, a frame is "a way of seeing and understanding the world that helps us interpret new information," and framing refers to "the process of shaping other people's frames, guiding how other people interpret new information."[60] They published a paper that analyzed #BlackLivesMatter discussions on Twitter regarding shooting events in 2016. Their research revealed a framing contest between the political left, which supported Black Lives Matter, and the political right, which was critical of the movement. The former operated within a frame that highlighted police violence against African Americans and explained the phenomenon as a product of systemic racism. In contrast, the latter highlighted violence within the African American community and cast police actions as a reasonable response to this reality. The paper noted the near-total division between the two sides and the toxic nature of the content.[61]

After the paper was published in late 2017, the House Intelligence Committee released a list of IRA-linked Twitter accounts to the public. The researchers cross-checked the IRA accounts with the accounts they had analyzed in their data set and discovered that dozens of the troll accounts were among the most retweeted in their analysis. They further noticed that retweets of the pro-BLM and anti-BLM troll accounts occurred within but not between the two communities they had identified. While in some of the cases, the IRA accounts were distorted, toxic exaggerations of Americans on both the left and right, many more still appeared to mimic Americans on both sides of the political divide accurately. Thus, the Russian actors were not creating these divides but instead actively encouraging them.

IRA efforts to impersonate Black Lives Matter activists were made all the more cynical by the fact that internal communications within the organization regarding the strategy and tactics behind their influence operations were explicitly racist. "Colored LGBT are less sophisticated than white; therefore, complicated phrases and messages do not work," read one internal IRA communique. "Be careful dealing with racial content. Just like ordinary Blacks, Latinos, and Native Americans, Colored LGBT are very sensitive toward #whiteprivilege and they react to posts and pictures that favor white people... Unlike with conservatives, infographics works well among LGBT and their liberal allies, and it does work very well. However, the content must be simple to understand consisting of short text in large font and a colorful picture."[62]

One example of an IRA effort targeting African Americans was the fictitious activist group Black Matters, which emphasized distrust of the media and a desire to create "Black independent media." On June 8th, 2015, the IRA established a Facebook page for the group. The total online presence of the group included its own website and accounts on Instagram, Twitter, YouTube, Google+, and a Tumblr account called SKWAD 55 with an associated SKWAD 55 podcast on Soundcloud. Its online presence was modest at best, with 28,466 followers on Instagram, 1,929,855 engagements, and only 5,841 followers on Twitter. However, the online reach of Black Matters was expanded by being promoted and shared both by false personas within the IRA online ecosystem as well as by actual activist influencers with significant followings, including Color of Change, Unapologetically Black, and YourAnonNews, all of which shared Black Matters articles on their Facebook pages.[63]

From Online to On the Streets:
IRA-Inspired Protests and Counter Protests

In the Spring of 2015, individuals within the IRA conducted an experiment. On one of their Facebook pages targeting New York City, the trolls advertised that free hot dogs would be provided to individuals who arrived at a certain place at a certain time. From their office on the 2nd floor of 55 Savushkina Street, funded by a one-time hot dog vendor, IRA employees watched via street web cameras as New Yorkers arrived and looked around quizzically for the free hot dogs on offer before leaving disappointed.[64] This was far more than a harmless prank. The implications were profound. The Russians could manifest activity on American streets using their growing online presence.

The earliest known attempt to organize a political rally

took place when an IRA Instagram account @stand_for_freedom promoted a "confederate rally" on November 14th, 2015, in Houston.[65] The account had 45,019 followers and an associated Facebook page, though it is unclear whether the rally ever occurred.[66] On March 27th, 2016, the IRA's Black Matters organized a "not my heritage" anti-confederate rally in Jackson, MI, which attracted dozens of protestors to rally against Confederate Heritage Month.[67] The IRA recruited a Los Angeles-based activist, Nolan Hack, who became an "official" member of Black Matters without knowing the truth behind it, to help organize the event. Black Matters contacted Hack in early 2016, and while he never actually met anybody from the organization, he did speak with them over the phone, by phone messages, and by text. He described the individuals posing as Black Matters activists as having "African" accents. Black Matters, or rather the IRA, paid for Hack's trip to Jackson, which he noted was a rare occurrence in the activist community. Hack eventually left the group in September when it failed to pay for one of his trips.[68]

Shortly after the Jackson protest, another IRA online persona targeting African Americans reached out to activists. The IRA creation Blacktivist had a Twitter account and a Facebook page, which at one point had 360,000 likes, nearly 60,000 more than the official Black Lives Matter Facebook page at the time.[69] Following the suspicious death of a young black woman named India Cummings while in police custody in Buffalo, NY, in February 2016, Blacktivist reached out to several local activists to attend an April 4th rally. A local civil rights activist, Dierra Jenkins, was contacted by Blacktivist, who she assumed was local given their focus on events that transpired in Buffalo. Craig Carson, a Rochester, NY-based civil rights attorney and activist, was recruited to print out and distribute flyers with specific visuals at the protest after three to four conversations over Facebook Messenger.[70]

On April 6th, two days after the Blacktivist promoted a protest in Buffalo, Black Matters purchased a Facebook ad calling for a "flashmob" of Americans to "take a photo with #HillaryClintonForPrison2016 or #nohillary2016."[71] Thus, the IRA used multiple interlocking accounts on different platforms to build an audience that it could subtly seed with anti-Clinton messages. This practice would only accelerate in the lead-up to the election.

On May 18th, the activist and co-creator of the 2011 Occupy Wall Street protests, Micah White, was contacted through his website by a man who said his name was Yan Big Davis and claimed to be working for Black Matters. Yan Big, writing in awkward English, requested an interview. While White hesitated, he agreed to be interviewed two weeks after the initial inquiry. "The interview with Yan Big was immediately uncomfortable," White later wrote. "The phone quality was terrible: it sounded like he was calling internationally or through a distant internet connection. He had a strange accent and an unusual way of phrasing questions. He was obviously not a typical American." White continued, "I rationalized that he must be an African immigrant living in America, and that was why he was interested in protesting against racism and police brutality. His attempts at flattery set off more alarm bells. I finished up the interview as quickly as possible and got off the phone."[72]

White's interview was posted on the Black Matters website to foster credibility with the activist community. Other individuals whose interviews were posted on the Black Matters site include Erica Huggins, a former leading member of the Black Panther Party, the mother of Ramarley Graham, a black teenager shot and killed by the NYPD in 2012, Jamal Joseph, a former member of the Black Panther Party and the Black Liberation Army and Godfather to Tupac Shakur and Ramona Africa, a former member of the black anarcho-primitivist group MOVE and survivor of a violent 1985 confrontation with the Philadelphia police that left 11 members, including five children, dead.[73] Yan Big reached out to Micah White several times after their interview to ask that he help promote a protest to free the MOVE 9 (a name for members of the MOVE above group who remained in prison) and for another incarcerated African American, Jerome "Skee" Smith, but White never replied.

Yan Big Davis's activities, beyond interviewing black activists, reveal the multifaceted tactics of the IRA. Posing as a spokesperson from Your Digital Face, a non-existent Los Angeles-based startup, Davis recruited predominantly African American business owners to pay a monthly fee in return for promoting their products on social media. One of the victimized companies, among over a dozen that *The Wall Street Journal* spoke with who had communicated with Davis, was Expression Tees, a

Pennsylvania t-shirt vendor noted for the progressive messaging on its apparel.[74] The IRA then used its accounts to promote the products, including @Blackstagram, which had over 300,000 followers and generated 28 million engagements on Instagram.[75] Intelligence officials have suggested that the "Your Digital Face" operation may have been designed to map out business networks. Other novel efforts by the IRA included attempting, with little apparent success, to target American teenage girls with a Chrome plug-in app called FaceMusic that contained malicious malware similar to that found on click-fraud scams that simulate clicks on online advertisements.[76]

On May 21st, an IRA-organized "Stop Islamization of Texas" rally took place outside the Islamic Da'wah Center in Houston.[77] The event was organized through an IRA-created "Heart of Texas" Facebook group, which attracted 250,000 followers and made repeated calls for Texas to secede.[78] Later in November, the IRA reached out via Facebook to the Texan Nationalist Movement, an actual organization calling for Texan independence led by Nathan Smith, who traveled to Moscow in 2015 for a conference attended by European Neo-Nazi and fringe right-wing groups. A spokesman for the group says they declined to participate.[79]

At the same time, a separate IRA Facebook page, "United Muslims for America," organized a counter-protest at the same location. The ensuing protests drew the attention of local media and led to verbal confrontations. The fictitious IRA creation, "United Muslims for America," was based on a real California-based nonprofit with no links to Russia and peddled conspiracy theories that Hillary Clinton had created and funded al Qaeda and the Islamic State terrorist organization and that Osama Bin Laden was a CIA agent.[80]

Four days after the dueling protests in Houston, the IRA promoted a counter-protest against the homophobic Westboro Baptist Church organized by the IRA-run Facebook page "LGBT United" to take place in Lawrence, Kansas.[81] Towards the end of the month, IRA operatives posing as activists and Facebook page administrators recruited Americans to stand before the White House holding signs. One of the signs being held by an unwitting protestor read "Happy 55th Birthday Dear Boss," a reference to Yevgeny Prigozhin, whose 55th birthday was on June 1st, 2016. The IRA imposters reportedly told the American holding the sign that it was for "someone who is our leader here and our boss... our founder."[82]

IRA-sponsored events and rallies continued into June and July. On June 1st, the IRA purchased Facebook ads for a "March for Trump," to be held in New York City on the 25th. The march was sponsored by an IRA Facebook group called "Being Patriotic" and promoted by the Twitter account @March_for_Trump. The IRA sent press releases to New York Media outlets to promote the event using allforusa@yahoo.com. A day later, the fictitious IRA online persona "Matt Skiber" contacted a Trump campaign volunteer who agreed to provide signs for the rally. "Matt Skiber" then contacted an unwitting US political activist to act as a recruiter for the March for Trump, offering them "money to print posters and get a megaphone." The march took place on June 25th.[83]

That same day, "LGBT United" organized a candlelight vigil following the mass shooting at the Pulse Nightclub in Orlando, Florida, which killed 49 mostly LGBT clubgoers. The vigil featured comments from the brother of one of the victims, attracting a dozen or more attendees and attention from local media.[84] On July 8th, the day after the police shooting of an unarmed black man named Philando Castile, the IRA Facebook group "Don't Shoot Us" promoted a protest outside of the police department where the officer who shot Castile worked. The "Don't Shoot Us" IRA effort was active on Facebook, Instagram, Twitter, YouTube, Tumblr, and even the augmented reality game Pokémon Go.

The "Don't Shoot Us" YouTube page contained over 200 videos relating to police brutality, which had been viewed over 368,000 times.[85] Overall, the IRA created 1,100 YouTube videos distributed over 17 channels, and 96% of the YouTube content was related to Black Lives Matter and police brutality.[86] The YouTube videos linked to the dedicated website donotshoot.us, which itself linked to a Tumblr page that promoted a contest in July 2016 that had participants play the game Pokémon Go, which allows users to travel to real locations to find and train digital Pokémon characters. The contest was designed for users to find Pokémon in locations where black men had been killed by police, offering Amazon gift cards as prizes. It is unclear whether anybody took part in the macabre game.

The IRA organized a rally in Minneapolis in support of

Philando Castile that attracted over 300 attendees on July 10th. That same day, the IRA arranged a "Blue Lives Matter" protest in Dallas, which was a reaction to the fatal shooting of five police officers at an anti-police violence protest held in the wake of Castile's death.[87] Less than a week later, the fictitious IRA group Blacktivist organized a protest in front of the Chicago Police Department's Homan Square office to protest the one-year anniversary of the death of Sandra Bland, an African American woman who died while in police custody in Texas. The protestors passed around a petition to get the Chicago City Council to pass a Civilian Police Accountability Council ordinance.[88]

Throughout July, the IRA anti-Hillary Clinton activities picked up pace. Shortly after the Pulse Nightclub shooting, which was perpetrated by an American admirer of the Islamic State terrorist organization, the IRA group "United Muslims of America" established a July 9th event on Facebook titled "Support Hillary. Save American Muslims!" The event page, which featured a picture of Clinton with her name written in Arabic-style font, claimed that she was "the only presidential candidate who refuses to 'demonize' Islam after the Orlando nightclub shooting" and further stated that "with such a person in White House [sic] America will easily reach the bright multicultural future."[89] The IRA contacted actual Americans to arrange for the production of posters for the rally, one of which depicted Clinton saying, "I think Sharia Law will be a powerful new direction in freedom."[90] On July 23rd, the same "Being Patriotic" IRA group that organized the "March for Trump" held a "Down with Hillary" rally in front of Trump Tower in New York. To publicize the event, they purchased Facebook ads and contacted over 30 media outlets using the email address joshmilton024@gmail.com.

IRA Interactions with Trump Supporters and Campaign Staff

"Hi there! I'm a member of [sic] Being Patriotic online community," the IRA persona "Matt Skiber" wrote in an August 2nd Facebook message to the real "Florida for Trump" Facebook page. "Listen, we've got an idea. Florida is still a purple state, and we need to paint it red. If we lose Florida, we lose America. We can't let it happen, right? What about organizing a YUGE pro-Trump flash mob in every Florida town? We are currently reaching out to local activists and we've got the folks who are okay to be in charge of organizing their events almost everywhere in FL. However, we still need your support. What do you think about that? Are you in?"

Throughout August 2nd and 3rd, the IRA used the stolen identity of a US citizen to reach out to various Florida-based pro-Trump grassroots organizations, describing their plans to "organize a flash mob across Florida to support Mr. Trump." On August 4th, the IRA purchased Facebook ads promoting the "Florida for Trump" events. The next day, using the @March_for_Trump Twitter account, the IRA recruited and later paid an American actress to portray Hillary Clinton in a prison uniform at a rally in West Palm Beach. They further paid another unwitting American, Harry Miller, as much as $1,000 to build a cage in the back of a flatbed truck for the Hillary impersonator to occupy. Miller had multiple conversations about the job with a man who he described as not speaking clear English.[91]

On August 15th, the chairwoman of the Trump Campaign in Broward County, Florida, Dolly Trevino Rump, reached out to one of the IRA's online personas and identified two locations for potential rallies. Unaware of who she was dealing with, Rump was a notable local Trump supporter and former Secretary of the Broward County Republican Party.[92] The IRA communicated with Rump to discuss logistics and an additional Florida rally. On August 16th, the IRA purchased ads on Instagram promoting the Florida rallies through their @Tea_Party_News fake account.[93] The Team Trump Broward County Facebook page, which real Trump supporters operated, posted numerous times promoting the pro-Trump flash mobs.[94]

Two weeks after their initial message to the "Florida for Trump" Facebook group, a Trump campaign employee overseeing the group responded and provided the IRA with the name and email address of Trump campaign Florida Communications Director Chad Tucker.[95] Posing as a "team leader" from the "Being Patriotic" group named Josh Milton, the IRA reached out to Tucker. "[W]e are organizing a state-wide event in Florida on August 20 to support Mr. Trump. Let us introduce ourselves first. "Being Patriotic" is a grassroots conservative online movement trying to unite people offline. . . . [W]e gained a huge lot of followers and decided to somehow help

Mr. Trump get elected. You know, simple yelling on the Internet is not enough. There should be real action. We organized rallies in New York before. Now we're focusing on purple states such as Florida."

"Josh Milton" told Tucker that they had thirteen "confirmed locations" in Florida for the rallies and asked if the Trump campaign could provide "assistance in each location." After receiving her contact information from the Trump campaign employee overseeing the "Florida for Trump" Facebook page, the IRA emailed Beatriz J. Ramos, the coalitions director for the Trump campaign in Florida. When later asked by *The New York Times*, Tucker and Ramos said they could not recall receiving the messages or if they responded. On the day the IRA emailed Ramos, an unwitting Trump supporter contacted their @March_for_Trump Twitter account and provided contact information for an as-yet-unnamed Florida Trump Campaign official. The IRA contacted the official using the joshmilton024@gmail.com email address, but there is no indication that they received a response.

The day before the "Florida for Trump" rallies, "Matt Skiber" contacted an unidentified Texas-based grassroots organization. The two parties had previously communicated with one another, with the unwitting Texas political group suggesting they focus on "purple states like Colorado, Virginia & Florida." Skiber wrote to the group, "We were thinking about your recommendation to focus on purple states, and this is what we're organizing in FL." The IRA then sent a link to a Facebook page for the Florida rallies, asking the grassroots organization to promote them among their followers, which they agreed to do.[96] While attendance at most locations was sparse, "Florida Goes Trump" rallies were held on August 20th in Fort Lauderdale and Coral Springs, both in Broward County, Florida.[97]

Four days later, the IRA updated an internal document that listed over 100 Americans that the group had contacted through fictitious online personas. The document monitored IRA recruitment efforts and outreach to these US citizens. More than this, the list summarized the political views of each of these Americans and laid out the activities they had been asked to perform by the IRA.[98]

Throughout September and October, the IRA creation Black Matters contacted and worked with an unwitting Raleigh,

North Carolina-based African American activist named Conrad James to organize more anti-police shooting rallies. James was told to contact a woman named Stephanie Williamson, who he would later describe as a spokeswoman for the organization. James met with Williamson, who was accompanied by an unnamed white man, and she provided him with a bankroll to cover expenses related to microphones and speakers. It remains unclear what role Williamson played with the IRA or whether she was tricked herself.[99]

While these IRA interactions were taking place with real people, attempting to organize rallies around actual episodes of police violence, IRA online ecosystems of false activists on platforms such as Tumblr were spreading rumors, in one instance promoting a false story about a black teenage girl being raped by NYPD officers using footage taken in South Africa.[100] In an attempt to suppress African American voter turnout, the IRA recruited two vloggers (video bloggers) who called themselves "Kalvin and Williams," purportedly from Nigeria but who expressed opinions on American domestic politics, to post YouTube videos attacking Obama's legacy, accusing Hillary Clinton of being a racist and defending Donald Trump, often over rap beats. The "Kalvin and Williams" Facebook page had 48,000 fans.[101]

IRA Activities Around the Election and Voter Suppression Strategies

As the election approached, the IRA placed a heavier emphasis on attempting to shape the outcome. On September 14th, in an internal IRA review of the activities of one of their Facebook pages designed to appeal to conservatives, "Secured Borders," the specialist who oversaw the group was criticized for a "low number of posts dedicated to criticizing Hillary Clinton" and was told "it is imperative to intensify criticizing Hillary Clinton" in future posts.[102] Later analysis showed that a significant portion of the political content produced by the IRA was anti-Clinton in thrust and, except for a single event organized by the "United Muslims of America" group, which was likely intended to undermine her campaign by associating her with Islam, there was no pro-Clinton content on Facebook or Instagram.[103]

On September 19th, Donald Trump personally responded to the IRA fake Twitter account @10_gop, a backup account for @TEN_GOP, which falsely claimed to be the "Unofficial Twitter Account of the Tennessee GOP."[104] In the lead-up to election day, @TEN_GOP relentlessly promoted the WikiLeaks email dumps and was listed in a *Fox News* article as a "Trump fan." The account was retweeted by Donald Trump Jr., Roger Stone, Trump political surrogate and later National Security Advisor Michael Flynn and his son Michael Flynn Jr., Trump Campaign Manager Kellyanne Conway, and Trump campaign digital director Brad Parscale.[105]

In the month before the election, many IRA online personas that they had spent years building followings for began pushing messages designed to discourage Americans from voting. This effort was most aggressively directed towards African Americans. On October 16th, the IRA Instagram account Woke Blacks posted, "[A] particular hype and hatred for Trump is misleading the people and forcing Blacks to vote Killary. We cannot resort to the lesser of two devils. Then we'd surely be better off without voting AT ALL." On November 3rd, the IRA Blacktivist account promoted a third-party candidacy in an attempt to siphon votes away from Clinton, writing on Instagram, "Choose peace and vote for Jill Stein. Trust me, it's not a wasted vote."[106] That same day, Blacktivist wrote, "NOT VOTING is a way to exercise our rights."[107]

African Americans were not the only subgroup targeted in voter suppression information operations by the IRA. American Muslims were also in their crosshairs. In early November, the IRA group "United Muslims of America" posted the following message to their Facebook page: "American Muslims [are] boycotting elections today, most of the American Muslim voters refuse to vote for Hillary Clinton because she wants to continue the war on Muslims in the middle east and voted yes for invading Iraq."[108]

Between November 5th and election day, November 9th, the IRA authored 32,000 posts across Twitter, Facebook and Instagram. The three primary groups targeted were Right-leaning, Left-leaning, and black voters. The IRA targeted right-wing voters with posts highlighting conspiracy theories, accusations of voter fraud, and the need to revolt if Clinton won the election openly. Left-leaning voters were targeted with anti-establishment messages, highlighting identity politics and promoting third-party candidates. Black voters, meanwhile, were primarily targeted with messages of social alienation and the ubiquity of police violence and racial injustice until, shortly before the election, the messages morphed into voter suppression narratives that attempted to dissuade African Americans from voting at all.[109]

Did the Internet Research Agency's efforts impact the outcome of the 2016 election? The question is hotly debated among scholars even to this day. Professor Thomas Rid, for example, falls firmly on the side that they did not. He points out the facts that the overall volume of IRA activity was over-reported in the press, that much of the activity was innocuous audience building and took place within echo chambers, and that only 8.4% of the overall activity was election-related.[110]

On the other hand, Professor Kathleen Hall Jamieson of the University of Pennsylvania, an expert in political communications, argues that "[t]hose alleging that Kremlin-tied trolls, bots, and hackers could not have affected enough voters to swing a close election are paddling against currents of scholarship showing that audiences are influenced by agenda setting, framing, and priming." She goes on to argue that by making specific issues, candidate characteristics, or concepts more important to voters' decision-making, by influencing the media narratives in ways that benefitted Trump and hurt Clinton, and by framing issues for voters in a similar dynamic, the IRA could have influenced the outcome of the election.[111]

While reasonable scholars disagree on this point, it may be the case that asking whether the efforts of the IRA in isolation impacted the outcome of the election is the wrong question. Perhaps it is more salient to view the IRA's social media disinformation and propaganda campaign as part of a broader confluence of separate but interrelated events that, taken in their totality, proved decisive in Trump's victory. These factors include the divisive nature of the Trump campaign itself and its voter suppression activities, as well as an attention-based business model at the core of the world's largest social media companies that encourages the spread of disinformation and divisive content.

Donald Trump's core strategy of dividing Americans by conspiratorial appeals to his base and demonizing his opponents, as well as his broad attack on the American political class and its institutions, neatly overlapped with the IRA's more comprehensive strategy. Witting or not, these efforts mutually reinforced each other. It is more useful to look at the cumulative impact these parallel efforts had on the election instead of trying to isolate and analyze them separately. One area where the Trump Campaign and the Internet Research Agency engaged in parallel efforts to achieve a similar goal was in African American voter suppression. This phenomenon, of course, had historically occurred in the United States as far back as Reconstruction. In a leaked data cache used by the Trump Campaign in 2016 of over 200 million American voters, 3.5 million African Americans distributed across 16 key battleground states were placed under the label of "Deterrence," which Trump's chief data scientist later publicly said described people the campaign "hope don't show up to vote."[112]

Finally, arguably the most important force driving division in the US body politic was the tech giants, whose advertising, attention-based business model has led to an extraordinary propagation of fake news and conspiracy theories and the Balkanization of the American information space. The IRA did not hack these platforms but instead used their essential functionality not to sell a product but to divide American society and destroy trust in institutions, and attack the idea of truth itself, which is vital to any functioning democracy. While the IRA pursued these goals consciously, it may ironically be the case that their efforts paled in comparison to the catastrophic unintended consequences of the business model driving some of America's largest and most widely subscribed to social media platforms

[1] Garmazhapova, Alexandra. "Where trolls live. How internet provocateurs work in St. Petersburg and who runs them," *Novaya Gazeta*. September 9th, 2013
[2] Atlantic Council's Digital Forensic Research Lab. "The Russians Who Exposed Russia's Trolls," *Medium*. May 7th, 2018
[3] Elder, Miriam. "Emails give insight into Kremlin youth groups priorities, means and concerns," *The Guardian*. February 7th, 2012
[4] Khazan, Olga. "Russia's Online-Comment Propaganda Army," *The Atlantic*. October 9th, 2013
[5] Klishin, Ilya. "The Kremlin's Trolls Go West," *The Moscow Times*. May 21st, 2014
[6] Atlantic Council's Digital Forensic Research Lab. "The Russians Who Exposed Russia's Trolls," *Medium*. May 7th, 2018
[7] Soldatov, Andrei; Borogan, Irina. *The Red Web: The Struggle Between Russia's Digital Dictators and the New Online Revolutionaries*. New York, NY: PublicAffairs, 2015. Pg. 282
[8] Klishin, Ilya. "The Kremlin's Trolls Go West," *The Moscow Times*. May 21st, 2014
[9] Elliott, Chris. "The readers editor on… pro-Russian trolling below the line on Ukraine stories," *The Guardian*. May 4th, 2014
[10] Seddon, Max. "Documents Show How Russia's Troll Army Hit America," *BuzzFeed News*. June 2nd, 2014
[11] Petlyanova, Nina. "The recipe for success for Putin's personal chef," *Novaya Gazeta*.

October 14th, 2011

[12] Zhegulev, Ilya. "Yevgeny Prigozhin's right to be forgotten: What does the restaurateur who served the presidents of Russia want to hide," *Meduza*. June 9th, 2016

[13] Zhegulev, Ilya. "Investigation: how Putin's personal chef will feed the army for 92 billion roubles," *Forbes Russia*. March 18th, 2013

[14] Knight, Amy. "American Murder-for-Hire Plot Has Kremlin Connections," *The Daily Beast*. February 8th, 2019

[15] Grove, Thomas. "Kremlin Caterer Accused in U.S. Election Meddling Has History of Dishing Dark Arts," *The Wall Street Journal*. February 16th, 2016

[16] MacFarquhar, Neil. "Yevgeny Prigozhin, Russian Oligarch Indicted by U.S., Is Known as 'Putin's Cook,'" *The New York Times*. February 16th, 2018

[17] Zhegulev, Ilya. "Investigation: how Putin's personal chef will feed the army for 92 billion roubles," *Forbes Russia*. March 18th, 2013

[18] Grove, Thomas. "Kremlin Caterer Accused in U.S. Election Meddling Has History of Dishing Dark Arts," *The Wall Street Journal*. February 16th, 2016

[19] MacFarquhar, Neil. "Yevgeny Prigozhin, Russian Oligarch Indicted by U.S., Is Known as 'Putin's Cook,'" *The New York Times*. February 16th, 2018

[20] Knight, Amy. "American Murder-for-Hire Plot Has Kremlin Connections," *The Daily Beast*. February 8th, 2019

[21] Kuprashevich, Maria. "Mata Hari. Who is spying on the Russia media," *Novaya Gazeta*. June 25th, 2013

[22] Korotkov, Denis. "Operative for "Putin's Chef" Shares Secrets, Vanishes - Then Reappears and Retracts," *Organized Crime and Corruption Reporting Project (OCCRP)*. December 17th, 2018

[23] Shoshnikov, Andrei. "Capital of political trolling," *Moy Rayon*. March 11th, 2015

[24] Atlantic Council's Digital Forensic Research Lab. "The Russians Who Exposed Russia's Trolls," *Medium*. May 7th, 2018

[25] "Trolling for Putin: Russia's information war explained," *AFP Network (YouTube)*. April 28, 2015

[26] Demirjian, Karoun. "A whistleblower is trying to bring down Russia's secret internet troll army," *The Washington Post*. June 4th, 2015

[27] Chen, Adrian. "The Agency," *The New York Times Magazine*. June 2nd, 2015

[28] Shimer, David. *Rigged: America, Russia, and One Hundred Years of Covert Electoral Interference*. New York, NY: Alfred A. Knopf. 2020, Pg. 210

[29] Chen, Adrian. "The Real Paranoia-Inducing Purpose of Russian Hacks," *The New Yorker*. July 27th, 2016

[30] Report of the Select Committee on Intelligence United States Senate on Russian Active Measures Campaigns and Interference in the 2016 U.S. Election, Volume 2: Russia's Use of Social Media With Additional Views. *116th Congress, 1st Session*. 2019. Pg. 51

[31] Howard, Philip N.; Bharath, Ganesh; Liotsiou, Dimitra; Kelly, John; François, Camille. "The IRA, Social Media and Political Polarization in the United States, 2012-2018," *Computational Propaganda Research Project, University of Oxford*. December 17th, 2018. Pg. 9

[32] United States of America v. Elena Alekseevna Khusyaynova, Criminal Complaint. *United States District Court for the Eastern District of Virginia*. Case No. 1:18-MJ-464. September 28th, 2018. Pg. 4 (Paragraph 8)

[33] Nemtsova, Anna. "After Mueller's Indictments, an Interview With a Mole Who Was Inside Russia's Pro-Trump Troll Factory," *The Daily Beast*. February 18th, 2018

[34] Korzova, Sofia. "Media: "Olga's Trolls" became "Savushkin,"" *Lenzidat*. October 28th, 2014

[35] Nechepurenko, Ivan; Schwirtz, Michael. "What We Know About Russians Sanctioned By the United States," *The New York Times*. February 17th, 2018

[36] United States of America v. Internet Research Agency LLC et al, Indictment. *United*

States District Court for the District of Columbia. February 16th, 2018. Pg. 4-8

[37] United States of America v. Elena Alekseevna Khusyaynova, Criminal Complaint. *United States District Court for the Eastern District of Virginia.* Case No. 1:18-MJ-464. September 28th, 2018. Pg. 9 (Paragraph 21, a.)

[38] Holland, Steve; Mason, Jeff. "Obama warns on Crimea, orders sanctions over Russian moves in Ukraine," *Reuters.* March 6th, 2014

[39] Rid, Thomas. *Active Measures: The Secret History of Disinformation and Political Warfare.* New York, NY: Farrar, Straus and Giroux, 2020. Pg. 402

[40] Nechepurenko, Ivan; Schwirtz, Michael. "What We Know About Russians Sanctioned By the United States," *The New York Times.* February 17th, 2018

[41] Kelly, John W. "Briefing for the United States Senate Select Committee on Intelligence," August 1st, 2018

[42] Mueller III, Robert S. *Report On The Investigation Into Russian Interference In The 2016 Presidential Election.* US Department of Justice. March 2019. Pg. 83

[43] United States of America v. Internet Research Agency LLC et al, Indictment. *United States District Court for the District of Columbia.* February 16th, 2018. Pg. 8-9

[44] Shane, Scott; Mazzetti, Mark. "Inside a 3-Year Russian Campaign to Influence U.S. Voters," *The New York Times.* February 16th, 2018

[45] United States of America v. Internet Research Agency LLC et al, Indictment. *United States District Court for the District of Columbia.* February 16th, 2018. Pg. 13

[46] Howard, Philip N.; Bharath, Ganesh; Liotsiou, Dimitra; Kelly, John; François, Camille. "The IRA, Social Media and Political Polarization in the United States, 2012-2018," *Computational Propaganda Research Project, University of Oxford.* December 17th, 2018. Pg. 8

[47] DiResta, Renee; Shaffer, Kris; Ruppel, Becky; Sullivan, David; Matney, Robert; Fox, Ryan; Albright, Jonathan; Johnson, Ben. *The Tactics & Tropes of the Internet Research Agency.* New Knowledge. December 18th, 2018. Pg. 7

[48] DiResta, Renee; Shaffer, Kris; Ruppel, Becky; Sullivan, David; Matney, Robert; Fox, Ryan; Albright, Jonathan; Johnson, Ben. *The Tactics & Tropes of the Internet Research Agency.* New Knowledge. December 18th, 2018. Pg. 63

[49] DiResta, Renee; Shaffer, Kris; Ruppel, Becky; Sullivan, David; Matney, Robert; Fox, Ryan; Albright, Jonathan; Johnson, Ben. *The Tactics & Tropes of the Internet Research Agency.* New Knowledge. December 18th, 2018. Pg. 80

[50] United States of America v. Internet Research Agency LLC et al, Indictment. *United States District Court for the District of Columbia.* February 16th, 2018. Pg. 17

[51] Windrem, Robert. "Russians launched pro-Jill Stein social media blitz to help Trump win election, reports say," *NBC News.* December 22nd, 2018

[52] Howard, Philip N.; Bharath, Ganesh; Liotsiou, Dimitra; Kelly, John; François, Camille. "The IRA, Social Media and Political Polarization in the United States, 2012-2018," *Computational Propaganda Research Project, University of Oxford.* December 17th, 2018. Pg. 12-14

[53] Report of the Select Committee on Intelligence United States Senate on Russian Active Measures Campaigns and Interference in the 2016 U.S. Election, Volume 2: Russia's Use of Social Media With Additional Views. *116th Congress, 1st Session.* 2019. Pg. 36

[54] Cobb, Jelani. "The Enduring Russian Propaganda Interests in Targeting African-Americans," *The New Yorker.* December 21st, 2018

[55] Braswell, Sean. "When The Soviet Union Tried To Woo Black America," *OZY.* February 17th, 2017

[56] Risen, James. "K.G.B. Told Tall Tales About Dallas, Books Says," *The New York Times.* September 12th, 1999

[57] Boghardt, Thomas. "Soviet Bloc Intelligence and Its AIDS Disinformation Campaign," *Studies in Intelligence, Vol. 53, No. 4.* December 2009

[58] Weiner, TIm. *The Folly and the Glory: America, Russia, And Political Warfare 1945-2020.*

New York, NY: Henry Holt and Company, 2020. Pg. 135

[59] Ewing, Philip. "Russia Targeted U.S. Racial Divisions Long Before 2016 And Black Lives Matter," *NPR*. October 30th, 2017

[60] Starbird, Kate. "The Surprising Nuance Behind the Russian Troll Strategy," *Medium*. October 20th, 2018

[61] Stewart, Leo G.; Arif, Ahmer; Nied, A. Conrad; Spiro, Emma S.; Starbird, Kate. "Drawing the Lines of Contention: Networked Frame Contests Within #BlackLivesMatter Discourse," *PACM on Human-Computer Interaction, Vol. 1. No. CSCW, Article 96*. November 2017

[62] United States of America v. Elena Alekseevna Khusyaynova, Criminal Complaint. *United States District Court for the Eastern District of Virginia*. Case No. 1:18-MJ-464. September 28th, 2018. Pg. 14 (Paragraph 27.)

[63] DiResta, Renee; Shaffer, Kris; Ruppel, Becky; Sullivan, David; Matney, Robert; Fox, Ryan; Albright, Jonathan; Johnson, Ben. *The Tactics & Tropes of the Internet Research Agency*. New Knowledge. December 18th, 2018. Pg. 43

[64] Rusyaeva, Polina; Zakharov, Andrey. "RBC investigation: how the "troll factory" worked in the US election," *RBC*. October 17th, 2017

[65] Mueller III, Robert S. *Report On The Investigation Into Russian Interference In The 2016 Presidential Election*. US Department of Justice. March 2019. Pg. 29

[66] Jordan, Jay R. "Houston Confederate rally 'earliest evidence' of Russian interference, says Mueller report," *Houston Chronicle*. April 19th, 2019

[67] "Protestors rally at Capitol against Confederate history month," *WAPT16 ABC*. March 27th, 2016

[68] Michel, Casey. "Here's how Russian operatives manipulated U.S. civil rights activists," *ThinkProgress*. October 19th, 2017

[69] O'Sullivan, Donie; Byers, Dylan. "Exclusive: Fake black activist accounts linked to Russian government," *CNN*. September 28th, 2017

[70] Ackerman, Spencer; Resnick, Gideon; Collins, Ben. "Leaked: Secret Documents From Russia's Election Trolls," *The Daily Beast*. October 26th, 2017

[71] Mueller III, Robert S. *Report On The Investigation Into Russian Interference In The 2016 Presidential Election*. US Department of Justice. March 2019. Pg. 25

[72] White, Micah. "I started Occupy Wall Street. Russia tried to co-opt me," *The Guardian*. November 2nd, 2017

[73] Rusyaeva, Polina; Zakharov, Andrey. "RBC investigation: how the "troll factory" worked in the US election," *RBC*. October 17th, 2017

[74] Holliday, Shelby; Barry, Rob. "Russian Operation Targeted U.S. Business Owners," *The Wall Street Journal*. December 20th, 2018

[75] Report of the Select Committee on Intelligence United States Senate on Russian Active Measures Campaigns and Interference in the 2016 U.S. Election, Volume 2: Russia's Use of Social Media With Additional Views. *116th Congress, 1st Session*. 2019. Pg. 49

[76] Poulsen, Kevin. "Russian Troll Farm Hijacked American Teen Girls' Computers for Likes," *The Daily Beast*. May 15th, 2018

[77] Report of the Select Committee on Intelligence United States Senate on Russian Active Measures Campaigns and Interference in the 2016 U.S. Election, Volume 2: Russia's Use of Social Media With Additional Views. *116th Congress, 1st Session*. 2019. Pg. 47

[78] Lister, Tim; Sebastian, Clare. "Stoking Islamophobia and secession in Texas -- From an office in Russia," *CNN*. October 6th, 2017

[79] Bertrand, Natasha. "Texas secession movement: Russia-linked Facebook group asked us to participate in anti-Clinton rallies," *Business Insider*. September 14th, 2017

[80] Poulsen, Kevin; Ackerman, Spencer; Collins, Ben. "Exclusive: Russians Impersonated Real American Muslims to Stir Chaos on Facebook and Instagram," *The Daily Beast*. September 27th, 2017

[81] Hlavacek, Joanne. "Facebook ad promoting 2016 Lawrence protest among those paid for by Russian trolls," *Lawrence Journal-World*. November 1st, 2017

[82] de Haldevang, Max. "Russian trolls convinced an American to hold a "Happy Birthday" sign for their oligarch boss," *Quartz*. February 16th, 2018

[83] United States of America v. Internet Research Agency LLC et al, Indictment. *United States District Court for the District of Columbia*. February 16th, 2018. Pg. 21-25

[84] Seetharaman, Deepa. "Russian-Backed Facebook Accounts Staged Events Around Divisive Issues," *The Wall Street Journal*. October 30th, 2017

[85] O'Sullivan, Donie; Byers, Dylan. "Exclusive: Even Pokémon Go used by extensive Russian-linked meddling effort," *CNN*. October 13th, 2017

[86] DiResta, Renee; Shaffer, Kris; Ruppel, Becky; Sullivan, David; Matney, Robert; Fox, Ryan; Albright, Jonathan; Johnson, Ben. *The Tactics & Tropes of the Internet Research Agency*. New Knowledge. December 18th, 2018. Pg. 16

[87] Seetharaman, Deepa. "Russian-Backed Facebook Accounts Staged Events Around Divisive Issues," *The Wall Street Journal*. October 30th, 2017

[88] Dahn, Andy. "Demonstrators Remember Sandra Bland, Demand Greater Police Accountability," *CBS Chicago*. July 16th, 2016

[89] Poulsen, Kevin; Ackerman, Spencer; Collins, Ben. "Exclusive: Russians Impersonated Real American Muslims to Stir Chaos on Facebook and Instagram," *The Daily Beast*. September 27th, 2017

[90] United States of America v. Internet Research Agency LLC et al, Indictment. *United States District Court for the District of Columbia*. February 16th, 2018. Pg. 21

[91] O'Sullivan, Donie; Griffin, Drew; Bronstein, Scott. "The unwitting: The Trump supporters used by Russia," *CNN*. February 20th, 2018

[92] Poulsen, Kevin; Ackerman, Spencer; Collins, Ben; Resnick, Gideon. "Exclusive: Russians Appear to Use Facebook to Push Trump Rallies in 17 U.S. Cities," *The Daily Beast*. September 20th, 2017

[93] United States of America v. Internet Research Agency LLC et al, Indictment. *United States District Court for the District of Columbia*. February 16th, 2018. Pg. 27

[94] O'Sullivan, Donie; Griffin, Drew; Bronstein, Scott. "The unwitting: The Trump supporters used by Russia," *CNN*. February 20th, 2018

[95] Vogel, Kenneth P. "How Russian Trolls Krept Into the Trump Campaign's Facebook Messages," *The New York Times*. March 8th, 2018

[96] United States of America v. Internet Research Agency LLC et al, Indictment. *United States District Court for the District of Columbia*. February 16th, 2018. Pg. 28-29

[97] Report of the Select Committee on Intelligence United States Senate on Russian Active Measures Campaigns and Interference in the 2016 U.S. Election, Volume 2: Russia's Use of Social Media With Additional Views. *116th Congress, 1st Session*. 2019. Pg. 47

[98] United States of America v. Internet Research Agency LLC et al, Indictment. *United States District Court for the District of Columbia*. February 16th, 2018. Pg. 29

[99] Adams, Rosalind; Brown, Hayes. "These Americans Were Tricked Into Working For Russia. They Say They Had No Idea." *BuzzFeed News*. October 17th, 2017

[100] Silverman, Craig. "Russian Trolls Ran Wild On Tumblr And The Company Refuses Yo Say Anything About It," *BuzzFeed News*. February 6th, 2018

[101] Ackerman, Spencer; Resnick, Gideon; Collins, Ben. "Exclusive: Russia Recruited YouTubers to Bash 'Racist B*tch' Hillary Clinton Over Rap Beats,"

[102] United States of America v. Internet Research Agency LLC et al, Indictment. *United States District Court for the District of Columbia*. February 16th, 2018. Pg. 17

[103] DiResta, Renee; Shaffer, Kris; Ruppel, Becky; Sullivan, David; Matney, Robert; Fox, Ryan; Albright, Jonathan; Johnson, Ben. *The Tactics & Tropes of the Internet Research Agency*. New Knowledge. December 18th, 2018. Pg. 9

[104] Mueller III, Robert S. *Report On The Investigation Into Russian Interference In The 2016 Presidential Election*. US Department of Justice. March 2019. Pg. 34

[105] Collins, Ben; Poulsen, Kevin; Ackerman, Spencer; Swan, Betsy. "Trump Campaign Staffers Pushed Russian Propaganda Days Before the Election," *The Daily Beast.* October 18th, 2017

[106] United States of America v. Internet Research Agency LLC et al, Indictment. *United States District Court for the District of Columbia.* February 16th, 2018. Pg. 17-18

[107] Howard, Philip N.; Bharath, Ganesh; Liotsiou, Dimitra; Kelly, John; François, Camille. "The IRA, Social Media and Political Polarization in the United States, 2012-2018," *Computational Propaganda Research Project, University of Oxford.* December 17th, 2018. Pg. 34

[108] United States of America v. Internet Research Agency LLC et al, Indictment. *United States District Court for the District of Columbia.* February 16th, 2018. Pg. 18

[109] DiResta, Renee; Shaffer, Kris; Ruppel, Becky; Sullivan, David; Matney, Robert; Fox, Ryan; Albright, Jonathan; Johnson, Ben. *The Tactics & Tropes of the Internet Research Agency.* New Knowledge. December 18th, 2018. Pg. 83

[110] Rid, Thomas. *Active Measures: The Secret History of Disinformation and Political Warfare.* New York, NY: Farrar, Straus and Giroux, 2020. Pg. 406

[111] Jamieson, Kathleen Hall. *Cyberwar: How Russian Hackers Helped Elect a President.* Oxford, UK: Oxford University Press, 2018. Pg. 38-45

[112] Channel Four News Investigation Team. "Revealed: Trump campaign strategy to deter millions of black Americans from voting in 2016," *Channel Four.* September 28th, 2020

Chapter 12:
Trump Tower Moscow, Eurasian Organized Crime, And the 2016 Election

Trump, the Agalarovs,
And the First Proposed Trump Tower Moscow Project

Donald Trump pursued several opportunities to build a Trump Tower in Moscow between the 2013 Miss Universe Pageant and his unlikely rise to the presidency. While Trump had dreamed since the late 1980s of scoring a major development in the Russian capital, the prospect of a presidential contender negotiating a major real estate deal with a foreign adversary during the heart of the campaign was unprecedented in American history. Trump and his negotiators understood well that a deal of this magnitude needed Putin's blessing. Furthermore, by publicly denying that he had any business interests in Russia while they were secretly underway, Trump provided the Kremlin with leverage it could use against him. However, when interpreted as the actions of a man who did not plan on winning the election but instead using the limelight to reignite his flagging business career, a method emerges to Trump's madness.

  While Trump's previous efforts to build a Trump Tower in Moscow have been chronicled in earlier chapters, a new opportunity arose through his business partnership with Aras Agalarov. Paula Shugart, the President of The Miss Universe Organization, recalled Trump and Emin Agalarov discussing partnering for a Trump Tower Moscow project during a tour of Crocus Hall on November 8th, 2013, the day before the facility hosted the Miss Universe Pageant.[1] On the day of the Pageant, Trump told *RT*, "I have plans for the establishment of business in Russia. Now, I am in talks with several Russian companies to establish this skyscraper." The same article quoted Aras Agalarov as telling a separate Russian news outlet, "We started talking about joint work in the field of real estate a few days ago."[2]

A day after the Pageant, Emin Agalarov exchanged emails with the architect William McGee and alluded to the project, writing, "We may do a tower with [Trump] now."[3] Trump thanked Emin and his father on Twitter and referred to the project, writing, "I had a great weekend with you and your family. You have done a FANTASTIC job. TRUMP-TOWER MOSCOW is next. Emin was WOW!"[4] Thus began another major Trump Organization push to score a Moscow development, a campaign that consisted of multiparty, clandestine negotiations that extended into the 2016 Presidential campaign. Throughout, Trump lavished Vladimir Putin with praise, as it was Putin who ultimately determined whether the project moved forward.

Donald Trump Jr. introduced himself to Emin Agalarov via email on November 19th, 2013, writing that his father had asked him to discuss the next steps on moving forward with a Trump Tower or hotel in Moscow. Emin replied within hours, enthusiastically agreeing to speak and see if they could shepherd the project forward. "I've spoken to my Father about our conversation, and all looks very positive," Emin wrote to Trump Jr. the next day. "[G]eneral terms are suitable for a negotiation, let's identify the land and building (we have a few options) and get the ball rolling contractually."[5]

On November 25th, *The Moscow Times* wrote that Trump had appeared in one of Emin's music videos.[6] At Trump's request, one of his employees printed a copy of the article. Trump scribbled a note onto the printout and sent it to Emin. It read: "Emin, You Are The Greatest! Trump Tower Moscow?" On December 5th, Donald Trump Jr. and Emin Agalarov signed a preliminary but formal agreement. The next day, Emin sent the signed agreement to Donald Trump Jr. and introduced him to Irakli Kaveladze via email. Kaveladze, as mentioned, was a Georgian-American Agalarov employee alleged to have been involved in money laundering activities related to Russian organized crime. After the introduction, Trump Jr. and Kaveladze agreed that the Trump Organization would receive a flat 3.5% fee on sales of any future Trump Tower Moscow project. Throughout January and February 2014, the two parties negotiated a letter of intent.[7]

On January 13th, 2014, Trump Jr. and Emin Agalarov dined at Nobu in New York City, where Emin's British publicist, Rob Goldstone, recalled that the two discussed Trump Tower Moscow. Ultimately, a proposal for an 800-unit, 194-meter skyscraper to be erected on the Agalarov-owned "Crocus City" was drawn up and submitted to the Trump Organization. Shortly after that, Ivanka Trump traveled to Moscow. Irakli Kaveladze met Ivanka at the Crocus Group office in Moscow before she visited the proposed building site. After the visit, Ivanka wrote to thank Emin, "I am very excited about our collaboration and am confident that our families will enjoy great success together. We look forward to meeting with you again in the US in March to review the details of the proposed Trump Tower with your architects."[8]

"When I went to Russia with the Miss Universe Pageant," Trump told *Fox and Friends* on February 10th, a week after Ivanka's trip to Moscow, "[Putin] contacted me and was so nice. I mean, the Russian people were so fantastic to us." Trump continued, "I'll just say this: they are doing – they're outsmarting us at many turns, as we all understand. I mean, their leaders are, whether you call them smarter or more cunning or whatever, but they're outsmarting us. If you look at Syria or other places, they're outsmarting us."[9]

While Trump engaged in a media blitz flattering Putin, which continued throughout his presidential campaign, negotiations between the Trump Organization and the Crocus Group continued throughout 2014. Shortly after the Russian invasion of Crimea in late February 2014, Emin Agalarov performed at Trump's Doral Golf Resort. However, discussions between the two parties seemed to stall by the late Summer and into the early Fall, and the project never developed past the planning stages.[10]

Trump's last known in-person meeting with Emin before running for president occurred on May 20th, 2015, at Trump Tower in Manhattan. According to Emin, Trump told him he would be running for President approximately six weeks before his public announcement. Rob Goldstone, who was present at the meeting, recalled that as they left, Trump said, "I'm going to be running for President, you know; so next time you won't be coming here; you'll be coming to see me at the White House."[11]

After Trump announced his candidacy on June 16th, 2015, Goldstone emailed Trump's longtime assistant, Rhona Graff, "Please pass on mine and Emin's best wishes and congratulations to Mr. Trump." Goldstone contacted Graff again on July 22nd with an invitation for Trump to travel to Moscow on November 8th, the day of the 2016 election, to attend Aras Agalarov's birthday party. Graff promised to pass the invitation on to Trump with the caveat that, given he was running for president, it was "highly unlikely" he would have time to attend a party on election day. Goldstone replied that he understood but offered "unless maybe he [Trump] would welcome a meeting with President Putin, which Emin would set up."[12]

Multiple discussions regarding a meeting with Putin occurred within the Trump Organization and Campaign. On September 10th, a reporter for *The New York Times* contacted Hope Hicks, the 26-year-old press secretary of the Trump Campaign, and inquired whether Trump would be meeting Putin during his visit to New York to attend the United Nations General Assembly. Hicks forwarded the email to Michael Cohen. Five days later, while speaking with Sean Hannity on his radio show, Cohen said there was "a better than likely chance" that Putin would meet with Trump during his stay in New York. Before the interview with Hannity, Cohen dialed a number that he found online for the Kremlin and spoke to a multilingual woman, asking her if there was "[a]ny chance when President Putin is in New York at the General Assembly he'd like to come by and have a burger with Mr. Trump at the [G]rille?" The woman replied that it was likely against "protocol" but that she would pass on the request.[13]

"Putin is the richest man in the world by a multiple," Cohen later claimed Trump often told him. According to Cohen, Trump was obsessed and in awe of Putin's wealth and power. "In fact, if you think about it," Trump told Cohen, "Putin controls twenty-five percent of the Russian economy, including every major business, like Gazprom. Imagine controlling twenty-five percent of the wealth of a country. Wouldn't that be fucking amazing?"[14]

By September 2015, Michael Cohen was running point on another potential Trump Tower Moscow project that was brought to him by Felix Sater.[15] Later that month, Sater reached out to a Russian contact of his, Andrey Rozov, to discuss the potential project. Rozov was the head of a Russian real estate firm, I.C. Expert. However, while Rozov may have served as the head of I.C. Expert, its actual ownership was opaque. The reporting of Scott Stedman of *Forensic News* provides insight into Rozov's sordid background and the company's ownership structure.

Sater met Rozov through a Russian real estate firm called Mirax. After a 2007 article in *The New York Times* had outed Sater's past involvement in a joint Italian and Russian mafia-backed pump-and-dump stock fraud scheme, he moved to Moscow and joined the board of Mirax in 2008.[16] Mirax worked on projects in Russia, the United States, Turkey, and Ukraine. The firm was headed by a flamboyant billionaire named Sergey Polonsky, who was convicted of fraud by a Russian court in 2017.[17] Sater and Rozov met while working for Polonsky.[18]

Before the Trump Tower Moscow proposal, I.C. Expert's largest real estate project was a suburban housing development built in Reutov, a suburb outside Moscow, called Novokosino-2. The project was plagued by lawsuits and delays, with the owners of 5000 units often protesting the developers' failure to complete projects on time. These problems were not secret but were actively being reported on during the time the Trump Organization was negotiating with I.C. Expert.[19] Nor was this the only red flag any company that performed due diligence would notice. In 2011, Rozov was charged with negligent homicide after causing a boat crash that led to the death of a nineteen-year-old boy and badly injured his girlfriend. In the spring of 2015, the Russian government granted Rozov amnesty for unknown reasons.[20]

Rozov was a close associate and business partner with Stalbek Mishakov, a man with significant ties to Oleg Deripaska.[21] Deripaska, an organized crime-linked Russian aluminum magnate and close Putin ally who played an important role in the 2016 Russian election interference effort, will be described in greater detail in the next chapter. Mishakov served as Deripaska's personal attorney and advisor and held management positions in Deripaska's various ventures, including his holding company En+ Group Plc and United Rusal.

*I.C. Expert's Opaque Ownership Structure
and Ties to Oligarchs and Organized Crime*

While Rozov served as the head of I.C. Expert, the actual ownership of the organization is obscured by a complex constellation of Russian and offshore corporate entities. As of early 2016, its shareholders included the Cyprus-based Colinsen Trading Limited LLC, which owned 60% of the company, the Marshall Islands-based Trianguli Limited LLC, which owned 25% of the company, with the remaining 15% of the company owned by a Russian LLC EKOPRESTIZH.[22]

Known as "Moscow on the Mediterranean," Cyprus has long been used by Russians as a "backdoor" to gain access to the European Union's financial system.[23] Cypriot shell companies often list lawyers as their owners to obscure their actual ownership. The owner listed for Colinsen Trading Limited was a Cypriot lawyer named Christodoulos Vassiliades. Vassiliades' clients have included Galina Telesh, Semyon Mogilevich's wife. Mogilevich has used Telesh to obscure his ownership stakes in various companies. Other Vassiliades clients include the Russian billionaires Vladimir Lisin, Sulieman Kerimov, and Alisher Usmanov.[24] Lisin was involved with Deripaska in the violent privatization of the Russian aluminum industry and was a business partner of Trump's friend Sam Kislin.[25] Usmanov has partnered with an alleged associate of the Solntsevskaya.[26] Both Mogilevich and Kerimov are alleged to have been involved in massive money laundering operations using Cypriot offshore vehicles, among other secrecy jurisdictions.

Scott Stedman uncovered links between Vassiliades and the Trump Ocean Club Hotel in Panama. The Panamanian law firm that advised the Trump Organization on the project, Alemán, Cordero, Galindo & Lee (ALCOGAL), has a Cypriot branch that shares the same office as Christodoulos G. Vassiliades & Co LLC. Vassiliades manages ALCOGAL's financial trust through another Cypriot shell company, Apex International. The Vassiliades-owned entity listed as director and

344

secretary of Apex International was a shell company called Ionic Nominees. In May of 2015, mere days after Rozov was granted amnesty by the Russian government, ownership of Colinsen Trading Limited LLC was transferred to Ionic Nominees, thus giving it 60% ownership over I.C. Expert.[27]

Just months before I.C. Expert engaged with the Trump Organization, it was majority-owned by Capilana Trading Limited, a shell company registered in the British Virgin Islands. The sole shareholder listed as owning Capilana was a Cypriot national named Ioanna Theofilou. While there is no direct evidence that Theofilou was representing Deripaska's ownership interests in Capilana, numerous offshore subsidiaries of Deripaska's companies, En+ and RUSAL, list Theofilou as director and secretary. Weeks after the Russian government granted Rozov amnesty, Capilana's ownership stake in I.C. Expert was transferred to the Vassiliades "owned" subsidiary Ionic Nominees.[28] Andrey Rozov's relationship with Deripaska associates Stalbek Mishakov and Pavel Lebedev and the Theofilou connection via Capilana Trading, are suggestive of Deripaska's involvement with, and potential ownership stake in, I.C. Trading. Further, Deripaska was known to have done business with Mirax, the Russian real estate firm whose board members included Felix Sater and Andrey Rozov.[29] Mirax was also involved in building a hotel and luxury villas for executives from Gazprom, Lukoil, and VTB Bank on the Bay of Kotor, an area of Montenegro heavily invested in by Deripaska.[30]

Michael Cohen and Felix Sater's
Trump Tower Moscow Negotiations Continue

In September 2015, Michael Cohen received permission from Trump to enter into negotiations with Andrey Rozov and I.C. Expert via Felix Sater. Throughout the heart of the presidential campaign, Cohen repeatedly briefed Trump on the progress of the negotiations.[31] On September 25th, Cohen, Sater, and Rozov held a conference call with Sater translating. Following the call, Cohen forwarded Rozov an email that contained architectural renderings for the proposed Tower.[32] Four days later, Rozov's "right-hand man" Dmitry Chizhikov sent Cohen a letter from Rozov which described I.C. Expert and stated that "the tallest building in Europe should be in Moscow, and I am prepared to build it." The letter suggested that the partnership between the Trump Organization and I.C. Expert would be "a shining example of business creating opportunities and significant goodwill between Russia and the US"

Rozov's letter to Cohen further alluded to a Manhattan building on 22 West 38th Street that I.C. Expert purchased in December 2014. Independent journalist Wendy Siegelman uncovered that Felix Sater represented Andrey Rozov in the resale of the building a year later, in December 2015, amid the Trump Tower Moscow negotiations. The accountant involved with the sale was a Russian-born, New York-based accountant named Ilya Bykov.[33] Bykov shared an office with Parason Inc., a Delaware LLC involved in a large-scale Russian money laundering scandal.[34] Bykov's clientele included Aras Agalarov and Igor Krutoy, a Russian composer noted for his vocal support of Vladimir Putin, who had written music for Emin Agalarov. In 2011, Krutoy entered into negotiations with the Trump Organization over building a Trump Tower in Riga, Latvia. Three years later, Latvian authorities contacted the FBI and asked that they investigate Krutoy and his partners for corruption related to the Trump Project.[35]

On October 5th, Cohen forwarded Sater a Letter of Intent (LOI), which set out the terms of a licensing agreement between the Trump Organization and I.C. Expert. The proposed tower was to be 120 stories tall and consist of "first-class, luxury residential condominiums with related amenities."[36] The license fee structure included a $4 million fee, to be paid in installments, as well as a percentage of fees from gross sales fees, rental fees, and revenue fees.[37] Three days later, Sater sent Cohen a revised version of the LOI, which designated the tower as "mixed-use" as opposed to just condos and had it located in Moscow City, an industrial zone housing some of Europe's tallest buildings located roughly three miles from the Kremlin.

On October 9th, Sater emailed Cohen that he would meet with a Russian real estate developer named Andrey Molchanov to discuss building Trump Tower Moscow "on his site."[38] Molchanov was a billionaire who founded LSR, one of Russia's leading real estate development companies. Sater described Molchanov as a "friend." He told Cohen that Molchanov's "stepfather was Gov of St. Petersburg and Putin worked for him."[39] Sater is referring to Molchanov's adopted father, Yuriy, who was Putin's first boss at Leningrad University, where Putin worked following his KGB stint in East Germany and where he continued to work for the agency recruiting and spying on students.[40]

As Deputy Director of Leningrad University, Yuriy Molchanov used his connections with city authorities to help Procter & Gamble (P&G) establish operations in the Soviet Union. Upon his return to St. Petersburg from Dresden, Putin helped Molchanov establish a joint venture between the university and the American multinational. P&G's first office in Russia was located at Leningrad University's rector's mansion, where Putin and Molchanov helped with staff recruitment, advertising, and land acquisition.[41] According to Russian press reports, Yuriy Molchanov was a KGB *rezident* at Leningrad University and was potentially even Putin's KGB superior.[42] Yuriy and his adopted son Andrey ultimately established LSR together. In 2004, Yuriy Molchanov became the deputy governor of St. Petersburg, where he oversaw public-private projects that included the restoration of Putin's palace in Strelna, located near St. Petersburg. He later became a Vice President at VTB Bank.

Sater claims to have met Andrey Molchanov via Maxim Temnikov, who he sat alongside on the board of Mirax.[43] Temnikov was accused in Russian court alongside Mirax Group head Sergey Polonsky of involvement in a 2.7 billion ruble embezzlement scheme.[44] Temnikov's first wife later remarried Andrey Molchanov, which is how Sater claims he was introduced to Molchanov. Temnikov and his second wife co-own a piece of real estate with Sater on Fisher Island, a 216-acre members-only island off the coast of Miami and one of the wealthiest zip codes in America. Aras Agalarov also owned a condo on Fisher Island, which mysteriously went into foreclosure in 2019.[45] Temnikov and Sater purchased the $5.1 million property via Fisher MB LLC, which was established by a Miami-based Russian lawyer named Michael Keifitz.[46] Keifitz has over 100 companies registered under the name Keyfitz, most of which are associated with Russian businesses. One company registered to "Keyfitz" purchased a $1,170,000 unit from Trump Towers II in Miami for the daughter of Vladimir Popovyan, a well-known member of the Russian Rostov-on-Don criminal organization.[47]

Sater believed that Andrey Molchanov, who once served in the Russian government, was "a phone call away from anyone he need[ed] to be in contact with."[48] While they hadn't previously worked together on a project, the two had often discussed Russian real estate. Sater met with Molchanov to discuss the possibility of constructing Trump Tower Moscow on the location of the ZiL factory, an out-of-use automobile and heavy equipment manufacturing facility. While they had several conversations and Molchanov was warm to the idea of Trump Tower Moscow, Sater later claimed they never arrived at a complete agreement before the project was put on hold after Trump won the Republican nomination.

On October 12th, Sater informed Cohen that Andrey L. Kostin, the CEO of VTB, who he described as "Putins [sic] top finance guy," was "on board" and willing to finance the project. Sater attached a Wikipedia bio of Kostin to the email. "This is major for us," Sater wrote Cohen, "not only the financing but Kostins position in Russia, extremely powerful and respected. Now all we need is Putin on board and we are golden, meeting with Putin and top deputy is tentatively set for the 14th. See buddy I can not only get Ivanka to spin in Putins [sic] Kremlin office chair on 30 minutes notice, I can also get a full meeting."

Kostin was a former Soviet diplomat who was once stationed in London. In 2002, he was made the President and Chairman of VTB, Russia's second largest bank. When Sater claims to have been in contact with Kostin, VTB was under US Sanctions. Despite Sater's emails to Cohen describing his interactions with Kostin, Kostin has denied that he or VTB ever negotiated with Sater.[49] The state-owned VTB is known to have financed intelligence operations and is suspected of using its international offices to engage in espionage.[50] One of the members of VTB's board, which was chaired by Kostin, was Denis Bortnikov, whose father, Alexander Bortnikov, was the head of the FSB.[51] Swedish economist and Russia expert Anders Åslund has described VTB as "a slush fund for Putin."[52]

VTB has a close relationship with Deutsche Bank, which has loaned over $2 billion to Donald Trump.[53] Andrey Kostin's son had worked at Deutsche Bank from 2000 until 2011 when he died in a motorcycle accident.[54] In 2007, Deutsche Bank issued a $1 billion long-term loan to VTB, allowing the Russian state bank to use the money as it pleased. At the time, 55 Deutsche Bank's CEO Josef Ackerman convinced Kostin to set up an investment banking division. After receiving the go-ahead from Putin, Kostin established VTB Capital.[55] In 2008, Kostin hired over 100 bankers from Deutsche to operate the new investment bank.[56]

While Kostin claims he never met Sater, Sater later testified that he contacted Kostin indirectly "through people in Moscow."[57] One of the individuals Sater tapped to contact Kostin was a former Russian intelligence officer in the GRU, Evgeny Shmykov.[58] Shmykov told *The Washington Post* that he worked "in a private capacity" for the anti-Taliban Northern Alliance in Afghanistan throughout the 1990s.[59] He may have served as an information conduit for Sater in his work for American intelligence. Shmykov connected Sater with sources on the ground in Afghanistan, and the two traveled the country together at one point.

"Lets [sic] make this happen and build a Trump Moscow," Sater wrote to Cohen in an October 13th email that contained the Trump Tower Moscow LOI signed by Rozov. "And possibly fix relations between the countries by showing everyone that commerce & business are much better and more practical than politics. That should be Putins [sic] message as well, and we will help him agree on that message. Help world peace and make a lot of money. I would say that's a great lifetime goal for us to go after."[60]

"You know, I've made a lot of money," Trump boasted at a political rally in Norfolk, Virginia. At the same time, Sater emailed Michael Cohen asking for him to send the LOI with Trump's signature. "Deals are people, deals are people," Trump continued. "And you have got to analyze people, and I can look at people. I can tell you, I'll get along with Putin. I was on 60 Minutes with Putin. He was my stablemate three weeks ago. We got the highest ratings in a long time on 60 Minutes. You saw that, right? He was my stablemate. I believe I'll get along with him. It was Trump and Putin, Putin and Trump. I'd even let him go first if it makes us friendly. I'll give up the name. I'll give up that place. But I was on 60 Minutes three weeks ago. I'll get along with him." Three days later, on November 2nd, Cohen sent Sater the LOI signed by Trump.[61]

"I think our relationship with Russia will be very good," Trump exclaimed at a press conference one day after Cohen sent the signed LOI to Sater. "Vladimir Putin was on 60 Minutes with me three weeks ago, right? Putin. And they have one of the highest ratings they had in a long time. So, I'm going to give him total credit. But we will have a very good relationship, I think, with Russia. Now maybe we won't, but I believe we will have a very good relationship with Russia. I believe that I will have a very good relationship with Putin."

"Loved Putin/Russia reference," Sater wrote to Cohen in an email 40 minutes after Trump's comments. "I need that part of the press conference cut into a short clip to be played for Putin. Please get it done . ... [Andrey] wants to send it to the Kremlin . ... I will get Putin on this program and we will get Donald elected . .. our boy can become President of the USA and we can engineer it. I will get all of Putins [sic] team to buy in on this . ... Get me that clip I will get it to Putin and his people quickly and it will help our cause and process." Sater sent a message minutes later, "2 boys from Brooklyn getting a USA president elected. This is good really good."[62]

Cohen later wrote that Trump saw Putin as a valuable ally, not for the United States but for himself. Trump believed that he could manipulate Putin's hatred of Hillary Clinton to his advantage. Cohen further maintains that neither he nor Trump ever expected to win the election and that Trump's sycophantic praise of the Russian leader was designed to push the Trump Tower Moscow deal along secretly and "to enable him to be able to borrow money from people in Putin's circle, and that meant sucking up to the Russians."[63]

To sweeten the deal for Putin, Sater suggested to Cohen that they give him a $50 million penthouse. "In Russia, the oligarchs would bend over backwards to live in the same building as Vladimir Putin," Sater later told *BuzzFeed News*. "My idea was to give a $50 million penthouse to Putin and charge $250 million more for the rest of the units. All the oligarchs would line up to live in the same building as Putin."[64] Cohen thought it was a great idea. It also would likely have violated the Foreign Corrupt Practices Act.

Sater added to his November 3rd message to Cohen, "[A] very close person & partner to Putins [sic] closest friend, partner, and advisor who has been with Putin ever since teenage years his friend and partner (on the largest shopping center in Moscow) is flying in to the private island in the Bahamas Andrey [Rozov] rented next week. Everything will be negotiated and discussed not with flunkies but with people who will have dinner with Putin and discuss the issues and get a go ahead."[65]

A week after Trump signed the LOI, Sater traveled with Andrey Rozov to Little Whale Cay, a private island in the Bahamas that Rozov had rented for $175,000.[66] Between bouts of diving and spearfishing, they met with Mikhail Zayats (AKA Mikhail Ziats), an individual with close links to Boris and Arkady Rotenberg, two billionaire brothers with deep personal connections to Putin.[67] Arkady Rotenberg had first met Putin in the 1960s when the two young men joined the same Sambo club. Over the years, the Rotenbergs have amassed a vast fortune in industries ranging from banking to construction, winning public contracts worth billions for construction projects for the Sochi Olympics and the World Cup and building a bridge from Russia to recently-occupied Crimea. Both were under US sanctions.[68]

Mikhail Zayats, who confusingly has the same name as a Russian mixed martial artist, partnered with the Rotenbergs on the Aviapark mall in Moscow, the largest mall in Europe. Gazprombank owned 30% of the billion-dollar project.[69] Sater saw Zayats, who was friends with Rozov, as his "ace in the hole" and a potential pathway to the Rotenbergs.[70] Ultimately, Sater hoped that the billionaire brothers would put up $400 to $500 million into the project, which he believed would lead to Putin green-lighting the project. According to Sater, Zayats was enthusiastic about the tower, particularly because he would have received a cut from the deal. He agreed to bring it to the Rotenbergs attention when the project was more advanced.

Sater hoped that Michael Cohen would travel to Moscow to further push the deal, and on December 1st, he requested a scanned copy of Cohen's passport "for the Russian Ministry of Foreign Affairs." Cohen sent a picture of his passport to Sater the next day. That same day, Donald Trump spoke to *Associate Press* reporter Jeff Horvitz over the phone. Horvitz asked Trump about his relationship with Sater. "Felix Sater, boy, I have to even think about it," Trump replied. Then he lied. "I'm not that familiar with him."[71]

On December 17th, Putin praised Trump during an interview with *ABC News*. "He's a very colorful person. Talented, without any doubt." Putin described Trump as "absolutely the leader in the American presidential race." He said he believed Trump wanted to "move to a more solid, deeper level of relations" between Russia and the United States. "How can Russia not welcome that? We welcome that."[72]

"Now is the time," Cohen wrote to Sater in an email that contained a Google alert showing the news of Putin's comments. "Call me."

Two days later, Sater emailed and texted Cohen requesting scanned copies of his and Donald Trump's passports. He explained that VTB Bank would issue them visas to discuss financing for the project and that Andrey Kostin would be present at the meetings. Sater also asked that Cohen call him because he had "Evgeny" on the other line.[73] While Sater would later try to mislead investigators and say he was referring to Evgeny Shmykov, it was subsequently discovered that, in fact, he was referring to Evgeny Dvoskin.[74]

Like Sater, Dvoskin was a Russian Jewish émigré who grew up in Brighton Beach, Brooklyn. The two were close friends from childhood.[75] Dvoskin and his family had moved to the United States from Odessa in 1977, where he lived under the name Eugene Slusker.[76] After being imprisoned for his role in a daisy chain fuel scam, he shared a prison cell with Vyacheslav Ivankov, the Mogilevich and Solntsevskaya-linked *vor* who once lived in Trump Tower and patronized the Trump Taj Mahal. Dvoskin and Ivankov returned to Moscow in 2004, where the former met and became an associate of Ivan Myazin, who stood at the center of FSB and organized crime money laundering efforts.[77] Through these relationships, Dvoskin became what Catherine Belton described as "the king of Russian black cash."[78]

Dvoskin received protection from the FSB General Ivan Tkachev, the head of the Directorate K, which was charged with investigating financial crimes but, in fact, masterminded and executed Russia's largest money laundering operations, funneling black cash into the West. After Semyon Mogilevich had been publicly tied to the Bank of New York scandal, Dvoskin played a key role in the next generation of Russian money laundering operations, with particular involvement in the Moldovan Laundromat and the Deutsche Bank mirror-trading scandal.

In 2006, Russian Ministry of Interior investigators launched a probe into a group of Russian banks involved in money laundering activities that exceeded one trillion rubles. The investigation found Dvoskin and his partner Ivan Myazin, along with their partners in organized crime, controlled dozens of small Russian banks through front men. Examples of banks they owned included Migros Bank, Siberian Bank of Development, and Falcon Bank, all of which had their licenses revoked between 2006-2007 for money laundering.[79] Kirill Kabanov, a former member of the FSB who now operates an anti-corruption watchdog group, has stated that Dvoskin "was involved in organizing serious schemes for *obnalichka*." *Obnalichka* consists of billions of dollars in off-the-books cash that sloshes through the Russian underground economy, which Putin ultimately sits atop.[80]

Following the Russian invasion of Crimea, most of the Ukrainian banking sector left the region. On April 4th, 2014, two weeks after Russia took control, Genbank was the first Russian bank to open its doors in Sevastopol. Dvoskin owns 4.8% of Genbank's share capital, and his wife sits atop its board. The bank has grown enormously since it opened, with its now over 175 branches making it the second largest bank in the region. Genbank is known for being under the protection of the FSB and is believed to be involved in funneling illicit cash to state officials and corporations.[81] Genbank is under US Government sanctions.

Russian intelligence may have been attempting to compromise Trump by involving him with criminal elements.[82] Sater's suggestion of offering Putin a $50 million penthouse, a likely FCPA violation, could have been part of this effort. Regardless of the intent of either party, the Republican candidate for the President was, through his personal attorney, using a convicted felon to pursue a real estate deal with a former GRU officer, FSB-linked criminal elements and oligarchs situated the highest echelons of power around Vladimir Putin.

Cohen sent Sater another copy of his passport but told him it was "premature" to send along Trump's. Over a week later, on December 29th, Cohen texted Sater asking if there was any response from Russia, thus beginning a terse back and forth in which Cohen lost patience at the lack of progress. Sater told Cohen that he was waiting to receive their official invitations to visit Russia sometime after New Year. "I have never steered you wrong," Cohen angrily texted Sater. "Or not been 100% upfront. When I return to the office, I am contacting my alternate and setting up the meeting myself." Cohen stated, "Not you or anyone you know will embarrass me in front of Mr. T when he asks me what is happening."[83]

The "alternate" Cohen referred to was another potential Trump Tower Moscow project he was exploring with Giorgi Rtskhiladze, a friend he had worked with on a potential Trump Towers in Georgia and Kazakhstan. Rtskhiladze had reached out to Cohen in late September of 2015 on behalf of Simon Nizharadze, a business associate of Rtskhiladze's who wanted to connect the Trump Organization with the Russian real estate developer Vladimir Mazur to partner on a project potentially.[84] On September 22nd, Cohen received architectural renderings from John Fotiadis, the same architect who had drawn up plans for the proposed "Trump Diamond" Tower in Astana, Kazakhstan.[85] Fotiadis had previously worked on projects for the Ukrainian oligarch Rinat Akhmetov, who had hired Paul Manafort as a political consultant for the Ukrainian pro-Russian Party of Regions.[86]

Two days later, Rtskhiladze emailed Cohen a draft letter written in Russian to Moscow's mayor Sergei Sobyanin, whom Rtskhiladze described as the "second guy in Russia." Rtskhiladze stated that Sobyanin was "aware of the potential project and will pledge his support." The letter claimed that the Trump Organization had been "approached by the Global Prospect LLC, a Moscow-based real estate development company co-founded by one of legendary Russian architects, developer, and statesman Mr. Michael Posokhin." The project was to be built in Moscow city and be of "monumental proportions." After inviting Sobyanin to New York, Rtskhiladze's letter stated that Trump Tower Moscow could "act as a symbol of stronger economic, business and cultural relationships between New York and Moscow and therefore the United States and the Russian Federation."[87] However, while Rtskhiladze and Cohen communicated several more times in late 2015 over the proposed Tower, and despite Cohen's threats to Sater that he would pursue the project, it never came to fruition.

"I have invested a lot of personal political capital, time, and energy into getting this done," Sater texted to Cohen, replying to his threat to pursue an "alternate" project. The two then engaged in a tense back and forth, with Cohen angry over their lack of progress and Sater complaining that Trump's public denial of knowing him had hurt his reputation. To troubleshoot the situation, Sater contacted his GRU contact Evgeny Shmykov, explaining that Cohen was "freaking out" and that he needed an invitation quickly. Despite it being a holiday in Russia, Shmykov produced what he described as a "placeholder" letter from Genbank. The next day, Sater texted Cohen a picture of the Genbank letter, falsely telling Cohen that he had received it three days earlier but that it had gone into his spam folder.[88] "Michael," Sater wrote, "this is thru Putins [sic] administration, and nothing gets done there without approval from the top."

"Who is Gen Bank?" Cohen asked. "I thought you were speaking to VTB?" Sater replied that Genbank was 50% owned by the Russian government, "is run like a junior for VTB," and that VTB's chairman (presumably Kostin) was away until January 11th, and the Russians didn't want to wait that long to issue the invitation. Cohen exploded, referring to Genbank as "3rd tier" and telling Sater that he would "take it from here." Sater attempted to explain that a lot of work had been put into the effort so far, that Cohen would be meeting with VTB's Chairman, and that if he wanted to wait until the 12th, he could arrange for an invitation from VTB. However, Cohen was unmoved. "Do you think I'm a moron," he asked. "Do not call or speak to another person regarding MY project."[89]

At this point, Cohen briefly stuck out on his own. On January 11th, 2016, Cohen emailed the office of Vladimir Putin's Press Secretary, Dmitry Peskov, asking to speak with Putin's then-chief of staff, Sergei Ivanov. Ivanov was a former KGB agent who had met Putin while both had studied at the Red Banner Institute. It remains unclear how Cohen got the email address, but he misspelled it, writing to pr_peskova@prpress.*gof.ru* *instead of* the correct *gov.ru*. The error prevented the email from being sent. The next day, a media contact sent Cohen a phone number for Peskov's office, and he sent another email to yet another address, info@prpress.gov.ru. By the 15th, Cohen realized his initial error and sent the email to the correct address. It contained the following letter: "Dear Mr. Peskov, Over the past few months, I have been working with a company based in Russia regarding the development of a Trump Tower-Moscow project in Moscow City. Without getting into lengthy specifics, the communication between our two sides has stalled. As this project is too important, I am hereby requesting your assistance. I respectfully request someone, preferably you; contact me so that I might discuss the specifics as well as arranging meetings with the appropriate individuals. I thank you in advance for your assistance and look forward to hearing from you soon."[90]

According to the Russian publication *The New Times*, Dmitry Peskov's father was a KGB officer responsible for conducting communist propaganda in what was then known as the Third World. Peskov himself has been suspected of working for Russia's foreign intelligence agency, the SVR, at one time.[91] On January 20th, Cohen received an email from Peskov's Chief of Staff and personal assistant, Elena Poliakova. Poliakova enjoyed exceptional access to the Kremlin. Writing from a personal email account, Poliakova informed Cohen that she had been trying to contact him. She provided him with a personal phone number, which Cohen dialed, and he and Poliakova spoke for twenty minutes.[92]

Cohen described himself and his position within the Trump Organization to Poliakova, and they discussed the Trump Tower Moscow project. Poliakova knew about the project and the Trump Organization's partnership with I.C. Expert. Cohen later described her as "extremely professional" and "very detailed in her questions regarding the project." Poliakova ended the conversation by saying she would assemble notes of what she had learned from Cohen and "pass them along," by which he assumed she meant to Peskov.[93]

Cohen informed Trump of his conversation with Poliakova, remarking she had comported herself professionally. They also discussed the potential for the presidential candidate to visit Moscow, which Trump did not see as problematic if it could help further the potential Trump Tower Moscow project. Trump instructed Cohen to speak with his then-campaign manager, Corey Lewandowski, about possible dates to visit Russia. Cohen went as far as requesting a copy of Trump's passport from his assistant, Rhona Graff, though there is no evidence that Trump's passport was ever passed to Sater.

On January 25th, Sater sent Cohen a letter signed by a Russian boxing and real estate magnate named Andrey Ryabinskiy, printed beneath the letterhead of a Russian company called MHG. "In furtherance of our previous conversations regarding the development of the Trump Tower Moscow project," the letter read, "we would like to respectfully invite you to Moscow for a working visit." It further called for Cohen to attend "round table discussions" and later arrange for dates for Trump to visit Moscow. The letter featured much of the same text that Sater and Trump had worked on just days earlier. Sater sent a follow-up email to Cohen requesting dates when he and Trump would travel to Moscow, claiming he had received "another call this morning asking for it." Cohen replied "will do."

"I need to speak to you very urgent [sic]," Sater texted Cohen the next day. "Can I put you on the phone with the guy coordinating to arrange all the calls so you can speak first person to everyone?" Cohen replied, "Now," to which Sater replied, "Ok, 2 minutes." The "guy" Sater referred to was the former GRU officer Evgeny Shmykov. It remains unknown what was discussed during the call, but Sater texted Cohen later that day, "it's set, they are waiting and will walk you into every office you need to make sure you are comfortable for DT trip."[94]

The following day, January 27th, communications between Cohen and Sater mysteriously ceased via text and email. However, it is known that during this period, at Cohen's suggestion, they clandestinely continued to discuss the Trump Tower Moscow project over Dust. This encrypted app automatically and permanently deletes its user's messages. As a result, the communication between Cohen and Sater between the crucial period of January 27th and early May appears to be lost forever. In April 2016, the Trump Organization sought extensions for six of its trademarks in Russia from Rospatent, the Russian government agency that oversees intellectual property. All of them were eventually granted.[95]

"Should I dial you now?" Sater texted Cohen on May 3rd, resuming their non-encrypted communications.[96] Sater wrote to Cohen the next day, "I had a chat with Moscow. ASSUMING the trip does happen, the question is before or after the convention. I said I believe, but don't know for sure, that it's probably after the convention. Obviously the pre-meeting trip (you only) can happen anytime you want but the 2 big guys where [sic] the question. I said I would confirm and revert. I explained that ONLY you will be negotiating all the details. I want to make sure no one tries to go around u, that's why I said that. Michael, it's completely in your hands, probably a quick trip by you would be the perfect move that locks it in, and no one else can elbow in at that point. Let me know about If I was right by saying I believe after Cleveland and also when you want to speak to them and possibly fly over."

"My trip before Cleveland," Cohen replied, referring to the Republican Convention. "Trump once he becomes the nominee after Cleveland."

"Peskov would like to invite you as his guest to the St. Petersburg Forum, which is Russia's Davos," Sater wrote to Cohen the next day, "June 16-19. He wants to meet there with you and possibly introduce you to either Putin or Medvedev, as they are not sure if 1 or both will be there. This is perfect. The entire business class of Russia will be there as well. He said anything you want to discuss, including dates and subjects, are on the table to discuss." Sater later testified that he had spoken with "Evgeny" (it remains unclear whether he meant Evgeny Shmykov or Dvoskin), and they had decided it would be better to portray Cohen's upcoming visit to Moscow more as a business trip than political.[97]

"Works for me," Cohen replied.

"Not only will you probably sit with #1 or #2, but the whole biz community is there," Sater explained to Cohen. "I'll be running around setting nice $100 mill deals. And you will come back, and the whole campaign team can kiss your ass. Keep this very very close to the vest, otherwise half a dozen idiots will try to jump on your coat tails. If it goes great you are a hero, if it doesn't all you did was go to an economic forum to check out the business. Bro this is why you got me working in the shadows. I will make sure you are clean as a whistle either way. For you 0 downside. But I know this is going to turn into 1. A major win for Trump, makes you the hero who bagged the elephant and 2. Sets up a stream of business opportunities that will be mind blowing. All from 1 short trip. I couldn't have dreamed of a better situation with no downside."

On May 26th, Donald Trump won enough delegates to secure the Republican nomination, an outcome still unthinkable to much of the American political elite. On June 9th, Sater informed Cohen that he was securing badges for the St. Petersburg forum and that "Putin is there on the 17th very strong chance you will meet him as well."[98] Four days later, he forwarded Cohen an invitation to the forum signed by the Director of Roscongress, the event organizer, and again asked

Cohen for his passport photos to arrange a visa.

Despite these preparations, Sater and Cohen met the next day, June 14th, in the atrium of Trump Tower. Cohen backed out of the Moscow trip at the last minute. Although Cohen had spoken with Trump ten or twelve times about the project, which the candidate considered an "active project," the effort ground to a halt in June. Sater later said there was "just no way that a presidential candidate could build a tower in a foreign country." Pursuing the project during the general election was deemed impossible. However, as Cohen maintains that Trump fully expected to lose the race, the opportunity to build Trump Tower Moscow would become viable after the Presidential election.

Additional Russian Overtures
To the Trump Organization During the Campaign

Aside from the Agalarov, Rtskhiladze, and Sater Trump Tower projects, several other Russians reached out to discuss similar matters with the Trump Organization and the Trump family. On November 16th, 2015, Ivanka Trump received an email from Lana Erchova, who was married to a Russian named Dmitry Klokov. Klokov was the director of communications at a giant Russian energy company and had once been an assistant to a Russian energy minister. Erchova offered Klokov's assistance to the campaign. "If you ask anyone who knows Russian to google my husband Dmitry Klokov," Erchova wrote to Ivanka, "you'll see who he is close to and that he has done Putin's political campaigns."[99]

Ivanka called Michael Cohen and informed him that she had received an email regarding the Trump Tower Moscow project. After forwarding the email from Erchova, Ivanka instructed Cohen to reach out to Klokov and report back to her.[100] Cohen proceeded to google Klokov's name, which is how he mistook his identity for a Russian Olympic weightlifter of the same name. Between November 18th and 19th, Cohen and Klokov exchanged emails and spoke over the phone at least once. During their phone conversation, Cohen learned that Klokov was aware of the Trump Tower Moscow project and that he had "relationships with the government," that he could "help with this Trump Moscow proposal, and it would be great if all parties were able to meet and to develop this property in Moscow."

Klokov pressed Cohen on traveling with Trump to Moscow, so they all could meet to discuss the project. While Cohen expressed interest in having Trump visit Moscow, he maintained that for any visit to occur, it would have to be "in conjunction with the development and an official visit."

The next day, Klokov sent a follow-up email to Cohen, describing himself as a "trusted person" focused on "political synergy." Klokov further wrote that "our person of interest," who Cohen then assumed and Erchova later confirmed was Vladimir Putin, was "ready to meet your candidate." To facilitate a meeting between Trump and Putin, Klokov told Cohen he would introduce him to a "close person" who, Klokov said, had spoken to Putin about meeting with Trump. The identity of this "close person" intermediary remains unknown. "Now, your client is a candidate, and hardly any other political move could be compared to a tete-a-tete meeting between them," Klokov wrote to Cohen about Trump and Putin. "If publicized correctly, the impact of it could be phenomenal, of course, not only in political but in a business dimension as well. I don't have to tell you that there is no bigger warranty in any project than consent of the person of interest [Putin]."

"[C]urrently our LOI developer is in talks with [Vladimir Putin's] Chief of Staff and arranging a formal invite for the two to meet," Cohen replied to Klokov in an email copied to Ivanka. Cohen told Klokov that he would be "honored" to meet with him in Moscow "to discuss any thoughts you might have that could enhance the project." This appears to be the last communication between the two, and there is no evidence that Cohen brought his interactions with Klokov to the attention of anyone in the Trump Organization or Campaign beyond Ivanka. The Special Counsel's office later received an email from someone claiming to be Lana Erchova, saying that her husband had instructed her to contact Ivanka Trump to "offer cooperation to Trump's team on behalf of the Russian officials." The email further claimed that these officials wanted to offer Trump "land in Crimea among other things and unofficial meeting [sic] with Putin." However, investigators could never determine the validity of the email or its claims.[101]

Yet another Trump Tower Moscow project was pitched to Trump's son, Eric. In the spring of 2016, a Soviet-born Trump Campaign surrogate and later employee named Boris Epshteyn was provided with a proposal for a hotel in Moscow by his contacts in Moscow's city government.[102] On October 28th, 2013, Epshteyn moderated a panel entitled "Invest in Moscow!" which featured Sergey Cheremin, the Minister of the Moscow City Government and Head of Moscow's Department for Foreign Economic and International Relations.[103] The blueprints of a proposed Trump Hotel in Moscow, which had originated from Cheremin, were shared with Epshteyn. Epshteyn, who had been friends with Eric Trump since both had attended Georgetown University, passed the plans over to Eric, who said he would "take a look" and that the proposed Moscow deal "could be interesting."[104] The proposal appeared to go no further.

Epshteyn routinely appeared on television to praise and defend the Trump campaign. In September of 2016, *MediaMatters* criticized outlets for failing "to disclose during discussions about Russia that Epshteyn has financial ties to the former Soviet Union," which included consulting for "entities doing business in Eastern Europe" and moderating a Russian-sponsored conference on "investment opportunities in Moscow."[105] The section of the Senate Counterintelligence Report regarding Epshteyn relaying the Cheremin-backed Trump hotel plan is heavily redacted. Two names, "Tarazov and Standik," stick out from an otherwise almost entirely redacted section. The Russian organization Rossotrudnichestvo is mentioned in the footnotes. "Standik" appears to be a misspelled reference to Alexander Stadnik, Moscow's Trade Representative to the United States, who was expelled from the country after the 2018 attempted assassination of the Russian Military Intelligence defector Sergei Skripal using a Novichok nerve agent.[106] Rossotrudnichestvo is a Russian government-run exchange program whose US Director, Yury Zaytsev, was investigated by the FBI in 2013 for being a Russian spy.[107]

The section is too redacted to make sense of, and it is unclear what Alexander Stadnik or Rossotrudnichestvo have to do with Boris Epshteyn or the Trump Moscow hotel deal he passed along to Eric Trump. In September 2016, Epshteyn received an email from Trump Campaign foreign policy advisor George Papadopoulos saying he wanted to connect him with his friend Sergei Millian.[108] Millian, a former Soviet émigré with ties to Trump and Michael Cohen, had come to the attention of the

FBI in 2011 after participating in a 2011 trip to Moscow organized by Rossotrudnichestvo that counterintelligence officials suspected had been used by Russian intelligence to recruit potential assets.[109] Epshteyn denies having met with Millian.

Yet another approach to candidate Trump from Russia took place in December of 2015, when an acquaintance of Ivanka Trump's from the fashion industry, Miroslava "Mira" Duma, passed along invitations on behalf of Russia's Deputy Prime Minister, Sergei Prikhodko, for Ivanka and Donald Trump to attend the St. Petersburg International Economic Forum, the same event Felix Sater attempted to get Michael Cohen to attend.[110] Ivanka had traveled to Moscow to visit Duma in the past.[111] Duma's father was a former Russian Senator, and her husband worked at the Russian Ministry of Trade and Industry.[112] On January 14th, Trump's assistant Rhona Graff emailed Duma and explained that while Trump was "honored to be asked to participate in the highly prestigious" Forum, he would "have to decline" the invitation due to his "very grueling and full travel schedule." Graff asked Duma if she should send a formal note to Prikhodko, the Deputy Prime Minister, to which Duma responded in the affirmative.

Graff appears to have not sent the note as on March 17th, 2016, she received an email from Prikhodko himself inviting Trump to the Forum. Two weeks later, Graff drafted a two-paragraph letter for Trump to sign stating that schedule has become extremely demanding" because of the presidential campaign, that he "already ha[d] several commitments in the United States" but "would have gladly given every consideration to attending such an important event." Graff sent the draft letter to another assistant at the Trump Organization for them to print out on paper with Trump letterhead for him to sign.

As this letter was being prepared, Graff was contacted by Robert Foresman, the vice chairman of UBS Investment Bank in New York, about securing an in-person meeting with Trump. Foresman maintains that he was asked by Anton Kobyakov, an advisor to Putin involved with the Roscongress Foundation, to invite Trump to speak at the St. Petersburg International Economic Forum. After a phone introduction to Graff via Mark Burnett, the producer of *The Apprentice*, Foresman emailed her on March 31st, writing that he had deep experience in Russia and was involved in establishing an early "private channel" between Putin and George W. Bush.

Foresman had headed Dresdner Bank's investment banking operations in Russia during the early 2000s. From 2001 to 2006, Foresman worked alongside Mattias Warnig, Dresdner Bank's president for Russia.[113] Warnig was a former member of the Stasi, East Germany's infamous intelligence agency and had been a friend of Putin's while he served in the KGB in Dresden. Before joining Dresdner, Warning had spied on it for the Stasi.[114] From 2006 to 2009, Foresman served as the vice chairman of the powerful Moscow investment bank Renaissance Capital. Internal Renaissance Capital emails leaked to *Reuters* reveal that in 2007, Foresman was among several Renaissance executives who secretly drew up an agreement that awarded an unspecified share of Renaissance to Warnig without him having to pay a dime.

Foresman told Graff he had received an "approach" from "senior Kremlin officials" about candidate Trump. He then asked her to arrange for him to meet with Trump, campaign chairman Corey Lewandowski, or "another relevant person" to discuss this "approach" as well as other "concrete things" that he didn't want to communicate over "unsecure email."[115]

Graff forwarded Foresman's meeting request to another Trump Organization assistant on April 4th. Foresman sent reminder emails to Graff on April 26th and 30th, forwarding his April 26th email to Lewandowski. In his April 30th email, Foresman suggested that he could meet with Donald Trump Jr. or Eric Trump so that they could convey the information he possessed "to [the candidate] personally or [to] someone [the candidate] absolutely trusts." Graff forwarded the email to Trump advisor Stephen Miller on May 2nd. It is unclear what happened next, and whether then-candidate Trump was made aware of Foresman's approaches remains unknown.

[1] Report of the Select Committee on Intelligence United States Senate On Russian Active Measures Campaigns And Interference in the 2016 US Election Volume 5: Counterintelligence Threats and Vulnerabilities. Pg. 290

[2] "US 'Miss Universe' billionaire plans Russian Trump Tower," *RT.* November 9th, 2013

[3] Report of the Select Committee on Intelligence United States Senate On Russian Active Measures Campaigns And Interference in the 2016 US Election Volume 5: Counterintelligence Threats and Vulnerabilities. Pg. 300

[4] Tweet. @realDonaldTrump. November 11th, 2013

[5] Report of the Select Committee on Intelligence United States Senate On Russian Active Measures Campaigns And Interference in the 2016 US Election Volume 5:

Counterintelligence Threats and Vulnerabilities. Pg. 301-304

[6] Golubock, D. Garrison. "Donald Trump in New Emin Video," *The Moscow Times.* November 25th, 2013

[7] Mueller, III, Robert S. *Report On The Investigation Into Russian Interference In The 2016 Presidential Election.* Department of Justice, Washington, DC. March 2019. Pg. 68

[8] Report of the Select Committee on Intelligence United States Senate On Russian Active Measures Campaigns And Interference in the 2016 US Election Volume 5: Counterintelligence Threats and Vulnerabilities. Pg. 308

[9] Kaczynsky, Andrew; Massie, Chris; McDermott, Nathan. "80 Times Trump talked about Putin," *CNN*

[10] Mueller, III, Robert S. *Report On The Investigation Into Russian Interference In The 2016 Presidential Election.* Department of Justice, Washington, DC. March 2019. Pg. 68

[11] Report of the Select Committee on Intelligence United States Senate On Russian Active Measures Campaigns And Interference in the 2016 US Election Volume 5: Counterintelligence Threats and Vulnerabilities. Pg. 311

[12] Report of the Select Committee on Intelligence United States Senate On Russian Active Measures Campaigns And Interference in the 2016 US Election Volume 5: Counterintelligence Threats and Vulnerabilities. Pg. 312

[13] Report of the Select Committee on Intelligence United States Senate On Russian Active Measures Campaigns And Interference in the 2016 US Election Volume 5: Counterintelligence Threats and Vulnerabilities. Pg. 420-421

[14] Cohen, Michael. *Disloyal: The True Story Of The Former Personal Attorney To President Donald J. Trump.* New York, NY: Skyhorse Publishing, 2020. Pg. 245

[15] Mueller, III, Robert S. *Report On The Investigation Into Russian Interference In The 2016 Presidential Election.* Department of Justice, Washington, DC. March 2019. Pg. 69

[16] Cormier, Anthony; Leopold, Jason. "How A Player In The Trump-Russia Scandal Led A Double Life As An American Spy," *BuzzFeed News.* March 12th, 2018

[17] Osborne, Andrew; Sichkar, Olga. "Russian tycoon, symbol of excess, convicted of fraud but walks free," *Reuters.* July 12th, 2017

[18] Sonne, Paul; Ballhaus, Rebecca; Berzon, Alexandra; Hodge, Nathan. "In Moscow Luxury-Tower Plan, Donald Trump Paired With Developer for Russia's Working Class," *The Wall Street Journal.* September 1st, 2017

[19] Sazonov, Alexander; Voreacos, David; Reznik, Irina. "Trump's Would Be Moscow Partner Faces Homebuyers' Ire," *Bloomberg.* September 1st, 2017

[20] Stedman, Scott. *Real News: An Investigative Reporter Uncovers The Foundations Of The Trump-Russia Conspiracy.* New York, NY: Skyhorse Publishing, 2019. Pg. 22-29

[21] Report of the Select Committee on Intelligence United States Senate On Russian Active Measures Campaigns And Interference in the 2016 US Election Volume 5: Counterintelligence Threats and Vulnerabilities. Pg. 423

[22] Stedman, Scott. *Real News: An Investigative Reporter Uncovers The Foundations Of The Trump-Russia Conspiracy.* New York, NY: Skyhorse Publishing, 2019. Pg. 26

[23] Colchester, Max; Patrick, Margot. "Hiding Russian Money Was Easy. Quitting Was Harder." *The Wall Street Journal.* August 4th, 2018

[24] Stedman, Scott. *Real News: An Investigative Reporter Uncovers The Foundations Of The Trump-Russia Conspiracy.* New York, NY: Skyhorse Publishing, 2019. Pg. 35

[25] "Bloomberg Billionaires Index #51 Vladimir Lisin," *Bloomberg.* August 17th, 2021

[26] Goodley, Simon; Harding, Luke; Elder, Miriam. "Man behind MegaFon pictured with alleged Russian gangsters," *The Guardian.* November 28th, 2012

[27] Stedman, Scott. *Real News: An Investigative Reporter Uncovers The Foundations Of The Trump-Russia Conspiracy.* New York, NY: Skyhorse Publishing, 2019. Pg. 41

[28] Stedman, Scott. *Real News: An Investigative Reporter Uncovers The Foundations Of The Trump-Russia Conspiracy.* New York, NY: Skyhorse Publishing, 2019. Pg. 47

[29] Humber, Yuriy; Miller, Hugo. "Determined Deripaska Casts Long Shadow," *The Moscow Times.* April 28th, 2008

[30] Bilefsky, Dan. "Montenegro becomes Russia's window of opportunity," *The New York Times*. October 31st, 2008

[31] Mueller, III, Robert S. *Report On The Investigation Into Russian Interference In The 2016 Presidential Election*. Department of Justice, Washington, DC. March 2019. Pg. 69

[32] Report of the Select Committee on Intelligence United States Senate On Russian Active Measures Campaigns And Interference in the 2016 US Election Volume 5: Counterintelligence Threats and Vulnerabilities. Pg. 425

[33] Siegelman, Wendy. "While Felix Sater pursued Trump Tower Moscow discussions, he did a deal with an accountant linked to Aras Agalarov," *Medium*. October 22nd, 2018

[34] "PARASON, INC," *The Organized Crime and Corruption Reporting Project (OCCRP)*. March 20th, 2017

[35] Swain, Jon. "FBI looked into Trump plans to build hotel in Latvia with Putin supporter," *The Guardian*. March 29th, 2018

[36] Ghorayshi, Azeen; Leopold, Jason; Cormier, Anthony; Loop, Emma. "These Secret Files Show How The Trump Moscow Talks Unfolded While Trump Heaped Praise On Putin," *BuzzFeed News*. February 5th, 2019

[37] Report of the Select Committee on Intelligence United States Senate On Russian Active Measures Campaigns And Interference in the 2016 US Election Volume 5: Counterintelligence Threats and Vulnerabilities. Pg. 425-426

[38] Ghorayshi, Azeen; Leopold, Jason; Cormier, Anthony; Loop, Emma. "These Secret Files Show How The Trump Moscow Talks Unfolded While Trump Heaped Praise On Putin," *BuzzFeed News*. February 5th, 2019

[39] Ghorayshi, Azeen; Leopold, Jason; Cormier, Anthony; Loop, Emma. "These Secret Files Show How The Trump Moscow Talks Unfolded While Trump Heaped Praise On Putin," *BuzzFeed News*. February 5th, 2019

[40] Hoffman, David. "Putin's Career Rooted In Russia's KGB," *The Washington Post*. January 30th, 2000

[41] Grozovsky, Boris; Trudolyubov, Maxim. "Capitalism the Kremlin Way," *The Russia File: A Blog of the Kennan Institute, The Wilson Center*. September 13, 2018

[42] Felshtinsky, Yuri; Pribylovsky, Vladimir. "Dossier on Putin in St. Petersburg. Drugs, bandits, theft and the KGB," Ruspress. January 15th, 2010

[43] Report of the Select Committee on Intelligence United States Senate On Russian Active Measures Campaigns And Interference in the 2016 US Election Volume 5: Counterintelligence Threats and Vulnerabilities. Pg. 426 [Note: the Senate report spells Maxim Temnikov as Maxim *Temikov*]

[44] Trifonov, Vladislav. "The share of the accused in the Mirax Group has grown," *Kommersant*. May 25th, 2016

[45] Brinkman, Paul. "Fisher Island condo belonging to Trump friend, billionaire Agalarov, hit by foreclosure," *The Real Deal*. January 17th, 2019

[46] "Russians in Miami," *Transparency International - Russia & The Sunlight Foundation*. September 2nd, 2020

[47] Shumanov, Ilya; Dobrovolskaya, Lily; Pavlovskaya, Yulia. "'Miami is ours': why Russian businessmen and bandits live in Trump Towers," *Forbes Russia*. July 11th, 2016

[48] Report of the Select Committee on Intelligence United States Senate On Russian Active Measures Campaigns And Interference in the 2016 US Election Volume 5: Counterintelligence Threats and Vulnerabilities. Pg. 426-427

[49] Schmidt, Michael S. "Russian Banker Denies Role in Planned Trump Building In Moscow," *The New York Times*. October 13th, 2017

[50] Enrich, David. *Dark Towers: Deutsche Bank, Donald Trump, And An Epic Trail of Destruction*. New York, NY: HarperCollins Publishers, 2020. Pg. 109

[51] Åslund, Anders. *Russia's Crony Capitalism: The Path from Market Economy to Kleptocracy*. New Haven and London: Yale University Press, 2019. Pg. 148

[52] Drucker, Jesse. "Kremlin Cash Behind Billionaire's Twitter and Facebook Investments," *The New York Times*. November 5th, 2017

[53] Enrich, David. "Deutsche Bank and Trump: $2 Billion in Loans and a Wary Board," *The New York Times*. March 18th, 2019

[54] Corcoran, Jason. "Deutsche Bank's Kostin, Son of VTB's Chief, Dies in Bike Crash," *Bloomberg*. July 4th, 2011

[55] Seddon, Max. "Cash flow and the Kremlin," *The Financial Times*. August 24th, 2016

[56] Enrich, David. *Dark Towers: Deutsche Bank, Donald Trump, And An Epic Trail of Destruction*. New York, NY: HarperCollins Publishers, 2020. Pg. 110

[57] Report of the Select Committee on Intelligence United States Senate On Russian Active Measures Campaigns And Interference in the 2016 US Election Volume 5: Counterintelligence Threats and Vulnerabilities. Pg. 428

[58] McIntire, Mike; Twohey, Megan; Mazzetti, Mark. "How a Lawyer, a Felon and a Russian General Chased a Moscow Trump Tower Deal," *The New York Times*. November 29th, 2018

[59] Hamburger, Tom; Troianovsky, Anton. "'I will answer every question': Onetime Trump business partner is set to tell a House panel new details about Moscow project," *The Washington Post*. January 20th, 2019

[60] Report of the Select Committee on Intelligence United States Senate On Russian Active Measures Campaigns And Interference in the 2016 US Election Volume 5: Counterintelligence Threats and Vulnerabilities. Pg. 429

[61] Report of the Select Committee on Intelligence United States Senate On Russian Active Measures Campaigns And Interference in the 2016 US Election Volume 5: Counterintelligence Threats and Vulnerabilities. Pg. 430

[62] Report of the Select Committee on Intelligence United States Senate On Russian Active Measures Campaigns And Interference in the 2016 US Election Volume 5: Counterintelligence Threats and Vulnerabilities. Pg. 432

[63] Cohen, Michael. *Disloyal: The True Story Of The Former Personal Attorney To President Donald J. Trump*. New York, NY: Skyhorse Publishing, 2020. Pg. 247-248

[64] Cormier, Anthony; Leopold, Jason. "The Trump Organization Planned To Give Vladimir Putin The $50 Million Penthouse In Trump Tower Moscow," *BuzzFeed News*. November 29th, 2018

[65] Report of the Select Committee on Intelligence United States Senate On Russian Active Measures Campaigns And Interference in the 2016 US Election Volume 5: Counterintelligence Threats and Vulnerabilities. Pg. 432

[66] Cormier, Anthony; Leopold, Jason. "Trump Moscow: The Definitive Story Of How Trump's Team Worked The Moscow Deal During The Campaign," *BuzzFeed News*. May 17th, 2018

[67] Report of the Select Committee on Intelligence United States Senate On Russian Active Measures Campaigns And Interference in the 2016 US Election Volume 5: Counterintelligence Threats and Vulnerabilities. Pg. 433

[68] Alexander, Dan; Behar, Richard. "The Truth Behind Trump Tower Moscow: How Trump Risked Everything For A (Relatively) Tiny Deal," *Forbes*. May 23rd, 2019

[69] Filatov, Anton. "Gazprombank became a co-owner of the Aviapark shopping mall," *Vedomosti*. January 27th, 2017

[70] Report of the Select Committee on Intelligence United States Senate On Russian Active Measures Campaigns And Interference in the 2016 US Election Volume 5: Counterintelligence Threats and Vulnerabilities. Pg. 434

[71] Isikoff, Michael; Corn, David. *Russian Roulette: The Inside Story Of Putin's War On America And The Election Of Donald Trump*. New York, NY: Hachette Book Group Inc., 2018. Pg. 78

[72] Reevell, Patrick. "Russian President Vladimir Putin Praises Donald Trump as "Talented" and "Very Colorful," *ABC News*. December 17th, 2015

[73] Ghorayshi, Azeen; Leopold, Jason; Cormier, Anthony; Loop, Emma. "These Secret Files Show How The Trump Moscow Talks Unfolded While Trump Heaped Praise On Putin," *BuzzFeed News*. February 5th, 2019

[74] Mueller, III, Robert S. *Report On The Investigation Into Russian Interference In The 2016 Presidential Election*. Department of Justice, Washington, DC. March 2019. Pg. 76

[75] Belton, Catherin. *Putin's People: How The KGB Took Back Russia And Took On The West*. New York, NY: Farrar, Straus and Giroux, 2020. Pg. 464

[76] Pismennaya, Evgenia; Reznik, Irina. "The Russian Ex-Con With a Thriving Banking Business in Crimea," *Bloomberg*. April 7th, 2016

[77] Reznik, Irina; Pismennaya, Evgenia; White, Gregory. "The Russian Banker Who Knew Too Much," *Bloomberg*. November 19th, 2017

[78] Belton, Catherin. *Putin's People: How The KGB Took Back Russia And Took On The West*. New York, NY: Farrar, Straus and Giroux, 2020. Pg. 408-409

[79] Zhuravlev, Evgeny; Nizovaya, Elena. "Controversial Russian Bankers Target Crimea," *The Organized Crime and Corruption Reporting Project (OCCRP)*. June 3rd, 2015

[80] Pismennaya, Evgenia; Reznik, Irina. "The Russian Ex-Con With a Thriving Banking Business in Crimea," *Bloomberg*. April 7th, 2016

[81] Galeotti, Mark; Arutunyan, Anna. "Commentary: Hybrid Business -- The Risks In The Kremlin's Weaponization Of The Economy," *RadioFreeEurope/RadioLiberty*. July 20th, 2016

[82] Belton, Catherin. *Putin's People: How The KGB Took Back Russia And Took On The West*. New York, NY: Farrar, Straus and Giroux, 2020. Pg. 474

[83] Ghorayshi, Azeen; Leopold, Jason; Cormier, Anthony; Loop, Emma. "These Secret Files Show How The Trump Moscow Talks Unfolded While Trump Heaped Praise On Putin," *BuzzFeed News*. February 5th, 2019

[84] Report of the Select Committee on Intelligence United States Senate On Russian Active Measures Campaigns And Interference in the 2016 US Election Volume 5: Counterintelligence Threats and Vulnerabilities. Pg. 453

[85] Michel, Casey. "Trump Diamond: An Unsuccessful Bid For The Astana Skyline," *The Diplomat*. June 30th, 2017

[86] Wilkie, Christina. "Meet the New York architect who was a key figure in Donald Trump's deals and connections in Eastern Europe," *CNBC*. June 6th, 2018

[87] Report of the Select Committee on Intelligence United States Senate On Russian Active Measures Campaigns And Interference in the 2016 US Election Volume 5: Counterintelligence Threats and Vulnerabilities. Pg. 453

[88] Report of the Select Committee on Intelligence United States Senate On Russian Active Measures Campaigns And Interference in the 2016 US Election Volume 5: Counterintelligence Threats and Vulnerabilities. Pg. 439

[89] Ghorayshi, Azeen; Leopold, Jason; Cormier, Anthony; Loop, Emma. "These Secret Files Show How The Trump Moscow Talks Unfolded While Trump Heaped Praise On Putin," *BuzzFeed News*. February 5th, 2019

[90] Report of the Select Committee on Intelligence United States Senate On Russian Active Measures Campaigns And Interference in the 2016 US Election Volume 5: Counterintelligence Threats and Vulnerabilities. Pg. 441-442

[91] Beshley, Olga; Ostalsky, Andray. "Man Of The Era of Press Secretaries," *The New Times*. December 9th, 2013

[92] Mueller, III, Robert S. *Report On The Investigation Into Russian Interference In The 2016 Presidential Election*. Department of Justice, Washington, DC. March 2019. Pg. 75

[93] Report of the Select Committee on Intelligence United States Senate On Russian Active Measures Campaigns And Interference in the 2016 US Election Volume 5: Counterintelligence Threats and Vulnerabilities. Pg. 444

[94] Cormier, Anthony; Leopold, Jason. "Trump Moscow: The Definitive Story Of How Trump's Team Worked The Russian Deal During The Campaign," *BuzzFeed News*. May 17th, 2018

[95] McIntire, Mike. "Russia Renewed Unused Trump Trademarks in 2016," *The New York Times*. January 18th, 2017

[96] Ghorayshi, Azeen; Leopold, Jason; Cormier, Anthony; Loop, Emma. "These Secret

Files Show How The Trump Moscow Talks Unfolded While Trump Heaped Praise On Putin," *BuzzFeed News*. February 5th, 2019

[97] Report of the Select Committee on Intelligence United States Senate On Russian Active Measures Campaigns And Interference in the 2016 US Election Volume 5: Counterintelligence Threats and Vulnerabilities. Pg. 448

[98] Mueller, III, Robert S. *Report On The Investigation Into Russian Interference In The 2016 Presidential Election*. Department of Justice, Washington, DC. March 2019. Pg. 78

[99] Mueller, III, Robert S. *Report On The Investigation Into Russian Interference In The 2016 Presidential Election*. Department of Justice, Washington, DC. March 2019. Pg. 72

[100] Report of the Select Committee on Intelligence United States Senate On Russian Active Measures Campaigns And Interference in the 2016 US Election Volume 5: Counterintelligence Threats and Vulnerabilities. Pg. 455

[101] Mueller, III, Robert S. *Report On The Investigation Into Russian Interference In The 2016 Presidential Election*. Department of Justice, Washington, DC. March 2019. Pg. 73

[102] Report of the Select Committee on Intelligence United States Senate On Russian Active Measures Campaigns And Interference in the 2016 US Election Volume 5: Counterintelligence Threats and Vulnerabilities. Pg. 458

[103] Hananoki, Eric. "Media Host Trump Advisor Boris Epshteyn On Russia Without Disclosing His Business Ties," *MediaMatters*. September 15th, 2016

[104] Meier, Barry; Craig, Suzanne. "The Obscure Lawyer Who Became Trump's TV Attack Dog," *The New York Times*. October 13th, 2016

[105] Hananoki, Eric. "Media Host Trump Advisor Boris Epshteyn On Russia Without Disclosing His Business Ties," *MediaMatters*. September 15th, 2016

[106] "Russian Trade Representative among Diplomats expelled from United States," *TASS Russian News Agency*. March 28th, 2018

[107] Redden, Molly. "FBI Probing Whether Russia Used Cultural Junkets to Recruit American Intelligence Assets," *Mother Jones*. October 23rd, 2013

[108] Helderman, Rosalind S.; DeYoung, Karen; Hamburger, Tom. "For 'Low-Level Volunteer,' Papadopoulos sought high profile as Trump advisor," *The Washington Post*. October 31st, 2017

[109] Belton, Catherine. "The shadowy Russian émigré touting Trump," *The Financial Times*. October 31st, 2016

[110] Mueller, III, Robert S. *Report On The Investigation Into Russian Interference In The 2016 Presidential Election*. Department of Justice, Washington, DC. March 2019. Pg. 78-79

[111] Report of the Select Committee on Intelligence United States Senate On Russian Active Measures Campaigns And Interference in the 2016 US Election Volume 5: Counterintelligence Threats and Vulnerabilities. Pg. 308 (Footnote #2006)

[112] Gonzales, Erica. "Fashion Influencer Miroslava Duma Is In The Mueller Report Because Of Her Link To Ivanka Trump," *Harpers Bazaar*. April 18th, 2018

[113] Belton, Catherine. "Exclusive: American banker and Putin ally dealt in access and assets, emails reveal," *Reuters*. June 9th, 2019

[114] Crawford, David. "Dresdener's Man in Russia," *The Wall Street Journal*. April 26th, 2005

[115] Mueller, III, Robert S. *Report On The Investigation Into Russian Interference In The 2016 Presidential Election*. Department of Justice, Washington, DC. March 2019. Pg. 79

Part IV
The Inside Story
Of the Trump Campaign

Chapter 13:
Roger Stone's Politics of Deception and Division
And the 2016 Trump Campaign

Roger Stone and the Genesis of the 2016 Trump Campaign

Roger Stone was one of Donald Trump's earliest, most vocal, and most controversial supporters during the 2016 election. Their relationship dates back decades. After their first meeting during the Reagan campaign, Stone deepened his relationship with Trump between 1980 and 2016. During this period, Trump's political career came slowly into focus, initially consisting of little more than stunt campaigns to wreak vengeance against his and Stone's mutual enemies and serve as publicity stunts. Stone also honed his style of politics, which consisted of an all-publicity-is-good publicity ethos inherited from Roy Cohn, Nixon-era "dirty tricks," and a divide-and-conquer electoral strategy articulated by Arthur Finkelstein. Finally, numerous individuals who later worked on the 2016 Trump campaign associated with Stone in this timeframe.

These 35 years of Stone's life can be divided into two parts. The first lasted from 1980 to 1996, when Stone operated within mainstream Republican politics. A tabloid sexual scandal involving Stone and his wife that broke during the 1996 Dole campaign marks a rupture in the political operative's career. In its aftermath, Stone became involved in fringe politics and masterminded a series of stunt campaigns designed to damage his enemies and line his and associates' pockets. Many of these campaigns involved Trump.

Following Reagan's victory, Stone and two other Reagan campaign alums, Paul Manafort and Charles Black, established the lobbying firm Black, Manafort, and Stone. Stone's bailiwick at the firm was in domestic affairs, and one of the earliest clients he brought on board was Trump. As the 1980s dawned, Stone and Trump were drawn to New Jersey. A 1976 state-wide referendum had legalized gambling in Atlantic City, the first place in the United States outside of Las Vegas to have done so in over four decades.

Though Trump initially opposed gambling in New Jersey, hoping that New York would legalize casinos first, he later aggressively moved to become the most prominent casino magnate in Atlantic City. Trump needed to curry favor with New Jersey's Governor to do so. The Governor appointed the Attorney General, who appointed the Division of Gaming Enforcement (DGE) and the Casino Control Commission (CCC), the two bodies whose stamp of approval was necessary to be awarded a casino license.

As Northeast coordinator of the 1980 Reagan campaign, Stone was responsible for campaign activities in New Jersey. A year after Reagan's election, Stone returned to New Jersey to manage Thomas H. Kean's gubernatorial campaign. After losing a statewide election in 1977, Kean enlisted Stone for the 1981 election.

Both Roy Cohn and Donald Trump were early supporters. Cohn hosted a fundraiser for Kean at his townhouse in January of 1981. Several attendees claimed that Trump was in attendance despite being legally barred from contributing because his application for a casino license was pending.[1] Stone contacted White House Chief of Staff James Baker III to arrange for Reagan to travel to New Jersey to support Kean's candidacy. Reagan made the trip, and years later, as we shall see, Baker would call on Stone to return the favor.

Election day in New Jersey was marred by Republican-backed voter suppression activities targeting African Americans. Kean narrowly won by 1,797 votes. After the election, Democrats sued the RNC and the New Jersey Republican Party for violating the 1964 Voting Rights Act. In a settlement, the RNC agreed to a federal consent decree that prohibited such activities. Stone denied any knowledge of voter suppression. Kean's campaign manager later stated that if Stone didn't directly arrange effort, it was "Stone-esque." [2]

Stone continued to lobby for Trump after the election. He worked on projects related to Treasury Department currency transaction rules pertinent to casinos and FAA limits on the height of skyscrapers that impacted a building Trump was planning in Chicago. Characteristically, Trump didn't always promptly pay Black, Manafort, and Stone. Charles Black often had to personally travel to New York to get a check from Trump. [3]

During Reagan's 1984 re-election campaign, Stone and Roy Cohn worked together to find dirt on the Democratic Vice Presidential candidate Geraldine Ferraro and her family. [4] Around this time, Stone began considering Trump's political prospects. Trump had been asked about running for president by celebrity journalists as early as 1980. A 1984 *New York Times Magazine* cover story explored the idea of a Trump candidacy. Trump stated in the article that he wouldn't want to run because of "false smiles and "red tape." [5] Stone met with Trump in Atlantic City to see if he would be interested in running against New York Governor Mario Cuomo in 1984. [6] Though Trump declined, Stone's aspirations were just beginning.

Stone began urging Trump to consider running in 1987. [7] In July of that year, Trump registered as a Republican for the first time. [8] That same month, Trump made his first visit to Moscow on a trip arranged by the Soviet State tourist agency, Goscomintourist, operated by the KGB. [9] Shortly after he returned from Moscow, Trump purchased a controlling interest in Resorts International. This company had funded the pro-legalization campaign during the 1976 referendum to allow casino gambling in Atlantic City.

Roger Stone wasn't the only party interested in a Trump presidential. A July 27th, 1987 edition of *Executive Intelligence Review*, published by the Lyndon LaRouche organization, wrote that "[t]he Soviets are reportedly looking a lot more kindly on a possible Presidential bid by Donald Trump, the New York builder who has amassed a fortune through real-estate speculation and owns a controlling interest in the notorious, organized crime linked Resorts International."

Stone had first met LaRouche, a perennial candidate for the US presidency known for outlandish conspiracy theories, in 1980, and many years later, would claim that he had come to embrace LaRouche's "extraordinary and prophetic thinking." [10]

In September of '87, Trump spent $94,801 to purchase full-page ads in *The New York Times*, *The Washington Post*, and *The Boston Globe*, which articulated a position he would maintain for decades: the United States was being cheated by its allies. Trump's first flirtation with a presidential run peaked the next month when, on October 22nd, he arrived by helicopter to an event in New Hampshire arranged by a Republican named Mike Dunbar, who supported a Trump presidential bid. Trump spoke at a local Rotary Club before a crowd of 500.

Trump didn't run in the 1988 election. Stone, on the other hand, was involved in several different capacities. During the primary, he advised Republican Jack Kemp. After Vice President George H.W. Bush got the nod, Stone served as a senior advisor to Bush. The Connecticut patrician's campaign was managed by another notorious hard-knuckled politico and Black, Manafort, and Stone partner, Lee Atwater. Paul Manafort served as Bush's director of operations. Donald Trump attended the 1988 Republican National Convention, telling Larry King he was there to see "how the system works."[11]

Stone divorced his first wife, Ann, and married Nydia Bertran in 1991. Bertran was the daughter of a diplomat in pre-Castro Cuba who had fled to the United States following the Cuban Revolution. In 1996, Stone worked on Republican Senator Bob Dole's presidential campaign. Dole's attacks on Bill Clinton centered on the Democratic incumbent's sexual scandals. Thus, it was a significant embarrassment when *The National Enquirer* reported, "Top Dole Aide Caught in Group Sex Ring." Stone had been placing ads in publications such as *Local Swing Fever* soliciting "well hung in shape men" to participate in "3-somes" with himself and his wife.

Stone initially claimed that the ads were made by a disgruntled domestic employee, though later admitted this was a lie. The scandal led to his resignation and exile from mainstream politics. With the benefit of hindsight, we can see that by forcing Stone out of the Republican mainstream and driving him to the political fringe, which would coalesce years later around the Trump presidential bid, the *Enquirer* scandal may have changed history.

In 2000, the St. Regis Mohawk tribe, located in Franklin County, NY, planned on opening a casino in the Catskills. The hitherto unknown New York Institute for Law and Society opposed the plan. The ostensibly grassroots, anti-gambling group claimed to be supported by 12,000 donors and attacked the tribe's planned casino with hard-hitting ad buys. In truth, the New York Institute for Law and Society was not a grassroots organization. It was the brainchild of Roger Stone and was funded by Trump.[12] Stone left Black, Manafort, and Stone in the 1990s and founded Ikon Public Affairs, which was behind the "Institute." Trump personally signed off on Stone's attack lines. "Roger — do it, Donald," Trump wrote in a memo.

It wasn't Trump's first battle with Indian gaming interests. Following a Supreme Court decision that allowed gambling on Indian reservations, Ronald Reagan signed the Indian Gaming Regulatory Act in 1988. The timing was terrible for Trump, whose real estate and casino empire was already reeling under a mountain of debt. His three casinos in Atlantic City were cannibalizing each other's business, and any additional competition was unwelcome.

In 1992, a year after the Trump Taj Mahal declared bankruptcy, the Mashantucket Pequot Tribal Nation partnered with the Malaysian gambling concern Genting. It opened the Foxwoods Resort and Casino in Connecticut. Trump filed a lawsuit against the Government, claiming it was discriminating against him.[13] "I think I might have more Indian blood than a lot of the so-called Indians that are trying to open up the reservations," Trump told shock jock radio host Don Imus.

Stone accompanied Trump to Washington, DC in 1993 where he testified before Congress.[14] In addition to claiming that the Mashantucket Pequot's didn't "look Indian," Trump stated that "Organized crime is rampant, is rampant — I don't mean a little bit — is rampant on the Indian reservations. It will blow sky-high. It will be the biggest scandal ever or one of the biggest scandals since Al Capone in terms of organized crime."

When Trump's appearance before Congress failed to defeat Indian gaming, Stone manufactured the New York Institute for Law and Society. Stone's campaign gained the attention of New York's Commission on Lobbying. The Commission found that Trump and Stone's attacks violated state law. Trump was fined $250,000, and Stone was fined $100,000. The settlement included a rare public apology from Trump.[15]

The fine infuriated Stone and whetted his appetite for revenge against New York Governor George Pataki, who he held responsible. Stone's first opportunity came during the 2000 presidential election. At the time, George W. Bush considered Pataki a running mate. Trump and Stone ran ads in New Hampshire, Texas, and South Carolina urging Bush to steer clear of Pataki, who they accused of supporting Indian gambling.

Stone was active during the 2000 election despite his banishment from mainstream politics. His first target was the Reform Party. Many Republicans ascribed Bill Clinton's 1992 victory to third-party candidate Ross Perot. The Texan billionaire received 18.5% of the vote. Encouraged by his showing, in 1995, Perot established the Reform Party and garnered 8.5% in the 1996 election. By the 2000 election, advisors around George W. Bush were concerned that another Reform Party candidate could threaten his chances of defeating Al Gore.

Stone encouraged former Nixon speechwriter Pat Buchanan to run as a third-party candidate, then sabotaged his campaign to improve Bush's election prospects. In June 1999, Stone lunched with Bay Buchanan, Pat's sister and campaign manager, and political aide Lyn Nofziger. According to Nofziger, having Buchanan run with the Reform Party was Stone's idea. He argued that if he did so, he would receive up to $13 million in federal matching funds.[16]

Meanwhile, Stone was simultaneously undercutting Buchanan's campaign. He spread a rumor that Buchanan had fathered an illegitimate child. One man who pursued the story and later refused to answer any questions regarding Stone's role in guiding his reporting was an *AP* reporter named John Solomon. Three decades later, Solomon came under severe criticism for reporting that smeared the American ambassador to Ukraine and peddling the discredited falsehood that Ukraine was behind the interference in the 2016 election as opposed to Russia.[17]

Another individual whom Stone had paid to spread the story was the consultant Mattie Lolavar. Lolavar was later involved in a lawsuit against Stone involving two contracts with his PR company. The first involved Argentinian President Fernando de la Rua. The second was to serve as a PR agent for the Secretary of Intelligence for Argentina. Lolavar fell out with Stone after he asked her to serve as an anonymous cutout in a transfer of funds to an official in Israel. The payment was to secure intelligence files from the Israeli government to assist de la Rua. Lolavar was to doctor the documents to make them look like they had come from Argentinian intelligence. Stone grew worried that the plot could be linked back to them and told Lolavar to blame the Gore campaign. Lolavar refused.[18] This episode indicates that Stone had links to Israeli officials with intelligence connections as far back as 2000.

Returning to the 2000 election, Stone had another card up his sleeve to derail the Reform Party: Donald Trump. Despite registering as a Republican in 1987, when Trump decided to flirt with a presidential run in 2000, it wasn't as a Republican but as the potential standard bearer for the Reform Party. It is no accident that at the same time Stone was encouraging Buchanan to enter the race under the Reform Party, he was doing the same with Trump.

Trump had considered running since 1998, when he asked Stone to "find the most eminent hack writer in America" to ghostwrite a book for him.[19] On October 7th, 1999, Trump met with the Governor of Minnesota, former professional wrestler Jesse Ventura, who had won an upset victory under the Reform Party banner.[20] Trump and Ventura had first met in 1988 at WrestleMania IV in Atlantic City. Both wanted to thwart Buchanan. Stone had paid close attention to Ventura's candidacy and saw an opening for unorthodox, populist candidates. A day after meeting Ventura, Trump announced that he was leaving the Republican Party for the Reform Party and was forming an exploratory committee to run for president.[21]

Trump began to attack Pat Buchanan aggressively, no doubt according to Stone's plans. Trump wrote an Op-Ed attacking Buchanan for his views on Adolf Hitler and Nazism. He told a gay news magazine that he didn't like how Buchanan talked about "Jews, blacks, gays, and Mexicans" and that, as President, he would extend the Civil Rights Act to include gay people and allow them to serve in the military, then-banned under "Don't Ask, Don't Tell."[22]

As he thrust the Reform Party into chaos, Trump went onto *Meet the Press* and said that he supported partial-birth abortion. After the show, Stone claimed that Trump admitted to him that he didn't know what partial birth abortion was. Trump later came out against the procedure. As part of his faux presidential run, Trump filmed an episode of *The Tonight Show* accompanied by Stone. "Hey Donald," host Jay Leno quipped, "you brought your bookie."

In addition to kneecapping the Reform Party, Trump's candidacy was a publicity stunt. On January 1st, 2000, he released his book *The America We Deserve*. Trump held a press conference at Trump Tower to promote the book. Despite the fanfare, Trump announced in a February 19th Op-Ed that he wouldn't run in the 2000 election.

Jesse Ventura put the nail in Buchanan's coffin when he pulled the support of the Minnesota branch of the party. The Reform Party was now a national joke. Supporters of George W. Bush could rest assured that there would be no repeat of 1992. Stone's involvement in the 2000 election, however, was far from over.

The election between Bush and Gore came down to Florida. On election night, the networks initially called the state for Gore before saying the race was "too close to call" and finally calling the state instead for Bush, who led on election night by 1,784 votes. An automatic recount followed, reducing Bush's lead to 900 votes. The issue was turned over to the courts, reaching the US Supreme Court.

Before the Bush v. Gore ruling, Stone attempted to pressure judges on the Florida Supreme Court. He secretly established the "Committee to Take Back Our Judiciary," fronted by a former chair of the Palm Beach Republican Party named Mary McCarty. Stone's "Committee" received a $150,000 loan, the source of which remains unknown. McCarty was determined to have violated campaign finance laws. Years later, McCarty received a pardon for an unrelated crime alongside Stone during the final days of the Trump presidency. [23]

Republican luminary James Baker III was in charge of managing the situation in Florida for the Bush campaign. Baker called in the favor Stone owed him dating back to getting Ronald Reagan to endorse Thomas Kean nineteen years earlier during the New Jersey gubernatorial campaign, which was decided by less than 2,000 votes.

"Get me Roger Stone," Baker ordered.

Several thousand pro-Bush protestors gathered in front of the Clark government center where the recount was taking place and insisted that it be stopped. Stone established himself in a Winnebago a block from the Clark Center and was in touch with activists in the building.

On November 22nd, Stone claims he heard that a Gore

supporter was attempting to remove 200–300 ballots from the count room. In reality, a Gore supporter named Joe Geller was carrying a single, unmarked sample ballot.

"I said, 'O.K., follow them," Stone explained. "Half you guys go on the elevator, and half go in the stairs.' Everyone got sucked up in this. They were trying to keep the doors from being closed. Meanwhile, they were trying to take the rest of the ballots into a back room with no windows. I told our guys to stop them — don't let them close the door! They are trying to keep the door from being closed. There was a lot of screaming and yelling."[24]

A rush of protestors flooded the Stephen P. Clark Government Center and stopped the recount, which was never continued after the Supreme Court's Bush v. Gore decision stopped the recount. As with many elements of Stone's biography, his role in the so-called "Brooks Brothers Riot" has been contested. Many allege that Stone has written himself into history as the villain to exaggerate his infamy and role in political history.

Roger Stone was out for revenge after his successful hijinks during the 2000 election. He hadn't forgotten the fines he and Trump suffered at the hands of New York's Commission on Lobbying. They blamed New York's Republican Governor George Pataki. Trump and Stone responded by running ads before the 2000 election, discouraging Bush from selecting Pataki as his running mate, but they were far from finished.

In the lead-up to the 2002 New York gubernatorial race, Stone challenged Pataki's bid to receive the New York's Conservative Party nomination. Despite its small size, no Republican candidate had won a statewide election in 25 years without its nomination. Stone managed the campaign of a former New York Giants receiver in a Conservative Party primary challenge. Pataki's advisors believed that Stone was acting at Trump's behest.[25]

Pataki was also attempting to gain the nomination of the New York Independence Party. Stone managed the Independence Party primary campaign of Tom Golisano, the billionaire founder of the party challenging Pataki for its nomination. Stone was introduced to Golisano by Trump, who was also intent on harming Pataki's electoral prospects. Golisano pledged to spend $75 million in his challenge to Pataki. Using Golisano's war chest, Stone ran a brutal slate of attack ads.

Though Pataki won re-election, he won with less than 50% of the vote.

Stone's activities during these revenge campaigns placed him in contact with people later involved in the 2016 election cycle. While working for Golisano, Stone befriended a left-wing comedian, radio host, and voice impressionist named Randy Credico. They bonded over their distaste for New York's drug sentencing laws. As we shall see, Stone and Credico would be in communication during the 2016 election regarding Julian Assange and WikiLeaks.

Pataki's advisors believed that Stone had played Golisano for a fool, convincing the billionaire to spend a fortune on a hopeless campaign that was, in reality, a revenge stunt. The claim that Stone took advantage of the candidates he worked with was echoed by Larry Klayman, founder of the vehemently anti-Clinton advocacy group Judicial Watch. Stone ran Klayman's 2004 Senate campaign for the state of Florida.

In his memoir, *Whores: How and Why I Came to Fight the Establishment*, Klayman alleges that Stone and a group of operatives he brought with him bilked his campaign of funds for their own personal enrichment. Many of the individuals Stone brought with him, whom Klayman calls the "Dirty Dozen," show up repeatedly in later campaigns managed by Stone and in Trump's 2016 presidential campaign.

The pollster Tony Fabrizio joined the Klayman campaign at Stone's behest. Fabrizio, who had cut his teeth working with Arthur Finkelstein, had conducted polls testing the waters for a Trump presidential run as far back as 1998 and later managed his 2016 polling operations. In 2004, Klayman met with Stone and Fabrizio in Miami to discuss the campaign.

"Isn't this great," Klayman recalled Stone saying as they looked over Biscayne Bay. "I feel like Hyman Roth." Stone referred to a character in The Godfather Part II, based on Meyer Lansky. According to Klayman, Lansky was one of Stone's heroes.[26]

Yet another Stone acolyte brought onto the Klayman campaign was Michael Caputo, who Klayman described as "a frequently well-lubricated press secretary who had once worked for Boris Yeltsin."[27] Caputo's past and experiences in Russia will be expanded upon in a later chapter. Like Fabrizio, Caputo was hired by Paul Manafort to manage the New York Primary for the

2016 Trump campaign.

Among Klayman's many complaints, Stone broke his promise not to work on any other campaigns. While Stone was working for Klayman, a hard right candidate, he was also quietly consulting the Reverend Al Sharpton, a progressive, African American firebrand considering running for President in the 2004 election.[28] Stone and Sharpton made for strange bedfellows. Sharpton was a civil rights activist and founded the National Action Network.

Stone's initial meeting with Sharpton to discuss his presidential campaign occurred in March 2004. Democratic consultant Hank Sheinkopf and the comedian/impressionist activist Randy Credico arranged it. According to Credico, Stone told him that he and Sharpton shared "a mutual obsession: We both hate the Democratic Party."[29]

Stone arranged for his friends, family members, and business associates to donate to the Sharpton campaign to ensure that Sharpton received Federal funding for his campaign. Among the donors was Michael Caputo, hitherto and afterward a lifelong Republican. Another Stone associate who donated to Sharpton was a lawyer named Paul Rolf Jensen, who was also serving as treasurer of the Larry Klayman campaign. Jensen later represented Stone and his infamous "Stop the Steal" group in 2016.

In the next sordid chapter of Roger Stone's political career, he waged war against George Pataki's successor as the Governor of New York, Democrat Eliot Spitzer. Stone began his assault against Spitzer by dredging up a dated story regarding a loan Spitzer's father had provided his campaign in 2008 while running for Attorney General. On August 6th, 2007, Bernard Spitzer, the Governor's 83-year-old father, who was suffering from Parkinson's disease, received a phone message from Stone.

"This is a message for Bernard Spitzer," Stone said. "You will be subpoenaed to testify before the senate committee on investigations on your shady campaign loans. You will be compelled by the senate sergeant at arms. If you resist this subpoena, you will be arrested and brought to Albany — and there's not a goddamn thing your phony, psycho, piece of shit son can do about it. Bernie, your phony loans are about to catch up with you. You will be forced to tell the truth. The fact that your son is a pathological liar will be known to all."

Bernard Spitzer responded by hiring private detectives, who traced the call to a telephone owned by Stone's wife. Stone denied having left the message, even floating the idea that Randy Credico, a known impressionist, may have impersonated him. The episode was mirrored years later, on a much grander scale, when Stone falsely claimed that Credico was his connection to Julian Assange and WikiLeaks.

On March 10th, 2008, *The New York Times* reported that Spitzer had been caught using a high-priced prostitution ring. Stone wrote himself into history as a critical player in the scandal and added a false detail to the story that became one of its more recognizable tidbits. *The Miami Herald* and *New York Post* published articles claiming that Stone had tipped off the FBI about Spitzer through a letter written by his lawyer, Paul Rolf Jensen. Jensen's letter claimed that Stone had learned of Spitzer's dalliances with prostitutes from "a social contact in an adult-themed club." The letter further alleged that "Governor Spitzer did not remove his mid-calf-length black socks during the sex act."[30]

The ridiculous sock allegation, for which there was no evidence other than Jensen's assertion, proved irresistible to the press and became part of the lore relating to Spitzer's spectacular fall. As it turned out, Jensen's letter had never been sent to the FBI. Instead, Stone disseminated it throughout the media in a successful effort to insert himself into the story.

During the 2010 New York governor's race, Stone had his hand in not one but two different campaigns simultaneously. Many of the same people Stone had placed on Larry Klayman's Senate campaign, whom Michael Caputo described as Stone's "traveling troupe of 'misfits,'" were involved, including Caputo himself.[31] One of the candidates Stone supported was a foul-mouthed Buffalo businessman and conservative activist named Carl Paladino, whose breaking of norms and racist antics in many ways foreshadowed the Trump campaign.

Stone was central in getting Paladino to run and staffing his campaign. While Stone claimed he was working *pro bono*, the associates he placed on Paladino's campaign were well-compensated. Paladino's pollster was Scott Fabrizio.[32] Michael Caputo was installed as Paladino's campaign manager. Over the campaign, Caputo was paid a staggering $407,190. Such generous compensation came just in the nick of time for Caputo. During the campaign, it was reported that he had failed to pay $53,000 in Federal taxes during the previous few years.[33]

Another of Stone's personal friends who was hired by the Paladino campaign was a woman named Dianne Thorne. Stone had also secured Thorne a paid position on his "Committee to Take Back the Judiciary" during the 2000 Florida recount and on the Larry Klayman campaign. The Paladino campaign paid two companies registered to Thorne $84,320. A remarkable sum, considering Thorne was described as Paladino's "scheduler."

Andrew Miller, Dianne Thorne's stepson and another Stone associate, was also involved in the 2010 New York gubernatorial election. Not for Paladino, however, but for his opponent. Miller served as the campaign manager for "Manhattan Madam" Kristin Davis, whose stunt gubernatorial campaign was another pet project of Stone's. After leaving a job at a hedge fund, Kristin Davis operated a high-priced prostitution ring. In March 2008, she was arrested for money laundering and promoting prostitution. Following her release after a four-month stint from Rikers Island, Davis appeared on a radio show with Stone, and the two became friends.[34]

The Davis candidacy was an extension of Stone's crusade to humiliate Eliot Spitzer. Without providing any evidence, she claimed that Spitzer had used her prostitution ring "dozens, maybe hundreds of times" and had been abusive to her workers. Stone further used her to "confirm" his made-up story that Spitzer wore thigh-high black socks during the act.

At the same time he was engaging in political shenanigans in New York, Roger Stone was also active in Florida. Stone and his wife live in Fort Lauderdale, located in the traditional Democratic stronghold Broward County. Sometime in the early-to-mid aughts, Stone came into contact with a local attorney named Scott Rothstein. Rothstein was the Bronx-born managing shareholder, chairman, and CEO of the law firm Rothstein Rosenfeldt Adler (RRA). During the early 2000s, the firm became one of the most prominent in South Florida.

Stone claims that he met Rothstein and then-Florida Republican Governor Charlie Crist at a dinner in 2006, during which Crist told Stone that he wanted to arrange a fundraiser with Donald Trump. Rothstein and Stone subsequently became partners, providing Stone with an office at RRA.[35] Rothstein paid Stone $400,000 to serve as his political director. RRA's server hosted Stone's now-defunct website, *The Stone Zone*.

Rothstein enjoyed close relations with the Broward County Sheriff's Office and the local police department. Twenty-eight police officials, including captains, majors, and undercover officers, guarded Rothstein's family, home, and office.[36] The Broward County Sheriff's Office has a tradition of corruption and ties to organized crime. From 1931 to 1950, the corrupt Sheriff Walter Clark held the office. In addition to being a racist, Clark turned a blind eye to illegal Syndicate casinos operated by Meyer Lansky.

In 2008, Stone became involved in the Broward County Sheriff's election. Rothstein supported the Republican incumbent Sheriff Al Lamberti. Governor Crist had appointed Lamberti after the previous sheriff, Ken Jenne, was indicted on Federal corruption charges.[37] Jenne, who had never served in law enforcement before being elected but rather was a politically connected lawyer, was known to have associations with several convicted felons with links to mobsters and drug smugglers.[38] Upon his release from prison, Jenne was hired by Rothstein to work at RRA, where Roger Stone kept an office.[39]

Lamberti's challenger was the Democrat Scott Israel. Stone agreed to help Lamberti at a private meeting at Rothstein's home. Before the election, a series of dirty tricks reeked of the Stone modus operandi. Purged court records surfaced revealing that Israel had fathered an out-of-wedlock child in the 1980s. Robocalls targeting Democrats featured impressions of Richard Nixon, George W. Bush, and other Republicans endorsing Israel. It was a classic Stone voter suppression technique. The impressionist turned out to be Stone's friend Randy Credico. Lamberti defeated Israel.

"I can tell you without a doubt that Roger Stone was involved in that campaign," Rothstein told Florida-based investigative reporter Bob Norman.[40]

Shortly after that, Rothstein's world collapsed around him when it was revealed that he was operating a $1.2 billion Ponzi scheme involving fabricated "structured settlements," the largest in the history of the State of Florida. Before being arrested, Rothstein fled to Morocco as it didn't have an extradition treaty with the United States or Israel. Remarkably, a Broward County Sheriff's Office lieutenant drove Rothstein to the airport.

Rothstein returned after his partner Stuart Rosenfeldt

talked him out of committing suicide. In his book, *The Ultimate Ponzi: The Scott Rothstein Story*, author Chuck Malkus ventures that Rothstein returned because of organized crime threats to his family. It was widely believed that elements of organized crime, who may have been laundering money through RRA, lost money after Rothstein's Ponzi scheme fell apart.

Rothstein was close to individuals with ties to Israeli organized crime. His friend and business partner, Ovadia "Ovi" Levy, was the son of multi-millionaire Israeli-American hotelier Shimon Levy.[41] Upon being released from prison in Israel for his associations with organized criminals accused of murder, Shimon Levy immigrated to Florida and set up the Sea Club Resort in Miami Beach. Levy's partner at the Sea Club Resort, Zvika Yuz, operated a Ponzi scheme of his own and was later murdered.[42] After turning himself in, Rothstein became an informant in a case involving the Italian Mafia and the Italian-American Gambino Crime Family.[43]

American Disinformation: Roger Stone, InfoWars, and Jerome Corsi

Stone, along with Michael Cohen and Sam Nunberg, formed core advisors around Trump during the earliest days of his presidential bid. Stone and Cohen reportedly did not get along in a campaign composed of warring personalities consumed by political infighting.[44] Nunberg, on the other hand, thought of Stone as a "mentor" and "like a surrogate father to him."[45] In an early contribution to Trump's messaging, Stone and Nunberg came up with the idea of "The Wall" as a way to keep Trump focused on issues related to the border.[46] Nunberg was later fired from the campaign in July when racist Facebook posts he had published surfaced.[47]

The following month, August 2015, Stone left his paid position on the campaign in disputed circumstances. During the first Republican Primary Debate, Trump had an intense exchange with *Fox News* moderator Megyn Kelly regarding his treatment of women. After the onstage blow-up, Trump proceeded to lay into the popular female reporter in public statements and on social media. Stone viewed the incident as an unnecessary self-sustained political wound and told Trump as much. Trump later claimed that he fired Stone over the incident.[48] Stone claimed he quit because of clashes with Trump campaign manager Corey

Lewandowski.

Despite this brief falling out, Stone remained involved as a shadow advisor to Trump, with whom he was in regular contact. He promoted Trump on alternative media sources such as *InfoWars*, a website and broadcast hosted by Alex Jones. Jones, who has been diagnosed with narcissistic personality disorder, was America's leading proponent of the New World Order conspiracy theory, which maintains that globalists are conspiring to rule under a totalitarian world government.[49] He has also claimed that the US Government was behind the 1995 Oklahoma City bombing, 9/11, and the Sandy Hook school shooting. Some portion of the content put out by *InfoWars* came from *RT*. Between May 2014 and 2017, over 1000 *RT* articles were republished on *InfoWars* without permission from the Russian broadcaster. *RT* does not appear to have acted to stop *InfoWars* from stealing their content.[50]

Jones' conspiracy-mongering has overlapped with Russian disinformation campaigns. Between July 15th and September 15th, 2015, the US Military held a training exercise in Texas called Jade Helm 15. Right-wing conspiracy theorists began making wild, unfounded claims online suggesting that the exercise was an Obama administration pretext to impose martial law, and Jones on InfoWars claimed that "Helm" was, in fact, an acronym for "Homeland Eradication of Local Militants."[51] Russian bots promoted the alt-right conspiracy theories, which gained so much traction that Texas Governor Gregg Abbot called out the state guard to observe the exercise. According to former CIA director Michael Hayden, the Russians saw the operation as such a success that it influenced their decision to direct a disinformation campaign toward the 2016 US election.[52] *McClatchy* later reported that the FBI investigated both *InfoWars* and *Breitbart News* (in addition to the Russian state-sponsored networks *RT* and *Sputnik*) for the roles they played in these disinformation campaigns.[53]

Stone understood that *InfoWars* received ratings comparable to the major networks and offered access to an untapped population that would find a political outsider like Trump appealing. On November 9th, 2015, Stone appeared on Jones's show and informed his viewers that "Trump is for real." Less than a month later, on December 2nd, Stone arranged for Trump himself to appear on the show.

"I know now, from top people, that you are for real," Jones said to Trump on the broadcast, parroting what he had heard from Stone, "and you understand you're in danger, and you understand what you're doing, is epic - it's George Washington level."

"Your reputation is amazing," Trump replied to Jones, "I will not let you down." From then on, Alex Jones enthusiastically supported Trump on *InfoWars* and helped shape his messaging. Jones was one of the first and loudest voices to claim that Hillary was going to steal the election and called on Trump to make it an election issue. Two days after he did so, Trump claimed that the election was going to be "rigged" at a rally in Columbus, Ohio.[54]

Stone's penchant for conspiracy theories brought him into contact with the infamous right-wing journalist and author Dr. Jerome Corsi, who would become a central figure in the mystery surrounding Stone's relationship with WikiLeaks. In February of 2016, Stone and Corsi dined together at the Harvard Club. While this was their first face-to-face meeting, the two had connected three years earlier while both were working on books about the JFK assassination to be released upon its fiftieth anniversary in 2013.

While often described in the media as a right-wing conspiracy theorist, a better description for Jerome Corsi would be a black propagandist and inveterate liar who uses weaponized half-truths and outright falsehoods to impact political outcomes. In 2004, he co-authored *Unfit for Command: Swift Boat Veterans Speak Out Against John Kerry*, a *New York Times* bestseller released during the 2004 presidential election that attacked Senator John Kerry's character and Vietnam War record. Corsi never served in Vietnam, and the book was denounced by those who served with Kerry as being simply "wrong."[55] Thereafter, "swift-boating" entered into the American political lexicon, referring to the targeting of a politician with untrue or unfair political attacks. Kerry narrowly lost the race to George W. Bush.

In the next election, Corsi targeted Barack Obama with yet another *New York Times* bestseller, *The Obama Nation*, which explored Obama's supposed ties to Islam and radical politics. The book opens with a quote from Andy Martin, the progenitor of the falsehood that Obama is secretly a Muslim.[56] Corsi appeared on Alex Jones' radio show to promote the book. While Obama cruised comfortably to victory, it was only the beginning of

Corsi's attacks against him. Corsi became a chief proponent of the false birther conspiracy theory, claiming that Obama had been born in Kenya and was, therefore, ineligible to be president. In May of 2011, Corsi released *Where's The Birth Certificate?: The Case That Barack Obama Is Not Eligible To Be President*. Corsi's birther crusade brought him into contact with Trump.

"Trump asked me what I thought of the controversy regarding Obama's birth certificate—not because he really wanted to know my opinion, because I think his opinion was already formed," Roger Stone explained to *The New Yorker*. "And Trump said, 'Do you know this guy Jerry Corsi?' I said, 'I only know of him. Why?' He said, 'Well, because I've been looking at his book'—he doesn't read books—but he said, 'I've been talking to him.'"[57]

Corsi first met Trump decades earlier as a guest at the Plaza Hotel, which Trump owned at the time.[58] Trump, who had been using the birther conspiracy to establish connections and burnish his reputation with the American right, received an advance copy of Corsi's book in April of 2011. Michael Cohen signed a non-disclosure agreement to acquire the book and described how Corsi and Trump had spoken on several occasions, explaining that "Jerome Corsi had reached out to Mr. Trump to explain certain facts that are in his book."[59]

Corsi described his interactions with Trump during an interview with Alex Jones, explaining how he pressed Trump to question the long-form birth certificate that Obama ultimately released to quell the controversy and to demand a forensic examination of the original document. At the time, not even Trump's efforts to promote birtherism were enough for Corsi and Jones, and they openly speculated whether he had dropped the issue because of a payout from NBC or perhaps was even working with the Obama White House.

Despite Trump not pursuing birtherism as vigorously as Corsi would have liked, Corsi later became an avid supporter of his candidacy. In September of 2015, he visited Trump Tower, where he met with Michael Cohen, who introduced him to Corey Lewandowski and Hope Hicks. Corsi was surprised that Lewandowski and Hicks were, at that time, the only occupants of the floor of Trump Tower that served as the campaign's headquarters.[60]

Beginning on February 22nd, 2016, Corsi started to have

recorded conversations with Roger Stone in his capacity as a reporter for WorldNetDaily (WND),[61] a right-wing news outlet notable for trafficking conspiracy theories.[62] During their discussions, Stone told Corsi that he was speaking with Trump every day and that while Trump didn't listen to everything he said, he described his hit rate as seven out of ten. "I'm really careful to pick my shots," Stone told Corsi. "I try to keep it to structural issues and important stuff, not trying him [sic] to get his picture taken with somebody's mother-in-law." There is evidence that Stone was telling Corsi the truth. The FBI later heard testimony that Stone was in daily contact with Trump over January and February of 2016 and kept contemporaneous notes of these conversations, the purpose of which was to provide later a "post mortem of what went wrong."[63] The location of these notes, doubtless of incalculable value, is unknown.

Throughout their conversations, Stone explained to Corsi his plans to damage Hillary Clinton's standing with women and African American voters by pushing stories related to Bill Clinton's alleged sexual assault victims and the unsubstantiated claim that he had a black child out of wedlock who he refused to recognize. As Corsi well understood and later wrote about: "A fundamental principle of the modern political campaign is that successful candidates must cut into the percentages their opponents expect to get from key voting blocs loyal to the opponents political party."

Stone and Corsi met for the first time in late February at the Harvard Club in New York City. It is important to note that Stone and Corsi provided the only accounts we have of this meeting. Over dinner, which included martinis, a bottle of French Bordeaux and London-style roast beef, Corsi agreed with Stone's strategy of targeting African Americans and female voters with anti-Clinton messaging. Corsi later introduced Stone to Candice Jackson, a Vancouver, WA-based attorney and author of the 2005 book *Their Lives: The Women Targeted By The Clinton Machine*. Jackson introduced Stone to several of Bill Clinton's accusers, including Juanita Broaddrick, Paula Jones, and Gennifer Flowers.[64] Stone used these contacts to write his book, *The Clinton's War On Women*, published on the eve of the presidential election in September of 2016.

Whether Stone or Corsi discussed WikiLeaks during this first meeting in late February is unknown. However, on March

10th, 2016, GRU Unit 26165 began targeting the Clinton campaign's Brooklyn headquarters.[65] Six days later, on March 16th, WikiLeaks released its first set of Clinton emails. This first release consisted not of stolen or hacked emails but emails from Clinton's time as Secretary of State that the State Department had released following a Freedom of Information Act request. WikiLeaks arranged the emails in a more searchable format, labeled the "Hillary Clinton Email Archive."[66]

Roger Stone, the "Stop the Steal" Scam, and Corruption in Broward County

In April of 2016, as Trump overtook Ted Cruz to become the Republican nominee, Stone established a (supposedly) independent non-profit called "Stop The Steal," the full importance of which wouldn't be appreciated until after the 2020 election when the phrase was trotted out again to spread the lie that the election had been stolen from Trump. In the lead-up to the 2016 convention, Stone used Stop The Steal to intimidate Republican delegates thinking of voting against Trump, threatening on its website "four days of non-violent demonstrations, protests, and lobbying delegates face to face... We must own the streets. In numbers there is strength."[67]

Stop The Steal was registered by Paul Rolf Jensen, the attorney involved in Stone's hijinks against Eliot Spitzer.[68] Stone wanted to use Stop The Steal to recruit volunteers to conduct exit polls at over 7,000 polling places to determine if there was a discrepancy between the exit polls and the official results. This "solid evidence" could then be used to show the election had been "rigged" if Trump lost.[69] Stop The Steal's efforts became the subject of litigation when Democrats sued, claiming Stone was engaging in voter intimidation.

Stop The Steal was closely affiliated with a Stone-founded Super PAC called the Committee to Restore American Greatness (CRAG), launched in December 2015. Upon first hearing of CRAG, Trump campaign head and bitter Stone rival Corey Lewandowski described the Super PAC as a "Big League Scam." While CRAG reported raising $587,000 during the 2016 election cycle, only $16,000 went towards two pro-Trump billboards. In April of 2016, CRAG donated $50,000 to Stop The Steal.[70]

Despite this initial infusion, IRS records show that Stop The Steal only raised $40,000. Perhaps this is because on July

12th, 2016, without explanation, Stop The Steal donated $63,000 back to CRAG. Other Stop The Steal expenditures included $4,000 to Steven Gray, the best friend of Danney Williams, the African American man who claimed to be Bill Clinton's out-of-wedlock child. $5000 went to Alejandro Vidal, a Florida-based rapper whose oeuvre includes "Clinton Crime Cartel" and a music video for the song "Justice for Danney Williams." $3,500 went to a PR firm Christian Josi, who operated the Clinton Rape T-shirt campaign for Stone which was promoted on *InfoWars*.[71]

CRAG paid $100,000 to Jensen Associates, Paul Rolf Jensen's law firm, for "legal and accounting" and "consulting" services. $130,000 went to Citroen Associates, operated by Stone's former driver and social media aide John Kakanis, supposedly for "voter fraud research and documentation." $12,000 went to Drake Ventures, a PR firm operated by Stone and his wife that shares an address with Citroen Associates. In July 2016, CRAG paid $5,000 to Cheryl Smith of Oroville, California, the "Manhattan Madam" Kristin Davis.[72] Upon being released from a halfway house in May 2016, Stone put Davis up in his Manhattan apartment on 71st Street.[73] In 2017, Stop The Steal, which IRS records show stopped raising money after the 2016 election, paid Davis two installments of $3,500.

Another Stone associate, Andrew Miller, was paid $9,000 by CRAG and another $5,000 from Stop The Steal. Miller, who worked for Stone for over a decade managing his schedule and travel, is the stepson of Stone's longtime assistant, Dianne Thorne.[74] Miller's father, Timothy Suereth, is a convicted felon immigrant smuggler who was caught by police transporting 19 illegal immigrants on a boat in Florida.[75]

Stone was behind a similar arrangement involving Thorne, Suereth, and Miller on Scott Israel's 2013 Broward County Sheriff campaign and later during his controversial tenure as Sheriff. Israel's campaign strategist, Ron Gunzberger, was a close friend and associate of Stone's and was subsequently hired by the Broward County Sheriff's Office (BSO) as its general counsel for $205,000 a year after Israel won. Israel then hired Dianne Thorne as his personal assistant. She later resigned after local press investigated allegations that she had falsified her college degree. Andrew Miller was later hired to operate Sheriff Israel's campaign website. Jenn Hobbs, Miller's fiancé, was hired by Israel and paid $60,000 to be a "community liaison." Mike

Colapietro, the co-author of Stone's book on the JFK assassination, also received a job at the BSO as a "community liaison."

Interestingly, in 2016, the Internet Research Agency targeted Broward County and interacted with real, unwitting Trump supporters who managed the Facebook page *Team Trump Broward Country.*[76] Stone's use of Stop The Steal to imply that the election would be stolen, as well as Alex Jones and later Donald Trump's suggestion that the election could be "rigged," overlapped with Russian efforts to cast doubt on the validity of the election. In 2016, the State Department became aware of Russian efforts to send election observers to polling sites in the United States, which included going outside traditional channels and directly approaching state and local officials with the request. These requests were denied.[77] Furthermore, GRU hackers could alter Florida's voter rolls.[78] As the full scope of the Russian election interference became apparent, the Obama White House worried that the Russians might make the election appear rigged by tampering with voter rolls in key precincts, which would lead to a kind of chaos that would seem to validate claims of a "rigged election."[79]

Stone's politics of deception and division achieved full-bloom during Trump's 2016 run for president. While he only officially worked on the Trump campaign for a short period, he exerted his influence in many subtle ways. In particular, he played a pivotal role in getting the campaign to hire his old friend and lobbying partner, Paul Manafort, as its chairman. It was a selection of historic significance and a dark omen of things to come.

---

[1] Barrett, Wayne. *Trump: The Deals and the Downfall.* New York, NY: HarperCollins, 1992

[2] Shearn, Ian T. "Voter suppression in New Jersey: a pivotal episode that still reverberates," *NJ Spotlight News.* November 3rd, 2020

[3] Roig-Franzia, Manuel. "The Swamp Builders: How Stone and Manafort Helped Create the Mess that Trump Promised to Clean Up," *The Washington Post.* November 29th, 2018

[4] Baram, Marcus. "Eavesdropping on Roy Cohn and Donald Trump," *The New Yorker.* April 14th, 2017

[5] Kruse, Michael. "The True Story of Donald Trump's First Campaign Speech – in 1987," *Politico Magazine.* February 5th, 2016

[6] Shearn, Ian T. "Roger Stone: The Ultimate Dirty Trickster, Formed by Watergate and Tempered in New Jersey," *NJ Spotlight News.* July 13th, 2020

[7] Longman, Martin. "Inside the Dirty Tricks of Roger Stone," *Washington Monthly.* April 19th, 2018

[8] Chasmar, Jessica. "Donald Trump changed political parties at least five times, report,"

The Washington Times. June 16th, 2016

[9] Harding, Luke. "The Hidden History of Trump's First Trip to Moscow," *Politico Magazine*. November 19th, 2017

[10] Shilpa, Jindia. "Here's an Insane Story About Roger Stone, Lyndon LaRouche, Vladimir Putin, and the Queen of England," *Mother Jones*. December 21st, 2018

[11] Samuels, Robert; Boburg, Shawn. "The man he's been waiting for," *The Washington Post*. July 13th, 2016

[12] Tanfani, Joseph. "Trump was once so involved in trying to block an Indian casino that he secretly approved attack ads," *The Los Angeles Times*. June 30th, 2016

[13] King, Wayne. "Trump, in a Federal Lawsuit, Seeks to Block Indian Casino," The New York Times. May 4th, 1993

[14] "Indian Gaming Issues Becoming More Work For Lobbyists," *The Hartford Courant*. October 10th, 1993

[15] Conason, Joe. "Pataki Camp Gets Stoned," Observer. October 28th, 2002

[16] Barrett, Wayne; Singer, Jessie. "The Sex Scandal That Put Bush In The White House," *The Village Voice*. May 11th, 2004

[17] Cheney, Kyle. "The Hill finds John Solomon 'failed' to identify key details of sources," *Politico*. February 19th, 2020

[18] Mattie Lolavar, T/a Triumph Communications International Group, Incorporated; Triumph Communications International Group, Incorporated, Plaintiffs-appellants, v. Fernando De Santibañes, Defendant-appellee, Andikon Holdings, Incorporated, T/a Ikon Public Affairs, T/a Ikon Public Affairs, Llc, T/a Ikon Public Affairs, Incorporated; Dick Morris; Roger Stone; Eileen Mcgann; John Does, # 1-10, Defendants, 430 F.3d 221 (4th Cir. 2005). US Court of Appeals for the Fourth Circuit - 430 F.3d 221 (4th Cir. 2005)

[19] Paschal, Olivia; Carlisle, Madeleine. "A Brief History of Roger Stone," *The Atlantic*. November 15th, 2019

[20] Orin, Deborah. "Trump Pumped to Hit Stump – Wants to Run with Oprah on Ticket," *New York Post*. October 8th, 1999

[21] Samuels, Robert; Boburg, Shawn. "The man he's been waiting for," *The Washington Post*. July 13th, 2016

[22] "READ: Donald Trump's ADVOCATE Interview Where He Defends Gays, Mexicans," *ADVOCATE*. November 28th, 2015

[23] Christensen, Dan. "Bush v Gore schemers Stone and McCarty together again on White House pardon list," *FloridaBulldog*. December 27th, 2020

[24] Toobin, Jeffrey. "The Dirty Trickster," *The New Yorker*. May 23rd, 2008

[25] Dicker, Frederic. "Golisano a $75M Man – Big$$ Campaign Gives Governor A Run For His Money," *New York Post*. May 20, 2002

[26] Klayman, Larry. "The Real Stone Cold Truth!" *Larry Klayman, Attorny At Law Blog*. February 4th, 2019

[27] Barrett, Wayne. "Carl Paladino: The Dirty Details in His Campaign Filings," *The Village Voice*. September 30th, 2010

[28] Slackman, Michael. "The 2004 Campaign: the Consultant – Sharpton's Bid Aided by an Unlikely Source," *The New York Times*. January 25th, 2004

[29] Barrett, Wayne; Hutton, Adam, LaGorio, Christine. "Sleeping With The GOP," *The Village Voice*. January 27th, 2004

[30] Adams Otis, Ginger. "Spitzer Tipster a GOP Swinger," *New York Post*. March 23rd, 2008

[31] Barrett, Wayne. "Carl Paladino: The Dirty Details in His Campaign Filings," *The Village Voice*. September 30th, 2010

[32] Hakim, Danny. "Opposing Campaigns, With One Unlikely Link," *The New York Times*. August 11th, 2010

[33] Barbaro, Michael. "Paladino Has Aides With Tainted Pasts," *The New York Times*. September 28th, 2010

34 Roig-Franzia, Manuel. "How an ex-madam, a political trickster and a toddler got tangled up in the Russia investigation," The Washinton Post. August 10th, 2018

35 Iannelli, Jerry. "Roger Stone Arrested: A Brief History of his Weirdest South Florida Antics," *Miami New Times*. May 29th, 2017

36 Wallman, Brittany. "High-ranking police officers guarded over Rothstein," *The Palm Beach Post*. March 31st, 2012

37 Aguayo, Terry. "Florida Sheriff Set To Admit Guilt In Corruption Case," *The New York Times*. September 5th, 2007

38 Norman, Bob. "The Sheriff's Criminal Association," *Broward/Palm Beach New Times*. October 15th, 1998

39 Norman, Bob. "Ken Jenne Back At Work At Rothstein's Firm," *Broward/Palm Beach New Times*. October 13th, 2008

40 Barrett, Wayne. "Roger Stone Backs Away From Paladino, But Can't Get Rid of the Stink of Scott Rothstein," *The Village Voice*. October 10th, 2010

41 Norman, Bob. "Attorney Confirms Some Stolen Rothstein Money Went to Business Partner," *Broward/Palm Beach New Times*. November 19th, 2009

42 Kidwell, David. "Who killed Broward hotel owner," The Miami Herald. July 7th, 1997

43 Norman, Bob "Scott Rothstein Was Informant in Mafia Case," *Broward/Palm Beach New Times*. March 15th, 2010

44 Palazzolo, Joe; Rothfeld, Michael. *The Fixers: The Bottom-Feeders, Crooked Lawyers, Gossipmongers, and Porn Stars Who Created the 45th President*. New York, NY: Penguin Random House, 2020. Pg. 132

45 Garcia, Catherine. "Sam Nunberg says he thinks Mueller is really focused on Trump's business," *The Week*. March 5th, 2018

46 Greene, Joshua. *Devil's Bargain: Steve Bannon, Donald Trump, And The Nationalist Uprising*. New York, NY: Penguin Books, 2017. Pg. 111

47 Walker, Hunter. "Sam Nunberg has a history of provocative and racial Facebook posts," Business Insider. July 31st, 2016

48 Toobin, Jeffrey. *True Crimes and Misdemeanors: The Investigation of Donald Trump*. New York, NY: DoubleDay, 2020. Pg. 167-168

49 Hartman, Ben. "Doctor: Alex Jones Diagnosed With Narcissistic Personality Disorder," *The Daily Beast*. May 5th, 2017

50 Lytvynenko, Jane. "InfoWars Has Republished More Than 1,000 Articles From RT Without Permission," *BuzzFeed News*. November 8th, 2017

51 Fernandez, Manny. "As Jade Helm 15 Military Exercise Begins, Texans Keep Watch 'Just in Case'," *The New York Times*. July 15th, 2015

52 Dart, Tom. "Obama martial law scare was stoked by Russian bots, say ex-director of CIA," *The Guardian*. May 3rd, 2018

53 Stone, Peter; Gordon, Greg. "FBI's Russian-influence probe includes a look at Breitbart, InfoWars news sites," McClatchy DC Bureau. March 20th, 2017

54 Neiwert, David. *Alt-America: The Rise Of The Radical Right In The Age Of Trump*. Brooklyn, NY: Verso, 2018. Pg. 282-283

55 Jones, Tim. "Swift boat skipper: Kerry critics wrong," *The Chicago Tribune*. August 22nd, 2004

56 Rutenberg, Jim. "The Man Behind The Whispers About Obama," *The New York Times*. October 12th, 2008

57 Toobin, Jeffrey. "Roger Stone's and Jerome Corsi's Time In The Barrel," *The New Yorker*. February 11th, 2019

58 Corsi, Jerome. *Silent No More*. New York, NY: Post Hill Press, 2019. Pg. 54-55

59 Isikoff, Michael. "Publisher of upcoming 'birther' book makes no apologies," *NBC News*. April 27th, 2011

60 Corsi, Jerome. *Silent No More*. New York, NY: Post Hill Press, 2019. Pg. 55 [Note: in the text of Corsi's e-book there appears to be a typo, Corsi claims Cohen introduced him to Lewandowski and Hicks in september of 2016. However, by that time

Lewandowksi had already left the Trump campaign. Thus, the only plausible alternative date for this meeting would have been September of 2015.]

[61] Corsi, Jerome. *Silent No More*. New York, NY: Post Hill Press, 2019. Pg. 33-38

[62] Foley, Jordan M. "Press Credentials and Hybrid Boundary Zones: The Case of WorldNetDaily and the Standing Committee of Correspondents," *Journalism Practice*. School of Journalism and Mass Communication, University of Wisconsin–Madison, Madison, WI, USA. September 30th, 2019

[63] United States District Court for the Southern District of New York. SEARCH AND SEIZURE WARRANT. January 24th, 2019. Agent Affidavit In Support of Application for Search and Seizure Warrant. Pg. 31

[64] Sherman, Gabriel. "How Donald Trump Decided to Make Bill Clinton's Accusers a Campaign Issue," *New York Magazine*. October 12th, 2016

[65] Rid, Thomas. *Active Measures: The Secret History of Disinformation and Political Warfare*. New York, NY: Farrar, Straus and Giroux, 2020. Pg. 379

[66] "Hillary Clinton Email Archive," *Wikileaks*. March 16th, 2016

[67] Rucker, Philip; Costa, Robert. "While the GOP worries about convention chaos, Trump pushes for 'showbiz' feel," *The Washington Post*. April 17th, 2016

[68] Bastone, William. "Roger Stone's Russian Hacking 'Hero,'" *The Smoking Gun*. March 8th, 2017

[69] Stone, Roger. *The Making of the President 2016: How Donald Trump Orchestrated A Revolution*. New York, NY: Skyhorse Publishing, 2017. Pg. 286

[70] Friedman, Dan. "Roger Stone's Super-PAC Paid the Manhattan Madam's Mom During the 2016 Campaign," Mother Jones. August 17th, 2018

[71] Bastone, William. "Roger Stone's Russian Hacking 'Hero,'" *The Smoking Gun*. March 8th, 2017

[72] Friedman, Dan. "Roger Stone's Super-PAC Paid the Manhattan Madam's Mom During the 2016 Campaign," Mother Jones. August 17th, 2018

[73] Roig-Franzia, Manuel. "How an ex-madam, a political trickster and a toddler got tangled up in the Russia investigation," *The Washington Post*. August 10th, 2018

[74] Rashbaum, William K. "Spitzer Antagonist Advises Ex-Madam's Campaign," *The New York Times*. April 16th, 2010

[75] Norman, Bob. "After resignation, BSO political hiring at issue," *Local10.com*. July 10th, 2014

[76] O'Sullivan, Donie; Griffin, Drew; Bronstein, Scott. "The unwitting: The Trump supporters used by Russia," *CNN*. February 20th, 2018

[77] *Report of the Senate Select Committee on Intelligence United States Senate on Russian Active Measures Campaigns and Interference in the 2016 U.S. Election Volume One: Russian Efforts Against Election Infrastructure With Additional Views*. 116th Congress 2nd Session. Pg. 30-31

[78] Robles, Frances. "Russian Hackers Were 'In a Position' to Alter Florida Voter Rolls, Rubio Confirms," *The New York Times*. April 26th, 2019

[79] Shimer, David. *Rigged: America, Russia, and One Hundred Years of Covert Electoral Interference*. New York, NY: Alfred A. Knopf. 2020, Pg. 178

Chapter 14:
Paul Manafort, Oligarchs, and Spies:
Global Corruption and the Politics of Ukraine

Meet Paul Manafort:
Influence Peddler and Future Chairman of the Trump Campaign

Paul Manafort's tenure as Chairman of the 2016 Trump Campaign will surely go down as the most corrupt in the history of American politics. However, before examining his activities during the 2016 campaign, you must understand his prior activities in Ukraine. To understand how he became involved in Ukrainian politics, you must understand his career as a political advisor and lobbyist in Washington. To truly understand Manafort, however, you must begin at the beginning, his upbringing in Connecticut and his introduction to politics and corruption.

Paul John Manafort Jr. was born on April 1st, 1949. Both sets of Manafort's grandparents immigrated from Italy to the United States around the turn of the century. His maternal grandparents arrived from Sicily, while his father's parents were from Naples. They settled in the blue-collar, industrial town of New Britain, Connecticut, which contained a large community of Italian and Polish immigrants. In 1919, Manafort's grandfather founded a demolition and construction company called New Britain House Wrecking. Decades later, when Manafort's uncles and cousins took control of the company, it was renamed Manafort Brothers.

Paul Manafort Sr. served as the mayor of New Britain

from 1965 to 1971. Manafort Sr.'s political career was closely interlinked with several local Republican power brokers. In particular, Manafort Sr. was closely associated with Thomas Meskill, who preceded him as mayor of New Britain and was elected Governor of Connecticut in 1971. Governor Meskill appointed Manafort Sr. as the state Commissioner of Public Works.

The younger Manafort had worked on Meskill campaigns since childhood and participated in Meskill's "Kiddie Corps."[1] Manafort Jr. had also volunteered on Meskill's Congressional campaigns. In the Summer of 1970, Manafort Jr. worked in Meskill's gubernatorial campaign headquarters.[2] Like his father, Manafort Jr. was also a member of the Young Republicans. In the Fall of 1970, Manafort Jr. attended the state convention of the Connecticut Young Republicans. According to *The Washington Post*, it was at this convention that Manafort met a Connecticut native and young high school student by the name of Roger J. Stone, Jr.[3]

"Hey, kid, how ya' doin'?" Manafort reportedly said to Stone upon meeting him at the 1970 Connecticut Young Republicans convention. "Why are you supporting Weicker?"

Manafort was referring to Lowell Weicker, a local Republican politician at that time who was running against Meskill in the primary. While Meskill would later be elected Governor, Weicker ran for the Senate successfully.

"You think I give a [fuck] about Weicker?" Stone replied. "I'm here to elect Meskill." Thus, one of the most infamous political partnerships in modern American history began supporting the candidacy of Thomas J. Meskill for the governorship of Connecticut.

Foreshadowing the later activities of his son, Paul Manafort Sr. was involved in two political scandals involving civic corruption and organized crime. In 1981, Manafort Sr. was charged with perjury, alleged to have lied during a municipal corruption investigation. The police department under his leadership was investigated for tolerating a Mafia-linked gambling racket and tampering with evidence to protect the man behind it, Joseph "Pippi" Guerriero.[4] Known as a "ruthless mob figure," Guerriero ran gambling operations out of New Britain on behalf of the DeCavalcante crime family and pleaded guilty to bribing a local police chief.[5]

Manafort Sr. was denounced as the person "most at fault" by a local attorney investigating New Britain's government. Whistle-blower testimony established that the elder Manafort explicitly hired someone "flexible" to manage his personnel office, which would not operate "100 percent by the rules." Manafort Sr. had received an envelope containing answers to an exam aspiring local police officers had to take. He delivered them to two of his preferred candidates. However, as the statute of limitations had passed, he was never charged with a crime.

The other organized crime-linked scandal that ensnared Paul Manafort's father also included gambling. Two weeks after being elected in 1971, Governor Meskill began to push for legalizing gambling in Connecticut. Among the various forms of gambling that were legalized was betting on a sport known as Jai-Alai, which was popular in Cuba and South Florida. Despite official promises that the mob would be kept out of the newly legitimized gambling establishments, a group of South Florida-based businessmen with links to some of the highest levels of organized crime attempted to cash in on the new gambling opportunity.

One was named David Friend, whose company Connecticut Sports Enterprises (CSE) attempted to open a Jai-Alai fronton (stadium) in Bridgeport, Connecticut.[6] At the time he did so, Paul Manafort Sr. was the Connecticut Commissioner of Public Works. Friend was a regular at Joe Sonken's Gold Coast Restaurant, a legendary South Florida mob hangout. Its proprietor, Joe Sonken, was a Chicago native and personal friend of Meyer Lansky's.

Austin McGuigan, a former lawyer in the Connecticut State Attorney's Office, testified to Congress that Friend was linked to senior members of the Genovese Crime Family, including John "Buster" Ardito and Anthony "Tony Pro" Provenzano, a member of the Teamsters Union suspected in the murder of Jimmy Hoffa. McGuigan testified that he saw Friend dining with Anthony Accardo, the head of the Chicago Outfit, and Johnny Roselli, a senior Chicago mobster who had assisted the CIA in its attempts to kill Fidel Castro.[7]

In February of 1974, a 24-year-old Paul Manafort Jr. accompanied his father to a meeting with Friend to discuss building a Jai Alai fronton in Bridgeport. Also present was Manafort's cousin, Frank Manafort. Frank represented Manafort

Brothers wrecking, which had been contracted to knock down the building where the new Jai Alai fronton was to be built. The meeting had been arranged by a member of the Operating Engineers Union, which had long been infiltrated by organized crime.[8]

In addition to Friend, another organized crime-linked participant in the meeting was named Lidzidio A. Renzulli, who was also a shareholder in CSE whom Connecticut investigators witnessed meeting with senior figures in the Genovese Crime Family, including John "Buster" Ardito.[9] According to court documents, Ardito was a leader in the Connecticut branch of the Genovese Crime Family.[10] It is not clear why Paul Manafort Jr. attended the meeting with his father, but a Grand Jury Report establishes that he was there.[11]

David Friend also communicated with the mob-linked Nixon political advisor Murray Chotiner. Chotiner had deep links to the Teamsters Union and assisted Friend in getting an $11 million loan from the Teamsters for the fronton. Frank Manafort Jr. and Manafort Brothers wrecking were critical in illicitly facilitating the Teamsters loan. Frank Manafort submitted false contracts and bills at Friend's request, which inflated the amount of the money Connecticut Sports Enterprises allegedly put into the project. Frank Manafort also handled over $200,000 in cash for alleged payoffs. He was later forced to testify about his activities.

The Fronton deal unraveled, derailed by investigators in the Connecticut State Attorney's office concerned about the infiltration of organized crime into legal gambling. Within a year of the February 1974 meeting between the Manaforts, Friend, and Renzulli, a bribery and public corruption scandal erupted, ensnaring the highest-ranking officials in Connecticut, including Manafort's father. However, the scandal that ensnared the father was hardly a speed bump for the son. He was well on his way to establishing himself in Washington, DC.

Manafort received his undergraduate degree from Georgetown University in 1971 and later graduated from its law school. His first foray into national politics occurred in Kansas City during the Republican National Convention in 1976, where he worked under Republican heavyweight James A. Baker III supporting Gerald Ford, unlike his friend Roger Stone, who supported Ronald Reagan. During the convention, Manafort huddled with Baker and learned how to whip delegates, a skill he would exercise for the Trump campaign.[12]

Both Manafort and Roger Stone were involved in establishing the National Conservative Political Action Committee (NCPAC), one of the first PACs ever to engage in hardcore, negative political campaigning. One of NCPAC's board members was the legendary Republican strategist Arthur Finkelstein.[13] Finkelstein was a key figure behind the conceptualization of negative campaigning and later managed the campaigns of Israeli Prime Minister Benjamin Netanyahu and the pro-Putin Hungarian populist Viktor Orbán.[14] NCPAC focused its fire on traditional liberal Senators like Frank Church of Iowa, whose Church Committee took on CIA abuses.

After Ford was defeated, Manafort joined the Reagan faction of the party. In 1977, Manafort managed Roger Stone's campaign to become the president of the Young Republicans. After Stone became Reagan's 1980 campaign director for the North East, Manafort was hired as Reagan's campaign director for the South. In this capacity, he supervised the "Southern Strategy," a Republican campaigning strategy that sought to exploit racial and cultural grievances to get white, conservative but traditionally Democratic voters across the South to switch their votes to the Republican Party. The Trump Campaign later used the tactic.

After the campaign, Manafort, Charles Black, and Roger Stone founded the political consulting and lobbying firm Black, Manafort, and Stone. All three occupied influential positions in the transition. Manafort was hired as the personnel director, Stone acted as deputy political director of the personnel office, and Black acted as a political advisor during the administration's staffing.[15] Black, Manafort, and Stone offered a one-stop-shop for campaign consulting, public relations, and political lobbying. In addition to his anti-regulation mantra, Reagan came into office determined to prosecute the Cold War with ferocity. Throughout the 1980s, the US increased its support for anti-communist "Freedom Fighters," often consisting of dictators and right-wing paramilitary groups. These interests desired representation in Washington, and Black, Manafort, and Stone were only too happy to fill the role.

With the 1984 hire of the DNC's finance chair, Peter G. Kelly, Black, Manafort, Stone, and Kelly (BMSK) was poised to become a foreign lobbying powerhouse, or what the Center for Public Integrity labeled "The Torturer's Lobby." Manafort aggressively expanded his foreign contacts and used his connection to Reagan to do so. He used his position as the political director of the 1984 Republican National Convention to provide Prince Bandar bin Sultan Al Saud with royal treatment, seeing to it that the Saudi Ambassador entered through the Presidential entrance and was seated in the Vice Presidential box.[16]

In 1985, BMSK took on Jonas Savimbi, leader of the Angolan guerilla rebel group UNITA, as a client and was paid $600,000.[17] Savimbi was a key player in the Angolan Civil War, a conflict that lasted for over 27 years and led to 500,000 deaths and one million internally displaced. Paul Manafort oversaw foreign accounts at BMSK and exhibited few scruples when it came to vetting the human rights records of new clients.[18] In 1988, it was revealed that BMSK represented the Bahamas, a well-known center for international money laundering, under Lynden Pindling, who has been accused of personal ties with drug traffickers.[19]

One of the more lucrative and mysterious relationships Manafort developed was with Ferdinand Marcos, the dictator of the Philippines. In 1985, the story broke that a $950,000 a year BMSK client, the Chamber of Philippines Manufacturers, Exporters and Tourist Associations, served as a front for Marcos. Marcos, at the time, stood accused of corruption, looting public resources, and human rights violations. After receiving approval from the Reagan White House to lobby for Marcos, Manafort spent weeks preparing for the upcoming elections in Manila. When they took place, the elections were marred by violence and intimidation at the polls, which observers largely blamed on Marcos supporters. Despite BMSK's effort to get the White House to issue a statement decrying election fraud on both sides and claim Marcos as the winner, a line which Reagan initially adopted, international outrage and disgust proved too much, and Marcos fled to the United States. Manafort had left Manila the day before.[20]

Several years later, Ed Rollins, a GOP political strategist, was working on a Philippine election, during which he attended a dinner alongside a former attorney for Marcos who signed the contract with BMSK and was involved with investing much of the money Marcos had pilfered. In his memoir, Rollins writes that "a prominent member of the Philippine congress" told him that he had delivered a suitcase with $10 million meant for the Reagan campaign to a "well-known Washington power lobbyist who was involved in the campaign." While on the one hand, Rollins claimed to be "stunned" by the revelation, on the other, he writes that he was "[n]ot in a total state of disbelief, though, because I knew the lobbyist well and I had no doubt the money was now in some offshore bank."[21] In a 2018 interview, Rollins admitted the "power lobbyist" he was referring to was Manafort.[22]

Manafort claimed in a 2022 interview with *Business Insider* that he served as a back channel and attempted to convince Marcos to step down from power at the behest of Reagan's National Security team, all the while feeding information to the head of the CIA at the time, Reagan's former campaign manager William Casey. He described Casey as a friend he grew close to during the 1980 Campaign.[23] As mentioned before, Casey was allegedly involved in the 1980 "October Surprise," in which the Reagan campaign convinced Iran to wait to release the American hostages until after the election to impact its outcome. Further, Casey, a former OSS clandestine operations enthusiast, was a central figure in the Iran-Contra scandal, which involved the illegal sales of arms to Iran, partially facilitated by Israeli intelligence, the proceeds of which were then illegally provided to the Nicaraguan right-wing Contra paramilitary group. These activities, particularly the "October Surprise," are reminiscent of Manafort's later activities during the 2016 election involving an American adversary.

The nature and extent of Manafort's relationship with the CIA, or rogue elements within it, during this period of his career, is mysterious and bears further inquiry. Among the international clients that BMSK is known to have represented, all of the following received funding and support from the CIA: Ferdinand Marcos of the Philippines, the dictator Mobutu Sese Sekou of the Congo, and the warlord Jonas Savimbi of Angola. Manafort also had extensive contacts within Israel and Saudi Arabia, whose intelligence agencies were accomplices in many of the illicit American intelligence activities of the 1980s and who, as we shall see, played a mysterious role in the 2016 election.

By the early 90s, Manafort had developed a taste for the high life. He drove a Mercedes and began buying and renting expensive properties in Virginia, Florida, and the Hamptons.

However, the man who introduced Manafort to an entirely different level of wealth and luxury lifestyle was a Lebanese international arms merchant named Abdul Rahman Al Assir (AKA El Assir). Al Assir was at one time the brother-in-law of Adnan Khashoggi, a billionaire Saudi arms dealer known for his role in the Iran-Contra scandal. Al Assir served as Khashoggi's representative in Spain and facilitated arms sales to Africa. Manafort brought Al Assir along as his guest to George H.W. Bush's inauguration, and their families vacationed together outside of Cannes in France.[24]

Manafort and Al Assir became embroiled in an international scandal known as the *Karachi Affair*. In 1993, Manafort hosted Al Assir and Pakistani Prime Minister Benazir Bhutto at a dinner in his Virginia home. Subsequently, Al Assir served as an intermediary in the sale of French Agosta 90B-class submarines to Pakistan, and it has been alleged that kickbacks related to the deal may have been routed into the unsuccessful French presidential campaign of Édouard Balladur. Manafort had been paid two payments of $52,000 and $34,975 for devising a campaign strategy for Balladur and conducting an opinion poll. However, instead of being paid directly by Balladur, the payments were routed through Al Assir.[25] A further $200,000 made its way to Manafort for serving as an interlocutor for the deal.[26] Manafort's relationship with Pakistan extended to its intelligence service, the ISI. From 1990 to 1995, BMSK was paid $700,000 to lobby for the Kashmiri American Council (KAC). While ostensibly a Washington, DC-based nonprofit, the FBI determined that the KAC was an ISI front designed to deflect attention away from the fact that Pakistan was funding terrorism in Kashmir.[27]

The Roots of Manafort's Ties to Oleg Deripaska, Russia, and Ukraine

Manafort's involvement in Ukraine can be traced to his relationship with Republican lobbyist and campaign guru Rick Davis. In 1996, Manafort left BMSK, and together, they set up the consulting and lobbying firm Davis Manafort Partners (DMP). Manafort and Davis worked on Bob Dole's 1996 presidential campaign. Manafort took charge of the convention, while Davis was Dole's Deputy Campaign Manager. Manafort's colleagues poked fun at his international man of mystery quality.

"We fondly used to refer to him as 'The Count' - 'The Count of Monte Cristo,'" recalled Dole's campaign manager. "It was just the whole air about him."[28]

Following Dole's loss to Bill Clinton, Manafort and Davis returned to lobbying. In 2003, Davis attended a secretive meeting at a hedge fund in Midtown Manhattan with the Honorable Nathaniel Philip Victor James Rothschild, scion and heir to the British branch of the Rothschild banking dynasty.[29] Nat was known as an Oxford-educated, jet-setting playboy with a reputation for youthful excesses that included eloping with a socialite and supermodel at the age of 23. The young Rothschild even briefly dated Ivanka Trump.[30]

Nat shed his youthful indiscretions and grew consumed by an ambition to live up to his family name. Opportunity arrived from the East. One of Rothschild's friends in London was the oligarch Roman Abramovich; the two were often seen together watching Chelsea football matches from Abramovich's private box. The Russian oil and metals billionaire owned the team. Through this relationship, Nat Rothschild met and became the chief advisor to one of Russia's richest and most controversial oligarchs, the aluminum magnate Oleg Deripaska.[31]

Deripaska was born to Jewish parents on January 2nd, 1968. His father died when he was four years old, and his grandparents raised him on a Cossack farm.[32] After a stint in the Russian military, Deripaska graduated from Moscow State University in 1993 with a degree in physics. While still an undergraduate, Deripaska grew fascinated with international metals trading and invested his life savings of $2500 to start his own company. Between October 1993 and May 1994,[33] Deripaska met and befriended Mikhail Chernoy in London.[34] Chernoy was a significant player in the post-Soviet metals market. Through this relationship, Deripaska became the most powerful player in the aluminum market, Russia's largest industry behind oil and natural gas. However, before he did so, he had to survive the Aluminum Wars. Of all the 90s-era privatizations in Russia, the aluminum market was the most deadly.

Chernoy was born in Tashkent, Uzbekistan, in 1952, when it was a Soviet Republic. After a brief stint with the Red Army, Chernoy returned to Tashkent and started an illegal gambling ring that made enough money that he had to pay off the local police. He soon became involved in a scheme that consisted of purchasing leftover raw materials from Soviet factory managers and using them in illegal private workshops to create products to sell on the black market. However, satisfying the local black market could only earn so much. The real money lay in establishing an international operation that could take advantage of the artificially low prices within the USSR and sell at a massive markup on the global market.[35]

In 1988, Chernoy partnered with Trump associate Sam Kislin, serving as the manager of Kislin's trading company Trans Commodities.[36] Reports by both the FBI and Interpol claim that Trans Commodities was used to launder money by both Mikhail and his brother Lev Chernoy as they set about seizing control of the Russian aluminum industry. The FBI report claimed that Mikhail Chernoy was "doing business as Transcommodities [sic], a New York based trading company which is known to have laundered millions of dollars from Russia to New York."[37]

Former FBI Agent and specialist in Eurasian organized crime Robert A. Levinson testified that Chernoy was "protected" outside of Russia by the Solntsevskaya and within Russia by the Izmaylovskaya. One of the Izmaylovskaya's leaders, Anton Malevsky, was a close partner and business associate of Chernoy's.[38] Thus, with strong trading contacts abroad and powerful criminal connections within Russia, Chernoy approached deep-pocketed foreign interests to help them swoop down upon the Russian aluminum industry from abroad.

Vast smelters in industrial centers such as Krasnoyarsk, Sayansk, Bratsk, and Novokuznetsk fed Soviet heavy industry aluminum. The dissolution of the USSR was catastrophic for Russia's aluminum industry for two primary reasons. First, the industry's traditional main customer, the Soviet military, no longer existed, and the new Russian military was a shell of its former self. Second, the primary sources of alumina necessary for the smelting process now exist outside the country in newly independent Kazakhstan and Ukraine. In this desperate situation, a London-based metals trader saw an opportunity. David Reuben was chairman of Trans World, a metals trading company that had purchased aluminum from the USSR since the 1970s.[39] He realized that if he provided the smelters with alumina, he could buy the aluminum they produced cheaply, sell it abroad at international prices, and make a fortune. The process was known as "tolling."[40]

Joined by his brother Simon, in 1992, the Reuben brothers set up a Trans World office in Moscow and were approached by Lev and Mikhail Chernoy.[41] In addition to Mikhail's criminal connections, the Chernoy's also enjoyed powerful political patrons, including Oleg Soskovets, the chairman of the Russian Committee on Metallurgy, and Shamil Tarpischev, an acquaintance from Tashkent who coached Boris Yeltsin in Tennis. With these alliances in place, Trans World set about buying stakes in and establishing tolling contracts with ten of the largest aluminum factories in Russia between August and September of 1992.[42]

The struggle for control of the various smelters across the country quickly turned deadly. The worst violence occurred in Krasnoyarsk, where Trans World came into conflict with the ruthless Anatoly Bykov. Bykov, a former high school PE teacher who set up a gang of former athletes, had initially been hired by Mikhail Chernoy to guard the Krasnoyarsk smelter. In this capacity, he wiped out the local *vor y zakone* in a ruthless murder campaign. However, Bykov soon took control of the plant, and bodies began to fall left and right. While Trans World was initially unable to root Bykov and his heavily armed minions out of the plant itself, potential buyers of their aluminum started conspicuously being assassinated.[43]

Under the threat of investigation and potential arrest in Russia, the Chernoy brothers and Anton Malevsky fled to Israel in the Spring of 1994. Later that year, Oleg Deripaska leveraged his alliance with Trans World to be made the manager of the Sayansk aluminum plant in Siberia.[44] Deripaska used his perch in Sayansk to establish the Sibirsky Aluminum Group in 1997. Shares of the company were held by a Liechtenstein foundation called Radom, with 40% owned by Deripaska, 40% by Mikhail Chernoy, 10% on Anton Malevsky's behalf by his brother Andrei and 10% by Sergei Popov.[45]

On November 26th, 2019, the *Transborder Corruption Archive*, a project run by the EU-Russia Civil Society Forum's Expert Group on Combating Transborder Corruption, posted an "undated unsigned report" made by Spanish law enforcement. "Michael Cherney [AKA Mikhail Chernoy] and Oleg Deripaska are directly related to the Russian organized crime group Izmaylovskaya, where Mr. Cherney is an absolute leader of the economic section. Mr. Deripaska built his first fortunes, firstly, through one or more controlled companies that were used to meet certain criminal purposes of the organization, and secondly, designing dirty money laundering schemes." The report continues, "Deripaska is currently making a special effort to dissociate himself entirely from the criminal circles with which he collaborated previously. And as indicated above this is the case of Cherney and Izmaylovskaya. To be exact, the main purpose of this attitude is to achieve a relevant role in the group of oligarchs closest to the Russian administration. For that he tries to play the same role as the oligarch Roman Abramovich who is attributed the role to manage the private economic interests of Vladimir Putin."[46]

After the height of the violence during the Aluminum Wars, the latter half of the 90s saw the industry's consolidation. Deripaska began pushing Trans World out of Sayansk and establishing himself as the premier executive in Russian aluminum. In 2000, Trans World sold its Russian holdings to Millhouse Capital, a company controlled by Roman Abramovich. Abramovich merged his aluminum assets with Deripaska, and Rusal was created, becoming what was, at the time, the largest aluminum company in the world. In 2001, Deripaska married Polina Yumasheva, daughter of Valentin Yumashev, the former head of Yeltsin's government. Yumashev had married Yeltsin's daughter Tatyana and made Deripaska's new wife Yeltsin's step-granddaughter. Thus, Deripaska married into "The Family," which had run Russia for nearly a decade. He would also make sure to keep on the good side of Putin.

"Deripaska enjoys a favorable relationship with President Putin," U.S. Ambassador to Moscow William Burns wrote in a leaked 2006 diplomatic cable. "[H]e is more or less a permanent fixture on Putin's trips abroad, and he is widely acknowledged by our contacts to be among the 2-3 oligarchs Putin turns to on a regular basis."[47]

Deripaska was now Russia's richest man, and Rusal controlled a significant stake in the global aluminum supply. However, he had one major problem. The US Department of Justice suspected Deripaska of ties to Anton Malevsky, a leader of the Izmaylovskaya. It had banned him from entering the US, infuriating the oligarch who was keen on gaining international respectability and launching Rusal on the London Stock Exchange.[48]

Deripaska set about buying himself legitimacy. In April 2003, he dropped an estimated £17 million on a six-story, 11-bedroom Regency townhouse in Belgrave Square, London. That same year, he met the British banker Lord Jacob Rothschild and befriended his only son Nat Rothschild. Deripaska and Nat Rothschild met regularly at an exquisite home next to St. James's Palace, owned by the Rothschilds, which served as Deripaska's de facto office in London. Nat became Deripaska's chief advisor, providing the oligarch with everything from investment advice to suggestions related to his American visa ban. However, it wasn't a one-way street. Rothschild needed Deripaska's connections to help his hedge fund, Atticus, gain access to lucrative opportunities in the former Soviet Union.[49] According to one London banker, the Rothschild name "was crucial in making Deripaska respectable."[50]

In addition to forging powerful connections in London, Deripaska used his immense wealth to throw his weight around Washington. In 2003, Deripaska paid $300,000 to the law firm Alston & Bird and hired former Republican presidential nominee Bob Dole as his lobbyist.[51] Dole lobbied lawmakers and the DOJ to reverse the visa ban. In this context, Rothschild, as Deripaska's advisor, met with Rick Davis, Dole's former Deputy Campaign Manager, and eventually hired Davis Manafort Partners.

In early 2004, Rothschild invited Rick Davis to the Moscow headquarters of Deripaska's holding company Basic Element. Nat introduced Davis to Igor Giorgadze, a former Georgian Minister of State Security.[52] The former intelligence chief stood accused by Georgian authorities of attempting to assassinate the previous Georgian President, Eduard Shevardnadze.[53] Since 1995, Giorgadze had remained in exile in Russia, where he had set up a Russian-backed political party. Following the Rose Revolution, Deripaska, likely under orders from the Kremlin, pursued a pro-Russia strategy within the country.

The first part of the plan consisted of Rothschild investing in Georgian vineyards and then lobbying the Georgian government to allow for Giorgadze's return. U.S. Ambassador to Georgia Kenneth Yalowitz noted that Giorgadze would have reliably worked in Russia's interest when Georgia sought a more Western-friendly path.[54] Later, in 2004, Davis and Rothschild traveled to Tbilisi to convince the new Georgian President

Mikheil Saakashvili over dinner to allow Giorgadze to return. Saakashvili, who had no love for the Russians, refused, effectively ending the lobbying effort.

While Manafort had no known involvement in the Georgia campaign, global events thrust him to the heart of Davis Manafort Partner's relationship with Deripaska. In November 2004, the Orange Revolution in Ukraine dominated headlines worldwide and sent shockwaves across the Russian political establishment. Both Rothschild and Deripaska had financial interests in Ukraine, the former in private equity investments, and the latter owned an aluminum smelter.[55] From then on, Davis Manafort Partners focused primarily on Ukraine, and Paul Manafort took the lead in the project.

In late 2004, while he was on his way home from Tbilisi, Phil Griffin, an associate at Davis Manafort Partners (DMP), received a phone call from his boss, Rick Davis. Instead of returning to DC, Griffin was to fly to Ukraine on behalf of two of the firm's top clients, Nat Rothschild and Oleg Deripaska. The Orange Revolution had just cast the Kremlin's preferred candidate, Viktor Yanukovych, into political exile. In the job Griffin held before joining DMP, working at the U.S. Congress-funded pro-democracy group the International Republican Institute, he would have stood behind the protestors on the Maidan. Now he worked for the other team.[56]

Paul Manafort took the lead on DMP's Ukraine work. Between Thanksgiving and Christmas 2004, he and Griffin held strategy sessions in Washington, DC. They met with political contacts knowledgeable about Ukraine and learned what they could about the prevailing attitudes within the U.S. capital towards the events unfolding in Kyiv. Finally, in late December, Oleg Deripaska sent Manafort to Donetsk in the far east of Ukraine to meet with Rinat Akhmetov, Ukraine's richest oligarch. Akhmetov had been Yanukovych's most enthusiastic supporter and had bankrolled the Party of Regions for years.

Manafort spent his first few months in Ukraine holed up in the Donbas Palace, a luxury hotel in the heart of the drab industrial center of Donetsk. He kept a low profile, hanging up on an *Urkainska Pravda* reporter who managed to get his hotel room phone number.[57] Manafort first met Yanukovych at an old-fashioned movie palace in Kyiv that had been converted into a Party of Regions headquarters. Yanukovych, who had just returned from self-imposed exile in the Czech Republic after the humiliation of the Orange Revolution, was assessed by most third parties to be politically dead.

Rinat Akhmetov ostensibly hired Manafort to represent his company System Capital Management (SCM), paying Davis Manafort Partners €10 million. The contract was a front to conceal his work for Viktor Yanukovych and the Party of Regions. This was made clear by Manafort in a *CONFIDENTIAL EYES ONLY* memo he prepared for Yanukovych.[58]

In the summer of 2005, Manafort and Griffin traveled to Moscow and met with Akhmetov, Yanukovych, and various high-level Party of Regions officials at the five-star Baltschug Kempinski Hotel. This was the same hotel that Trump had partied at years earlier in 1996, believed by the FBI to be owned by Semyon Mogilevich. According to flight records, Manafort traveled to Moscow at least 18 times between 2004 and 2011 while advising Yanukovych, with most of the trips taking place in the 2005-20006 timeframe.[59]

That autumn, Manafort rented an office at 4 Sophia Street in Kyiv and established operational headquarters opposite the 16 and 18 trolley buses. Residents noted that the office blinds were generally drawn.[60] The first test of Manafort's campaign skills and Yanukovych's electoral durability would come with the 2006 parliamentary elections.

Manafort's Manafort:
Konstantin Kilimnik, Russian Intelligence, and Ukraine

Konstantin Kilimnik was an early figure of central importance to Manafort's efforts in Ukraine. He started as a translator but became the director of Manafort's operations in Kyiv. Manafort leaned on Kilimnik's linguistic skills and insights into Ukrainian and Russian culture to such an extent that he referred to him to others in the office as "my Russian brain."[61] The FBI has assessed that Kilimnik "has ties to Russian intelligence."[62] According to the US Department of Treasury, Kilimnik is an agent of the Russian Intelligence Services.[63] The Senate Intelligence Committee described him as a "Russian intelligence officer."

Born a dual Russian-Ukrainian citizen in 1970 in

Dnepropetrovsk, the diminutive Kilimnik stands at 5-foot-3 inches and goes by the nickname Kostya, or occasionally just KK. Kilimnik attended the Soviet military's leading university for languages in the 1990s and later worked as a translator for the Russian military.[64] The academy was considered a training ground for the GRU, Russian military intelligence.[65] Through this experience, Kilimnik grew fluent in English and Swedish. In 1995, Kilimnik's language skills landed him a job at the International Republican Institute (IRI) office in Moscow. During his interview, when asked how he had become fluent in English, Kilimnik replied, "Russian military intelligence." An IRI official speaking with *Politico* later quipped, "I never called GRU headquarters for a reference."[66]

The IRI had been chaired by Republican Senator John McCain since January 1993 and had offices in over 70 countries.[67] David A. Merkel, who headed IRI's Moscow office when Kilimnik was hired, said that Kilimnik "took the job for the money. Not because he believed in the mission of the IRI or in advancing the principle of free-market democracy."[68] Fiona Hill, who in the 1990s worked for the Kennedy School of Government and interacted with Kilimnik, stated in sworn congressional testimony that "all of my staff thought he was a Russian spy."[69]

Despite these suspicions, which Kilimnik has denied, IRI officials in Washington grew so reliant on Kilimnik that they eventually named him acting director of the Moscow office. During the lead-up to the 2004 Ukrainian election, the IRI worked to help Yushchenko and the Orange coalition. However, according to the Russian investigative news outfit *Proekt*, Kilimnik was already working for Yanukovych in 2004 without the knowledge of his colleagues at the IRI.[70] According to Taras V. Chernovyl, a former member of the Party of Regions, Kilimnik was "known as the representative of Russia" within the party.[71]

A source within IRI told *Proekt* that Kilimnik's work in Ukraine was organized through Oleg Deripaska. Between late 2004 and early 2005, Kilimnik sent IRI employees to the offices of Deripaska's company Basic Element in Moscow at least twenty times. They were handed envelopes full of cash or air tickets for Kilimnik and his designated political consultants.[72] Sometime in early 2005, Manafort Davis Partners associate Phil Griffin, who had worked with Kilimnik at the IRI, hired him to join Manafort's effort in Ukraine.[73]

By the spring of 2005, officials at the IRI learned that Kilimnik was working to support Yanukovych. There were also suspicions that he had leaked information about an IRI conference held in Bratislava to the FSB.[74] Stephen Nix, a senior IRI official in Washington, fired Kilimnik. Kilimnik, known for avoiding email and photographs, wiped his IRI computer before he left.[75] In April, FSB head Nikolai Patrushev denounced the IRI in a speech before the Duma, accusing the organization of planning the "continuation of velvet revolutions in the post-Soviet territory." Patrushev's speech contained information from an IRI meeting in Bratislava where Kilimnik had been one of only two non-Americans in attendance.[76]

Now, with Kilimnik as his full-time deputy, Manafort brought the most sophisticated American campaign methodology to Ukraine, hiring 40 political consultants for the job, many based out of Washington. He polled the Ukrainian electorate to establish what the most pressing social and economic issues were. Manafort and his team shaped the Party of Regions advertising campaign.[77] Overall strategy for the pro-Russian Party of Regions party was placed in the hands of a man once at the vanguard of the Reagan Revolution.

Yanukovych had confidence in Manafort because he believed the Orange Revolution was the product of secret American machinations.[78] American diplomats in Kyiv soon took note of Manafort's activities. "As part of an effort to transform its image into that of a democratic political force," wrote U.S. Ambassador John Herbst in a confidential leaked cable a month before the 2006 parliamentary elections, "Ukraine's Party of Regions -- long a haven for Donetsk-based mobsters and oligarchs -- is in the midst of an 'extreme makeover.'" The cable continued, "The effort enlists the help and advice of veteran K street political tacticians."[79]

Manafort rebranded Yanukovych in his own image. Yanukovych began wearing finely tailored Italian suits and changed his hairstyle to one similar to Manafort's. Yanukovych's new look, in addition to the change in strategy masterminded by Manafort, seemed to achieve the impossible by lifting his political fortunes out of an early grave. Following the March 26th, 2006 parliamentary elections, the Party of Regions won a plurality of the vote with 32.1%. The Yulia Tymoshenko bloc, bitter foes of Yanukovych and his oligarch backers, particularly the natural gas magnate Dmytro Firtash, came in a distant second place with only 22.3%. Yanukovych was once again Prime Minister of Ukraine, poised to run for President in 2010 from a position of strength.

The Manafort-Deripaska-Putin Axis and the Montenegro Connection

In June 2005, Manafort sent Oleg Deripaska a confidential strategy proposal to influence politics and media coverage in a way that would promote Vladimir Putin. "We are now of the belief that this model can greatly benefit the Putin government if employed at the correct levels with the appropriate commitment to success," Manafort wrote to Deripaska. The project, Manafort continued, "will be offering a great service that can re-focus, both internally and externally, the policies of the Putin government."

As part of his pitch, Manafort explained to Deripaska that in the course of his Ukraine work, he was utilizing contacts "at the highest levels of the U.S. government - the White House, Capitol Hill, and the State Department." Without naming the firm, Manafort also said he had hired a "leading international law firm with close ties to President Bush to support our client's interests." Manafort claimed he had employed legal experts from top universities and think tanks, including NYU, Duke, and the Center for Strategic and International Studies.

Manafort suggested to Deripaska that he could employ a similar strategy to benefit both him and Putin's Government and that he extend the work he was currently doing in Ukraine to Uzbekistan, Tajikistan, and Georgia. Manafort eventually signed a $10 million contract with Deripaska starting in 2006. However, instead of using Davis Manafort Partners, Manafort had the money funneled through a Delaware shell company, LOAV Ltd., which he had registered in 1992 and was listed as having the same address as his Alexandria, Virginia home.[80]

Manafort's next project for Deripaska took place in the tiny, mountainous Balkan statelet of Montenegro. In 2005, Deripaska's Rusal purchased KAP, an aluminum smelter whose output accounted for nearly half of Montenegro's exports.[81] Overnight, Deripaska became one of the most influential men in the country. However, he wasn't acting independently. Deripaska told a close associate that he had bought the plant "because Putin encouraged him to do it" and that "the Kremlin wanted an area of influence in the Mediterranean."[82]

Russia had been opposed to Montenegrin independence from its traditional ally Serbia. However, following Deripaska's purchase of KAP, the Kremlin had reasons to drop its opposition as Deripaska would enjoy immense influence in the newly independent country. Davis Manafort Partners signed on for a multimillion-dollar contract to help manage the pro-independence campaign in the lead-up to a referendum that would take place in 2006. Both Rick Davis and Paul Manafort participated in the effort.

It was in Montenegro that Manafort became acquainted with Victor Boyarkin.[83] Boyarkin had served as an assistant naval attaché at the Russian embassy in Washington, DC, and was now just one of many Deripaska employees with military and intelligence backgrounds. According to the U.S. Treasury Department, Boyarkin "is a former GRU officer who reports directly to Deripaska and has led business negotiations on Deripaska's behalf."[84] Manafort and Boyarkin would cross paths again during the 2016 election.

In addition to Davis and Manafort's pro-independence efforts in-country, the Montenegrin government had paid Bob Dole $1.38 million since 2001 to lobby in Washington.[85] By 2005, Dole's lobbying finally paid off, and Deripaska was awarded a U.S. multi-entry visa. At the time, he was looking into a series of acquisitions that would have given him a stake in the US automaker Chrysler.[86] In return for receiving the visa, Deripaska sat down for an FBI interview.[87] The interview went poorly, and the visa ban was reinstated after he left the US. US officials reinstated the ban partially due to worries that Deripaska would try to launder illicit profits through U.S. real estate.[88]

Following Deripaska's trip to the U.S., Manafort and Davis turned to an unlikely ally in their push for Montenegrin independence, Arizona Senator John McCain. Davis, who later served as McCain's campaign manager for his 2008 presidential bid, was close with the Senator. McCain was one of Putin's most vehement critics on Capitol Hill. In January 2006, McCain and two other Republican senators, Saxby Chambliss of Georgia and John E. Sununu of New Hampshire gathered for drinks in an apartment near Davos, Switzerland, when Davis and Deripaska greeted them. The entourage left for a ski chalet owned by the Hungarian-born billionaire Peter Munk, who owned Barrick Gold, the world's largest gold-mining company. At the gathering, Munk delivered remarks before the guests in which he complimented Deripaska.[89] Munk served as a board member of Deripaska's company, Rusal.

As the May 21st, 2006 independence referendum drew near, Manafort and Davis ratcheted up the pressure and used powerful Deripaska allies to help do so. Nat Rothschild arrived in Montenegro three weeks before the referendum and promised $1 million to counter a threat by Serb authorities to revoke scholarships to Montenegrin students. Peter Munk also arrived in Montenegro with pledges of support for Montenegrin students from Canadian universities. Aides of Bob Dole arranged for a teleconference between McCain's Senate office and Montenegro's visiting foreign minister. McCain issued a statement saying that Montenegro's independence was "the greatest European democracy project since the end of the Cold War."[90]

The referendum passed by a 0.5% margin. In August of 2006, McCain and Davis were back in Montenegro celebrating McCain's 70th birthday at a yacht party hosted by an Italian businessman, Raffaello Follieri, and his movie starlet girlfriend, Anne Hathaway.[91] Following dinner, the group took boats out across Kotor Bay to the Queen K, Oleg Deripaska's 238-foot superyacht, where they enjoyed champagne and pastries in honor of McCain's birthday.[92] In March 2008, in the run-up to the presidential election, Nat Rothschild and his father held a fundraiser for McCain at the Rothschild's mansion at Spencer House in London.[93] Oleg Deripaska was reportedly in attendance.[94] As far back as 2005, McCain had been warned by a staffer on the National Security Council that Rick Davis and Manafort were working to undermine the Orange Revolution, a cause McCain championed. McCain eventually cut ties with Manafort completely and nearly fired Davis from his campaign, but relented after Davis tearfully begged him to reconsider.[95]

In addition to entertaining politicians and plutocrats on his yacht, Oleg Deripaska also entered into business dealings with Paul Manafort and his new deputy, Rick Gates. Gates had interned at Black, Manafort, and Stone and was close with Rick Davis.[96] As Davis became more involved with the McCain presidential campaign, Gates took over his responsibilities and worked closely with Manafort in Ukraine. Gates, who later worked on the Trump Campaign, also played a pivotal role in Manafort's business dealings with Deripaska.

On March 26th, 2007, Pericles Emerging Market Partners, L.P. was registered in the Cayman Islands. Rick Davis, Rick Gates, and Paul Manafort were listed as the initial members of the company's investment committee.[97] Responsibility for the day-to-day operations of Pericles fell to Gates. Konstantin Kilimnik was involved with the company's investment program, as well as Party of Regions member Alexander Balanutsa. Pericles was ostensibly formed to make private equity investments in countries within the former Soviet Union, Montenegro, and eastern and southern Europe.[98]

Deripaska was the sole investor in Pericles and pledged to invest up to $200 million. While Pericles was supposed to make numerous investments, it only ever made one. In July of 2007, Deripaska created a company called Surf Horizon Ltd, registered in Cyprus, and provided Pericles with $18,938,400.[99] The money was used to purchase a stake in Black Sea Cable, a Ukrainian telecom company based in Odessa that reportedly controlled 45% of the city's telecommunications infrastructure.[100]

Manafort structured the investment in a peculiar way. Deripaska was to send the money to a Cyprus-based shell company, which would then "loan" the money to yet another Cypriot legal structure known as a "special purpose vehicle" (SPV). Transferring the money as a loan allowed them to avoid Cypriot taxation. The SPV would then be transferred to another Manafort-owned holding company, owned by a UK-based "controlling" company, Colberg Projects LLP. Colberg Projects was then supposed to purchase Black Sea Cable. Manafort charged Deripaska a remarkable $7.35 million in management fees.[101]

Colberg Projects LLP is part of a network of 127 UK-based shell companies registered to the same handful of London offices. When asked, no one at these offices had ever heard of Colberg or any of the other companies. Nearly a third of the companies, which have extensive links to companies and individuals in Ukraine and the former Soviet Union, face accusations of tax evasion, fraud, and corruption.[102] The companies in the shell network share the same corporate structure. They were first established and operated by two firms based in the British Virgin Islands, Ireland & Overseas Acquisitions and Milltown Corporate Services. Both have been linked to money laundering schemes related to the theft of state assets in Ukraine, Russia, and Azerbaijan.[103] These firms were then replaced by two shell companies registered in the Seychelles, Intrahold A.G. and Monohold A.G. Lastly, the shell network was taken over by Talberg Ltd. and Uniwell Inc., two companies registered in the Caribbean offshore haven Nevis.

According to *BuzzFeed*, court documents suggest that after the money went to Colberg Projects LLP, Manafort never actually purchased Black Sea Cable. Black Sea Cable's management was close to the Party of Regions, and its assets were controlled at various times by different shell companies linked to Viktor Yanukovych. One such entity was Milltown Corporate Services, which set up Colberg Projects LLP. Other entities that owned Black Sea Cable at one time or another were the very same companies that at one point also owned Colberg Projects, Monohold A.G, and Intrahold A.G. Both companies were investigated by the Seychelles Financial Intelligence Unit in 2014 for money laundering related to the embezzlement of state resources by the Yanukovych government.[104]

The Black Sea Cable deal gives every impression of being a money laundering scheme through which Russia, via Deripaska, provided Viktor Yanukovych and the Party of Regions cash in the lead-up to the 2010 election. If true, Manafort's $7.35 million management fees could be interpreted as a payoff. By structuring the payments as "loans" they avoided Cypriot taxes and provided Deripaska with potential leverage over Manafort, should he ever choose to collect his debt. Money launderers often disguise payments as loans.

The Black Sea Cable deal was the only investment ever made by Pericles. Regardless of whether Deripaska ever intended to collect on the loan, events conspired to disrupt his plans. After the 2008 global financial crisis, Deripaska's financial representatives contacted Manafort and asked that he liquidate Pericles and return his share of the money. Rick Gates, who had visited Deripaska's office twice in Moscow and was the contact for all Pericles-related matters, maintained that an audit of Black Sea Cable was underway, but the results never arrived. By 2011, Manafort had stopped responding to Deripaska's entreaties. A 2014 Cayman Island court filing made on behalf of Deripaska's investment vehicle, Surf Horizon, against Pericles, stated, "[i]t appears that Paul Manafort and Rick Gates have simply disappeared."[105]

Oleg Deripaska wasn't the only oligarch Manafort tried to go into business with. In 2008, Manafort attempted to partner with both Deripaska and the Ukrainian natural gas billionaire Dmytro Firtash in an aborted $850 million deal to purchase the Drake Hotel in New York and convert it into a 70-story luxury office and residential space called Bulgari Tower. In a July 2008 memo, Rick Gates wrote that the planned tower would generate "over $3 billion in value as a result of the unique combination of retail, smart office space, residential, and a luxury hotel."[106] Firtash is an alleged front for Semyon Mogilevich's Ukrainian energy holdings.

On June 9th, 2008, the real estate development company CMZ Ventures was incorporated in Delaware and listed its controllers as Paul Manafort, Arthur & Karen B. Cohen, and Brad S. Zackson. Zackson was a convicted felon who had worked as Fred Trump's real estate developer. In 1981, Zackson was arrested on charges of possession of a weapon and attempted murder after he tried to shoot a nightclub bouncer and was sentenced to seven years in prison. After serving his time, Zackson became a rental broker and successfully rented out units in several of Fred Trump's buildings. One day, the elder Trump summoned him to his office in his limo and placed him in charge of the Trump Organization Queens buildings.[107]

Manafort had known Donald Trump since Roger Stone had brought him on as a client for Black, Manafort, and Stone. In 2006, Manafort purchased a Trump Tower apartment for $3,675,000 using an LLC called John Hannah. Manafort's middle name is John, and Hannah is the middle name of Rick Davis.[108] According to Franklin Foer, Manafort "would kibitz with his old client [Trump] when they'd run into one another on the elevator." McCain aides suspected that Oleg Deripaska had purchased the Trump Tower apartment for Manafort and Davis and went as far as to mention it to the Senator. The claim, however, remains unsubstantiated.[109]

Manafort, Cohen and Zackson looked at billions of dollars worth of properties, including Manhattan House, the Helmsley Hotel and two Bahamian islands. However, they ultimately negotiated a deal with real estate investor and developer Harry B. Macklowe to purchase the Drake Hotel site for $850 million. In his search to secure financing for the deal, Manafort met and discussed the deal with Deripaska on June 30th, 2008.[110]

While Deripaska didn't end up financing the project, Manafort made more progress with Dmytro Firtash. On November 6th, Group DF [Dmytro Firtash] Real Estate, a subsidiary of Firtash's holding company Group DF, wrote to Manafort that Firtash was willing "to provide $112 million in equity for the project." He continued, "Group DF has executed a deposit of $25 million into escrow for the project." The cash funds arrived via wire transfer and were placed into an escrow account accessible to Manafort.

By March of 2009, the project was in trouble, and Zackson even considered attempting to bring Donald Trump into the deal, writing in an email, "I have an idea to bring Trump in on the Drake. I think it solves a lot of issues right away."[111] Trump was never involved in the deal, which eventually fell through. However, in a subsequent lawsuit filed by former Ukrainian Prime Minister Yulia Tymoshenko, it was alleged that Manafort and Firtash had never intended for the deal to go through but used it as a faux investment to launder money.

Tymoshenko's RICO lawsuit alleged that the Drake funds provided by Firtash had been "skimmed" from RosUkrEnergo. The lawsuit listed Semyon Mogilevich as Firtash's "silent partner." Tymoshenko's lawsuit was dismissed. Judge Kimba Wood didn't dispute the facts laid out in the case, but wrote, "[w]ithout specifying the particular contribution of each defendant to the money-laundering scheme, plaintiffs fail to establish the requisite directness of relationship between each defendant's conduct and the harm suffered by Tymoshenko."

Manafort's attention never strayed too far from Ukraine. After engineering Yanukovych's Lazarus-like rise from the political grave to the office of Prime Minister in 2006, Manafort enjoyed his absolute confidence. With the Ukrainian presidential elections fast approaching in 2010, the next step was to permanently annul the already faltering Orange Revolution by having Yanukovych return to the highest office in the land, which protestors and the courts had prevented him from occupying six years earlier.

Ukrainian politics between 2006 and 2010 was characterized by shifting alliances and chaotic infighting among the factions of the Orange Revolution. This political warfare was personified by the intense rivalry between President Viktor Yushchenko and Prime Minister Yulia Tymoshenko, who narrowly edged out Yanukovych for the job in the 2007 elections. Yanukovych was appointed chairman of the Government Chief Council of the Commonwealth of Independent States and prepared for his presidential run in 2010.

Having transformed Yanukovych's appearance, Manafort set about honing his message and modernizing his campaign methodology. Polling told him that Yanukovych could motivate his base by inflaming divisions over the perceived mistreatment of Russian language speakers. Manafort also encouraged Yanukovych to criticize NATO, particularly its exercises in Crimea.[112] American diplomats in Ukraine grew concerned over Yanukovych's rhetoric and Manafort's role in promoting it. The American Ambassador to Ukraine, William Taylor, called Manafort into his office and requested that he use his influence with Yanukovych to have him tamp down his anti-NATO rhetoric. Manafort refused, saying that the rhetoric polled too well.[113]

Manafort then added firepower to his team and hired long-time Democratic Party political consultants. Among them were Tad Devine and Julian Mulvey. Devine would go on to manage Senator Bernie Sanders's 2016 presidential bid, while Mulvey worked as the creative director of Sanders' TV advertising operation. Manafort also brought Democratic media consultants Daniel Rabin and Adam Strasberg on board. Rabin had developed ad campaigns for Democratic candidates for decades, and Strasberg had worked on the Kerry campaign and would go on to work on the Sanders campaign.[114] Manafort rounded off the new additions with the veteran public relations giant Edelman, which celebrated Yanukovych's "accomplishments in economic development" for $35,000 a month.[115]

Viktor Yanukovych accepted the Party of Regions nomination for president at a party convention much like the ones Manafort had organized for Republican nominees for years. As confetti rained down, rapturous supporters raised portraits of the transformed leader.[116] On January 17th, 2010, Yanukovych came in first in early voting returns with 35.8% of the vote, with Tymoshenko coming in second with 24.7%. In a runoff election less than a month later, on February 7th, Yanukovych was elected the President with 48.95% of the vote.

Yanukovych and his oligarch allies acted quickly to consolidate their power. In September of 2010, Yanukovych reshaped the Ukrainian Constitutional Court. A month later, the court repealed reforms from 2004 that had been made to limit executive power. Yanukovych emerged as the most powerful president since Kuchma. His financial backers, primarily Rinat Akhmetov and Dmytro Firtash, were thrust into the highest echelons of power.

Serhiy Lyovochkin, a close ally of Firtash and the gas lobby, was appointed the head of the Presidential Administration. Firtash and Lyovochkin own villas next to one another on the CÔTE D'AZUR in the French Riviera, and it is believed that through a complex web of offshore shell companies, Lyovochkin had financial interests in the Mogilevich-linked RosUkrEnergo.[117] Another Firtash ally and member of RUE's coordinating council, Yuriy Boyko, was appointed Minister of Energy. Lastly, a Firtash confidant was made the head of the SBU, Ukraine's state security service.[118] The group around Yanukovych that engaged in industrial-scale looting and larceny under his tenure came to be known, in an echo of Yeltsin-era Russia, as "The Family."

Later, Ukrainian authorities accused Yanukovych of stealing $37 billion from the state during his tenure as president. The forms this gargantuan theft took were manifold. There was the tried-and-true Ukrainian tradition of rent-seeking and skimming off the natural gas trade. Yanukovych also dispensed infrastructure contracts entirely at his discretion. Swedish economist Anders Åslund has estimated that infrastructure-related corruption alone provided "The Family" with $2 billion in illicit yearly proceeds. Yanukovych also engaged in outright embezzlement from the State Tax Administration and the State Customs Committee, stealing between $3 and $5 billion during his time in office.[119]

Ukraine's ousted Prime Minister, Yulia Tymoshenko, had been a thorn in Yanukovych's side since the Orange Revolution. Now, she was vulnerable to selective prosecution by Ukraine's corrupt prosecutor general's office. During the summer and autumn of 2010, Ukrainian prosecutors under Yanukovych's direction began charging Tymoshenko with a series of crimes that prevented her from leaving the country or engaging in political activity. In June of 2011, Tymoshenko was accused of abuse of power and embezzlement. Finally, in October 2011, Tymoshenko was sentenced to seven years in jail and fined $186 million. While the EU denounced Yanukovych's persecution of political opponents and said that such acts threatened Ukraine's entry into the EU, the Ukrainian president argued that Tymoshenko's trial was simply part of a general anti-corruption campaign.

As Ukraine received billions of dollars in foreign aid, Yanukovych couldn't afford to let the West drift too far away. He had been managing a balancing act between Europe and the United States on the one hand and Russia on the other. Lucky for him, Paul Manafort had a plan. After Yanukovych's victory, he gained unparalleled access to the innermost sanctums of the new President's administration, being granted "walk-in" privileges to his offices at any time. Manafort became a regular at the Mezhyhirya Residence, a luxurious 350-acre former monastery that had been retrofitted with a golf course, equestrian club, yacht pier, and ostrich farm, among other extravagances that served as Yanukovych's home. The two would play tennis together and occasionally swim naked with one another outside Yanukovych's banya.[120]

Manafort's lobbying plan unfolded against a backdrop of negotiations between the EU and Ukraine over a proposed Association Agreement that, were it signed, would strengthen ties between the two. Russia, under Putin, was developing its own Customs Union that it desired Ukraine to join and was vociferously opposed to further Ukrainian integration with Europe. The EU Association Agreement had its roots back in 2008 when Tymoshenko was still Prime Minister. Her arrest in

2011 outraged much of Europe and threatened to derail the agreement entirely.[121] Manafort's job was to manage Western perceptions.

First, Manafort arranged for the Ukrainian oligarch Viktor Pinchuk, ironically a major donor to the Clinton Foundation, to pay the powerhouse American law firm Skadden, Arps, Slate, Meagher & Flom to have former Obama White House Counsel Gregg Craig oversee the production of a report on the government's prosecution of Yulia Tymoshenko. Craig was guided on the ground in Ukraine by Konstantin Kilimnik, and the report that was produced was seen by most as a legalese whitewash.[122]

Manafort also enlisted the help of a former reporter named Alan Friedman to put together an online black PR campaign against not only Tymoshenko but also Hillary Clinton, at one point arranging for press articles to suggest that they were antisemitic and pushing them out through friendly media organs in the United States in the hopes of upsetting "Obama Jews."[123] According to later court papers, they coordinated the effort with a "senior Israeli Government official" that both *Haaretz*[124] and *The Jerusalem Post*[125] speculated was Avigdor Lieberman. Lieberman, who was born in the former Soviet Union before moving to Israel, denied any involvement with Manafort.[126] He is the founder of the secular nationalist Yisrael Beiteinu party, whose membership was initially dominated by Russian-speaking Israelis,[127] and is known for his warm relations with Vladimir Putin.[128]

Critical to these efforts was the establishment of phony think tanks and NGOs such as the Center for the Study of Former Soviet Socialist Republics (CXSSR),[129] and the Brussels-based European Centre for a Modern Ukraine. These served as a channel to publish disinformation about political enemies, often using non-existent "reporters." They also allowed Manafort to pay for lobbying services in Washington on behalf of Yanukovych without registering as a foreign agent with the Justice Department as required by law.[130] Manafort used them to pay for the services of the Washington lobbying firm the Podesta Group,[131] founded by John Podesta's brother Tony Podesta, and the PR heavyweight Mercury Public Affairs.[132]

The final piece in Manafort's global influence campaign on behalf of Yanukovych was the establishment of the

"Hapsburg Group," described by Manafort in a June 2012 email to Rick Gates, Konstantin Kilimnik, and Alan Friedman as "a small group of high-level European highly influential champions and politically credible friends who can act informally and without any visible relationship with the Government of Ukraine." The concept had been developed by Friedman, who proposed that former Austrian Chancellor Alfred Gusenbauer lead the group.[133] Gusenbauer agreed to help for €300,000 per year. According to court documents, he successfully recruited Romano Prodi, former prime minister of Italy, and Aleksander Kwaśniewski, a former president of Poland, into the lobbying effort.[134]

The money used to pay for the black PR campaign against Tymoshenko and Clinton and the members of the Hapsburg Group came from the Ukrainian oligarch and Dmytro Firtash ally Serhiy Lyovochkin.[135] Manafort would later be in contact with Lyovochkin and provide him inside information at critical moments during the 2016 election. Between 2010 and 2013, Lyovochkin provided Manafort with $42,042,307 for his efforts on behalf of Yanukovych.[136] Some amount of it, doubtless, made its way into Manafort's pockets.

One of the contradictory aspects of Manafort's lobbying campaign on behalf of Yanukovych and the Ukrainian government was that it supported the Ukrainian adoption of the EU Association Agreement, a measure that Yanukovych ultimately rejected in a move that would spell the end of his regime. The simplest explanation for Manafort's support of the Association Agreement is that it served as the primary justification for his lucrative lobbying effort to take place at all. Had the Ukrainians rejected it outright, there would have been no reason to spend millions lobbying authorities in the United States and Europe. Ultimately, the Maidan Revolution put an end to Manafort's double game of lobbying on behalf of the corrupt, Kremlin-preferred Yanukovych while also pushing him to adopt the Association Agreement. However, political developments in the United States soon attracted Manafort's full attention.

Manafort's Friends in Ukraine:
Roger Stone and the Michael Caputo Enigma

Paul Manafort was not the only American political consultant in
Ukraine. In 2007, two of his old friends joined him in the country
to consult for a candidate running for the Ukrainian Rada. One
we know already: Roger Stone. The other was their mutual
longtime associate, Michael Caputo.

In the book *Russian Roulette: The Inside Story of Putin's War
on America and the Election of Donald Trump*, David Corn and
Michael Isikoff relate a story Stone told them regarding his
experience in Ukraine. According to Stone, while dining at a
restaurant in Kyiv, Phil Griffin, a member of Manafort's team in
Ukraine, confronted him. Shortly afterward, Stone claims that
Manafort called him demanding to know, "What are you doing in
my country?"

As with most Stone stories, this one is colorful,
irresistible, and unsubstantiated. In later Congressional testimony,
Stone and Caputo went to great lengths to describe their
candidate as "pro-Western." They emphasized that they were
working against Manafort's client, Viktor Yanukovych. "I worked
in one cycle for the splinter party of Volodymyr Lytvyn," Stone
testified, "a pro-Western candidate who opposed Paul Manafort's
candidate, Viktor Yanukovych, in the 2006–2007 parliamentary
elections in Ukraine."

If Stone is to be believed, it was simply friendly
competition abroad between old friends. However, Stone and
Caputo's activities in Ukraine give every appearance that they
were engaging in the political "dirty trick" of splitting the political
opposition with a hopeless, artificially boosted candidate and that
this was done to benefit Viktor Yanukovych. Stone had a long
history with this kind of political stunt, a history that involved
Roy Cohn.

Roger Stone first met Cohn while working on the Reagan
campaign and has stated that he suggested to Cohn that if they
could get the candidate John B. Anderson to run on behalf of
New York's Liberal Party, it would split the vote between Carter
and Anderson and deliver the New York to Reagan. "Let me
look into it," Roy replied. Shortly after that, Cohn told Stone,
"You need to go see this lawyer… and see what his number is."

"Roy, I don't understand," Stone replied.

"How much cash he wants, dumbfuck," Cohn shouted. Stone claims the lawyer wanted $125,000 cash. Thinking the number was outlandish, Stone returned to Cohn. "That's not the problem," Cohn responded. "How does he want it?"

"There's a suitcase," Stone explained. "I don't look in the suitcase… I don't even know what was in the suitcase… I take the suitcase to the law office. I drop it off. Two days later, they have a convention. Liberals decide they're endorsing John Anderson for president. It's a three-way race now in New York State. Reagan wins with 46 percent of the vote. I paid his law firm. Legal fees. I don't know what he did for the money, but whatever it was, the Liberal party reached its right conclusion out of a matter of principle."[137]

Stone and Caputo were in Ukraine working on behalf of a candidate named Volodymyr Lytvyn. Despite Stone's attempts to paint Lytvyn as a "pro-Western candidate," his history is much more complex. Lytvyn was a member of the Ukrainian Communist Party. In 1994, he was selected by the second president of independent Ukraine, Leonid Kuchma, to serve as his aide.

Kuchma's administration, which lasted from 1994 to 2005, oversaw the establishment of the Ukrainian oligarchic ruling system and the criminalization of large sections of the Ukrainian economy and its politics. Between 1996 and 1999, Lytvyn served as Kuchma's first assistant and speech writer. In 1999, Lytvyn became Head of the Presidential Administration.

On the evening of September 16th, 2000, a Georgian-Ukrainian journalist named Georgiy Gongadze went missing. Gongadze founded the muckraking website *Ukrainska Pravda* and was well known for reporting corruption in Ukraine. On November 3rd, Gongadze's decapitated corpse was discovered outside of Kyiv. His body bore the signs of torture and mutilation.

A scandal erupted when an opposition politician revealed the existence of tapes purportedly recorded by Kuchma's bodyguard, Mykola Melnychenko. The most explosive revelations contained within the tapes related to the kidnapping and murder of Gongadze. Ukrainian President Kuchma was recorded speaking to Lytvyn and his interior minister, Yuriy Kravchenko, about the need to silence Gongadze.[138] Lytvyn was recorded as saying, "In my opinion, let loose Kravchenko to use alternative methods."[139]

In the aftermath, protests erupted in Ukraine. Kuchma fired several officials. In 2013, former Kyiv police chief Oleksiy Pukach was convicted of killing Gongadze. After Pukach was declared guilty, the court asked him if he accepted the verdict. "I will accept it when Kuchma and Lytvyn join me in this cage," Pukach replied.[140]

In September 2007, before the Ukrainian parliamentary elections, Stone's consulting partner Michael Caputo wrote an editorial in *The Washington Times* that mentioned Lytvyn.[141] It didn't mention that he and Stone were working on Lytvyn's campaign. Caputo criticized Yulia Tymoshenko, Viktor Yanukovych's chief domestic political rival. Tymoshenko had been urging Ukrainians not to waste their votes on the many smaller parties vying for a place in the Ukrainian parliament but rather to focus on voting on parties that had a shot of winning, such as her own.

"Yulia urged the electorate to choose among mega-blocks instead of wasting votes on smaller parties," Caputo wrote. Then, without mentioning his conflict of interest, he plugged Lytvyn. "[R]eliable research shows other parties may pass the 3 percent minimum threshold and join the Rada. Among them are the communists and the party of democratic reformer Volodymyr Lytvyn, former speaker of the Rada who kept the rowdy legislature from devolving into anarchy during the Orange Revolution. Rested and ready after losing re-election in 2006, he is a fresh face in a tired crowd of self-interested politicians."

There is a distinct possibility that Stone and Caputo supported the so-called "democratic reformer" Lytvyn to siphon votes away from Tymoshenko. This redounded to the benefit of Manafort's client, Viktor Yanukovych. Following the election, the Party of Regions won a plurality of the vote, while the Lytvyn bloc won 3.97%, enough to be seated in parliament.

A year after the election, Lytvyn joined a fractious "pro-West" coalition with Ukrainian President Viktor Yushchenko and Prime Minister Yulia Tymoshenko.[142] Ukraine was reeling from the 2008 financial crisis and desperately needed Western financial aid. After Yanukovych triumphed in the 2010 Ukrainian presidential election, Lytvyn switched sides. Tymoshenko accused Lytvyn of illegally exploiting a loophole to cause the collapse of her coalition.[143] Days later, the Lytvyn Bloc joined the Party of

Regions in a parliamentary coalition that solidified Yanukovych's control over Ukraine.[144] Lytvyn was awarded the Order of Friendship in Russia a year later.[145]

Stone and Caputo's experience in Ukraine was marred by violence. While Stone and Caputo had served as general consultants, their local campaign manager was a Ukrainian named Oleg Sheremet.[146] On election day, Sheremet was shot six times by an AK-47. He was assassinated in front of his children. It is unclear why Sheremet was murdered in such a gruesome fashion. It may have had something to do with a land dispute.

"In former Soviet Union races, nobody wants to see American faces," Caputo later wrote. "So global experts hide behind local managers who execute Western-standard campaign plans."

Caputo would know. He had more experience inside former Soviet states, including Russia, than both Manafort and Stone combined. Michael Caputo was born in Fort Bragg, NC, on March 4th, 1962. He joined the military and served as an enlisted public affairs specialist for the 25th Infantry Division in the U.S. Army from 1980 to 1983. While in the military, he came to support Ronald Reagan and joined the Republican Party.[147]

After leaving the Army, Caputo studied journalism and foreign affairs at the State University of New York (SUNY). In 1985, *The Buffalo News* reported that Caputo was among eight SUNY Buffalo students involved in secretly monitoring and taping "radical and liberal professors."[148] This was done at the behest of a group called Accuracy in Academia. Caputo acted as a liaison between SUNY Buffalo students and the Washington, DC-based group.

While he was liaising with Accuracy in Academia, Caputo formed a relationship with General Rahmatullah Safi, a senior figure with the Afghan mujahideen who fought against the Soviet invasion and later became an ambassador for the Taliban.[149] While Caputo described the time he knew Safi as his "college days," he was by that time a military veteran. Caputo claims that he first met Safi in 1984 at a conference in Washington, DC.

Following the Soviet invasion of Afghanistan, Safi was involved with Islamic resistance fighters known as the Mujahideen. Specifically, he was allied with The National Islamic Front of Afghanistan. The group was used by Pakistan's Inter-Services Intelligence (ISI) service to distribute CIA-funded weapons. Safi was also friends with Congressman Charlie Wilson (D-TX), a key figure behind U.S. funding of the mujahideen.

Caputo assisted Safi on a speaking tour that took him to various American universities, including SUNY Buffalo. In 1985, photos show that Caputo traveled to Peshawar with Safi. Caputo also traveled with Safi to London and Amsterdam. Their relationship extended into the 1990s, before allegedly coming to an end when Caputo moved to Moscow.

Around the time Caputo traveled to Peshawar with Safi, he met Roger Stone. It is unclear whether this was in 1985 or 1986. Their introduction was made possible by Caputo's connection to Buffalo Congressman Jack Kemp, a former quarterback for the Buffalo Bills. Caputo traveled to Washington, DC, in 1986 to work on Kemp's 1988 Presidential campaign. Stone has a long history in Buffalo politics. He worked on Jack Kemp's successful 1984 Congressional campaign and later advised Kemp's unsuccessful 1988 presidential campaign. Caputo claims he took a side job working for Black, Manafort, and Stone as a driver, where he met Stone.[150] The meeting made an enormous impression on Caputo, who describes Stone as his "best friend."[151]

Caputo also met Paul Manafort. The two bumped into each other in the office of Jack Kemp's political action committee. Their relationship has lasted thirty years and includes a number of business collaborations. Though Kemp's 1988 campaign failed, Caputo attended the Republican convention in New Orleans, where he first met Donald Trump.

In 1988, Caputo began working on the ground in Nicaragua, Honduras, and Costa Rica for the Reagan Administration's Council for Inter-American Security. The Council funded and supported the Nicaraguan Contras, a right-wing paramilitary organization accused of involvement in multiple atrocities. Caputo's role at the Council was to "craft the [Reagan] administration's anti-communism propaganda in Central and South America."[152]

Caputo "rubbed elbows" with Oliver North.[153] North was a member of Reagan's National Security Council and the central figure in the Iran-Contra Affair. A website for Caputo's PR company featured a photo of him standing with General Enrique Bermudez, the founder of the Contras. Another showed him standing on a tarmac with Oliver North in Central America.

Stone and Trump had brushes with individuals linked to Iran-Contra. Stone worked under William Casey, who became the CIA director under Reagan during the Iran-Contra period. Roger Stone's first wife, Ann Stone, was a specialist in direct-mail fundraising and had been mentored by Richard Viguerie, a pioneer of the practice. She and Viguerie engaged in direct-mail fundraising for the Contras.[154] Adolfo Calero, head of the Contras and their chief lobbyist for funds, specifically mentioned Ann Stone while testifying before Congress.[155] Calero was an associate of Oliver North. Following North's appearance before Congress, Ann Stone and Viguerie used North's testimony to raise funds for the Contras.

Trump interacted with another key figure Iran-Contra scandal, Saudi arms dealer Adnan Khashoggi. Khashoggi facilitated the Saudi-U.S. intelligence relationship, brokering billions of dollars of arms sales between the two countries.[156] In the late 70s, Trump attended a party in Khashoggi's Olympic Tower penthouse and subsequently ordered his architect to ensure that the dimensions of his penthouse in Trump Tower were larger. In 1989, Trump told *Vanity Fair* that he "read every word" he could about Khashoggi.[157] Trump purchased a 280-foot yacht from the Sultan of Brunei that belonged to Khashoggi, which he renamed the Trump Princess. Stone lobbied Atlantic City authorities to dredge the city's harbor so the yacht could be anchored outside of the Trump Castle.[158] Paul Manafort lobbied on behalf of the Saudis and was friends with Khashoggi's one-time brother-in-law and arms-dealing partner, Abdul Rahman al-Assir.

Caputo also worked on the presidential campaign of Alfredo Cristiani, a hard-right politician elected President of El Salvador in 1989.[159] In May of 1989, Caputo was working in Panama. A former SUNY Buffalo classmate of Caputo's named David Chodrow was forced the flee the country after Panamanian authorities caught him photographing polling locations. Caputo was coordinating with Chodrow while he was in Panama.[160] Chodrow, who died in 2021, was involved in the same Accuracy in Academia monitoring effort at SUNY Buffalo as Caputo.

In 1994, Caputo traveled to Moscow as a staffer for USAID.[161] Specifically, Caputo worked for the International Foundation for Electoral Systems (IFES), which was funded by

USAID. Roger Stone is connected to IFES's founder, F. Clifton White. In his book *Nixon's Secrets*, Stone states that he worked for F. Clifton White in New York in the 1970s. Stone may have met White through the Young Republicans. Roger and Ann Stone participated alongside White in the 1975 Young Republican Leadership Conference. In 1977, Stone was elected President of the Young Republicans. Paul Manafort had managed his campaign.

White worked with CIA director William Casey and CIA officer Walter Raymond on Project Democracy, a pro-Contra propaganda network.[162] In 1982, Reagan named F. Clifton White as the head of Radio Marti, a U.S. initiative meant to counter anti-American radio broadcasts coming out of Cuba.[163] Radio Marti had been set up by the United States Information Agency. USIA was a government agency with close ties to the intelligence community devoted to "public diplomacy" during the Cold War. On April 20th, 1982, Roy Cohn co-hosted a lunch in honor of USIA's director Charles Z. Wick. Attendees included Roger Stone and Richard Viguerie, who employed Stone's wife in pro-contra mailing campaigns.[164]

On January 18th, 1983, Cohn attended a meeting in the Oval Office and introduced Ronald Reagan to Rupert Murdoch. Murdoch's company News Corp., which owns Fox News, was one of Black, Manafort, and Stone's top corporate clients. Murdoch was recruited to support Casey's and Raymond's propaganda effort supporting Reagan's policies in Central America.[165] This was the very same effort F. Clifton White was also supporting.

A November 1986 memorandum from Walter Raymond, a former CIA officer and expert on clandestine overseas media operations, to National Security Advisor John Poindexter called for White to establish an organization that would focus on Central America. A year later, White founded the International Foundation for Electoral Systems (IFES).[166] Michael Caputo joined IFES sometime around 1994 when it had turned its attention from Central America to Russia.

While in Moscow, Caputo became fluent in Russian and married a Russian astrophysics student. The marriage ended in divorce. Caputo lived next to a Moscow cafe owned by the local mafia.[167] "Organized crime is everywhere in the former Soviet Union," Caputo wrote. "In the 1990s, I lived right next to my *krysha* — Russian for "roof," or the guy who doesn't let it rain on you. Businesses in our area of Moscow paid him monthly to stay dry. Apparently he liked me, because I got a pass. And our street was the safest in the area, if you could wheel your way through the dozen-plus black Mercedes lined up outside the local don's lair."

Caputo interacted with the highest levels of the Russian government. His main contact was Nikolai Ryabov, the first Deputy Prime Minister and chairman of the Federal Elections Commission. He also met with Boris Yeltsin and then-Deputy Mayor of St. Petersburg, Vladimir Putin. Caputo shared the dais with Putin at an event in St. Petersburg, ironically, on election law development. Caputo has claimed that he hosted Putin at a reception at his house in Russia.[168]

Caputo's tenure with IFES was short and controversial. In the lead-up to the 1996 election, the Russian Federal Election Commission took the controversial step of disqualifying several parties on the basis of a technicality.[169] This included Yabloko, a pro-reform party. The move inspired protests within Russia and without. Stanford professor Michael McFaul, the future American ambassador to Russia, described the decision as "totally concocted," and said that Nikolai "Ryabov would never do it without the approval of higher-ups."

Caputo, who was close to Ryabov and his aides, had a different take. "Just because Yabloko is the darling of the West doesn't mean they can operate with impunity," Caputo told *The Washington Post*. "If you violate the rules, you're out. That's democracy."

Caputo's defense of Ryabov's actions ran counter to the US State Department's policies in Russia. Embassy officials in Moscow requested that Caputo be removed from his position at IFES. Caputo's phone, fax machine, and office keys were confiscated and he was fired.[170] Despite being terminated from IFES, Caputo stayed in Russia and established his own public relations firm called the Florence Group. Florence represented various Russian politicians as well as companies seeking to do business in the former Soviet Union.

Caputo worked on Yeltsin's 1996 campaign, serving as his youth-vote director. He established "Choose or Lose," a televised program based on MTV's "Rock the Vote." Following Yeltsin's 1996 victory, Caputo pursued his PR business in Russia, describing himself as "the only executive in history who has worked for both the White House and the Kremlin."

In 2000, he returned to the United States and began working as a publicist on behalf of Renaissance Capital, Russia's largest private investment firm. Caputo's closest connection at Renaissance was a Russian-American billionaire named Boris Jordan. Jordan was a central figure in devising the "loans-for-shares" program, which led to the seizure of vast portions of Russia's natural resource wealth by a small group of oligarchs following Yeltsin's 1996 victory.

In February of 2001, on the recommendation of Boris Jordan, Caputo was hired by Gazprom Media, a subsidiary of Gazprom. Caputo represented Gazprom media's CEO Alfred Koch, working to improve his image in Washington, DC. Koch had served as a Deputy Prime Minister under Yeltsin. Despite technically working on behalf of Koch, Caputo was hired to convince American lawmakers that Putin wasn't consolidating his power over Russian media. In fact, that is exactly what Putin was doing. "I'm not proud of the work today," Caputo said in 2016. "But at the time, Putin wasn't such a bad guy."

In 2004, Paul Manafort enlisted Caputo to work on a project for Oleg Deripaska. According to Caputo, he worked on the project for ten days. Caputo attempted to get positive stories into the press on Deripaska's behalf but appears to have met with limited success.

In 2013, Caputo was involved in an effort to enlist Donald Trump to run for governor of New York. Roger Stone arranged for Caputo and a host of other Republicans to meet with Trump in December of 2013 at Trump Tower to discuss the possibility of him running against Andrew Cuomo in the upcoming New York gubernatorial race. While Trump claimed he only had five minutes, the meeting reportedly stretched into five hours.[171]

Trump decided against running but soon had use for Caputo in another venture: his attempt to purchase the Buffalo Bills NFL team. In 2014, Ralph Wilson, the owner of the Bills, died at the age of 95. Hardly a week passed before speculation began as to who would become the team's next owner. The list quickly narrowed down to three: Donald Trump, the billionaire owner of Buffalo's NHL team Terry Pegula, and 1980s rock icon Jon Bon Jovi, who represented a consortium of investors from

Toronto, Canada.

Aware he couldn't outbid Bon Jovi and his Canadians, Trump hired Caputo in the Spring of 2014 to manage a campaign to turn local Buffalo residents against the Bon Jovi bid. As part of this mission, Caputo created a "grass-roots" organization of Bills fans he originally named "12th Man Thunder" to attack Bon Jovi and support the Trump bid. The practice of creating artificial grassroots movements is known as "Astroturfing."

Around this time, Caputo and Bills Fan Thunder came into conflict with an eccentric, local Buffalo area blogger named James Kriger. The ensuing online conflict would lead to one of the more bizarre and intriguing episodes in the entire Caputo story. Kriger was a Buffalo Bills fan and wrote a blog called BuffaloBruises.com. After initially decrying Bon Jovi, Kriger set his sights on Caputo's 12th Man Thunder.[172] The conflict eventually got so bad that Caputo personally got involved in the spat. The group later successfully sued Kriger for defamation

Kriger's online war of words against Caputo gained the notice of an unusual third party. In November 2015, an anonymous Twitter account claiming to belong to an American intelligence officer in Belgium reached out to Kriger after having seen Caputo's tweets attacking him. "Figured it out," the anonymous account wrote to Kriger, "you're going to blog about him and it's good for our designs if you do."[173]

Between November and December of 2015, the anonymous Twitter account sent Kriger over 100 messages. According to *The Buffalo News*, the source possessed "surprisingly detailed knowledge of Caputo's movements in Russia and Europe and was familiar with some of his childhood friends and current partners."

The information the source sent to Kriger consisted of known facts about Caputo's life mixed in with unsubstantiated assertions. For example, the source told Kriger that Caputo had worked in Ukraine in 2007 on behalf of the Russian Federal Security Service. The account sent Kriger a copy of a supposedly Top Secret CIA document that described Caputo as a "Specialized Skills Officer" who retired from the CIA in July of 2006 after having defied orders. While the document reflected known facts, such as Caputo's relationship with General Rahmatullah Safi, it ventured into unsubstantiated allegations that Safi was affiliated with al-Qaeda.

After sharing the document with Kriger, the source suggested 19 specific Twitter accounts that he tweet the document to. Kriger ultimately only sent a single tweet about the document. Afterward, two anonymous Twitter accounts forwarded Kriger's tweet to various local, state, and national reporters who had written about Caputo in the past. The only publication that decided to write about the curious incident was *The Buffalo News*. When Kriger told the anonymous source that a reporter wanted to contact them, the source deleted their private Twitter correspondence.

The author of the article concluded that the document was a forgery. The Afghanistan experts she spoke with told her that there was no evidence Safi had any connection to al-Qaeda. The CIA sources she spoke with told her that the document contained irregularities, such as the wrong font and a lack of codenames, that established its inauthenticity. The only named source in the story is retired CIA officer Gary Berntsen. While Berntsen claimed the document was a forgery, he added, "Whoever is perpetrating this hoax is clearly a student of American intelligence work and spent considerable time building the damaging story."

This raises the obvious questions. Who was behind the stunt? We are left only to speculate. Presumably not Bills fans in Toronto. While the document might be a forgery, what is the nature of Caputo's relationship with the American intelligence community?

Berntsen told Tan that Caputo had never been a CIA agent. It's perhaps only a tiny detail, but the official term used within the CIA is "officer" rather than "agent." The article describes Berntsen as being "acquainted" with Caputo. In fact, Berntsen had known Caputo since at least 2010. At that time, Berntsen was running in the Republican Senate primary and hoping to take on Democrat Chuck Schumer in the general election. "Gubernatorial candidate Carl Paladino and I had grown close to Berntsen, a military and CIA veteran decorated for combat heroism in Afghanistan," Caputo wrote in his blog.

Berntsen had a remarkable career in the CIA, which spanned from 1982 to 2006. He served as CIA head of station three times, including in Latin America.[174] Most notably, he was part of the CIA team that pursued Osama Bin Laden and al-Qaeda to the cave complex of Tora Bora in Afghanistan.

Berntsen wrote about the experience in *Jawbreaker: The Attack on Bin Laden and Al-Qaeda: A Personal Account by the CIA's Key Field Commander.*

In 2016, the Associated Press reported that Berntsen was a co-owner of a business partnership called Denx LLC. The other owners were another former CIA officer, Scott Modell, and an Iranian-born American citizen, Farzad Azima. According to AP, Azima was a CIA-linked gunrunner who had been involved in the Iran-Contra Affair.

The strange story of the "CIA document" never traveled beyond the local Buffalo press. Donald Trump failed in his bid to buy the Bills, but Caputo succeeded in derailing Bon Jovi anyway. In fact, he succeeded in souring the 80s rocker on Buffalo altogether. "I won't ever go back to the city of Buffalo," Bon Jovi stated in an interview. "You will never see my face in Buffalo ever. I have knocked it off the map."

Donald Trump now had bigger fish to fry. He was running to be the President of the United States. When Paul Manafort became Trump's chairman, the first person he hired to manage the New York State Primary was his and Roger Stone's old friend Michael Caputo. In May 2016, Caputo reached out to Stone to let him know that he had learned through a Russian business partner that another Florida-based Russian claimed to possess derogatory information on Hillary Clinton.[175] Caputo arranged an in-person between Stone and a Florida-based Russian national named Henry Oknyansky (AKA Henry Greenberg), who claimed to have access to derogatory information related to Hillary Clinton.[176]

Oknyansky had a colorful past. After marrying a Russian actress and moving to Los Angeles, in 1994 he was arrested and charged with assault with a deadly weapon, after which he entered a plea in which he was convicted without accepting guilt. After returning to Russia in 2000, he shared a fashionable Moscow address with John Daly, a British film producer[177] In 2002, Moscow authorities arrested Oknyansky on charges related to a $2.7 million fraud, and he was reportedly found with three fake passports under assumed names. According to a court filing, Oknyansky cooperated with the FBI for 17 years, though that cooperation ended in 2013. There is no evidence to suggest that his interactions with Caputo and Stone were done at the behest or with the knowledge of the FBI.

Oknyansky was accompanied to his meeting with Stone at a restaurant in Sunny Isles, FL, by a Ukrainian named Alexei Rasin, who had worked with Oknyansky in Florida real estate. According to *The Washington Post*, Rasin told Stone that he had been fired from the Clinton Foundation and possessed damaging information on Hillary. The Clinton Foundation has claimed that it never employed anyone named Alexei Rasin. The Special Counsel's Office, which found no evidence that Rasin had any connection to the Clintons, wrote that Rasin told Stone that he had possessed documents showing that Hillary Clinton had used his companies for money laundering purposes. Raisin offered to sell the materials to the Trump campaign.

"You don't understand Donald Trump," Stone replied. "He doesn't pay for anything."

"How crazy is the Russian," Caputo texted Stone following the meeting.

"Wants big [$] for info," Stone replied. "[W]aste of time."

"The Russia way," Caputo wrote back. "Anything at all interesting."

"No," Stone replied. Stone's interactions with Russians, however, were only beginning.

[1] Foer, Franklin. "Paul Manafort, American Hustler," *The Atlantic*. March 2018 Issue
[2] Stewart, Patricia. "Young Interns Work For Central Committee," *The Hartford Courant*. August 21st, 1971
[3] Roig-Franzia, Manuel. "The Swamp Builders," THE WASHINGTON POST. November 29th, 2018
[4] Foer, Franklin. "Paul Manafort, American Hustler," *The Atlantic*. March 2018 Issue
[5] "Joseph 'Pippi' Guerrier; Gambler," *The Hartford Courant*. April 9th, 1993
[6] Dorman, Michael. "Malaise In High Places (Part 1)," CONNECTICUT MAGAZINE. March 1976
[7] Austin McGuigan's Congressional Testimony: https://www.govinfo.gov/content/pkg/CHRG-107hhrg78662/html/CHRG-107hhrg78662.htm
[8] REPORT TO THE PRESIDENT AND THE ATTORNEY GENERAL — THE EDGE: ORGANIZED CRIME, BUSINESS, AND LABOR UNIONS. President's Commission on Organized Crime. September 29th, 1986
[9] "It's Not Me — Manafort," The Journal, October 10th, 1975
[10] "Oversight Hearing on Organized Crime Strike Forces," Hearing Before the Subcommittee on Criminal Justice of the Committee on the Judiciary, House of Representatives, One Hundred First Congress, First Session, June 20, 1989
[11] "Text of the Grand Jury Report on Jai Alai Hearing," *The Hartford Courant*, January 13th, 1976, Pages 6–8
[12] Foer, Franklin. "Paul Manafort, American Hustler," *The Atlantic*. March 2008
[13] Alan, Emory. "Democrats Doubt the Independence of Conservative Money-Baggers," The Washington Post. December 31st, 1981
[14] Gross, Terry. "How the American right became aligned with Hungary and its authoritarian leader," *NPR*. July 13th, 2022

[15] Choate, Pat. *Agents of Influence: How Japan's Lobbyists In The United States Manipulate America's Political And Economic System.* New York, NY: Alfred A. Knopf, 1990. Pg. 124

[16] Foer, Franklin. "Paul Manafort, American Hustler," *The Atlantic.* March 2008

[17] Shear, Michael D.; Birnbaum, Jeffrey H. "McCain Advisor's Work As Lobbyist Criticized," *The Washington Post.* May 22nd, 2008

[18] Brogan, Pamela. "The Torturer's Lobby: How Human Rights-Abusing Nations Are Represented in Washington," *The Center for Public Integrity.* 1992. Pg. 1

[19] Ho, Catherine. "From Ukraine to Trump Tower, Paul Manafort unafraid to take on controversial jobs," *The Washington Post.* April 7th, 2016

[20] Vogel, Keneth P. "Paul Manafort's Wild and Lucrative Philippine Adventure," *Politico Magazine.* June 10th, 2016

[21] Vogel, Keneth P. "Paul Manafort's Wild and Lucrative Philippine Adventure," *Politico Magazine.* June 10th, 2016

[22] Roig-Franzia, Manuel. "The Swamp Builders: How Stone and Manafort helped create the mess Trump promised to clean up," *The Washington Post.* November 29th, 2018

[23] Schwartz, Mattathias. "Paul Manafort Isn't Sorry," *Business Insider.* August 7th, 2022

[24] Foer, Franklin. "Paul Manafort, American Hustler," *The Atlantic.* March 2008

[25] "US consultant admits role in France's 'Karachi Affair,'" *France 24.* April 8th, 2013

[26] Foer, Franklin. "The Quiet American," *Slate.* April 28th, 2016

[27] Isikoff, Michael. "Top Trump aide lobbied for Pakistani spy front," *Yahoo News.* April 18th, 2016

[28] Burns, Alexander; Haberman, Maggie. "Mystery man: Ukraine's U.S. fixer," *Politico.* March 5th, 2014

[29] Foer, Franklin. "Paul Manafort, American Hustler," *The Atlantic.* March 2008

[30] Brennan, Zoe. "The richest Rothschild of them all," *The Daily Mail.* April 1st, 2007

[31] Dovkants, Keith. "Nat the ex-playboy set to be central character in Corfu holiday saga," *The Evening Standard.* October 21st, 2008

[32] Hollingsworth, Mark; Lansley, Stewart. *Londongrad: From Russia With Cash The Inside Story Of The Oligarchs.* London, UK: Fourth Estate, 2009. Pg. 56

[33] HIGH COURT OF JUSTICE, QUEENS BENCH DIVISION, COMMERCIAL COURT. MICHAEL CHERNEY (Claimant) - and - OLEG VLADIMIROVICH DERIPASKA (Defendant). CLAIMANT'S WRITTEN OPENING SUBMISSIONS FOR TRAIL. Case No 2006 Folio 1218

[34] Multiple spelling variations of Mikail Chernoy's name can be found used in various court documents and publications , including Michael Cherney, Mikhail Cherney, Mikhail Chernoi, Mikhail Chornoy, Mikhail Chorny, etc. The author has selected Mikhail Chernoy for continuity sake.

[35] Bell, Simon. "First oligarch claims his due," *The Guardian.* June 2nd, 2007

[36] Royce, Knut. "FBI Tracked Alleged Russian Mob Ties of Giuliani Campaign Supporter," *Center for Public Integrity.* December 14th, 1999

[37] Royce, Knut. "FBI Tracked Alleged Russian Mob Ties of Giuliani Campaign Supporter," *Center for Public Integrity.* December 14th, 1999

[38] UNITED STATES DISTRICT COURT FOR THE DISTRICT COURT OF DELAWARE. Davis International LLC et al. (Plaintiffs) -against- New Start Group Corp, et al. (Defendants). No. 44-1482-GMS. DECLARATION OF ROBERT A. LEVINSON

[39] Robinson, James. "Pack up your roubles…," *The Guardian.* June 26th, 2004

[40] Satter, David. *Darkness At Dawn: The Rise Of The Russian Criminal State.* New Haven, CT: Yale University Press, 2003. Pg. 183

[41] Behar, Richard. "Capitalism In A Cold Climate," *Fortune Magazine.* June 12th, 2000

[42] Satter, David. *Darkness At Dawn: The Rise Of The Russian Criminal State.* New Haven, CT: Yale University Press, 2003. Pg. 184

[43] Satter, David. *Darkness At Dawn: The Rise Of The Russian Criminal State.* New Haven, CT: Yale University Press, 2003. Pg. 185-189

44 Barnes, Andrew. *Owning Russia: The Struggle Over Factories, Farms, And Power*. Ithaca and London: Cornell University Press, 2006. Pg. 192

45 Belton, Catherine. "Rusal: a lingering heat," *The Financial Times*. January 25th, 2010

46 "Spanish report on Deripaska and Chernoy's connection to organized crime and Russian political power, (English Translation)" *Transborder Corruption Archive*. November 26th, 2019

47 06MOSCOW12713_a. Public Library of US Diplomacy - Wikileaks

48 Glenny, Misha; Booth, Robert; Parfitt, Tom. "US refused oligarch visa over alleged criminal associations," *The Guardian*. October 30th, 2008

49 Hollingsworth, Mark; Lansley, Stewart. *Londongrad: From Russia With Cash The Inside Story Of The Oligarchs*. London, UK: Fourth Estate, 2009. Pg. 329-330

50 Mattews, Owen. "The Frightening Fall of Russia's Richest Man," *Newsweek*. April 3rd, 2009

51 Simpson, Glenn R.; Jacoby, Mary. "How Lobbyists Help Ex-Soviets Woo Washington," *The Wall Street Journal*. April 17t, 2007

52 Forrest, Brett. "Paul Manafort's Overseas Political Work Had a Notable Patron: A Russian Oligarch," *The Wall Street Journal*. August 30th, 2017

53 Cathcart, Will. "Who Blew Out a CIA Spy's Brains? A New Book Fingers His Best Friend," *The Daily Beast*. December 2nd, 2018

54 Forrest, Brett. "Paul Manafort's Overseas Political Work Had a Notable Patron: A Russian Oligarch," *The Wall Street Journal*. August 30th, 2017

55 Foer, Franklin. "Paul Manafort, American Hustler," *The Atlantic*. March 2008

56 Forrest, Brett. "Paul Manafort's Overseas Political Work Had a Notable Patron: A Russian Oligarch," *The Wall Street Journal*. August 30th, 2017

57 Kovensky, Josh. "In Manafort's World, Everyone Had A Price," *The Kyiv Post*. October 12th, 2018

58 UNITED STATES OF AMERICA v. PAUL J. MANAFORT, JR. (Defendant). CRIMINAL NO. 17-201-1 (ABJ_(S-5) SUPERSEDING CRIMINAL INFORMATION. GOVERNMENT EXHIBIT 532

59 Bertrand, Natasha. "Newly obtained flight records shed light on Paul Manafort's extensive Russia ties," Business Insider. November 25th, 2017

60 Harding, Luke. "How Trump's campaign chief got a strongman elected president of Ukraine," *The Guardian*. August 16th, 2016

61 Foer, Franklin. "The Astonishing Tale of the Man Mueller Calls 'Person A,'" *The Atlantic*. June 6th, 2018

62 Vogel, Kenneth. P. "Mueller Adds Obstruction Charge on Manafort and Indicts His Right-Hand Man," *The New York Times*. June 8th, 2018

63 Press Release. "Treasury Escalates Sanctions Against the Russian Government's Attempts to Influence U.S. Elections," US Department of the Treasury. April 15th, 2021

64 Miller, Christopher. "'Person A' In His Own Words: On The Record With Shadowy Operative In Russia Probe," *RadioFreeEurope/RadioLiberty*. April 6th, 2018

65 Vogel, Kenneth P.; Kramer, Andrew E. "Russian Spy or Hustling Political Operative? The Enigmatic Figure at the Heart of Mueller's Inquiry," *The New York Times*. February 23rd, 2019

66 Vogel, Kenneth P. "Manafort's man in Kiev," *Politico*. August 18th, 2016

67 Mcintire, Mike, "Democracy institute gives donors access to McCain," *The New York Times*. June 28th, 2008

68 Vogel, Kenneth P.; Kramer, Andrew E. "Russian Spy or Hustling Political Operative? The Enigmatic Figure at the Heart of Mueller's Inquiry," *The New York Times*. February 23rd, 2019

69 PERMANENT SELECT COMMITTEE ON INTELLIGENCE joint with the COMMITTEE ON OVERSIGHT AND REFORM and the COMMITTEE ON FOREIGN AFFAIRS, U.S. HOUSE OF REPRESENTATIVES, WASHINGTON,

DC. DEPOSITION OF: FIONA HILL. October 14th, 2019

[70] Zholobova, Maria; Badanin, Roman. "The Absolute Soviet Man: A Portrait of Konstantin Kilimnik, Russian patriot and Paul Manafort's Buddy," *Proekt*. August 22nd, 2018

[71] Vogel, Kenneth P.; Kramer, Andrew E. "Russian Spy or Hustling Political Operative? The Enigmatic Figure at the Heart of Mueller's Inquiry," *The New York Times*. February 23rd, 2019

[72] Zholobova, Maria; Badanin, Roman. "The Absolute Soviet Man: A Portrait of Konstantin Kilimnik, Russian patriot and Paul Manafort's Buddy," *Proekt*. August 22nd, 2018

[73] Vogel, Kenneth P. "Manafort's man in Kiev," *Politico*. August 18th, 2016

[74] Vogel, Kenneth P.; Kramer, Andrew E. "Russian Spy or Hustling Political Operative? The Enigmatic Figure at the Heart of Mueller's Inquiry," *The New York Times*. February 23rd, 2019

[75] Stone, Peter. "Konstantin Kilimnik: elusive Russian with ties to Manafort faces fresh Mueller scrutiny," *The Guardian*. November 9th, 2018

[76] Foer, Franklin. "The Astonishing Tale of the Man Mueller Calls 'Person A,'" *The Atlantic*. June 6th, 2018

[77] Forrest, Brett. "Paul Manafort's Overseas Political Work Had a Notable Patron: A Russian Oligarch," *The Wall Street Journal*. August 30th, 2017

[78] Bateson, Ian. "What Exactly Did Paul Manafort Do to Earn That $66 Million?" *New York Magazine*. November 11th, 2018

[79] 06KIEV473_a. Library of American Diplomacy - Wikileaks

[80] Horwitz, Jeff; Day, Chad. "AP Exclusive: Before Trump job, Manafort worked to aid Putin," *The Associated Press*. March 22nd, 2017

[81] Shuster, Simon. "Exclusive: Russian Ex-Spy Pressured Manafort Over Debts to an Oligarch," *Time Magazine*. December 29th, 2018

[82] Ames, Mark; Berman, Ari. "McCain's Kremlin Ties," *The Nation*. October 1st, 2008

[83] Shuster, Simon. "Exclusive: Russian Ex-Spy Pressured Manafort Over Debts to an Oligarch," *Time Magazine*. December 29th, 2018

[84] "Treasury Targets Russian Operative Over Election Interference, World Anti-Doping Agency Hacking, And Other Malign Activities," Press Release. *U.S. Department of the Treasury*. December 19th, 2018

[85] Ames, Mark; Berman, Ari. "McCain's Kremlin Ties," *The Nation*. October 1st, 2008

[86] Wolf, Jim. "U.S. revoked Deripaska visa - State Dep't official," *Reuters*. May 11th, 2007

[87] Ames, Mark; Berman, Ari. "McCain's Kremlin Ties," *The Nation*. October 1st, 2008

[88] Goldman, Adam; Benner, Katie. "Bruce Ohr Fought Russian Organized Crime. Now He's a Target of Trump." *The New York Times*. August 27th, 2018

[89] Birnbaum, Jeffrey H.; Solomon, John. "Aide Helped Controversial Russian Meet McCain," *The Washington Post*. January 25th, 2008

[90] Ames, Mark; Berman, Ari. "McCain's Kremlin Ties," *The Nation*. October 1st, 2008

[91] Swan, Betsy. "The Wacky Tale of Paul Manafort, Anne Hathaway's Fraudster Ex-Boyfriend, and a Vatican Land Scam," *The Daily Beast*. March 13th, 2019

[92] Birnbaum, Jeffrey H.; Solomon, John. "Aide Helped Controversial Russian Meet McCain," *The Washington Post*. January 25th, 2008

[93] Nasaw, Daneil. "McCain accused of accepting improper donations from Rothschilds," *The Guardian*. April 28th, 2008

[94] Hollingsworth, Mark; Lansley, Stewart. *Londongrad: From Russia With Cash The Inside Story Of The Oligarchs*. London, UK: Fourth Estate, 2009. Pg. 336

[95] Foer, Franklin. "The Quiet American," *Slate*. April 28th, 2016

[96] Confessore, Nicholas; Meier, Barry. "How the Russia Investigation Entangled Rick Gates, a Manafort Protégé," *The New York Times*. June 16th, 2017

[97] Foer, Franklin. "Paul Manafort, American Hustler," *The Atlantic*. March 2008

[98] IN THE GRAND COURT OF THE CAYMAN ISLANDS. FINANCIAL SERVICES DIVISION. CAUSE NO. 0131 OF 2014

[99] Mufson, Steven; Hamburger, Tom. "Inside Trump adviser Manafort's world of politics and global financial dealmaking," *The Washington Post*. April 26th, 2016

[100] Angerer, Drew. "Trump's campaign manager haunted by business past," *The Kyiv Post*. July 8th, 2016

[101] Angerer, Drew. "Trump's campaign manager haunted by business past," *The Kyiv Post*. July 8th, 2016

[102] Bradley, Jane; Bullough, Oliver; "The Ghost Companies Connected To Suspected Money Laundering, Corruption, And Paul Manafort," *BuzzFeed News*. August 23rd, 2018

[103] Biscevic, Tanya. "Swedbank's Shady business in Estonia," *Organized Crime and Corruption Reporting Project (OCCRP)*. March 19th, 2019

[104] Uranie, Sharon. "Seychelles investigates reports of money laundered in the country by former Ukrainian President," *Seychelles News Agency*. April 13th, 2014

[105] IN THE GRAND COURT OF THE CAYMAN ISLANDS. FINANCIAL SERVICES DIVISION. CAUSE NO. 0131 OF 2014. Pg. 12

[106] Ackerman, Spencer; Markay, Lachlan. "Paul Manafort South $850 Million Deal With Putin Ally and Alleged Gangster," *The Daily Beast*. August 14th, 2017

[107] Clarke, Katherine; Parker, Will. "Meet Paul Manafort's real estate fixer," *The Real Deal*. August 31st, 2017

[108] Dilanian, Ken; Winter, Tom; Abou-Sabe, Kenzi. "Ex-Trump Aide Manafort Bought New York Homes With Cash," *NBC News*. March 29th, 2017

[109] Foer, Franklin. "The Quiet American," *Slate*. April 28th, 2016

[110] Eckel, Mike; Miller, Christopher. "The Metals Magnate and Manafort: A Kremlin Confidant Is Drawn Into The Trump Investigation," *RadioFreeEurope/RadioLiberty*. September 22, 2017

[111] Kusisto, Laura. "Unmasking Three Mismatched Heavies Who Won and Lost the Drake," *Commercial Observer*. June 7th, 2011

[112] Abou-Sabe, Kenzi; Winter, Tom; Tucker, Max. "What Did Ex-Trump Aide Paul Manafort Really Do in Ukraine?" *NBC News*. June 27th, 2017

[113] Foer, Franklin. "The Quiet American," *Slate*. April 28th, 2016

[114] Baker, Stephanie. "Democratic Consultants to Get Dragged Into Manafort Trial," *Bloomberg*. July 20th, 2018

[115] Burns, Alexander; Haberman, Maggie. "Mystery man: Ukraine's U.S. fixer," *Politico*. March 5th, 2014

[116] Bateson, Ian. "What Exactly Did Paul Manafort Do to Earn That $66 Million?" *New York Magazine*. November 11th, 2018

[117] Leshchenko, Serhiy. "Cote d'Azur: how Lyovochkin's villa near Nice led to the deal with Ukrtelecom," *Ukrainska Pravda*. January 16th, 2016

[118] Matuszak, Sławomir. "The Oligarchic Democracy: The Influence of Business Groups On Ukrainian Politics," OSW Studies, Number 42. Centre for Eastern Studies. September 2012. Pg. 37-28

[119] Åslund, Anders. "The Maidan and Beyond: Oligarchs, Corruption, And European Integration," *Journal of Democracy, Volume 25, Number 3*. July 2014

[120] Foer, Franklin. "Paul Manafort, American Hustler," *The Atlantic*. March 2008

[121] Interfax-Ukraine. "EU-Ukraine association deal might hit ratification problems if Tymoshenko situation remains unchanged," *The Kyiv Post*. September 5th, 2011

[122] Gerstein, Josh. "Craig worked with Manafort aide that FBI links to Russian intelligence," *Politico*. June 24th, 2019

[123] United States of America v Paul J. Manafort Jr. (Defendant). STATEMENT OF THE OFFENSES AND OTHER ACTS. September 14th, 2018. Pg. 7-8

[124] Tibon, Amir. "Manafort and Senior Israeli Official Meddled in Ukraine, Obama Foreign Policy," *Haaretz*. September 14th, 2018

[125] Wilner, Michael. "Mueller: Manafort used 'Obama's Jews' to smear Ukrainian leader," *The Jerusalem Post*. September 14th, 2018

[126] TOI Staff. "Liberman blames anti-Russian racism for accusation he aided Manafort scheme," *The Times of Israel*. September 20th, 2018

[127] Mitnick, Joshua. "Meet Israel's New Kingmaker," *Foreign Policy*. August 18th, 2019

[128] Levy, Clifford J. "Israel's Foreign Minister Cozies Up To Moscow," *The New York Times*. June 13th, 2009

[129] Swan, Betsy; Markay, Lachlan. "Inside the Shadowy Think Tank Tied to Paul Manafort," *The Daily Beast*. September 19th, 2018

[130] United States of America v Paul J. Manafort Jr. (Defendant). STATEMENT OF THE OFFENSES AND OTHER ACTS. September 14th, 2018. Pg. 10

[131] Vogel, Kenneth P. "Russia Scandal Befalls Two Brothers: John and Tony Podesta," *The New York Times*. November 10th, 2017

[132] Swan, Betsy. "How a Champion of Democracy Became a Manafort Flack," *The Daily Beast*. March 3rd, 2018

[133] Meyer, Theodoric; Gerstein, Josh. "Manafort associate proposed hiring German, Spanish politicians to lobby on Ukraine," *Politico*. June 13th, 2018

[134] Meyer, Theodric; Gerstein, Josh. "Former Austrian chancellor appears to have lobbied as part of Manafort scheme," *Politico*. February 23rd, 2018

[135] Stack, Graham. "Exposed: The Ukrainian Politician Who Funded Paul Manafort's Secret EU Lobbying Campaign," *Organized Crime and Corruption Reporting Project*. November 4th, 2019

[136] Kovensky, Josh. "Dirty Money: Manafort trial exposes seedy realities of Ukrainian politics," *The Kyiv Post*. August 10th, 2018

[137] Labash, Matt. "Roger Stone, Political Animal," *The Washington Examiner*. November 5th, 2007

[138] "Key Suspect in Gongadze Murder Arrested: Pukach Allegedly Strangled Journalist, But Who Gave Order?" *The Kyiv Post*. July 22nd, 2009

[139] "Ex-Minister Linked to Journalist Slaying Found Dead in Ukraine," *The New York Times*. March 5th, 2005

[140] Olearchyk, Roman. "Kiev police chief jailed for Gongadze murder," *The Financial Times*. January 29th, 2013

[141] Caputo, Michael. "Ukraine Elections," The Washington Times. September 12th, 2007

[142] Olearchyk, Roman. "Ukraine unveils pro-west coalition," *The Financial Times*. December 9th, 2008

[143] Olearchyk, Roman. "Ukraine's ruling coalition collapses," *The Financial Times*. March 2nd, 2010

[144] Olearchyk, Roman. "Yanukovych tightens grip on Ukraine," *The Financial Times*. March 11th, 2010

[145] Interfax-Ukraine. "Lytvyn awarded Order of Friendship in Russia," *The Kyiv Post*. May 16th, 2011

[146] Caputo, Michael. "Crimea River, Kiev," *Artvoice*. March 27th, 2014

[147] Graham, Tim. "Michael Caputo emerges from high-stakes testimony on Capitol Hill unbowed," *The Buffalo News*. July 16th, 2017

[148] Anzalone, Charles. "Students Secretly Monitor UB Professors for Liberal Bias," *The Buffalo News*. December 1st, 1985

[149] Tan, Sandra. "The strange (made-up) story of Caputo the spy," *The Buffalo News*. March 6th, 2016

[150] McCarthy, Thomas J. "Michael Caputo banned from Roger Stone's Buffalo fundraiser," *The Buffalo News*. September 12th, 2019

[151] "Transcript: Former Trump campaign aide Michael Caputo's interview on "The Investigation" podcast," ABC News. April 30th, 2019

[152] Williams, Zach. "How Michael Caputo learned the dark art of politics," *City & State*

New York. September 15th, 2020

153 Tan, Sandra. "The radical adventures of conservative radio host Michael Caputo," *The Buffalo News*. March 5th, 2016

154 Edsall, Thomas B. "Conservative Fundraisers Face Red Ink," *The Washington Post*. January 15th, 1986

155 Senate Report No. 2016. IRAN-CONTRA INVESTIGATION, Appendix B, Vol. 3. Depositions. Pg. 194

156 Isikoff, Michael. "Arms, Harems, and a Trump-owned Yacht: How a Khashoggi family member helped mold the U.S.-Saudi relationship," Yahoo News. June 17th, 2021

157 Dunne, Dominick. "Khashoggi's Fall," *Vanity Fair*. September 1989

158 Breslow, James M. "The FRONTLINE interview: Roger Stone," PBS. September 27th, 2016

159 Jordan, Rob. "Commie Book Ban," *Miami New Times*. August 10th, 2006

160 Turner, Douglas. "Ex-UB Student Flees Panama Poll Observer Learned That His Arrest Was Planned," *The Buffalo News*. May 12th, 1989

161 Miller, James. "Trump and Russia: All the Mogul's Men," The Daily Beast. November 7th, 2016

162 Robinson, William I. *A Faustian Bargain: U.S. Intervention in Nicaraguan Elections and American Foreign Policy in the post-Cold War Era*. Westview Press. San Francisco, CA. 1992

163 "Radio Marti Head Named," *The New York Times*. January 20th, 1982

164 https://consortiumnews.com/wp-content/uploads/2015/01/Cohn-Wick4.pdf

165 Parry, Robert. "How Roy Cohn Helped Rupert Murdoch," Consortium News. January 28th, 2015

166 "International Foundation for Electoral Systems," *Militarist Monitor*. Published by the International Relations Center/Interhemispheric Resource Center. January 11th, 1989

167 Tan, Sandra. "The radical adventures of conservative radio host Michael Caputo," *The Buffalo News*. March 5th, 2016

168 Graff, Garrett M. "Former Trump Campaign Aide: My Russia Ties Are Not Nefarious!" *Wired*. May 25th, 2018

169 Hockstader, Lee. "Russia Election Board Disqualifies Reform Party," *The Washington Post*. October 30th, 1995

170 Kamen, Al. "Toasting Democracy in Moscow," *The Washington Post*. November 27th, 1995

171 McCarthy, Robert J. "David DiPietro Knows N-27 and says Trump loyalty is ticket in," *The Buffalo News*. November 23rd, 2019

172 Sesom, J.B. "Blogger Nightmare: No Good Deed Goes Unpunished," *Artvoice*. January 28th, 2016

173 Tan, Sandra. "The strange (made-up) story of Caputo the spy," *The Buffalo News*. March 6th, 2016

174 Faddis, Charles. *Beyond Repair: The Decline and Fall of the CIA*. Lyons Press: New York, NY. 2009. Pg. 11

175 Roig-Franzia, Manuel; Helderman, Rosalind S. "Trump associate Roger Stone reveals new contact with Russian national during 2016 campaign," *The Washington Post*. June 17th, 2018

176 Mueller, III, Robert S. *Report On The Investigation Into Russian Interference In The 2016 Presidential Election*. Department of Justice, Washington, DC. March 2019. Pg. 61

177 Roig-Franzia, Manuel; Helderman, Rosalind S. "Trump associate Roger Stone reveals new contact with Russian national during 2016 campaign," *The Washington Post*. June 17th, 2018

Chapter 15:
Roger Stone, Russian Military Intelligence, and WikiLeaks

By April or May of 2016, months before WikiLeaks released the DNC and John Podesta's emails, Roger Stone repeatedly told Donald Trump and senior members of his campaign that WikiLeaks would release information harmful to Clinton.[1] Stone was in contact with Guccifer 2.0, the online cutout for the GRU. He was also in contact with WikiLeaks both before and after the election. Due to Stone's use of encrypted messaging applications during this timeframe, the full extent of these communications is impossible to determine.

The Trump Campaign saw Stone as an "access point" to WikiLeaks.[2] On August 21st, 2016, over a month before WikiLeaks released John Podesta's emails, Stone tweeted: "Trust me, it will soon the [sic] Podesta's time in the barrel." This tweet, in tandem with Stone's public claims of having an "intermediary" with WikiLeaks, as well as claims Stone made of speaking to Assange, inspired suspicions and later investigations into Stone's relationship with WikiLeaks.

Stone was later convicted of having lied to the House Intelligence Committee regarding his supposed "intermediary" with WikiLeaks, among several other matters. These lies raise the simple question: *what does Roger Stone have to hide?* Federal and Congressional investigations were unable to provide a satisfactory answer to this question. On July 10th, 2020, Trump pardoned Stone for multiple crimes, including lying to Congress and witness tampering.

As always with Stone, his pathological dishonesty and courting of infamy muddy the waters. It is possible that he had no real connection to WikiLeaks, but rather was attempting to attract media attention and curry favor with the Trump campaign by claiming that he did. However, his prescience raises serious questions. As we shall see, he interacted with multiple individuals with varying degrees of access to WikiLeaks. He may also have learned about the GRU and WikiLeaks' plans from other sources, including Israelis linked to Benjamin Netanyahu, or perhaps even from Russian military intelligence itself.

Potential WikiLeaks Intermediaries and the Redacted Israelis

In the Spring of 2016, before Julian Assange made any announcements regarding Clinton-related email releases, Stone began informing the Trump campaign that WikiLeaks would release materials damaging to Hillary's campaign.[3] According to Trump's Deputy Campaign Manager, Rick Gates, as early as April 2016, Stone stated that WikiLeaks would release Democratic documents that would help the Trump campaign.[4] "Mr. Stone indicated that WikiLeaks would be submitting or dropping information but no information on dates or anything of that nature," Gates later testified in court.[5]

In mid-May, Jerome Corsi introduced Stone to Theodore Roosevelt Malloch, a conservative American author and consultant living in the UK. Corsi had been involved in publishing Malloch's memoir, which *The Financial Times* found to be riddled with exaggerations and inaccuracies.[6] Malloch arrived in New York on May 15th hoping to meet with Trump and or campaign chairman Paul Manafort, whom Stone played a role in getting hired.

Malloch, who was friendly with pro-Brexit politicians with links to Julian Assange, later came under scrutiny over whether he served as Stone and Corsi's connection to WikiLeaks. Malloch wanted a policy role in the Trump campaign, so Corsi connected him with Stone.[7] Corsi forwarded Stone a message from Malloch asking about the possibility of going to Trump Tower and meeting either Trump or Manafort.

"May meet Manafort," Stone replied, "guarantee nothing."[8]

Stone, Corsi, and Malloch dined at the New York

restaurant Strip House. Stone has given conflicting accounts of their discussion, telling *Business Insider* they discussed "Brexit and globalism" but that Julian Assange and WikiLeaks were not brought up.[9] However, Stone later told ABC News that Malloch "had dropped Assange's name."[10] Stone then told Fox News that Malloch "mentioned that he knew Assange."[11]

When asked during his first interview with the Special Counsel's Office whether he had communicated with Corsi and Stone, Malloch lied and said he had never done so. However, Malloch was allowed to "correct" his statement during his second interview.[12] In addition to Brexit, globalism, and Malloch's relationship with Assange, Stone asked Malloch to look into claims that Bill Clinton had been dismissed from the Rhodes Scholar program at Oxford after raping a female graduate student.[13]

The next day, Corsi and Malloch travelled to Trump Tower, where they met with as-yet unidentified Trump campaign staffers. "[Malloch] and I did manage to see Mr. Trump for a few minutes today as we were waiting in Trump Tower to say hello to Mike Cohen." Corsi wrote in an email to Stone later that day. "Mr. Trump recognized us immediately and was very cordial. He would look for this memo from you this afternoon." It isn't clear what memo Corsi refers to, though he appears to have added an attachment to his email for Stone to review.[14]

Contemporaneous with his meetings with Corsi and Malloch, Stone also interacted with foreign nationals from Israel. This information comes from a redacted FBI search warrant. On May 17th, Stone was contacted by an Israeli whose name is redacted. The Redacted Israeli knew Jerome Corsi, a rabid supporter of Israel. In his book, *SPYFAIL: Foreign Spies, Moles, Saboteurs, and the Collapse of America's Counterintelligence*, James Bamford suggests that the profile of the redacted Israeli is similar to that of Isaac Molho, an attorney used by Israeli Prime Minister Benjamin Netanyahu for sensitive intelligence and diplomatic assignments.[15]

"Hi Roger, I hope all is well," the Redacted Israeli wrote to Stone on the evening of May 17th. "Our dinner tonight for 7 PM is confirmed. I arrive at 4 PM. Please suggest a good restaurant that has privacy. Thank you. See you soon."

Stone and the Redacted Israeli dined together on either May 17th or 18th. The FBI later uncovered evidence that Stone may have learned of the GRU plan to use the Guccifer 2.0 online persona during this timeframe. Between May 17th and June 15th, the date GRU Unit 74455 launched Guccifer 2.0, Google records show that searches for the terms "dcleaks," "guccifer" and "guccifer june" were conducted from IP addresses within one of two ranges: 172.56.26.0/24 and 107.77.216.0/24. Comparable to a postal address, an IP address, short for internet protocol address, is a label used to identify devices on the internet. The searches were conducted from Florida, where Stone resides. The FBI found that Stone had used multiple IP addresses within the ranges in question to log onto his Twitter account. On June 13th, two days before Guccifer 2.0 went public, Stone used an IP address within the range 172.56.26.0/24 to purchase a Facebook ad.[16] Bamford notes that this raises the possibility that Stone learned details about the GRU's hack and leak operation and their dissemination plans from an Israeli source.

"Hi Roger," the Redacted Israeli wrote to Stone on May 19th. "It Was Great Seeing You Again Last Night At Dinner. Did You Talk To Trump This Morning? Any News? Thank You."

"Contact made - interrupted - mood good," Stone replied. Stone and the Redacted Israeli then exchanged texts about arranging a meeting with Trump.

A month later, Stone was involved in arranging a secret meeting between an Israeli government minister and Trump. According to FBI search warrants, the Redacted Israeli sent Stone a message with the subject line "RS: Secret I[sraeli] Cabinet Minister in NYC Sat. June 25. Available for [Donald J. Trump] meeting." *The Times of Israel* has suggested that the cabinet minister was Tzachi Hanegbi, a member of the Likud party appointed by Benjamin Netanyahu in May of 2016 as a minister without a portfolio.[17] Hanegbi denies being the individual in question.[18]

According to his official Knesset biography: "In 2004, Hanegbi was appointed by Prime Minister Sharon as Minster in the Prime Minister's Office, which is in charge of secret services and strategic dialogue between Israel and the United States. Within these confines, he was responsible for forming the stance of the Prime Minister to audits of the State Comptroller on the intelligence community, the Mossad and special positions, General Security Services, and the Atomic Energy Commission."[19]

On June 25th, the Redacted Israeli messaged Stone again.

"Roger, Minister left. Sends greetings from [Prime Minister]. When am I meeting [Donald J. Trump]? Should I stay or leave Sunday as planned? Hope you are well."

"I am better but turn out to have been poisoned. Completely out of action for 3 days- apologize to Minister for me," Stone replied to the Redacted Israeli the next day. It is unclear what Stone meant by suggesting he had been poisoned. "I would not leave as we hope to schedule the meeting Mon or Tues."

"RETURNING TO DC AFTER URGENT CONSULTATIONS WITH [PRIME MINISTER] IN ROME," the Redacted Israeli wrote to Stone on June 28th. "MUST MEET WITH YOU WED[NESDAY] EVE[NING] AND WITH [DONALD J. TRUMP] THURSDAY IN NYC." Benjamin Netanyahu was in Rome on a state visit in late June 2016.[20]

Roger Stone, WikiLeaks, the Emergence of Guccifer 2.0, And the DNC Leak

Throughout June 2016, Stone continued to tell the Trump campaign that WikiLeaks was preparing to release materials that would be damaging. On June 12th, Julian Assange gave an interview on *ITV* in which he claimed that WikiLeaks was planning upcoming leaks related to Hillary Clinton and the US presidential election.[21] Weeks before Assange's announcement, Stone told Rick Gates that something "big" was coming related to leaks of information and that he believed that Assange had Clinton's emails. Gates asked Stone when they would be released, and Stone suggested it would happen very soon.[22]

In addition to Gates, Stone told Manafort that he was dealing with a source close to WikiLeaks and that the release of Clinton's emails was imminent. Manafort claimed that at some point in June, Stone told him that "a source close to WikiLeaks confirmed that WikiLeaks had the emails from Clinton's server." While WikiLeaks would later release emails the GRU stole from the DNC and John Podesta, it never released any non-publicly available emails from Clinton's time as Secretary of State. If Manafort is correct that Stone specifically mentioned Clinton's server emails, it would indicate that Stone was confused as to which set of Clinton-related emails WikiLeaks both possessed and planned to release.

While Manafort never specified when this discussion occurred, phone records show that Stone and Manafort spoke with one another on June 4th, June 12th (the day of Assange's announcement), June 20th, and June 23rd. Manafort told Gates to check in with Stone "from time to time" to see if the information he was providing on WikiLeaks was "real and viable." Following Assange's June 12th announcement, Manafort told Gates that Stone received "half-credit" as his prediction had been vindicated, but the emails had still yet to be released.[23]

On June 14th, 2016, two days after Assange's *ITV* interview, the DNC announced that it had been compromised by hackers linked to the Russian government. That evening, Stone spoke with Trump twice over the phone for two and a half and two minutes, respectively. They likely discussed WikiLeaks and the DNC hack. Rick Gates told investigators later that he had a phone call with Stone during this period in which Stone claimed that the information WikiLeaks received could have come from the Russians.

The Trump campaign was pleased to learn about the DNC hack. While Gates suggested that some on the campaign didn't believe the news about the Russians, he also said that given "what we were told that information might be about," it was "felt it would give [the campaign] a leg up" if the hacked materials were released. The Trump campaign planned a "press strategy, a communications campaign, and messaging based on the possibility the emails existed." Conversations occurred "about what the campaign could plan for in the way of emails."

On June 15th, Stone asked Gates for Jared Kushner's contact information so he could "debrief" Trump's son-in-law on developments related to the hacked emails.[24] That same day, Unit 74455 of the GRU launched the online persona Guccifer 2.0 at 7 pm Moscow time in an attempt to deflect from reports that hackers linked to the Russian government had hacked the DNC.[25] Seven days earlier, the GRU had set up DCLeaks, their first attempt to release the hacked materials before handing over that task to WikiLeaks.[26]

Shortly after midnight on June 16th, hours after Guccifer 2.0 went public, Gates and Stone discussed the DNC hack over a 30-minute phone call, during which Stone told Gates that "more information would be coming out of the DNC hack." Following the call, Gates provided Stone with Kushner's contact information. It is unclear whether Stone ever connected with Kushner, who told later investigators that he had only met Stone once during the transition.[27]

Roger Stone traveled to Cleveland in July to attend the Republican National Convention. Traveling with him in his entourage was a group of filmmakers working on a Netflix documentary called *Get Me Roger Stone*. At the convention, Stone connected with Alex Jones.

Stone and Jones dined at an Italian restaurant with Nigel Farage. Farage was a pro-Brexit British politician with links to WikiLeaks that will be explored further in a later chapter. One of the documentarians trailing Stone later told *The Guardian*, "We got to the restaurant, and Farage's people were: 'No, no, no! You can't film. You can't film.' It was weird. Jones and Stone were totally open to it. But Farage was 'No way'. He didn't want any record of it. We didn't know what to make of it."

"It was the first time that Alex Jones, Roger Stone, and Nigel Farage met face to face. We'd had a wire on Roger everywhere we went, but when we turned up to meet Farage and his guy, he [Farage's aide] was absolutely adamant," another *Get Me Roger Stone* said. "What was so noticeable was how Alex Jones was so pumped up afterwards about the leaks that were coming. He was saying it openly on his show. And then days later, the DNC leaks dropped [on July 22] and blew apart the Democratic National Convention."[28]

Michael Cohen recalled that the following event occurred on either the day of or the day before Stone met with Farage. "I was sitting in Mr. Trump's office when Rhona Graff yelled out: 'Mr. Trump, Roger Stone on line 1.' And as the way Mr. Trump's habit is, he doesn't use the handset of the phone. He uses a little black box. A speaker box that [he] maintains on his desk. And without telling Roger Stone that I was in the office, Mr. Trump hit the power button and Roger Stone responded: 'Mr. Trump,' he said. 'Roger, how are you?' He says: 'Good, I just want to let you know I got off the telephone a moment ago with Julian Assange. And in a couple of days, there's going to be a massive dump of emails that's going to be extremely damaging to the Clinton campaign.' Mr. Trump said: 'Uh, that's good. Keep me posted.' To which point, after they hung up, Mr. Trump looked at me and he said to me: 'Do you believe him? Do you think Roger really spoke to Assange?' And I responded: 'I don't know.

Roger is Roger, and for all you know, he was looking on his Twitter account. I don't know the answer.'[29] On July 22nd, the eve of the Democratic National Convention, WikiLeaks released the DNC hacked emails for maximum political impact. Upon learning the news, Trump turned to Cohen and said, "'I guess Roger was right.'"[30] Neither the Special Counsel's Office nor the Senate Intelligence Committee ever determined who, if anyone, Roger Stone's source of information on the July 22nd WikiLeaks release was.

Manafort and Trump discussed how the campaign could use the leaked DNC emails against Chairwoman Debbie Wasserman Schultz. Cohen and Trump discussed "the usefulness of the released emails" and how they might sow division between Bernie Sanders, Donna Brazile, and Wasserman Shultz. Gates witnessed Trump on his private jet working the contents of the emails into his next speech.[31]

That same day, Stone held a conference call with Manafort and Gates. An excited Manafort congratulated Stone. Stone informed Manafort that "additional information would be coming out down the road."

Gates later testified that "Manafort thought that would be great."[32]

Manafort spoke to Trump, reminding him of Stone's accurate prediction that WikiLeaks would release Clinton-related emails as well as his claim to be in contact with the anti-secrecy organization. Trump told Manafort to keep in contact with Stone to see if there would be any additional email releases, a message Manafort relayed to Stone on July 25th. Manafort further informed Stone that he wished to be fully apprised of any new developments related to WikiLeaks and directed Gates to keep in touch with Stone regarding the matter. A week later, Manafort held his meeting with Konstantin Kilimnik at the Grand Havana Room.

The next day, July 23rd, Trump tweeted: "The WikiLeaks e-mail release today was so bad to Sanders that it will make it impossible for him to support her unless he is a fraud!"

Get to Assange: Roger Stone's Byzantine Connections to WikiLeaks

In late July, Stone and Corsi discussed the latter's "ability to get to Assange."[33] On July 25th, Stone emailed Corsi the subject "Get to Assange." The body contained the same message in bold: **"Get to Assange."**

Three days earlier, on the day of the WikiLeaks DNC release, Corsi and Malloch spoke over FaceTime, and Corsi had asked "if he could facilitate an interview with Julian Assange" or if he knew anybody around Nigel Farage who could help. Upon receiving Stone's "Get to Assange" email, Corsi forwarded it to Malloch with the message, "From Roger Stone." Corsi later claimed that he never heard back from Malloch regarding the request and gave conflicting accounts on whether he had informed Stone of his WikiLeaks conversation with Malloch,.[34]

On July 25th, Julian Assange claimed during an interview that there was "no proof whatsoever" that WikiLeaks had received the DNC emails from Russia. "The real story is what these emails contain, and they show collusion at the very top of the Democratic Party," Assange said. "Would Hillary Clinton have won anyway? Maybe, maybe not. I think that it's completely up in the air now, and so the result of the nomination process has no political legitimacy."[35]

On July 28th, Corsi traveled to Italy with his wife. Four days later, he sent the following email to Stone: "Word is friend in embassy plans 2 more dumps. One shortly after I'm back. 2nd in Oct[ober]. Impact planned to be very damaging… Time to let more than Podesta to be exposed as in bed w[ith] enemy if they are not ready to drop HRC. That appears to be the game hackers are now about. Would not hurt to start suggesting HRC old, memory bad, has stroke - neither he nor she well. I expect much of next focus, setting stage for Foundation debacle."[36]

Corsi's email presaged WikiLeaks October 7th email dump. More suspicious still, Corsi mentions John Podesta, who two months later was revealed as the primary subject of the hack. He further learned that Assange planned to "release the emails seriatim and not all at once."

Stone was later convicted of lying to Congress to hide his communications with Corsi during this critical period. This raises the obvious questions: how did Corsi come across this information, and why did Stone later lie to Congress, a felony, to hide his interactions with Corsi? To add to the confusion, even if Corsi had provided Stone with inside information he had obtained on the nature of the materials Julian Assange possessed and his plans on what to do with them, it is unlikely such an act would have constituted a crime. Thus, the motivations for Stone's lies and evasions, which opened him up to prosecution, appear even more mysterious.

Neither the Special Counsel's Office nor the Senate Intelligence Committee could ever determine how Corsi learned that WikiLeaks possessed John Podesta's emails and would be releasing them in batches. In addition to deleting his email communications with Stone, which the Special Counsel's Office was able to retrieve, Corsi provided conflicting accounts on how he came into the knowledge that he shared with Stone on the August 2nd email.

At first, Corsi falsely claimed that he had never been in contact with Stone regarding WikiLeaks. After being confronted with evidence to the contrary, Corsi claimed that a "man" had told him about Assange's plans while in Italy. However, he subsequently walked that claim back and concocted an elaborate story that he had deduced that WikiLeaks possessed Podesta's emails. His story failed to convince prosecutors, and his repeated false statements and "memory lapses" rendered him useless as a witness.[37]

On July 29th, Stone messaged Manafort saying that there was "good shit happening" and that the two needed to find a time to speak. The next day, they spoke for 68 minutes. Stone and Manafort spoke again the next day, after which Stone called Rick Gates. Stone spoke with Trump twice over the phone ten minutes after that, each conversation lasting over ten minutes. Following his discussions with Trump, Stone emailed eight draft tweets to Trump's assistant, Jessica Machia, with the subject "Tweets Mr. Trump requested last night." Stone's ghost tweets criticized Hillary Clinton's stances vis-a-vis Russia, with one in particular stating, "I want a new detente with Russia under Putin."

On August 3rd, the day after Stone received Corsi's email regarding Assange's plans, Stone attempted to call Manafort, but the call didn't go through. Afterward, he sent Manafort an email with the subject "I have an idea" and wrote in the body of the email, "to save Trump's ass." Manafort called Stone later in the day, presumably to learn what Stone's cryptic idea was. While what they discussed remains unknown, it is clear that Stone did not want to put the idea down in writing.

On August 4th, Stone told Sam Nunberg that he was

returning from London, where he had dined with Julian Assange. "I dined with my new pal Julian Assange last nite," Stone wrote to Nunberg.[38] Nunberg recalled that Stone had told him that he had "met with Julian Assange about the emails" and that he believed the next batch of emails WikiLeaks released would pertain to the Clinton Foundation. In addition to Nunberg, an unnamed source described by *The Washington Post* as a Stone associate told the paper that sometime in the Spring of 2016, Stone had said to them that he had learned that WikiLeaks possessed and would release emails about John Podesta and other top Democrats.[39]

Stone denied ever having met Assange or traveling to London during this time and claimed he had been joking with Nunberg.[40] Nunberg did not take Stone's statement regarding meeting Assange as a joke. Stone later produced Airline and Credit Card statements showing that on August 1st, he flew JetBlue from Miami to Los Angeles. He stayed at the London Hotel in West Hollywood on August 1st and 2nd, returning to Miami on the 3rd, the day he claimed to have "dined" with Assange.[41]

The same day he told Sam Nunberg that he had dined with Assange, Stone appeared on *InfoWars,* where he discussed WikiLeaks and claimed to have spoken with Trump the day before. "The Clinton campaign narrative that the Russians favor Donald Trump and the Russians are leaking this information, this is inoculation because, as you said earlier, they know what is coming, and it is devastating," Stone said. "Let's remember that their defense to all the Clinton Foundation scandals is not that 'we didn't do,' but 'you have no proof.'" Stone continued, "Julian Assange has that proof, and I think he is going to furnish it for the American people."

Roger Stone's Communications with the GRU: Knowns and Unknowns

On August 5th, Stone wrote an opinion piece for *Breitbart* entitled "Dear Hillary: DNC Hack Solved, So Now Stop Blaming Russia."[42] He embraced the GRU cover story that Guccifer 2.0 was a lone hacker unaffiliated with the Russian government. Stone also showed that he was familiar with Guccifer's activities before WikiLeaks released the DNC emails, providing links to Guccifer 2.0's WordPress and various tweets sent from Guccifer

2.0's account. Furthermore, by publishing his denial that Guccifer 2.0 was not related to the Russian government in the right-wing press, Stone drew further attention to Guccifer 2.0.

On August 8th, Stone spoke before the Southwest Broward Republican Organization. Responding to a question during the Q&A, Stone said, "I actually have communicated with Assange. I believe the next tranche of his documents pertain to the Clinton Foundation, but there's no telling what the October surprise may be." It was the first time Stone publicly claimed to have communicated with Assange. The next day, WikiLeaks tweeted: "We are not aware of having communicated with Roger Stone. We do however take, and verify, anonymous tips"[43]

At this point, the mysterious Redacted Israeli re-emerges in the timeline. "Roger - As per [Prime Minister], we have one last shot before moving on," the Redacted Israeli wrote to Stone on August 9th, referring to Benjamin Netanyahu. "Can you deliver? History will not forgive us. TRUMP IN FREE FALL. OCTOBER SURPRISE COMING!" It is not clear what the Redacted Israeli meant by an October Surprise. "Roger, hello from Jerusalem," the Redacted Israeli wrote on August 12th. "Any progress? He is going to be defeated unless we intervene. We have critical intell. The key is in your hands! Back in the US next week."

What kind of intervention the Redacted Israeli was contemplating is unknown, as is the exact nature of the "critical intell" they claimed to possess. That same day, Corsi returned to the United States from his trip to Italy. Also, Guccifer 2.0 leaked information the GRU had stolen from the Democratic Congressional Campaign Committee.[44] The information included the email addresses and phone numbers of every Democratic member of the House of Representatives.

Guccifer 2.0 tweeted at Stone, "thanks that u believe in the real #Guccifer2."[45]

Breitbart writer Lee Stranahan reached out to Guccifer 2.0 via Twitter DM. Stranahan, who later worked for the Russian state-owned news agency Sputnik, first reached out to Guccifer 2.0 ten days earlier. After seeing Guccifer 2.0's tweet thanking Stone, Stranahan wrote to Guccifer 2.0 again, referring to Stone's recently published piece in *Breitbart* denying Russian involvement in the DNC hack. "I worked with Roger [Stone] on that piece and was actually the one who pointed out what was going on with him in the first place."[46] Stranahan claims he ghostwrote Stone's op-ed.[47]

Stranahan's boss at *Breitbart*, Steve Bannon, was made the Trump campaign's CEO the next day. Bannon later testified that before being hired on as CEO, "Stone told him that he had a connection to Assange" and "implied that he had inside information about WikiLeaks." After Bannon got the job on August 13th, Stone explained to him that he "had a relationship with Assange and said that WikiLeaks was going to dump additional materials that would be bad for the Clinton Campaign."[48]

The day Bannon was hired, Twitter suspended Guccifer 2.0. WikiLeaks tweeted, "@Guccifer_2 has account completely censored by Twitter after publishing some files from Democratic campaign #DCCC." Stone tweeted that the suspension was "outrageous" and that Guccifer 2.0 was a "HERO." The next day, after Twitter reinstated Guccifer 2.0's account, Stone sent a Direct Message to Guccifer 2.0 saying that he was "delighted" by the reinstatement.

"wow," Guccifer 2.0 replied to Stone. "thank u for writing back, and thank u for an article about me!!! do you find anyting [sic] interesting in the docs i posted?"[49]

"Give me a call today if you can," Corsi wrote to Stone on the same day. "Despite MSM [Mainstream Media] drumroll that HRC is already elected, it's not over yet. More to come than anyone realizes. Won't really get started until after Labor Day."[50]

On August 16th, Stone sent a Twitter Direct Message to Guccifer 2.0 requesting they retweet a column he wrote predicting that the election could be "rigged against Donald Trump."

Guccifer 2.0 replied, "done."[51]

That same day, Ted Malloch sent Corsi an email with the subject "Vladimir Putin Has Already Won Our Election." The body of the email contained two words: "VENONA" and "Observer."[52] VENONA is a reference to a top-secret effort by US intelligence in the 1940s to decrypt messages sent by the NKVD, KGB, and GRU. Three days earlier, John R. Schindler of *The Observer* had published an article with the same title as the subject of Malloch's email to Corsi, "Vladimir Putin Has Already Won Our Election."

The subtitle of Schindler's article states, "It's time to face facts: Kremlin spies and hackers are undermining American politics." The article went on to say, "WikiLeaks, nowadays a transparent Kremlin front, disseminated some 20,000 purloined DNC emails that were stolen by Russian intelligence." Schindler noted that the "Kremlin is weaponizing stolen information for political effect."[53]

Corsi emailed Stone a link to a *WND* piece he had written entitled "Trump advisor: WikiLeaks plotting email dump to derail Hillary."[54] The article stated that Stone had "told WND in an interview that he has communicated directly with Assange."[55] Later that day, Stone told Alex Jones on *InfoWars* that he had "backchannel communications" with Assange, who possessed "political dynamite" about the Clintons, which he was planning to release.[56]

The next day, August 17th, Guccifer 2.0 publicly tweeted at Stone, writing, "@RogerJStoneJR paying him back." The GRU then sent Stone a Twitter Direct Message from the Guccifer 2.0 account. "i'm pleased to say u r great man," Guccifer 2.0 wrote. "please tell me if I can help u anyhow. it would be a great pleasure to me."[57]

Stone didn't reply via Twitter. FBI Search Warrants reveal that on August 18th, Stone downloaded the end-to-end encryption application Signal and the encrypted email service ProtonMail.[58] Signal uses cell phone numbers for secure, encrypted communications. ProtonMail uses client-side encryption. The timing of Stone's downloading of these encryption services, coming within 24 hours of Guccifer 2.0's offer to "help," is highly suggestive.

"Trump can still win - but time is running out," Stone wrote to Steve Bannon in an email on August 18th, the same day he downloaded Signal and ProtonMail. "Early voting begins in six weeks. I do know how to win this but it ain't pretty. Campaign has never been good at playing the new media. Lots to do -- let me know when you can talk."

"Let's talk ASAP," Bannon replied. When later asked under oath about what he thought Roger meant by the statement that he knew how to win but it "ain't pretty," Bannon stated, "Roger is an agent provocateur, he's an expert in opposition research. He's an expert in the tougher side of politics. And when you're this far behind, you have to use every tool in the toolbox." When asked to elaborate about what kind of "tools", Bannon said, "opposition research, dirty tricks, the types of things that campaigns use when they have got to make up some ground." When asked if Stone's stated relationship with Assange was included in this, Bannon replied, "I don't know if I thought it at the time, but he could - you know, I was led to believe that he had a relationship with WikiLeaks and Julian Assange."[59]

On the morning of August 19th, Bannon texted Stone asking if he was available to speak.[60] Stone also had a lengthy phone call with Paul Manafort, who had just resigned from the campaign.[61] "[W]hen can you talk???" Stone replied to Bannon's text the next day, August 20th. It is unclear whether they ended up connecting that day.

At 9:24 am on August 21st, Stone published the most scrutinized tweet of the 2016 election cycle: "Trust me, it will soon the [sic] Podesta's time in the barrel. #CrookedHillary." The tweet provided the most tantalizing indication yet that Stone had obtained inside information that WikiLeaks possessed and was planning to release emails related to John Podesta.

Twelve hours after Stone's Podesta tweet, Guccifer 2.0 replied to *Breitbart* reporter Lee Stranahan over Twitter. "[H]i man," the GRU-controller of the Guccifer 2.0 account, "how's life?" The GRU then sent Stranahan memos stolen from the DCCC describing the Black Lives Matter movement and "Tactics" on how to deal with BLM activists.[62]

On August 30th, Stone realized his Podesta tweet from nine days earlier would be a problem and contacted Jerome Corsi to attempt to concoct a cover story. According to Corsi, Stone told him he was getting "heat" for his tweet and required a cover story.[63] Corsi and Stone then conspired to falsely make it look as though Stone learned from Corsi's own research and writing on Podesta that WikiLeaks had Podesta's emails.[64]

On August 31st, Corsi drafted a nine-page memo regarding Podesta and made it seem as though it was written on behalf of Stone to counter a *CNN* story two weeks earlier about Manafort's activities in Ukraine. Later, in March of 2017, when the Trump-Russia storyline was reaching a fevered pitch in the American media, Stone requested that Corsi write an article fabricating a story about how he, Stone, came to know that WikiLeaks possessed Podesta's emails, which Corsi dutifully did and published on *InfoWars*.

Stone later suggested that his tweet ("Trust me, it will

soon the Podesta's time in the barrel") was not referring to the WikiLeaks release of John Podesta's emails but to John and his brother Tony Podesta's lobbying activities. However, his conspiring with Corsi to create a cover story for the tweet undermines this explanation. In addition to fabricating a cover story for his August 21st Podesta tweet, Stone was also later convicted of lying to Congress about his intermediary to WikiLeaks, which constituted a felony. In his September 2017 testimony before the House Intelligence Committee, Stone falsely claimed that he gained information on the materials in WikiLeaks possession and Assange's plans on what to do with them from a longtime acquaintance named Randy Credico.

While Credico wasn't Stone's intermediary to WikiLeaks, he did have a connection to the organization. Credico had served as the director of the William Moses Kunstler Fund for Racial Justice and was friends with its founder, William Kunstler.[65] Working alongside Credico at the Fund was Kunstler's widow, Margaret Ratner Kunstler, an attorney who, throughout 2015 and 2016, assisted Julian Assange with his legal strategy and media appearances.[66] Kunstler assisted Credico in getting Assange on his radio show but never passed information between the two.[67]

"Kunstler's wife is [Assange's] lawyer or one of them," Credico texted Stone on August 19th, 2016, marking the beginning of their interactions regarding Assange and WikiLeaks. Credico contacted Stone to inform him that he was about to host Assange on his radio program on August 25th. Two days before the Assange interview, Stone himself appeared on the program. "What about the October surprise?" Credico asked Stone during the interview. "I mean, you've been in touch indirectly with Julian Assange. What- can you give us any kind of insight? Is there an October surprise happening?"

"Well, first of all, I don't want to intimate in any way that I control or have influence with Assange, because I do not," Stone replied. "We have a mutual friend, somebody we both trust and therefore I am a recipient of good information."[68]

Two days later, when Assange appeared on Credico's radio show, Credico asked about Stone's claim. "Roger Stone is a rather canny spin master," Assange replied, "and we have not had any communications with him whatsoever."[69]

On September 9th, Guccifer 2.0 sent Stone another Twitter Direct Message, sharing a link to a post by the conservative Florida blogger Aaron Nevins that contained an "exclusive report" about the Democratic Party voter turnout model that the GRU had stolen and provided to Nevins. The GRU wrote to Stone, "what do u think of the info on the turnout model for the democrats entire presidential campaign?"

"Pretty standard," Stone replied.

This was the last message exchanged between Stone and the GRU via Twitter.[70] A week later, Stone continued to make public statements about the impending WikiLeaks release. During a September 16th interview with *Boston Herald Radio*, he claimed that he expected WikiLeaks to "drop a payload of new documents on a weekly basis fairly soon. And that of course will answer the question of exactly what was erased on that email server."[71]

The Road to October 7th and the Final Days of the Campaign

Around the time of the first Presidential Debate on September 26th, Stone provided Paul Manafort with a private briefing regarding WikiLeaks. "John Podesta was going to be in the barrel," Stone explained to Manafort, further telling him that "there were going to be leaks of John Podesta's emails." The next day, news broke that Julian Assange planned to make a big announcement from the Ecuadorian Embassy on September 30th.

A day before the announcement, Rick Gates was riding in a limo with Trump on their way to LaGuardia airport when he overheard a phone call between Trump and Stone. Trump had tried calling Stone three times before 10 am that morning but couldn't connect until the car ride with Gates. Trump used his bodyguard Keith Schiller's phone for the conversation with Stone. After he hung up, Trump told Gates that "more releases of damaging information would be coming."

Assange's announcement was canceled the next day due to "security concerns." That same day, Credico texted Stone a picture of him in front of the Ecuadorian Embassy. He had gone to London to visit a friend and had agreed to deliver a letter to the Embassy on behalf of Berthold Reimers, the manager of the WBAI radio station. Credico never got past the door of the Embassy nor spoke to Assange but instead passed the letter over to someone in the doorway. On the evening of October 1st,

Credico texted Stone that there would be "big news Wednesday," October 5th, and that "Hillary's campaign will die this week." He finished by writing, "now pretend u don't know me."

"U died 5 years ago," Stone replied.[72]

The next day, October 2nd, Stone tweeted: "Wednesday @HillaryClinton is done. #WikiLeaks."[73] Andrew Surabian, who was in charge of the Trump campaign war room, emailed Stone's Twitter prediction to Steve Bannon, Kellyanne Conway, and the Trump campaign press office. However, later in the day, there was more confusion related to Assange's announcement. Stone texted Credico later that day, "WTF?" and linked to an article suggesting WikiLeaks had canceled the announcement again due to security concerns.

"[H]ead fake," Credico replied.[74]

Later that day, it was clarified that the Assange announcement would still be taking place but that they would change venues from the Ecuadorian Embassy in London to a press conference in Berlin.[75] That evening, Stone appeared on *The Alex Jones Show* and told viewers that he had been "assured" by his intermediary with Assange that "the mother lode is coming Wednesday." However, despite his outward confidence, the following day, on October 3rd, Stone wrote to Credico, "Did Assange back off?"

"I can't talk about it," Credico replied. "I think it's on for tomorrow."

Stone then tweeted: "I have total confidence that @wikileaks and my hero Julian Assange will educate the American people soon #LockHerUp."

"Why can't you get Trump to come out and say that he would give Julian Assange Asylum[?]" Credico texted Stone. "Off the Record Hillary and her people are doing a full-court press they [sic] keep Assange from making the next dump ... That's all I can tell you on this line ... Please leave my name out of it."

"So nothing will happen tonight?" Stone replied.

"[T]uesday," Credico responded. "There is so much stuff out there… There will be an announcement but not on the balcony."

Shortly after that, WikiLeaks tweeted: "WikiLeaks press conference Tuesday [October 4th] 10:00 am Berlin time on the past, present & future of WikiLeaks."

Dan Scavino, the Trump Campaign's social media

director, emailed Bannon about the WikiLeaks tweet. Bannon then contacted *Breitbart* editors Wynton Han and Peter Schweitzer to see if they could be available "to get what he [Assange] has live." Yet another *Breitbart* editor, Matthew Boyle, forwarded Bannon an email thread between himself and Stone from earlier that day. "Assange-what's he got?" Boyle asked Stone. "Hope it's good."

"It is," Stone replied. "I'd tell Bannon but he doesn't call me back."

Boyle suggested to Bannon that he call Stone, to which Bannon replied that he had important things to worry about. "Well clearly he knows what Assange has," Boyle responded. "I'd say that's important."

Stone was also in contact with Erik Prince via email on October 3rd. "Spoke to my friend in London tonight. Payload still coming."[76] Stone told Prince, "[y]ou are a great American."[77]

On Tuesday, October 4th, WikiLeaks' 10th anniversary, Julian Assange announced that, starting that week, WikiLeaks would be releasing materials "affecting three powerful organizations in three different states as well as, of course, information previously referred to about the US election process," which he described as "significant," and that from that point on they would be releasing materials weekly for the next ten weeks. He further promised that "all the US-election related documents" would be released before November 8th.

"Assange made a fool of himself," Corsi wrote to Stone after the announcement. "Has nothing or he would have released it. Total BS hype."[78]

"When is the other stuff coming out?" Trump complained to Rick Gates, having expected actual Clinton-related documents to be released. His multiple conversations with Stone almost certainly stoked his expectations.

"What was that this morning???" Bannon emailed Stone.[79]

"Fear," Stone replied. "Serious security concern. He thinks they are going to kill him and the London police are standing [down]."

Erik Prince also emailed Stone that day, asking if Assange had "chicken[ed] out." Stone replied that he was "not sure" and was "checking." Prince texted Stone later that day, asking whether he had "hear[d] any more from London?" Stone replied, "Yes - want to talk on a secure line - got WhatsApp?" Stone further suggested that the WikiLeaks materials were "good." FBI search warrants show that Stone downloaded a copy of WhatsApp, which offers end-to-end encryption, on his iPhone the next day.[80] When asked about his conversation with Stone, Prince told investigators that Stone had told him that WikiLeaks would be releasing materials damaging to Clinton and that Stone had the equivalent of "insider stock trading" information on Assange.[81]

There were no WikiLeaks releases on Wednesday, October 5th, as Stone and Credico had expected. Stone maintained outward confidence, tweeting, "Libs thinking Assange will stand down are wishful thinking. Payload coming #Lockthemup." On October 6th, WikiLeaks again failed to leak any election-related documents. Still, Stone remained undeterred, tweeting, "Julian Assange will deliver a devastating expose on Hillary at a time of his choosing. I stand by my prediction. #handcuffs4hillary." Later that afternoon, he received a call from Trump bodyguard Keith Schiller's phone. Stone and almost certainly Trump spoke for six minutes, likely discussing the impending WikiLeaks release.

At some point on October 7th, Stone may have gained foreknowledge that *The Washington Post* was preparing to release the explosive *Access Hollywood* tape.[82] While one unnamed witness later told the Special Counsel's Office that WikiLeaks release of the Podesta emails on October 7th "may have come at the behest of, or in coordination with, Roger Stone," they were never able to establish whether or not that was the case.[83]

At 11:27 am, Jerome Corsi attempted to call Stone, and call logs show that the call lasted for only one minute. According to an affidavit attached to an FBI search warrant application, Stone didn't pick up the phone.[84] However, Corsi later told the Special Counsel's Office that Stone did answer the phone, and they discussed the "status of the WikiLeaks publication of the Podesta emails and Roger's concern that Assange should start publishing immediately the Podesta emails."[85]

Stone received a call from *The Washington Post* at 11:53 am, which may have been where he learned of the upcoming story. However, the Special Counsel's Report notes that phone records alone do not indicate that Stone spoke with any of the *Post* reporters who broke the story and that investigators could not uncover the exact content of the conversation.[86] Stone's conversation with the *Post* lasted for approximately 20 minutes.

Stone then spoke with Corsi twice over the phone, informing him about the explosive nature of the *Access Hollywood* tape soon to be released. He claimed that Stone "[w]anted the Podesta stuff to balance the news cycle" either "right then or at least coincident." Stone told Corsi he wanted him to have WikiLeaks "drop the Podesta emails immediately."[87]

At approximately 3 pm, Trump was with his debate prep team when he learned that the release of the *Access Hollywood* tape was imminent.[88] At 3:32 pm, the Department of Homeland Security and the Office of the Director of National Intelligence issued a joint statement attributing the recent hacks of the DNC and election interference efforts to the Russian government.[89] Less than thirty minutes later, at 4 pm, *The Washington Post* published its story. Thirty-two minutes after that, WikiLeaks tweeted out its first link to the John Podesta emails purloined by the GRU, the first in a staggered set of releases that would last the election.

"Lunch postponed - have to go see T," Stone messaged Corsi on October 8th regarding Trump.[90] According to Corsi, he and Stone believed they deserved "credit" for the leaks and that Trump should "reward" them.[91] Stone, however, was concerned about having indicated that he had advance information on the Podesta email release. He instructed Corsi to delete all emails they exchanged regarding the Podesta emails. However, while he worried about the public learning about his apparent foresight into WikiLeaks release of the Podesta emails, he boasted about it to the Trump campaign. Rick Gates later testified that following the release, Stone exclaimed, "I told you this was coming."[92]

Meanwhile, Stone promoted the leaked materials through a social media campaign. He directed a small team to purchase hundreds of new and existing Facebook accounts, and bloggers working for Stone created what appeared to be real Facebook accounts. The team also created Twitter accounts for the same purpose: to push the leaked Podesta emails.[93]

On October 12th, John Podesta gave an interview with C-SPAN in which he claimed that it was "a reasonable assumption to - or at least a reasonable conclusion - that [Stone] had advanced warning [of the release of his emails] and the Trump campaign had advanced warning about what Assange was going to do. I think there's at least a reasonable belief that

[Assange] may have passed this information on to [Stone]."

The day after Podesta's claim on C-SPAN that Stone and WikiLeaks may have collaborated, WikiLeaks tweeted "As we have already stated clearly: WikiLeaks has had no contact wiith [sic] Roger Stone." Shortly after that, Stone sent a private Twitter DM to @WikiLeaks. "Since I was all over national TV, cable and print defending wikileaks and assange against the claim that you are Russian agents and debunking the false charges of sexual assault as trumped up bs you may want to rexamine [sic] the strategy of attacking me."

"We appreciate that," WikiLeaks' Twitter account responded. "However, the false claims of association are being used by the democrats to undermine the impact of our publications. Don't go there if you don't want us to correct you."

"Ha!" Stone replied. "The more you 'correct' me the more people think you're lying. Your operation leaks like a sieve. You need to figure out who you[r] friends are."[94]

Stone's last known communication between Stone and the Redacted Israeli occurred on October 30th. "Roger, you are doing a great job!!!" the Redacted Israeli wrote to Stone on October 30th. "I am in NY-met with [Donald J. Trump] and helping. Victory is in sight."

Four days later, on November 3rd, the Redacted Israeli wrote another cryptic message to Stone. "Roger, European country ready to release secret tapes to DESTROY objective. Can we meet ASAP? 4 star General will join."

"Yes let's talk thurs," Stone replied.

On November 7th, the day before the election, Person 2 wrote to Stone: "ROGER,JERRY- SORRY, BUT DUE TO AN UNEXPECTED EMERGENCY I HAVE TO CANCEL TODAY'S MEETING AT 9. THANKS .. HAVING a TIA. Early Stroke."

"You can't die until after we elect Donald," Stone wrote in their last communication.

Roger Stone, the GRU, and WikiLeaks: The Final Analysis

Did Roger Stone have advanced information regarding WikiLeaks' releases of John Podesta's emails? And if so, how? Was it through an intermediary with Assange? Did sources from Israel provide him with the answer? Was he informed by Russian military intelligence directly? Neither the Special Counsel's Office nor the Senate Intelligence Committee were able to answer these questions. In November 2019, a jury convicted Stone on five counts of false statements, one count of witness tampering, and one count of obstruction of a Congressional proceeding.[95] President Trump, however, commuted his longtime friend's sentence and, in his last days in office, offered him a full pardon. Trump's corrupt pardon of Stone is critically important in understanding the investigators inability to get to the bottom of Stone's activities during the election. Stone understood perfectly well that the man he had helped elect to the highest office in the land would use the power of that office to pardon him as long as he didn't cooperate.

Then-President Trump's dangling of the pardon power over Stone wasn't the only challenge facing investigators and prosecutors. After providing false testimony to the House Intelligence Committee, Stone exercised his Fifth Amendment right against self-incrimination and refused to testify before the Senate Intelligence Committee. During the campaign, Stone utilized encrypted applications and email services that made his communications with key individuals unavailable to investigators. However, Stone's lies and usage of encryption offer certain clues and circumstantial evidence of interest.

Stone's attempt to cover up his apparent foreknowledge that WikiLeaks possessed John Podesta's emails began on August 30th, 2016. On that day, nine days after Stone's August 21st tweet about "Podesta's time in the barrel," Stone and Corsi fabricated the story that Stone's tweet was based upon a public article Corsi had written and a subsequent memorandum he had prepared for Stone. Corsi later told investigators that this story was "bullshit" and that he had been Stone's direct source.[96] Corsi provided conflicting explanations on how he came across this information, first claiming that he learned it from a "man" while in Italy, and later, even more dubiously, that he had come into the knowledge through his own powers of deduction.

A second cover-up occurred after Trump's election and during the many investigations into the 2016 election. Stone lied to the House Intelligence Committee, telling them that his intermediary with Assange was Randy Credico. He also used Credico in an apparent attempt to cover up his relationship with Jerome Corsi. During his trial, Stone's defense attorney made the interesting two-part argument that, despite his lies to Congress, 1.) Stone's outreach to WikiLeaks hadn't been successful, and, 2.) even if it had been, it would not have been illegal.

This raises the obvious question: *if Stone learning from Jerome Corsi details about WikiLeaks upcoming plans was not illegal, why did Stone bother to lie about this and expose himself to a potential felony?* One potential answer is that Roger Stone did not learn that WikiLeaks possessed John Podesta's emails from Jerome Corsi, which wouldn't have been a crime, but rather from an alternative source that he was willing to go to great lengths to hide, possibly from Israel or from Russian military intelligence itself.

On August 5th, Stone published an article in *Breitbart* linking to Guccifer 2.0's Twitter and WordPress sites and advancing the cover story devised by Russian military intelligence that Guccifer 2.0 was a lone hacker responsible for the hack of the Democratic National Committee. Four days later, the Redacted Israeli wrote to "OCTOBER SURPRISE COMING," and on the 12th said that they had "Critical Intell." One day later, Stone protested Guccifer 2.0's banning from Twitter, calling "him" a "HERO." On August 14th, Stone established direct contact with Russian military intelligence by sending a private Twitter Direct Message to Guccifer 2.0.

By this time, it had been widely reported that the account was a Russian intelligence cutout. Rick Gates testified that in June 2016, Stone told him that the WikiLeaks information could have come from the Russians.[97] Stone and Guccifer 2.0 exchanged messages via Twitter between August 14th and August 17th, culminating in the GRU's offer of "help" to Stone on the 17th. The very next day, August 18th, Stone downloaded the encrypted communications applications Signal and ProtonMail. Three days after that, Stone tweeted: "Trust me, it will soon the Podesta's [sic] time in the barrel."

[1] Report of the Select Committee on Intelligence United States Senate On Russian Active Measures Campaigns And Interference in the 2016 US Election Volume 5: Counterintelligence Threats and Vulnerabilities. Pg. 222

[2] Samuelsohn, Darren; Gerstein, Josh. "Steve Bannon: Roger Stone was our unused WikiLeaks 'access point'," *Politico*. November 8th, 2019

[3] Report of the Select Committee on Intelligence United States Senate On Russian Active Measures Campaigns And Interference in the 2016 US Election Volume 5: Counterintelligence Threats and Vulnerabilities. Pg. 172

[4] LaFraniere, Sharon; Montague, Zach. "Trump Predicted More Leaks Amid WikiLeaks Releases in 2016, Ex-Aide Testifies," *The New York Times*. November 12th, 2019

[5] Samuelsohn, Darren; Gershtein, Josh. "What Roger Stone's trial revealed about

Donald Trump and WikiLeaks," *Politico.* November 12th, 2019

[6] Mance, Henry. "Oxford distances itself from Trump favourite Ted Malloch," *The Financial Times.* February 23rd, 2017

[7] Kovensky, Josh. "Meet Ted Malloch, Jerome Corsi's Alleged Wikileaks Contact In London," *TalkingPointsMemo.* December 10th, 2018

[8] United States District Court for the Southern District of New York. SEARCH AND SEIZURE WARRANT. July 12th, 2018. AMENDED AFFIDAVIT IN SUPPORT OF AN APPLICATION FOR A SEARCH WARRANT. Pg. 14

[9] Sheth, Sonam. "A 'significant figure' linked to Roger Stone has been compelled to testify in the Russia probe as Mueller homes in on the DNC hack," *Business Insider.* March 30th, 2018

[10] Dukakis, Ali. "Emails about WikiLeaks publisher Julian Assange being 'mischaracterized': Roger Stone," *ABC News.* December 2nd, 2018

[11] "Roger Stone: I never talked to Julian Assange," *Fox News.* November 28th, 2018

[12] Report of the Select Committee on Intelligence United States Senate On Russian Active Measures Campaigns And Interference in the 2016 US Election Volume 5: Counterintelligence Threats and Vulnerabilities. Pg. 235 [Footnote 1537]

[13] Corsi, Jerome. *Silent No More.* New York, NY: Post Hill Press, 2019. Pg. 82

[14] United States District Court for the Southern District of New York. SEARCH AND SEIZURE WARRANT. July 12th, 2018. AMENDED AFFIDAVIT IN SUPPORT OF AN APPLICATION FOR A SEARCH WARRANT. Pg. 14

[15] Bamford, James. *SPYFAIL: Foreign Spies, Moles, Saboteurs, and the Collapse of America's Counterintelligence.* New York, NY: Hachette Book Group, 2023. Pg. 266

[16] United States District Court for the District of Columbia. SEARCH AND SEIZURE WARRANT. July 27TH, 2018. AFFIDAVIT IN SUPPORT OF AN APPLICATION FOR A SEARCH WARRANT. Pg. 25

[17] "Redacted FBI document hints at Israeli efforts to help Trump in 2016 campaign," *The Times of Israel.* April 29th, 2020

[18] Shalev, Chemi. "No Stone Unturned in Trump-Netanyahu Mutual Intervention Alliance," *Haaretz.* April 30th, 2020

[19] Tzachi Hanegbi Likud Knesset Bio

[20] "Redacted FBI document hints at Israeli efforts to help Trump in 2016 campaign," *The Times of Israel.* April 29th, 2020

[21] "Assange on Peston on Sunday: 'More Clinton leaks to come,'" *ITV.* June 12th, 2016

[22] Mueller, III, Robert S. *Report On The Investigation Into Russian Interference In The 2016 Presidential Election.* Department of Justice, Washington, DC. March 2019. Pg. 52

[23] Report of the Select Committee on Intelligence United States Senate On Russian Active Measures Campaigns And Interference in the 2016 US Election Volume 5: Counterintelligence Threats and Vulnerabilities. Pg. 223-226

[24] Balsamo, Michael; Barakat, Matthew; Tucker, Eric. "Stone trial testimony ends with talk of outreach to Kushner," *The Associated Press.* November 12th, 2019

[25] Rid, Thomas. *Active Measures: The Secret History of Disinformation and Political Warfare.* New York, NY: Farrar, Straus and Giroux, 2020. Pg. 387-388

[26] USA v. Netyksho, et al. Indictment. United States District Court for the District of Columbia. July 13th, 2018. Pg. 14

[27] Report of the Select Committee on Intelligence United States Senate On Russian Active Measures Campaigns And Interference in the 2016 US Election Volume 5: Counterintelligence Threats and Vulnerabilities. Pg. 226

[28] Cadwalladr, Carole. "Who is the real Nigel Farage... and why won't he answer my questions?" *The Guardian.* November 25th, 2018

[29] Report of the Select Committee on Intelligence United States Senate On Russian Active Measures Campaigns And Interference in the 2016 US Election Volume 5: Counterintelligence Threats and Vulnerabilities. Pg. 229-230

[30] Mueller, III, Robert S. *Report On The Investigation Into Russian Interference In The 2016*

Presidential Election. Department of Justice, Washington, DC. March 2019. Pg. 53

[31] Report of the Select Committee on Intelligence United States Senate On Russian Active Measures Campaigns And Interference in the 2016 US Election Volume 5: Counterintelligence Threats and Vulnerabilities. Pg. 231

[32] Hsu, Spencer S.; Weiner, Rachel; Zapotosky, Matt. "Roger Stone trial: Former top Trump official details campaign's dealings on WikiLeaks, and suggests Trump was in the know," *The Washington Post.* November 12th, 2019

[33] Report of the Select Committee on Intelligence United States Senate On Russian Active Measures Campaigns And Interference in the 2016 US Election Volume 5: Counterintelligence Threats and Vulnerabilities. Pg. 234

[34] Report of the Select Committee on Intelligence United States Senate On Russian Active Measures Campaigns And Interference in the 2016 US Election Volume 5: Counterintelligence Threats and Vulnerabilities. Pg. 234-236

[35] Johnson, Alex. "WikiLeaks' Julian Assange: 'No Proof' Hacked DNC Emails Came From Russia," *NBC News.* July 25th, 2016

[36] Report of the Select Committee on Intelligence United States Senate On Russian Active Measures Campaigns And Interference in the 2016 US Election Volume 5: Counterintelligence Threats and Vulnerabilities. Pg. 236-238

[37] Report of the Select Committee on Intelligence United States Senate On Russian Active Measures Campaigns And Interference in the 2016 US Election Volume 5: Counterintelligence Threats and Vulnerabilities. Pg. 233-239

[38] Holliday, Shelby; Barry, Rob. "Roger Stone's Claim of a 2016 Julian Assange Meeting Draws Scrutiny," *The Wall Street Journal.* April 2nd, 2018

[39] Hamburger, Tom; Dawsey, Josh; Leonnig, Carole D.; Harris, Shane. "Roger Stone claimed contact with WikiLeaks founder Julian Assange in 2016, according to two associates," *The Washington Post.* March 13th, 2018

[40] Report of the Select Committee on Intelligence United States Senate On Russian Active Measures Campaigns And Interference in the 2016 US Election Volume 5: Counterintelligence Threats and Vulnerabilities. Pg. 236-238

[41] Kaczynski, Andrew; Borger, Gloria. "Stone, on day he sent Assange dinner email, also said 'devastating' WikiLeaks were forthcoming," *CNN.* April 4th, 2018

[42] Stone, Roger. "Dear Hillary: DNC Hack Solved, So Now Stop Blaming Russia," *Breitbart.* August 5th, 2016

[43] Report of the Select Committee on Intelligence United States Senate On Russian Active Measures Campaigns And Interference in the 2016 US Election Volume 5: Counterintelligence Threats and Vulnerabilities. Pg. 239

[44] United States District Court for the District of Columbia. APPLICATION FOR A SEARCH WARRANT. August 3rd, 2018. AFFIDAVIT IN SUPPORT OF AN APPLICATION FOR SEARCH WARRANTS. Pg. 4-5

[45] Report of the Select Committee on Intelligence United States Senate On Russian Active Measures Campaigns And Interference in the 2016 US Election Volume 5: Counterintelligence Threats and Vulnerabilities. Pg. 195

[46] Twitter DMs between Lee Stranahan and Guccifer 2.0 (Released during Roger Stone Trial)

[47] Swan, Betsy; Suebsaeng. "Will Trump Keep Pushing Putin's Lies About Attacking America?" *The Daily Beast.* July 13th, 2018

[48] Report of the Select Committee on Intelligence United States Senate On Russian Active Measures Campaigns And Interference in the 2016 US Election Volume 5: Counterintelligence Threats and Vulnerabilities. Pg. 241

[49] Report of the Select Committee on Intelligence United States Senate On Russian Active Measures Campaigns And Interference in the 2016 US Election Volume 5: Counterintelligence Threats and Vulnerabilities. Pg. 195

[50] United States District Court for the District of Columbia. SEARCH AND SEIZURE WARRANT. July 12th, 2018. AMENDED AFFIDAVIT IN SUPPORT

OF AN APPLICATION FOR A SEARCH WARRANT. Pg. 16

[51] Report of the Select Committee on Intelligence United States Senate On Russian Active Measures Campaigns And Interference in the 2016 US Election Volume 5: Counterintelligence Threats and Vulnerabilities. Pg. 195

[52] United States District Court for the District of Massachusetts. APPLICATION FOR A SEARCH WARRANT. March 27th, 2018. AFFIDAVIT IN SUPPORT OF AN APPLICATION FOR SEARCH WARRANTS. Pg. 16

[53] Schindler, John R. ""Vladimir Putin Has Already Won Our Election," *The Observer*. August 13th, 2016

[54] United States District Court for the District of Columbia. APPLICATION FOR SEARCH AND SEIZURE WARRANT. October 17th, 2017. AFFIDAVIT IN SUPPORT OF AN APPLICATION FOR A SEARCH WARRANT. Pg. 11

[55] Corsi, Jerome. "Trump advisor: Wikileaks plotting email dump to derail Hillary," *WorldNetDaily*. August 15th, 2016

[56] Kaczynski, Andrew; McDermott, Nathan; Massie, Chris. "Trump adviser Roger Stone repeatedly claimed to know of forthcoming WikiLeaks dumps," *CNN*. March 20th, 2017

[57] United States District Court for the District of Columbia. APPLICATION FOR SEARCH AND SEIZURE WARRANT. August 7th, 2017. AFFIDAVIT IN SUPPORT OF AN APPLICATION FOR A SEARCH WARRANT. Pg. 5

[58] United States District Court for the District of Columbia. APPLICATION FOR SEARCH AND SEIZURE WARRANT. February 13th, 2019. AFFIDAVIT IN SUPPORT OF AN APPLICATION FOR A SEARCH WARRANT. Pg. 29

[59] Wheeler, Marcy. "ROGER STONE'S 2016 "STOP THE STEAL" EFFORT MAY HAVE BEEN COORDINATED WITH RUSSIA," *EmptyWheel*. November 14th, 2020

[60] United States District Court for the District of Columbia. APPLICATION FOR SEARCH AND SEIZURE WARRANT. AFFIDAVIT IN SUPPORT OF AN APPLICATION FOR A SEARCH WARRANT. Pg. 12

[61] Report of the Select Committee on Intelligence United States Senate On Russian Active Measures Campaigns And Interference in the 2016 US Election Volume 5: Counterintelligence Threats and Vulnerabilities. Pg. 242 [Footnote 1596]

[62] Guccifer2. "DCCC Docs from Pelosi's PC," *GUCCIFER 2.0 WordPress*. August 31st, 2016

[63] Corsi, Jerome. *Silent No More*. New York, NY: Post Hill Press, 2019. Pg. 83

[64] Holliday, Shelby; Nicholas, Peter; Ballhaus, Rebecca. "Jerome Corsi Says Roger Stone Sought 'Cover Story' for 2016 Tweet," *The Wall Street Journal*. November 28th, 2018

[65] Ross, Chuck. "Randy Credico Claimed Not To Know Any WikiLeaks Lawyers. Turns Out He Is Represented By One," *The Daily Caller*. November 20th, 2018

[66] Kocieniewski, David. "The Civil Rights Warrior Who May Have Linked Roger Stone to WikiLeaks," *Bloomberg*. January 30th, 2019

[67] Toobin, Jeffrey. "Roger Stone's and Jerome Corsi's Time in the Barrel," *The New Yorker*. February 11th, 2019

[68] Report of the Select Committee on Intelligence United States Senate On Russian Active Measures Campaigns And Interference in the 2016 US Election Volume 5: Counterintelligence Threats and Vulnerabilities. Pg. 242-243

[69] Kaczynski, Andrew; McDermott, Nathan. "Special counsel's office has radio interviews between Roger Stone and alleged WikiLeaks 'back channel'" *CNN*. October 5th, 2018

[70] Mueller, III, Robert S. *Report On The Investigation Into Russian Interference In The 2016 Presidential Election*. Department of Justice, Washington, DC. March 2019. Pg. 44

[71] United States District Court for the District of Columbia. APPLICATION FOR A SEARCH WARRANT. August 7th, 2017. AFFIDAVIT IN SUPPORT OF AN APPLICATION FOR A SEARCH WARRANT. Pg. 6

[72] Report of the Select Committee on Intelligence United States Senate On Russian Active Measures Campaigns And Interference in the 2016 US Election Volume 5: Counterintelligence Threats and Vulnerabilities. Pg. 246-247

[73] Boccagno, Julia. "WikiLeaks changes venue for "October surprise" announcement," *CBS News*. October 3rd, 2016

[74] United States District Court for the District of Columbia. APPLICATION FOR A SEARCH WARRANT. February 13th, 2019. AFFIDAVIT IN SUPPORT OF AN APPLICATION FOR A SEARCH WARRANT. Pg. 12

[75] Kirkland, Allegra. "WikiLeaks Cancels, Then Hints At Clinton-Related October Surprise," *TalkingPointsMemo*. October 3rd, 2016

[76] Report of the Select Committee on Intelligence United States Senate On Russian Active Measures Campaigns And Interference in the 2016 US Election Volume 5: Counterintelligence Threats and Vulnerabilities. Pg. 247-248

[77] Samuelsohn, Darren; Gerstein, Josh. "Insults, threats and 'Godfather' impressions: Feds parade Roger Stone witness-tampering evidence," *Politico*. November 7th, 2019

[78] United States District Court for the District of Columbia. APPLICATION FOR A SEARCH WARRANT. July 12th, 2018. AMENDED AFFIDAVIT IN SUPPORT OF AN APPLICATION FOR A SEARCH WARRANT. Pg. 17

[79] United States District Court for the District of Columbia. APPLICATION FOR A SEARCH WARRANT. March 14th, 2018. AFFIDAVIT IN SUPPORT OF AN APPLICATION FOR A SEARCH WARRANT. Pg. 13-14

[80] United States District Court for the District of Columbia. APPLICATION FOR A SEARCH WARRANT. February 13th, 2019. AFFIDAVIT IN SUPPORT OF AN APPLICATION FOR A SEARCH WARRANT. Pg. 29

[81] Report of the Select Committee on Intelligence United States Senate On Russian Active Measures Campaigns And Interference in the 2016 US Election Volume 5: Counterintelligence Threats and Vulnerabilities. Pg. 248-249

[82] Ross, Chuck. "EXCLUSIVE: Jerome Corsi Testified That Roger Stone Sought WikiLeaks' Help To Rebut 'Access Hollywood' Tape," *The Daily Caller*. November 27th, 2018

[83] Mueller, III, Robert S. *Report On The Investigation Into Russian Interference In The 2016 Presidential Election*. Department of Justice, Washington, DC. March 2019. Pg. 176

[84] United States District Court for the District of Columbia. APPLICATION FOR A SEARCH WARRANT. July 12th, 2018. AMENDED AFFIDAVIT IN SUPPORT OF AN APPLICATION FOR A SEARCH WARRANT. Pg. 18-19

[85] Report of the Select Committee on Intelligence United States Senate On Russian Active Measures Campaigns And Interference in the 2016 US Election Volume 5: Counterintelligence Threats and Vulnerabilities. Pg. 249 [Footnote 1667]

[86] Mueller, III, Robert S. *Report On The Investigation Into Russian Interference In The 2016 Presidential Election*. Department of Justice, Washington, DC. March 2019. Pg. 58-59

[87] Report of the Select Committee on Intelligence United States Senate On Russian Active Measures Campaigns And Interference in the 2016 US Election Volume 5: Counterintelligence Threats and Vulnerabilities. Pg. 249-250

[88] Report of the Select Committee on Intelligence United States Senate On Russian Active Measures Campaigns And Interference in the 2016 US Election Volume 5: Counterintelligence Threats and Vulnerabilities. Pg. 250

[89] DHS Press Office. "Joint Statement from the Department Of Homeland Security and Office of the Director of National Intelligence on Election Security," *The Department of Homeland Security*. October 7th, 2016

[90] United States District Court for the District of Columbia. APPLICATION FOR A SEARCH WARRANT. July 12th, 2018. AMENDED AFFIDAVIT IN SUPPORT OF AN APPLICATION FOR A SEARCH WARRANT. Pg. 19

[91] Report of the Select Committee on Intelligence United States Senate On Russian Active Measures Campaigns And Interference in the 2016 US Election Volume 5:

Counterintelligence Threats and Vulnerabilities. Pg. 251

[92] United States District Court for the District of Columbia. APPLICATION FOR A SEARCH WARRANT. February 13th, 2019. AFFIDAVIT IN SUPPORT OF AN APPLICATION FOR A SEARCH WARRANT. Pg. 13-14

[93] United States District Court for the District of Columbia. APPLICATION FOR A SEARCH WARRANT. August 2nd, 2018. AFFIDAVIT IN SUPPORT OF AN APPLICATION FOR A SEARCH WARRANT. Pg. 22

[94] Report of the Select Committee on Intelligence United States Senate On Russian Active Measures Campaigns And Interference in the 2016 US Election Volume 5: Counterintelligence Threats and Vulnerabilities. Pg. 251-252

[95] Tau, Byron; Holliday, Shelby. "Roger Stone Found Guilty of Lying to Congress, Witness Tampering," *The Wall Street Journal*. November 15th, 2019

[96] Report of the Select Committee on Intelligence United States Senate On Russian Active Measures Campaigns And Interference in the 2016 US Election Volume 5: Counterintelligence Threats and Vulnerabilities. Pg. 241-242

[97] Report of the Select Committee on Intelligence United States Senate On Russian Active Measures Campaigns And Interference in the 2016 US Election Volume 5: Counterintelligence Threats and Vulnerabilities. Pg. 224

Chapter 17:
Black Caviar: Manafort on the Trump Campaign

Paul Manafort's Family and Financial Crises Before the Campaign

Following the Maidan Revolution, Manafort vanished from the DC circuit, prompting Roger Stone to distribute an email with the subject line, "Where is Paul Manafort?" Stone listed multiple choice options: 1.) *Was seen chauffeuring Yanukovych around Moscow,* 2.) *Was seen loading gold bullion on an Army Transport plane from a remote airstrip outside Kyiv and taking off seconds before a mob arrived at the site,* and 3.) *Is playing golf in Palm Beach.*[1]

Manafort had unfinished business in Ukraine. In September of 2014, he returned to Kyiv to salvage what he could of his business and political relationships.[2] Ukraine had changed profoundly. Viktor Yanukovych had fled to Russia. In March 2014, Dmytro Firtash was arrested by Austrian authorities in Vienna on an FBI warrant for bribery charges.[3] With few allies left in the country, Manafort re-established contact with Serhiy Lyovochkin.[4]

Lyovochkin offered to pay Manafort to reorganize what was left of the Party of Regions into a new political entity that he recommended be called the Opposition Bloc (OB). According to Manafort's thinking, the newly minted OB could more effectively recruit members from the ranks of those critical of the new Western-friendly government in Kyiv. Another individual key to the establishment of OB was Rinat Akhmetov, the wealthiest oligarch in Ukraine, whom Manafort had met years earlier through a recommendation from Oleg Deripaska.[5]

Konstantin Kilimnik managed Manafort's office in Ukraine. While Manafort was shadow-managing the OB's campaign to win seats in the upcoming October 2014 parliamentary election, Lyovochkin wanted to attack the OB's political opponents. Kilimnik brought on Sam Patten for the job, a Republican political consultant he had met at the International Republican Institute in Moscow.[6] The campaign was a relative success, with the OB winning 10% of the parliamentary seats, outperforming by roughly twice its expected results.

Shortly after that, Paul Manafort's personal life descended into a sordid crisis. In November of 2014, Manafort's wife Kathleen and their two daughters discovered that he had been carrying on an extramarital affair.[7] In the aftermath, Kathleen Manafort explained to her daughters that he had been pressuring her against her wishes to engage in group sex activities that he would watch and film.[8] The "gang bangs," as the disgusted daughters referred to them in a series of texts, occurred when Paul and Kathleen Manafort traveled abroad.[9]

A series of professional and legal setbacks compounded Paul Manafort's personal problems. He and Kilimnik believed their new Ukrainian sponsors had failed to pay them nearly $2.4 million.[10] In yet another unwelcome development, Oleg Deripaska began legal proceedings to collect "debts" of up to $18.9 million related to the suspect Pericles investment.[11]

Deripaska's pursuit of legal action against Manafort can be interpreted in several ways. If you assume that their original business dealings were above board, it may be exactly as it appears: simply a businessman trying to collect his debts. However, suppose you interpret the Black Sea Cable deal as an elaborate method to disguise money laundering or a bribe. In that case, Deripaska's legal actions can be seen as a disingenuous means of exerting pressure on Manafort. Either way, Manafort was placed in an uncomfortable position. Manafort's deputy, Rick Gates, later recalled that Manafort and Deripaska met several times between 2009 and 2014, though he did not know the substance of the meetings.

Nor were Deripaska's attorneys the only people poking around Manafort's financial affairs. During his tenure as President of Ukraine, Manafort came to the attention of the Justice Department's Money Laundering and Asset Recovery Section (MLARS) as part of a probe into Viktor Yanukovych's theft and laundering of tens of billions of dollars. DOJ investigators were interested in whether Manafort had used offshore accounts to launder funds and evade U.S. taxes. Manafort was interviewed by the FBI twice, first in March 2013 and then in July 2014.[12] Manafort admitted that he maintained offshore accounts in Cyprus at the suggestion of the Ukrainian oligarchs who paid him. Manafort further told the FBI that he had engaged in significant work for Rinat Akhmetov and Oleg Deripaska over the years.[13] *NBC News* estimated that the business dealings between Manafort and Deripaska amounted to nearly $60 million.[14]

The DOJ investigation was a pitiful affair that obtained neither Manafort's foreign banking records nor his tax returns.[15] Had investigators obtained these documents, they would have discovered that Manafort and Rick Gates were involved in numerous illegal money laundering and tax evasion schemes. Between 2008 and 2014, Manafort and his Ukrainian patrons engaged in an elaborate shell game, moving large amounts of money from offshore into various Manafort and Gates-controlled accounts. Manafort and Gates were instructed to use Cypriot shell companies by their Ukrainian oligarch sponsors, all of whom were linked to the Party of Regions, including Rinat Akhmetov, Serhiy Lyovochkin, Serhiy Tihipko, Boris Kolesnikov, and Andriy Klyuyev.[16] One of the shell companies Manafort used to wire millions of dollars to the US, Lucicle Consultants, received money from a Ukrainian businessman and parliamentarian named Ivan Fursin, a known close associate of Semyon Mogilevich.[17]

Manafort and Gates were assisted in these matters by an elite Cypriot lawyer named Kypros Chrysostomides, who listed Oleg Deripaska among his clients. Konstantin Kilimnik was also involved, conducting a final review of all the payments made.[18] Manafort and Gates then laundered the money. They evaded U.S. taxes through a variety of means, including "loaning" the money to themselves, using offshore vehicles to make expensive purchases on their behalf from vendors in the United States, and engaging in a complex set of real estate transactions that included purchasing and taking out loans on properties and paying for costly renovations.[19] Ultimately, more than $75 million passed through Manafort's various offshore accounts, with more than $30 million concealed from the US Department of Treasury.

In March 2015, Deripaska instructed his US-based lawyer, Adam Waldman, to "look into" the Pericles matter. Despite his best efforts, Waldman's quest to locate Manafort proved remarkably difficult. He left Manafort several voicemails and sent emails but was initially unable to establish contact. Manafort, stricken with cascading personal and financial difficulties, seemed to go underground. He eventually responded to Waldman, directing him to Rick Gates. The two held an inconclusive meeting at Waldman's home in Washington, DC, where Gates nervously gave a meandering explanation about the Black Sea Cable deal.[20]

Gates was deposed later on the matter, and Manafort's mysterious conflict with Deripaska continued into 2016. Nor was this his only problem; in addition to the Opposition Bloc in Ukraine withholding millions of dollars of fees that Manafort felt he was owed, he faced an unexpected tax bill. On April 17th, 2015, Gates emailed Manafort, informing him that he owed an additional $509,000 in taxes for the previous year. "WTF?" Manafort replied. "How could I be blindsided by this? You told me you were on top of this. We need to discuss options. This is a disaster."[21]

Konstantin Kilimnik emailed Gates promising to send $500,000 to "calm down Paul," but Manafort was on a downward spiral.[22] The difficulties facing Manafort reached a crescendo in the Spring of 2015, and he appeared to suffer a breakdown, with his daughters speculating that he might even be suicidal.[23] He checked himself into a clinic in Arizona for what one of his daughters described as "sex addiction." However, despite this low point, Manafort emerged from the clinic with what he described to his daughters as a new sense of self-awareness. The influence peddler and international man of mystery was preparing to embark on a journey that would take him to the heights of the most infamous presidential campaign in American history.

Thomas Barrack and Roger Stone
Get Manafort Hired onto the Trump Campaign

Manafort began seeking a role on the Trump Campaign in January 2016. According to Gates, Manafort believed holding such a position would be "good for business" and help them collect their debts in Ukraine. He used his connections with

Roger Stone and the billionaire financier, real estate investor, and Trump friend Thomas Barrack to send initial feelers to the campaign.[24] Manafort and Barrack had met 40 years earlier in Beirut while the former was doing business for a Saudi construction company, and the two became fast friends. Barrack, a Lebanese Christian who had grown up in California, had close ties to the Saudi royal family and leveraged the relationship to gain access to the Reagan White House.[25] Barrack was indicted for failing to register as a foreign agent for the United Arab Emirates, obstruction of justice, and lying to investigators. He was subsequently acquitted.[26]

Manafort met with Barrack at the Montage Hotel in Beverly Hills on January 30th, 2016, and requested that he use his influence with Trump to win him a position on the campaign.[27] Barrack emailed Jared and Ivanka, suggesting that Manafort could help.[28] By February 25th, he had spoken twice with Trump and argued that Manafort could help him secure the nomination at the convention against any last-ditch efforts by the Republican establishment. Manafort sent Barrack two sets of memos that Rick Gates helped him prepare articulating arguments in support of his joining the campaign. Barrack added a personal cover letter that described Manafort as "the most experienced and lethal of managers" and "a killer."

"I have managed Presidential campaigns around the world," Manafort wrote to Trump. "I have had no client relationships dealing with Washington since around 2005. I have avoided the establishment in Washington since 2005." He continued, "I will not bring Washington baggage." Manafort highlighted the fact that he owned a condo in Trump Tower and initially pitched himself as occupying the role of convention manager. Lastly, in what would ultimately prove to be his most persuasive argument, Manafort wrote, "I am not looking for a paid job."[29]

Following Trump's commanding wins on Super Tuesday, March 1st, 2016, Barrack continued to promote Manafort to Trump, Jared and Ivanka. Throughout this period, Manafort and Barrack were in close and continuous contact with Roger Stone. "You are the only one who can do this," Stone wrote to Barrack. "Donald sees you as a peer - the rest of us are just vassals. [H]e has no research or plan. [H]is handlers reinforce his worst instincts ... I think Ivanka and Jared and Don [Jr] and Eric have had their fill of Corey. We will know Tues if we are headed to a brokered convention- if so he needs Manafort or he will get robbed."[30]

Stone pressed his case with Trump, holding ten phone calls with him between March 1st and 16th. Throughout the same period, Manafort spoke with Stone over the phone eleven times. By the evening of March 16th, Stone and Barrack's efforts paid off, and the Trump campaign hired Manafort. "You are the Best!!!" Manafort wrote in the subject line of an email to Barrack. "[W]e are going to have so much fun and change the world in the process."

Six days earlier, on March 10th, GRU Unit 26165 had begun targeting the Clinton campaign in its data exfiltration operations. The Senate Intelligence report states that Konstantin Kilimnik "may be connected to the GRU hack-and-leak operation." The section describing the "fragmentary evidence" of his involvement is almost entirely redacted. The report further describes Manafort's involvement in the hack and leak as "largely unknown." However, it points towards "two pieces of information" that suggest he could have been involved. The following section describing the information is nearly entirely redacted, except for a small part mentioning Jeffrey Yohai, Manafort's now incarcerated ex-son-in-law who was married to one of his daughters at the time. Curiously, Manafort and Yohai were engaged in a series of highly suspect real estate and financial transactions at key moments during the 2016 election involving several financial institutions with tantalizing links to Eurasian organized crime. What this had to do with the GRU's hack-and-leak campaign is a mystery. Unfortunately, at the time of this writing, there is not enough publicly available information to write about these matters with any authority. This is an important avenue for future investigators.[31]

According to *The Wall Street Journal*, in August of 2016, the billionaire sex offender Jeffrey Epstein scheduled Thomas Barrack to join him for lunch with Vitaly Churkin, Russia's Ambassador to the UN, and the former Israeli Prime Minister Ehud Barak. Epstein and Barrack's relationship went back years. Epstein scheduled two more meetings with Barrack in September of 2016, including at a large get together at his Manhattan townhouse that also included Vitaly Churkin and Ehud Barak. Also in September, Epstein scheduled a meeting with Nicholas

Ribis, a former Trump employee who worked with him at his casinos in Atlantic City and as the CEO of Trump Hotels and Casino Resorts in the 1990s. Ribis later worked for Thomas Barrack at NorthStar Capital. Ribis and Epstein had met several times between 2011 and 2017.[32]

Manafort, Kilimnik, Pro-Kremlin Oligarchs, and the Trump Campaign

Manafort joined Trump for dinner at Mar-a-Lago on March 24th, and five days later, the campaign officially announced that Manafort had been hired. That same day, March 29th, Rick Gates sent Konstantin Kilimnik an email with five attachments, four of which consisted of personal memoranda drafted by Gates and signed off by Manafort personally addressed to Oleg Deripaska and three Ukrainian members of the pro-Kremlin Opposition Bloc: Serhiy Lyovochkin, Rinat Akhmetov and Akhmetov's right-hand man, Borys Kolesnikov. All had been involved with Manafort's activities in Ukraine. Gates also included a press release announcing the Trump campaign's hiring of Manafort for Kilimnik to translate and distribute.[33]

"I am hopeful that we are able to talk about this development with Trump where I can brief you in more detail," Manafort wrote to Deripaska, "I look forward to speaking with you soon." Rick Gates believed Manafort was attempting to confirm that Deripaska was dropping the Pericles matter. He further believed that Manafort didn't need to address this explicitly in writing in the memo to Deripaska as he had already discussed the matter with Kilimnik.

Kilimnik knew of Manafort's courting of the Trump campaign. He spoke of the matter with Sam Patten before Manafort was officially hired, prompting Patten to believe that Kilimnik had communicated with Manafort about the Trump campaign. While Patten had thought the idea of Trump hiring Manafort was ridiculous, Kilimnik believed it was likely and forwarded the press release of the news to Patten to emphasize how wrong his skepticism had been.

"In late 2015, Lyovochkin asked me whether it was true that Trump was going to hire Manafort to run his campaign," Patten wrote in a 2019 article for *Wired*. "I told Lyovochkin that was an absurd notion; that Trump would have to be nuts to do such a thing."[34] If Patten's timeline is to be trusted, Lyovochkin knew Manafort's plans to join the Trump campaign months before Tom Barrack. Given that Lyovochkin was close to both Manafort and especially Kilimnik, it seems plausible that they could have discussed this possibility for months.

"Dad and Trump are literally living in the same building, and mom says they go up and down all day long hanging and plotting with each other," Jessica Manafort wrote to her sister in an April 7th text. The sisters' feelings about their father's position on Trump's campaign veered between disgust and pride. One described Manafort and Trump's relationship as the "most dangerous friendship in America."

"I assume you've shown our friends my media coverage, right?" Manafort wrote to Kilimnik on April 10th, referring to reports that he had joined the Trump campaign.[35]

"Absolutely," Kilimnik replied. "Everyone."

"How do we use to get whole?" Manafort replied. "Has ovd [Oleg Vladimirovich Deripaska] operation seen?"

"Yes," Kilimnik responded. "I have been sending everything to Victor [Boyarkin], who has been forwarding the coverage directly to OVD."

The US Treasury Department describes Victor Boyarkin as "a former GRU officer who reports directly to Deripaska and has led business negotiations on Deripaska's behalf."[36] The Senate Intelligence report described Boyarkin as "a Russian intelligence officer affiliated with the GRU."[37] Throughout the 1990s, Boyarkin served at Russian embassies in the United States and Mexico, dealing in military affairs. By the 2000s, Boyarkin worked for Deripaska's company, Rusal, where he used his unique skill set to negotiate with foreign dictators to gain access to natural resources for the Russian metals company. Boyarkin had known Manafort since they worked together on Deripaska's behalf in Montenegro in 2006.

"He owed us a lot of money," Boyarkin told *Time* in late 2018, referring to his interactions with Manafort during the 2016 campaign. "And he was offering ways to pay it back." Boyarkin stated that Deripaska had tasked him with collecting the money Manafort owed him. "I came down hard on him," Boyarkin claimed.[38]

The full extent of the communications between Paul Manafort and Konstantin Kilimnik are not publicly available. Contemporaneous with their email correspondence, they also used encrypted applications such as Viber, Signal, and WhatsApp to communicate. In addition to encrypted apps, Manafort and Kilimnik engaged in foldering, which consists of writing email drafts without sending them in a shared email account where two parties can read messages without ever having sent them. They used code words such as check the "tea bag" or the "updated travel schedule" to indicate when new messages should be read.[39]

No known communications between Manafort and Kilimnik have ever been uncovered between April 11th and May 6th, though they may have communicated over encrypted apps. However, there are indications that the two were in contact. On April 22nd, Kilimnik sent a series of emails to an associate in which he claimed that Manafort had a "clever plan" to defeat Hillary Clinton. Kilimnik expressed confidence that Trump would win, describing Manafort as a good strategist and claiming that there could be surprises even in American politics. Kilimnik reiterated that Manafort was confident that Trump would win and had "a clever plan of screwing Clinton."[40]

Konstantin Kilimnik Provides Internal Trump Polling Data To Russian Intelligence

In a May 5th email to Gates, Manafort wrote that Kilimnik was "coming to DC for a wedding" and "wanted to meet up." Later, investigators were unable to determine how Manafort knew about Kilimnik's trip, nor has any evidence surfaced that Kilimnik did, in fact, attend a wedding at this time. Manafort and Kilimnik's use of coded language has led some to speculate that Manafort meant something else by "wedding." After arriving in DC on the 5th, the next evening, Kilimnik visited the "Off the Record" bar in the basement of the Hay Adams hotel, across the street from the White House.[41] He appears to have had drinks with, among others, Jon Finer, the chief of staff to then-Secretary of State John Kerry. Kilimnik, who was unimpressed or disagreed with his views on Ukraine, wrote in a later email that he had met with "Finer or whatever the fuck is his name. In total space."[42]

That same evening, Kilimnik communicated with Manafort and Gates to arrange a 7:30am meeting with Manafort at the Peninsula Hotel in New York. Before the meeting, Kilimnik had been collecting information on political developments in Ukraine. As part of this preparation, he met with the former Minister of Fuel and Energy under Yanukovych, Yuriy Boyko. The pro-Russian Boyko was a close associate of Dmytro Firtash and the Putin-ally Viktor Medvedchuk, who was later accused by Ukrainian authorities of treason.[43] Boyko had just returned from a trip to Moscow where he likely met with senior leaders from the Kremlin and told Kilimnik of a plan to increase election participation in Eastern Ukraine. Kilimnik, also in contact with Serhiy Lyovochkin throughout this period, reportedly shared the plan with Manafort during their May 7th meeting.

At the Peninsula Hotel meeting, Manafort described his vision for Trump's path to victory to Kilimnik and the margins by which he thought Trump might win. He did so with the understanding that Kilimnik would pass the information to their contacts in Russia and Ukraine, including Oleg Deripaska. Kilimnik returned to DC after the meeting. Gates and Kilimnik spoke over the phone at 5:26 pm, before he departed from Washington Dulles at 6:50 pm. Shortly after Gates and Kilimnik's 13-minute phone call, Gates spoke with Roger Stone for approximately 34 minutes. It remains unknown what Gates and Stone spoke about or if it had to do with Kilimnik's meeting with Manafort that morning. Kilimnik later told Sam Patten that he and Manafort had discussed whether Trump "[has] a shot; if he has a shot, why."[44] The next day, May 8th, Patten flew to Kyiv to meet with Kilimnik.

Shortly after that, Manafort instructed Gates to send Kilimnik internal Trump campaign polling data, which he expected to be forwarded to Deripaska and oligarchs in Ukraine, including Lyovochkin and Akhmetov.[45] The polling data was prepared by Tony Fabrizio, the pollster who had worked with Manafort in Ukraine and a disciple of Arthur Finkelstein. Gates sent Kilimnik "topline" data, which included information such as the states polled, the dates the polls took place, and the voter information gathered (i.e. how many are undecided, decided GOP, etc.). Gates copied and pasted the information from Fabrizio's summaries to messages he sent Kilimnik via the encrypted WhatsApp and then deleted the messages daily. According to the US Treasury Department, Kilimnik shared the polling data with Russian intelligence.[46]

The polling data generated by Fabrizio, the Trump campaign's primary pollster, was highly valued by the campaign.

According to Brad Parscale, the Trump campaign digital director, 98% of the campaign's resource allocation was determined by polling and data. Manafort took polling very seriously and, on several occasions, emphasized that the data they generated should not be shared, describing it as "sensitive stuff."[47] At the end of one email Manafort received containing Fabrizio's polling data, he wrote, "I don't want these results shared with anyone outside of the recipients of this email."[48]

Kilimnik knew very well the importance that Manafort attached to polling. "Manafort is a guy who can merge, you know, strategy and messages into something that will work for victory," Kilimnik told a reporter in 2018. "I've seen him work in different countries, and...he really does take seriously his polling and can spend, you know, two weeks going through the data, and he'll come [up] with the best strategy you can ever have."[49]

On May 19th, Manafort was promoted to campaign Chairman, replacing Corey Lewandowski, who was distrusted by the Trump children and personally despised by Michael Cohen and Roger Stone. Rick Gates also joined the Trump campaign as Manafort's deputy. Two days later, on May 21st, Manafort was contacted by a young and ambitious, if virtually unknown, Trump foreign policy advisor based out of London named George Papadopoulos. Papadopoulos forwarded an email he had received from a Russian claiming to have contacts with the Foreign Ministry who were open to meeting with Trump.[50] "Russia has been eager to Mr. Trump for quite sometime [sic]," Papadopoulos wrote to Manafort, "and have been reaching out to me to discuss."

"We need someone to communicate that DT [Trump] is not doing these trips," Manafort wrote, forwarding the email to Gates. "It should be someone low-level on the campaign so as not to send any signal."[51]

No communications between Manafort and Kilimnik from May 7th to July 7th are publicly available, nor appear to have ever been unearthed by investigators. However, Gates sent Kilimnik internal polling data throughout this period. May 25th is the last known date hackers from the GRU exfiltrated data from the DNC. The following month of June saw several significant developments. On June 9th, Manafort participated in the infamous Trump Tower meeting, which will be covered at length shortly. Three days after that meeting, on June 12th, Julian

Assange announced during an interview on ITV that WikiLeaks would be publishing previously unreleased Hillary Clinton emails. Two days after that, *The Washington Post* ran a story about how the cyber security firm CrowdStrike had assessed that it was Russian hackers who had breached the DNC.

Interest within the Trump campaign in Hillary's missing emails had been ramping up over the spring. Sometime in May, Roger Stone alerted Manafort and Gates that WikiLeaks would be releasing Hillary's emails but didn't provide an exact date for the release. Throughout April and May, Stone spoke over the phone with Gates 67 times and Manafort 64 times. Gates later testified that at Trump family meetings he attended, Donald Trump Jr. regularly inquired about Hillary's emails. Other campaign officials Gates heard ask about the emails included Jared Kushner, Michael Flynn, Corey Lewandowski, Senator Jeff Sessions, and Trump campaign co-chair Sam Clovis. By June, Stone told Manafort that "a source close to WikiLeaks confirmed that WikiLeaks had the emails from Clinton's server." Manafort instructed Gates to follow up with Stone "from time to time" to see if his WikiLeaks insider knowledge was "real and viable."[52]

Nor was it only individuals within the Trump campaign who were interested. Following Assange's June 12th announcement, Gates spoke with Republican National Committee head Reince Priebus and later described the RNC as being "energized" by a potential WikiLeaks dump of Clinton emails. Based on a conversation he had with Manafort, Gates learned that the RNC was planning "to run the WikiLeaks issue to ground." In anticipation of the release, the RNC planned to issue press releases to amplify their political impact. Gates later told the FBI that the RNC "indicated they knew the timing of the upcoming releases." He claimed to be unaware of how the RNC could have this information.[53]

It was around this time that Manafort, parroting a view held by Kilimnik and later pushed by Russian intelligence, pushed the false notion that forces in Ukraine carried out the hack of the DNC. The Trump campaign surrogate Lieutenant General Michael Flynn shared the view that the Russians were not responsible for the cyber attack. Flynn, who Gates described as having more Russian contacts than even Manafort, was "adamant" that the Russians didn't carry out the hack because he doubted that US Intelligence could determine who had conducted the hack.[54] Roger Stone, on the other hand, informed Gates that the Russians might have conducted the hack.

Manafort's history in Ukraine soon caused him serious problems. Already in April, Manafort had told Hope Hicks to disregard questions sent by *The Washington Post* about his business relationships in Ukraine and with Oleg Deripaska.[55] However, that wouldn't be the end of the inquiries into those matters. On July 7th, Josh Kovensky, a reporter from the *Kyiv Post*, reached out to Manafort for comments regarding his past business activities, including the Pericles venture with Deripaska.[56] Manafort forwarded Kovensky's inquiry to Kilimnik with an "FYI" and asked if there was "any movement on this issue with our friend?" By "our friend," Manafort was referring to Deripaska.

"I am carefully optimistic on the question of our biggest interest," Kilimnik replied to Manafort. "Our friend V [Boyarkin] said there is lately significantly more attention to the campaign in his boss' [Deripaska's] mind, and he will be most likely looking for ways to reach out to you pretty soon, understanding all the time sensitivity. I am more than sure that it will be resolved, and we will get back to the original relationship with V's boss."[57]

"[T]ell V[ictor Boyarkin's] boss [Deripaska] that if he needs private briefings, we can accommodate," Manafort wrote back to Kilimnik eight minutes later. Despite Manafort's offer, he later denied ever having briefed Deripaska. When Kovensky's article was published the next day, Kilimnik emailed a copy to Manafort. Manafort responded that Kilimnik "should cover V[ictor Boyarkin] on this story and make certain that V understands this is all BS and the real facts are the ones we passed along last year."[58]

Despite the unavailability of communications between Manafort and Kilimnik, Kilimnik's correspondence during this period indicates that he had insider knowledge regarding the Trump campaign. Kilimnik's response to an email from Sam Patten sent in mid-July regarding the selection of Mike Pence as Trump's choice for Vice President suggests that he was discussing these matters with Manafort contemporaneously as the decisions were being made. "You know Paul," Kilimnik wrote to Patten, "he is focused on winning the elections and then dealing with foreign policy or whatever. The choice of VP is purely electoral, as I understand."

Black Caviar, the Grand Havana Room,
And a Mysterious Ukrainian Peace Plan

On July 28th, Kilimnik traveled from Kyiv to Moscow. The next day, he sent Manafort an email with "Black caviar" as the subject. "I met today with the guy who gave you your biggest black caviar jar several years ago," Kilimnik wrote. Manafort later identified the man who gave him the "black caviar" as Viktor Yanukovych, who then lived in exile in Moscow. According to Manafort, in 2010, Yanukovych gave him a $30-40,000 jar of black caviar at a lunch to celebrate his victory in the presidential election.[59] "We spent about 5 hours talking about his story," Kilimnik continued, "and I have several important messages from him to you. He asked me to go and brief you on our conversation. I said I have to run it by you first, but in principle, I am prepared to do it, provided that he buys me a ticket. It has to do about the future of his country and is quite interesting. So, if you are absolutely not against the concept, please let me know which dates/places will work, even next week, and I could come and see you."

"Tuesday's best," Manafort replied, "Tues or Weds in NYC." They settled on the evening of Tuesday, August 2nd. Kilimnik returned to Kyiv from Moscow on July 31st and emailed Manafort explaining that he needed "about two hours" to meet with him as "it is a long caviar story to tell."

Kilimnik passed through US customs at JFK International Airport at 7:43 pm on August 2nd. After wrapping up a 5:30 pm meeting with Trump and Rudy Giuliani, Manafort made his way to his rendezvous with Kilimnik scheduled for 9 pm at the Grand Havana Room, a private cigar lounge located in a building once owned by Jared Kushner, 666 Fifth Avenue in Manhattan. Manafort and Kilimnik met for dinner sometime after 9 pm, with Rick Gates arriving late.

There is no definitive account of what was discussed at the August 2nd Grand Havana Club meeting. Gates and Manafort's accounts differ slightly, and Manafort is known to have lied to subsequent Federal investigators about several matters, so his testimony is unreliable. However, at least three topics of conversation seem to have been broached: internal Trump campaign polling numbers and strategy, a potential peace plan for Ukraine that would create an autonomous republic in the

East, and Manafort's debts and business disputes with Deripaska and various figures in Ukraine related to the Opposition Bloc.

Manafort briefed Kilimnik, who had been receiving internal polling data via WhatsApp from Rick Gates since at least May, on the status of the presidential campaign. Kilimnik was keen on understanding Manafort's strategy to win. Walking him through the polling data, Manafort explained that the polls had identified swaths of voters in blue-collar, democratic-leaning states that Trump could peel away if he focused on economics and established a strong campaign ground game. Manafort emphasized these efforts in the following battleground states: Michigan, Wisconsin, Pennsylvania, and Minnesota.

Days earlier, on July 27th, Fabrizio sent Manafort an email with the subject "CONFIDENTIAL - EYES ONLY." Fabrizio's firm had just conducted a large round of polling in seventeen "target states" over mid-July. It detected what they viewed as a significant shift in the public view of the candidates images, with Trump having a 7-point net positive swing while Clinton suffered a 7-point swing downward. Manafort suggested to Kilimnik at the Grand Havana Club meeting that Clinton's high unfavorable ratings could tip the election toward Trump.[60]

Manafort and Kilimnik also discussed a potential resolution to the conflict between the Western-backed Ukrainian government and pro-Russian separatists in the East supported by the Russian military. According to Gates, Kilimnik delivered an "urgent" message to Manafort from Yanukovych asking if he would run his comeback campaign. Kilimnik then outlined a plan, which he had already run by a member of the Russian government, to have Eastern Ukraine declared an autonomous republic led by Yanukovych. Manafort recognized the plan as a "backdoor" means for Russia to control the Eastern industrial regions of Ukraine.[61]

Manafort, who later violated a plea agreement with prosecutors by lying, told investigators that he had informed Kilimnik that the plan was "crazy." He claimed that had he not cut off the discussion regarding Yanukovych's plan, Kilimnik would have asked him to have Trump come out in favor of the plan. Despite Gates and Manafort's testimony to the contrary, there are reasons to believe that Manafort did not dismiss Kilimnik's Ukrainian peace plan. Manafort and Kilimnik continued discussing and working on elements of the plan after

Trump was elected president. As late as 2018, Manafort and Kilimnik worked together to draft a poll to test out aspects of the plan.

Manafort and Kilimnik may have also spoken about how the Trump campaign formulated its policy vis-a-vis Russia and Ukraine. In an August 18th email sent to a reporter for *The Wall Street Journal*, Kilimnik wrote that he had "seen Manafort last week" and "got a sense that everything that Trump says about Russia and Ukraine is Trump's own emotional opinion, not campaign strategy." Kilimnik maintained that Manafort was not determining policy related to Russia; "otherwise, the message would have been much more balanced."

The third topic discussed related to financial disputes Manafort had with Oleg Deripaska and Ukrainian members of the Opposition Block that Manafort believed owed him money. According to Gates, Kilimnik told Manafort that Deripaska's lawsuit against him had been dismissed and that Kilimnik was working on getting the paperwork to confirm this outcome. Kilimnik also updated Manafort on what was happening with Lyovochkin, Akhmetov, and other of their "friends" in Ukraine." Kilimnik suggested that Akhmetov would pay Manafort what he was owed but was having trouble getting his money out of Ukraine.

Gates and Manafort left the Grand Havana Club separately from Kilimnik because they knew the press was tailing Manafort and they didn't want to be seen together.[62] Important unanswered questions remain about the August 2nd meeting. What little is known is solely based upon the testimony of Rick Gates and Paul Manafort. Gates arrived at the meeting significantly late, Manafort and Kilimnik were nearly finished with their dinner, and Manafort was convicted of repeatedly lying to subsequent investigators. Kilimnik later fled to Russia and was never able to be questioned. What was actually discussed between Manafort and Kilimnik may never be fully known. One obvious question is whether Manafort or the Trump campaign would have requested anything in return for supporting the Ukrainian peace plan. Curiously, on the evening of August 2nd, Oleg Deripaska's private jet landed at New Jersey's Teterboro airport. Customs and Border Protection records reported that its only passengers were Deripaska's wife, daughter, mother and father-in-law. Records obtained by later investigators show that

Kilimnik flew to New York on a commercial flight.[63]

The Black Ledger and Manafort's Final Days on the Campaign

While Manafort was in the thick of his intrigues, events were transpiring in Ukraine that would ultimately doom his position on the Trump campaign. A Ukrainian parliamentarian and investigative journalist named Serhiy Leshchenko was preparing to reveal to the world a portion of a hand-written "Black Ledger," which listed secret, illegal payments made by the Yanukovych regime that would eventually implicate Manafort.[64]

In February of 2016, Leshchenko received an envelope delivered to his parliamentary mailbox containing 22 pages supposedly from the ledger, though none of the payments listed in them were to Manafort. Unable at that time to verify the veracity of the documents, Leshchenko initially refrained from publishing them. Three months later, Leshchenko learned via Ukrainian media that Viktor Trepak, the former deputy head of Ukraine's security services, was in possession of the full ledger. At that point, on May 31st, Leshchenko held a press conference in which he released the portion of the Black Ledger he had received months earlier.[65]

According to Leshchenko, the National Anti-Corruption Bureau of Ukraine (NABU) eventually confirmed to *New York Times* reporter Andrew Kramer and an unnamed British journalist who was unable to publish because of UK libel laws that Manafort was listed on the ledger. On August 14th, less than two weeks after his meeting with Kilimnik at the Grand Havana Club, *The New York Times* published the sensational story revealing that Manafort had received $12.7 million in illicit, potentially illegal payments, from the Yanukovych regime.[66] None of this came as a surprise to Manafort.

Earlier that day, hours before the publication of the piece in the *Times*, Manafort attended a meeting in Trump Tower with Steve Bannon, Roger Ailes of *Fox News*, Rudy Giuliani, Chris Christie and Trump Himself. According to Bob Woodward, Manafort had troubles within the Trump campaign that were entirely unrelated to the impending Ukraine story. Trump's poll numbers were 12-16 points underwater and as campaign chairman Manafort was shouldering much of the blame. A story in the *Times* published on August 13th featured 20 unnamed

Republican sources and painted a dismal picture of chaos and dysfunction in the Trump camp.[67] Rebekah Mercer, daughter of the billionaire hedge fund manager and top Trump donor Robert Mercer, had described Manafort as a "disaster" to Bannon and urged the Breitbart firebrand to usurp his position on the campaign. Trump, infuriated by what he perceived as leaks to the *Times*, angrily attacked Manafort during the meeting.[68] Bannon was brought on as the CEO of the campaign that very day, with the understanding that Manafort wouldn't be fired, but rather would be able to "stick around as a figurehead."[69]

Following the contentious meeting, Manafort invited Bannon up to his condo in Trump Tower and showed him a draft copy of the Ukrainian Black Ledger story about to go live on *The New York Times* website. Manafort explained to Bannon, who believed the article was "a kill shot," that he had known that the article was in the works for two months.[70] This would have placed the time that Manafort learned of the article roughly around the same time he was elevated to the position of campaign chairman on June 20th, 2016. Manafort denied to Bannon that he had been the recipient of the cash, claiming that the money was distributed to people who worked for him in Ukraine. After the story was published, Trump, reportedly having received no advanced warning, was furious.[71] Manafort later told the FBI that he had previously discussed his work in Ukraine with Trump so that he wouldn't be blindsided if news related to Ukraine or Oleg Deripaska were to come out, but that Trump at the time was uninterested.[72]

Accounts of Manafort's final days on the Trump Campaign are primarily based upon the testimony of Paul Manafort and Steve Bannon. As mentioned, Manafort was convicted of violating his plea agreement by lying to the Special Counsel's office. The Senate Intelligence Committee made a criminal referral to DOJ regarding their suspicions that Bannon had lied to Congressional investigators.[73] Bannon is also believed to have been a key source for Bob Woodward's book *Fear*, which also describes this moment in the campaign.[74] While Manafort's and Bannon's unreliable testimony doesn't mean that the current account is wrong, it does raise questions. While it is certainly possible that Manafort was de facto replaced by Bannon mere hours *before* the Black Ledger story broke, when nobody on the campaign aside from Manafort and later Bannon knew about the impending story, it is a remarkable coincidence.

On August 18th, Konstantin Kilimnik emailed James Marson of *The Wall Street Journal* and explained that he was in "almost daily contacts with Manafort these days on this 'Ukraine crisis.'" Kilimnik further indicated that he was in contact with Rick Gates. As these communications were presumably made via encrypted apps, they are not part of the public record. "What others do not see," Kilimnik explained to Marson, "is that Manafort is building a parallel system of HQ, pretty similar to what he has done in Ukraine for [the Party of Regions], which plays a crucial role in key moments. Whether he has time to finish it is a key story."[75]

Kilimnik was not alone in this belief. Rick Gates told later investigators that Manafort, much as he had done with the Party of Region in Ukraine, established a "parallel system" of loyal contacts on the Trump campaign that included Digital Media Director Brad Parscale, pollster Tony Fabrizio and Jeff Sessions' chief of staff Rick Dearborn, among others. Gates believed that Manafort maintained these contacts after he officially left the Trump campaign.

On the same day Kilimnik emailed Marson, *Politico* published an article by Kenneth P. Vogel about Kilimnik that described him as "a Russian Army-trained linguist who has told a previous employer of a background with Russian intelligence."[76] It was the first time any hint of Kilimnik's connection with Russian intelligence was mentioned in the Western press. While the story largely vanished into the media maelstrom surrounding the campaign, the article led to an investigation into Kilimnik being launched in Ukraine.[77] The next day, on the 19th, *CNN* reported that the FBI and Justice Department had been looking into Manafort as part of a sprawling investigation into the corruption of the deposed Viktor Yanukovych regime.[78] Finally succumbing to negative press, Manafort tendered his resignation from the campaign that day.

However, while Manafort may no longer have held an official position on the Trump Campaign, he was not out of the picture. His subordinate Rick Gates stayed on with the campaign under Steve Bannon. Between his resignation and election day, Manafort also continued to speak with Donald Trump, Jared Kushner and Steve Bannon, among others.[79] Manafort later claimed that he spoke with Trump "a few times" and provided him with advice regarding his debate performances. In addition to speaking with Trump, Manafort claimed to have met with Kushner "once or twice" and to have spoken with him on the phone "five or six times." According to an email sent by Tony Fabrizio, he was aware that Manafort was scheduled to have breakfast with Kushner on September 13th, less than a month after his resignation. Manafort exchanged messages of encouragement via text with Bannon, but internally Bannon warned of further communication with the former campaign chairman.[80]

"We need to avoid [M]anafort like he has a disease," Bannon wrote in an email to RNC head Reince Priebus. "Dems will say that the Russians are helping us win."

Despite Bannon's concerns, Manafort kept in contact with the campaign. Kilimnik was aware of these communications, telling Sam Patten that Manafort kept up his contacts with Trump whilst remaining in the background. In particular, Manafort was involved in discussions that took place in mid-September between Rick Gates and former State Department official Frank Mermoud regarding a potential meeting or phone discussion between Trump and then-Ukrainian President Petro Poroshenko. While there is no indication that Trump ever spoke with Poroshenko, Mermoud later said that he understood Manafort was "still talking to candidate Trump quite a bit." According to Mermoud, Gates told him that Manafort was "still involved, particularly at this juncture, on political issues relating to the campaign."[81]

On October 21st, in the midst of WikiLeaks' staggered releases of John Podesta's emails, Manafort emailed Kushner a strategy memo that argued that the campaign should portray Clinton as "as the failed and corrupt champion of the establishment." He further argued that "WikiLeaks provides the Trump campaign the ability to make the case in a very credible way – by using the words of Clinton, its campaign officials and DNC members."[82]

On November 5th, three days before election day, Manafort emailed Trump, Kushner and Priebus a message, which he forwarded separately to *Fox News* Anchor Sean Hannity, with the subject line "Securing Victory." In the email, Manafort predicted a Trump victory in the election. Manafort advised that the Trump team devise a strategy to prepare the public and media for such a shocking and unexpected outcome or they would face severe backlash. Following a Trump victory, Manafort argued that the Clinton campaign would "'move immediately to discredit the DT victory and claim voter fraud and cyber-fraud, including the claim that the Russians have hacked into the voting machines and tampered with the results."

Three days later, Donald Trump was elected President of the United States. Records indicate that Manafort and Trump spoke on the night of the election.[83] What words passed between the influence peddler and the President-Elect remain unknown.

Manafort's Mystery Real Estate Transactions
And Potential Links to the Hack-and-Leak Operation

At key moments during the 2016 election, Paul Manafort and members of his family engaged in a series of mysterious and highly suspect financial and real estate transactions. As many, if not most, of these transactions may have been legal in the narrow sense, the un-redacted sections of the report produced by Special Counsel Robert Mueller do not address these activities. Prosecutors later established that Manafort used real estate transactions to launder money he received from his work in Ukraine.[84] The portions of the Senate Intelligence Committee report on counterintelligence that deal with these matters are heavily redacted and allude to a potential connection with the hack-and-leak campaign conducted by Russian military intelligence.[85]

At the heart of the Russian effort to benefit Donald Trump was a hack-and-leak operation targeting the Democratic National Committee (DNC). According to Volume 5 of the Senate Intelligence Committee's mammoth report into Russian Active Measures Campaigns and Interference in the 2016 US Election, "Manafort's involvement with the GRU hack-and-leak operation is largely unknown." The report continues: "Two pieces of information, however, raise the possibility of Manafort's potential connection to the hack-and-leak operations."

The following section describing these pieces of information is nearly entirely redacted except for a small section that mysteriously refers to Manafort's interactions with his then-son-in-law Jeffrey Yohai "during key periods in 2016." Why Manafort's relationship and communications with Yohai were mentioned in this critically important section, which goes to the heart of the question of what relationship the Trump campaign had with the Russian active measures operation, remains redacted.

An analysis of publicly available financial information indicates that Paul Manafort experienced liquidity crises on two separate occasions, between 2003-04 and in 2016. Each time, the liquidity crisis led to mortgage defaults, foreclosures, and legal actions. On both occasions, in order to make mortgage payments, Manafort took out loans on properties he owned that, in certain cases, appeared to exceed their market value. These two periods of apparent liquidity crisis for Manafort preceded events transpiring internationally that he could have reasonably assumed would lead to investigations into his finances by prosecutors and other authorities.

Manafort's first liquidity crisis was preceded by a May 2002 suicide bombing in Karachi, Pakistan, that killed eleven French naval engineers who were in the country working on a billion-dollar military contract involving submarines. The attack led to a 15-year investigation that came to be known in France as the "Karachi Affair." The scandal involved alleged kickbacks to French and Pakistani officials following a nearly $1 billion sale in 1994 of French submarines to the Pakistani Navy, some amount of which may have funded the 1995 Presidential campaign of then-Prime Minister Edouard Balladur in violation of French campaign finance law.

French investigators suspected the bombing may have been retaliation following France's decision to end the payment of kickbacks to military and intelligence figures in Pakistan. Paul Manafort was paid $272,000 by the Balladur campaign for consulting services.[86] French authorities also discovered that between 1994 and 1995, one of the two key intermediaries in the arms deal, Abdul Rahman Al Assir, paid Manafort $400,000 from Swiss bank accounts.[87]

At this time, Manafort owned four properties: a home in Alexandria, VA; a vacation home in Bridgehampton, NY; a horse farm in Lorton, VA; and a horse farm in Wellington, FL. In October 2003, Manafort, who by then had built a lucrative international political consulting career, failed to make a monthly mortgage payment to BB&T Bank on the horse farm in Wellington, FL. The property went into default. In February of

2004, he took out a $2.8 million loan from BB&T Bank, secured on the home he owned in Alexandria, Virginia. As the Virginia property sold eleven years later for only $1.5 million, it appears as though the loan greatly exceeded the market value property.

In March of 2004, Manafort borrowed $250,000 from Abdul Rahman Al Assir using the Alexandria, VA, property as collateral. Manafort sold the Wellington horse farm in July of 2004 for $1.55 million, causing BB&T to drop its foreclosure action. That same month, Thomas Barrack, the man who later got Manafort a job on the Trump campaign, assumed a $1,370,997 mortgage on Manafort's Bridgehampton vacation home. Barrack then turned around and loaned Manafort $389,002.

The nature of these loans, which in certain cases exceeded the market value of the properties used to secure them, raises questions. Publicly available documentation suggests that a large amount of cash was used by Manafort as collateral. While this is obviously justifiable from the lender's perspective, the use of cash as collateral would seem to obviate Manafort's need for liquidity. There are several potential explanations for this apparent contradiction. It does seem to resemble the loan-back scheme, by which individuals with access to dirty cash arrange for loans from friendly financial institutions in order to explain their wealth and liquidity to investigators.

Over the course of the 2016 election and immediately afterward, Manafort engaged in similar activities. While this could have been a continuation of his efforts to launder the money he earned in Ukraine, it seems possible that he could have used these methods to conceal additional payments or other forms of illicit financial activity. In the years leading up to the 2016 election, Manafort entered into a real estate investment partnership with his then-son-in-law Jeffrey Yohai, which was surprising given that he had initially opposed the union between his daughter Jessica and Yohai.

While Yohai had enjoyed a privileged upbringing, he had long been troubled by a gambling addiction and substance abuse, first using cocaine by the age of twelve and experimenting with heroin by sixteen. Despite Manafort's misgivings about Yohai, they entered into a real estate partnership together. According to hacked texts, Jessica Manafort believed her father and Yohai were in a 50/50 partnership. Beginning in 2014, Yohai began purchasing and taking out loans on a series of Los Angeles properties, ostensibly with the intent of flipping them for a profit. LLCs controlled by Yohai purchased four properties in Los Angeles.

According to *Bloomberg News*, Manafort, as well as his wife and daughter, provided Yohai with over $4 million in loans to make the purchases. The only other investor was the Oscar-winning actor Dustin Hoffman, who invested $3 million into a home Yohai was planning to flip on Blue Jay Way in Los Angeles.[88] By 2016, Yohai initially appeared flush with cash. In January, he offered to buy a mansion for $7 million cash from an as-yet unidentified Russian businessman who was in debt to several individuals in Russia who had liens on the house. Yohai put down a $160,000 deposit on the house but later backed out of the deal and lost the deposit.

In July 2016, Yohai appeared on the TV show "Million Dollar Listing" and offered to purchase three New York apartments for $15 million cash. The broker on the show claimed to have "seen proof of funds." Hacked texts reveal that when Andrea Manafort was asked whether her sister and Yohai had access to such funds, she responded, "Of course they don't."

"Her hubby is running a Ponzi scheme," Andrea wrote. "I'm sure of it."[89]

At the same time Yohai was willing to lose a $160,000 deposit and was publicly presenting himself as cash rich, LLCs related to his and Manafort's real estate partnership took out a series of loans on their various Los Angeles properties through a private money lender called Genesis Capital. One loan for $5,950,000 was made on January 28th, the same month Manafort began seeking a position on the Trump campaign, for an $8.5 million home on Stradella Road in Los Angeles.

Less than a month later, on February 18th, a Manafort/Yohai-linked LLC borrowed an additional $3,737,100 from Genesis secured by a Los Angeles property they purchased on Nottingham Avenue. On March 4th, Genesis provided yet another multimillion-dollar loan to a Yohai/Manafort-linked LLC, this time with a property located at 377 Union Street in Brooklyn as collateral. On June 1st, 2016, nineteen days before Manafort was elevated to the position of chairman of the Trump campaign, the Yohai/Manafort-linked MC Brooklyn Holdings, LLC failed to make a scheduled monthly payment on a Genesis

Capital loan.[90]

Over the summer of 2016, it became known around Kyiv that Manafort was receiving messages threatening to reveal his potential malfeasance.[91] Manafort learned about the existence of the Black Ledger sometime in June. It is possible that, in anticipation of further financial scrutiny, Manafort engineered a liquidity crisis to justify loans meant to hide illicit cash, as he did over a decade earlier during the investigations into the "Karachi Affair."

On August 16th, two days after *The New York Times* ran the Black Ledger story, Genesis Capital filed a notice of default on the Stradella Road property and filed two more on separate properties on the 18th, 19th, and 30th. On August 19th, the day he resigned from the Trump campaign, Manafort established a holding company, Summerbreeze LLC, and filed a notice of default on one of his investment properties. Less than two weeks later, on September 12th, Manafort, through Summerbreeze LLC, borrowed $3.5 million from SIII Capital Group LLC, a subsidiary of Spruce Capital.[92]

The co-founder and principal of Spruce Capital, Joshua Crane, worked with the Trump Organization to develop the Trump International Hotel and Tower at Waikiki Beach Walk.[93]

Spruce Capital is financially backed by a Brooklyn-based fertilizer billionaire named Alexander Rovt. Born Sándor Róth in Ukraine, Rovt identifies as Carpathian and moved to New York City in the mid-1980s. In 1988, Rovt joined IBE Trade (International Barter Exchange), which had been founded by a Korean war veteran, major Republican party donor and former intelligence operative named Sheldon Silverston. A Facebook post from the United Veterans Council, Inc. claims that First Lieutenant Sheldon Silverston served as a guerrilla leader in North Korea during the Korean War.[94] On November 14th, 1952, *The New York Times* published a letter from Silverston arguing for the re-armament in Japan. The article claims that Silverston had just returned from East Asia after having worked for eighteen months for "an American Strategic Intelligence Service."[95]

IBE Trade sold goods to pariah states with little hard currency; examples include Uganda after its civil war in the 1980s and Romania under Ceausescu in exchange for commodities. Silverston used Rovt's contacts to access the Soviet Union when it opened up under Gorbachev, where they bartered for vast quantities of fertilizer. Rovt and a partner, Imre Pákh, bought out Silverston. By the late '90s, IBE Trade controlled over 85% of the fertilizer in Russia and Ukraine.[96] According to the Senate Intelligence Committee, Imre Pákh has ties to Russian organized crime.[97] In 1999, IBE Trade purchased a fertilizer factory in Bulgaria.

To provide the plant with a steady gas supply, Rovt partnered with Igor Makarov. Makarov is a natural gas tycoon from Turkmenistan who established ITERA, the Gazprom-linked intermediary and predecessor to Eural Trans Gas (ETG) and RosUkrEnergo (RUE), all of which sold Turkmen gas to Ukraine and have been associated with corrupt Gazprom officials, Vladimir Putin, Semyon Mogilevich and Eurasian organized crime. In return, Makarov received a 25% ownership stake in the plant.

Rovt got into a dispute with some of his other partners in the plant, and one accused him and Pákh, without providing evidence, of having old ties to the KGB. Rovt sold his overseas assets to Dmytro Firtash, the Ukrainian billionaire and suspected front for Semyon Mogilevich, who was listed as part owner of ETG and RUE. On the election day, Rovt donated $10,000 to the Trump campaign. All but $2,700 was returned, as the rest exceeded the legal limit.

Manafort received two more loans from the Chicago-based Federal Savings Bank following his resignation from the Trump campaign, the first made on December 9th, 2016, and the second on January 17th, 2017, for a total of $16 million.[98] The chairman and chief executive officer of Federal Savings Bank, Stephen Calk, was a former Army helicopter pilot who had met Trump years earlier at a charity event and enjoyed a relationship with Manafort that predated the campaign. Federal Savings Bank received a "seven-figure" cash investment from the Vector Group, whose CEO Howard Lorber traveled with Trump to Moscow in 1996 and has been described as one of Trump's closest friends.[99]

Trump and Lorber were joined in Moscow by the Vector Group's founder and chairman Bennett LeBow, where they visited a factory that LeBow had purchased to see if it might be developed into a Trump Tower. Among Lorber's business associates was Vadim Rabinovich, a Ukrainian oligarch with alleged ties to organized crime. Rabinovich had worked as the Ukrainian representative of Nordex, a commodities trading firm and suspected Russian intelligence front run by Grigori Loutchansky, who was described in a 1996 Swiss Federal Police Report as a KGB recruit. [100] In September 1995, Rabinovich, while on a State Department Watch List, attended a Clinton-Gore fundraiser as Bennett LeBow's guest at the Bel Harbor Hotel in Miami. Former CIA Director John Deutch described Nordex as "an example of an organization associated with Russian criminal activity moving out of Russia."[101]

"Is there any evidence that former KGB officials are involved in the Russian organized crime syndicates?" the chairman of the House Committee on International Relations asked then-FBI director Louis J. Freeh during a hearing in 1997.

"Yes, sir, there is," Freeh replied, "both in investigations in Russia, as well as in other parts of Europe, in companies such as Nordex, which is a Vienna-based company, a multinational company. There are strong indications of former KGB officers working directly with some of these organized crime groups, and that poses an additional level of threat and sophistication to these people."

According to bank employee Dennis Raico, Manafort first contacted Federal Savings to inquire about loans relating to his real estate projects in April 2016. In May, Manafort, Calk, and Raico dined together in New York and discussed politics and loans. On July 27th, Manafort and Yohai held a meeting with Raico, which Calk attended via videoconference to discuss refinancing loans related to a Los Angeles property of theirs. Calk expressed interest in participating in the Trump campaign, and Manafort replied that he would get back to him.

The next day, Calk met with several officials at the bank to discuss the Manafort loan. Several bank officials noticed red flags; for example, Manafort claimed he earned $4 million in business income for 2015, yet other documents showed that he had made at most $400,000. As a result, some wanted to reject the loan application. In a highly unusual move, they were overruled by Calk himself. Employees such as Raico had never seen Calk approve a loan before, nor was a one-day turnaround usual practice. According to later testimony, Calk hoped he would be rewarded with a cabinet position by issuing the loan if Trump won.

The $16 million in loans extended to Manafort ultimately constituted the bank's largest loan, representing nearly a quarter of its capital equity. On August 3rd, the day after Manafort met with Konstantin Kilimnik, Manafort emailed Calk and requested that he send his resume. After Manafort sent a follow-up message the next day, Calk sent him his resume. "Per our conversation," Manafort replied, "I want to add you to the National Economic Advisory Committee for Donald Trump. Is that something you would be able to do?"

"I am happy and willing to serve," Calk responded. Two days later, his name was released on the Trump Campaign's Economic Advisory Committee list, alongside Howard Lorber, who was also named to the committee. Calk's goal of receiving a position in the Trump campaign never came to fruition. By the time of the transition, Paul Manafort was already beginning to feel the heat of multiple investigations into his own and the Trump campaign's affairs. So, too, would Stephen Calk.

Whether these loans concealed hidden payments to Manafort remains conjecture. The only known official investigation into these matters remains heavily redacted in the Senate Intelligence Report. Much of the information on these matters that is publicly available is due to the efforts of citizen journalists and investigators. Attorneys Julian Russo and Matthew Termine conducted critically important original research into Manafort's real estate activities, which can be viewed at www.377union.com.

The Escort and the Oligarch: Oleg Deripaska and Nastya Rybka

In February of 2018, a leader of the Russian opposition to the Putin regime, Alexei Navalny, released an online video in which he described the strange story of a Belorussian escort and self-described "sex coach" named Nastya Rybka, who, at a critical moment during the 2016 election was present on a yacht with Oleg Deripaska and then-Russian Deputy Prime Minister, Putin-ally and noted foreign policy expert Sergei Eduardovich Prikhodko. This was the same Sergei Prikhodko who had invited Trump to attend a conference in St. Petersburg.[102]

Rybka later claimed from a Thai prison to have audio recordings that established connections between Russian officials, Paul Manafort and Donald Trump and would provide evidence of Russian interference in the US Presidential election.[103] While the claims of an obscure Belorussian escort relating to matters of geopolitical and historic importance might otherwise be summarily dismissed, Navalny and his team, renowned for their investigations into Russian corruption, were able to establish to a certainty through a careful analysis of photographic and video evidence on her social media profiles that Rybka *did* know Deripaska and *was* present with him and Deputy Prime Minister Prikhodko at the time she claimed.

Rybka, whose real name is Anastasia Vashukevich, chronicled her interactions with Deripaska in three Russian language books, one of which remains unpublished but has been seen by Russian media outlets and through her highly active social media accounts.[104] Through thorough analysis, it has been determined that she had at least three extended interactions with Deripaska. The earliest of these took place during a critical moment during the American presidential election in August of 2016. Photos and videos from Rybka's Instagram account confirm that, mere days after Paul Manafort met with Konstantin Kilimnik at the Grand Havana Club in New York, Rybka and several other escorts traveled alongside Deputy Prime Minister Prikhodko as guests on Deripaska's yacht on a multi-day trip off the coast of Norway.

The late Prikhodko had a distinguished career at the highest levels of the Russian foreign policy establishment. A graduate of the Moscow State Institute for International Relations, he began his career in 1980 as a Soviet diplomat to Czechoslovakia, where he eventually rose to become the Soviet embassy's First Secretary. In 1997, after having risen through the ranks of Russia's top foreign policy officials, Prikhodko became an advisor to Boris Yeltsin. He continued his rise through the ranks throughout Vladimir Putin's Presidency and the Medvedev interregnum. When he was seen on Deripaska's yacht, Prikhodko was considered one of Russia's top foreign policy officials with deep links to the Kremlin.[105]

In the Summer of 2016, the 26-year-old Rybka decided she wanted to seduce a billionaire. Under the guidance of a self-described seduction coach, Alexander Kirillov, she signed up with an escort service and was sent to spend time on Deripaska's yacht while on a trip up the Norwegian coast. According to Rybka, she and Deripaska began an affair that lasted for several months.[106]

In a video Rybka uploaded onto Instagram as part of a montage of the trip, Deripaska can be heard discussing Russian-American relations. "We've got bad relations with America," Deripaska says while sitting beside Prikhodko, "because the friend of Sergey Eduardovich [Prikhodko], Nuland's her name, is responsible for them." Here, Deripaska refers to Victoria Nuland, the Assistant Secretary of State for European and Eurasian Affairs, who was widely blamed in Russia at the time for souring diplomatic relations. "When she was your age, she spent a month on a Russian whaling boat. She hates our country after this. Why is that?"[107]

According to Rybka's unpublished book, a copy of which was reviewed by the Russian publication *The Bell*, Rybka next met with Deripaska sometime in the September-October timeframe in the Fall of 2016. Rybka claims that one of Deripaska's assistants flew her from Moscow to one of the billionaire's country homes in Krasnodar, where she spent three days with the oligarch. At one point, Rybka claims that Deripaska met with an "important-looking man" who arrived in an all-terrain vehicle with tinted windows. Though Deripaska and this man spoke privately, Rybka claims to have hidden her phone behind a book in the library and recorded the conversation. Though this recording has never been released, if indeed it exists at all, the fact that Rybka possessed separate photos and recordings of Deripaska lends at least some credence to a claim that might otherwise be reflexively dismissed.[108]

In her book *Eurotrash: How to Seduce the Rich for the Poor*, Rybka chronicles another meeting with Deripaska on January 7th, 2017, at a ski resort in Lech, Austria. Once again, a video posted on social media establishes Rybka was present with Deripaska when and where she said she was. Also present was Deripaska's American lobbyist since 2009, Adam Waldman, and his wife.[109] Less than a week later, Waldman met twice with his other client at the Ecuadorian embassy in London, Julian Assange.[110] The content of their meetings and whether they had anything to do with Oleg Deripaska remain unknown.

Rybka's story and connections with Deripaska would likely have been lost to obscurity as her books used pseudonyms, and the photos and videos she posted on social media were not presented in any cohesive narrative were it not for a fortunate accident. In September of 2017, Rybka, along with several other scantily clad women, barged into Alexei Navalny's campaign office in what he interpreted as an attempt to embarrass him. Curious about who these strange women were, Navalny and his team began researching their social media presence, where they discovered Nastya Rybka.[111] Intrigued, Navalny and his researchers searched Rybka's social media presence until they found her photos and videos with Deripaska and Prikhodko. After getting a hold of her books, Navalny and his researchers were able to piece together the story and eventually put together a video chronicling their discoveries, which they released online, gaining international notoriety.

The response in Russia to the release of the Navalny video was swift. Within days, Oleg Deripaska filed a lawsuit, and Roskomnadzor, the Russian state media and telecommunications watchdog agency, demanded that both YouTube and Instagram take down videos and posts related to Nastya Rybka and Alexei Navalny or face investigation themselves. Russian language publications were also ordered to remove content related to Navalny's claims.[112] While the video remained on YouTube, Instagram, owned by Facebook, bowed to the pressure exerted by the Russian government and removed the posts.[113] Within days, Russian internet providers blocked access to Navalny's website.[114]

At the time the video was released, Nastya Rybka and her sex coach Kirillov were in Pattaya, Thailand, where they were teaching a seminary on sex and seduction. On February 25th, they were arrested by Thai authorities initially for working without a permit, but the charges were later changed to soliciting sexual services.[115] Immediately following her arrest, Rybka posted a shaky video onto Instagram made from a police van in which she claimed that if she were to be released from Thai prison, she would be able to provide evidence of Russian interference in the 2016 American presidential election, as well as detail the connections between Russian officials, Paul Manafort, and Donald Trump.[116]

While in prison, Rybka claimed that she had 16 hours of audio recordings that could provide evidence of Russian meddling in the election. She further contended that Oleg Deripaska discussed these matters with three fluent English speakers, whom she assumed were American. "They were discussing elections," Rybka told *The New York Times*. "Deripaska had a plan for elections."

"If America gives me protection, I will tell everything I know," Rybka continued. "I am afraid to go back to Russia. Some strange things can happen."[117]

One of the individuals whom Deripaska appears to have sent to help clean up the Nastya Rybka situation was Viktor Boyarkin, the same Russian military intelligence officer whom he had tasked with pursuing Paul Manafort for the money he owed him. A video later leaked onto YouTube by unknown sources, which was treated as authentic by the Senate Intelligence Committee, features a recording made after Rybka and her associates' arrest in Thailand.[118] The conversation is between Georgy Oganov, Tatiana Monaghan, and an attorney named William Sein. During the discussion, Oganov says, "What we are interested in is that these people be kept in jail." The group then proceeds to discuss the case.

Georgy Oganov once worked in the Russian Embassy in the United States and is a senior advisor to Deripaska. In January 2017, Oganov met Paul Manafort in Madrid in a meeting that evidence from text messages suggests was set up by Konstantin Kilimnik and Viktor Boyarkin, both individuals affiliated with Russian military intelligence and with strong links to Deripaska.[119] Tatiana Monaghan is the President of the Russian National Committee of the International Chamber of Commerce (ICC) and is another Deripaska associate. In March and May of 2016, she co-hosted two ICC events with Viktor Boyarkin.

According to *Intelligence Online*, another individual to whom Deripaska turned to handle the Rybka situation was a former Israeli military intelligence officer named Walter Soriano, who operates a private intelligence firm called USG Security. The article further claims that Deripaska and Soriano are primarily in contact through a former SVR officer and now director of international cooperation at Deripaska's holding company En+, Evgeny Fokin. Soriano is reportedly close to Israeli Prime Minister Benjamin Netanyahu and Nathaniel Rothschild.[120]

Through a handwritten letter written by Kirillov, Rybka attempted to get into contact with the US Embassy in Thailand, asking for asylum for herself and her fellow sex workers and writing that she had "very important information for the USA."[121] The FBI contacted the Thai Immigration Bureau to organize a meeting with Rybka but was turned down by Thai authorities.[122] One individual who gained access to Rybka was Vladimir Pronin,

Russia's newly appointed Consul to Pattaya. After improving the conditions in which she was kept, Rybka later suggested that it was Pronin who arranged for her to be deported after pleading guilty to the charges against her in Thai court.[123]

As a citizen of Belarus, Rybka had intended to return to Minsk. However, during a stop-over in Moscow, she was arrested in a dramatic and physical confrontation with plainclothes Russian officers that was captured on video and posted online. Rybka was detained on charges of coercing people into prostitution. After being released from custody, Rybka claimed she sent her audio recordings to Deripaska. Though she remains at liberty in Russia, Rybka was warned by the FSB not to return to her native Belarus.[124] She has made no further comments on the existence or nature of the audio recordings.

[1] Burns, Alexander; Haberman, Maggie. "Mystery man: Ukraine's U.S. fixer," *Politico*. March 5th, 2014

[2] Lee Myers, Steven; Kramer, Andrew E. "How Paul Manafort Wielded Power In Ukraine Before Advising Donald Trump," *The New York Times*. July 31st, 2016

[3] Shield, Michael; Gruber, Angelika. "Ukrainian gas oligarch Firtash arrested in Vienna on FBI warrant," *Reuters*. March 13th, 2014

[4] Stack, Graham. "Exposed: The Ukrainian Politician Who Funded Paul Manafort's Secret EU Lobbying Campaign," *Organized Crime and Corruption Reporting Project (OCCRP)*. November 4th, 2019

[5] Report of the Select Committee on Intelligence United States Senate On Russian Active Measures Campaigns And Interference in the 2016 US Election Volume 5: Counterintelligence Threats and Vulnerabilities. Pg. 48

[6] Patten, Sam. "Kostya and Me: How Sam Patten Got Ensnared in Mueller's Probe," *Wired*. August 14th, 2019

[7] Foer, Franklin. "Paul Manafort, American Hustler," *The Atlantic*. March 2018

[8] Gurantz, Maya. "Kompromat: Or, Revelations From The Unpublished Portions Of Andrea Manafort's Hacked Texts," *Los Angeles Review of Books*. February 18th, 2019

[9] Cockburn. "'Has mom been tested for STDs?' The Manaforts' home life and why it matters," *The Spectator*. July 31st, 2018

[10] Report of the Select Committee on Intelligence United States Senate On Russian Active Measures Campaigns And Interference in the 2016 US Election Volume 5: Counterintelligence Threats and Vulnerabilities. Pg. 50

[11] Mufson, Steven; Hamburger, Tom. "Inside Trump advisor Manafort's world of politics and financial dealmaking," *The Washington Post*. April 26th, 2016

[12] Helderman, Rosalind S. "Manafort interviewed twice by the FBI before joining Trump's 2016 campaign, new documents show," *The Washington Post*. April 24th, 2018

[13] AFFIDAVIT IN SUPPORT OF AN APPLICATION FOR A SEARCH WARRANT. Criminal N. 1:17-sw-449. United States District Court Eastern District of Virginia. Pg. 4

[14] Petropoulos, Aggelos; Engel, Richard. "Manafort Had $60 Million Relationship With a Russian Oligarch," *NBC News*. October 13th, 207

[15] Weissmann, Andrew. *Where Law Ends: Inside The Mueller Investigation*. New York, NY: Random House, 2020. Pg. 13

[16] Orphanides, Stelios. "The Curious Case of Dr. K and Mr. Christomides," *Organized Crime and Corruption Reporting Project (OCCRP)*. June 28th, 2019

[17] Swan, Betsy. "Mueller Reveals New Manafort Link to Organized Crime," *The Daily Beast.* November 2nd, 2017

[18] Buchman, Brandi; Ryan, Tim. "Gates Recounts Ups & Downs of Manafort Finances," *Courthouse News Service.* August 7th, 2018

[19] United States of America v. Paul J. Manafort, Jr. and Richard W. Gates, III. Superceding Indictment. February 2018

[20] Report of the Select Committee on Intelligence United States Senate On Russian Active Measures Campaigns And Interference in the 2016 US Election Volume 5: Counterintelligence Threats and Vulnerabilities. Pg. 52

[21] 4/17/15 Email from Paul Manafort to Rick Gates

[22] LaFraniere, Sharon; Vogel, Kenneth P.; Haberman, Maggie. "The Rise and Fall of Paul Manafort: Greed, Deception and Ego," *The New York Times.* August 12th, 2018

[23] Foer, Franklin. "Paul Manafort, American Hustler," *The Atlantic.* March 2018

[24] Report of the Select Committee on Intelligence United States Senate On Russian Active Measures Campaigns And Interference in the 2016 US Election Volume 5: Counterintelligence Threats and Vulnerabilities. Pg. 53

[25] Kranish, Michael. "'He's Better Than This,' says Thomas Barrack, Trump's loyal whisperer," *The Washington Post.* October 11th, 2017

[26] LaFraniere, Sharon; Rashbaum, William K. "Thomas Barrack, Trump Fund-Raiser, Is Indicted on Lobbying Charge," *The New York Times.* July 20th, 2021

[27] Thrush, Glenn. "To Charm Trump, Paul Manafort Sold Himself as an Affable Outsider," *The New York Times.* April 8th, 2017

[28] Kranish, Michael. "'He's Better Than This,' says Thomas Barrack, Trump's loyal whisperer," *The Washington Post.* October 11th, 2017

[29] Thrush, Glenn. "To Charm Trump, Paul Manafort Sold Himself as an Affable Outsider," *The New York Times.* April 8th, 2017

[30] Report of the Select Committee on Intelligence United States Senate On Russian Active Measures Campaigns And Interference in the 2016 US Election Volume 5: Counterintelligence Threats and Vulnerabilities. Pg. 55

[31] Report of the Select Committee on Intelligence United States Senate On Russian Active Measures Campaigns And Interference in the 2016 US Election Volume 5: Counterintelligence Threats and Vulnerabilities. Pg. 85-91

[32] Safdar, Khadeeja; Benoit, David. "How Jeffrey Epstein Tried to Tap Into Trump's Circle," The Wall Street Journal. August 30th, 2023

[33] Report of the Select Committee on Intelligence United States Senate On Russian Active Measures Campaigns And Interference in the 2016 US Election Volume 5: Counterintelligence Threats and Vulnerabilities. Pg. 59-60

[34] Patten, Sam. "Kostya and Me: How Sam Patten Got Ensnared in Mueller's Probe," *Wired.* August 14th, 2019

[35] Ioffe, Julia; Foer, Franklin. "Did Manafort Use Trump to Curry Favor With a Putin Ally," *The Atlantic.* October 2nd, 2017

[36] "Treasury Targets Russian Operatives over Election Interference, World Anti-Doping Agency Hacking, and Other Malign Activities," (Press Release) US Department of the Treasury. December 19th, 2018

[37] Report of the Select Committee on Intelligence United States Senate On Russian Active Measures Campaigns And Interference in the 2016 US Election Volume 5: Counterintelligence Threats and Vulnerabilities. Pg. 140

[38] Shuster, Simon. "Exclusive: Russian Ex-Spy Pressured Manafort Over Debts to an Oligarch," *Time Magazine.* December 29th, 2018

[39] LaFraniere, Sharon; Barnes, Julian. E. "Report Details Manafort's Ties During 2016 Trump Campaign to a Russian Agent," *The New York Times.* August 18th, 2020

[40] Report of the Select Committee on Intelligence United States Senate On Russian Active Measures Campaigns And Interference in the 2016 US Election Volume 5: Counterintelligence Threats and Vulnerabilities. Pg. 67

[41] Vogel, Kenneth P.; Kramer, Andrew E. "Russian Spy or Hustling Political Operative? The Enigmatic Figure at the Heart of the Mueller Inquiry," *The New York Times*. February 23rd, 2019

[42] Report of the Select Committee on Intelligence United States Senate On Russian Active Measures Campaigns And Interference in the 2016 US Election Volume 5: Counterintelligence Threats and Vulnerabilities. Pg. 68

[43] "Ukraine charges Putin ally Medvedchuk with treason," *The Associated Press*. May 11th, 2021

[44] Report of the Select Committee on Intelligence United States Senate On Russian Active Measures Campaigns And Interference in the 2016 US Election Volume 5: Counterintelligence Threats and Vulnerabilities. Pg. 80

[45] Mueller, III, Robert S. *Report On The Investigation Into Russian Interference In The 2016 Presidential Election*. Department of Justice, Washington, DC. March 2019. Pg. 136

[46] Press Release. "Treasury Escalates Sanctions Against the Russian Government's Attempts to Influence U.S. Elections," U.S. Department of the Treasury. April 15th, 2021

[47] Report of the Select Committee on Intelligence United States Senate On Russian Active Measures Campaigns And Interference in the 2016 US Election Volume 5: Counterintelligence Threats and Vulnerabilities. Pg. 79

[48] Report of the Select Committee on Intelligence United States Senate On Russian Active Measures Campaigns And Interference in the 2016 US Election Volume 5: Counterintelligence Threats and Vulnerabilities. Pg. 71

[49] Miller, Christopher. "'Person A' In His Own Words: On The Record With Shadowy Operative In Russia Probe," *RadioFreeEurope/RadioLiberty*. April 6th, 2018

[50] Yourish, Karen; Buchanan, Larry; Watkins, Derek. "A Timeline Showing the Full Scale of Russia's Unprecedented Interference in the 2016 Election, and Its Aftermath," *The New York Times*. September 20th, 2018

[51] Bump, Philip. "Timeline: How a Trump advisor tried to work with the Russian government," *The Washington Post*. October 30th, 2017

[52] Report of the Select Committee on Intelligence United States Senate On Russian Active Measures Campaigns And Interference in the 2016 US Election Volume 5: Counterintelligence Threats and Vulnerabilities. Pg. 223-224

[53] FD-302 Richard Gates Interview 4/10/2018. Pg. 4-6

[54] Tillman, Zoe. "Trump's Campaign Was Talking About The Conspiracy Theory That Ukraine Was Involved In The DNC Hack Back In 2016," *BuzzFeed News*. November 2nd, 2019

[55] Hamburger, Tom; Helderman, Rosalind S.; Leonnig, Carol D.; Entous, Adam. "Manafort offered to give Russian billionaire 'private briefings' on 2016 campaign," *The Washington Post*. September 20th, 2017

[56] Kovensky, Josh. "Trump's campaign manager haunted by past business," *The Kyiv Post*. July 8th, 2016

[57] Mueller, III, Robert S. *Report On The Investigation Into Russian Interference In The 2016 Presidential Election*. Department of Justice, Washington, DC. March 2019. Pg. 137

[58] Report of the Select Committee on Intelligence United States Senate On Russian Active Measures Campaigns And Interference in the 2016 US Election Volume 5: Counterintelligence Threats and Vulnerabilities. Pg. 72

[59] Mueller, III, Robert S. *Report On The Investigation Into Russian Interference In The 2016 Presidential Election*. Department of Justice, Washington, DC. March 2019. Pg. 139

[60] Report of the Select Committee on Intelligence United States Senate On Russian Active Measures Campaigns And Interference in the 2016 US Election Volume 5: Counterintelligence Threats and Vulnerabilities. Pg. 81

[61] Mueller, III, Robert S. *Report On The Investigation Into Russian Interference In The 2016 Presidential Election*. Department of Justice, Washington, DC. March 2019. Pg. 140

[62] Mueller, III, Robert S. *Report On The Investigation Into Russian Interference In The 2016*

Presidential Election. Department of Justice, Washington, DC. March 2019. Pg. 141

[63] Mueller, III, Robert S. *Report On The Investigation Into Russian Interference In The 2016 Presidential Election*. Department of Justice, Washington, DC. March 2019. Pg. 139

[64] Groll, Elias. "The Ukrainian Who Sunk Paul Manafort," *Foreign Policy*. August 27th, 2018

[65] Leschenko, Serhiy. "Sergii Leschenko: the true story of Yanukovych's black ledger," *The Kyiv Post*. November 24th, 2019

[66] Kramer, Andrew E.; McIntire, Mike; Meier, Barry. "Secret Ledger in Ukraine Lists Cash for Donald Trump's Campaign Chief," *The New York Times*. August 14th, 2016

[67] Burns, Alexander; Haberman, Maggie. "Inside the Failing Mission to Tame Donald Trump's Tongue," *The New York Times*. August 13th, 2016

[68] Woodward, Bob. *Fear*. New York, NY: Simon & Schuster, 2018. Pg. 9-14

[69] Report of the Select Committee on Intelligence United States Senate On Russian Active Measures Campaigns And Interference in the 2016 US Election Volume 5: Counterintelligence Threats and Vulnerabilities. Pg. 91

[70] Woodward, Bob. *Fear*. New York, NY: Simon & Schuster, 2018. Pg. 21

[71] Woodward, Bob. *Fear*. New York, NY: Simon & Schuster, 2018. Pg. 22

[72] Report of the Select Committee on Intelligence United States Senate On Russian Active Measures Campaigns And Interference in the 2016 US Election Volume 5: Counterintelligence Threats and Vulnerabilities. Pg. 92

[73] Demirjian, Karoun; Nakashima, Ellen; Zapotosky, Matt. "Senate panel told Justice Dept. of Suspicions over Trump family members' Russia testimony," *The Washington Post*. August 15th, 2020

[74] Vernon, Pete. "The devil's bargain in Bob Woodward's *Fear*," *Columbia Journalism Review*. September 12th, 2018

[75] Report of the Select Committee on Intelligence United States Senate On Russian Active Measures Campaigns And Interference in the 2016 US Election Volume 5: Counterintelligence Threats and Vulnerabilities. Pg. 92

[76] Vogel, Kenneth P. "Manafort's man in Kiev," *Politico*. August 18th, 2016

[77] Vogel, Kenneth P.; Stern, David. "Authorities looked into Manafort's protege," *Politico*. March 8th, 2017

[78] Perez, Evan. "First on CNN: Feds investigate Manafort firm as part of Ukraine probe," *CNN*. August 19th, 2016

[79] Mueller, III, Robert S. *Report On The Investigation Into Russian Interference In The 2016 Presidential Election*. Department of Justice, Washington, DC. March 2019. Pg. 141

[80] Report of the Select Committee on Intelligence United States Senate On Russian Active Measures Campaigns And Interference in the 2016 US Election Volume 5: Counterintelligence Threats and Vulnerabilities. Pg. 93

[81] Report of the Select Committee on Intelligence United States Senate On Russian Active Measures Campaigns And Interference in the 2016 US Election Volume 5: Counterintelligence Threats and Vulnerabilities. Pg. 94-96

[82] Mueller, III, Robert S. *Report On The Investigation Into Russian Interference In The 2016 Presidential Election*. Department of Justice, Washington, DC. March 2019. Pg. 141

[83] Report of the Select Committee on Intelligence United States Senate On Russian Active Measures Campaigns And Interference in the 2016 US Election Volume 5: Counterintelligence Threats and Vulnerabilities. Pg. 93

[84] Andrews, Wilson; Parlapiano, Alicia. "How a Federal Inquiry Says Paul Manafort Laundered $18 Million, and How He Spent It," *The New York Times*. October 31st, 2017

[85] Report of the Select Committee on Intelligence United States Senate On Russian Active Measures Campaigns And Interference in the 2016 US Election Volume 5: Counterintelligence Threats and Vulnerabilities. Pg. 103

[86] Foer, Franklin. "Paul Manafort, American Hustler," *The Atlantic*. March 2018

[87] Labrouillère, François; Le Bailly, David. "INFO Match. Un politologue américain au cœur de l'affaire Karachi," *Paris Match*. April 7th, 2012

[88] Martin, Andrew; Petersson, Edvard. "Manafort's Ex-Son-in-Law Pleads Guilty, Is Helping Government, Source Says," *Bloomberg*. May 17th, 2018

[89] McIntire, Mike. "F.B.I. Investigating Deals Involving Paul Manafort and Son-in-Law," *The New York Times*. June 23rd, 2017

[90] Russo, Julian; Termine, Matthew. "Real Estate, Karachi & Friendly Lending," *377Union.com*. October 29th, 2017

[91] Vogel, Kenneth P.; Stern, David; Meyer, Josh. "Manafort's Ukrainian 'Blood Money' caused qualms, hack suggests," *Politico*. February 28th, 2017

[92] Winter, Tom; Abou-Sabe, Kenzi. "Feds Subpoena Records for $3.5M Mystery Mortgage on Manafort's Home," *NBC News*. May 16th, 2017

[93] Ignatius, David. "We know an awful lot about Manafort and Russia. Trump can't make it disappear." *The Washington Post*. April 24th, 2018

[94] https://z-upload.facebook.com/unitedwarveterans/posts/10158574918946761

[95] Silverston, Sheldon. "Rearming of Japan; People Said to Realize Necessity and to Desire Material Aid," *The New York Times*. November 14th, 1952

[96] Rice, Andrew. "Alex Rovt, the Fertilizer Baron of Manhattan," *Bloomberg*. September 6th, 2012

[97] Report of the Select Committee on Intelligence United States Senate On Russian Active Measures Campaigns And Interference in the 2016 US Election Volume 5: Counterintelligence Threats and Vulnerabilities. Pg. 345

[98] Rothfeld, Michael. "Paul Manafort Received Loans From Another Former Trump Advisor's Bank," *The Wall Street Journal*. March 29th, 2017

[99] Reel, Monte; McCormack, John. "Behind Manafort's Loans, a Chopper Pilot Who Flew Into Trump's Orbit," *Bloomberg*. July 25th, 2017

[100] Tavernise, Sabrina. "At Russian Paper, A New Hint of Intrigue; Buyer of New York Daily Must Read It From Afar," *The New York Times*. December 11th, 2003

[101] Anin, Roman; Shmagun, Olesya; Vasic, Jelena. "Ex-Spy Turned Humanitarian Helps Himself," *Organized Crime and Corruption Reporting Project*. November 4th, 2015

[102] Mueller, III, Robert S. *Report On The Investigation Into Russian Interference In The 2016 Presidential Election*. Department of Justice, Washington, DC. March 2019. Pg. 78

[103] Paddock, Richard C. "Seeking Asylum, an Escort Has a Tale of Trump and Russia to Offer," *The New York Times*. March 2nd, 2018

[104] Stognei, Anastasia. "Revelations to come? A deep dive into what Nastya Rybka might know," *The Bell*. January 26th, 2019

[105] Bekbulatova, Taisiya. "The man with the golden shoes: The key figure in Alexey Navalny's "Russiagate" investigation is Deputy Prime Minister Sergei Prikhodko. Just who is he?" *Meduza*. February 16th, 2018

[106] Paddock, Richard C. "She Gambled on Her Claim to Link Russians and Trump. She Is Losing." *The New York Times*. August 31st, 2018

[107] Prokop, Andrew. "The escort claiming to have tapes proving Russian interference in the US election, explained," *Vox*. April 3rd, 2018

[108] Stognei, Anastasia. "Revelations to come? A deep dive into what Nastya Rybka might know," *The Bell*. January 26th, 2019

[109] "American lobbyist Adam Waldman met with Oleg Deripaska before visiting Julian Assange in London," *Proekt*. December 11th, 2018

[110] Kirchgaessner, Stephanie; Harding, Luke. "US lobbyist for Russian oligarch visited Julian Assange nine times last year," *The Guardian*. June 20th, 2018

[111] Prokop, Andrew. "The escort claiming to have tapes proving Russian interference in the US election, explained," *Vox*. April 3rd, 2018

[112] Luxmoore, Matthew. "Russia Threatens to Block YouTube and Instagram, After Complaints From an Oligarch," *The New York Times*. February 12th, 2018

[113] Kharpal, Arjun. "Facebook complies with Russia's request to take down an Instagram post linked to Putin's rival," *CNBC*. February 16th, 2018

[114] Report of the Select Committee on Intelligence United States Senate On Russian

Active Measures Campaigns And Interference in the 2016 US Election Volume 5: Counterintelligence Threats and Vulnerabilities. Pg. 143

[115] Zotova, Nataliya; Boldyrev, Oleg. "Nastya Rybka: model who got caught up in Trump-Russia row," *BBC News*. January 31st, 2019

[116] Paddock, Richard C. "Seeking Asylum, an Escort Has a Tale of Trump and Russia to Offer," *The New York Times*. March 2nd, 2018

[117] Paddock, Richard C. "Escort Says Audio Recording Show Russian Meddling in U.S. Election," *The New York Times*. March 5th, 2018

[118] Report of the Select Committee on Intelligence United States Senate On Russian Active Measures Campaigns And Interference in the 2016 US Election Volume 5: Counterintelligence Threats and Vulnerabilities. Pg. 143

[119] Mueller, III, Robert S. *Report On The Investigation Into Russian Interference In The 2016 Presidential Election*. Department of Justice, Washington, DC. March 2019. Pg. 142

[120] "FBI report could find Soriano exposed again," *Intelligence Online*. December 24th, 2019

[121] Paddock, Richard C. "Seeking Asylum, an Escort Has a Tale of Trump and Russia to Offer," *The New York Times*. March 2nd, 2018

[122] Watson, Ivan; Olarn, Kocha. "FBI tried to contact 'sex coaches' in Thai jail," *CNN*. March 13th, 2018

[123] Vailyeva, Nataliya. "Belorussian model: I gave info on Trump to Russian tycoon," *The Associated Press*. February 1st, 2019

[124] RFE/RL Belarus Service, "'Nastya Rybka' Says FSB Warned Her Not To Go Home To Belarus," *RadioFreeEurope/RadioLiberty*. February 25th, 2019

Chapter 17:
George Papadopoulos, Carter Page
And the Mayfair Hotel Speech

George Papadopoulos and the Professor:
A Trump Campaign Advisor Learns Of Russian Dirt

George Papadopoulos, the son of Greek immigrants, was born in
Chicago on August 17th, 1987. In the Summer of 2015, the 27-
year-old foreign policy neophyte sought a position on a
Republican presidential campaign. In mid-July, he contacted
Corey Lewandowski via LinkedIn to inquire whether any
positions were available. Lewandowski put Papadopoulos in
touch with the campaign's National Political Director, Michael
Glassner, who informed Papadopoulos that the campaign wasn't
hiring foreign policy advisors at that time.[1]

Between 2011 and 2015, he interned at the Hudson
Institute, a Washington, DC-based conservative think tank. His
work consisted of promoting the idea that Israel should exploit
the Leviathan gas field located off its coast and sell the natural
gas to Europe in partnership with Greece and Cyprus while
avoiding any dealings with Turkey.[2] The Special Counsel's Office
later considered charging him with being an unregistered agent
for Israel.[3] No charges were ever filed. The Hudson Institute has
long-standing ties to Israeli Prime Minister Benjamin Netanyahu
and is closely linked with the energy firms seeking to exploit the
Leviathan gas field.[4] Papadopoulos was managed at Hudson by
Richard Weitz.[5] Weitz sits on the board of Wikistrat, an Israeli
geopolitical analysis firm known to employ former members of

Israeli intelligence.[6] The Special Counsel's Office investigated Wikistrat's outreach to the Trump campaign.[7]

Papadopoulos eventually connected with Sam Clovis, who had been tasked with assembling a team of foreign policy advisors. Clovis was a former F-16 fighter pilot turned Iowa-based Academic and conservative talk radio host who had emerged as a supporter of Trump. In his interview with Papadopoulos, Clovis explained that an improved US relationship with Russia was a principal foreign policy focus for the campaign.[8] Clovis later dissembled over his emphasizing of the importance of Russia to the Trump campaign in his testimony to the Senate Intelligence Committee, which sent the DOJ a criminal referral accusing him of lying under oath.[9] Clovis recruited Papadopoulos over the phone for the unpaid position.

At the same time he was interacting with Clovis, Papadopoulos also reached out to the London Centre of International Law Practice (LCILP).[10] After being hired, Papadopoulos moved to London and traveled on a work trip to Rome. He and several other LCILP members visited Link Campus University, a for-profit subsidiary of the University of Malta. Link was famous for its close ties to Italian intelligence.[11] During the visit, Papadopoulos was introduced to a Maltese Professor who worked at Link named Joseph Mifsud. While Mifsud was initially uninterested in Papadopoulos, his tune changed when he learned the young American was working on the Trump campaign. Mifsud described himself as a former Maltese diplomat with extensive access to European leaders. In particular, he emphasized that he had "substantial connections" with the Russian government. Recalling Clovis' emphasis on Russia, Papadopoulos believed that Mifsud could help him improve his status in the Trump campaign.

Mifsud never actually worked as an official diplomat for Malta. From 2006 to 2007, he acted as the Head of the Private Secretariat for Malta's Foreign Affairs Minister. [12] In 2012, Mifsud became the director of an obscure for-profit graduate school for embassy officials living in the UK called the London Academy of Diplomacy.[13] It was here that Mifsud cultivated contacts within Russia. In April 2014, he attended a conference in Moscow called the Global University Summit. Upon his return to the UK, Mifsud was invited to meet with the Russian Ambassador to the United Kingdom, Alexander Yakovenko, at his private residence.[14]

Two years earlier, Ambassador Yakovenko hosted a launch party for the Conservative Friends of Russia, a British organization consisting of Tory peers and Members of Parliament dedicated to fostering a better relationship between Russia and the UK.[15] Sergey Nalobin, one of the Russian diplomats who regularly liaised with the Conservative Friends of Russia, was the son of a high-ranking spy. Nalobin had received orders from Moscow to deepen the relationship between the Tories and Putin's political party.[16] According to *Mail on Sunday*, Yakovenko was expelled from the United States in the 1980s during a purge of Russian intelligence assets.[17]

Mifsud brought on a 24-year-old Russian intern, Natalia Kutepova-Jamrom, to work for him at the Academy. She had previously worked as a legislative aide in the Russian government and introduced him to senior Russian officials. She even managed to secure him a speaking slot at the Valdai Discussion Club, a Russian state-funded think tank that holds an annual meeting and often features Vladimir Putin.[18] Mifsud was present when Putin addressed the 2014 Valdai Discussion Club.[19] Following the meeting, Mifsud informed Kutepova-Jamrom that he had used her introductions to arrange "a short private meeting" with Putin.[20] According to a Ukrainian woman with whom Mifsud was romantically involved, he also claimed to have dined with Russia's foreign minister, Sergey Lavrov, who he described as a friend.[21]

Mifsud published articles on Valdai's website that praised Putin and kept to the Kremlin line. In March of 2015, he lauded Putin's controversial intervention in Syria.[22] That same year, Mifsud served as an observer for the elections held in Kazakhstan, then ruled over by the corrupt Putin ally Nursultan Nazarbayev. Even though independent election watchdogs criticized the election, Mifsud told Kazakh media that the election had been "consistent with international norms."[23]

After meeting Mifsud in Rome and learning of his potential high-level contacts in the Russian government, Papadopoulos returned to London. He next heard from Mifsud on March 22nd, the day after Trump had publicly announced that Papadopoulos was officially a campaign foreign policy advisor, mentioning him by name. Mifsud sent Papadopoulos a text, providing his phone number, and followed up with an email, writing, "It's very important for us to meet in London. I have to introduce you to somebody very important."[24]

Papadopoulos met with Mifsud two days later at the Holborn Hotel in London. Accompanying Mifsud was a beautiful young Russian woman named Olga Polonskaya, whom he introduced as a student with close connections to Vladimir Putin.[25] Papadopoulos was told that Polonskaya was Putin's niece.[26] While he appears to have believed this, Putin does not have a niece. Papadopoulos noted that Polonskaya had been escorted to the meeting by an unidentified man who didn't join them. The three discussed US-Russian trade relations. Polonskaya, who spoke poor English, explained that she could connect Papadopoulos with contacts in the Russian government and that she was friends with Ambassador Yakovenko. He left the meeting believing he had established contact with the Russian government.[27]

"I just finished a very productive lunch with a good friend of mine, Joseph Mifsud," Papadopoulos wrote in an email titled "Meeting with Russian Leadership--including Putin," to the members of the Trump foreign policy team. "[Mifsud] introduced me to both Putin's niece and the Russian ambassador in London--who also acts as the Deputy Foreign Minister." Papadopoulos lied about meeting the Russian ambassador. "The topic of the lunch was to arrange a meeting between us and the Russian leadership to discuss US-Russia ties under President Trump," Papadopoulos continued. "They are keen to host us in a "neutral" city, or directly in Moscow. They said the leadership, including Putin, is ready to meet with us and Mr. Trump should there be interest."

Following their meeting at the Holborn, Polonskaya began communicating with Papadopoulos via email. "Then all of a sudden," Papadopoulos later testified, "I'm talking to who I think is the same person, but she's writing in more fluent English. And now she goes from a seemingly obscure girl who... I thought might have been... Putin's niece, to now the interlocutor with Mifsud to the Russian government for me."[28]

Papadopoulos didn't know that Mifsud had drafted Polonskaya's initial email outreach to him following their meeting. In the email chain between Mifsud and Polonskaya, he refers to her as "Baby," which indicates they may have enjoyed something beyond a student-teacher relationship.[29] The Senate Intelligence report described Mifsud as using Polonskaya as a "proxy for his activities," consistent with intelligence tradecraft.[30]

A week later, on March 31st, Papadopoulos was in Washington, DC, to attend the first in-person meeting of Trump's foreign policy advisors chaired by Alabama Senator Jeff Sessions. The meeting was attended by Trump, the only known time that Papadopoulos ever met the candidate. After introducing himself, Papadopoulos explained that he had learned through contacts in London that Putin wanted to meet with Trump and that these contacts could help facilitate a meeting. Papadopoulos interpreted Trump and Sessions' reactions as favorable to the idea and left the meeting determined to pursue a meeting with Putin.

Papadopoulos reached out to Polonskaya and suggested they meet again. He expressed interest in arranging a meeting with Ambassador Yakovenko and attached an interview of himself published in *The Jerusalem Post* in which he said that Trump was interested in striking deals with Putin. The next day, Papadopoulos had breakfast with Mifsud at the Andaz Hotel in London. Polonskaya wrote that she had "alerted my personal links to our conversation and your request. The Embassy in London is very much aware of this. As mentioned we are all very excited by the possibility of a good relationship with Mr. Trump: The Russian Federation would love to welcome him once his candidature [sic] would be officially announced."

On April 18th, Mifsud traveled to Moscow and connected Papadopoulos with Ivan Timofeev, the Director of Programs at the Russian International Affairs Council (RIAC). RIAC's President, Igor Ivanov, was a former Russian Foreign Minister. Ivanov's replacement as Foreign Minister, Sergey Lavrov, also sits on the board of RIAC.[31] Another board member is Sergei Prikhodko.[32] Timofeev has been a professor at the Academy for Military Science in Russia since 2013. Starting in 2015, Timofeev led the "Euro-Atlantic Security" program at the Valdai Discussion Club. It appears likely that Mifsud met Timofeev in this capacity.

Papadopoulos contacted Timofeev, and they scheduled a Skype meeting. What exactly they discussed during their initial April 22nd Skype conversation remains unknown. Papadopoulos, who was later convicted of lying to the FBI, told investigators that they likely discussed relations between Russia, Israel, Cyprus, and China. Two days after the conversation, Papadopoulos searched the name of Alisher Usmanov on LinkedIn, indicating that Usmanov may have come up during the conversation. Usmanov is an Uzbek-born billionaire oligarch with investments in precious metals and Gazprom who developed his early fortune through his relationship with the Russian gangster Andrei Skoch, who is tied to the Solntsevskaya.[33]

Between April 25th and 27th, Papadopoulos and Timofeev exchanged emails and set up another Skype conversation to discuss arranging a Trump trip to Moscow via the Russian Embassy in Washington, DC. Also, on the 25th, Papadopoulos connected with Dmitry Andreyko, First Secretary of the Russian Embassy in Ireland. This was the first of several Russian diplomats that Papadopoulos connected with on LinkedIn, including Sergey Nalobin.[34]

On April 26th, Mifsud and Papadopoulos met again at the Andaz Hotel. Papadopoulos later described thinking that Mifsud seemed "giddy… like he had something to get off his chest." Mifsud explained to Papadopoulos that while in Moscow, he had met with senior Russian government officials as well as various Russian academics, among others. Mifsud told him that the Russians had "dirt" on Hillary Clinton in the form of "thousands of emails." Mifsud delivered this news just over a month after the GRU had exfiltrated John Podesta's emails. When Papadopoulos asked how he could know such information, Mifsud replied, "They told me."[35]

The day after Papadopoulos learned this information, he spoke again with Timofeev over Skype. The contents of this conversation are not publicly known. Papadopoulos later described the call to investigators as being "strange" and that he felt Timofeev was being overly formal. Timofeev's awkward manner and the static sound in the call's background led Papadopoulos to believe that the call might have been recorded. The timing of the call could indicate that the Russians were hoping to record a conversation in which Papadopoulos admitted that he was aware that the Russians had "Hillary's" emails. Such a recording could give them leverage over Papadopoulos and the Trump campaign. According to Papadopoulos, the subject never came up. Despite this, Papadopoulos spent much of the rest of the campaign, ultimately unsuccessfully, attempting to arrange a meeting between Trump and Putin. His primary conduit for trying to arrange the meeting was Timofeev.

Whether Papadopoulos shared information with anyone on the Trump campaign about the Russians having dirt on Hillary Clinton remains unknown. Papadopoulos never denied having told somebody on the campaign about the information. Instead, after confronted with previous demonstrable falsehoods that he had told investigators, he claimed that *he couldn't recall* having told any Trump campaign officials. Among the Trump campaigners asked if Papadopoulos had ever spoken to them regarding the matter, responses ranged from outright denials to claims of inability to remember.

Trump campaign policy director John K. Mashburn recalled that Papadopoulos had sent an email to the campaign in the first half of 2016 alerting it that Russia had damaging information on Clinton. Mashburn, who said other campaign officials would have been copied, claimed he didn't take Papadopoulos seriously.[36] Despite Mashburn's recollection under oath, neither the Senate Intelligence Committee nor the Special Counsel's Office could find the email he referred to. The Committee would later write of this crucial issue: "The Committee could not determine if Papadopoulos informed anyone on the Trump Campaign of the information, though the Committee finds it implausible that Papadopoulos did not do so."[37]

The subject of Russian dirt on Clinton came up during a meeting on May 10th between Papadopoulos and the Australian diplomat Alexander Downer. Papadopoulos and Downer met at the Kensington Wine Bar on May 10th, 2016. Over Gin-and-Tonic's, how many remains unclear, Downer asked Papadopoulos whether he thought Trump would win the election. After affirming he did, Papadopoulos told Downer that Russia possessed "damaging" material on Clinton and was prepared to release it in the final stages of the election.

Papadopoulos did not seem to treat this revelation as groundbreaking, nor did Downer appear to have either. In a report Downer sent to the Australian Foreign Ministry in Canberra describing the meeting, written per his regular diplomatic duties, Downer didn't mention Papadopoulos' claim of the Russians possessing damaging material related to Clinton until midway through the report.[38] However, following the public release of DNC-related emails later in the Summer, Downer's report was submitted to the FBI and used as a predicate to open its investigation into the Trump campaign's links with Russia during the campaign.

Shortly after the Downer meeting, Papadopoulos contacted Corey Lewandowski again, writing, "[t]he Greek and Cyprus governments, the EU Parliament and Russian governments have also relayed to me that they are interested in hosting Mr. Trump." Papadopoulos forwarded the email to Sam Clovis the next day. Clovis then emailed Lewandowski, writing "[s]till working on the ins and outs of going to Russia as a candidate."

Clovis, who was subject to a criminal referral by the Senate Intelligence Committee for lying under oath, claimed that this reference was unrelated to Papadopoulos's email from the day earlier but was related to other internal discussions that were taking place in the context of a potential trip by Trump to Europe. The documentary evidence points to the fact that the Trump campaign *was* actively considering a trip to Russia.[39]

On May 17th, Papadopoulos traveled to Greece. The country was then under the leadership of Syriza, an ideologically populist left/nationalist party. Syriza was infamous for its close connections to the Putin regime.[40] Then-Greek Prime Minister and Syriza leader Aléxis Tsípras was an opponent of sanctioning Russia for its invasion of Ukraine. One of the first individuals Papadopoulos met in Greece was Defense Minister Panagiotis Kammenos, noted for his many connections to Russia and sympathy for Putin. Since becoming Defense Minister, Kammenos advocated closer military ties with Russia.[41]

Kammenos was an associate of the Russian Orthodox billionaire Konstantin Malofeev.[42] Malofeev linked pro-Russian militants in Ukraine to the political establishment in Moscow and propagated the lie that the West was behind the shooting down of flight MH17.[43] He founded Tsargrad, a monarchist political movement and Russian Orthodox pro-Putin television station.[44] The Russian Eurasianist and neo-fascist Aleksandr Dugin has been described as the "mastermind" behind Tsargrad's ideology. Malofeev also has links with Marine Le Pen in France and US Republican Senator Rand Paul.[45]

Papadopoulos got buzzed drinking ouzo with Kammenos, who complained to him that President Obama and US Secretary of Defense Ash Carter thought he was a Russian stooge.[46] On May 26th, Papadopoulos met with Greek Foreign

Minister Nikos Kotzias. Kotzias, once a Piraeus University professor, had also cultivated a relationship with Aleksandr Dugin during his various visits to Moscow. In 2013, Kotzias invited Dugin to Piraeus University to speak on how Orthodox Christianity could unite Greeks and Russians.

Papadopoulos and Kotzias discussed geopolitics over fruit and coffee. In a remarkable coincidence, Vladimir Putin was scheduled to arrive in Greece for high-level meetings with Greek government officials the next day. During his meeting with Papadopoulos, Kotzias stated, "Tomorrow, Putin will be sitting right where you are sitting." The remark supposedly took Papadopoulos by surprise, leading to the first instance he could later "recall," in which he mentioned the information he had learned from Mifsud.

"I heard the Russians have Clinton's emails," Papadopoulos said.

"[D]on't tell this to anyone," Kotzias, who didn't appear shocked by the news, responded in Greek. Papadopoulos interpreted his response to mean that Kotzias already knew this information. He claims to have never brought the matter up again. When Putin arrived in Athens the next day, he was warmly greeted by Kammenos.[47]

On July 15th, Papadopoulos received a LinkedIn message from Sergei Millian.[48] Millian introduced himself as the "President of [the] New York-based Russian American Chamber of Commerce" and boasted that he had "insider knowledge and direct access to the top hierarchy in Russian politics (president circle, ministers, governors level)."[49] Born in Belarus under the name Siarhei Kukuts, Millian attended Minsk State Linguistic University. According to an online biography, he studied to be a military translator. At some point in the early 2000s, Millian immigrated to the US, changed his name, and established himself in Atlanta. He initially worked in real estate and set up a translation company that counted the Russian Ministry of Foreign Affairs among its clients.[50] In 2006, Millian founded the Russian American Chamber of Commerce (RACC). While receiving little annual donations and showing no trace at its listed office address, the chamber has arranged trips for visiting Russian regional governors to the US. In January 2015, the Russian government awarded Mr. Millian a prize for developing ties between Russian and American businesspeople."[51]

Shortly after he founded RACC, Millian claims to have met Donald Trump. Millian claims he was first introduced to Trump after a "mutual acquaintance" facilitated Trump's attendance at the 2007 Millionaire's Fair in Moscow. Despite these claims, there is no evidence that Trump visited Moscow in 2007. While their introduction remains mysterious, Trump did invite Millian to join him at a horse race at Gulfstream Park in Florida. Millian posted photos of him at the race with Trump on Facebook and used them in RACC promotional literature. Following that meeting, Millian claimed that he traveled to New York and Trump put him in touch with Michael Cohen, at which point he signed a contract with the Trump Organization to sell units in Florida.[52]

Millian came to the attention of the FBI in 2011 through his affiliation with Rossotrudnichestvo, a Russian government organization dedicated to promoting Russian culture abroad. The US director of Rossotrudnichestvo, Yury Zaytsev, was investigated by the FBI for attempting to recruit American intelligence assets through cultural exchange trips to Russia. The FBI reportedly came to believe that Zaytsev was a Russian foreign intelligence officer.[53] Millian collaborated with Rossotrudnichestvo and Zaytsev, helping them organize a 10-day exchange trip that took 50 American entrepreneurs to a forum held in Moscow.[54]

Before reaching out to Papadopoulos, Millian attended several conferences and events in Moscow where he was photographed with senior Russian officials. At one of the events, Millian spoke on a panel featuring the Vice Presidents of Rosneft, Lukoil, and Gazprom. The panel was moderated by Sergey Belyakov, a Russian military veteran trained by Russian intelligence who worked six years as a "Chief Specialist" at Oleg Deripaska's company Basic Element.[55] Millian has been photographed speaking with Deripaska.[56]

On July 31st, Papadopoulos met with Millian in New York City. While the contents of their meeting remain unknown, the next day Papadopoulos reached out to Trump campaign official Bo Denysyk, informing him that he had been contacted "by some leaders of Russian-American voters here in the US about their interest in voting for Mr. Trump," and asked if he wanted to be put in touch "with their group (US-Russia chamber of commerce)."

Denysyk thanked Papadopoulos for "taking the initiative" but asked that he "hold off with outreach to Russian-Americans" because there were "too many articles" painting the campaign, its chairman Paul Manafort, and Trump himself as "being pro-Russian."[57]

Papadopoulos met Millian again on August 1st. Four days later, Papadopoulos emailed Anthony Livanios, the CEO of Energy Stream, a company Papadopoulos had briefly worked for in 2015. In the message, which Millian was copied to, Papadopoulos suggested to Livanios that they have a Skype call with his "friend" Sergei Millian. Three days after that, Millian sent Papadopoulos an email that contained the details and agenda for an energy conference in Moscow. Throughout their conversations, Millian invited Papadopoulos to speak at two international energy conferences, one in Moscow.

Papadopoulos provided his bio to Millian and then reached out to the Trump campaign for permission to present the campaign's positions in his presentations but was rebuffed. Despite this, Papadopoulos continued to interact with Millian. Millian also corresponded with Michael Cohen over email. On March 15th, five days after the GRU started targeting the Clinton Campaign, Millian wrote to Cohen asking if he could join Trump's foreign policy team, boasting about his official connections in Russia. Cohen appears to have ignored the request. Jared Kushner was copied to Millian's later correspondence with Cohen.[58] Rick Gates told the FBI that Millian's name was on a special access "Friends and Family" list that granted access to Trump campaign events to individuals selected by the Trump children, close friends, and staff. Gates didn't know who added Millian's name to the list but noted that Michael Cohen would have been able to. The list was kept by Trump's personal assistant, Rhona Graff.[59]

Sometime in September, Papadopoulos attempted to put Millian in touch with senior Trump Campaign advisor Boris Epshteyn, describing him as a friend in an email to Epshteyn. It is unknown whether Millian and Epshteyn ever spoke or met. Earlier that Spring, Epshteyn had attempted to put Trump in contact with his associates in Moscow to discuss a potential Trump Tower Moscow deal. The Senate Intelligence Report heavily redacts the section that describes the interactions related to this building proposal. In one of the few unredacted footnotes, the front for Russian intelligence, Rossotrudnichestvo, is mentioned.[60] Why it is mentioned, what it has to do with Boris Epshteyn, and whether there is any connection to Millian is unknown.

On November 5th, Papadopoulos received an odd message from Sergei Millian, "I have no doubt that forces that invested so much into H[illary] will try to steal the elections. Otherwise, all the money they paid will go to waste." He continued, "Please be very cautious these last few days. Even to the point of not leaving your food and drinks out of eye sight. I saw you in my dream with two men in black with angry faces hiding behind your back."[61]

Three days later, Donald J. Trump was elected President of the United States.

Carter Page, Russian Foreign Intelligence, and the Trump Campaign

Born in 1971, Carter Page's interest in Russia started early in life. In 1986, Page watched the meeting between Ronald Reagan and Mikhail Gorbachev in Reykjavik, Iceland, on television. Five years later, he visited Moscow for the first time as a midshipman in the Naval Academy. After graduating from the Naval Academy in 1993, Page served as a Marine intelligence officer based in the Western Sahara.[62] He would also serve several tours as a surface warfare officer in the Middle East and Europe and work at the Pentagon on arms control issues.[63]

After leaving the Navy, Page became a fellow at the Council on Foreign Relations (CFR), where he researched economic development in the former Soviet Union and the Middle East.[64] Columbia professor Stephen Sestanovich met Page several times at CFR events related to Russia. "His view of how the world worked seemed to have an edgy Putinist resentment to it," Sestanovich later said of Page. "I think Carter genuinely felt an affinity for Putin's critique of the US foreign-policy establishment and its unfairness to Russia because he wasn't doing any better with that establishment than Putin was."[65]

In 2000, Page went into investment banking after being hired by Merrill Lynch and joining their capital markets group based out of London. He was transferred in 2004 to the Merrill Lynch branch in Moscow after impressing a colleague by having a relationship with the Ukrainian Billionaire Victor Pinchuk.[66]

Between 2004 and 2007, Page served as the deputy branch manager of Merrill Lynch's Moscow office. Page worked with Gazprom and befriended its Deputy Chief Financial Officer Sergey Yatsenko.[67] He was introduced to Gazprom through a Russia-based American investor and colleague at Merrill Lynch named Allen Vine.[68] After working at Merrill, Vine moved on to become the "right-hand man" of Suleiman Kerimov, a Kremlin-connected Russian oligarch with strong links to Gazprom.[69] In 2018, the US added Kerimov to the list of Russians under sanctions, accusing him of laundering money by purchasing villas in France.[70]

Upon his return to the United States in 2008, Page met a Russian intelligence officer named Aleksandr Bulatov, who was then working undercover as a Trade official at the Russian consulate in New York.[71] Page and Bulatov's relationship lasted for a year, during which time Page offered to provide introductions to Bulatov with his political and business contacts. He also provided Bulatov with Merrill Lynch's annual report, which was not publicly available.[72] Page, who later learned that Bulatov was an SVR agent, claims that he only provided "immaterial non-public information" to him.[73]

In April of 2008, Page met with the CIA. Between 2008 and 2013, Page was classified as an "operational contact," which meant that the agency could ask him about activities that took place during the normal course of his activities but couldn't specifically assign him to go out and gather information.[74] While he was in contact with the CIA during his interactions with Bulatov, which ended two months after Bulatov returned to Moscow in August of 2008, Page didn't mention their relationship to the agency until August 2010. At this point, Page claimed to have met with Bulatov four times, described his interest in meeting a specific "US Person," who remains unidentified, and described him as a "compelling, nice guy."[75]

In 2008, Page established an emerging market energy consulting firm called Global Energy Capital LLC (GEC). Its office was in a co-working space at 590 Madison Avenue, a building linked to Trump Tower via a glass atrium. His partners in the company were James Richard and Sergey Yatsenko, who left Gazprom in 2010 to work at GEC as a semi-retired senior advisor on a contingency basis. At the same time, Yatsenko and his wife moved to London and went on a high-end European real estate buying spree, purchasing a £3 million flat in Chelsea and a £6.2 million six-bedroom home in Kensington.[76]

In June of 2009, Page was interviewed by an agent from the FBI's New York Field Office. Page told the agent that he "knew and kept in regular contact with" Bulatov "and provided him with a copy of a non-public annual report." Page also explained to the FBI agent that, due to his overseas work, he had previously been questioned by the CIA and provided them with information on an ongoing basis.[77] The FBI and CIA do not appear to have exchanged information regarding their interactions with Page.

Shortly after that, Page was once again in contact with Russian intelligence. In January 2013, Page met a Russian junior attaché named Victor Podobnyy at the Russian consulate in New York City. Podobnyy's position at the Russian Consulate was a cover for his real job as an economic intelligence agent for the SVR. Podobnyy worked alongside another SVR agent named Igor Sporyshev. Both worked undercover as trade representatives of the Russian Federation in New York. Evgeny Buryakov, another SVR colleague, worked out of the New York office of the Russian state-controlled Vnesheconombank under "non-official cover."[78] Podobnyy, Sporyshev, and Buryakov were tasked with gathering information on potential US sanctions against Russia and American efforts to exploit alternative energy resources.[79] One of the sources they attempted to recruit was Page.[80] The FBI knew that Podobnyy had replaced Page's previous Russian intelligence contact, Alexander Bulatov.[81]

Page and Podobnyy met again in March. Page later recollected that they met only once again over coffee or coke. On April 8th, 2013, Podobnyy was recorded by the FBI having a conversation with Igor Sporyshev about his attempts to recruit Page. "[Carter] wrote that he is sorry, he went to Moscow and forgot to check his inbox, but he wants to meet when he gets back. I think he is an idiot and forgot who I am. Plus he writes to me in Russian [to] practice the language. He flies to Moscow more often than I do. He got hooked on Gazprom thinking that if they have a project, he could be [sic] rise up. Maybe he can. I don't know, but it's obvious he wants to earn a lot of money."

A month later, FBI Agent Gregory Monaghan interviewed Page at the Plaza Hotel in New York. During the January meeting, page told Monaghan that Podobnyy had provided him with a business card and two email addresses. Page explained that he and Podobnyy exchanged emails over several months and met in person "on occasion" so Page could tell him about his views on the energy industry's future and provide him with documents about the energy business.[82] The FBI could never definitively determine whether Page was aware that he was interacting with Russian intelligence officers at the time of the interactions. Witting or not, Page touted his relationship with the Kremlin. "Over the past half year," Page wrote, "I have had the privilege to serve as an informal advisor to the staff of the Kremlin in preparation for their Presidency of the G-20 Summit next month, where energy issues will be a prominent point on the agenda."[83]

Page continued to publish his pro-Kremlin views in various formats and settings. In the online journal *Global Policy*, Page wrote that the war in Ukraine had been "precipitated by US meddling." He also wrote that Igor Sechin, the head of Rosneft, friend of Putin, and former KGB agent, had "done more to advance US-Russian relations than any individual in or out of government from either side of the Atlantic over the past decade."[84] In a 2015 blog post, Page likened the National Security Council's rationale for the imposition of sanctions on Russia to an 1850 publication informing slaveholders on how to produce "the ideal slave."[85]

In late January 2015, Podobnyy, Sporyshev, and Buryakov were indicted by the Southern District of New York. Page was mentioned in the criminal complaint as "Male-1" and was able to identify himself as such by the description of his interactions with Podobnyy.[86] At some point after he read the criminal complaint, Page attended an event sponsored by United National where he met with a Russian Minister and various other Russian officials. During their discussion, Page told the Russians that he was the "Male-1" that the recent indictment against the Russian intelligence officers alluded to.[87]

Towards the end of 2015, Page began his efforts to contact the Trump campaign. He reached out to Ed Cox, Richard Nixon's son-in-law. Page had met Cox while volunteering on the McCain campaign. In his capacity as head of the New York Republican Party, Cox interacted extensively with Trump in 2013 when he was considering and ultimately decided against, running against Andrew Cuomo to become the Governor of New York.[88]

"[I'm] cautiously optimistic that the next administration might finally offer a change in direction in US-Russia relations," Page wrote to Cox, stating further that "recent statements by Trump give me renewed hope." He then asked Cox if he could provide insights "as to how one might be able to support [Trump], including by becoming one of his delegates." Included in his email was a paper Page had written titled "Trump, Putin and the Possible End of the Second Cold War."[89]

Cox forwarded Page's email and the attached article to Corey Lewandowski, and they set up a meeting at Trump Tower. Page met with Lewandowski, Sam Clovis, and Trump campaign political director Michael Glassner at the meeting. Judging from subsequent communications between Page and Clovis, they discussed Russia at the meeting. At this point, Page began volunteering with the Trump campaign on an informal, unpaid basis.[90]

"Following up on our discussions about Russia earlier this month," Page wrote to Clovis, Glassner, and Lewandowski in an email titled "J.P. Morgan Securities: GAZPROM INVESTOR DAY," "I spent the past week in Europe and have been in discussions with some individuals with close ties to the Kremlin... Through my discussions with these high-level contacts, it is their belief that a direct meeting in Moscow between Mr. Trump and President Putin could be arranged."[91] On February 7th, Page emailed Clovis, Glassner, and Lewandowski, noting that *Forbes* had just selected Putin as its most powerful world leader. "As I have alluded to before," Page wrote, "there is no question that a Trump visit to Moscow and related meetings with Putin would prove to be the most important campaign event in the history of US politics."[92]

On February 17th, Page reached out to Clovis, Glassner, and Lewandowski again, letting them know that he had heard Trump was assembling a foreign policy advisory team. Page attached his bio. Clovis asked Page to call him to receive additional information.

Less than two weeks later, Page was interviewed by a Counterintelligence Agent from the FBI's New York Field Office (NYFO), as well as by Assistant United States Attorneys from the SDNY who were preparing for their upcoming trial of SVR Agent Evgeny Buryakov. During the interview, Page explained that he knew he was the "Male-1" mentioned in court documents describing Podobnyy's efforts at recruiting sources. He said that he had also provided this information to Russian diplomatic officials. Following the interview, the NYFO agent discussed opening a counterintelligence investigation into Page with her supervisor because he had informed Russian officials of his identity as "Male-1." The supervisor contacted the Counterespionage section at FBI headquarters in Washington, DC, to see if Page held any security clearances and to inquire what type of investigation they should open up into him. The NYFO Counterintelligence Supervisor would later claim she believed she should have opened up a counterintelligence investigation into Page. However, her squad had been too busy working on the upcoming trial of Buryakov (as well as Podobnyy and Sporyshev in absentia).[93]

Page was eventually hired onto Trump's foreign policy advisor team. On April 1st, the FBI Counterespionage Section in Washington, DC, contacted the NYFO Supervisor who had inquired a month earlier about opening up an investigation into Page and instructed her to do so. This is not to be confused with the FBI's Crossfire Hurricane investigation into the Trump campaign's links with Russia, a separate investigation opened later. Five days later, on April 6th, the NYFO officially opened a counterintelligence investigation into Page, attempting to see if any more foreign intelligence officers would contact him.[94]

On April 25th, Page was contacted by an old acquaintance from Moscow, Andrej Krickovic. A professor at Moscow's Higher School of Economics, Krickovic had been an intern at the US Embassy in Moscow when he first met Page while the latter was working at Merrill Lynch. Both had a mutual acquaintance in a Defense Attaché stationed at the Embassy.[95] The Higher School of Economics offers a Joint Bachelor of Economics Program with the New Economic School (NES). Krickovic learned from an HSE colleague, Yuval Weber, that Shlomo Weber, Yuval's father and the Rector of NES, was looking for speakers for the NES's 2016 commencement ceremony. Krickovic put Shlomo in contact with Page. Shlomo later claimed his invitation to Page to speak at the commencement was a publicity stunt as "there was incredible interest in Moscow related to the Donald J. Trump presidential campaign."[96]

Page was cautious, replying that he did want to discuss

Trump's foreign policy before it had been officially formed. Despite these concerns, he eventually reached out to Trump campaign Director of National Security J.D. Gordon on May 9th, informing him that he had received invitations for "speaking engagements in Russia and the Middle East." In this email to Gordon, instead of mentioning Shlomo Weber, Page wrote that he had received a speaking invitation from a "close advisor of President Putin," Sergey Karaganov. Why exactly he did so, and if Karaganov actually reached out to Page, is unclear. In his initial April 25th email chain introducing Page to Weber, Krickovic had ended his correspondence by writing: "Perhaps we can even arrange a private meeting with our dean, Sergei Karaganov. As you know, he has quite some influence in high places here. It would be really good to get a dialogue going."

In 1992, Karaganov, a Russian nationalist intellectual, gave a highly influential speech in the aftermath of the collapse of the Soviet Union in which he laid out what came to be known as the "Karaganov Doctrine." The doctrine has influenced Putin. In the speech, Karaganov argued that instead of seeing the fact that the collapse of the Soviet Union had left millions of Russian speakers outside of Russia's borders as irretrievably lost, they should be seen as a means to cultivate Russian influence over former Soviet satellite states.[97]

Karaganov was close to Putin, Yevgeny Primakov, a former KGB and then SVR intelligence chief, and Russian Deputy Prime Minister Sergei Prikhodko.[98] He has served as the Chairman of the Valdai Discussion Club since 2004.[99] Karaganov also sat on the board of the Russian International Affairs Committee (RIAC) alongside Ivan Timofeev.[100] The nature of Page's relationship with Karaganov is unclear. Page met Karaganov in the late 1990s and again when he lived in Moscow and worked for Merrill Lynch. He has never explained why he suggested to J.D. Gordon that Karaganov had invited him.

On May 16th, Page emailed Sam Clovis, J.D. Gordon, and Walid Phares, proposing that Trump speak in his stead at the Moscow event. There does not seem to be any initial campaign response to Page's suggestion that Trump travel to Moscow. On May 18th, Page submitted a speech request form to J.D. Gordon. Gordon later testified that he told Page the trip would be a bad idea. However, there is no evidence that he did so.[101] On his last day on the campaign, Corey Lewandowski told Page that he could speak at the event but had to do so outside his capacity on the Trump campaign.

Page arrived in Moscow on July 4th, 2016. Page joined Shlomo Weber, Krickovic, and several others for dinner early in the trip. Weber arrived at the dinner two hours late and was later unable to remember the content of the discussions that took place with any specificity. However, he did recall that Page continually spoke about "Igor Ivanovich, Igor Ivanovich, Igor Ivanovich," which was how he referred to Rosneft CEO and former KGB agent Igor Sechin.[102]

On July 5th, Page emailed Weber and asked him to remove any mention of his involvement with the Trump campaign from the webpage announcing his role in the commencement. Despite this request, Page continually gave the impression that he was an adviser to Donald Trump and, according to Weber, "[n]obody ever doubted" that Page worked for the Trump campaign. Before his speech, Weber wasn't sure whether Page wanted to be introduced as a Trump campaign adviser.

The next day, July 6th, NES staffer Denis Klimentov emailed the Director of the Russian Ministry of Foreign Affairs Press Department, Maria Zakharova, informing her that he desired to bring Page's presence in Moscow to the attention of the Russian government and offering to put him in contact with her.[103] Klimentov then contacted Putin's press secretary, Dmitry Peskov, to see if he was interested in introducing Page to Russian government officials.[104]

"I have read about [Page]," Peskov replied the next day. "Specialists say that he is far from being the main one. So I better not initiate a meeting in the Kremlin."

On the evening of the 6th, Page attended a J.P. Morgan social event to watch a European Cup match and met there with a friend from his days in Moscow named Andrey Baranov. Baranov had once worked for Gazprom but was then the Head of Investor Relations for Rosneft. Page later told the FBI that he and Baranov discussed "immaterial non-public information," using the same language he used to describe his previous interactions with Russian intelligence agents. He believed that he and Baranov discussed Igor Sechin in passing and recalled that Baranov may have briefly mentioned the possible upcoming sale of a stake in Rosneft.[105]

On July 7th, Page delivered his first of two scheduled speeches before the NES. He used the opportunity to critique America's policy vis-a-vis Russia, stating, "Washington and other Western capitals have impeded potential progress through their often hypocritical focus on ideas such as democratization, inequality, corruption, and regime change." According to Shlomo Weber, NES students were disappointed by Page's speech, and nobody at the time believed that Trump would win the election.[106]

Page's speech was attended and promoted by several infamous Russian nationalists, some with connections to Russian intelligence. Maria Katasonova, a 21-year-old Russian nationalist, attended the event and asked Page a question regarding Trump and US-Russian relations.[107] Katasonova was at the time running to represent a Russian ultra-nationalist party in the State Duma and was known for her ardent support of Putin, French right-wing politician Marine Le Pen, and Donald Trump, in addition to publicly bashing Hillary Clinton. She often expressed her political views through PR stunts such as protesting in front of the American Embassy in Moscow and releasing white doves in favor of Trump.[108]

Aleksandr Dugin also promoted Page's speech via his now-deleted Twitter account. As described earlier, Dugin is affiliated with the sanctioned billionaire Konstantin Malofeev's *Tsargrad* television station. *Tsargrad* was one of the few stations to cover Page's trip to Russia. *Tsargrad* is affiliated with the Russian nationalist think tank KATEHON, which features Malofeev and Dugin on its board. Following Page's speech, an article covering it from KATEHON read: "After the reunification of Crimea with Russia and the beginning of operations in Ukraine, he was one of the few American experts who called for understanding the actions of Russia."[109]

Another ardent Russian nationalist, Konstantin Rykov, published a Facebook post on July 7th praising Page's speech. Rykov has numerous links to Russian intelligence and is a Kremlin-backed online propagandist. He began receiving Russian government support in 2003 and initially focused his online propaganda on the Russian domestic audience. Eventually, his efforts turned to international targets, including the US and its allies.[110] Rykov is also a close associate of two Aras Agalarov employees, Artem Klyushin and his then-wife Yulya Klyushina, both of whom spent time with Donald Trump during the 2013

Miss Universe Pageant in Moscow. Klyushin and Rykov were involved in Kremlin-backed efforts to flood Ukrainian social media with pro-Russian propaganda in 2014.[111] Following Trump's announcement to run for President, Rykov's pro-Kremlin website *Vzglyad* contacted Hope Hicks attempting to arrange an interview with Trump that never came to fruition. In August of 2015, Rykov registered the domain trump2016.ru, which he used as a content aggregator.

Rykov organized numerous pro-Trump events in Russia around the 2016 election, some of which were attended by Maria Katasonova and Artem Klyushin. Another attendee at these events included Anton Korobkov-Zemlyanskiy, a pro-Kremlin bot developer and social media operative who had worked with Rykov and Klyushin in their efforts in Ukraine and was known to have targeted the United States in the past. Jack Hanick, a former Fox News producer and director of Sean Hannity's program who works for Malofeev's Tsargrad television station, also attended Rykov's election events.[112]

On July 8th, Page delivered his second speech in Moscow at the NES commencement ceremony, though he was not the keynote speaker. One of the main speakers at the event was Russian Deputy Prime Minister and head of the NES board, Arkady Dvorkovich. At some point during the ceremony, Page greeted Dvorkovich, and the two spoke briefly. While Page later maintained their interaction only lasted a few seconds, Weber recalled that they spoke for several minutes. Dvorkovich reportedly mentioned working together with Page in the future.[113] The two later had a private dinner together when Page returned to Moscow in December.

The Senate Intelligence Committee had counterintelligence concerns about Dvorkovich. He was known to be close to the former Russian president Dmitri Medvedev.[114] In November 2016, the Russian newspaper *Vedomosti* claimed that Dvorkovich had been under surveillance by Russian domestic intelligence agencies on suspicion of graft.[115] In 2018, he became the chairman of the Skolkovo Foundation, a Russian organization dedicated to developing and commercializing technology. The FBI's Boston office issued a warning that the Skolkovo Foundation may be a means by which the Russian government stole American technology.[116] Dvorkovich was later sanctioned by the US.

Carter Page was in Moscow from July 4th to July 9th. Later, investigators let it be known that due to Page's own vague and contradictory testimony and the inability to compel testimony from several key individuals in Russia, there remain unanswered questions as to what he did while he was in Moscow, as well as who he met with and what they spoke about.[117] These questions are pertinent given Page's own descriptions, which he provided to members of the Trump campaign, of speaking with Russian legislators and senior members of the Presidential administration. In his later interview with the FBI, Yuval Weber claimed that rumors were floating around Moscow while Page was in town that he had met with Igor Sechin.[118]

Page later left the campaign after a *Yahoo! News* story by the reporter Michael Isikoff, informed by extremely controversial opposition research paid for by the Democratic Party, much of which was later debunked, reported that US intelligence was looking into Page due to suspicions that he had been in communication with senior Russian officials, including a meeting with Igor Sechin. There is no evidence that any such meeting took place.

The Mayflower Hotel Speech:
Jared Kushner, Dmitri Simes, and Trump's First Foreign Policy Address

On April 27th, 2016, Donald Trump delivered his campaign's first foreign policy address at the Mayflower Hotel in Washington, DC. The genesis of the speech dates back to a March 14th luncheon at Manhattan's Time Warner Center organized by the DC-based think tank the Center for the National Interest (CNI) for its honorary chairman Henry Kissinger.[119] Jared Kushner was in attendance and connected with CNI's President and CEO, Dimitri Konstantinovich Simes.[120]

Born in Moscow in 1947, Simes immigrated to the United States in 1973 and became a US citizen. In his youth, he served as First Secretary of Komsomol, the communist political youth organization in the Soviet Union.[121] Simes graduated from Moscow University and studied at the Institute of the World Economy and International Relations.[122] The Institute was led by Yevgeny Primakov, who was later appointed the First Deputy Chairman of the KGB.[123] Simes' parents were lawyers who defended Soviet dissidents and had to flee the country after his father was discovered to be working an exposé of corruption in Soviet society.[124]

Simes worked his way into the Washington foreign policy establishment. He served as the Chairman of the Center for Russian and Eurasian Programs and a Senior Associate at the Carnegie Endowment for International Peace. After writing an op-ed in 1985 "re-appraising" Richard Nixon and describing him as "a very impressive President," Simes met Nixon and became his informal foreign policy advisor.[125] Simes accompanied the former president on several trips to Moscow, later claiming that Nixon helped him find a wife, acted as his best man at the wedding, and personally appointed him head of The Nixon Center.

Simes was a controversial figure in Washington, DC. Rumors circulated that he was a spy. To supporters, he was a foreign policy realist, while to others, he constantly parroted Kremlin propaganda. He gained enemies when he suggested in a 1979 article that the motivations for what he described as Washington's neoconservative "anti-Soviet brigade" could be explained by their "Jewish connection."[126] Simes, who is Jewish, has used that fact, along with his parents' story, to bolster his argument that he was a Soviet.[127]

The most in-depth analysis of Simes that concludes he is "an agent of the Kremlin embedded into the American political elite" was done by the Russian historian Yuri Felshtinsky for the Ukrainian publication GORDON.[128] Craig Unger spoke with two KGB defectors, Yuri Shvets and Oleg Kagin, who indicated that they believed Simes was connected with Russian intelligence. According to Shvets, while he was an acting KGB officer, he had wanted to attempt to recruit Simes but was told to "stand down" because "[h]e was being taken care of," which meant he was already a KGB contact. Kalugin relayed a story in which Simes had called him a "traitor" after he had defected to the United States.[129]

Simes was noted for his wide array of contacts among current and former Russian government officials.[130] However, upon Vladimir Putin's ascension to the Presidency, Simes courted controversy for his perceived sympathies with the authoritarian Russian leader. CNI and *The National Interest*, its flagship publication, became known in certain circles in Washington as "two of the most Kremlin-sympathetic institutions in the nation's capital."[131]

In December of 2005, *The Moscow Times* and *Kommersant* reported that Simes was in discussions with the Putin advisor Gleb Pavlovsky about establishing a Washington, DC-based think tank funded with Russian money to combat negative views of Russia in America. *The Moscow Times* reported that Oleg Deripaska also discussed being involved with the project.[132] Deripaska employee Georgy Oganov is quoted saying that the potential Russian-backed NGO "was discussed... on many occasions among Mr. Deripaska and people living in the States, including people at the Nixon Center."

In 2013, Simes attended the Valdai Discussion Summit, where he shared the stage with Vladimir Putin. He attended again in 2014 alongside Joseph Mifsud. In February 2015, Simes traveled to Moscow and met with Putin and other Russian officials.[133] The purpose of the meeting remains unknown. Shortly after that, Simes began interacting with Maria Butina, who was convicted of being an unregistered agent of Russia in 2018, and her handler Alexander Torshin, a Russian Central Bank deputy governor alleged to have links to the Moscow-based Taganskaya criminal organization.[134] Butina became infamous for infiltrating the National Rifle Association. David Keene, the former President of the NRA, is a board member of CNI.[135]

Simes put Butina in touch with the Editor-in-Chief of CNI's publication, *The National Interest*. Butina submitted an essay titled "The Bear and the Elephant."[136] On June 12th, *The National Interest* published Butina's article. It began as follows: "It may take the election of a Republican to the White House in 2016 to improve relations between the Russian Federation and the United States. As improbable as it may sound, the Russian bear shares more interests with the Republican elephant than the Democratic donkey."[137]

On March 24th, Kushner and Simes spoke over the phone and then met in person at Kushner's New York Office on the 31st. Simes encouraged Kushner to enlist a foreign policy advisory group that would offer Trump their counsel and establish policies acceptable to the candidate.[138] It was agreed that CNI would host a speech and its board members would provide their expertise to the campaign. Kushner put Simes in touch with Stephen Miller, who was responsible for drafting the speech. Simes provided Miller with a set of suggested themes outlined by himself, CNI executive director Paul Saunders, and board member Richard Burt.

After being appointed the Ambassador to West Germany by Reagan, Richard Burt helped facilitate a spy exchange between the US and USSR across the Glienicke Bridge in Berlin.[139] Under George H.W. Bush, Burt was appointed as the chief negotiator for the Strategic Arms Reduction Treaty.[140] In 2000, he became the chairman of a private intelligence and risk assessment firm called Diligence.[141] In 2005, Diligence was hired by the lobbying firm Barbour, Griffith & Rogers (BGR), who in turn represented one of the largest privately owned Russian conglomerates, Alfa Group Consortium. Some of Russia's wealthiest oligarchs, including Mikhail Fridman, Petr Aven, and German Khan sit on its Supervisory Board.

In 2007, Nathaniel Rothschild purchased a stake in the company.[142] Oleg Deripaska became a Diligence client[143] Burt left Diligence in 2007 and joined Kissinger McLarty Associates, a consulting firm established by Henry Kissinger.[144] He is a Non-Executive Director at LetterOne, an investment company established by Alfa Group Consortium leader Mikhail Fridman. According to Stratfor, Fridman is tied to the Solntsevskaya.[145]

At the time Bert helped draft the bullet points for Trump's speech, he was in the midst of a $365,000 lobbying job representing New European Pipeline AG, a holding company 50% owned by Gazprom that was attempting to build the NORD Stream 2 natural gas pipeline, a top geopolitical priority of the Putin regime.[146] While Simes, Bert, and Saunders provided the Trump campaign with bullet point suggestions for the speech, the primary speech writer was Stephen Miller. Other individuals who provided notes included Paul Manafort, Rick Gates, Corey Lewandowski, George Papadopoulos, and Carter Page. Suggested passages by former New Jersey Governor Chris Christie and Admiral Chuck Kubic that contained language challenging Russia or supporting NATO were nixed.[147]

On the day of the speech, April 27th, CNI arranged a VIP reception. Simes introduced Trump to the Russian Ambassador Sergey Kislyak, and the two exchanged pleasantries. Kislyak also met and shook hands with Jared Kushner. "I really like what he's saying," Kislyak told Kushner. "America and Russia should have a good relationship; we don't have one now with the current administration, and I hope if President Trump wins, that will change."

Kushner and Simes also kept in contact after the speech. Russia was often the subject of their conversations. Simes, who denied that Kushner ever asked him to establish a back channel line of communication with the Kremlin, later claimed that he warned Kushner that it would be "bad optics" for the campaign to develop hidden Russian contacts and that they should steer clear of Russia as an issue in the campaign.

On August 17th, 2016, Kushner met with Simes to discuss the Clinton campaign's Russia-related attacks against Trump. Before the meeting, Simes sent Kushner an email with the subject line *Russia Policy Memo* describing "what Mr. Trump may want to say about Russia." In the email, Simes wrote of a "well-documented story of highly questionable connections between Bill Clinton" and the Russian government. According to Simes, the story was familiar to the CIA, FBI, and Kenneth Starr, the special counsel who investigated Clinton in the 1990s. Kushner forwarded Simes' email to Paul Manafort, who scheduled a meeting with Simes but resigned from the campaign before the meeting could take place. However, Simes did meet with Kushner.

During the meeting, Simes told Kushner of rumors that had circulated within the US intelligence community that the Russians and recordings of Bill Clinton and Monica Lewinsky engaging in sexually explicit phone calls.[148] Simes explained that he had learned this from a former CIA Soviet analyst.[149] Kushner considered the item "old news" and unable to be "operationalized." Simes' relationship with Trump and those around him continued into the transition.

[1] Report of the Select Committee on Intelligence United States Senate On Russian Active Measures Campaigns And Interference in the 2016 US Election Volume 5: Counterintelligence Threats and Vulnerabilities. Pg. 471

[2] Missy, Ryan; Mufson, Steven. "One of Trump's foreign policy advisers is a 2009 college grad who lists model UN as credential," *The Washington Post*. March 22nd, 2016

[3] Helderman, Rosalind S. "Mueller was investigating Trump advisor as unregistered agent of Israel, his wife says," *The Washington Post*. June 5th, 2018

[4] Horn, Steve. "Holy Gas: Donald Trump's Foreign Policy Team Member Pushed Offshore Drilling in Israel," *DeSmog*. March 29th, 2016

[5] Sanders, Linley. "George Papadopoulos Lied on His Resume to Get Trump Campaign Foreign Policy Job, Former Employer Says," *Newsweek*. November 1st, 2017

[6] Report of the Select Committee on Intelligence United States Senate On Russian Active Measures Campaigns And Interference in the 2016 US Election Volume 5: Counterintelligence Threats and Vulnerabilities. Pg. 518 [Footnote 3386]

[7] Klippenstein, Ken. "Inside Wikistrat, the Mysterious Intelligence Firm Now in

Mueller's Sites," *The Daily Beast*. March 4th, 2019

[8] United States of America v. George Papadopoulos, Defendant. Statement of Offense. October 5th, 2017. Pg. 3

[9] Dilanian, Ken. "Senate committee made criminal referral of Trump Jr., Bannon, Kushner, two others to federal prosecutors," *NBC News*. August 18th, 2020

[10] Whitaker, Brian. "The Trump-Russia affair and an odd company in London," *Medium*. November 6th, 2017

[11] Kirchgaessner, Stephanie; Phipps, Claire; Rawlinson, Kevin. "Joseph Mifsud: more questions than answers about mystery professor linked to Russia," *The Guardian*. October 31st, 2017

[12] Nardelli, Alberto. "These Are The Contradictions Surrounding The Professor At The Center Of The Trump-Russia Probe," *BuzzFeed News*. November 4th, 2017

[13] Helderman, Rosalind S.; Harris, Shane; Nakashima, Ellen. "'The enigma of the entire Mueller probe,': focus on origins of the Russia probe puts spotlight on Maltese professor," *The Washington Post*. June 30th, 2019

[14] Press Release. "Ambassador Alexander Yakovenko met Director London Academy of Diplomacy," *The Embassy of the Russian Federation to the United Kingdom of Great Britain and Northern Ireland*. May 30th, 2014

[15] Harding, Luke; Watt, Nicholas. "Conservative Friends of Russia under fire for launch after Pussy Riot verdict," *The Guardian*. August 22nd, 2012

[16] Harding, Luke. "Tory blushes deepen over activities of Conservative Friends of Russia," *The Guardian*. November 30th, 2012

[17] Lazarus, Ben. "Kicked out for being a SOVIET AGENT: The damning evidence that Putin's man in London, who mocks Britain at every turn as his countrymen murder their enemies on our soil, was expelled from the US in a Cold War spy purge," *Mail On Sunday*. March 2nd, 2019

[18] LaFraniere, Sharon; Kirkpatrick, David D.; Higgins, Andrew; Schwirtz, Michael. "A London Meeting of an Unlikely Group: How a Trump Adviser Came to Learn of Clinton 'Dirt,'" *The New York Times*. November 10th, 2017

[19] Anishchuck, Alexei. "Putin accuses United States of damaging world order," Reuters. October 24th, 2014

[20] Adam, Karla; Krohn, Jonathan; Witte, Griff. "Professor at center of Russia disclosures claims to have met Putin," *The Washington Post*. October 31st, 2017

[21] Nardellie, Alberto. "The Professor At The Center Of The Trump-Russia Probe Boasted To His Girlfriend In Ukraine That He Was Friends With Russian Foreign Minister Sergey Lavrov," *BuzzFeed News*. February 27th, 2018

[22] Mifsud, Joseph. "Vienna Talks on Syria: Diplomacy at Work," *Valdai Discussion Club*. March 11th, 2015

[23] Adam, Karla; Krohn, Jonathan; Witte, Griff. "Professor at center of Russia disclosures claims to have met Putin," *The Washington Post*. October 31st, 2017

[24] Report of the Select Committee on Intelligence United States Senate On Russian Active Measures Campaigns And Interference in the 2016 US Election Volume 5: Counterintelligence Threats and Vulnerabilities. Pg. 474

[25] Mueller, III, Robert S. *Report On The Investigation Into Russian Interference In The 2016 Presidential Election*. Department of Justice, Washington, DC. March 2019. Pg. 84

[26] Executive Session. Committee of the Judiciary, Joint with the Committee on Government Reform and Oversight, U.S. House of Representatives, Washington, DC. Interview of George Papadopoulos. October 25th, 2018. Pg. 17

[27] Report of the Select Committee on Intelligence United States Senate On Russian Active Measures Campaigns And Interference in the 2016 US Election Volume 5: Counterintelligence Threats and Vulnerabilities. Pg. 475

[28] Executive Session. Committee of the Judiciary, Joint with the Committee on Government Reform and Oversight, U.S. House of Representatives, Washington, DC. Interview of George Papadopoulos. October 25th, 2018. Pg. 18

[29] Mueller, III, Robert S. *Report On The Investigation Into Russian Interference In The 2016 Presidential Election*. Department of Justice, Washington, DC. March 2019. Pg. 193

[30] Report of the Select Committee on Intelligence United States Senate On Russian Active Measures Campaigns And Interference in the 2016 US Election Volume 5: Counterintelligence Threats and Vulnerabilities. Pg. 465

[31] Hamburger, Tom; Leonnig, Carol D.; Helderman, Rosalind S. "Trump campaign emails show aides repeated efforts to set up Russia meetings," *The Washington Post*. August 14th, 2017

[32] Russian International Affairs Council, Board of Trustees

[33] Goodley, Simon; Harding, Luke; Elder, Miriam. "Man behind MegaFon pictured with alleged Russian gangsters," *The Guardian*. November 28th, 2012

[34] Mueller, III, Robert S. *Report On The Investigation Into Russian Interference In The 2016 Presidential Election*. Department of Justice, Washington, DC. March 2019. Pg. 88 [Footnote 458]

[35] Report of the Select Committee on Intelligence United States Senate On Russian Active Measures Campaigns And Interference in the 2016 US Election Volume 5: Counterintelligence Threats and Vulnerabilities. Pg. 485-486

[36] Fandos, Nicholas; Schmidt, Michael S. "Tantalizing Testimony From a Top Trump Aide Sets Off a Search for Proof," *The New York Times*. May 15th, 2018

[37] Report of the Select Committee on Intelligence United States Senate On Russian Active Measures Campaigns And Interference in the 2016 US Election Volume 5: Counterintelligence Threats and Vulnerabilities. Pg. x-xi

[38] Miller, Greg. *The Apprentice: Trump, Russia and the Subversion of American Democracy*. New York, NY: Custom House, 2018. Pg. 136-139

[39] Report of the Select Committee on Intelligence United States Senate On Russian Active Measures Campaigns And Interference in the 2016 US Election Volume 5: Counterintelligence Threats and Vulnerabilities. Pg. 496-497

[40] Jones, Sam; Kerin, Hope; Weaver, Courtney. "Alarm bells ring over Syriza's Russian links," *The Financial Times*. January 28th, 2015

[41] Prothero, Mitch; Bergengruen; Vera. "Key Trump Officials Met With A Putin Ally During Inauguration Weekend," *BuzzFeed News*. March 26th, 2018

[42] Marson, James. "Deepening Ties Between Greece and Russia Sow Concerns in West," *The Wall Street Journal*. February 13th, 2015

[43] Weaver. Courtney. "Malofeev: the Russian billionaire linking Moscow to the rebels," *The Financial Times*. July 24th, 2014

[44] Seddon, Max. "The Russian oligarch who wants Vladimir Putin to be Tsar," *The Financial Times*. March 12th, 2020

[45] Weaver, Courtney. "God's TV, Russian style," *The Financial Times*. October 16th, 2015

[46] Kakaounaki, Marianna. "Trump, Hilary's Emails and me," *ekathimarini*. March 25th, 2019

[47] Report of the Select Committee on Intelligence United States Senate On Russian Active Measures Campaigns And Interference in the 2016 US Election Volume 5: Counterintelligence Threats and Vulnerabilities. Pg. 498-499

[48] Mueller, III, Robert S. *Report On The Investigation Into Russian Interference In The 2016 Presidential Election*. Department of Justice, Washington, DC. March 2019. Pg. 94

[49] Report of the Select Committee on Intelligence United States Senate On Russian Active Measures Campaigns And Interference in the 2016 US Election Volume 5: Counterintelligence Threats and Vulnerabilities. Pg. 507

[50] Helderman, Rosalind S.; Hamburger, Tom. "Who is 'Source 'D'? The man said to be behind the Trump-Russia dossier's most salacious claims," *The Washington Post*. March 29th, 2017

[51] Belton, Catherine. "The shadowy Russian émigré touting Trump," *The Financial Times*. October 31st, 2016

[52] Helderman, Rosalind S.; Hamburger, Tom. "Sergei Millian, identified as an unwitting source for the Steele Dossier, sought proximity to Trump's world in 2016," *The Washington Post*. February 7th, 2019
[53] Redden, Molly. "FBI Probing Whether Russia Used Cultural Junkets to Recruit American Intelligence Assets," *Mother Jones*. October 23rd, 2013
[54] Corn, David. "Investigator's on the Trump-Russia Beat Should Talk to This Man," *Mother Jones*. January 19th, 2017
[55] ROSCONGRESS: Sergey Belyakov Bio
[56] Stedman, Scott. "FBI actively investigating Papadopoulos days after his release from prison," *Medium*. December 14th, 2018
[57] Mueller, III, Robert S. *Report On The Investigation Into Russian Interference In The 2016 Presidential Election*. Department of Justice, Washington, DC. March 2019. Pg. 94
[58] Bertrand, Natasha. "Jared Kushner received emails from Sergei Millian - an alleged dossier source who was in touch with George Papadopoulos," *Business Insider*. November 17th, 2017
[59] Report of the Select Committee on Intelligence United States Senate On Russian Active Measures Campaigns And Interference in the 2016 US Election Volume 5: Counterintelligence Threats and Vulnerabilities. Pg. 875
[60] Report of the Select Committee on Intelligence United States Senate On Russian Active Measures Campaigns And Interference in the 2016 US Election Volume 5: Counterintelligence Threats and Vulnerabilities. Pg. 459 [Footnote 2990]
[61] Report of the Select Committee on Intelligence United States Senate On Russian Active Measures Campaigns And Interference in the 2016 US Election Volume 5: Counterintelligence Threats and Vulnerabilities. Pg. 508
[62] Mufson, Steven; Hamburger, Tom. "Trump adviser's public comments, ties to Moscow stir unease in both parties," *The Washington Post*. August 5th, 2016
[63] Hall, Kevin G. "Why did FBI suspect Trump campaign advisor was a foreign agent?" *McClatchy DC Bureau*. April 14th, 2017
[64] Horn, Steve. "Carter Page, Trump Aide With Russia Ties, Is Also An Energy Scholar: Here's What He's Written," *DESMOG*. March 30th, 2017
[65] Zengerle, Jason. "What (if anything) Does Carter Page know?" *The New York Times Magazine*. December 18th, 2017
[66] Mider, Zachary. "Trump's New Russia Adviser Has Deep Ties to Kremlin's Gazprom," *Bloomberg*. March 30th, 2016
[67] Mueller, III, Robert S. *Report On The Investigation Into Russian Interference In The 2016 Presidential Election*. Department of Justice, Washington, DC. March 2019. Pg. 96
[68] Report of the Select Committee on Intelligence United States Senate On Russian Active Measures Campaigns And Interference in the 2016 US Election Volume 5: Counterintelligence Threats and Vulnerabilities. Pg. 528
[69] Belton, Catherine. "Suleiman Kerimov, the secret oligarch," *The Financial Times*. February 10th, 2012
[70] Press Release. "Treasury Designates Russian Oligarchs, Officials, and Entities in Response to Worldwide Malign Activity," *U.S. Department of the Treasury*. April 6th, 2018
[71] Mueller, III, Robert S. *Report On The Investigation Into Russian Interference In The 2016 Presidential Election*. Department of Justice, Washington, DC. March 2019. Pg. 96
[72] FISA Warrant Application for Carter Page, Pg. 12
[73] Carter Page FBI 302, 3/30/2017. Pg. 6
[74] Harris, Shane; Leonnig, Carol D.; Helderman, Rosalind S. "In opening an investigation of the Trump campaign, the FBI felt it had reached a 'tipping point,' IG finds," *The Washington Post*. December 9th, 2019
[75] Office of the Inspector General. *Review of Four FISA Applications and Other Aspects of the FBI'S Crossfire Hurricane Investigation*. U.S. Department of Justice. December 2019. Pg. 158 [Note: "Russian Intelligence Officer 1 is Bulatov]
[76] Hettena, Seth. "Exclusive: who is Sergey Yatsenko?" *Trump/Russia*. September 9th,

2019

[77] Office of the Inspector General. *Review of Four FISA Applications and Other Aspects of the FBI'S Crossfire Hurricane Investigation.* U.S. Department of Justice. December 2019. Pg. 61 [Note: "Russian Intelligence Officer 1 is Bulatov]

[78] Press Release. "Attorney General Holder Announces Charges Against Russian Spy Ring in New York City," Office of Public Affairs, US Department of Justice. January 26th, 2015

[79] United States of America v. Evgeny Buryakov, AKA "Zhenya," Igor Sporyshev, and Victor Podobnyy. Criminal Complaint. Southern District of New York

[80] Watkins, Ali. "A Former Trump Advisor Met With A Russian Spy," *BuzzFeed News.* April 3rd, 2017

[81] Carter Page FBI 302, 3/30/2017. Pg. 6

[82] Miller, Greg. *The Apprentice: Trump, Russia and the Subversion of American Democracy.* New York, NY: Custom House, 2018. Pg. 59-60

[83] Calabresi, Massimo; Abramson, Alana. "Carter Page Touted Kremlin Contacts in 2013 Letter," *Time Magazine.* February 3rd, 2018

[84] Shane, Scott; Mazzetti, Mark; Goldman, Adam. "Trump Adviser's Visit to Moscow got F.B.I.'s Attention," *The New York Times.* April 19th, 2017

[85] Mufson, Steven; Hamburger, Tom. "Trump adviser's public comments, ties to Moscow stirs unease in both parties," *The Washington Post.* August 5th, 2016

[86] Mueller, III, Robert S. *Report On The Investigation Into Russian Interference In The 2016 Presidential Election.* Department of Justice, Washington, DC. March 2019. Pg. 97

[87] Office of the Inspector General. *Review of Four FISA Applications and Other Aspects of the FBI'S Crossfire Hurricane Investigation.* U.S. Department of Justice. December 2019. Pg. 62

[88] Freedlander, David. "How the New York State Republicans Could Have Derailed Trump's White House Run," *New York Magazine.* January 7th, 2016

[89] Report of the Select Committee on Intelligence United States Senate On Russian Active Measures Campaigns And Interference in the 2016 US Election Volume 5: Counterintelligence Threats and Vulnerabilities. Pg. 533

[90] Mueller, III, Robert S. *Report On The Investigation Into Russian Interference In The 2016 Presidential Election.* Department of Justice, Washington, DC. March 2019. Pg. 97

[91] Sam Clovis HPSCI Testimony. December 12th, 2017. Pg. 21

[92] Report of the Select Committee on Intelligence United States Senate On Russian Active Measures Campaigns And Interference in the 2016 US Election Volume 5: Counterintelligence Threats and Vulnerabilities. Pg. 537-538

[93] Office of the Inspector General. *Review of Four FISA Applications and Other Aspects of the FBI'S Crossfire Hurricane Investigation.* U.S. Department of Justice. December 2019. Pg. 62

[94] Office of the Inspector General. *Review of Four FISA Applications and Other Aspects of the FBI'S Crossfire Hurricane Investigation.* U.S. Department of Justice. December 2019. Pg. 62-63

[95] Andrej Krickovic FBI-302. August 22nd, 2017. Pg. 1

[96] Shlomo Weber FBI-302. July 28th, 2017. Pg. 3

[97] MacKinnon, Mark. "Sergey Karaganov: The man behind Putin's pugnacity," *The Globe and Mail.* March 30th, 2014

[98] Feifer, Gregory. "Putin's Foreign Policy A Private Affair," *The Moscow Times.* April 2nd, 2002

[99] Report of the Select Committee on Intelligence United States Senate On Russian Active Measures Campaigns And Interference in the 2016 US Election Volume 5: Counterintelligence Threats and Vulnerabilities. Pg. 540

[100] Russian International Affairs Council. Sergei Karaganov Biography

[101] J.D. Gordon HPSCI Testimony, July 26th, 2017. Pg. 61-62

[102] Shlomo Weber FBI-302. July 28th, 2017. Pg. 4

[103] Mueller, III, Robert S. *Report On The Investigation Into Russian Interference In The 2016 Presidential Election*. Department of Justice, Washington, DC. March 2019. Pg. 99-100

[104] Report of the Select Committee on Intelligence United States Senate On Russian Active Measures Campaigns And Interference in the 2016 US Election Volume 5: Counterintelligence Threats and Vulnerabilities. Pg. 548

[105] Mueller, III, Robert S. *Report On The Investigation Into Russian Interference In The 2016 Presidential Election*. Department of Justice, Washington, DC. March 2019. Pg. 100-101

[106] Shlomo Weber FBI-302. July 28th, 2017. Pg. 3

[107] Report of the Select Committee on Intelligence United States Senate On Russian Active Measures Campaigns And Interference in the 2016 US Election Volume 5: Counterintelligence Threats and Vulnerabilities. Pg. 548 [Footnote 3613]

[108] Mackey, Robert. "Russian Alt-Right Candidate Hopes to Get Elected by Loving Trump and Hating Clinton," *The Intercept*. September 16th, 2016

[109] Hall, Kevin G. "Why did FBI suspect Trump campaign adviser was a foreign agent?" *The Sacramento Bee (McClatchy News)*. April 14th, 2017

[110] Report of the Select Committee on Intelligence United States Senate On Russian Active Measures Campaigns And Interference in the 2016 US Election Volume 5: Counterintelligence Threats and Vulnerabilities. Pg. 400-402

[111] Report of the Select Committee on Intelligence United States Senate On Russian Active Measures Campaigns And Interference in the 2016 US Election Volume 5: Counterintelligence Threats and Vulnerabilities. Pg. 395-397

[112] Gettys, Travis. "A former director for Sean Hannity left Fox News to build a pro-Kremlin propaganda network in Russia," *Salon*. April 19th, 2018

[113] Mueller, III, Robert S. *Report On The Investigation Into Russian Interference In The 2016 Presidential Election*. Department of Justice, Washington, DC. March 2019. Pg. 100

[114] Stanovaya, Tatiana. "Grudges Before Politics: Arrests in Russia Are Increasingly Random," *Carnegie Moscow Center*. May 4th, 2019

[115] Korsunskaya, Darya; Reiter, Svetlana; Soldatkin, Vladimir. "Minister's arrest leaves Russians asking, who's next?" *Reuters*. November 18th, 2016

[116] Ziobro, Lucia. "FBI's Boston office warns businesses of venture capital scams," *Boston Business Journal*. April 4th, 2014

[117] Mueller, III, Robert S. *Report On The Investigation Into Russian Interference In The 2016 Presidential Election*. Department of Justice, Washington, DC. March 2019. Pg. 101

[118] Yuval Weber FBI-302. 6/1/2017. Pg. 5

[119] Mueller, III, Robert S. *Report On The Investigation Into Russian Interference In The 2016 Presidential Election*. Department of Justice, Washington, DC. March 2019. Pg. 104

[120] Melby, Caleb; Kocieniewski, David; Smith, Gerry. "Kushner Foreign Policy Role Grew After Kissenger Lunch," *Bloomberg*. August 13th, 2018

[121] Grove, Lloyd. "RUSSKY BUSINESS," *The Washington Post*. April 7th, 1995

[122] Center for the National Interest. DIMITRI K. SIMES

[123] IMEMO. Yevgeny Maksimovich Primakov

[124] Sullivan, Patricia. "Konstantin Simis; Critic Of Soviet Corruption," *The Washington Post*. December 17th, 2006

[125] Kotkin, Stephen. "Book Reviews: After the Collapse: Russia Seeks Its Place as a Great Power," *The Milken Institute Review*. Second Quarter 1999

[126] Smith, Ben. "Divorce for Nixon Center, Foundation." *Politico*. April 19th, 2011

[127] Kotkin, Stephen. "Book Reviews: After the Collapse: Russia Seeks Its Place as a Great Power," *The Milken Institute Review*. Second Quarter 1999

[128] Felshtinsky, Yuri. "Who is Dimitri Simes And Why Is He Trying To Sink Mayflower? Investigation By Yuri Felshtinsky," *GORDON*. August 22nd, 2018

[129] Unger, Craig. *American Kompromat: How the KGB Cultivated Donald Trump and Related Tales of Sex, Greed, Power and Treachery*. New York, NY: DUTTON. 2021. Pg. 14-15

[130] Mueller, III, Robert S. *Report On The Investigation Into Russian Interference In The 2016 Presidential Election*. Department of Justice, Washington, DC. March 2019. Pg. 104

[131] Kirchick, James. "Donald Trump's Russia Connections," *Politico*. April 27th, 2016

[132] Boykewich, Stephen. "A U.S. NGO Made in Moscow," *The Moscow Times*. December 5th, 2005

[133] Lynch, Sarah N. "Exclusive: Alleged Russian agent Butina met with U.S. Treasury, Fed officials," *Reuters*. July 22nd, 2018

[134] Duarte, Esteban; Meyer, Henry; Pismennaya, Evgenia. "Mobster or Central Banker? Spanish Cops Allege This Russian Both," *Bloomberg*. August 8th, 2018

[135] Center for the National Interest. Profile: David Keene

[136] Swan, Betsy. "Maria Butina: Private Messages Reveal Accused Russian Spy's True Ties to D.C. Wise Man," *The Daily Beast*. April 29th, 2018

[137] Butina, Maria. "The Bear and the Elephant," *The National Interest*. June 12th, 2015

[138] Mueller, III, Robert S. *Report On The Investigation Into Russian Interference In The 2016 Presidential Election*. Department of Justice, Washington, DC. March 2019. Pg. 104

[139] Schreckinger, Ben; Ioffe, Julia. "Lobbyist advised Trump campaign while promoting Russian pipeline," *Politico*. October 7th, 2016

[140] Gordon, Michael R. "SUMMIT LINKED TO ARMS PACT, RUSSIAN INSISTS," *The New York Times*. August 21st, 1986

[141] Gonzalo, Vina. "Shakers: Former Tory leader to head risk firm," *International Herald Tribune*. June 19th, 2006

[142] Thomas Jr., Landon. "The Man Who May Become the Richest Rothschild," *The New York Times*. March 9th, 2007

[143] Ames, Mark; Berman, Ari. "McCaine's Kremlin Ties," *The Nation*. October 1st, 2008

[144] McLarty Associates: Richard Burt Bio

[145] MIKHAIL FRIDMAN: Background Information. *Stratfor*. August 2nd, 2007. Pg. 19

[146] Schreckinger, Ben; Ioffe, Julia. "Lobbyist advised Trump campaign while promoting Russian pipeline," *Politico*. October 7th, 2016

[147] Report of the Select Committee on Intelligence United States Senate On Russian Active Measures Campaigns And Interference in the 2016 US Election Volume 5: Counterintelligence Threats and Vulnerabilities. Pg. 562-563

[148] Bertrand, Natasha. "Mueller report reveals Kushner's contacts with 'pro-Kremlin' campaign adviser," *Politico*. April 29th, 2019

[149] Mueller, III, Robert S. *Report On The Investigation Into Russian Interference In The 2016 Presidential Election*. Department of Justice, Washington, DC. March 2019. Pg. 109

Chapter 18:
Kremlin Influence Campaigns
And the June 9th Trump Tower Meeting

The June 9th meeting at Trump Tower held between senior figures in the Trump campaign and Russians promising compromising material on Hillary Clinton can only be understood as but one part of a larger influence campaign pursued by the Russian government to overturn the 2012 Magnitsky Act. While the Trump team looked no further than the upcoming election, the Kremlin played a longer game. The meeting on June 9th amounted to a self-inflicted counterintelligence nightmare for the Trump campaign and the later Trump presidency.

The Magnitsky Act sanction regime was inspired by a 2007 scheme to defraud Russian taxpayers of $230 million. The case involved predatory actions taken by members of the Russian state and organized crime against Hermitage Capital Management, the largest foreign investment fund in Russia at that time. Fund manager Bill Browder had his tax advisor Sergei Magnitsky look into the case. Magnitsky discovered a vast tax fraud perpetrated by members of the Russian government allied with organized crime. He was later imprisoned by Russian authorities, deprived of medical care, and, according to Browder, beaten to death.

In large part due to Browder's advocacy, in 2012, the United States passed the Magnitsky Act. While the original act targeted Russian officials involved in Magnitsky's death with sanctions, it has been built upon over time to target those in the power structure around Putin. Infuriated by the law, Putin responded by banning Americans from adopting Russian children, depriving tens of thousands of Russian orphans of a chance for a better life. With the emergence of the Trump candidacy, the Russians saw an opportunity to have the act overturned. As we shall see, the Trump Campaign was more than willing to play ball.

Aras Agalarov and Origins of the June 9th Trump Tower Meeting

"Good morning," British publicist Rob Goldstone wrote to Donald Trump Jr. on June 3rd, 2016. "Emin just called and asked me to contact you with something very interesting." Goldstone had been contacted earlier that morning by Emin Agalarov, who asked if he would contact the Trumps and explain that his father, Aras Agalarov, had met with a Russian lawyer who claimed to have access to information showing that illicit Russian funding may have made its way into the coffers of the Democratic Party and its nominee for president, Hillary Clinton.

"Could you articulate," Goldstone asked. "[W]hat does that mean? Who is this person?"

"It doesn't matter; all you need to do is get the meeting," Emin replied. "There's information, it's potentially damaging to the Democrats and Hillary, and I think you should contact the Trumps; my dad would really like this meeting to take place."

Crocus employee Irakli "Ike" Kaveladze, who years earlier had been implicated in suspected money laundering in the United States and had months earlier gone back and forth on a potential Trump Tower Moscow project, learned of his boss's request for Emin to reach out to the Trump's shortly after it was made. He understood that Aras Agalarov was "directly and personally involved" in the effort and knew that the potential meeting between the Trump team and the Russian lawyer was Agalarov's "initiative and project." He suspected it was being done as a favor, but to whom and for what reason, he couldn't say.[1]

Goldstone had been in contact with the Trumps throughout the campaign. Six months earlier, Goldstone put Don Jr. and Trump's assistant Rhona Graff in contact with Konstantin Sidorkov, the Partner Relations Manager at VKontakte (VK), Russia's largest social media site. Sidorkov had reached out to Goldstone and explained that VK had 2.7 million profiles created by Russian-Americans living in the United States, in other words, potential voters.

"We want to invite Donald Trump to set up an official page on VK, which will have the latest updates from Donald and maybe Russian translation," Sidorkov wrote to Goldstone, who forwarded the message to Don Jr. "Also we will make a huge promotion for it with our marketing instruments and put this page to user's recommendation [including] targeting to all of our audience."[2] Rhona Graff put Dan Scavino, the head of social media for the Trump campaign, in touch with Goldstone and Sidorkov. However, it does not appear that the discussions yielded any tangible results. There are strong reasons to believe that VK is under the influence of the Russian intelligence services. Sidorkov's proposal to promote Trump was broadly in keeping with Russian efforts to assist his campaign. The founder of VK was forced to sell his company shares due to pressure from the FSB.[3] The shares were sold to Alisher Usmanov,[4] an Uzbek-born Russian oligarch with links to the Solntsevskaya.[5]

"The Crown prosecutor of Russia met with his father Aras this morning," Goldstone wrote to Donald Trump Jr. on June 3rd, even though no such position existed in Russia. Goldstone was attempting to refer to the Russian Prosecutor-General, similar to the Attorney General position in the United States. Goldstone continued, "and in their meeting offered to provide the Trump campaign with some official documents and information that would incriminate Hillary and her dealings with Russia and would be very useful to your father. This is obviously very high level and sensitive information but is part of Russia and its government's support for Mr. Trump - helped along by Aras and Emin."

"Thanks, Rob. I appreciate that," Don Jr. replied. "I am on the road at the moment but perhaps I just speak to Emin first. Seems we have some time and if it's what you say I love it especially later in the summer. Could we do a call first thing next week when I am back?"

Natalia Veselnitskaya's Connections
To Russia's Government and Intelligence Services

The lawyer Aras Agalarov introduced Donald Trump Jr. to was Natalia Veselnitskaya. The Senate Intelligence Committee assessed her to have "significant connections" to the Russian government and intelligence services.[6] Veselnitskaya was a prosecutor for the Central Administrative District of the Russian Prosecutor's Office from 1998 to 2001.[7] In 2003, she established her law firm, Kamerton Consulting. Veselnitskaya further cemented her connection to the Russian Prosecutor's Office through her marriage to Alexander Mitusov, the former deputy prosecutor for the Moscow Region.[8]

Moscow Region, where Veselnitskaya operated, included the administrative district surrounding Moscow but not the city itself and was famous for its corruption. It contained valuable land where the previous Soviet nomenklatura kept country residences. In the post-Soviet period, land that once consisted of collective farms was purchased for pennies on the dollar. Ruthless battles took place between corporate raiders to seize control of the land in a practice known in Russian as *reiderstvo*. The disputes that arose, often between members of the Russian government or between the oligarchs, is where Veselnitskaya made her mark.[9]

She claimed to have won over 300 cases, often threatening her foes with action by the Russian government.[10] Through her husband, who left the Russian Prosecutor's Office to become the deputy transport minister, Veselnitskaya met the Russian Transport Minister Pyotr Katsyv. According to Damir Marusic and Karina Orlova, "Katsyv was born in Khmelnitsky Oblast in Ukraine, in a small Jewish town, in 1953. He may have been recruited by the KGB to watch over his community (the Fifth Directorate had a special Jewish Department for keeping an eye on Jewish dissidents), and gained his earliest connections that way."[11]

Veselnitskaya has represented Katsyv in several cases and has been accused of participating in land-raiding schemes with Katsyv and her husband.[12] A Russian anti-corruption nonprofit called Spravedlivost accused Veselnitskaya's husband and Pyotr Katsyv of using their government positions to corruptly seize valuable land. An attorney who ran Spravedlivost claimed that Veselnitskaya told him that she was working with the FSB and the Russian Prosecutors Office and threatened him with prison.[13]

Between 2005 and 2013, Veselnitskaya represented "military unit 55002" of the FSB in a property dispute. The FSB hoped to evict private companies from an office building and seize control of the land.[14] At the time, it was understood that elements of the FSB, which were supposed to be investigating economic crimes, were involved in the land raiding. Frequently, government officials ordered the FSB to confiscate the land in the first place.[15]

Starting in 2013 or 2014, Veselnitskaya performed the same work for Aras Agalarov.[16] Agalarov was also a close associate of Pyotr Katsyv, who in 2014 was made the Vice President of Russian Railways, the Russian state rail company with annual revenues comprising nearly 2% of the Russian GDP. In 2006, Putin elevated a senior KGB officer, Vladimir Yakunin, as the President of Russian Railways. It was part of a process known as "Kremlin Inc," in which Putin placed his fellow KGB officials in charge of strategic sectors of the Russian economy.[17]

Natalia Veselnitskaya, Yury Chaika,
And the Prevezon Money Laundering Case

Veselnitskaya was in New York in early June 2016, working on a case involving Russian money laundering into the United States. In September 2013, United States Attorney Preet Bharara launched a civil forfeiture complaint against Prevezon Holdings, a Cyprus-based company with real estate holdings in Manhattan owned by Denis Katsyv, Pyotr Katsyv's son. Bharara accused Prevezon of laundering money that was part of the alleged $230 million tax fraud discovered by Sergei Magnitsky. To help with their legal defense, the Kastyvs turned to Natalia Veselnitskaya.

Some money stolen in the $230 million tax fraud had been diverted to Prevezon Holdings.[18] In December 2015, Denis Katsyv was made the beneficial owner of Prevezon. An Israeli citizen, in 2005 Katsyv was forced to pay a 35 million shekel settlement payment to Israeli authorities after being indicted for laundering money from a company called Martash Investment Holdings.[19] While Denis Katsyv became the official beneficiary of Prevezon months after Magnitsky fraud money sloshed through its accounts, the previous beneficiary owner was a Russian citizen named Alexander Litvak. Katsyv and Litvak were partners in Martash Investment Holdings, a minority shareholder in Prevezon.

While advising Prevezon, Veselnitskaya represented to the American court overseeing the case that she was acting privately. However, she was, in fact, illegally working on behalf of the Russian government. In March 2014, the US government sent a Mutual Legal Assistance Treaty (MLAT) request to Russia for information regarding Prevezon. Veselnitskaya helped the Russian Prosecutor's Office draft their response. She then colluded with the Russian Prosecutor's Office to conceal her role in the MLAT response, which she later used in court as a supposed independent party in her defense of Prevezon.[20]

Veselnitskaya was a close associate of the Prosecutor General of Russia, Yury Chaika, the man Goldstone was alluding to in his message to Don Jr. Chaika, who is also close to Aras Agalarov, played a pivotal role in Vladimir Putin's rise to power. In his role on the Russian Security Council, he is deeply enmeshed in Russia's security and intelligence establishment. Sitting alongside Chaika on the Security Council are former FSB Director Nikolai Patrushev and current FSB head Alexander Bortnikov. Throughout the Prevezon case, Veselnitskaya regularly took calls from Chaika and briefed him on legal developments.[21]

Chaika was hired by Russian Prosecutor General Yuri Skuratov and served as his first deputy from 1995 to 1999. Skuratov played a central role in the *kompromat* operation that led to Boris Yeltsin's designation of Vladimir Putin as his heir apparent. To unseat Skuratov, who was investigating Yeltsin and Putin, a tape of a man who looked like Skuratov cavorting with prostitutes was released on Russian state television and later "authenticated" by Putin, who was at that time the head of the FSB. After Skuratov was forced out, Chaika became the acting Prosecutor General and confirmed the legality of the proceedings against Skuratov.

Once Putin became President, he moved Chaika to the Justice Ministry, where he busied himself with rubber stamping Putin's swift centralization of power. He consistently rejected attempts by opposition groups to register as official political parties and led an attack against NGOs working to foster civil society and democracy within Russia. By 2006, he was elevated to Skuratov's old position as Prosecutor General. In this capacity, he acted as Putin's loyal servant. In 2011, he declared that the protests against Putin were paid for with foreign money.[22]

In October 2015, Veselnitskaya provided Chaika with a report that turned the Prevezon allegations on their head and accused Bill Browder of committing tax fraud against the Russian Federation.[23] She accused Browder's Hermitage Capital Management and its American investors, the billionaire Ziff Brothers, of illegally purchasing shares in Gazprom and then evading $16 million in Russian taxes.[24] This report was later not only used in the June 9th Trump Tower meeting but was the centerpiece of a highly coordinated, Kremlin-led influence campaign to undermine the American sanctions regime.

Prevezon, BakerHostetler, and Rinat Akhmetshin: Agents of Influence

While Veselnitskaya was a critical intermediary between Prevezon and the Russian government, she spoke little English and could not practice law in American courts. As a result, Prevezon hired the law firm BakerHostetler to lead its defense. The firm also assisted in developing an anti-Magnitsky Act lobbying campaign, part of which culminated in the Trump Tower Meeting and another that reached into the hallways of Congress.

In September 2015, BakerHostetler retained the services of the Russian-born American citizen and Washington lobbyist Rinat Akhmetshin, who later attended the Trump Tower meeting.[25] A former Soviet counterintelligence officer in the late 1980s, Akhmetshin worked for the *Kommandant* service, which provided protection and support to a KGB unit attached to the Soviet military designed to ferret out foreign spies. While Akhmetshin has described his role as little more than ferrying around documents and a brief stint serving in Afghanistan, little is known about his actual duties.[26]

In 1994, Akhmetshin immigrated to the United States to attend graduate school. Four years later, he entered the Washington lobbying world after answering an ad to run the International Eurasian Institute for Economic and Political Research."[27] Edward Lieberman, a DC-based lawyer with extensive professional ties to Russia, arranged the position.[28] Lieberman's wife, Evelyn S. Lieberman, served as Bill Clinton's deputy chief of staff from 1996-1997 and had known Hillary Clinton as far back as the 1980s.[29] Through this connection, Akhmetshin met Hillary Clinton in passing during several parties at the Lieberman's.[30]

While at the International Eurasia Institute, Akhmetshin lobbied on behalf of Akezhan Kazhegeldin, the Prime Minister under Kazakhstan's authoritarian leader, Nursultan Nazarbayev.[31] After making a fortune in the privatization of Kazakhstan's major industries, Kazhegeldin rebranded himself as a democracy activist and took on Nazarbayev without much success. In 1998, Akhmetshin leaked a trove of documents to *The New York Times* linking millions of dollars in payments from oil companies to Nazarbayev's Swiss bank accounts. The leak led to a *Times* story and an investigation by the DOJ and established Akhmetshin's modus operandi of strategically leaking materials to the press on behalf of his clients.[32]

Between 2009 and 2014, Akhmetshin worked closely with Viktor Ivanov, a former KGB agent who later served as the deputy head of the FSB. At the time, Ivanov was traveling regularly to Washington to promote a joint Russian and American endeavor to combat the narcotics trade coming out of Afghanistan. In October of 2010, Akhmetshin guided Ivanov throughout Washington. The anti-narcotics initiative was shelved after the Russian annexation of Crimea. Akhmetshin later testified that he had been in email contact with Ivanov on matters ranging "from narco-trafficking and terrorism in Afghanistan to surveillance of undercover agents, suspected undercover agents, and their identities."[33]

In a parallel to the GRU's 2016 election activities, Akhmetshin has been linked to at least two alleged hack and leak operations. In 2011, he gained the former Russian Finance Minister Andrey Vavilov as a client. Vavilov and an alliance of Russian businessmen that included the suspected money launderer Suleiman Kerimov hired Akhmetshin to derail the US visa application of a Russian businessman named Ashot Egiazaryan. Egiazaryan accused Akhmetshin of coordinating a black PR campaign slandering him in the media as being antisemitic. Egiazaryan's lawyers received emails containing malware that allowed computers later traced back to an office belonging to a Kerimov company to open sensitive documents.

Akhmetshin was later accused of overseeing a hack and leak operation in a bitter internecine turf battle between powerful forces within the Russian power structure. In 2015, International Mining Resources (IMR), owned by the Kazakh trio of oligarchs Alexander Mashkevich, Patokh Chodiev, and Alijan Ibragimov, sued Akhmetshin and the clients he represented. Akhmetshin was retained by a law firm representing an IMR competitor,

Eurochem. IMR accused Akhmetshin of orchestrating a hacking campaign against it and providing the stolen data via a thumb drive to his clients and the press.[34]

Before the Maidan Revolution, Akhmetshin attempted to gain business representing Viktor Yanukovych and the Party of Regions. According to Sam Patten, who had been friends with Akhmetshin for 15 to 20 years, Akhmetshin arranged a meeting with Serhiy Lyovochkin while Yanukovych was visiting New York to attend a meeting of the UN General Assembly. Lyovochkin was serving as Yanukovych's chief of staff at the time. According to Patten, the meeting was interrupted by Manafort and Konstantin Kilimnik, who acted to defend their business.[35] Patten later told the Senate Intelligence Committee that Akhmetshin and Kilimnik may have met outside of his presence more than once.[36] According to *The New York Times*, Akhmetshin described himself as a longtime acquaintance of Manafort. However, Akhmetshin later testified that he had never met Manafort before June 9th.

In October 2015, Akhmetshin met with Natalia Veselnitskaya and her translator, Anatoli Samochornov, at BakerHostetler's offices in New York to strategize about the Prevezon case and the lobbying campaign against the Magnitsky Act.[37] In November, Veselnitskaya filed the Russian Prosecutor's Office report into Bill Browder and Hermitage with the US Court, illegally failing to disclose her role in its drafting. Akhmetshin's friend and business partner Ed Lieberman suggested that to lobby against the Magnitsky sanctions effectively, they should establish a foundation for American families impacted by Russia's adoption ban.[38]

In February of 2016, Ed Lieberman and lawyers from BakerHostetler established the Human Rights Accountability Global Initiative Foundation (HRAGI), registering it in Delaware. Despite ostensibly being an American Foundation, funding came from Russians with connections to Pyotr Katsyv. Denis Katsyv donated $150,000 to the organization. His Russian business partners Mikhail Ponomarev and Albert Nasibulin gave $100,000 each. Vladimir Lelyukh, the deputy general director of a subsidiary of the Russian state-owned Sberbank, Sberbank Capital LLC, donated $50,000.[39] Bill Browder later testified that HRAGI was established to help Akhmetshin and BakerHostetler avoid having to register under the Foreign Agent Registration Act

(FARA).[40] In addition to sidestepping FARA, leaked emails show that lawyers at BakerHostetler looked into ways of cloaking Russian donations to the Foundation.[41]

The presence of Lelyukh on the small list of HRAGI funders and his role at Sberbank raises a few interesting connections to Donald Trump. During the 2013 Miss Universe Pageant in Moscow, Trump enjoyed a two-hour private dinner with Sberbank CEO Herman Gref and the Agalarovs.[42] Sberbank Capital's CEO, Ashot Khachaturyants, is a former high-ranking FSB official. In 2016, Gref, Khachaturyants, and Sberbank Capital were sued for seizing control of a Russian granite company. The lawyer who defended them was Marc Kasowitz, who also served as Donald Trump's attorney and later defended him during the Russia investigations during his presidency.[43]

In early 2016, the Russian billionaire oligarch Vasily Anisimov sought to hire the former Director of the FBI-turned Washington lobbyist Louis Freeh to work with Natalia Veselnitskaya on the Prevezon case.[44] Through his ownership stake in the Russian mining and metallurgy company Metalloinvest, Anisimov is a business partner with Alisher Usmanov and Andrei Skoch, the latter of whom has links to the Solntsevskaya.[45] Freeh attended numerous meetings in Moscow, at least one of which was attended by senior Russian government officials and another that Veselnitskaya attended. Pyotr Katsyv and Yury Chaika attended his first meeting in Moscow. Chaika suggested that Freeh meet with Veselnitskaya. They later met at an undisclosed location before he returned to the United States. Freeh later went on to help Prevezon negotiate a settlement with the SDNY following Trump's victory in the election.[46]

Dana Rohrabacher and Kremlin Influence Campaigns Old and New

After establishing the HRAGI Foundation, there was a concerted effort to make inroads into the US Congress. This effort centered around Republican Congressman Dana Rohrabacher and his close aide Paul Behrends. In April of 2016, Rohrabacher and Behrends traveled to Moscow as part of a Congressional delegation. While there, they held meetings outside the officially sanctioned itinerary with Veselnitskaya, Akhmetshin, and high-level officials.

Rohrabacher had been warned of Russia's intelligence

service's interest in him. During a 2012 meeting in a secure room in the United States Capitol, an FBI agent told Congressman Rohrabacher that Russian intelligence was attempting to recruit him as an "agent of influence."[47] The agent further informed Rohrabacher that the Kremlin had given him a code name.[48] The news didn't seem to make much of an impression on Rohrabacher. "I remember them telling me, 'You have been targeted to be recruited as an agent,'" Rohrabacher later recalled of the incident to *The New York Times*. "How stupid is that?"

Rohrabacher's path from his beginnings in politics to being told by the FBI he was being cultivated by Russian intelligence is a tale of dramatic transformation. During his youth in California, Rohrabacher was known more for body surfing, drinking tequila, writing screenplays, and writing folk songs than politics.[49] However, after coming across the radical libertarian Richard LeFevre, Rohrabacher dedicated himself to right-wing politics. After joining the Young Republicans, Rohrabacher became an early admirer of Ronald Reagan, which led him to serve as Reagan's assistant press secretary from 1976 to 1980. During this time, he became involved in the American policy to support the Afghan Mujahideen in their war against the Soviet Union. In this capacity, Rohrabacher met a young Marine named Paul Behrends.[50]

Behrends, a devout Catholic, joined the Marines out of college. Working together, he and Rohrabacher assisted in the effort to provide weapons to the Afghan mujahideen. To this day, Behrends' friends are unsure exactly how he was involved in the effort. In addition to his activities in Afghanistan, Behrends traveled to Poland during the period of Communist martial law, pretending to be an American student. According to his friends, there were rumors that he even "ran secret reconnaissance missions inside the Soviet Union."[51]

In 1988, Rohrabacher, bearded and dressed in Afghan attire, hiked from Pakistan into Afghanistan to see the front lines for himself.[52] Later that year, Rohrabacher ran for a newly vacant California seat in the House of Representatives and won with the support of Oliver North of Iran-Contra infamy. Behrends went on to serve as a foreign policy advisor for Congressman Rohrabacher.[53] After the collapse of the Soviet Union, Rohrabacher and those in his orbit lost interest in anti-Communist crusades and focused on making money, institutionalizing expensive lobbying and bending, or in some cases breaking election laws.

In 1995, Rohrabacher's campaign director, Rhonda Carmony, illegally arranged to place a decoy candidate to split the Democratic vote to ensure that Rohrabacher's friend Scott Baugh won a seat in the California State Assembly. Two years later, Carmony pled guilty to two felony charges, which were reduced to misdemeanors. She was sentenced to three years of probation and 300 hours of community service.[54] Rohrabacher went on to marry Carmony, and the newly named Rhonda Rohrabacher eventually gave birth to triplets.[55]

Another friend of Rohrabacher's who fell afoul of the law was Jack Abramoff. Abramoff's lobbying adventures in Russia between 1997 and 1998 led to him raising a million dollars for the US Family Network from the Russian oil company Naftasib. Ed Buckham, the former Chief of Staff to the Republican House Majority Leader Tom DeLay, had founded the US Family Network. DeLay, a close political ally of Abramoff's, was later indicted on money laundering charges. While in Russia, Abramoff interacted extensively with a Naftasib executive named Marina Nevskaya.[56] Years later, in 2019, someone who knew her told the press that Nevskaya had described herself as a "colonel-lieutenant in the GRU."[57]

Rohrabacher had known Abramoff since the latter had served as the chairman of the Young Republicans.[58] In 2000, Abramoff listed Rohrabacher as a personal reference when he purchased a casino boat.[59] In 2004, Paul Behrends became the Alexander Strategy Group's chief lobbyist, a firm Ed Buckham founded. Alexander Strategy Group shared the same offices as the US Family Network. Most of the $3.2 million raised for the US Family Network came from Abramoff clients, including $1 million from Naftasib.[60]

In 2005, the Rohrabachers were in a cash squeeze, with Rhonda going on shopping sprees and bouncing checks. On September 18th, 2005, Rohrabacher emailed Marina Nevskaya, the Naftasib executive and alleged GRU officer, not using any of his six personal and professional email addresses but his wife's email address. Rohrabacher offered to work behind the scenes to assist Naftasib with its "major investment" in a Ukrainian shipping port. "I may be able to lead a congressional delegation to Berlin on the first four days of October," Rohrabacher wrote to Nevskaya. "Is there a chance that we could meet the contact you had in mind at that time and place? All the best, Dana."

"Dear Dana," Nevskaya replied. "Thank you so much for [contacting Kateryna]. . . . Please, let me know your schedule when you know. Kisses for Rhonda and the kids. Marina."[61]

Who the contact Marina Nevskaya suggested Rohrabacher meet with, and whether he ever did so in Berlin or anywhere else, and for what purpose, are all questions without answers. In 2006, the Abramoff scandal exploded across the headlines, and he was convicted and served time in prison. It is likely that after having Nevskaya's name featured in the press, Rohrabacher chose not to pursue future business dealings.

In the following years, Dana Rohrabacher became known in Washington as "Putin's favorite Congressman." Before meeting with Natalia Veselnitskaya in Moscow in April 2016, Rohrabacher had made several other trips to the Russian capital. In 2013, Rohrabacher traveled to Moscow alongside five other members of Congress. Separating from the official delegation, Rohrabacher connected with the actor Steven Seagal. Russia's Deputy Prime Minister Dmitry Rogozin had been attempting to use Seagal to help Russian companies break into the American gun market. Rohrabacher, who had known Seagal for years, had the actor join him during several meetings with Rogozin and, to the discomfort of State Department diplomats, several high-level FSB officials. Seagal attempted to arrange for Rohrabacher to meet with Ramzan Kadyrov, the dictator of Chechnya whose father had been installed by Putin. It took a call from House Majority Leader John Boehner to dissuade Rohrabacher from taking the meeting.[62]

In September 2014, Rohrabacher returned to Moscow, this time with Paul Behrends. Two months earlier, Behrends had surprised colleagues after taking a major pay cut by leaving his independent lobbying gig to return to his job on the Hill with Rohrabacher. After traveling through Europe and Asia alongside Representative Gregory Meeks, Rohrabacher and Behrends took a private side trip to Russia, where they spent three days and met with Mikhail Margelov, then-Chairman of the Foreign Affairs Committee of the upper house of Russia's Parliament.[63] Margelov, a confidant of Putin's with a background in the Russian intelligence services, once taught Arabic at the Higher School of the KGB.[64] In addition to being the Vice President of the Russian oil company Transneft, where he worked just beneath the company's President Nikolay Tokarev, a former KGB officer who served alongside Vladimir Putin in East Germany,[65] Margelov also worked at the Russian International Affairs Council (RIAC).[66] The purpose of Rohrabacher and Behrend's 2014 meeting with Margelov is unclear.

When Rohrabacher and Behrends traveled to Moscow in April of 2016, they met on multiple occasions with individuals who were either members of or had links to Russian intelligence. As they had on previous trips, Rohrabacher and Behrends ignored the concerns of the US Embassy in Moscow and once again broke away from the official delegation and met with the Russian oligarch Vladimir Yakunin at Café Pushkin. At the time of the meeting, Yakunin was under US sanctions.[67]

As a former KGB senior officer, Yakunin was once a covert operative at the United Nations in New York. He later became a close ally of Putin's while the latter was the deputy Mayor in St. Petersburg. Yakunin became a member of the Ozero Cooperative and played a vital role in the takeover of Bank Rossiya, the financial institution most associated with Putin's personal wealth.[68] In 2000, shortly after Putin ascended to the Presidency, Yakunin was made the Deputy Transport Minister of Russia. Five years later, as part of a broader move by Putin to place his former colleagues at the KGB in positions to control the Russian economy, Yakunin became the President of the state-owned Russian Railways, where Pyotr Katsyv, father of Prevezon-owner and Veselnitskaya client Denis Katsyv, worked beneath him as Vice President.

During his term as President, vast sums of cash stolen from Russian Railways was washed through a money laundering scheme operating out of Moldova that came to be known as the Moldovan Laundromat.[69] Between 2010 and 2014, over $3 billion was siphoned away from the state transport company by Russian Railway contractors with links to Yakunin. The Moldovan Laundromat washed over $20 billion, much of which came from Russian businessmen evading taxes and customs duties. Moldovan prosecutors came to believe that a portion of the money was being used to fund Russian intelligence influence operations abroad and went towards funding foreign far-right and far-left political parties.[70]

Yakunin has been involved in numerous Kremlin-backed

influence operations. Known as an "Orthodox Chekist," a reference to both his Russian Orthodox religion and his past in the KGB, he has supported culturally conservative organizations that promote the Kremlin's policy goals. Yakunin and his wife are the directors of the Foundation of St. Andrew the First-Called, which associates cultural and Orthodox conservatism with support for the Russian state under Putin. In 2002, Yakunin founded the "Dialogue of Civilizations" annual forum in Rhodes, which not only promoted traditional family values but also political orthodoxy in support of Putin's government in Moscow.[71] Fourteen years later, in 2016, Yakunin established the Dialogue of Civilizations Research Institute in Berlin, the goal of which is to coordinate the activities of Russian NGOs around the world to counter American influence and soft power abroad.[72]

Rohrabacher told later investigators that Ambassador Sergey Kislyak may have arranged his April 2016 meeting with Yakunin. During their discussion, Yakunin invited Rohrabacher to participate in the annual Dialogue of Civilizations event in Rhodes. He also brought up the Magnitsky Act sanctions. "Look," Rohrabacher claimed Yakunin said to him, "our prosecutors have done an investigation into this Magnitsky thing and would you - were you willing to look at the material, their report?"

"I'll look at any report," Rohrabacher replied.[73]

Rohrabacher and Behrends next met with the Chairman of the Council of Federation Committee of Foreign Affairs, Konstantin Kosachev. Kosachev has a history of involvement in Russian influence operations. In the late 1990s, he served as an advisor to three Russian prime ministers, two of whom, Yevgeny Primakov and Sergei Stepashin, were former heads of Russian security services. Kosachev sits on the boards of numerous Kremlin-linked "NGOs," which are used to promote Kremlin priorities abroad.[74] Kosachev is also a member of the RIAC.[75] In 2012, Kosachev was promoted to head Rossotrudnichestvo, which was investigated by the FBI a year later for attempting to cultivate Americans as intelligence assets.[76]

As his meeting with Rohrabacher was wrapping up, Kosachev slid Rohrabacher a note that contained the message: "Would you be willing to accept sensitive documents?" After showing the note to Behrends, Rohrabacher said that he would.[77] At that point, a top deputy working under Yury Chaika provided

Rohrabacher with a dossier that contained some of the material Veselnitskaya had secretly written in cooperation with Chaika's office and provided to US courts while representing herself as a third party in the course of her defense of Prevezon.[78]

Rinat Akhmetshin, who had known and worked with Rohrabacher as a lobbyist, was in Moscow at the same time as Rohrabacher and Behrends. During the trip, he introduced Rohrabacher to Natalia Veselnitskaya in the lobby of the Ritz Carlton near Red Square, where the Congressman was staying.[79] It was their first meeting to discuss the Magnitsky sanctions, but it would not be the last. They met two months later in Washington, DC, mere days after Veselnitskaya and Akhmetshin had attended a fateful meeting to discuss similar issues with Donald Trump Jr.

The June 9th Trump Tower Meeting

In May of 2016, Natalia Veselnitskaya met with Aras Agalarov. After she described her role in the Prevezon case, Agalarov suggested that she should meet with Donald Trump Jr.[80] The Senate Intelligence Committee later determined that Agalarov likely pushed for the meeting on behalf of individuals affiliated with the Russian Government.

As Agalarov and likely Veselnitskaya knew, Michael Cohen and Felix Sater had been negotiating with various Russians with links to organized crime and money laundering operations to build a Trump Tower Moscow. In addition to being Veselnitskaya's former client, Agalarov is a close associate of Yury Chaika.[81] Like Prevezon, Agalarov and his employee at Crocus, Irakli Kaveladze, have been implicated in money laundering.[82] Agalarov and Prevezon used the same New York-based accountant, Ilya Bykov. Several Prevezon companies allegedly used in money laundering activities were registered to Bykov's office.[83] Bykov also worked for Felix Sater and Andrey Rozov, the owner of I.C. Expert.[84]

On June 3rd, 2016, Emin Agalarov contacted Rob Goldstone, who reached out and suggested to Donald Trump Jr. that the "Crown prosecutor of Russia" was willing to provide the Trump campaign with information that would "incriminate Hillary." Three days later, Emin followed up with Goldstone, asking if there was any news regarding the meeting. Goldstone reached out to Don Jr. via email and asked if he was "free to talk with Emin about this Hillary info." Throughout June 6th and 7th, Don Jr. and Emin held several brief phone conversations. While the contents of these discussions are unknown, it seems safe to assume the meeting was discussed.[85]

Aras Agalarov contacted Irakli Kaveladze and instructed him to attend what he described as an "important meeting" at Trump Tower. While Kaveladze claimed that Agalarov informed him that the meeting would be with "Trump people," he maintains that he wasn't provided with a description of what the meeting was to be about. Agalarov told Kaveladze to contact Veselnitskaya and arrange to get together before the meeting to review what would be discussed. Kaveladze called Veselnitskaya and coordinated a time and date to meet.[86]

"Emin asked that I schedule a meeting with you and [t]he Russian government attorney who is flying over from Moscow," Rob Goldstone wrote to Don Jr. on June 7th. The meeting was scheduled for 3 pm at Trump Tower on Thursday, June 9th. Don Jr. informed Goldstone that he, Paul Manafort, and Jared Kushner would all attend the meeting. Goldstone was surprised that so many Trump campaign heavyweights would be present. Kaveladze, who also claimed to be "puzzled" upon learning that Manafort and Kushner would be there, contacted Emin Agalarov's assistant, Roman Beniaminov, and asked what the purpose of the meeting was, to which Beniaminov replied that it was to convey "negative information on Hillary Clinton."[87]

The presence of Jared Kushner at a meeting raises interesting questions. Kushner had conducted real estate deals with a business partner of Denis and Pyotr Katsyv, Lev Leviev. In 1996, Leviev, a successful diamond merchant, purchased the Africa Israel Investments (AFI Group) holding company for $400 million and expanded into real estate and construction. By 2007, the company was worth over $7 billion.[88] Rotem Rosen, the former CEO of AFI USA, attended the Miss America Pageant in Moscow, where he was photographed with Trump.[89]

Pyotr and Denis Katsyv began doing business with Leviev as early as 2003 when Denis Katsyv was made the CEO of an offshore Cypriot shell company owned by Leviev. In 2008, a Netherlands-based, Leviev-owned company, AFI Europe NV, sold 30% of four subsidiary companies to Prevezon for $3 million. The assets sold to Prevezon appear to have consisted of approximately $20 million worth of property in Germany. As it was sold for a fraction of that price, it raises suspicions that the Katsyv-Leviev business relationship may involve money laundering. When Prevezon attempted to sell the shell company-owned assets back to Leviev, Dutch financial authorities froze the transaction. A Leviev-owned company, AFI USA, sold Prevezon the Manhattan real estate that formed the core of the SDNY money laundering case.[90]

In 2015, Kushner Companies purchased several floors of retail space in the old New York Times building on 43rd Street in Manhattan from Leviev's Africa Israel Investments and its partner Five Mile Capital for $295 million.[91] When Kushner took over, the floors were 25% occupied. The Kushner Company went about recruiting tenants, offering, in some cases, a full year rent-free to secure contracts. During the height of the 2016 election, Kushner approached Deutsche Bank for refinancing. A subsequent appraisal valued the building at $470 million, a remarkable 59% increase in the space of a year.

In October 2016, Kushner Companies took out a $370 million loan, $285 million from Deutsche Bank, and $85 million from SL Green Realty, $74 million more than the purchasing price. Shortly after the loan, Deutsche Bank paid a series of settlements to US authorities, including $425 million, to New York authorities for failing to track money laundering out of their Moscow branch properly.[92] Deutsche Bank also loaned Prevezon $90 million.[93] The extent of Kushner's knowledge regarding Veselnitskaya's representation of Prevezon and the relationship between Prevezon and their mutual business partner, Lev Leviev, is unclear.

In the days before June 9th, possibly on June 6th, a "Family Meeting" occurred between the Trump children and top campaign staff. Rick Gates testified that he was present at the family meeting along with Don Jr., Eric Trump, Paul Manafort, and Hope Hicks, with Jared Kushner and Ivanka Trump arriving late. According to Gates, Don Jr. explained that a friend had connected him to a group from Kyrgyzstan that would provide the campaign with damaging information about the Clinton Foundation. While Aras Agalarov's company, the Crocus Group, had been contracted to provide services in Kyrgyzstan, it is unclear why Don Jr. would have referred to them in this fashion.[94] Manafort cautioned that the meeting would not likely yield important information and that they should proceed cautiously.[95]

Don Jr. claims that he never mentioned the meeting to his father. However, the Senate Intelligence Committee later issued the DOJ a criminal referral, arguing that Don Jr. provided misleading testimony under oath.[96] On either June 6th or 7th, Michael Cohen recalled being present in Donald Trump's office when Don Jr. entered, approached his father's desk, leaned over, and whispered, "The meeting, it's all set."

"Okay. Keep me posted," Trump replied.[97] According to the Special Counsel's Report, the interaction led Cohen to believe that Trump and his son had already discussed the meeting, though he had not personally witnessed them do so.[98] However, Cohen is more explicit in the Senate Intelligence Counterintelligence report.

"Trump Jr. said to Trump that he was setting up a meeting in order to get dirt on Hillary Clinton," Cohen told the Senate Intelligence Committee. He further claimed that upon learning this news, Trump replied, "That's great. Let me know."

On June 7th, Trump made a public statement to the media that could indicate foreknowledge of the meeting and its purpose. "I'm going to give a major speech on probably Monday [June 13th] of next week and we're going to be discussing all of the things that have taken place with the Clintons. I think you're going to find it very informative and very, very interesting." The speech was ultimately postponed. Stephen Miller later claimed the postponement may have been due to the Pulse Nightclub in Florida. However, it is also possible that the speech was changed because, as we shall see, the meeting with Veselnitskaya didn't yield the kind of damaging information on the Clinton's that the Trump campaign had hoped for.

On the morning of June 8th, Jared Kushner emailed his assistant and asked to discuss a 3pm meeting he was scheduled to have with Don Jr. the next day. Kushner, who was also the subject of a criminal referral by the Senate Intelligence Committee for providing misleading testimony under oath, later claimed that he couldn't recall discussing the June 9th meeting with his assistant. That same morning, Rob Goldstone emailed Don Jr. and asked that the meeting be pushed back to 4pm the next day. Don Jr. agreed and then forwarded his entire email correspondence with Rob Goldstone, which had the subject line "FW: Russia - Clinton - private and confidential" and included

Goldstone's description of the "Crown prosecutor of Russia" providing information that would "incriminate Hillary," to Kushner and Manafort.[99]

On the morning of June 9th, Veselnitskaya met in the lobby of her Manhattan hotel with her translator Anatoli Samochornov. During their drive to a Prevezon related court proceeding, Samochornov first learned that they would be attending a meeting later that day at Trump Tower. Around this time, Veselnitskaya contacted Rinat Akhmetshin, who in a remarkable coincidence claims he was in New York to watch a relative perform on Broadway that evening.[100] Veselnitskaya invited Akhmetshin to join her for lunch and told him that she wanted to discuss something important. He agreed to meet with her.

That morning at Trump Tower, Trump and Manafort were scheduled to hold a meeting together at 10:30 am. Manafort has testified that he didn't mention the meeting to Trump, and Trump claimed that he couldn't remember his June 9th meeting with Manafort at all. Don Jr. and Kushner later suggested that they never treated the meeting as significant, downplaying that a major part of the campaign leadership attended the meeting by suggesting that they all happened to be in the building at the time.

"The reason why Jared and Manafort were in that meeting is because Mr. Trump would never have allowed Junior to be in that meeting by himself," Michael Cohen later testified. "Mr. Trump was very quick to tell everybody that he thinks Don Jr. has the worst judgment of anyone he's ever met in the world. And I can assure you that when that meeting, conversation, took place, that Mr. Trump turned around and said: Make sure that Jared and Paul are part of the meeting. Because he would never let Don Jr. handle that meeting by himself."[101]

Veselnitskaya and Samochornov ate lunch in Manhattan at a restaurant near Trump Tower, where Akhmetshin joined them. Irakli Kaveladze was also present. During lunch, Veselnitskaya provided Kaveladze with documents that he assumed would be distributed at the meeting. After allegedly first learning from Emin Agalarov's assistant Roman Beniaminov that the Trump Tower meeting was to be used to transmit damaging information about Hillary Clinton, which he claims made him nervous, Kaveladze later suggested that upon reviewing the documents provided, he was relieved to see that they contained no new information about Clinton. Instead, they appeared to be focused on the charges related to Browder that Veselnitskaya had been peddling to discredit the Magnitsky Act.

According to Rinat Akhmetshin's later testimony, he only learned about Veselnitskaya's meeting with Donald Trump Jr. upon joining them at lunch. He further claims that Veselnitskaya asked him what he thought she should mention to Don Jr., to which he responded that Russian-American relations had been a significant part of the campaign so far and a place where Clinton and Trump diverged. Akhmetshin suggested making the Magnitsky Act, which Clinton supported, a campaign issue and linking it to the Russian adoption ban.[102]

After lunch, the group walked to Trump Tower, where Rob Goldstone greeted them in the lobby. Goldstone led them through security and up to the 25th floor. After providing introductions of the Russian entourage, Goldstone prepared to leave, but Don Jr. invited him to stay for the meeting and show everybody out upon its completion. They were seated around a conference table, with Don Jr. and Manafort at the head of the table, while Kushner sat across from Veselnitskaya, Akhmetshin, Kaveladze, Samochornov, and Goldstone.

"So, what brings you here?" Don Jr. asked, officially opening the meeting. "We hear you have some important information for the campaign."

Veselnitskaya took the floor and launched into a three to four-minute speech in Russian, which Samochornov translated. In her rambling and disjointed presentation, which Samochornov found "completely unconvincing," Veselnitskaya claimed that through her research into Bill Browder, she had discovered that investors into Hermitage Capital, the Ziff brothers, had laundered money and failed to pay taxes in both the United States and Russia. She then said that the Ziff Brothers had been donors to either the Democratic National Committee or Hillary Clinton herself.

Veselnitskaya's accusations against the Ziff brothers appear to have been largely irrelevant. According to public records, Hermitage Capital Management had donated between $10,000-$25,000 to the Clinton Global Initiative a decade before the June 9th meeting took place. Of the three Ziff brothers, only one, Daniel Ziff, donated between $50,000-$100,000 to CGI. Both of these donations were dwarfed by the $250,000-$500,000 donated to CGI at one point by Charles Kushner, Jared Kushner's father.[103]

'That's very interesting," Don Jr. interjected, "but so could you show how money goes to Hillary's campaign? Do you think it goes to Hillary's campaign or just DNC?" Don Jr. asked again, "Could you show us how the money goes to Hillary's campaign?"

Veselnitskaya responded by saying that was all the information she had and suggested that the campaign pursue its own research on the project. At that moment, Akhmetshin later recalled, the light went out of the Trump team's eyes, and they checked out from the meeting.

"Why are we here?" Jared Kushner reportedly asked, evidencing a growing frustration. "Why are we listening to this Magnitsky Act story?" After Veselnitskaya again mentioned the Ziff brothers, Kushner interrupted. "I have no idea what you 're talking about." Kushner then asked, "What are you saying? Can you be more specific? I don't understand."

Veselnitskaya responded by rehashing the presentation she had just delivered. Again, varying recollections and testimony complicate the reconstruction of events. According to Samochornov, her focus throughout the meeting was disparaging the Magnitsky Act. Manafort later claimed that Veselnitskaya suggested that candidate Trump call for repealing the Magnitsky Act and suggested that, in return, Russia would be willing to lift the adoption ban.

"This is nothing," Manafort reportedly said of Veselnitskaya's allegations regarding the Ziff brothers, "people give money to all kinds of people."

Put off balance by Manafort's disparaging remarks, Veselnitskaya switched subjects to focus on the adoption ban for roughly five minutes. As she did so, the Trump campaign attendees became visibly more disinterested, appearing restless and regularly checking and typing things into their phones. Akhmetshin, sensing the meeting was going off the rails, took the floor and addressed the group in English. He mentioned his role representing HRAGI and continued to focus more specifically on the issue of Russian adoptions.

"Waste of time," Kushner sent to Manafort in a text at 4:26 pm. A minute later, Kushner emailed two separate assistants, asking them to call him on his cell so he would have an excuse to leave the meeting. Kushner left the meeting to take a call and never returned.

"Look, we're at the electoral stage; we're not there yet," Don Jr. interrupted, referencing any suggestion to change policy presumably related to the Magnitsky Act and Russian adoptions. "[W]e don't know if we'll ever win this campaign; if we win the campaign, we could get back to the topic and continue this topic, continue discussion; but at this point we're busy with other things, we're in the electoral campaign."

The meeting lasted between 20 and 30 minutes, with both sides leaving feeling like it had not met expectations. As they left the conference room, the meeting participants ran into Ivanka Trump and said a brief hello on their way to the elevator. Goldstone, embarrassed that the meeting did not yield smoking gun information against Hillary Clinton as he had promised, apologized to Don Jr. as they left the meeting. He then called Emin Agalarov and told him the meeting had been an embarrassment, which surprised Emin. Goldstone also described the meeting to Kaveladze as an embarrassment, but both recognized that their mutual boss, Aras Agalarov, had vigorously sought it.

After the meeting, Veselnitskaya, Akhmetshin, Kaveladze, and Samochornov retreated to the Trump Tower bar. After Veselnitskaya expressed disappointment in how the meeting went, Akhmetshin and Kaveladze suggested that it was worth it to have introduced the Trump team to the topics of the Magnitsky Act and Russian adoptions that she had wanted to get across. As they drank, Aras Agalarov called Kaveladze and asked how the meeting went. Claiming he could not speak freely in Veselnitskaya's presence, Kaveladze said it went well. Veselnitskaya asked to be placed on the phone and thanked Agalarov for setting up the meeting. After they left the bar and parted ways, Kaveladze said he spoke with Agalarov and explained that the meeting was a disaster and a waste of time.[104]

It violates Federal law for a foreign national to provide anything of value to a campaign in a US election. While it is conceivable that Don Jr. and Jared Kushner, as relative political novices, may not have been aware of Federal election law, Paul Manafort, as a seasoned campaign veteran, certainly would have. As evidenced by the explicit mention of information provided by a Russian prosecutor that would incriminate Hillary, the rapidity with which Don Jr. accepted the meeting, and the fact that the top-tier campaign leadership sat in on it, there can be no doubt that the Trump campaign expected to receive something of value.

Former CIA director Michael Hayden has described the June 9th Trump Tower meeting as having "the classic outlines of a Russian intelligence soft approach."[105] Simply agreeing to take a meeting, the Trump team provided Russian intelligence with valuable insights. The meeting makes even more sense if, like the Trump Tower Moscow negotiations, it is seen in the context of a Russian intelligence operation as much targeting the Trump campaign as it was intending to help it. By creating an incriminating situation that was only known by the Trump team and the Russians, Russian intelligence lured Don Jr. and, by extension, his father into a counterintelligence and potential blackmail trap. Furthermore, investigators did not uncover news of the June 9th Trump Tower meeting; instead, news of it was leaked to the press by the Russians involved in the meeting. It could be that the leak was a Russian active measure intended to roil American politics and society.

On June a14th, *The Washington Post* broke the story that the DNC had been hacked. Later that morning, Goldstone emailed Emin Agalarov and Irakli Kaveladze with a *CNN* article attached that reported the cybersecurity firm FireEye attributed the cyberattack to hackers linked to the Russian government. "Top story right now," Goldstone wrote, "seems eerily weird based on our Trump meeting last week with the Russian lawyers, etc."

The day before, on the 13th, Paula Shugart, the President of the Miss Universe Organization, met with Rob Goldstone and later recalled what he told her. "He did say that he saw Don at a ridiculous meeting, where he went and they supposedly had emails from the Democrats and dirt on Hillary and then it turned out to be something about adoptions," Shugart later told the Senate Intelligence Committee. By testifying that Goldstone mentioned "emails from the democrats" only days after the meeting and a day *before* the *Post* story, Shugart contradicts the testimony of the attendees of the June 9th meeting, none of whom ever claimed that emails related to Hillary or the Democrats had been mentioned during the meeting.

Veselnitskaya and Akhmetshin continued to pursue the anti-Magnitsky Act influence campaign. Upon returning from his

April trip to Moscow, Dana Rohrabacher held up the passage of the Global Magnitsky Act, a law designed to expand the sanctions regime established by the first Magnitsky Act in 2012 to deal with human rights abusers the world over. Using information that had been gleaned from the documents provided to him by the Russian Prosecutor's Office, Rohrabacher attempted to have Magnitsky's name removed from the legislation.

With the help of Rinat Akhmetshin, Rohrabacher and Paul Behrends attempted to arrange for a subcommittee hearing that would screen an anti-Browder documentary, *Magnitsky Act: Behind the Scenes*. Following the screening, Veselnitskaya was to be a witness. The hearing was only canceled when the committee chairman, Ed Royce (R-CA), shut it down to avoid an embarrassing debacle. He rescheduled it as a general committee hearing on relations with Russia, which was to take place on June 14th.

The groundwork for the Capitol Hill lobbying campaign had been laid shortly after Rohrabacher and Behrends had returned from Moscow. Behrends had for some time acted as Veselnitskaya's and Akhmetshin's chief contact in the US Capitol.[106] Akhmetshin visited Rohrabacher's Congressional office on May 17th, with the lobbyist Ron Dellums in tow. Behrends led Akhmetshin and Dellums around the Congress to meet with top committee Democrats. Akhmetshin's appearance did not go unnoticed, either. House Foreign Affairs Committee staffer Kyle Parker sent an email around to his colleagues warning that Akhmetshin had spied for the Soviets and that he "specializes in active measures campaigns."[107]

On the day of the hearing, which took place on the day the *Post* broke the Russian involvement in the DNC hacking story, Rohrabacher compared Trump to Putin as though it were a compliment and submitted into the congressional record testimony that suggested the Russian security services were not behind the assassination of Alexander Litvinenko.[108] The hearing was attended by Veselnitskaya, who sat next to a Republican consultant named Lanny Wiles, a mutual acquaintance of Rinat Akhmetshin and Paul Manafort, who had reserved her seat at the hearing. Wiles' wife Susie was chair of the Trump campaign in Florida at the time.[109]

Later that evening, Rohrabacher, Behrends, Veselnitskaya, and Akhmetshin dined at the Capitol Hill Club. Veselnitskaya and

Akhmetshin had much to celebrate; it had been a busy few days between meeting the top leadership of the Trump campaign in New York and gallivanting around the United States Congress flogging Kremlin talking points. Not that these antics had been lost of Rohrabacher and Behrends Republican colleagues. The next day, June 15th, House Majority Leader Kevin McCarthy was recorded as saying: "There are two people I think Putin pays: Rohrabacher and Trump."

McCarthy's fellow Republican Congressmen laughed.

[1] Report of the Select Committee on Intelligence United States Senate On Russian Active Measures Campaigns And Interference in the 2016 US Election Volume 5: Counterintelligence Threats and Vulnerabilities. Pg. 347-348

[2] Report of the Select Committee on Intelligence United States Senate On Russian Active Measures Campaigns And Interference in the 2016 US Election Volume 5: Counterintelligence Threats and Vulnerabilities. Pg. 313-317

[3] Monaghan, Jennifer. "VKontakte Founder Says Sold Shares Due to FSB Pressure," *The Moscow Times*. April 17th, 2014

[4] Razumovskaya, Olga. "Alisher Usmanov Cements Control of Social Network," *The Wall Street Journal*. January 25th, 2014

[5] Goodley, Simon; Harding, Luke; Elder, Miriam. "Man behind Megafon pictured with alleged Russian gangsters," *The Guardian*. November 28th, 2012

[6] Report of the Select Committee on Intelligence United States Senate On Russian Active Measures Campaigns And Interference in the 2016 US Election Volume 5: Counterintelligence Threats and Vulnerabilities. Pg. 260

[7] Mueller, III, Robert S. *Report On The Investigation Into Russian Interference In The 2016 Presidential Election*. Department of Justice, Washington, DC. March 2019. Pg. 112

[8] Vasilyeva, Natalia. "Pop star, lobbyist: The cast of Trump's Russia connections," *The Associated Press*. July 15th, 2017

[9] Bershidsky, Leonid. "Trump's Low-Level Russian Connection," *Bloomberg*. July 11th, 2017

[10] MacFarquhar, Neil; Kramer, Andrew E. "Natalia Veselnitskaya, Lawyer Who Met Trump Jr., Seen as Fearsome Moscow Insider," *The New York Times*. July 11th, 2017

[11] Marusic, Damir; Orlova, Karlina. "All The Dots, Connected," *The American Interest*. July 25th, 2017

[12] Vasilyeva, Natalia. "Pop star, lobbyist: The cast of Trump's Russia connections," *The Associated Press*. July 15th, 2017

[13] Isikoff, Michael; Corn, David. *Russian Roulette: The Inside Story Of Putin's War On America And The Election Of Donald Trump*. New York, NY: Hachette Book Group, 2018. Pg. 120

[14] Tsvetkova, Maria; Stubbs, Jack. "Exclusive: Moscow lawyer who met Trump Jr. had Russian spy agency as client," *Reuters*. July 21st, 2017

[15] Harding, Luke. "Raiders of the Russian Billions," *The Guardian*. June 23rd, 2008

[16] Report of the Select Committee on Intelligence United States Senate On Russian Active Measures Campaigns And Interference in the 2016 US Election Volume 5: Counterintelligence Threats and Vulnerabilities. Pg. 338

[17] Belton, Catherine. *Putin's People: How The KGB Took Back Russia And Then Took On The West*. New York, NY: Farrar, Straus and Girox, 2020. Pg. 310-311

[18] OCCRP. "The Wall Street Connection," *Organized Crime and Reporting Project*. June 9th, 2013

[19] Shalev, Chemi. "The Countless Israeli Connections to Mueller's Probe of Trump and Russia," *Haaretz*. May 26th, 2018

[20] United States of America v. Natalia Veselnitskaya. SEALED INDICTMENT. UNITED STATES DISTRICT COURT SOUTHERN DISTRICT OF NEW YORK. Pg. 4-11

[21] Report of the Select Committee on Intelligence United States Senate On Russian Active Measures Campaigns And Interference in the 2016 US Election Volume 5: Counterintelligence Threats and Vulnerabilities. Pg. 338

[22] Smirnov, Sergei. "Investigating Russia's top prosecutor: The life and career of Yuri Chaika," *Meduza*. December 25th, 2015

[23] LaFraniere, Sharon; Kramer, Andrew E. "Talking Points Brought To Trump Tower Meeting Were Shared With Kremlin," *The New York Times*. October 27th, 2017

[24] Kocieniewski, David; Farrell, Greg; Robison, Peter; Van Voris, Bob. "Russian Lawyer Who Met Trump Jr. Saw a Clinton Scandal in Tax Inquiry," *Bloomberg*. July 12th, 2017

[25] Rinat Akhmetshin House HPSCI Testimony, Pg. 55

[26] Manson, Katrina. "Russian lobbyist Rinat Akhmetshin on that notorious meeting at Trump Tower," *The Financial Times*. September 1st, 2017

[27] Eckel, Mike. "Russian 'Gun-for-Hire' Lurks In Shadows Of Washington's Lobbying World," *RadioFreeEurope/RadioLiberty*. July 17th, 2017

[28] Sullivan, Eileen; Vogel, Kenneth P.; Goldman, Adam; Becker, Jo. "Russian-American Lobbyist Attended Meeting Organized by Trump's Son," *The New York Times*. July 14th, 2017

[29] Langer, Emily. "Evelyn Lieberman, White House deputy chief of staff under Clinton, dies at 71," *The Washington Post*. December 15th, 2015

[30] Rinat Akhmetshin House HPSCI Testimony, Pg. 165-166

[31] Levin, Steve. "In Election, Kazakhstan Gets a Dose of the West," *The New York Times*. October 25th, 1998

[32] Levin, Steve. "Meet the ex-Soviet intel officer at Don Jr.'s Trump Tower meeting," *Axios*. July 14th, 2017

[33] Sullivan, Eileen; Vogel, Kenneth P.; Goldman, Adam; Becker, Jo. "Russian-American Lobbyist Attended Meeting Organized by Trump's Son," *The New York Times*. July 14th, 2017

[34] International Mineral Resources BV v. Rinat Akhmetshin, et al. COMPLAINT. Supreme Court of the State of New York County of New York. Pg. 10-14

[35] Patten, Sam. "Kostya and Me: How Sam Patten Got Ensnared In Mueller's Probe," *Wired*. August 14th, 2019

[36] Report of the Select Committee on Intelligence United States Senate On Russian Active Measures Campaigns And Interference in the 2016 US Election Volume 5: Counterintelligence Threats and Vulnerabilities. Pg. 344-345

[37] Anatoli Samochornov HPSCI Testimony. November 28th, 2017. Pg. 8-9 & 14-15

[38] Baker, Stephanie; Reznik, Irina. "Mueller Is Looking Into a U.S. Foundation Backed By Russian Money," *Bloomberg*. December 21st, 2017

[39] Baker, Stephanie; Reznik, Irina. "Mueller Is Looking Into a U.S. Foundation Backed By Russian Money," *Bloomberg*. December 21st, 2017

[40] Browder, William. *Testimony of William Browder to the Senate Judiciary Committee on FARA violations connected to the anti-Magnitsky Campaign by Russian government interests*. July 26th, 2017. Pg. 6

[41] Satter, Raphael. "Emails: lawyer who met Trump Jr. tied to Russian officials," *The Associated Press*. July 27th, 2018

[42] Pismennaya, Evgenia; Kravchenko, Stepan; Baker, Stephanie. "The Day Trump Came To Moscow: Oligarch's Miss Universe and Nobu," *Bloomberg*. December 21st, 2016

[43] Markey, Lachlan. "Donald Trump Jr.'s Russian Connection Has Ties to Former Kremlin Spies," *The Daily Beast*. July 11th, 2017

[44] Report of the Select Committee on Intelligence United States Senate On Russian

Active Measures Campaigns And Interference in the 2016 US Election Volume 5: Counterintelligence Threats and Vulnerabilities. Pg. 331-332

[45] Goodley, Simon; Harding, Luke; Elder, Miriam. "Man behind MegaFon pictured with alleged Russian gangsters," *The Guardian*. November 28th, 2012

[46] Bertrand, Natasha. "Former FBI director represented Russian firm at center of major money-laundering probe," *Business Insider*. November 16th, 2017

[47] Apuzzo, Matt; Goldman, Adam; Mazzetti, Mark. "F.B.I. Once Warned GOP Congressman That Russian Spies Were Recruiting Him," *The New York Times*. May 19th, 2017

[48] Fandos, Nicholas. "He's a Member of Congress. The Kremlin Likes Him So Much It Gave Him a Codename," *The New York Times*. November 21st, 2017

[49] May, Clifford D. "Washington Talk; Two House Freshman Reflect Clash of Cultures," *The New York Times*. May 11th, 1989

[50] Weinberger, Sharon. "The Life and Death of the Most Notorious Man in Washington," *New York Magazine*. January 1st, 2021

[51] Waller, J. Michael. "We lost an extraordinary friend and ally: Paul Behrends, 1958-2020," *Center for Security Policy*. December 17th, 2020

[52] Schulman, Daniel. "Dana Rohrabacher's War," *Mother Jones*. March/April 2010

[53] Hines, Nico. "GOP Lawmaker Got Director From Moscow, Took It Back to DC," *The Daily Beast*. July 19th, 2017

[54] Warren, Peter M. "Carmony Pleads Guilty in Baugh Case," *The Los Angeles Times*. December 5th, 1997

[55] Coker, Matt. "The List of Dana Rohrabacher's Convicted Friends and Lovers Grows Ever Longer," *OC Weekly*. January 18th, 2017

[56] Smith, R. Jeffrey; Grimaldi, James V. "A 3rd DeLay Trip Under Scrutiny," *The Washington Post*. April 6th, 2005

[57] Mason, Cass. "Whatever happened to our 'billionaire' Khimich," *newsroom*. July 12th, 2019

[58] Pasco, Jean O. "Rohrabacher Defends Abramoff, a Friend," *The Los Angeles Times*. January 10th, 2006

[59] Smith, R. Jeffrey. "Abramoff's Holiday Cheer His 2001 Shopping List Included Lavish Gifts for Congressmen," *The Washington Post*. December 20th, 2006

[60] Smith, R. Jeffrey. "Former DeLay Aide Enriched By Nonprofit," *The Washington Post*. March 26th, 2006

[61] Moxley, R. Scott. "Was Ex-Rep Dana Rohrabacher A Pig On Vladimir Putin's Animal Farm," *OC Weekly*. November 6th, 2019

[62] Seddon, Max; Gray, Rosie. "Putin's Action Hero: How Steven Seagal Became The Kremlin's Unlikeliest Envoy," *BuzzFeed News*. April 20th, 2015

[63] Schreckinger, Ben. "The Hill Staffer at the Center of the Russia Intrigue," *Politico*. July 20th, 2017

[64] Brady, Rose. "Online Extra: Russia's Goal: 'To Make Iraq Disarm,'" *Bloomberg*. March 9th, 2003

[65] Bachman, Jessica. "Transneft Boss - from KGB to oil diplomat," *Reuters*. September 14th, 2010

[66] Mikhail Margelov, Russian International Affairs Council Bio

[67] Report of the Select Committee on Intelligence United States Senate On Russian Active Measures Campaigns And Interference in the 2016 US Election Volume 5: Counterintelligence Threats and Vulnerabilities. Pg. 323-324

[68] Belton, Catherin. *Putin's People: How The KGB Took Back Russia And Took On The West*. New York, NY: Farrar, Straus and Giroux, 2020. Pg. 105-109

[69] Anin, Roman. "The Russian Laundromat Superusers Revealed," *Organized Crime and Corruption Reporting Project*. March 20th, 2017

[70] Belton, Catherin. *Putin's People: How The KGB Took Back Russia And Took On The West*. New York, NY: Farrar, Straus and Giroux, 2020. Pg. 402-404

[71] Laruelle, Marlene. "Russian Soft Power in France: Assessing Russia's Cultural and Business Para-Diplomacy," *Carnegie Council for Ethics in International Affairs.* January 8th, 2018

[72] "Putin's Asymmetric Assault on Democracy In Russia And Europe: Implications For U.S. National Security," *Committee on Foreign Relations, United States Senate.* January 10th, 2018. Pg. 49

[73] Report of the Select Committee on Intelligence United States Senate On Russian Active Measures Campaigns And Interference in the 2016 US Election Volume 5: Counterintelligence Threats and Vulnerabilities. Pg. 325-326

[74] "Putin's Asymmetric Assault on Democracy In Russia And Europe: Implications For U.S. National Security," *Committee on Foreign Relations, United States Senate.* January 10th, 2018. Pg. 19-20

[75] Vojtiskova, Vladislava; Novotny, Vit; Schmid-Schmidsfelden, Herbertus; Potapova, Kristina. "The Bear In Sheep's Clothing: Russia's Government-Funded Organisations in the EU," *Wilfried Martens Centre for European Studies.* July 19th, 2016. Pg. 36-38

[76] Redden, Molly. "FBI Probing Whether Russia Used Cultural Junkets to Recruit American Intelligence Assets," *Mother Jones.* October 23rd, 2013

[77] Report of the Select Committee on Intelligence United States Senate On Russian Active Measures Campaigns And Interference in the 2016 US Election Volume 5: Counterintelligence Threats and Vulnerabilities. Pg. 328

[78] Seddon, Max. "Did Russia's top prosecutor Yuri Chaika want to help Donald Trump?" *The Financial Times.* July 12th, 2017

[79] Rinat Akhmetshin House HPSCI Testimony, Pg. 66-69

[80] Yaffa, Joshua. "How Bill Browder Became Russia's Most Wanted Man," *The New Yorker.* August 13th, 2018

[81] Report of the Select Committee on Intelligence United States Senate On Russian Active Measures Campaigns And Interference in the 2016 US Election Volume 5: Counterintelligence Threats and Vulnerabilities. Pg. 260-261

[82] Cheney, Kyle; Samuelsohn, Darren; Hutchins, Ryan. "Eight person in Trump Tower meeting was linked to money laundering," *Politico.* July 18th, 2017

[83] Swaine, Jon; Stedman, Scott. "Revealed: Russian billionaire set up US company before Trump Tower meeting," *The Guardian.* October 18th, 2018

[84] Siegelman, Wendy. "While Felix Sater pursued Trump Tower Moscow discussions he did a deal with an accountant linked to Aras Agalarov," *Medium.* October 22nd, 2018

[85] Mueller, III, Robert S. *Report On The Investigation Into Russian Interference In The 2016 Presidential Election.* Department of Justice, Washington, DC. March 2019. Pg. 113-114

[86] Report of the Select Committee on Intelligence United States Senate On Russian Active Measures Campaigns And Interference in the 2016 US Election Volume 5: Counterintelligence Threats and Vulnerabilities. Pg. 351-352

[87] Mueller, III, Robert S. *Report On The Investigation Into Russian Interference In The 2016 Presidential Election.* Department of Justice, Washington, DC. March 2019. Pg. 114

[88] Green, David B. "Who Is Lev Leviev, the Israeli Billionaire With Ties to Jared Kushner and Putin," *Haaretz.* July 25th, 2017

[89] Dukakis, Ali; Bruggerman, Lucien. "Who are the mystery men photographed sharing cigars with Michael Cohen," *ABC News.* April 18th, 2018

[90] Marusic, Damir; Orlova, Karlina. "All The Dots, Connected," *The American Interest.* July 25th, 2017

[91] Dent, Wendy; Pilkington, Ed; Walker, Shaun. "Jared Kushner sealed real estate deal with oligarch's firm cited in money-laundering case," *The Guardian.* July 24th, 2017

[92] Kranish, Michael. "Kushner firm's $285 million Deutsche Bank loan came just before election day," *The Washington Post.* June 25th, 2017

[93] Protess, Ben; Silver-Greenberg, Jessica; Drucker, Jesse. "Big German Bank, Key to Trump's Finances, Faces New Scrutiny," *The New York Times.* July 19th, 2017

[94] MacFarquhar, Neil. "A Russian Developer Helps Out the Kremlin on Occasion. Was

He a Conduit to Trump?" *The New York Times.* July 16th, 2017

[95] Report of the Select Committee on Intelligence United States Senate On Russian Active Measures Campaigns And Interference in the 2016 US Election Volume 5: Counterintelligence Threats and Vulnerabilities. Pg. 349

[96] Dilanian, Ken. "Senate committee made criminal referral of Trump Jr., Bannon, Kushner, two others to Federal prosecutors," *NBC News.* August 18th, 2020

[97] Report of the Select Committee on Intelligence United States Senate On Russian Active Measures Campaigns And Interference in the 2016 US Election Volume 5: Counterintelligence Threats and Vulnerabilities. Pg. 357

[98] Mueller, III, Robert S. *Report On The Investigation Into Russian Interference In The 2016 Presidential Election.* Department of Justice, Washington, DC. March 2019. Pg. 115

[99] Report of the Select Committee on Intelligence United States Senate On Russian Active Measures Campaigns And Interference in the 2016 US Election Volume 5: Counterintelligence Threats and Vulnerabilities. Pg. 355-356

[100] Report of the Select Committee on Intelligence United States Senate On Russian Active Measures Campaigns And Interference in the 2016 US Election Volume 5: Counterintelligence Threats and Vulnerabilities. Pg. 361-362

[101] Report of the Select Committee on Intelligence United States Senate On Russian Active Measures Campaigns And Interference in the 2016 US Election Volume 5: Counterintelligence Threats and Vulnerabilities. Pg. 360

[102] Report of the Select Committee on Intelligence United States Senate On Russian Active Measures Campaigns And Interference in the 2016 US Election Volume 5: Counterintelligence Threats and Vulnerabilities. Pg. 362-363

[103] Kocieniewski, David; Farrell, Greg; Robison, Peter; Van Voris, Bob. "Russian Lawyer Who Met Trump Jr. Saw a Clinton Scandal in Tax Inquiry," *Bloomberg.* July 12th, 2017

[104] Report of the Select Committee on Intelligence United States Senate On Russian Active Measures Campaigns And Interference in the 2016 US Election Volume 5: Counterintelligence Threats and Vulnerabilities. Pg. 363-373

[105] Manchester, Julia. "Hayden: Trump Tower meeting had "classic outlines of a Russian intelligence soft approach," *The Hill.* August 24th, 2018

[106] Schreckinger, Ben. "The Hill Staffer at the Center of the Russia Intrigue," *Politico.* July 20th, 2017

[107] Arnsdorf, Isaac; Oreskes, Benjamin. "Putin's favorite congressman," *Politico.* November 23rd, 2016

[108] Hines, Nico. "GOP Lawmaker Got Direction From Moscow, Took It Back to D.C." *The Daily Beast.* July 19th, 2017

[109] Helderman, Rosalind S.; Hamburger, Tom. "Russian-American lobbyist was present at Trump Jr.'s meeting with Kremlin-connected lawyer," *The Washington Post.* July 14th, 2017

Chapter 19:
Steve Bannon, Cambridge Analytica, And the Bad Boys of Brexit

Months before the election of Donald Trump, political events in the United Kingdom presaged the populist uprising that would shake the foundations of the West to the core. The factors that drove a slim majority of Britons to vote to separate the UK from the European Union, popularly known as Brexit, were interpreted by Donald Trump and his supporters to mean that his campaign had emerged at the perfect moment to ride a wave of popular discontent across Europe and the United States. However, more than shared themes and ideological underpinnings connected the Brexit referendum and the Trump candidacy.

The British consulting and data analytics firm Cambridge Analytica (CA) was a nexus between the Trump campaign and a flamboyant cast of British politicians and businessmen associated with Brexit. The company was partly founded by a group of Americans who formed the central pillars of support for the Trump campaign. While the exact nature and efficacy of the work performed by CA on both Brexit and the Trump campaign is disputed, an exploration of the facts is useful insofar as it reveals the risks posed by data-informed psychological operations to democracy. There was a remarkable overlap between the techniques used by CA and the Internet Research Agency.[1] An analysis of CA also provides a prism to explore the suspicious interactions between the Trump campaign and several prominent Brexiters with links to Russia and, more broadly, the remarkable infiltration of Russian money, as well as its intelligence apparatus and organized crime, into British social, political and economic life.

Nigel Oakes, SCL Group, and Vincent Tchenguiz

Both the separation of the United Kingdom from Europe and the election of Donald Trump as the President of the United States were foreign policy goals held by the Kremlin. Suspicious linkages between CA and its parent company, SCL Group, with Russian actors and interests, as well as those of the prominent Brexiters who later became active supporters of Trump, demand further scrutiny. "Cambridge Analytica," according to a report issued by the US Senate Intelligence Committee, "had a degree of intersection with and proximity to Russia, and specifically Russia's intelligence services."[2]

CA was one part of a complex and opaque corporate ownership structure. Its parent company, Strategic Communication Laboratories (SCL), was founded by an old Etonian named Nigel Oakes.[3] Oakes was fascinated with the science behind shaping behavior and mass psychology. In 1989, he established the Behavioral Dynamics Institute (BDI) with the psychologists Adrian Furnham and Barrie Gunter. The academics later distanced themselves from Oakes after determining that he was overselling what their understanding of psychology at the time could substantiate.[4]

At Strategic Communication Laboratories, Oakes applied his new methodology to foreign elections, primarily in Africa, Asia, and Eastern Europe.[5] Following 9/11, there were populations across the Islamic world that the US sought to influence. Strategic Communication Laboratories was soon deluged with US government contracts, including from the Department of Homeland Security, NATO, the CIA, the FBI, and the State Department.[6]

According to a part of its website now offline, in 2004 Strategic Communication Laboratories worked on behalf of the Orange coalition in Ukraine.[7] If true, it may have come to the attention of Russian intelligence. Vladimir Putin and the Russian security establishment believed that outside instigators had initiated the Color Revolutions.[8]

In 2005, Oakes set up SCL Group, which claimed expertise in "influence" and "psychological" operations.[9] Oakes founded SCL Group with fellow Etonian Alexander Nix. Nix had been hired by Strategic Communication Laboratories in 2003 as a director. Other shareholders included members of Britain's Conservative Party and military establishment.[10]

SCL Group's largest shareholder between 2005 and 2015 was Vincent Tchenguiz. Born in Tehran to Iraqi-Jewish parents, Vincent and his brother Robert are some of Britain's most prominent property moguls.[11] In 2002, the Tchenguiz brothers purchased the Art Deco Shell-Mex House for £350 million. They co-owned the building with the Reuben brothers, former business partners with Mikhail Chernoy, an alleged senior member of the Izmaylovskaya.[12]

In 2005, Tchenguiz's company, Consensus Business Group, purchased 22,533 shares of SCL Group, making him the largest investor in the company. His shares were then transferred to an entity called Wheddon Ltd. Another Tchenguiz investment vehicle, Vantania Holdings Ltd, invested in a soil regeneration company called Zander Group Ltd. Between 2006 and 2011, the largest shareholder in Zander was Semyon Mogilevich-linked Dmytro Firtash.[13] Tchenguiz transferred his ownership stake in Zander to Wheddon Ltd, thus housing both his investments in SCL Group and the Firtash-linked Zander Group Ltd under the same holding company.

In 2010, Tchenguiz was seen multiple times attending the London nightclub Annabel's with Anna Chapman.[14] Chapman was the daughter of a KGB agent and served as an undercover illegal Russian intelligence agent working for the SVR. She lived in London between 2001 and 2006, working at the Mayfair hedge fund for a friend of Tchenguiz's. After moving to the US, Chapman was arrested with ten other illegals and deported back to Russia.[15]

In 2011, Vincent and Robert Tchenguiz were arrested in a raid by the British Serious Fraud Office in relation to their alleged role in the collapse of the Icelandic Kaupthing Bank in the wake of the 2008 financial crisis. Two weeks before it failed, Kaupthing's credit committee engaged in an orgy of lending that exceeded 100% of the bank's equity base. Among those who received the questionable loans were Robert Tchenguiz and Alisher Usmanov.[16] Usmanov has done business with alleged associates of the Solntsevskaya and was a major investor in Facebook.[17] Usmanov's office in Mayfair was next door to the

Tchenguiz brothers' office.[18]

Following his and Robert's arrest, Vincent Tchenguiz sought advice from Meir Dagan, former head of Mossad.[19] Dagan connected Tchenguiz with Dan Zorella and Avi Yanus, and Tchenguiz later provided seed funding to establish the private intelligence firm Black Cube, which he became the first client of.[20] The firm employed former members of Mossad, Shin Bet, and Israeli military intelligence and featured Dagan on its board as well as another former Mossad chief. Black Cube used the Tchenguiz's Mayfair office as their UK headquarters. From December 2011 to December 2012, it gave him weekly reports on their work. The SFO's case against the Tchenguiz brothers eventually collapsed, marred by errors in the information used to procure search warrants against Vincent.[21] Vincent Tchenguiz and Black Cube later had a falling out over payment issues and traded lawsuits that ultimately settled.

How separate Black Cube is from Israeli intelligence is open to question. Between 2012 and 2013, it was hired out by the Israeli Defense Ministry, and several of its employees reportedly operated out of an IDF intelligence base full-time.[22] The firm later became infamous for its work on Harvey Weinstein's behalf.[23] Black Cube also spied on a state prosecutor of the Romanian Anti-corruption directorate,[24] secretly recorded individuals affiliated with George Soros-linked NGOs during the re-election campaign of the pro-Putin Hungarian Prime Minister Viktor Orbán,[25] and targeted the Russian anti-corruption activists including Alexei Navalny.[26]

SCL Group engaged in dirty tricks abroad, particularly in African elections. In Nigeria, it engineered a campaign for the ruling party that counterintuitively pushed the narrative to voters that the elections would be rigged, with the idea that when it, in fact, was rigged, voters would respond with cynical resignation instead of outrage.[27] It was an early example of suppression techniques aimed at black voters that would be mirrored by the Trump campaign and the Internet Research Agency in the 2016 American election.

In 2010, SCL Group was contracted to undertake a research project in Afghanistan and survey twelve war-torn provinces.[28] According to a report in *Fast Company*, the work was overseen by Michael Flynn, then the director of intelligence for the international security assistance force in Afghanistan.[29] Flynn later served as advisor to SCL Group as it bid for government and defense contracts with the Trump administration.[30]

In 2010, Alexander Nix grew intrigued by Google Analytics and considered opening up a data analytics division at SCL Group.[31] By 2012, Nix and Oakes began to have competing visions for SCL Group. Nix wanted to develop the elections side of the business, while Oakes wished to promote the defense side. Ultimately, a solution was found with Nix taking control of a new SCL Group subsidiary, SCL Elections.[32]

In 2013, Sophie Schmidt, the daughter of Google CEO Eric Schmidt, became an intern at SCL. After absorbing all the information he could from her about Google's efforts in data analytics, Nix became determined to incorporate data analytics into SCL's suite of services. He realized early on that the United States would be an ideal place to establish a business with its lax data and privacy regulations relative to Europe.[33] Nix also saw that the Democratic Party enjoyed a decisive advantage over the Republicans at the time in the sophistication of their data operations. This created a business opportunity.[34]

In June 2013, Nix hired 24-year-old Canadian data whiz Christopher Wylie.[35] Wylie's role at SCL was to figure out ways to digitize the traditional information warfare techniques. He suggested that SCL reorient its focus toward gathering more accurate data. This would allow them to build more effective algorithms to target specific people using online mediums.[36] One of their earliest projects that sought to incorporate data into their psychological operations occurred in Trinidad and Tobago. The company already had a shockingly unethical history of activities on the dual-island Caribbean nation. As it had in Nigeria, SCL Elections devised a clandestine psychological campaign involving subtle messaging and a fake grassroots movement to dissuade the island nation's black youth from voting.[37]

Robert Mercer, Steve Bannon, and the Birth of Cambridge Analytica

At some point in 2013, a fateful meeting on an airplane set in motion events that would lead to the birth of Cambridge Analytica. On a flight from Los Angeles to New York, Republican political strategists Mark Block and Linda Hansen sat next to a military contractor who had done work with SCL.[38] The contractor effusively praised SCL and inspired Block to contact

Nix.[39]

Nix explained how SCL had pioneered the practice of *psychographics* to utilize the data it collected more effectively.[40] *Psychographics*, Nix explained, was the process by which SCL applied personality scoring to the individuals within the company's data set. Through *behavioral microtargeting*, SCL tailored messaging to groups of individuals with similar personality traits, thus theoretically improving the efficacy of the messaging. SCL utilized the OCEAN model to classify its data, which established the "Big Five" personality traits as being (O)pen, (C)onscientious, (E)xtroverted, (A)greeable and (N)eurotic.[41] Block was thrilled by Nix's presentation. However, credible experts have argued that the methodology was oversold by Nix and others who had a financial incentive to exaggerate the firm's data prowess.

Block introduced Nix to the billionaire Rebekah Mercer, one of the most prolific donors to conservative causes in the US. Over lunch in Manhattan, Nix delivered his well-polished spiel to Mercer. Nix next met with Rebekah's father, Robert Mercer, on his 203-foot Yacht, the Sea Owl, where he was introduced to Mercer's right-wing political Svengali, Steve Bannon.[42]

Robert Mercer, an arch-conservative eccentric and recluse, was the billionaire co-CEO of Renaissance Technologies, considered the most successful and secretive hedge fund on earth.[43] In the 1970s, he researched speech recognition software as an employee at IBM. James Simons, a mathematician who founded Renaissance Technologies, believed Mercer's research could be applied to his attempts to use quantitative models to inform systematic trading across financial markets. Simons convinced Mercer to join him at Renaissance. The crown jewel of their efforts was the Medallion Fund. Established in 1988 and open only to employees of RenTec, it is arguably the most successful fund in history.[44]

While Mercer is a notorious recluse, many of his colleagues at Renaissance realized that he held profoundly conservative views. Despite being a scientist, Mercer was a climate change skeptic. His views on race and civil rights disturbed some. A RenTec employee claimed that Mercer had told him that African-Americans were doing "fine" in the 1950s and 1960s and that the Civil Rights Act had "infantilized" them. The employee further claimed that Mercer told him that the only racist people remaining in the US were black.[45]

After the election of Obama in 2008, Mercer and his daughter Rebekah became increasingly politically active. While the Mercers initially backed traditional Republican organizations, Robert's tendency to distrust the establishment found a fellow traveler in 2011 when he became acquainted with right-wing provocateur, online news entrepreneur, and television personality Andrew Breitbart. The founder of *Breitbart News*, Breitbart is perhaps best known for his belief that "politics is downstream from culture."[46]

The Mercers purchased 50% of *Breitbart News*. Nine months later, Andrew Breitbart unexpectedly dropped dead of a heart attack, but not before introducing the Mercers to his friend and fellow conservative iconoclast Steve Bannon. Bannon drew up the business plan that led to the Mercer's dropping $10 million into *Breitbart News*.

A Navy veteran, Harvard Business School graduate, former Goldman Sachs employee, and conservative Hollywood filmmaker, Bannon took over as Editor-in-Chief of *Breitbart News*. As a devout Catholic, he was influenced by the French intellectual René Guénon's philosophy of Traditionalism, which rejected liberalism and secular modernity and characterized the West as being in spiritual decline. A key follower of Guénon was the Italian fascist intellectual and radical traditionalist Julius Evola. Evola's ideas later partially inspired the Eurasianist philosophy of Aleksandr Dugin.[47] In remarks given at the Vatican in 2014, Bannon synthesized many of Guénon's and Evola's ideas into his own fears of what he viewed as the existential threat posed by Islamic encroachment into the West through the European migrant crisis.[48]

After Nix delivered his pitch, Mercer sent Bannon to the UK to explore the opportunity further. In October 2013, Bannon met Christopher Wylie at a hotel near Cambridge University. Wylie explained SCL's activities in Trinidad and Tobago to Bannon, highlighting their ability to see in real-time what Trinidadians were looking at online and incorporate that information into their data set. When Bannon asked if such a thing could be replicated in the US, Wylie replied that he didn't see why not. Backed with Mercer money, Bannon oversaw the founding of Cambridge Analytica in partnership with SCL Elections.

In 2012, a Cambridge academic named John Stillwell arrived at the insight that social media could be used to gather valuable psychometric data.[49] In early 2014, Christopher Wylie contacted Stillwell to discuss partnering with SCL Group, but Stillwell ultimately decided against it. Wylie then turned to another academic at Cambridge, Aleksandr Kogan. Kogan had been using macro-level datasets from Facebook since early 2013 and offered to replicate Stillwell's work and harvest his own data set.[50]

At the time, Facebook's policy allowed third-party apps that received permission from a user to access their Facebook friends' data. Using an online personality test, Kogan gained access to the data of 50 million users. They matched 30 million with other gathered data, allowing them to form psychographic profiles. Facebook later claimed that upwards of 87 million of its users may have had their data harvested.[51]

Kogan also worked at St. Petersburg University.[52] According to Wylie, Kogan's work in St. Petersburg was funded by the Russian state.[53] Employees of SCL Group were aware of Kogan's work in Russia. In an email dated March 14th, 2014, an SCL Group employee wrote to Nix and Wylie about "the interesting work Alex Kogan has been doing for the Russians," as it related to the "predictive crime-based CRM [customer relationship management]" and "criminal psychographic profiling" analytics being gathered for SCL's work in Trinidad and Tobago.[54]

According to Wylie, Kogan's research at St. Petersburg State University was focused on the link between narcissism, Machiavellianism, and psychopathy, known as the dark triad of personality traits, and online behavior such as cyberstalking, cyberbullying, and trolling.[55] Kogan's work in St. Petersburg brings to mind the fact that the IRA was operating in the same city. In May 2014, Kogan signed a contract with SCL Elections. That same month, the IRA began targeting the US.[56] Nonetheless, there is no evidence that Kogan was involved in, or aware of, the activities of Yevgeny Prigozhin's troll factory.

Lukoil, Russian Intelligence, and Polling Americans About Putin

In the Spring of 2014, CA was contacted by Lukoil, Russia's

second-largest privately held corporation. Later that year, the company was placed on the US sanctions list.[57] Nix sent a white paper drafted by Christopher Wylie to Lukoil's CEO Vagit Alekperov, an Azerbaijani billionaire and former Soviet oil minister. Alekperov is an ally of Vladimir Putin and close to Russian intelligence. Lukoil's co-founder, Andrei Pannikov, was a former member of the KGB.[58]

Around this time, Wylie grew suspicious of how SCL and CA operated. Shortly after Lukoil's outreach, Wylie saw a memo that claimed: "SCL retains a number of retired intelligence and security agency officers from Israel, USA, UK, Spain, and Russia." The memo further detailed SCL strategies, such as leaking damaging stories to the press and how the company infiltrated opposing campaigns using "intelligence nets" to gather "damaging information." All of this was on his mind when he attended a meeting alongside Nix with Lukoil executives.

"In reality," Wylie later wrote, "when Nix and I met with these "Lukoil executives," we were almost certainly speaking to Russian intelligence. They likely were interested in finding out more about this firm that was also working for NATO forces. That's likely also why they wanted to know so much about our American data, and Nix probably struck them as someone who could be flattered into saying pretty much anything."[59] There is no direct evidence supporting Wylie's claim. However, Lukoil does have a relationship with Russian intelligence and has been used as a tool of the Russian state in the past.

Another strange coincidence links CA to Russian intelligence. Alexander Nix hired the American political consultant Sam Patten in early 2014 to perform work in the United States.[60] Patten was a friend and longtime associate of Konstantin Kilimnik.[61] In February 2015, Patten established a DC-based political consulting firm with Kilimnik called Begemot Ventures International LLC.[62]

Patten was sent to Oregon in the Spring of 2014, where CA worked on three local campaigns while preparing for the presidential election.[63] Patten was tasked with conducting focus groups, data collection, and writing polling questions. Wylie was surprised to find that the questions were about Russia. The Oregon team asked questions like, "Is Russia entitled to Crimea?" or "What do you think about Vladimir Putin as a leader?" Photos of Putin were projected against the wall, and the American focus group participants were asked what it felt like to see a strong leader. Wylie was disturbed by the number of Americans who admired Putin's "strength." He was also surprised that Putin was the only foreign leader asked about.[64]

Wylie later testified that Steve Bannon had authorized the focus groups and that Bannon and Konstantin Kilimnik were two of three individuals responsible for the idea.[65] While the claim regarding Kilimnik has yet to be corroborated, we know Patten and Kilimnik were in contact during this period. Following his work in Oregon, Kilimnik invited Patten and Paul Manafort to join them in their work on behalf of the Opposition Bloc in Ukraine.[66] While there is no evidence that Bannon ever met or spoke with Kilimnik, in July of 2016, he featured Sam Patten on his Sirius FM radio show.[67]

Around the time CA was conducting its Russian messaging research, Steve Bannon gave a speech at the Vatican. Bannon painted a grim picture of a Judeo-Christian West sapped by secularism and a crony form of capitalism. These corrosive trends were occurring, according to Bannon, just as the West faced a cataclysmic and civilizational struggle against radical Islam. During the Q&A, he expounded upon his views of Vladimir Putin. "When Vladimir Putin, when you really look at some of the underpinnings of some of his beliefs today, a lot of those come from what I call Eurasianism; he's got an adviser who harkens back to Julius Evola and different writers of the early 20th century who are really the supporters of what's called the traditionalist movement, which really eventually metastasized into Italian fascism. A lot of people that are traditionalists are attracted to that." The advisor Bannon referred to is Aleksandr Dugin. "I'm not justifying Vladimir Putin and the kleptocracy that he represents, because he eventually is the state capitalist of kleptocracy. However, we, the Judeo-Christian West, really have to look at what he's talking about as far as traditionalism goes..."

"You know, Putin's been quite an interesting character. He's also very, very, very intelligent. I can see this in the United States, where he's playing very strongly to social conservatives about his message about more traditional values, so I think it's something that we have to be very much on guard of. Because at the end of the day, I think that Putin and his cronies are really a kleptocracy, that are really an imperialist power that want to expand. However, I really believe that in this current environment, where you're facing a potential new caliphate that is very aggressive, that is really a situation — I'm not saying we can put it on a back burner — but I think we have to deal with first things first."[68]

Cambridge Analytica and the Bad Boys of Brexit

The role CA played in Brexit is the source of enormous controversy in the United Kingdom—part of the scandal concerned questions regarding British campaign finance and election laws. SCL's diffuse corporate structure enabled British officials to announce that CA hadn't violated the letter of the law. There was also speculation over the impact of CA's psychographic methodology on the outcome. While these are worthwhile questions, this section will provide a more basic description of the interactions between CA and prominent members of the pro-Brexit movement and the latter's manifold ties to Russia.

Sometime around 2010 or 2011, Steve Bannon was introduced to the founding member of the United Kingdom Independence Party (UKIP), Nigel Farage.[69] Bannon and Farage found kindred spirits in one another and discussed establishing a British Tea Party-style populist movement.[70] Bannon invited Farage to visit him in New York in the Summer of 2012.[71] In 2013, Bannon established *Breitbart London*. Farage was enlisted to write a column for the publication. In a video filmed after the successful Brexit vote, Farage raises a pint and says, "Well done, Bannon. Well done, *Breitbart*. You helped with this. Hugely."[72]

Earlier in 2013, then-British Prime Minister David Cameron had pledged to hold a simple yes/no referendum on whether Britain would remain in the EU. Nigel Farage and UKIP jumped on the Brexit bandwagon. In May of that year, Farage met with the Russian Ambassador Yakovenko and discussed the Russia-UK bilateral relationship.[73]

Farage was a regular commentator on the Russian state-backed channel *RT*. In March of 2014, Farage raised eyebrows when he told *GQ* magazine that the leader he most admired, as an "operator" if not a "human being," was Vladimir Putin.[74] In a televised debate, Farage argued that the EU had blood on its hands for "forcing" Ukraine to choose between itself and Russia.

Farage had been elected as a "Eurosceptic" Member of

the European Parliament (MEP) in 1999. A Maltese national named Kevin Ellul Bonici was a senior Farage staff member at the European Parliament. Bonici, a fluent Russian speaker educated in the former Soviet Union, frequently visited the Russian Embassy in Brussels, where he had relationships with Russian officials. "I was told in June 2015 that this gentleman had a relationship with the Russian embassy in Brussels and that every time he came back from the Russian embassy, he would return with a bootload of propaganda," a former Farage staffer told *The Guardian*.[75]

Farage also has links to Julian Assange. In February of 2011, when a European Arrest Warrant had been issued against Assange regarding a sexual assault allegation in Sweden, the office of UKIP founding member and MEP Gerrard Batten emailed Assange's lawyer, Mark Stephens, about "the possibility of meeting Mr. Julian Assange." Farage and other UKIP leaders met with UKIP donors and denounced the European Arrest Warrant against Assange. Emails later leaked to *Business Insider* suggest that Farage spoke with Assange's lawyer at the event.[76] He also reportedly attended Assange's 40th birthday party.[77]

In the Summer of 2014, Farage was introduced to a British insurance magnate named Arron Banks, who became the main financial backer of the Leave campaign. The introduction was facilitated by Farage's friend Jim Mellon, a millionaire and Oxford-educated hedge fund manager at various times based out of Russia, Hong Kong, and eventually the notorious tax haven the Isle of Man.[78] Mellon donated up to £100,000 to pro-Brexit causes.[79]

Jim Mellon earned a fortune in Russia during the privatizations of the 1990s. He has insisted that he was not involved in the investment decisions of the firm most responsible for the Russia deals, Charlemagne Capital.[80] However, he was a co-founder, non-executive director, and major shareholder. Mellon also established a firm called Regent Pacific, which, by 1997, had over $1.1 billion invested in Russia.[81]

Regent Pacific became the second largest shareholder in Uralmash, a machine-making plant in Yekaterinburg.[82] By the 1990s, when Mellon became a shareholder, the Uralmash plant was controlled by the Uralmashskaya organized crime group.[83] Regent Pacific also owned a stake in Lukoil. At one point, it engaged in a scheme to illicitly sell shares of Gazprom to foreigners. However, the scheme was discovered, and Gazprom's board was so upset that Mellon left Russia, worried that he "might end up at the bottom of the Moscow River."[84] In 2012, two oil companies based out of Trinidad and Tobago, Bayfield and Trinity, merged to form one company. Andrei Pannikov, a former KGB agent and co-founder of Lukoil, owned 20% of Bayfield, while Regent Pacific was a large investor in Trinity.[85]

Mellon connected with Arron Banks through his investment in the Isle of Man-based Conister Bank, which Banks owned. Conister was renamed Manx Financial, and they became business partners.[86] It is in Banks' personal life that we find connections to Russia. In 2001, Banks married his second wife, a Russian national named Ekaterina Paderina, known better as Katya Banks. A linguist who speaks six languages, Katya's mother worked at a language school, and her father, Evgeny Paderin, was the head of government property in Yekaterinburg.[87]

Katya's marriage to Banks was her second marriage. Three years earlier, she had married a retired merchant sailor from Portsmouth named Eric Butler. They met when Butler stumbled across Katya sunbathing topless on Portsmouth's waterfront.[88] At the time, she faced visa problems and the prospect of being deported.[89] After a whirlwind romance, Paderina suggested that Butler marry her. When Butler asked if the marriage was about love or a passport, she told him love. However, after their wedding ceremony, Paderina told him, "I do not love you. I am not married to you in Russia. And, if you ever disobey me, you will feel the full force of my father's connections." When her father arrived from Yekaterinburg to visit after the marriage, Butler claims that he bragged "about his connections with the Russian Mafia."[90]

Butler was visited by Britain's Special Branch officers, who informed him that Katya had aroused suspicion by depositing large sums of money into various private bank accounts. Butler eventually filed for divorce, and Katya was charged with assault after smashing a lampshade over his head. However, the case fell apart after Butler refused to give evidence. A local Russian threatened him on Katya's behalf, and he subsequently fled the UK.[91]

As Katya's marriage to Butler ended, she received a deportation notice. She turned to a local Liberal Democrat MP named Jack Hancock for help. Hancock provided Katya with a flat to live in. In 2010, the same year he was kicked out of a Parliamentary Group on Russian Affairs because of his "pro-Putin and pro-Medvedev" views, Hancock was revealed to be having an affair with his Parliamentary assistant, a Russian named Ekaterina Zatuliveter.

MI5 believed that the Kremlin targeted Hancock because of his many contacts and access to sensitive documents.[92] Zatuliveter also had a relationship with a diplomat from the Netherlands and a German NATO officer. After seeing her interact with an SVR officer in London, British officials came to suspect that Zatuliveter was a member of Russia's foreign intelligence agency and attempted to have her deported. However, she appealed her deportation to a special immigration panel, which determined that "on the balance of probabilities," she wasn't a Russian intelligence officer. When asked about the Zatuliveter case, former GRU agent Boris Volodarsky described the panel's findings as violating "all logic and common sense." Volodarsky believed that the SVR "were in this or that way involved in the life and further career development" of both Ekaterina Paderina (now Katya Banks) and Ekaterina Zatuliveter. Both reminded him of the Soviet practice of having beautiful women, referred to as "swallows," influence "important and promising foreign targets."[93] Arron Banks and Ekaterina Paderina were wed in 2001.

In 2014, Banks donated £1 million to UKIP. Two years later, the Banks-owned company Better for the Country Ltd (BFTC) purchased £2 million worth of pro-Brexit merchandise, which it then donated to the pro-Brexit group Grassroots Out. In the largest political donation in British history, Banks donated £6 million to a pro-Brexit campaign organization called Leave.EU. The media organization *openDemocracy* has estimated Banks' wealth to be around £21 million, while *Bloomberg* estimated his net worth to be around £25 million.[94] Given the size of the donations relative to his overall wealth, questions have been raised about whether Banks was simply a front for the money.

The UK Electoral Commission found that it had "reasonable grounds" to suspect that Banks was not the true source of the donated money and referred the matter to the National Crime Agency (NCA).[95] For unknown reasons, perhaps because it didn't want to know the answer, the NCA ignored the question of whether Banks was the true source of the donations but instead narrowed the investigation to focus solely on the legality of whether Banks could loan money to himself from Rock Holdings, which was a shareholder alongside Mellon in Manx Financial, and then have its British subsidiary Rock Services make the actual donation to BFTC and Leave.EU.[96] The NCA interpreted Banks' actions in this narrow context as legal.

In September 2015, Banks attended UKIP's annual convention with Andy Wigmore, a Eurosceptic activist and friend of both Farage and Banks. Banks and Wigmore met at the convention with a Russian diplomat and intelligence officer named Alexander Udod. Years earlier, as an undercover FSB agent, Udod had worked closely with SVR and was tasked with ensuring Western businessmen in the Far East were not spies. In 2012, Udod was transferred to Moscow and a year later sent to London as a diplomat.[97] In 2018, he was expelled from the UK along with other suspected Russian agents after the poisoning of the former GRU agent Sergei Skirpal.

While in Doncaster, Banks, Wigmore, and Udod discussed meeting with Ambassador Yakovenko. Banks and Wigmore were interested in providing Yakovenko with a briefing on Brexit.[98] On October 10th, Udod emailed Banks, informing him that Ambassador Yakovenko "would be happy to invite you for lunch at his residence" scheduled for November 6th.[99] Before their meeting with Yakovenko, Banks and Wigmore met with Cambridge Analytica.

The nature and extent of the work CA did for the leave campaign later became a matter of much controversy in the UK but is beyond the purview of this book. Suffice it to say that CA business development director Brittany Kaiser was present at the launch of Leave.EU and CA data scientists did some uncompensated work that likely did not do much to sway the outcome of the vote. Nonetheless, there were numerous interactions between the parties. Meanwhile, as Brexit approached, Banks and Wigmore had extensive meetings and discussions with Russian diplomats, businessmen, and suspected intelligence agents.

On November 6th, 2015, Banks and Wigmore traveled to Ambassador Yakovenko's residence in Kensington Gardens and had a "six-hour boozy lunch." Yakovenko poured them glasses of vodka from a bottle, one of only three specially produced for Joseph Stalin. Yakovenko wanted "the inside track" on the Brexit campaign, and Banks explained that he believed the world was "in for a shock."[100] There is no definitive account of the six-hour meeting. At some point, Yakovenko invited Banks to meet with a Russian mining magnate named Siman Povarenkin to discuss a deal regarding Russian goldmines.[101] Povarenkin had known Alexander Udod from his days working in the Russian Far East for the FSB.[102]

Banks had mining interests in South Africa and Lesotho. In 2018, *Channel 4 News* traveled to a mine Banks controlled in Lesotho and spoke to employees who told them that no diamonds had been found in the three years the mine had been operational. *Channel 4* further uncovered an allegation made in a South African court by one of Banks' business partners claiming that Banks had traveled to Russia to discuss investment in his mining operations.[103]

The South African Hawks, akin to the FBI, investigated Banks for using his mines to launder diamonds from other parts of Africa, a practice known as "salting the mines."[104] As of this writing, Britain's National Crime Agency is investigating whether Banks was sourcing black market diamonds from Zimbabwe. Banks' partner claimed that he was "dealing with Russians" and trying "to marry... illegally gotten diamonds" with the low output of his own mining operations.[105] Officials in both South Africa and Zimbabwe believe that Russian intelligence has controlled the underground diamond trade in Zimbabwe's capital, Harare, for over a decade.[106]

On November 17th, Banks and Wigmore had tea with Yakovenko and Siman Povarenkin, owner of GeoProMining.[107] A presentation titled "Russian gold sector consolidation play" outlined a proposal in which GeoProMining would merge with competing mining firms to form an $8 billion gold mining giant. The deal was to be backed by Sberbank.[108] The next day, Leave.EU kicked off its official pro-Brexit campaign, with representatives from CA present at the launch press conference. Banks wrote to Povarenkin later that day, informing him that he had alerted his business partner and fellow Brexiter James Mellon of the opportunity.[109]

Povarenkin also offered Banks a different sweetheart deal involving the Russian diamond mining giant Alrosa. The Russian government, Alrosa's largest shareholder, planned to sell a 10% stake in the company. The sale was to be offered to a private group of investors and was expected to raise $800 million.[110] Since 2013, Alrosa, the world's largest diamond producer by output, had been conducting geological surveys and mining in Zimbabwe. However, in 2016, Alrosa briefly lost its licenses due to reforms in the country's diamond industry.[111]

Banks visited Russia in February of 2016.[112] Documents leaked to the press suggest that Banks met with high-level officials from Sberbank.[113] He claimed that his trip to Moscow was a family vacation and that he held no meetings but instead visited the Hermitage and went on a river cruise.[114] It has been pointed out that the Moscow River is mostly frozen in February, and the Hermitage is in St. Petersburg. On March 15th, 2016, Banks donated his first £1 million to Leave.EU, which by April 21st ballooned to £6 million in donations.

In April 2016, Banks received an offer regarding the sale of a goldmine in Guinea. The owner of the mine, Ilya Karas, CEO of the Moscow-based Farafina Gold Group, met with Banks in Bristol in "mid-2016" to discuss a $3.5 million investment into the mine. Karas claimed that nothing came of the deal.[115] Three days before the referendum, Andy Wigmore invited Yakovenko and Udod to attend a results watch party. Udod said the Ambassador would be on a flight to Moscow but that he would love to attend.[116]

Britain's domestic security services asked then-Foreign Secretary Theresa May for permission to investigate Banks. May quashed the investigation as it was too politically explosive.[117] The referendum was held on June 23rd, 2016. That day, Russian troll accounts linked to the Internet Research Agency tweeted 1,104 messages with the hashtag #ReasonsToLeaveEU.[118] To the shock of much of the world, voters in the UK voted to leave the European Union 51.9% to 48.1%.

While Banks didn't pursue any Russian mining deals, the Russian government sold a 10.9% stake in Alrosa three weeks after the Brexit vote. Among the investors allowed to participate in the sale was James Mellon's Charlemagne Capital.[119] Between 2017 and 2018, Banks' ownership stake in Manx Financial, which he held through Rene Nominees (IOM) Ltd, went up from 25.76% in 2016[120] to 29.1% in 2017.[121]

Cambridge Analytica started working on Ted Cruz's presidential campaign in the fall of 2014.[122] Three weeks before CA joined the American presidential race, Vincent Tchenguiz sold his shares of SCL Group, potentially indicating they foresaw problems with his association with the company.[123] The Cruz campaign didn't have them sign a non-compete agreement, so Alexander Nix was free to pursue other opportunities in America. One of those candidates was Trump.

Steve Bannon had been introduced to Donald Trump in 2011 by David Bossie, the head of the conservative 501(c)(4) Citizens United. Bannon met with Trump in Trump Tower to discuss a potential run against Obama. While Trump ultimately decided against it, he and Bannon stayed in contact, and Breitbart provided Trump with favorable coverage.[124] Bannon pushed for CA to meet with Trump and his team even before he announced his candidacy. By May 2015, CA had internal discussions about possibly signing a commercial agreement with the Trump Organization to support its business interests.[125]

In mid-September 2015, Alexander Nix and Brittany Kaiser traveled to Washington to meet with Bannon. During the meeting, Bannon received a call from Trump, who was still in the early stages of his presidential run. The following day, a meeting with Corey Lewandowski was scheduled for Nix and Kaiser. On the train ride to New York, Nix told Kaiser that Trump was only "technically" running for President and that, in fact, what Trump was really doing was a promotional stunt to prepare the way for the launch of Trump TV. Bannon reportedly had been involved in the conception of Trump TV, and the funding was to come from the Mercers, all of whom hoped to use it to promote their unique brand of right-wing politics.[126]

Nix and Kaiser pitched Corey Lewandowsky the following day, but it would be months before the campaign officially hired Cambridge Analytica. In the Spring of 2016, CA began yet again to aggressively pursue work on behalf of the Trump campaign. Following Lewandowsky's dismissal from the campaign, Nix was in discussions with Trump's campaign leadership, including Paul Manafort, Jared Kushner, and Brad Parscale.[127] Despite Manafort and Gates's skepticism, CA's connections to the Mercers proved convincing, and it was eventually hired to work with Parscale's digital operation. CA set up offices in New York and San Antonio, where Parscale had established the campaign's digital headquarters. When CA staff arrived, they found Parscale's operation in disarray, with no voter models, without a functioning marketing apparatus, and five separate pollsters working at cross purposes.[128]

After negative press about Manafort's activities in Ukraine roiled an already chaotic campaign, Rebekah Mercer called Trump personally. She arranged for Manafort to be replaced by Steve Bannon as the head of the campaign.[129] With Bannon and the Mercers now firmly ensconced at the top of the Trump campaign, CA's position was secure.

Even though CA had amassed a vast trove of data about American voters, much of which came from Facebook, the data they used on the Trump campaign came from the RNC's database. Nor was its much-vaunted psychographic modeling used, deemed to take too long. Instead, CA data scientists focused on modeling qualities like "propensity to donate."[130]

CA paid for surveys to be conducted in sixteen swing states, then used the data to divide the voters into various pro-Trump and pro-Clinton segments of voters. A major category within the Clinton segment of voters was labeled under *deterrence*. These were Clinton supporters who CA and the Trump Campaign believed could be dissuaded from voting. In this way, the Trump campaign's tactics dovetailed perfectly with those of the IRA in St. Petersburg.

"We have three major voter suppression operations underway," a senior Trump official told *Bloomberg* in the final days of the Campaign. The three groups targeted were idealistic white liberals, young women, and African Americans. The Trump campaign trumpeted the WikiLeaks emails to turn Bernie Sanders supporters away from Clinton. It used Bill Clinton's sexual improprieties to target women. Finally, it hammered away at Hillary Clinton's comments in the 1990s about "Super Predators" to hurt her standing in the black community.[131] *Channel 4 News* later revealed that 3.5 million African Americans were categorized under *deterrence*.[132]

Meanwhile, the "Bad Boys of Brexit" were taking a victory lap following Brexit. On the eve of the Republican National Convention in Cleveland, Nigel Farage, Andy Wigmore, and a young Farage advisor and head of fundraising for UKIP named George Cottrell flew to the convention from London. Banks had intended to go but was prevented by illness.[133]

During the Convention, Roger Stone arranged to have dinner with Farage and Wigmore, along with Alex Jones, the notorious American conspiracist and host of *InfoWars*. A group of documentary filmmakers was trailing stone at the time. A Farage aide insisted they not film the dinner. What Stone, Jones, and Farage discussed that evening is not known. The fact that the dinner took place days before the WikiLeaks DNC email leaks, that Roger Stone claimed to be in contact with Assange via an intermediary, and that Farage was known to have associated with Assange in the past has led to speculation that WikiLeaks was discussed. "What was so noticeable," one of the documentarians later said, "was how Alex Jones was so pumped up afterwards about the leaks that were coming. He was saying it openly on his show. And then days later, the DNC leaks dropped and blew apart the Democratic National Convention."[134]

On the final night of the Republican Convention, Farage and Wigmore went for a late-night drink at the bar of the Hilton Hotel, where they had a chance encounter with a group of staffers for the Republican governor of Mississippi, Phil Bryant, who had been an avid Brexit supporter from afar.[135] A formal invitation from Governor Bryant for Farage to visit Mississippi was emailed to Farage's staff the next day.[136]

On their way back to London from the convention, Farage's chief of staff and UKIP's deputy treasurer, an aristocratic 22-year-old named George Cottrell, was arrested at Chicago O'Hare on charges of blackmail and money laundering.[137] "Posh George" hailed from a wealthy family. His mother had once been romantically linked to Prince Charles. His uncle, Lord Hesketh, was a former Conservative Party treasurer who joined UKIP in 2011.[138]

In 2014, Cottrell had been in contact with undercover IRS agents on a Tor network black-market website. Posing as drug traffickers, the undercover agents got Cottrell to agree to launder between $50-150,000 per month by transferring it to offshore accounts.[139] He later blamed his crimes on a gambling addiction. At 19, Cottrell helped set up a multi-billion dollar private office in Mayfair for a well-known "international family," whose identity is unknown. The job taught him about shadow banking, offshore accounts, and constructing elaborate financial structures using international secrecy jurisdictions.[140]

Cottrell went on to become what *The Telegraph* described as "a London-based banker for an offshore private bank (which was under investigation by the US authorities as a 'foreign financial institution of primary money-laundering concern')." While the paper didn't name the bank, Cottrell listed Banca Privada d'Andorra (BPA) amid his "Interests" on LinkedIn.[141] In March 2015, the US listed BPA as a "primary money laundering concern," accusing the bank of laundering money on behalf of Russian and Chinese organized crime. A manager at BPA had assisted the Russian money launderer Andrei Petrov, who was arrested by Spanish authorities in 2013 and suspected of having links to Semyon Mogilevich.[142]

Cottrell was one of only 71 people to list an interest in Moldindconbank, which had been involved in a multi-billion dollar money laundering scheme known as the Russian Laundromat.[143] Yet another Russian-linked Interest of Cottrell's on LinkedIn was the bank FBME, a Tanzanian-registered entity with offices in Cyprus and Russia that was later linked to Syria's chemical weapons program, the Russian government, and major figures within international organized crime.[144] Other Russian financial institutions listed among Cottrell's interests included VTB and Alfa Bank. Cottrell pleaded guilty in December of 2016 and spent eight months in American prison before being released and returning to the UK.

On August 19th, 2016, Banks and Wigmore visited Ambassador Yakovenko at his London residence.[145] Three weeks earlier, Yakovenko attended a polo match with Alexander Nix.[146] He had much to discuss with the victorious backers of Brexit. Banks and Farage's friend Steve Bannon had just been installed as CEO of the Trump campaign. Farage had learned that Trump would be in Mississippi at the same time he was.[147] The three talked about the Trump campaign and that Banks and Wigmore would be traveling to Mississippi in the coming days with Farage, where they would meet with Donald Trump. The content of their discussions is unknown. However, George Cottrell's recent arrest was a topic of conversation. The next day, Wigmore sent an email with the subject "Fw Cottrell Docs - Eyes Only" to Sergey Fedichkin, the third secretary at the Russian Embassy, with the message, "Have fun with this." The email contained six attachments of legal documents related to Cottrell's case in

Arizona.[148] Why Banks and Wigmore shared these documents with the Russian embassy remains unknown.

Two days later, Banks, Wigmore, and Farage were going to Mississippi to meet Donald Trump. After three "filthy cappuccino martinis" each and four bottles of wine drunk in transit, the three Brits arrived in Jackson.[149] Farage was first scheduled to speak at a fundraiser dinner. Trump sought Farage out at a cocktail reception before their speeches. "Donald says a few words," Farage later recalled to *The New Yorker*. "And he says, 'Where's that? Where's Nigel? Where's the Brexit guy?' So I go up. He gives me a big hug, and he says, 'This guy is smart. This guy is smart. We've got to do what he does.'"

Later in the trip, Trump introduced Farage at a rally before 15,000 supporters. Farage, who had discussed his planned remarks with Steve Bannon before making them, electrified the crowd by thundering, "If I was an American citizen, I wouldn't vote for Hillary Clinton if you paid me. In fact, I wouldn't vote for Hillary Clinton if SHE paid me!" He then hammered away at the populist message he and Bannon had delivered to the British electorate to devastating effect. "Folks, the message is clear, the parallels are there. . . . Remember, anything is possible if enough decent people are prepared to stand up against the establishment."

Farage made several other stops on the campaign, attending the Presidential Debates in St. Louis and Las Vegas and another Trump rally in Michigan. Farage's expenses were covered by Banks, who accompanied him to the debate in Las Vegas.[150] "We are in daily contact with the Trump campaign—Brexit playbook!" Banks wrote in a Twitter direct message (DM).[151]

On the night of the election, Banks, Wigmore, and Farage stayed at the Waldorf Astoria Hotel in Manhattan, again on Banks' dime, to watch the returns come in. That evening, Brittany Kaiser, Alexander Nix, Robert and Rebekah Mercer of Cambridge Analytica huddled together at the Trump campaign party in New York. Kaiser claims that she and Nix were convinced Trump would lose. At 2 am, she tapped Rebekah on the shoulder to show her a television monitor reporting that *The Washington Post* had called the election for Trump.[152] The Mercers were now arguably the most influential political donors in the United States. One man who doesn't appear to have been surprised by Trump's victory was Vincent Tchenguiz, who collected £1.2 million after betting that Donald Trump would be the next President of the United States.[153]

Following Trump's victory, Banks boasted of their access to the incoming administration. "Nigel and Donald love each other," Banks wrote in a Twitter DM soon after Trump won the election. "The media don't really get how deep the links go."

[1] Report of the Select Committee on Intelligence United States Senate On Russian Active Measures Campaigns And Interference in the 2016 US Election Volume 5: Counterintelligence Threats and Vulnerabilities. Pg. 663

[2] Report of the Select Committee on Intelligence United States Senate On Russian Active Measures Campaigns And Interference in the 2016 US Election Volume 5: Counterintelligence Threats and Vulnerabilities. Pg. 663

[3] Cadwalladr, Carrole. "Robert Mercer: the big data billionaire waging war on mainstream media," *The Guardian*. February 26th, 2017

[4] Knight, Sam. "Life Inside S.C.L., Cambridge Analytica's Parent Company," *The New Yorker*. March 26th, 2018

[5] Kaiser, Brittany. *Targeted: The Cambridge Analytica Whistleblower's Inside Story of How Big Data, Trump, and Facebook Broke Democracy and How It Can Happen Again.* New York, NY: HarperCollins, 2019. Pg. 26

[6] Kaiser, Brittany. *Targeted: The Cambridge Analytica Whistleblower's Inside Story of How Big Data, Trump, and Facebook Broke Democracy and How It Can Happen Again.* New York, NY: HarperCollins, 2019. Pg. 26

[7] "Cambridge Analytica: The data firm's global influence," *BBC News*. March 22nd, 2018

[8] Nikitina, Yulia. "The 'Color Revolutions' and 'Arab Spring' in Russian Official Discourse," Partnership for Peace Consortium of Defense Academies and Security Studies Institutes, *Connections*, Winter 2014, Vol. 14, No. 1 (Winter 2014), pp. 87-104

[9] Weinberger, Sharon. "You Can't Handle The Truth: Psy-Ops propaganda goes mainstream," *Slate*. September 19th, 2005

[10] Watt, Holly; Osborne, Hilary. "Tory donors among investors in Cambridge Analytica parent firm," *The Guardian*. March 21st, 2018

[11] Davidson, Andrew. "Fraudbusters can shell out £100m for my next party," *The Sunday Times*. June 24th, 2012

[12] Behar, Richard. "Capitalism In A Cold Climate," *Fortune*. June 12th, 2000

[13] Marlowe, Ann. "Will Donald Trump's Data-Analytics Company Allow Russia To Access Research On U.S. Citizens?" *Tablet*. August 22nd, 2016

[14] Hill, Amelia; Syal, Rajeev; Harding, Luke; Harris, Paul. "Anna Chapman: Diplomat's daughter who partied with billionaires," *The Guardian*. June 30th, 2010

[15] Baker, Peter; Weiser, Benjamin. "Russian Spy Suspects Plead Guilty as Part of a Swap," *The New York Times*. July 8th, 2010

[16] Davíðsdóttir, Sigrún; Mason, Rowena. "Kaupthing approved £1.69bn loans for Arsenal backer Alisher Usmanov prior to collapse," *The Telegraph*. January 20th, 2011

[17] Weaver, Courtney. "Partner breaks silence over Usmanov deals," *The Financial Times*. November 22nd, 2012

[18] Bowers, Simon. "Tchenguiz and friend trade blows over 'consultancy' payments," *The Guardian*. March 8th, 2012

[19] Entous, Adam; Farrow, Ronan. "Private Mossad For Hire," *The New Yorker*. February 11th, 2019

[20] "Cambridge Analytica-linked businessman helped start Black Cube, lawsuit claims," *The Times of Israel.* August 23rd, 2018

[21] Hammond, Ed. "SFO errors in Vincent Tchenguiz probe," *The Financial Times*. December 23rd, 2011

[22] Ron, Omri. "Black Cube was hired out by the Defense Ministry, operated out of intel base," *The Jerusalem Post*. August 24th, 2019

[23] Farrow, Ronan. "Harvey Weinstein's Army of Spies," *The New Yorker*. November 6th, 2017

[24] Megiddo, Gur. "Black Cube, a Late Mossad chief, and a Rogue Op Against a Top Romanian Official," *Haaretz*. October 21st, 2020

[25] Bayer, Lili. "Israeli intelligence firm targeted NGO's during Hungary's election campaign," *Politico*. July 6th, 2018

[26] Hope, Bradley; McNish, Jacquie. "Black Cube: The Bumbling Spies of the 'Private Mossad,'" *The Wall Street Journal*. June 18th, 2019

[27] Hilder, Paul. "'They were planning on stealing the election': Explosive new tapes reveal Cambridge Analytica CEO's boasts of voter suppression, manipulation and bribery," *openDemocracy*. January 28th, 2019

[28] Christopher Wylie Background Papers, Provided to UK Parliament. Pg. 117

[29] Witt, Jesse; Pasternak, Alex. "Before Trump, Cambridge Analytica quietly built "Psy Ops" for militaries," *Fast Company*. September 25th, 2019

[30] Day, Chad; Braun, Stephen. "Flynn files new financial form reporting ties to data firm," *The Associated Press*. August 4th, 2017

[31] Report of the Select Committee on Intelligence United States Senate On Russian Active Measures Campaigns And Interference in the 2016 US Election Volume 5: Counterintelligence Threats and Vulnerabilities. Pg. 664

[32] Knight, Sam. "Life Inside S.C.L., Cambridge Analytica's Parent Company," *The New Yorker*. March 26th, 2018

[33] Kaiser, Brittany. *Targeted: The Cambridge Analytica Whistleblower's Inside Story of How Big Data, Trump, and Facebook Broke Democracy and How It Can Happen Again*. New York, NY: HarperCollins, 2019. Pg. 96-99

[34] Report of the Select Committee on Intelligence United States Senate On Russian Active Measures Campaigns And Interference in the 2016 US Election Volume 5: Counterintelligence Threats and Vulnerabilities. Pg. 664

[35] Wylie, Christopher. *Mindf*ck: Cambridge Analytica And The Plot To Break America*. New York, NY: Random House, 2019. Pg. 43

[36] Wylie, Christopher. *Mindf*ck: Cambridge Analytica And The Plot To Break America*. New York, NY: Random House, 2019. Pg. 47-50

[37] Hilder, Paul. "'They were planning on stealing the election': Explosive new tapes reveal Cambridge Analytica CEO's boasts of voter suppression, manipulation and bribery," *openDemocracy*. January 28th, 2019

[38] Witt, Jesse; Pasternak, Alex. "Before Trump, Cambridge Analytica quietly built "Psy Ops" for militaries," *Fast Company*. September 25th, 2019

[39] Kaiser, Brittany. *Targeted: The Cambridge Analytica Whistleblower's Inside Story of How Big Data, Trump, and Facebook Broke Democracy and How It Can Happen Again*. New York, NY: HarperCollins, 2019. Pg. 101

[40] Kroll, Andy. "Cloak and Data: The Real Story Behind Cambridge Analytica's Rise and Fall," *Mother Jones*. May/June 2018

[41] Kaiser, Brittany. *Targeted: The Cambridge Analytica Whistleblower's Inside Story of How Big Data, Trump, and Facebook Broke Democracy and How It Can Happen Again*. New York, NY: HarperCollins, 2019. Pg. 82-85

[42] Kroll, Andy. "Cloak and Data: The Real Story Behind Cambridge Analytica's Rise and Fall," *Mother Jones*. May/June 2018

[43] Dewey, Richard; Moallemi, Ciamac. "The Unsolved Mystery of the Medallion Fund's Success," *Bloomberg*. November 12th, 2019

[44] Zuckerman, Gregory. *The Man Who Solved The Market: How Jim Simons Launched The Quant Revolution*. New York, NY:Portfolio/Penguin, 2019. Pg. xvi

[45] Boag, Keith. "Money man: Reclusive U.S. billionaire Robert Mercer helped Trump win the presidency. But what is his ultimate goal?" *CBC*

[46] Friedersdorf, Connor. "How Breitbart Destroyed Andrew Breitbart's Legacy," *The Atlantic*. November 14th, 2017

[47] Green, Joshua. *Devil's Bargain: Steve Bannon, Donald Trump, And The Nationalist Uprising*. New York, NY: Penguin Books, 2017. Pg. 204-208

[48] Horowitz, Jason. "Steve Bannon Cited Italian Thinker Who Inspired Fascists," *The New York Times*. February 10th, 2017

[49] Lapowsky, Issie. "The Man Who Saw The Danger Of Cambridge Analytica Years Ago," *Wired*. June 19th, 2018

[50] Report of the Select Committee on Intelligence United States Senate On Russian Active Measures Campaigns And Interference in the 2016 US Election Volume 5: Counterintelligence Threats and Vulnerabilities. Pg. 669

[51] Kang, Cecilia; Frenkel, Sheera. "Facebook Says Cambridge Analytica Harvested Data of Up to 87 Million Users," *The New York Times*. April 4th, 2018

[52] Cadwalladr, Carole; Graham-Harrison, Emma. "Cambridge Analytica: links to Moscow oil firm and St. Petersburg university," *The Guardian*. March 17th, 2018

[53] Wylie, Christopher. *Mindf*ck: Cambridge Analytica And The Plot To Break America*. New York, NY: Random House, 2019. Pg. 78

[54] Report of the Select Committee on Intelligence United States Senate On Russian Active Measures Campaigns And Interference in the 2016 US Election Volume 5: Counterintelligence Threats and Vulnerabilities. Pg. 669

[55] Wylie, Christopher. *Mindf*ck: Cambridge Analytica And The Plot To Break America*. New York, NY: Random House, 2019. Pg. 138

[56] United States of America v. Elena Alekseevna Khusyaynova, Criminal Complaint. *United States District Court for the Eastern District of Virginia*. Case No. 1:18-MJ-464. September 28th, 2018. Pg. 4

[57] Roberts, Dan. "Sweeping new US and EU sanctions target Russia's banks and oil companies," *The Guardian*. September 12th, 2014

[58] Belton, Catherine. *Putin's People: How The KGB Took Back Russia And Then Took On The West*. New York, NY: Farrar, Straus and Giroux, 2020. Pg. 218

[59] Wylie, Christopher. *Mindf*ck: Cambridge Analytica And The Plot To Break America*. New York, NY: Random House, 2019. Pg. 151

[60] Report of the Select Committee on Intelligence United States Senate On Russian Active Measures Campaigns And Interference in the 2016 US Election Volume 5: Counterintelligence Threats and Vulnerabilities. Pg. 668

[61] Patten, Sam. "Kostya and Me: How Sam Patten Got Ensnared in Mueller's Probe," *Wired*. August 14th, 2019

[62] Markay, Lachlan. "Accused Russian Intel Asset Teamed Up With GOP Operative," *The Daily Beast*. April 4th, 2018

[63] Patten, Sam. "Kostya and Me: How Sam Patten Got Ensnared in Mueller's Probe," *Wired*. August 14th, 2019

[64] Wylie, Christopher. *Mindf*ck: Cambridge Analytica And The Plot To Break America*. New York, NY: Random House, 2019. Pg. 137

[65] Report of the Select Committee on Intelligence United States Senate On Russian Active Measures Campaigns And Interference in the 2016 US Election Volume 5: Counterintelligence Threats and Vulnerabilities. Pg. 668

[66] Report of the Select Committee on Intelligence United States Senate On Russian Active Measures Campaigns And Interference in the 2016 US Election Volume 5: Counterintelligence Threats and Vulnerabilities. Pg. 49 [Footnote 213]

[67] Bertrand, Natasha. "A Suspected Russian Spy, With Curious Ties to Washington," *The Atlantic*. April 6th, 2018

[68] Feder, J. Lester. "This Is How Steve Bannon Sees The Entire World," *BuzzFeed News*. November 15th, 2016

[69] Jukes, Peter. "Nigel Farage and Boris Johnson Adviser Steve Bannon Implicated in Mueller Investigation," *Byline Times*. January 25th, 2019

[70] Jukes, Peter. "The Trans-Atlantic Triumph of Trumpism: Boris Johnson A Plan Years In The Making," *Byline Times*. June 21st, 2019

[71] Knight, Sam. "Nigel Farage On The Story Behind His Friendship With Trump," *The New Yorker*. November 30th, 2016

[72] "Watch deleted video of Nigel Farage thanking Steve Bannon and Breitbart for Brexit," *The New European*. April 6th, 2018

[73] Press Release. "Ambassador Yakovenko Meets Nigel Farage," *The Embassy of the Russian Federation to the United Kingdom of Great Britain and Northern Ireland*. May 13th, 2013

[74] "Nigel Farage: I admire Vladimir Putin," *The Guardian*. March 31st, 2014

[75] Kirchgaessner, Stephanie. "The Farage Staffer, the Russian Embassy and a smear campaign against a Kremlin critic," *The Guardian*. December 18th, 2017

[76] Bienkov, Adam. "Leaked emails reveal Nigel Farage's long-standing links to Julian Assange," *Business Insider*. March 10th, 2017

[77] Patrick, James. "We Need To Talk About Nigel…" *Byine*. November 6th, 2017

[78] Campbell, Iain. "Revealed: How Arron Banks's campaign 'ambassador' made his millions in Russia," *openDemocracy*. November 10th, 2018

[79] Hope, Christopher. "Millionaire Jim Mellon backs £20million 'anti-politics' campaign to leave EU as name revealed," *The Telegraph*. July 11th, 2015

[80] "8 key myths and inconsistencies in the Open Democracy article about Jim Mellon," *JimMellonRussia*. January 31st, 2020

[81] Clifford, Mark Lambert. "The Bad Boys Of Emerging Markets," *Bloomberg*. June 22nd, 1997

[82] Campbell, Iain. "Revealed: How Arron Banks's campaign 'ambassador' made his millions in Russia," *openDemocracy*. November 10th, 2018

[83] Handelman, Stephen. "Inside Russia's Gangster Economy," *The New York Times*. January 24th, 1993

[84] Campbell, Iain. "Revealed: How Arron Banks's campaign 'ambassador' made his millions in Russia," *openDemocracy*. November 10th, 2018

[85] Campbell, Iain. "Revealed: How Arron Banks's campaign 'ambassador' made his millions in Russia," *openDemocracy*. November 10th, 2018

[86] Campbell, Iain. "Revealed: How Arron Banks's campaign 'ambassador' made his millions in Russia," *openDemocracy*. November 10th, 2018

[87] Harper, Tom. "From Urals to Ukip: racy tale of Arron Banks's Russian wife," *The Times of London*. September 10th, 2017

[88] Caesar, Ed. "The Chaotic Triumph Of Arron Banks, The "Bad Boy Of Brexit," *The New Yorker*. March 18th, 2019

[89] Swinford, Steven. "Russian 'spy' case: Liberal Democrat MP 'helped second Russian girl'," *The Telegraph*. December 7th, 2010

[90] Caesar, Ed. "The Chaotic Triumph Of Arron Banks, The "Bad Boy Of Brexit," *The New Yorker*. March 18th, 2019

[91] Harper, Tom. "From Urals to Ukip: racy tale of Arron Banks's Russian wife," *The Times of London*. September 10th, 2017

[92] Kennedy, Dominic. "Arron Banks profile: The Brexiteer, his Russian wife and their family runabout: MI5 SPY," *The Times of London*. November 1st, 2018

[93] Caesar, Ed. "The Chaotic Triumph Of Arron Banks, The "Bad Boy Of Brexit," *The New Yorker*. March 18th, 2019

[94] Metcalf, Tom; Baker, Stephanie. "The Mysterious Finances of the Brexit Campaign's Biggest Backer," *Bloomberg*. February 23rd, 2019

[95] "Public statement on NCA investigation into suspected EU referendum offences," *UK National Crime Agency*. September 24th, 2019

[96] Rudolph, Josh; Morley, Thomas. "Covert Foreign Money: Financial loopholes exploited by authoritarians to fund political interference in democracies," *alliance for securing democracy*. August 2020. Pg. 19

[97] Harding, Luke. *Shadow State: Murder, Mayhem, and Russia's Remaking of the West*. New

York, NY: HarperCollins Publishers, 2020. Pg. 178-179

[98] Roig-Franzia, Manuel; Helderman, Rosalind S.; Booth, William; Hamburger, Tom. "How the 'Bad Boys of Brexit' forged ties with Russia and the Trump campaign — and came under investigators' scrutiny," *The Washington Post.* June 28th, 2018

[99] "Email trail shows how Arron Banks and Andy Wigmore were cultivated," *The Sunday Times.* June 10th, 2018

[100] Banks, Arron. *The Bad Boys of Brexit: Tales Of Mischief, Mayhem & Guerrilla Warfare In The EU Referendum Campaign.* London, UK: Biteback Publishing Ltd, 2016, 2017. Pg. 95-97

[101] Kirkpatrick, David D.; Rosenberg, Matthew. "Russians Offered Business Deals to Brexit's Biggest Backer," *The New York Times.* June 29th, 2018

[102] Harding, Luke. *Shadow State: Murder, Mayhem, and Russia's Remaking of the West.* New York, NY: HarperCollins Publishers, 2020. Pg. 178-188

[103] "Long Read: The Arron Banks allegations," *Channel 4 News.* July 27th, 218

[104] Caesar, Ed. "The Chaotic Triumph Of Arron Banks, The "Bad Boy Of Brexit," *The New Yorker.* March 18th, 2019

[105] Harper, Tom; Wheeler, Caroline; Ostanin, Iggy. "Smuggling claims cast shadow over Brexit's £8m diamond geezer Arron Banks," *The Sunday Times.* August 11th, 2019

[106] Rudolph, Josh; Morley, Thomas. "Covert Foreign Money: Financial loopholes exploited by authoritarians to fund political interference in democracies," *alliance for securing democracy.* August 2020. Pg. 20

[107] Farand, Chloe. "The Russian Magnate, 'Goldfinger' and Ex-Army Chief Discussing Siberian Gold Mine Deals With Arron Banks," *DeSmogUK.* June 13th, 2018

[108] Harding, Luke. "Revealed: details of exclusive Russian deal offered to Arron Banks in Brexit run-up," *The Guardian.* August 9th, 2018

[109] "The Banks Files: How Brexit 'bad boy' Arron Banks was eyeing a massive Russian gold deal," *Channel 4 News.* March 5th, 2019

[110] Kirkpatrick, David D.; Rosenberg, Matthew. "Russians Offered Business Deals to Brexit's Biggest Backer," *The New York Times.* June 29th, 2018

[111] "Russia's Alrosa returns to diamond exploration in Zimbabwe," *Reuters.* January 14th, 2019

[112] "Email trail shows how Arron Banks and Andy Wigmore were cultivated," *The Sunday Times.* June 10th, 2018

[113] Cadwalladr, Carole; Jukes, Peter. "Arron Banks 'met Russian officials multiple times before Brexit vote'," *The Guardian.* June 9th, 2018

[114] Kerbaj, Richard; Wheeler, Caroline; Shipman, Tim; Harper, Tom. "Revealed: Brexit backer Arron Banks's golden Kremlin connection," *The Times of London.* June 10th, 2018

[115] Harding, Luke. *Shadow State: Murder, Mayhem, and Russia's Remaking of the West.* New York, NY: HarperCollins Publishers, 2020. Pg. 191-192

[116] Harding, Luke. *Shadow State: Murder, Mayhem, and Russia's Remaking of the West.* New York, NY: HarperCollins Publishers, 2020. Pg. 196

[117] Pendlebury, Richard; Middleton, Joe. "Theresa May STOPPED security services probing Arron Banks in run-up to Brexit referendum - as ex-Culture Secretary says PM 'has serious questions to answer'," *The Daily Mail.* November 1st, 2018

[118] Field, Matthew; Wright, Mike. "Russian trolls sent thousands of pro-Leave messages on day of Brexit referendum, Twitter data reveals," *The Telegraph.* October 17th, 2017

[119] Kirkpatrick, David D.; Rosenberg, Matthew. "Russians Offered Business Deals to Brexit's Biggest Backer," *The New York Times.* June 29th, 2018

[120] Manx Financial Group Annual Report 2016. Pg. 6

[121] Manx Financial Group Annual Report 2017. Pg. 7

[122] Kaiser, Brittany. *Targeted: The Cambridge Analytica Whistleblower's Inside Story of How Big Data, Trump, and Facebook Broke Democracy and How It Can Happen Again.* New York, NY: HarperCollins, 2019. Pg. 69

[123] Vendor/Receipt Profile: Cambridge Analytica, 2016. OpenSecrets.org. Center for

Responsive Politics.

[124] Mayer, Jane. "The Reclusive Hedge-Fund Tycoon Behind The Trump Presidency," *The New Yorker*. March 17th, 2017

[125] Report of the Select Committee on Intelligence United States Senate On Russian Active Measures Campaigns And Interference in the 2016 US Election Volume 5: Counterintelligence Threats and Vulnerabilities. Pg. 673

[126] Kaiser, Brittany. *Targeted: The Cambridge Analytica Whistleblower's Inside Story of How Big Data, Trump, and Facebook Broke Democracy and How It Can Happen Again*. New York, NY: HarperCollins, 2019. Pg. 119

[127] Alexander Nix HPSCI Interview. December 14th, 2017. Pg. 9

[128] Kaiser, Brittany. *Targeted: The Cambridge Analytica Whistleblower's Inside Story of How Big Data, Trump, and Facebook Broke Democracy and How It Can Happen Again*. New York, NY: HarperCollins, 2019. Pg. 192

[129] Woodward, Bob. *Fear: Trump In The White House*. New York, NY: Simon & Schuster, 2018. Pg. 9.

[130] Kaiser, Brittany. *Targeted: The Cambridge Analytica Whistleblower's Inside Story of How Big Data, Trump, and Facebook Broke Democracy and How It Can Happen Again*. New York, NY: HarperCollins, 2019. Pg. 218-223

[131] Green, Joshua; Issenberg, Sasha. "Inside the Trump Bunker, With Days to Go," *Bloomberg*. October 27th, 2016

[132] "Revealed: Trump campaign strategy to deter millions of Black Americans from voting in 2016," *Channel 4 News*. September 28th, 2020

[133] Banks, Arron. *The Bad Boys Of Brexit: Tales of Mischief, Mayhem & Guerrilla Warfare In The EU Referendum Campaign*. London, UK: Biteback Publishing Lt. 2017. Pg. 323

[134] Cadwalladr, Carole. "Who is the real Nigel Farage... and why won't he answer my questions?," *The Guardian*. November 25th, 2018

[135] Roig-Franzia, Manuel; Helderman, Rosalind S.; Booth, William; Hamburger, Tom. "How the 'Bad Boys of Brexit' forged ties with Russia and the Trump campaign — and came under investigators' scrutiny," *The Washington Post*. June 28th, 2018

[136] Ganuchaeu, Adam. "How Donald Trump and Nigel Farage met in Mississippi," *Mississippi Today*. November 15th, 2016

[137] "Ukip aide indicted in US on charges of blackmail and money laundering," *The Guardian*. August 13th, 2016

[138] Henry, Robin; Harnden, Toby. "My crooked son was saved by Ukip," *The Times of London*. January 8th, 2017

[139] United States of America v.s George Swinfen Cottrell. Indictment. The United States District Court For The District Of Arizona. July 19th, 2016. Pg. 1-2

[140] Cash, William. "Nigel Farage's fixer and convicted fraudster, George Cottrell, on how he survived US prison," *The Telegraph*. July 14th, 2017

[141] Hines, Nico. "Meet 'Posh George': The Shady Money Man Tangled Up With Brexit, Russia, and Trump," *The Daily Beast*. December 28th, 2017

[142] Press Release. "FinCEN Names Banca Privada d'Andorra a Foreign Financial Institution of Primary Money Laundering Concern," *U.S. Department of the Treasury's Financial Crimes Enforcement Network (FinCEN)*. March 10th, 2015

[143] "The Russian Laundromat Exposed," *Organized Crime and Corruption Reporting Project*. March 20th, 2017

[144] Warren, Tom; Campbell, Alex. "Revealed: The Secrets Of One Of The World's Dirtiest Banks And Its Powerful Western Protectors," *BuzzFeed News*. December 12th, 2017

[145] Cadwalladr, Carole; Jukes, Peter. "Arron Banks 'met Russian officials multiple times before Brexit vote'" *The Guardian*. June 9th, 2018

[146] "Here (Was Once) a Photo of Cambridge Analytica's CEO With the Russian Ambassador to the UK," *Mother Jones*. March 20th, 2018

[147] Knight, Sam. "Nigel Farage On The Story Behind His Friendship With Trump," *The*

New Yorker. November 30th, 2016

[148] Cadwalladr, Carole; Jukes, Peter. "Leave.EU faces new questions over contacts with Russia," *The Guardian.* June 16th, 2018

[149] Banks, Arron. *The Bad Boys Of Brexit: Tales of Mischief, Mayhem & Guerrilla Warfare In The EU Referendum Campaign.* London, UK: Biteback Publishing Lt. 2017. Pg. 334

[150] "Nigel Farage's funding secrets revealed," *Channel 4 News.* May 16th, 2019

[151] Hines, Nico. "Leak: Man Who Bankrolled Brexit Boasted of WikiLeaks Backchannel," *The Daily Beast.* February 3rd, 2020

[152] Kaiser, Brittany. *Targeted: The Cambridge Analytica Whistleblower's Inside Story of How Big Data, Trump, and Facebook Broke Democracy and How It Can Happen Again.* New York, NY: HarperCollins, 2019. Pg. 212

[153] Mills, Jen. "Vincent Tchenguiz wins £1.2 million after betting on a Trump victory," *METRO.* November 9th, 2016

Chapter 20:
Erik Prince, Psy Group,
And the Israeli/Gulf States Connection

George Birnbaum, Arthur Finkelstein, and the Israeli Connection

On August 3rd, Donald Trump Jr met with Joel Zamel, the head of the Israeli private intelligence firm Psy Group, and George Nader, an emissary representing the Gulf monarchies of Saudi Arabia and the United Arab Emirates. The meeting had been arranged and was attended by Erik Prince, America's most infamous private military and intelligence contractor and an ardent supporter of Donald Trump. Zamel, with the support of Prince and Nader, offered to assist Trump's candidacy through a sophisticated online and social media influence campaign.

The genesis of the meeting began months earlier. On March 29th, 2016, the conservative political consultant George Birnbaum met with Rick Gates at the Mandarin Oriental Hotel in Washington, DC. The two had been introduced by Eckart Sager,[1] a former CNN producer who had assisted Manafort and Gates in a black PR campaign on behalf of Viktor Yanukovych.[2] Sager listed the government of Azerbaijan among his clients and received over $2.6 million from a shell company that sat at the heart of a $2.5 billion money laundering operation known as the Azerbaijani Laundromat.[3]

Their meeting took place in the lead-up to the convention, and Gates mentioned "the challenge of the delegates" and asked Birnbaum if there was "any Israel[i] technology that could help us with some of these goals?" Gates needed help identifying which delegates were pro-Trump, anti-

Trump, and which hadn't decided yet. Regarding the latter category, he wanted to know whether they could use social media to influence their decision and get them to support Trump. Gates was also interested in gathering opposition research on Clinton and "up to ten of her closest circle."

Birnbaum had deep connections to Israel. In 1996, he worked beneath the Republican strategist Arthur Finkelstein to support the right-wing Likud Party challenger Benjamin Netanyahu's successful run to become the Israeli Prime Minister. Birnbaum later served as Netanyahu's chief of staff. Netanyahu's use of American political consultants provided an important lesson to future campaigns worldwide. "It's not so easy to replicate America to any country, let alone Israel, a multiparty parliamentary system with so many dividing lines," Birnbaum later told *The Jerusalem Post*. "But the 1996 race changed the dynamics of elections. No one thought Netanyahu would win, and everyone attributed it to Arthur."[4]

Birnbaum's association with Netanyahu makes it unsurprising that he supported Trump. For years, Netanyahu's relationship with Barack Obama had been deteriorating. According to *The New Yorker*, the Israeli Prime Minister believed that Obama had "no special feeling" for the Jewish state.[5] Obama, having won a majority of American Jewish voters, resented the charge. Obama and Netanyahu's relationship further soured when the latter supported Mitt Romney, Obama's 2012 Republican challenger. Despite Netanyahu's denials, the Obama team was convinced the Israeli leader had attempted to interfere in the election.[6] Relations reached a nadir after Obama signed a nuclear treaty with Iran, which Netanyahu vehemently opposed.[7]

Netanyahu also had ties to the Trump clan. He was close friends with Jared Kushner's father, Charles Kushner. The Kushners had for years donated to Israeli causes, including to the yeshiva at the Beit El settlement, located in the West Bank. Netanyahu often visited the Kushner family home in New Jersey, sometimes staying over for the night and sleeping in Jared's bedroom, while the younger Kushner found lodging in the basement.

Netanyahu and his party, Likud, were closely connected to the Republican Party. Arthur Finkelstein was his campaign manager in 1996 and George Birnbaum's mentor. The late Finkelstein, who died of lung cancer in 2017, was legendary among political strategists despite being notoriously private and camera-shy. While at Columbia, he studied with Ayn Rand.[8] In the 1970s, Finkelstein was among the first to understand the implications of a Supreme Court decision allowing independent political committees to spend money on candidates and causes. He developed advanced demographic analyses of primary voters, used exit polling, and applied the marketing strategy known as microtargeting to political campaigns.[9] He worked for numerous Republicans ranging from Richard Nixon to Ronald Reagan. In an echo of Roy Cohn, Finkelstein was gay and later married his long-term partner, all the while supporting opponents of gay rights and gay marriage.

Finkelstein was famous for turning the term "liberal" into a dirty word in American politics.[10] In the 1970s, he developed the "Six-Party Theory," which divided the electorate into ideological and racial groupings and predicted that Republicans could win elections if they peeled off support from Conservative Democrats. As early as 1996, Finkelstein encouraged Republican candidates to go negative and "polarize the electorate."[11] At its core, Finkelstein's strategy relied on demoralizing his opponents' supporters to keep them from voting.

In a rare recording of Finkelstein dating back to a 2011 presentation made in Prague, he presages not only the rise of right-wing populism but also the candidacy of Donald Trump. According to Finkelstein, the economic crisis that shook the world after 2008 "appears, at least from my travels around, to be much worse than it feels to most of us. There is real anger." He continued, "The anger is at the Mexicans. Not even all Hispanics - the Mexicans." Finkelstein predicted that "from nowhere politicians" could rise to the fore in such an environment. Finkelstein then suggested, "We're looking at business people to become leaders." He then brought up Trump. "I don't know if anybody here is watching Donald Trump in the US, but it's mind-boggling. It's just pure personality."[12]

Finkelstein didn't just predict the rise of right-wing populists; he helped make it happen. He and George Birnbaum had been working on political campaigns across Eastern Europe since 2003. In 2008, after an introduction provided by Netanyahu, Finkelstein and Birnbaum worked to help re-elect Viktor Orbán to power in Hungary. According to Steve Bannon, Orbán's populist political rhetoric made him "Trump before

Trump."[13] Orbán had once been a pro-democracy critic of Russia and Putin. However, after 2009, the Hungarian leader notably changed his tune and became a right-wing populist and arguably the number one Putin cheerleader within the EU. According to the Russian publication *The Insider*, Semyon Mogilevich, who for years used Budapest as the base of his operations, possessed *kompromat* in the form of a video of Orbán accepting a suitcase full of cash as a bribe that he may have turned over to Putin.[14]

After Orbán's initial victory, Finkelstein landed on a critical insight that he would use to devastating effect in Orbán's future campaigns: he needed to invent an enemy for Orbán to run against that personified the collective fears of the electorate. According to George Birnbaum, the man Finkelstein settled on to fill this role was the Hungarian-born Jewish financier, Holocaust survivor, and liberal philanthropist George Soros, founder of the Open Societies Foundation. Soros' financial support of liberal causes had already made him a despised figure on the American right. His support of civil society and liberal democracy initiatives in Eastern Europe made him an enemy of Vladimir Putin and the Kremlin.

By the time the Trump campaign got into gear, Finkelstein had not only laid the intellectual foundations for the electoral strategy it pursued but sat at the nexus of many key figures backing Trump's improbable run. Finkelstein had reportedly done work for the Trump Organization, though what exactly and when is unclear.[15] Finkelstein got the job working for Netanyahu after being recommended by the billionaire Ronald Lauder.[16]

Lauder has known Donald Trump personally for decades. Lauder's mother, the cosmetics magnate Estée Lauder, socialized with Trump and Roy Cohn.[17] In *The Art of the Deal*, Trump claimed that he first met the Soviet Ambassador to the United States, Yuri Dubinin, at a luncheon held by Ronald's brother, Leonard Lauder. As Trump tells it, the surreptitious meeting led to a series of events culminating in Trump's first visit to Moscow. Ronald Lauder later became a major donor to the 2016 Trump campaign and Trump-supporting Super PACs.[18]

Lauder became politically involved during the Reagan years and, in 1986, was made the US Ambassador to Austria. Three years later, he unsuccessfully ran to be the Mayor of New York City against Rudy Giuliani. Lauder's campaign was managed by Finkelstein and the later chairman and CEO of Fox News, Roger Ailes.[19] In addition to funding Netanyahu's first run for Israeli Prime Minister in 1996, Ronald Lauder introduced him to Finkelstein, who subsequently joined his campaign and played a decisive role in its victory.

In the late 1990s, Lauder also negotiated with Syria on behalf of Israel. During this time of shuttle diplomacy between Jerusalem and Damascus, he was accompanied by George Nader, a convicted pedophile representing the interests of the UAE and Saudi Arabia who would later accompany Erik and Prince and Joel Zamel in their meeting with Donald Trump Jr.

Following the collapse of the Soviet Union, Lauder used connections he gained as an Ambassador in Vienna to pursue business opportunities in Eastern Europe, some of which brought him into contact with individuals with ties to Eurasian organized crime. In 1995, he established Central European Media Enterprises (CME), which purchased dozens of commercial television stations across Eastern Europe. That same year, while attempting to buy a television station in Ukraine, Lauder met with an advisor to Ukraine's famously corrupt President Leonid Kuchma named Oleksandr Volkov, who was later investigated for money laundering and corruption.[20]

Oleksandr Volkov, a close aide of Kuchma's, was a representative of an international company called Seabeco, owned by the Russian Boris Birshtein.[21] Birshtein has been linked to organized crime by the FBI and, according to a former KGB officer who spoke with *The Financial Times*, and the book *Putin's Kleptocracy* by Karen Dawisha, among other sources, Birshtein was one of the businessmen cultivated by the KGB to launder Communist Party funds out of Russia and to develop international business interests.[22] Birshtein's (now former) son-in-law, Alexander Shnaider, invested in Trump Tower Toronto.

On Volkov's suggestion, Lauder's CME purchased a stake in Studio 1 + 1, then co-owned by the Ukrainians Vadim Rabinovitch and Boris Fuchsmann. According to the FBI, Boris Fuchsmann was a gold smuggler and embezzler with links to organized crime. Vadim Rabinovich is a Ukrainian ex-convict and alleged organized crime boss who worked as the Ukrainian representative of Nordex, a commodities firm established by Grigori Loutchansky that is allegedly associated with both Russian intelligence and Eurasian organized crime.[23] In 1994,

Rabinovich attended a meeting in Tel Aviv with Semyon Mogilevich, Solntsevskaya criminal syndicate head Sergei Mikhailov, and other prominent Eurasian organized crime figures, including Viktor Averin, Boris Birshtein, and Arnold Tamm, where the sharing of criminal assets in Ukraine was discussed.[24]

Lauder's company CME was later investigated for offering up to $1 million in bribes to Ukrainian officials, though no charges ever appear to have been filed. Though Rabinovich sold his stake in the television station, he remained closely connected to its investors. In 2007, the Ukrainian oligarch Ihor Kolomoyskyi purchased 3% of the company. Kolomoyskyi was accused by the Department of Justice of involvement in a massive international money laundering scheme.[25] In 2011, he co-founded the European Jewish Union with Rabinovich.[26]

When later attempting to explain how they could have gone into business with Rabinovich, CME executives claimed to have been impressed by a picture he had on his wall showing him with then-President Bill Clinton and Vice President Al Gore at a 1995 Democratic fundraiser in Miami. The man who brought Rabinovich to the event, Bennet S. LeBow, traveled to Moscow with Donald Trump in 1996 to look into investing in a Trump Tower Moscow.[27]

The Rabinovich-LeBow axis is not the only link Lauder has had with corrupt figures from the former Soviet Union who have interacted with Trump. In his capacity as the President of the World Jewish Congress (WJC), Lauder has had multiple interactions with Alexander Mashkevich, the Israeli-Kazakh billionaire who served as the President of the Euro-Asian Jewish Congress until 2011, a regional subsidiary of the WJC.[28] Mashkevich once worked for the suspected KGB money laundering outfit Seabeco, underneath the alleged KGB-linked organized criminal Boris Birshtein, whose former son-in-law invested in Trump Tower Toronto.[29] Mashkevich was also listed as an investor in Trump Tower Soho.[30]

Returning the influence of Arthur Finkelstein, Roger Stone, Trump's oldest political advisor, and Tony Fabrizio, the Trump campaign pollster brought on by Paul Manafort whose data was shared with Konstantin Kilimnik, were both part of a group of Republic consultants known as "Arthur's kids," meaning they had learned the tricks of the trade under

Finkelstein's tutelage.[31] Peter Geoghegan writes that Finkelstein, who had done campaign work in Ukraine, had introduced Manafort to several "pro-Russian Ukrainian oligarchs."[32]

Prosecutors later accused Manafort of coordinating with a "senior Israeli official" in 2012 to spread a story accusing Yulia Tymoshenko of antisemitism during his work supporting Viktor Yanukovych.[33] *Haaretz* and *The Jerusalem Post* speculated that the official in question was the Soviet-born Israeli official Avigdor Lieberman.[34] According to *The Times of Israel*, Finkelstein "masterminded" the October 2012 alliance between Netanyahu's Likud Party and Lieberman's Yisrael Beiteinu party.[35]

Psy Group, iVote Israel, and the Israeli Private Intelligence Industry

A day after Birnbaum met with Gates, he contacted Eitan Charnoff, a project manager at Psy Group. Birnbaum had been connected to Charnoff just by Kory Bardash, the head of Republicans in Israel. In addition to his role at Psy Group, Charnoff was the director of iVote Israel, an ostensibly nonpartisan get-out-the-vote campaign encouraging Israeli-Americans to vote.[36] Founded in 2012, iVote Israel is registered in the United States as a 501(c)(4) "dark money" non-profit that is not required to disclose its donors. According to the Sunlight Foundation, the nonprofit behind iVote Israel shares the same address as the Ronald S. Lauder Foundation.[37]

iVote Israel's first campaign strategist, Aron Shaviv, was a former campaign staffer for Avigdor Lieberman.[38] In 2016, Shaviv worked as a consultant for the Democratic Front, a pro-Russian political opposition party in Montenegro that was later involved in an attempted Kremlin-backed coup.[39] Montenegrin prosecutors believe Shaviv was one of the conspirators in the planned violent overthrow of the government.[40] The failed coup involved the GRU and was funded by Oleg Deripaska, who owned significant aluminum assets in the country.[41] Paul Manafort, who had done work in the country on behalf of Deripaska years earlier, also appears to have been in discussions with Montenegrin opposition officials in 2016. However, it is unclear whether he provided them with any services.[42] Victor Boyarkin, an ex-GRU agent whom Deripaska had tasked with pressuring Manafort over his debts to the oligarch, has been accused by the US Treasury Department of providing funding for the Democratic Front and the coup.[43]

"I have spoken to both of you about the other," Kory Bardash wrote to Birnbaum and Charnoff. "Hopefully you can have a mutually beneficial chat." In connecting with Psy Group via Charnoff, Birnbaum was reaching out to the world of Israeli private intelligence firms.

"These guys came out of the military intelligence army unit, and it's like coming out with a triple Ph.D. from MIT," Birnbaum later testified.[44]

Mossad and the Israeli Defense Force's (IDF) Unit 8200, an elite signals intelligence unit, had been tracking and conducting influence operations on terrorists and perceived enemies of Israel for years. Multiple successful technology startups and several private intelligence firms emerged from this milieu. The first of these, Terrogence, was established in 2004 by Gadi Aviran, the former head of an Israeli military intelligence team.[45] Four years later, in 2008, Shalev Hulio and Omri Lavie established NSO Group, which gained infamy for providing the Saudi government with software that allowed it to track dissidents, including Jamal Khashoggi, who was later murdered by the regime.[46] 2011 saw the founding of Black Cube by ex-Israeli intelligence officers Dan Zorella and Avi Yanus, with the help of Victor Tchenguiz.[47]

Operating under the motto "Shape Reality," Psy Group was founded in 2014. The firm specialized in collecting and analyzing information, particularly online and on social media, and offered services related to online reputation management and sophisticated, targeted influence campaigns. Psy Group was founded by Joel Zamel, an Israeli born in Australia in 1986. Zamel's co-founders included Daniel Green and Elad Schaffer. Psy Group's CEO, Royi Burstein, was a lieutenant colonel in Israeli military intelligence. According to the Psy Group's promotional literature, the company's capabilities included financial intelligence, cyber intelligence, targeting & monitoring, online reputation management, offline/online campaigns, and "Honey Traps."[48]

Psy Group was not Zamel's first foray into private intelligence. In 2010, he co-founded a "crowdsourced" geostrategic consulting firm, Wikistrat. Elad Schaffer, who later founded Psy Group alongside Zamel, served as Wikistrat's COO. Most of Wikistrat's clients were foreign governments, yet it was well-connected to senior officials within the US intelligence community. Its board members included former CIA and NSA director Michael Hayden, former national security advisor James L. Jones, former deputy director of the National Security Council Elliott Abrams, and the former acting director of the Defense Intelligence Agency (DIA) David Shedd.[49] Shedd had worked for Michael Flynn.[50]

In 2015, Wikistrat ran simulations exploring what would happen if a foreign government attempted to interfere in the American political process and compiled a report. The report discussed the possibility that Russian trolls might target the United States. "At the time we were discussing the subject of cyber-interference in democratic processes, it seemed and felt like just another idle intellectual exercise and scenario planning project for political scientists," a Wikistrat analyst who worked on the report told *The Daily Beast*. "But retrospectively, it feels a bit too on-the-nose not to be disturbing."[51]

Wikistrat's 2015 report contained prescient analysis at a time when the Internet Research Agency (IRA) was already targeting the US. The report refers to the "Internet Research Group," almost certainly a reference to the IRA. "[T]hese 'cyber-trolls' are trained controversialists: they openly engage in public controversy...People are drawn to the excitement of controversy and these cyber-trolls are experts in sensationalizing a political issue. The objective of cyber-trolls is not to convince explicitly, but rather subconsciously, by inserting a seed of doubt that leads to confusion and encourages fact-skepticism. They are not afraid to use provocative and confrontational language, as it is to their advantage if it leads to an emotional rise in the reader because the reader is then more likely to engage in debate, which in-turn, creates more buzz and attracts a greater audience, increasing the potential number of people exposed to this misinformation campaign."

Psy Group's Opaque Corporate Structure,
And Links to Russia and Walter Soriano

According to Zamel, Psy Group was composed of a Cyprus-registered parent company, IOCO Ltd., and a subsidiary company based in Israel called Invop Ltd. Zamel described himself as the majority shareholder for IOCO Ltd, which was responsible for business development, contracting and marketing.

Invop was responsible for operations in Israel.[52] Zamel did not explain why the company was structured this way, nor did he explain several other oddities, most of which seemed to point to a remarkable number of connections to Russia.

IOCO Ltd was managed by a Cyprus-based holding company administered by two Cypriot directors named Ria Christofides and Giannakis Ermogenous, who also served as the official affiliates of the Russian state-owned Vozrozhdenie Bank and Promsvyazbank and the privately held Avtovazbank. Through an analysis of incorporation documents, Scott Stedman found that Christofides and Ermogenous "have the power to decide over the activities and conduct of the company. They are involved in all of the decisions concerning the company and have to fulfill certain duties towards the enterprise and its other members."[53]

From its inception in 2014 until July 2016, IOCO Ltd was owned by a rotating cast of shell companies. Two of these companies, Prime Nominees Ltd and Sea Holdings Ltd, were registered in the British Virgin Islands. Both companies were under the control of a Swiss lawyer named Judith Hamburger. Hamburger worked for two UK-based companies which, from 2010-2016, listed their ultimate beneficiary as the Russian national Alina Zolotova, wife of the Russian banker Georgy Bedzhamov, who fled to Monaco in December of 2015 after being accused of embezzling $3.4 billion from Vneshprombank.

In July 2016, ownership over IOCO Ltd was transferred to a British Virgin Islands-based shell company called Protexer Ltd. Protexer-owned MGMT Financial Services Limited is controlled by a multi-billion dollar Russian consortium called the Metropole Group. Based out of Moscow, Metropole Group is owned by a Russian billionaire and former member of the state Duma for Vladimir Putin's party, United Russia, named Mikhail Slipenchuk. Protexer Ltd is a subsidiary of the Cyprus-based Trident Trust, which provides corporate trust and fund services. Protexer is just one of sixteen subsidiaries owned by Trident. Of those, five were owned by Slipenchuk, three featured Directors affiliated with numerous Russian banks, and one used the same Cyprus-based secretarial services as Paul Manafort.[54]

According to *The Times of Israel*, Protexer is associated with Gazprombank and Gazprom Media, Russia's largest media holding company and a subsidiary of Gazprom. The connection is through yet another sister company to Psy Group, the Protexer-owned Benton Solutions Ltd. Registered in Cyprus, Benton's shareholder was listed as Ecofran Marketing, Consulting, and Communication Services Company Limited, itself a subsidiary of Gazprom Media, which Gazprombank owns. Russian corporate documents show that Ecofran provided millions of dollars in loans to various companies owned by Gazprom Media.[55]

In or around 2015, Psy Group was hired by Oleg Deripaska to conduct an intelligence operation codenamed "Project Starbuck" that involved a business dispute Deripaska was having with a large Austrian company possibly involving real estate. Deripaska enlisted Psy Group to dig up derogatory information on the Austrian company. However, Psy Group CEO Royi Burstein, who may have met with Deripaska in Switzerland to discuss the project, told the Senate Intelligence Committee that Psy Group was unable to do so. Publicly available details of Psy Group's work for Deripaska remain scant.

Another Russian oligarch who hired Psy Group was Dmitry Rybolovlev. As previously covered, Rybolovlev purchased a Florida mansion from Donald Trump in 2008 for $95 million, approximately $50 million more than Trump had bought it for at the height of a recession.[56] Rybolovlev engaged Psy Group to perform an intelligence project involving a dispute the billionaire Russian oligarch was having with the Swiss art dealer Yves Bouvier. Psy Group was paid $150,000 to collect derogatory information on Bouvier.

Oleg Deripaska was put in touch with Psy Group by a mysterious British-Israeli citizen named Walter Tzvi Soriano, who had worked in the past for Deripaska and was also present at Psy Group's meetings with Rybolovlev.[57] Soriano is an Argentinian-born, former Israeli intelligence officer who operates a London-based consultancy, USG Security.[58] He enjoys elite connections to the Israeli government and powerful Russian oligarchs.

Soriano is a close friend and associate of Benjamin Netanyahu's. He produced a documentary about the Prime Minister's brother, who died while leading an Israeli raid on Entebbe Airport in Uganda in 1976.[59] After losing to Ehud Barak in 1999, Netanyahu briefly left politics and entered the private sector with Soriano, where they invested in several US-based technology ventures. In 2002, Soriano arranged for Netanyahu to deliver lectures at a Mexico City-based charity, the Lev Malka Organization, for which he was paid $180,000. Soriano had described his and Netanyahu's relationship as being based on "years of deep friendship, devoid of any external interests."[60] In an explosive allegation that both Soriano and Netanyahu deny, the Israeli press has reported that the Israeli police believed that Netanyahu hired Soriano to surveil police officers who were investigating the Prime Minister on corruption charges.[61]

Soriano's relationships with Russian oligarchs are extensive. According to the journalist Raviv Drucker, whom Soriano unsuccessfully sued for defamation, Oleg Deripaska hired Soriano while he was involved in a legal dispute with Mikhail Chernoy in British court. In 2014, USG Security was hired by a Deripaska-linked company to provide security at Sochi Airport during the 2014 Winter Olympics.[62] According to *Intelligence Online*, Soriano was also involved in Oleg Deripaska's attempts to silence Nastya Rybka while she was imprisoned in Thailand.[63]

In addition to working for Oleg Deripaska and Dmitry Rybolovlev, Psy Group has also done work for an as yet unknown client attempting to discredit Ukrainian anti-corruption activists, which would have been in the interests of the Kremlin and its supporting oligarchs in Ukraine. In the Summer of 2017, Psy Group was allegedly behind a disinformation campaign targeting the Anti-Corruption Action Center (AntAC) run by a Ukrainian activist named Daria Kaleniuk.[64] AntAC was a key proponent of establishing the National Anti-Corruption Bureau of Ukraine (NABU), a law enforcement body dedicated to rooting out corruption.[65] Kaleniuk is also an associate of Serhii Leshchenko,[66] the Ukrainian lawmaker and investigative journalist who helped publicize the "Black Ledger" of illicit payments made by the Yanukovych regime that led to Paul Manafort's resignation from the Trump campaign.[67]

Project Rome: Psy Group Devises a Plan for the Trump Campaign

After meeting with Rick Gates, George Birnbaum contacted Psy Group project manager Eitan Charnoff. On March 30th, Charnoff emailed his Psy Group colleagues Royi Burstein and Arnon Epstein to alert them to the new opportunity to work for an American presidential campaign. Charnoff said that he and

Epstein had been in touch with "a major American campaign consultant who [had] been tasked by the [T]rump campaign." He explained that "[t]hey want us to [use] social platform analytical tools as well as our Rubik department capabilities to identify who is truly with [T]rump and who isn't and then run an influence campaign to impact their decision using avatars and creating third party assets and outreach." Charnoff ended by saying, "[b]y the end of today, they want a rough estimate of what it will cost," as well as a timeline and more exact cost estimate within three days.

Charnoff divided the potential work for the Trump campaign into two distinct projects. The first involved gathering opposition research on "the female opposing candidate," meaning Hillary Clinton, by means of "dig[ging] up dirt as well as active [information] gathering on associates." The second project would consist of looking into state delegates voting at the Republican National Convention to determine which delegates were "pro [T]rump, against and unknown." The delegates who fit into the latter two categories would be targeted by a social media influence campaign designed to get them "to support [T]rump and not change the convention rules."

On April 1st, Arnon Epstein sent an email with the subject line "Project D-Day" in which he suggested that Psy Group had been authorized to "move to the planning phase of the activity" following "several conversations last night with George [Birnbaum]" Epstein included a screenshot of Birnbaum's communications suggesting that the Trump Campaign was not "intimidated" by the budget numbers being discussed and was anxious to receive proposals from Psy Group within days. Epstein also elaborated on the oppo research against Clinton. "As for the intel on the lady and her team, he's talking about up to 10 people in her inner-inner circle," Epstein wrote. "We told him an estimate of 10 people and her would be around $250K for passive work + very light active. We explained we suggest not to go heavy active at the moment because of the issues we discussed. We spun it a bit and said we are not concerned for us, but wish to prevent any blow back or flags raising pointing to him at this point."

In another email sent April 1st, Birnbaum offered guidance to Charnoff and Epstein on how to draft the proposal for the Trump team, suggested that they "run intensive influence campaigns on the unknown delegates themselves and on the influencers of the delegates," and "[f]or the Clinton Proposal... run an intensive, deep open source opposition research campaign on Hillary and her 10 closest associates (names to be supplied by [the] campaign). Depending on information found, apply a second layer of info gathering to make sure no stone was left unturned. Anything else you might want to add as well."

"Project D-Day" initially envisioned up to 53 Psy Group employees being involved in the effort, divided into four teams: Team Black, Team Rubik, Team Blue and Team Red. Four days later, on April 5th, Epstein reached out to Birnbaum with an updated plan, now referred to as "Project Rome." According to the renamed proposal, Psy Group would conduct "influence services" for the Trump campaign targeting Republican convention delegates. The proposal also called for conducting "opposition intelligence research" on the Clinton camp. The cost estimate for the "influence services" targeting the Republican delegates was $3.1 million, plus $100k for media expenses, while the opposition research was priced at $400k.

In addition to these proposals, Epstein's email to Birnbaum included a "sample report" on an actual California Republican delegate named Felicia Michelle Tweedy. Psy Group's "sample report" included biographical data related to Tweedy, including her place of residence, employment status, marital status, political and religious beliefs, and personal interests. According to the report, while Tweedy was "a strong supporter of Donald Trump, and therefore no active influence is required at this point," it recommended "infrequent monitoring (monthly) to check whether any changes in opinions or sentiments towards Trump." It was explained that the information contained in the sample report had been gathered through "available OSINT (Open Source Intelligence)" and promised that "[i]n the event that additional information is required, Psy Group can carry out various active intelligence activities to extract additional information based on the needs and directions."[68]

Psy Group promised that "veteran intelligence officers" would look through social media accounts and other publicly available information to produce similar dossiers on the psychology of every persuadable Republican delegate. Upwards of 40 Psy Group employees would target up to 2,500 individuals with tailored messages to sway them towards Trump. The messages would also target Trump's chief rival for the Republican nomination, Senator Ted Cruz of Texas. Targeted messages appearing to come from former Cruz supporters or influential people within the Republican Party would highlight Cruz's "ulterior motives or hidden plans." The influence campaign would consist of "online and offline approaches" and potentially involve telephone calls. Psy Group further promised that it could gather "unique intel" through both "covert sources" and "tailored avatars."[69]

George Birnbaum informed Rick Gates that he had received proposals from Psy Group. Gates then told Birnbaum to send the proposals to Scott Wilkerson. Though Birnbaum wasn't familiar with Wilkerson, he sent the information to him anyway. Conversations regarding the project continued with Psy Group. In a May 8th email chain under the subject "campaign work," Psy Group employees discussed developing "psyop campaigns" against Trump's "opposition," which would consist of "[h]undreds of avatars driving negative messaging" and "physical world ops like counter protests, hecklers, etc."[70]

Despite these discussions, the initial communications between Psy Group and the Trump campaign do not appear to have led to the two moving forward with "Project Rome." Birnbaum later claimed to have never heard back from Gates or the Trump campaign and subsequently canceled his meetings with Psy Group. However, Joel Zamel and Psy Group continued their efforts to offer their services to the Trump campaign. In May of 2016, Zamel emailed the former Republican Speaker of the House, Newt Gingrich, who had only just endorsed Trump for President that month, suggesting that he could offer the Trump campaign powerful tools to utilize social media to help it in the election. Zamel suggested that they meet to discuss the issue. Gingrich forwarded Zamel's email to Jared Kushner, who ran the idea by Brad Parscale, the Trump campaign's digital director. Parscale reportedly rebuffed the offer.[71]

Joel Zamel Meets George Nader in St. Petersburg

Zamel's most successful attempt to access the Trump campaign began with an unusual individual in an unlikely place: St. Petersburg, Russia. While attending the St. Petersburg Economic Forum in June of 2016, Zamel was introduced to a politically connected Lebanese-American named George Nader. Nader enjoyed close ties to Arab leaders in the Gulf, including the Crown Prince of the Emirate of Abu Dhabi, Mohammed Bin Zayed al-Nahyan (MBZ), and the powerful Saudi prince Mohammed bin Salman (MBS). Zamel's introduction to Nader was facilitated by John Hannah, a former national security advisor to Vice President Dick Cheney, who currently serves as the senior counselor to the pro-Israel nonprofit the Foundation for the Defense of Democracies and as a member of the advisory board of Wikistrat. Hannah also worked with Nader during the former's time in the George W. Bush administration.[72]

In the 1990s, George Nader edited *Middle East Insight*. This Washington, DC-based magazine occasionally served as a forum for Arab, Israeli, and Iranian officials to express opinions directed toward an American audience.[73] In 1998, Nader became involved in a diplomatic exchange between Israel and Syria over the Golan Heights. Nader traveled to Damascus multiple times alongside Israel's informal diplomatic representative, Ronald Lauder, a longtime friend of Trump's.[74] By 2003, Nader was hired by the American military contractor Blackwater to help generate business in Iraq, which had just undergone an American invasion that had toppled the government of Saddam Hussein and unleashed an insurgency.

Nader established high-level contacts within the Iraqi government, which in turn provided him access to influential parties within Russia. In 2012, he helped broker a $4.2 billion arms deal between Russia and Iraq by traveling to Moscow and informing the Russians that he represented the Iraqi government of Nouri al-Maliki. Sources knowledgeable about the deal in Iraq found it suspicious as Maliki appeared to be using Nader to go around the official channels that typically negotiated such deals. A month after the deal was signed, the Iraqi acting Defense Minister pulled the plug on the deal, citing possible corruption.[75]

Also in 2012, Nader first attended the St. Petersburg Economic Forum, the same Davos-like conference where, four years later, he would meet with Joel Zamel. It was also around this time that Nader moved to the United Arab Emirates and became an advisor and representative to its' powerful de facto ruler, Crown Prince Mohammed bin Zayed, often referred to in the West by his initials, MBZ. Nader often traveled to Russia, acting as a representative for MBZ and the United Arab Emirates (UAE).

Looming in the shadows behind his political activities was the fact that Nader was a convicted pedophile and consumer of child pornography. In 1985, he was indicted in the US on charges of importing obscene materials, including photos of nude boys "engaging in a variety of sexual acts." The charges were brought after a US Customs inspector opened a package that was destined for Nader's office and discovered the materials, which led to a search warrant being drawn up and further illegal pornographic materials being found. Despite the government's argument that the searches had been justified because Nader, "a suspected pedophile, was likely to seek to contact children," the charges were thrown out on procedural grounds.[76] In 1991, a federal court in Virginia convicted Nader of transporting videos from Germany of "pre and post-pubescent boys" engaging in sexually explicit acts and sentenced him to six months. Prosecutors put the case under seal "due to the extremely sensitive nature of Mr. Nader's work in the Middle East."[77] In 2003, Nader served a year in prison in the Czech Republic after being convicted by a court in Prague of sexually abusing ten boys.[78] How Nader managed to continue finding himself in politically sensitive positions even though he was a convicted pedophile with a compromised past remains a mystery.

In June of 2016, Joel Zamel approached Nader for a meeting while both were attending the St. Petersburg Economic Forum. A representative for Nader later told *The New Yorker* that Zamel told Nader he was trying to raise money for a social media campaign to support the candidacy of Donald Trump and thought that the Gulf Princes might be interested.[79] However, Zamel denied to both *The New Yorker* and the Senate Intelligence Committee that any such conversation took place or that US politics was discussed during the St. Petersburg meeting. Zamel did recall that several days after they had met, Nader sent him a picture of himself standing with Vladimir Putin, which Zamel interpreted as a means to emphasize Nader's high level of access. Following their initial meeting, Zamel and Nader began communicating with increased frequency, speaking multiple times a week or even daily.[80]

Despite the mystery surrounding the content of Joel Zamel and George Nader's conversation in St. Petersburg, Zamel would have been on firm footing had he assumed that Nader's patrons MBZ and the ferociously ambitious Prince Mohammed bin Salman (MBS), then serving as Saudi Arabia's Second Deputy Prime Minister and Minister of Defense, preferred Donald Trump over Hillary Clinton. According to a report in *Middle East Eye* by David Hearst, in late 2015, Nader convened a remarkable summit of Middle Eastern leaders on a yacht in the Red Sea. Among those present were MBZ, MBS, Egyptian President Abdel Fatah al-Sisi, Prince Salman bin Hamad Al Khalifa of Bahrain, and King Abdullah of Jordan.

Nader used the Summit to propose that the combined leaders replace the Gulf Cooperation Council (GCC) and the Arab League with a new, elite institution that consisted of their five countries plus Libya, which did not have a representative at the meeting. The purpose of this bloc was to back the United States and Israel and, through doing so, further isolate and damage their chief regional rival, the Islamic Republic of Iran. According to Hearst, it was at that meeting that the Arab leaders decided that a Trump presidency was their best hope of reversing President Obama's efforts to engage Iran in diplomacy, in particular through the Joint Comprehensive Plan of Action (JCPOA), colloquially known as the Iran Nuclear Deal.[81]

Like Netanyahu, MBZ and MBS opposed Obama's foreign policy in the Middle East. The arch-conservative monarchies in the Gulf were horrified when Obama chose to side with the protesters in Cairo over America's traditional ally, Hosni Mubarak, and clandestinely worked to overthrow the subsequently elected Muslim Brother government of Mohammed Morsi and have it replaced with the military dictatorship led by al-Sisi. Relations between the Obama administration further deteriorated when he opted against imposing his so-called "Red Line" after the Iranian-backed government of Bashar al-Assad used chemical weapons against his own people during the Syrian Civil War. However, it was Obama's direct diplomatic overtures to Iran that angered Israel and the Gulf States and drew the traditional enemies closer together.

George Nader met with Joel Zamel of Psy Group on multiple occasions in New York, Washington, DC, and several other locations. In July 2016, Nader informed Zamel that he was interested in setting up a meeting with either the Trump campaign or the Trump family. To facilitate such a meeting, Zamel reached out to Erik Prince, a conservative activist and billionaire founder of the infamous military contracting and security firm Blackwater, who was himself attempting to establish ties to the Trump campaign.[82]

The Aggrieved Warrior:
Erik Prince's Journey to Supporting the Trump Campaign

Erik Prince was the scion of a wealthy, conservative, and devoutly religious family. His father, Edgar D. Prince, founded the auto parts supplier, the success of which made him one of the wealthiest men in Michigan. After an injury forced him to leave the Naval Academy, Prince attended Hillsdale College, where his conservative views crystallized. Around this time, Prince also became an intern at the George H.W. Bush White House. He was disillusioned by the experience, convinced that Bush was abandoning conservative principles.

Prince had a fateful, chance encounter at a DC bowling alley with a Republican member of the House of Representatives from California: Dana Rohrabacher. After Prince explained that he was unhappy interning at the White House, Rohrabacher offered him an unpaid position in his office on Capitol Hill. Prince accepted and quickly befriended Paul Behrends. It began an enduring friendship that would last for many years. Behrends became so close to Prince that he influenced his decision to become a Catholic.[83]

Rohrabacher sent Prince and Behrends on several Congressional fact-finding trips abroad. Prince and Behrends traveled to Nicaragua in the aftermath of a civil war where the United States had covertly funded the right-wing rebel group the Contras against the Marxist Sandinista government.[84] In what became known as the Iran Contra Affair, the funding of the Contras had been organized by elements of the Reagan administration in contravention of a prohibition by Congress and was facilitated by the illegal sales of arms to Iran.

After his brief stint in Washington, Prince joined the Navy SEALS. Following his father's death in 1995, Prince left the SEALS and established Blackwater Worldwide, which became the world's most infamous military contractor. In 2002, following the American invasion of Afghanistan, Blackwater was awarded a classified contract by the CIA to provide security for its station in Kabul and other facilities it operated across the country.[85] Prince's relationship with the CIA was partially facilitated by

Behrends, who had valuable contacts in Afghanistan.[86]

After 9/11, George W. Bush signed orders authorizing the CIA to pursue a secret assassination program targeting members of al-Qaeda.[87] The template for Bush's order was a memo authored by Cofer Black, the head of the CIA's Counterterrorist Center (CTC).[88] Working beneath Black was Enrique "Ric" Prado, who oversaw the CTC's "targeted assassination program." In 2004, Black and Prado left the CIA and joined Blackwater. According to sources who spoke to Vanity Fair, Prince was a fully-fledged asset of the Agency. Prado appears to have brought the assassination program that he had overseen while at the CIA with him to Blackwater, providing the Agency with plausible deniability.[89] Blackwater participated in some of the CIA's most secretive operations in both Afghanistan and Iraq.[90]

Following the 2003 American invasion of Iraq, Blackwater was awarded many more US government contracts. Through Blackwater's work in Iraq, Prince became acquainted with George Nader.[91] Blackwater quickly found itself at the heart of some of the most controversial episodes of the war. On March 31st, four Blackwater contractors were ambushed and killed while driving through the Iraqi city of Fallujah. The contractors were dragged from their cars, and the bodies were burned and desecrated before being hung from a bridge. The incident received widespread media attention and precipitated the First Battle of Fallujah.

The day after the ambush Prince turned to Paul Behrends. Behrends, who had lobbied for Blackwater since 1998, was by 2004 working at the Alexander Strategy Group. Within days of the ambush, Behrends was shuttling Prince around the halls of Congress, arranging for meetings with congressional leaders and the heads of the committees in charge of awarding government contracts and establishing the rules of conduct for military contractors operating in warzones.[92]

Shortly after Obama succeeded Bush, Prince's relationship with the US Government took a turn for the worse. On June 23rd, 2009, Obama's new head of the CIA, Leon Panetta, was informed of the existence of the CIA paramilitary assassination program.[93] He further learned of Blackwater's involvement in the program.[94] Panetta canceled the program. The next day, he revealed its existence in a special, closed-door session of Congress.

The move infuriated Prince, who believed he had been betrayed and that Panetta had outed him as a CIA asset.[95] Nor was his deteriorating relationship with the CIA Prince's only problem. The Department of Justice was investigating Blackwater for federal weapons trafficking violations. In 2008, the Bureau of Alcohol, Tobacco, and Firearms raided Blackwater's complex in Moyock, North Carolina. Even though the government's case mostly collapsed, Prince began to believe that he was being intentionally targeted.[96]

Prince left the US and resettled in the United Arab Emirates. He wasted no time reorienting his company towards a clientele that included foreign governments and private corporations. Prince established himself as a close ally of MBZ, serving as a foreign policy and military advisor and convincing him to invest millions in a mercenary army that would act as a kind of Praetorian Guard for the Gulf monarchies.

By 2011, Prince started running into trouble again. His business in the UAE dried up after MBZ balked at the unwelcome attention following a *New York Times* blockbuster report on his private army.[97] Prince then moved into private equity, establishing Frontier Resource Group (FRG), which invested in extracting African natural resources such as oil and minerals in countries like Guinea, South Sudan, and the Democratic Republic of Congo. However, after losing his income stream from the UAE, Prince began having cash flow problems.[98]

In 2013, Prince sold the Hong Kong entrepreneur Johnson Ko a controlling interest in another company he established called Frontier Services Group (FSG) and remained chairman. FSG's executives comprised a group of Americans, including a Blackwater alum named Gregg Smith, and Chinese executives from state-owned CITIC Group, which held a 20% stake in FSG.[99] Prince entered the Chinese market when the country's communist government was investing in its Belt and Road Initiative, a global infrastructure project. FSG focused on protecting Chinese foreign ventures, primarily in Africa.[100] Prince's proximity to the Chinese government stirred discomfort in American intelligence circles.[101]

While Prince publicly presented himself as out of the mercenary game, privately, he offered mercenary services to various unsavory foreign actors. As early as 2013, Prince developed plans to build a small army in Libya. Code-named "Operation Lima," Prince proposed to put together an armed ground force to help stabilize eastern Libya. Though the proposal fell through, Prince returned to Libya in 2015 and pitched the plan again, this time promising that the armed force of private contractors could be used to stem the flow of refugees and economic migrants using Libya as a launch pad to enter the European Union.

By May 2015, Prince pitched Operation Lima to individuals and government authorities in Germany and Italy. He proposed to pay for the project using money from the Libyan Investment Authority, which European Banks had frozen. However, after the Europeans failed to support the plan and the banks refused to unfreeze the Libyan cash, Prince sought alternatives. According to *The Intercept*, Prince was being investigated by the US Government for potentially illegal weapons sales in Africa. Investigators surveilled Prince and discovered that, after being rebuffed by the Europeans, he had discussed the possibility of opening up a bank account in China for his Libyan associates. Prince traveled to Macau and attempted to open a bank account at a branch of a European bank but was denied after the bank's European headquarters reviewed the request. Prince then traveled to Beijing, where he reportedly met with Ministry of State Security agents, China's intelligence agency. By January 2016, Prince returned to Macau, where he opened up an account with the Bank of China that US intelligence officials believed could have been used to facilitate the laundering of Libyan money to fund Operation Lima.

Thus, by the beginning of 2016, Prince was reportedly under investigation by the Department of Justice and other federal agencies not only for offering potentially illegal military services and arms sales to Libya and other African countries but also for setting up a Chinese bank account, with the possible assistance of Chinese intelligence, for the purpose of laundering money to fund his Libyan operations.[102] To add to his problems, Prince was also facing a potential revolt from the American executives working at Frontier Services Group.

At a tense, two-day meeting in Hong Kong in March of 2016, FSG's American executives expressed their worries that the company risked running afoul of US laws regulating the sale of weapons to foreign governments. Gregg Miller, FSG's Chief

Executive, had learned that in 2015, Prince had ordered that two of the company's crop duster aircraft, which were supposed to be used for scouting purposes, be modified so they could be outfitted with either guns, rockets, or hellfire missiles. After learning that the planes were intended to be used by the Government of Azerbaijan in a campaign against ethnic Armenians, Miller came to worry that such an action could violate U.S International Arms Trafficking Regulations (ITAR).[103]

Prince's plans to build weaponized crop dusters dated back to 2013. A month after becoming FSG's chairman, Prince purchased two Thrush 510G crop dusters, which he told his colleagues would be used for non-lethal reconnaissance missions. Prince informed executives at FSG that the plans would be used by the government of Mali for surveillance purposes in their battle against a local al-Qaeda militant group. He then hired an Austrian company called Airborne Technologies to install surveillance equipment on the crop dusters.

Unbeknownst to FSG's executives, Prince secretly owned 25% of Airborne Technologies. His purchase of a portion of the company had been brokered by an Israeli named Dorian Barak, who served as Prince's attorney and represented his interests on Airborne's board. The planes were flown to Vienna, where Prince arranged for them to be modified into paramilitary aircraft. The project was overseen by a former Australian Special Forces pilot named Christiaan "Serge" Durrant, whom Prince had placed in charge of FSG's "specialty aviation division." To get around Austria's strict defense export regulations, Prince and associates at Airborne Technologies established a Bulgarian front company called LASA (an acronym for "Light Armed Surveillance Aircraft") Engineering Ltd. Bulgaria was chosen due to its lax export laws.

In May 2014, Prince traveled to Bulgaria and toured the Arsenal factory in Kazanlak, Bulgaria's largest arms manufacturer. He was interested in Arsenal's line of "aerial weaponry." A month later, an FSG contractor named Shawn Matthews traveled to Bulgaria and met with Peter Mirchev, a Bulgarian arms dealer who had supplied weapons to Viktor Bout, a Russian weapons dealer known as the "Merchant of Death."[104] According to Nicholas Schmidle of *The New Yorker*, Mirchev had told him that Bout worked for the GRU.[105] Mirchev is also believed to have been a major Bulgarian node in Semyon Mogilevich's extensive international illegal arms sales network.[106] It is not known what Matthews and Mirchev discussed.

While most of the weaponized modifications were done to the planes in Austria, the crop dusters were brought to Bulgaria for a simple installation process. One of the planes was outfitted with Russian-made mounted machine guns and engineered to utilize both Russian and NATO-designed munitions. While the first plane was meant to be used in a contract with the President of South Sudan that ultimately fell apart, Prince and Airborne Technologies moved forward with arming the second plane. Two Airborne employees visited weapons manufacturers in Bulgaria and Ukraine to look into various weapons systems that could be added to the second modified aircraft.[107]

Prince offered the use of the planes to the government of Azerbaijan, which was building up its military in anticipation of a conflict with Armenia over the disputed territory of Nagorno-Karabakh. According to *The Intercept*, Prince was connected to the Azerbaijanis through a "former Russian weapons supplier," whose identity remains unknown.[108] Suspicious of Prince's tendency to have FSG sign contracts with companies in which he held secret stakes, and worried that they might be in violation of US ITAR laws, FSG executives hired the firm King & Spalding to investigate what Prince had been up to. The King & Spalding investigation uncovered that Prince had been using his position at FSG to privately court the former Soviet county of Azerbaijan's Ministry of Defense, proposing to offer security services under the codename "Project Zulu," which included the use of the secretly weaponized aircraft. King & Spalding further determined that the services Prince offered Azerbaijan were not in the interests of FSG.[109] The internal scrutiny of the deal at FSG led to it falling apart.

In February of 2016, representatives at FSG reportedly traveled to Washington, where they met with officials at the Department of Justice, including the head of DOJ's National Security Division and a senior prosecutor with expertise in export control in the DOJ's counterespionage section. At the meeting, the FSB executives disclosed evidence related to the modified crop dusters and Prince's activities in China and Azerbaijan.[110] At the FSG board meeting held the following month in March, the company's American executives confronted Prince. However,

Johnson Ko and the company's Chinese executives leaped to Prince's defense. The disagreement over Prince ultimately led to numerous resignations among FSG American executives, fearing their work for the company conflicted with US interests.[111]

It was in this context that Prince began to support Trump. Having a friend in the White House selecting the next Attorney General and the heads of the various American intelligence agencies would have been very much in Prince's interest. During this time, Prince became acquainted with Psy Group owner Joel Zamel. Zamel claims that he was introduced to Prince by Cofer Black, the former No. 3 at CIA turned Blackwater executive and Chairman of the Prince-linked Total Intelligence Solutions.[112]

Prince, Zamel, and Nader Meet Don Jr:
The Second Trump Tower Meeting

Prince's interactions with Zamel led to Psy Group developing a project designed to improve Prince's online reputation, referred to as "Black Jack" or "Jack Black." Despite meeting several times to discuss the project, Zamel claims that Psy Group never went ahead with it. In July 2016, Zamel contacted Prince about setting up a meeting with the Trump team for himself and George Nader, whom Prince had known since Iraq.

In the context of these discussions, Psy Group CEO Royi Burstein sent Zamel an email on August 1st with a two-page document titled "Project Rome" that described the suite of services Psy Group could offer the Trump campaign related to the 2016 election. While the proposal had the same name as the offer Psy Group had made several months earlier to George Birnbaum, it contained subtle differences. The services offered included "generat[ing] influence through various online and offline platforms, assets and techniques," as well as setting up and promoting "tailored third-party messaging directed toward optimizing impact and acceptance within the target audience(s)." The proposal further promised to "focus on select voter groups/segments that may not be susceptible to campaign messaging originating from the candidate or organizations known to be affiliated with the candidate." Minority voters, suburban women, and undecided voters were all specifically mentioned as targets.[113]

Two days later, on August 3rd, Zamel and Nader were together at a hotel in Midtown Manhattan when, at roughly 4 pm, they received a call from Erik Prince instructing them to head over to Trump Tower. Upon their arrival, Prince, Zamel, and Nader were shuttled into Donald Trump Jr.'s office. Prince reportedly took charge and led the meeting. According to *The New York Times*, he explained to the candidate's son, "We are working hard for your father."[114]

Prince and Don Jr. started by discussing matters related to the campaign. Nader explained to Don Jr. that the Saudi and Emirate Crown Princes MBS and MBZ, whom he repeatedly called "my friends," wanted his father to win the election. To emphasize his point, Nader showed Don Jr. photos of himself in friendly poses with MBS and MBZ. He also discussed matters related to Middle Eastern politics, mentioning issues such as the Islamic State and the risks posed by Iran and explaining how the Gulf Princes believed that Trump could fill a vacuum that President Obama had left in the region. About 25 minutes into the meeting, Stephen Miller entered and joined the discussion.

Toward the end of the meeting, Joel Zamel described his work through his private intelligence firms Psy Group and Wikistrat. The exact nature of his description, and whether it included discussing "Project Rome" or any of the other pro-Trump proposals generated over the past months at Psy Group, is unknown. Zamel then asked Don Jr. whether a Psy Group campaign conducted to benefit his father that Nader paid for would present a conflict to the campaign. Trump Jr. replied that it would not, further stating that a Psy Group social media campaign wouldn't conflict with the Trump campaign's social media efforts.

What transpired in the immediate aftermath of the meeting is hazy, with the various players involved later providing conflicting testimony. Zamel testified that Nader "circumvented" him and continued communicating with Donald Trump Jr. alone, leaving him "cut out." However, Zamel also admitted that Erik Prince encouraged Nader to pay Zamel for the services he outlined to Trump Jr., explicitly telling Nader, "[y]ou should pay him."

Zamel later claimed that he offered Nader a "five to ten [million dollars]" quote to begin the work and that Nader agreed to pay up to $5 million. Despite this, Zamel denies that Psy

Group did any work for the Trump Campaign during the 2016 election. However, a few days after the November election, Zamel testified that Nader reached out to him and asked that he prepare a presentation on social media's impact on the outcome of the presidential contest. Curiously, Zamel claims not to have utilized experts on these matters employed at Psy Group to prepare the presentation but instead delegated the task to a minority owner of Psy Group named Daniel Green, despite Green having no expertise in data analytics, polling, or political analysis. Stranger still, Zamel maintained that Green simply "Googled a bunch of articles" during his research, and the presentation he produced was prefaced by the statement: "This is an academic study based on open source materials."

In January 2017, Zamel delivered the presentation to Nader in New York. He claims that he never provided Nader with a physical or electronic copy of the presentation. Zamel further claims that the presentation was transported from Israel to New York on a thumb drive, presented to Nader on an individual laptop, and returned to Israel on the thumb drive. After delivering the presentation to Nader, Zamel claims that Nader told him that he planned to share its content with "the young man," which Zamel interpreted to mean Donald Trump Jr.

After delivering the presentation to Nader in New York, Zamel returned to Israel with the thumb drive. He claims Nader never again asked about the presentation, which is strange as Zamel informed the Senate Intelligence Committee that Nader had paid him "over a million dollars" for it. A source speaking to *The New York Times* characterized the amount as "up to $2 million."[115] Zamel claimed Nader's payment was made "from his personal account to a business entity related to me" and that the payment was made before Nader heard the presentation.[116]

According to Zamel, Nader never asked about the presentation again. Zamel further claims that he deleted the presentation from the thumb drive and the laptop. It seems strange, even unbelievable, that George Nader would spend $1-2 million to hear a single presentation based on publicly available information, not even bother to get a copy of it, and never ask about it again. Obvious questions sprout from these inexplicable circumstances. Given that Joel Zamel explicitly asked Donald Trump Jr. if it would pose a conflict to the campaign for George Nader to pay for a social media campaign as outlined by Psy

Group to be conducted on behalf of Donald Trump's candidacy, that Donald Trump Jr. explicitly told him that it would not and that Erik Prince encouraged Nader to do so, is that in fact what happened? No evidence of such a campaign has been uncovered. Still, more questions remain. What information was contained in the January presentation by Zamel to Nader, and why did Zamel delete it without any backup copies? What exactly was George Nader paying for when he sent Zamel $1-2 million?

Erik Prince's support of the Trump campaign continued after the August 3rd Trump Tower meeting. In September, he donated $100,000 to the pro-Trump Super PAC Make America Number 1, which was led by Rebekah Mercer, the daughter of the billionaire recluse and top Trump supporter and money man, Robert Mercer.[117] However, in addition to political contributions, Erik Prince would provide further clandestine services to both the Trump campaign and, later, the Trump administration. During the transition, Erik Prince clandestinely traveled to the Seychelles where he met with Kirill Dmitriev, the CEO of the Russian Direct Investment Fund, to discuss setting up a backchannel between Trump and Putin.

---

[1] Report of the Select Committee on Intelligence United States Senate On Russian Active Measures Campaigns And Interference in the 2016 US Election Volume 5: Counterintelligence Threats and Vulnerabilities. Pg. 684-685

[2] Shubber, Kadhim. "Prosecutors expose dark arts of Manafort lobbying," *The Financial Times*. September 15th, 2018

[3] Eckart Sager, *Organized Crime and Corruption Reporting Project (OCCRP)*, September 4th, 2017

[4] Hoffman, Gil. "Record in US strategists advising Israeli election," *The Jerusalem Post*. March 7th, 2021

[5] Entous, Adam. "Donld Trump's New World Order," *The New Yorker*. June 11th, 2018

[6] Baker, Peter. "As Trump vs. Clinton Captivates World, Netanyahu Unusually Silent," *The New York Times*. September 1st, 2016

[7] Goldberg, Jeffrey. "The Crisis in U.S.-Israel Relations Is Officially Here," *The Atlantic*. October 28th, 2014

[8] Shirley, Craig. "Not Just Good at National Politics, but the Best," *National Review*. January 26th, 2017

[9] Roberts, Sam. "Arthur Finkelstein, Innovative, Influential Conservative Strategist, Dies at 72," *The New York Times*. August 19th, 2017

[10] Posner, Sara. "Right Makes Might," *The New Republic*. March 25th, 2019

[11] "Don't Look Now," *Newsweek*. November 17th, 1996

[12] Kuper, Simon. "Secrets of the populist playbook," *The Financial Times*. March 13th, 2019

[13] Krastev, Ivan. "Steve Bannon Has Found His Next Trump," *The New York Times*. August 19th, 2018

[14] Kirilenko, Anastasia. "A suitcase full of cash from the Solntsevo mafia: does Putin have a video kompromat on the Hungarian leader?" *The Insider*. April 7th, 2018

[15] Berkowitz, Bill. "Arthur Finkelstein is Hunting Hillary Clinton," *Media Transparency*.

January 9th, 2005

[16] Pfeffer, Anshel. "The little-known strategist who changed the course of Israel's history," *The Jewish Chronicle*. August 22nd, 2017

[17] Manso, Peter. "My Bizarre Dinner Party with Donald Trump, Roy Cohn, and Estee Lauder," *Politico Magazine*. May 27th, 2016

[18] Tindera, Michela. "Meet the Billionaire Couple Who Had Donated to Both Trump and Biden," *Forbes*. October 14th, 2020

[19] Lynn, Frank. "Lauder's Mayoral Campaign Is a Bonanza for Consultants," *The New York Times*. July 23rd, 1989

[20] Bonner, Raymond. "Lauder Media Company Faces a Federal Inquiry," *The New York Times*. June 12th, 2001

[21] Byrne, Peter. "Lazarenko trail leads FBI to Kyiv," *The Kyiv Post*. November 25th, 1999

[22] Burgis, Tom, "Tower of secrets: the Russian money behind a Donald Trump skyscraper," *The Financial Times*. July 11th, 2018

[23] Woodward, Bob. "White House Gave DNC Top-Secret Intelligence," *The Washington Post*. April 8th, 1997

[24] OCCRP Archive Research, "Semion Mogilevich Organization: Eurasian Organized Crime," Eurasian Organized Crime, Department of Justice and the Federal Bureau of Investigation, August 1996

[25] Dasgupta, Shirso; Loginova, Olena. "A made-in-Miami money laundering saga develops even deeper Ukrainian roots," *The Miami Times*. April 7th, 2021

[26] Axelrod, Toby. "European Jewish Parliament Off to Semi-Comedic Start," *The Jewish News of Northern California*. November 4th, 2011

[27] Frantz, Douglas; Bonner, Raymond. "A Cosmetics Heir's Joint Venture is Tainted by Ukrainian's Past," *The New York Times*. April 5th, 1997

[28] Berkman, Jacob. "Three hats in JWC ring?" *Jewish Telegraphic Agency*. May 17th, 2007

[29] MacKinnon, Mark. "World leaders, spies, and mafia dons: Who's who in Boris Birshtein's World," *The Globe and Mail*. December 29th, 2018

[30] Champion, Marc. "How a Trump Soho Partner Ended Up With Toxic Mining Riches From Kazakhstan," *Bloomberg*. January 11th, 2018

[31] Posner, Sara. "Right Makes Might," *The New Republic*. March 25th, 2019

[32] Geoghegan, Peter. "Dark money, dirty politics and the backlash against human rights," *openDemocracy*. August 20th, 2020

[33] Tibon, Amir. "Manafort and Senior Israeli Official Meddled in Ukraine, Obama Foreign Policy," *Haaretz*. September 14th, 2018

[34] Wilner, Michael. "Mueller: Manafort used 'Obama's Jews' to smear Ukrainian leader," *The Jerusalem Post*. September 14th, 2018

[35] Podolsky, Phillip. "Likud-Beytenu campaign guru Finkelstein leaves Israel," *The Times of Israel*. January 18th, 2013

[36] Weinglass, Simona; Horovitz, David; Ahren, Raphael. "Israeli firm under FBI scrutiny in Trump probe allegedly targeted BDS activists," *The Times of Israel*. June 6th, 2018

[37] Ahren, Raphael. "iVoteIsrael has strong ties to Ron Lauder, report says," *The Times of Israel*. October 17th, 2012

[38] Weinglass, Simona. "Israeli pitched covert pro-Trump plan while leading 'nonpartisan' iVote Israel," *The Times of Israel*. August 31st, 2020

[39] Barnes, Julian E. "Ex-C.I.A. Officer's Brief Detention Deepens Mystery in Montenegro," *The New York Times*. November 23rd, 2018

[40] Kajosevic, Samir. "Montenegro Prosecution Suspects Israeli Consultant of Coup Role," *Balkan Insight*. July 31st, 2019

[41] Report of the Select Committee on Intelligence United States Senate On Russian Active Measures Campaigns And Interference in the 2016 US Election Volume 5: Counterintelligence Threats and Vulnerabilities. Pg. 147

[42] Shuster, Simon. "Exclusive: Russian Ex-Spy Pressured Manafort Over Debts to an

Oligarch," *TIME*. December 29th, 2018

[43] Press Release. "Treasury Targets Russian Operative over Election Interference, World Anti-Doping Agency Hacking, and Other Malign Activities," *U.S. Department of the Treasury*. December 19th, 2018

[44] Report of the Select Committee on Intelligence United States Senate On Russian Active Measures Campaigns And Interference in the 2016 US Election Volume 5: Counterintelligence Threats and Vulnerabilities. Pg. 682-685

[45] Entous, Adam; Farrow, Ronan. "Private Mossad for Hire," *The New Yorker*. February 11th, 2009

[46] Mazzetti, Mark; Goldman, Adam; Berman, Ronen; Perlroth, Nicole. "A New Age of Warfare: How Internet Mercenaries Do Battle for Authoritarian Governments," *The New York Times*. March 21st, 2019

[47] Bolshaw, Liz. "A new breed of commercial intelligence company," *The Financial Times*. March 25th, 2015

[48] "Reality Is A Matter Of Perception," PSY GROUP Promotional Materials

[49] Klippenstein, Ken. "Inside Wikistrat, the Mysterious Intelligence Firm Now in Mueller's Sights," *The Daily Beast*. June 4th, 2018

[50] Miller, Greg; Goldman, Adam. "Head of Pentagon intelligence agency forced out, officials say," *The Washington Post*. April 30th, 2014

[51] Swan, Betsy; Banco, Erin. "Mueller Witness' Team Gamed Out Russian Meddling… in 2015," *The Daily Beast*. January 30th, 2019

[52] Report of the Select Committee on Intelligence United States Senate On Russian Active Measures Campaigns And Interference in the 2016 US Election Volume 5: Counterintelligence Threats and Vulnerabilities. Pg. 680

[53] Stedman, Scott. *Real News: An Investigative Reporter Uncovers The Foundations Of The Trump-Russia Conspiracy*. New York, NY: Skyhorse Publishing, Inc. 2019. Pg. 77

[54] Stedman, Scott. *Real News: An Investigative Reporter Uncovers The Foundations Of The Trump-Russia Conspiracy*. New York, NY: Skyhorse Publishing, Inc. 2019. Pg. 77-83

[55] Ivanidze, Vladimir; Weinglass Simona; Gryvnyak, Natalie. "How an Israeli intel firm allegedly harassed pro-democracy activists in Ukraine," *The Times of Israel*. May 15th, 2020

[56] Crowley, Michael. "Trump and the Oligarch," *Politico Magazine*. July 28th, 2016

[57] Report of the Select Committee on Intelligence United States Senate On Russian Active Measures Campaigns And Interference in the 2016 US Election Volume 5: Counterintelligence Threats and Vulnerabilities. Pg. 683-684

[58] Mendick, Robert. "I'm being smeared, says Diego Maradona's ex-agent in row over Senate inquiry into Russian election interference," *The Telegraph*. January 25th, 2020

[59] Bertrand, Natasha. "Senate Intelligence Committee summons mysterious British security consultant," *Politico*. June 5th, 2019

[60] Betito, Merav; Yehezkeli, Zadok. "Million Shekel Bibi," *Yedioth Ahronoth*. March 9th, 2010 [Hebrew Language Publication]

[61] Schneider, Tal; Maanit, Chen. "Soriano Riddle: Who is the man whose name is linked in the conflict between the commissioner and the prime minister," *Globes*. December 2nd, 2018

[62] Stedman, Scott; Coleman, Jess. "Walter Soriano: The covert operative for Russian and Israeli elite," *Forensic News*. July 14th, 2019

[63] "FBI report could find Soriano exposed again," *Intelligence Online*. December 24th, 2019

[64] Ivanidze, Vladimir; Weinglass Simona; Gryvnyak, Natalie. "How an Israeli intel firm allegedly harassed pro-democracy activists in Ukraine," *The Times of Israel*. May 15th, 2020

[65] Marson, James; Forrest, Brett. "Ukrainian Corruption Showdown Sets State for Impeachment Inquiry," *The Wall Street Journal*. November 12th, 2019

[66] Leshchenko, Serhii; Kalaniuk, Daria; Sobolov, Yehor. "Daria Kaleniuk, Sergii

Leshchenko, Yehor Sobolev: Ukraïne should become a normal European country," *The Kyiv Post*. April 1st, 2016

[67] Vasilyeva, Natalia. "Ukraine lawmaker: Manafort tried to hide $750,000 payment," *The Associated Press*. March 21st, 2017

[68] Report of the Select Committee on Intelligence United States Senate On Russian Active Measures Campaigns And Interference in the 2016 US Election Volume 5: Counterintelligence Threats and Vulnerabilities. Pg. 684-687

[69] Mazzetti, Mark; Bergman, Ronen; Kirkpatrick, David D.; Haberman, Maggie. "Rick Gates Sought Online Manipulation Plans From Israeli Intelligence Firm for Trump Campaign," *The New York Times*. October 8th, 2018

[70] Report of the Select Committee on Intelligence United States Senate On Russian Active Measures Campaigns And Interference in the 2016 US Election Volume 5: Counterintelligence Threats and Vulnerabilities. Pg. 688

[71] Entous, Adam; Farrow, Ronan. "Private Mossad for Hire," *The New Yorker*. February 11th, 2009

[72] Banco, Erin; Swan, Betsy. "Top Cheney Aide in Mueller's Sights as Probe Expands," *The Daily Beast*. November 16th, 2018

[73] Mazzetti, Mark; Kirkpatrick, David D.; Haberman, Maggie. "Mueller's Focus on Advisor to Emirates Suggests Broader Investigation," *The New York Times*. March 3rd, 2018

[74] Akkad, Dania; Cobaine, Ian. "George Nader: how a convicted paedophile became key to an Emirati hook-up with Trump," *Middle East Eye*. July 15th, 2019

[75] Rozen, Laura. "The dealmaker: Mueller witness helped broker $4.2 billion Iraq-Russia arms deal," *Al-Monitor*. March 8th, 2017

[76] Bertrand, Natasha. "Why Was George Nader Allowed Into the White House?" *The Atlantic*. March 8th, 2018

[77] Gerstein, Josh. "Mueller witness was convicted on child porn charge," *Politico*. March 16th, 2018

[78] Klapper, Bradley; Janicek, Karel. "Mueller witness is convicted pedophile with shadowy past," *The Associated Press*. March 15th, 2018

[79] Entous, Adam; Farrow, Ronan. "Private Mossad for Hire," *The New Yorker*. February 11th, 2009

[80] Report of the Select Committee on Intelligence United States Senate On Russian Active Measures Campaigns And Interference in the 2016 US Election Volume 5: Counterintelligence Threats and Vulnerabilities. Pg. 680-689

[81] Hearst, David. "EXCLUSIVE: The secret yacht summit that realigned the Middle East," *Middle East Eye*. December 27th, 2018

[82] Report of the Select Committee on Intelligence United States Senate On Russian Active Measures Campaigns And Interference in the 2016 US Election Volume 5: Counterintelligence Threats and Vulnerabilities. Pg. 689

[83] Prince, Erik. *Civilian Warriors: The Inside Story of Blackwater and the Unsung Heroes of the War on Terror*. New York, NY: PORTFOLIO/PENGUIN. 2013. Pg. 20

[84] Simons, Suzanne. *Master of War: Blackwater USA's Erik Prince and the Business of War*. New York, NY: HarperCollins Publishers, 2009. Pg. 19-25

[85] Miller, Greg. "Revolving door from CIA to Blackwater," *The Los Angeles Times*. August 21st, 2009

[86] Prince, Erik. *Civilian Warriors: The Inside Story of Blackwater and the Unsung Heroes of the War on Terror*. New York, NY: PORTFOLIO/PENGUIN. 2013. Pg. 52-53

[87] Mazzetti, Mark; Black, Shane. "C.I.A. Had Plan to Assassinate Qaeda Leaders," *The New York Times*. July 13th, 2009

[88] Mayer, Jane. *The Dark Side: The Inside Story Of How The War On Terror Turned Into A War On American Ideals*. New York, NY: DoubleDay, 2008. Pg. 38-40

[89] Ciralsky, Adam. "Tycoon, Contractor, Soldier, Spy," *Vanity Fair*. January 2010

[90] Risen, James; Mazzetti, Mark. "Blackwater Guards Tied to Secretive C.I.A. Raids,"

The New York Times. December 10th, 2009

[91] Mazzetti, Mark; Kirkpatrick, David D.; Haberman, Maggie. "Mueller's Focus on Advisor to Emirates Suggests Broader Investigation," *The New York Times.* March 3rd, 2018

[92] Scahill, Jeremy. *Blackwater: The Rise Of The World's Most Powerful Mercenary Army.* New York, NY: Nation Book, 2007. Pg. 147-150

[93] Mazzetti, Mark; Black, Shane. "C.I.A. Had Plan to Assassinate Qaeda Leaders," *The New York Times.* July 13th, 2009

[94] Cole, Matthew. "The Complete Mercenary," *The Intercept.* May 3rd, 2019

[95] Nissenbaum, Dion. "Blackwater's Founder Blames U.S. for Its Troubles," *The Wall Street Journal.* November 17th, 2013

[96] Ciralsky, Adam. "Tycoon, Contractor, Soldier, Spy," *Vanity Fair.* January 2010

[97] Mazzetti, Mark; Hager, Emily B. "Secret Desert Force Set Up by Blackwater Founder," *The New York Times.* May 14th, 2011

[98] Cole, Matthew. "The Complete Mercenary," *The Intercept.* May 3rd, 2019

[99] Fisher, Marc; Shapira, Ian; Rauhala, Emily. "Behind Erik Prince's China Venture," *The Washington Post.* May 4th, 2018

[100] Cole, Matthew; Scahill, Jeremy. "Erik Prince In The Hot Seat," *The Intercept.* March 24th, 2016

[101] Fisher, Marc; Shapira, Ian; Rauhala, Emily. "Behind Erik Prince's China Venture," *The Washington Post.* May 4th, 2018

[102] Cole, Matthew; Scahill, Jeremy. "Erik Prince In The Hot Seat," *The Intercept.* March 24th, 2016

[103] Fisher, Marc; Shapira, Ian; Rauhala, Emily. "Behind Erik Prince's China Venture," *The Washington Post.* May 4th, 2018

[104] Scahill, Jeremy; Cole, Matthew. "Echo Papa Exposed," *The Intercept.* April 11th, 2016

[105] Schmidle, Nicholas. "Disarming Viktor Bout," *The New Yorker.* August 27th, 2014

[106] Busch, Gary K. "Uncivil Aviation in Africa," *Academia.edu.* March 9th, 2012

[107] Scahill, Jeremy; Cole, Matthew. "Echo Papa Exposed," *The Intercept.* April 11th, 2016

[108] Cole, Matthew. "The Complete Mercenary," *The Intercept.* May 3rd, 2019

[109] Scahill, Jeremy; Cole, Matthew. "Before He Was FBI Director, Chris Wray Supervised An Investigation That Found Erik Prince Likely Broke U.S. Law," *The Intercept.* March 19th, 2018

[110] Scahill, Jeremy; Cole, Matthew. "Echo Papa Exposed," *The Intercept.* April 11th, 2016

[111] Fisher, Marc; Shapira, Ian; Rauhala, Emily. "Behind Erik Prince's China Venture," *The Washington Post.* May 4th, 2018

[112] Report of the Select Committee on Intelligence United States Senate On Russian Active Measures Campaigns And Interference in the 2016 US Election Volume 5: Counterintelligence Threats and Vulnerabilities. Pg. 683

[113] Report of the Select Committee on Intelligence United States Senate On Russian Active Measures Campaigns And Interference in the 2016 US Election Volume 5: Counterintelligence Threats and Vulnerabilities. Pg. 689

[114] Mazzetti, Mark; Bergman, Ronen; Kirkpatrick, David D. "Trump Jr. and Other Aides Met With Gulf Emissary Offering Help to Win Election," *The New York Times.* May 19th, 2018

[115] Mazzetti, Mark; Bergman, Ronen; Kirkpatrick, David D. "Trump Jr. and Other Aides Met With Gulf Emissary Offering Help to Win Election," *The New York Times.* May 19th, 2018

[116] Report of the Select Committee on Intelligence United States Senate On Russian Active Measures Campaigns And Interference in the 2016 US Election Volume 5: Counterintelligence Threats and Vulnerabilities. Pg. 689-691

[117] Swan, Betsy. "Blackwater Founder Erick Prince, Who Got Rich Off Iraq, Now Backs 'Anti-War' Donald Trump," *The Daily Beast.* October 22nd, 2016

Chapter 21:
Michael Flynn, Colt Ventures,
And the Search for the "Missing" Clinton Emails

The Alienation of Michael Flynn:
From the War on Terror to Russia to Trump

"Russia, if you're listening, I hope you are able to find the 30,000 emails that are missing," intoned the Republican nominee for President. Donald Trump made this statement in Miami on July 27th, 2016. Five days earlier, WikiLeaks had released 20,000 internal DNC emails. Russian military intelligence was listening. Within five hours of his making the statement, hackers from the GRU's Unit 26165 targeted Hillary Clinton's personal office for the first time.

Trump turned to three-star Lieutenant General Michael T. Flynn to pursue a parallel effort.[1] After being asked "repeatedly" by Trump to find Hillary's "missing" 30,000 emails, Flynn told Trump that he "had people" who could find them.[2] However, beyond these efforts, Flynn engaged in further activities to aid the Trump, many of which remain shrouded in mystery.

Michael Thomas Flynn was one of nine siblings born to a middle-class, Irish-American Catholic family in Middleton, Rhode Island. His father had enjoyed a distinguished military career during the Second World War.[3] Flynn's mother was a noted lawyer and activist for the Rhode Island Democratic Party.[4] In his memoir, Flynn describes having engaged in "some serious and unlawful activity" as a youth. He later dropped out of college, leaving his freshman year with a 1.2 GPA. However, his life turned around upon joining the military and becoming an Army intelligence officer.[5]

He made his mark in Iraq as a colonel in charge of intelligence gathering at the Joint Special Operations Command (JSOC). At the time, Iraq was consumed by a violent insurgency. Under the leadership of General Stanley McChrystal, Flynn revolutionized the military's interrogation process, expanding the use of digital technology and information sharing that led to a dynamic intelligence-gathering process followed by special forces operations.[6]

In 2009, Flynn followed McChrystal to Afghanistan. McChrystal was at loggerheads with Obama, who was skeptical of escalating the eight-year-old conflict. The Obama White House came to believe that his generals were attempting to box him in after a 60-day assessment of the Afghan War's progress made by McChrystal arguing that the war was being lost and that the number of American forces should be increased was leaked to the press.[7] It was Flynn's first disagreement with his commander and chief, but far from the last.

Flynn oversaw an assessment of intelligence efforts in Afghanistan. He argued that the US military was focusing on meaningless metrics while neglecting to gain a fundamental understanding of social and cultural currents. According to Flynn, the solution to this problem could be found in "Big Data."[8] DARPA implemented a program in Afghanistan to predict insurgent attacks known as *Nexus 7*. Press reports described Flynn as a "godfather" of the program. In this timeframe, SCL Group began applying its analysis on the Afghan population under Flynn's auspices.[9]

Flynn's views of Obama further deteriorated after the latter fired General McChrystal following an article in *Rolling Stone* in which McChrystal spoke disparagingly of several Obama administration officials. In 2011, Flynn moved to Washington, DC, where he worked at the Office of the Director of National Intelligence (ODNI) under the Obama-appointed James Clapper. Despite Flynn's disdain, Obama nominated him to become the 18th Director of the Defense Intelligence Agency (DIA), and he officially took command in July of 2012.

Drawing from his experience in Afghanistan, Flynn also attempted to modernize DIA's utilization of data and analytics.[10]

Despite this, his tenure at DIA was turbulent. Flynn's colleagues noticed that he made strange and unsubstantiated claims using what some within the agency began referring to dismissively as "Flynn Facts."[11] Flynn's critics accused him of engaging in politically motivated, speculative, or even in some cases, outright conspiratorial thinking that aligned with his preconceived notions.[12]

One of Flynn's more controversial actions was becoming the first DIA Director to visit the Aquarium, the headquarters of the GRU. Flynn was invited by Russia's chief of military intelligence, Major General Igor Sergun, who died in mysterious circumstances in early 2016.[13] The Russian Ambassador to the US, Sergei Kislyak, helped arrange the trip.[14]

Flynn's visit to GRU headquarters occurred in the context of several other discreet meetings between American and Russian intelligence officials throughout 2012-2013.[15] However, the high-profile nature of Flynn's visit made it controversial among American intelligence officials. Flynn, who claimed to be aware of Russian efforts to manipulate joint counterterrorism efforts in the past, persisted in his desire to foster increased collaboration between Russia and the United States when it came to fighting Islamic extremism.[16]

James Clapper, who had been asked to visit the GRU's headquarters after he had retired as DIA director in 1995 but declined the invitation, warned Flynn over the trip. "One time I had a little chat with him," Clapper later said, "sort of for some fatherly advice, to 'just be careful.'"[17]

Flynn arrived in Moscow in June of 2013. He laid a wreath at Russia's Tomb of the Unknown Soldier before being shuttled to the GRU's headquarters, where he gave a presentation on leadership and intelligence before a gathering of young GRU officers. According to the Attaché to the Russian Federation Peter Zwack, the young officers asked questions that indicated they had never met an American intelligence official before. Later that evening, Sergun and two other GRU officials dined with Flynn and Zwack at the US Embassy in Moscow.[18] Flynn left Russia believing he had established a rapport with Sergun.[19] Within months, the GRU's cyber warriors were busily at work supporting Russia's annexation of Crimea.

Upon returning to the US, Flynn wanted to invite Sergun to Washington. After Crimea, James Clapper nixed the idea.

Eventually, Clapper and the Under Secretary of Defense for Intelligence, Michael Vickers, decided that Flynn wasn't up to managing DIA and informed him that he wouldn't be serving out the customary three years but would be forced into retirement after only two.[20] Clapper later suggested that Flynn became "an angry man" after his removal from office.[21] Flynn believed that he had been silenced by an administration that did not want to hear the truth about Islamic terrorism. During his retirement speech, Flynn stated that the US was less safe from Islamist terror than it was before 9/11.[22]

Flynn's Links to Russia, Trump,
And the Israeli Private Intelligence Industry

In October 2014, Flynn established the Flynn Intel Group.[23] He signed a contract with the speakers bureau Leading Authorities shortly after that. By the Summer of 2015, in remarkably close succession, Flynn began to be courted by various interests connected to Russia and the newly launched Trump campaign. On July 31st, Flynn was paid $11,250 by an American subsidiary of the Russian cyber security firm Kaspersky Lab to make a speech. The company's founder, Eugene Kaspersky, was educated at the High School of the KGB, where he studied cryptography. Kaspersky then served as a Soviet intelligence officer before founding his cyber security company.[24] Kaspersky Lab has developed software for the FSB and even accompanied its agents on raids.[25] The US later banned Federal agencies from using Kaspersky software.[26]

That same day, July 31st, Flynn was paid $11,250 by the Russian company Volga-Dnepr Airlines to make a speech at an event in Washington, DC. In 2007, Volga-Dnepr was found to have been involved in an illegal kickback scheme involving a United Nations procurement officer. The UN suspended the company as a vendor.[27] In May of 2015, two months before Flynn received payment, the Pentagon deemed the airline "[u]nsuitable for use."[28]

Less than a month later, Flynn received his first outreach from the Trump campaign. On August 17th, an as-yet unidentified individual put Flynn in contact with Steve Bannon. Bannon connected Flynn to Corey Lewandowski.[29] Flynn traveled to New York to meet with Trump. While only scheduled to meet for thirty minutes, they spoke for ninety. Flynn left the meeting enraptured. "I knew he was going to be the President of the United States," he recalled.[30]

In early September, Flynn corresponded with Bannon and Erik Prince.[31] Flynn and Prince discussed how the US could work with Russia on issues such as Libya, where Prince had significant mercenary interests. Flynn and Prince also discussed the United Arab Emirates (UAE), which they believed had been helpful in Afghanistan. When later asked if he and Prince had discussed a potential back channel to Russia through the UAE, Flynn replied that he "did not remember any such discussion." Flynn also recalled that Prince had "carte blanche" at Trump Tower, and he often saw him there speaking with Bannon and Jared Kushner.[32] After its investigation, the Senate Intelligence Committee wrote to DOJ requesting an inquiry into Bannon and claiming that he may have lied about his interactions with Eric Prince.[33]

On October 5th, Flynn appeared on *RT* and attacked the US strategy being pursued against the Islamic State, arguing that the US and Russia should confront the group together. Following the broadcast, a Washington-based representative from *RT* contacted Flynn's son, Michael G. Flynn Jr., who served as his father's chief of staff. The *RT* representative told Flynn Jr. that she had "discussed with [the] General an opportunity for him to visit Moscow this coming December as a guest of honor of *RT*'s conference that will mark the 10th anniversary of our news broadcast" and that he "looked very interested in it and asked me to check with you [on] his plans for December."[34]

Flynn agreed to speak at the event for $45,000, which would be routed to him through his speakers bureau.[35] After signing the contract with *RT* on November 11th, the total amount of money paid to him from Russian sources throughout 2015 approached $70,000. *RT* also offered to pay for business class travel to Moscow for Flynn and his son and to put them up at the Metropole, a luxurious five-star historic hotel in the heart of the Russian capital.[36]

Before leaving for Moscow, Flynn and his son met with Ambassador Kislyak at his residence.[37] Flynn also received a courtesy classified briefing on Russia from DIA. Officials later claimed that Flynn failed to disclose all the relevant details as to the nature and purpose of his trip.[38] Flynn stayed in Moscow from December 8th-11th, 2015. On the evening of the gala, he was seated at the head table next to Vladimir Putin. Seated around them were the former KGB agent Sergei Ivanov, Putin's then chief-of-staff and fellow classmate at the Red Banner Institute, Kremlin spokesman Dmitry Peskov, *RT* Editor-in-Chief Margarita Simonyan, and Jill Stein, the Green Party candidate for the upcoming US presidential election.[39]

During the conference, Flynn was interviewed by *RT* and argued that Russia and the United States had shared interests in fighting the Islamic State. Other speakers included Julian Assange, beamed via telecast from the Ecuadorian Embassy in London.[40] Flynn later met with the CIA's station chief in Moscow and lectured him about Russian-American relations, suggesting that the US needed to "ease back." When Flynn asked for a follow-up meeting, the station chief refused, worried that Flynn had met with Russian officials in the interim and either had un-asked for suggestions or possibly even information he wanted to collect.

Nine days after he returned from Moscow, Flynn wrote to Trump campaign chief Corey Lewandowski on December 19th. Attached to his email was an article from *Sputnik*, another Russian-state-backed news organization, entitled "US Must Cooperate With Russia, Arabs to Defeat ISIL." Flynn argues for increased US and Russian cooperation in Syria in the article. Flynn wrote to Lewandowski that this was "something Mr. Trump should at least be aware of... I have been very outspoken on this issue." Flynn continued, "I met with President Putin last Thursday in Moscow. We actually sat at dinner together."[41]

On March 20th, Flynn emailed Trump campaign policy advisor Sam Clovis, copying Corey Lewandowski. "Below is a recent OPED from Russian Foreign Minister [Sergey] Lavrov," Flynn wrote. "I strongly recommend Trump read this." Flynn then suggested that Trump speak with Henry Kissinger. "Regarding Russia," Flynn continued, "we lack any serious strategic thinking in our current administration - they see Russia as an enemy - as long as we do that, nothing good will come of it. We have to directly confront Russia and take collective steps to figure out how we are going to deal with them going forward. We don't need to be friends, but we need to start somewhere - and there are good and valid starting points that do exist."[42]

In February 2016, Flynn joined the advisory board of

Brainwave Science, which developed technology designed to measure brainwaves to determine whether a subject under interrogation was lying. One of Brainwave's two main directors, an Indian engineer named Sabu Kota, pleaded guilty in 1996 to attempting to sell stolen biotech material to the KGB.[43] According to prosecutors, Kota, whose name was only removed from Brainwave's website after news of his activities surfaced in the press in late 2016, had been involved in a spy ring attempting to sell sensitive technologies to the KGB between 1985 and 1990.[44] As part of a deal in which he testified against another defendant, he was only convicted of tax evasion and theft.[45]

In addition to Russia, Flynn has connections to the Israeli private intelligence industry. In May 2016, he was hired as an advisory board member for OSY Technologies, an offshoot of NSO Group, a technology conglomerate founded by veterans of the IDF's Unit 8200. NSO Group gained notoriety after developing surveillance software used by, among others, Saudi Arabia and the United Arab Emirates to track the regime dissidents.[46] As of this writing, NSO Group is under investigation by the FBI[47] Scott Stedman has reported that OSY Technologies has been contracted to work for the Moscow-based law firm Egorov Puginsky Afanasiev & Partners (EPAP) and that EPAP was operating as a stand-in for Oleg Deripaska.[48]

OSY Technologies is the parent company of another surveillance firm called Circles.[49] The founders of Circles, Boaz Goldman and Nadia Ropleva, also work at the cyber security firm FloLive. Two individuals with ownership stakes in FloLive, Shlomo Rechtschaffen and Doron Cohen, are the personal lawyer and business partner, respectively, of the former Israeli military intelligence officer Walter Soriano. One potential connection between Flynn and Soriano is Richard Frankel, described by *ABC News* as a "friend" of Flynn's, who went to work for Soriano's company, USG Security, in early 2016.[50]

The Senate Intelligence Committee wrote to Soriano requesting that he provide documents related to any communications he had with Oleg Deripaska, Konstantin Kilimnik, Paul Manafort, Steve Bannon, Erik Prince, and Michael Flynn. Soriano does not appear to have complied with the Committee's request, and his name appears only once in the non-redacted portions of its report. It is unclear why the Senate Intelligence Committee was interested in Soriano's relationship with Flynn.

Michael Flynn, the Montenegro Connection, and Voter Suppression

The Committee also requested Soriano provide any
communications he may have had with Darren Blanton, a Texan
venture capitalist, biotech investor, and founder of Colt Ventures.
During the 2016 election, Blanton regularly contacted Steve
Bannon and frequently visited Trump Tower. Colt Ventures was
an investor in VizSense, a Dallas-based social media and "micro-
influencer" company that provided the Trump campaign with
$200,000 worth of services in the campaign's final month. What
precisely these services were remains a mystery. Stranger still, the
campaign paid the money to Colt Ventures, which then remitted
a portion of it to VizSense, raising questions as to whether the
Trump campaign attempted to conceal its relationship with
VizSense or violated campaign finance law.[51]

VizSense was founded in 2015 by former Navy SEAL Jon
Iadonisi and a nuclear engineer and former submariner named
Tim Newberry. On its website, VizSense promised to "weaponize
your brand's influence" through "military-grade influencer
marketing and intelligence services." Flynn served with Iadonisi
in Iraq and has described him as "one of the best problem solvers
I have ever worked with." In August 2016, Tim Newberry was
CEO of the Flynn Intel Group subsidiary FIG Cyber. VizSense
was a spin-off of another Iadonisi and Newberry joint project
called White Canvas Group, a technology company described as
"a privatized DARPA" with expertise in social media, cyber
operations, and digital influence. Flynn Intel Group rented office
space from White Canvas Group.[52]

"Social media is a new form of signals intelligence," Flynn
said in one of his final interviews as Director of DIA. At that
time, the US invested heavily in various methods of collecting
and examining social media data as a source of overseas
intelligence.[53] In July 2016, Jon Iadonisi spoke with Flynn about
the critical role "influencers" would play in the upcoming
election. Flynn then put Iadonisi in contact with the Trump
campaign.[54]

On August 18th, Iadonisi began discussions with the
Trump campaign's digital director, Brad Pascale, providing him
with examples of VizSense's work. He offered an example of a

"persuasion campaign using organically created content to drive a conversation ... using influencers to spread the message." Iadonisi explained to Parscale that the "same technique can be used in politics, where the content and influencers are surgically designed to deliver a political message to a specific audience, creating a digital bonfire of conversation."

Later, in mid-September, Iadonisi sent Steve Bannon a $769,000 proposal to pursue an online campaign to mobilize Trump voters in critical voting districts. Bannon asked Darren Blanton to meet with Iadonisi and review the proposal. Iadonisi connected Blanton with Michael Flynn. While this initial offer was rejected after the campaign decided to use Brad Parscale's team, Blanton continued to pursue Bannon, writing him an email with the subject line "Did call on foreign voters this is the week they request ballots. Got to act quick." Blanton wrote that he "spoke to Jesse at [GOP] about foreign voters and have a strategy. He's getting me as many digital addresses as he can find. We need to send out a video request from [then-candidate Trump] via social [media] to ask for their votes." It is unclear who "Jesse" is, but he appears to have been involved with the Republican Party's outreach on behalf of Trump to American voters living overseas.

The portion of the Senate Counterintelligence report about Colt Ventures and VizSense contains a subsection entitled "[REDACTED] and Overseas Voters." It is entirely redacted but for a single footnote that directs readers to an article by *Balkan Insight*, which reports that Montenegrin prosecutors suspected that a British-Israeli political consultant named Aron Shaviv had been involved in an October 2016 GRU-assisted and Deripaska-backed coup attempt in Montenegro.[55] While there is no publicly available information on what Shaviv or the coup in Montenegro have to do with Colt Ventures or VizSense, the redacted section of the report follows a description of Blanton's interest in targeting overseas voters with social media. An analysis of Shaviv and his activities in Montenegro reveals a remarkable nexus of Russian and American figures involved in the American election, which occurred less than a month after the attempted coup.

Before becoming involved in politics, Shaviv was a captain in the Israeli Defense Forces and a "field agent for a civilian intelligence agency."[56] He started politics in 2006, working for Yisrael Beiteinu, a center-right party founded by the

Soviet-born Israeli Avigdor Lieberman.[57] Lieberman has been investigated for potentially receiving illegal bribes from individuals close to Putin and individuals suspected of links to organized crime.[58]

Shaviv later established a political consulting firm and worked for right-wing candidates across Central and Eastern Europe, including in Ukraine, Cyprus, Bulgaria, Romania, Serbia, Croatia, Slovakia, and, later, Montenegro. He worked on both the campaigns of Netanyahu and Britain's Conservative Prime Minister David Cameron.[59] Shaviv's mentor, Arthur Finkelstein, arranged for a political merger between Yisrael Beiteinu and Likud in 2012.[60] Shaviv credits Finkelstein and George Birnbaum with getting him a start in politics.[61] As covered, Birnbaum introduced Rick Gates to Psy Group via Eitan Charnoff. In addition to being a project manager for Psy Group, Charnoff was also the head of iVote Israel, an ostensibly non-partisan group dedicated to increasing absentee voting in the US elections by eligible Israelis.[62] During the 2016 election, both Democratic and Republican voters in Israel complained that iVote Israel failed to send them their ballots.[63] The author believes, though cannot prove, that the title of the redacted section of the Senate Intelligence Committee report in question is, in fact, "[iVote Israel] and Overseas Voters."

Founded in 2012 during the lead-up to the Obama-Romney race, iVote Israel was initially run by Elie Pieprz, a former member of the Republican Jewish Coalition who later immigrated to Israel and joined the group Republicans Abroad Israel. At its founding, iVote Israel's campaign strategist was Aron Shaviv.[64] As a 501(c)4 so-called "dark money" nonprofit, iVote Israel is not required to list its donors. As mentioned previously, the group has been linked to the American billionaire heir Ronald Lauder.

When iVote Israel's former campaign strategist Aron Shaviv worked on behalf of the pro-Kremlin Democratic Front (DF) opposition party in Montenegro, several disparate threads relating to the Russian interference in the 2016 US election and figures within the Trump campaign came together. International investigators from *Bellingcat* have confirmed that the GRU was involved in the plot.[65] Oleg Deripaska supported the coup.[66] Paul Manafort, who had worked on behalf of Deripaska's interests in Montenegro as far back as 2005, was also in contact with figures in the DF in the Fall of 2016.[67] Victor Boyarkin, the former GRU officer who worked for Deripaska and chased down Manafort over his debts to the oligarch, was also involved in funding the DF.[68]

Despite the placement of "[Redacted] and Overseas Voters," with its reference to Aron Shaviv, in the part of the Senate Counterintelligence report describing the activities of Colt Ventures and VizSense, there is no public information linking either company to iVote Israel or the events in Montenegro. However, the analysis of iVote Israel, Aron Shaviv, and the events surrounding the coup attempt in Montenegro is useful insofar as they appear to serve as a nexus of intersecting relationships between individuals involved with the Trump campaign and Russians involved in the 2016 US election interference effort coming together in the context of a yet another national election being interfered with by agents of the Kremlin.

Shortly after Blanton inquired about a proposal regarding overseas voters, Michael Flynn sent Brad Parscale a contract from Colt Ventures. It was a crucial moment in the campaign, a day after the release of the *Access Hollywood* tape. Between October 8th-9th, VizSense appears to have engaged in a social media campaign around the second presidential debate that focused on denigrating Hillary Clinton and attacking former President Bill Clinton as a "rapist," a not-so-subtle means of deflecting attention away from Trump's own sexual indiscretions.

In mid-October, Steve Bannon put Blanton and Iadonisi in touch with Bruce Carter, an African American political activist who had previously supported Bernie Sanders but had switched to supporting Trump. Carter created the group *Trump For Urban Communities*, which he later claimed was tasked by the Trump campaign with getting black voters to either switch their vote to Trump or to sit out the election entirely. Carter put together a $160,000 proposal for the group, and to facilitate funding, Bannon put him in contact with Blanton.

Blanton and Iadonisi met with Carter in Dallas, and Blanton said he would provide him with funding while Iadonisi would amplify his message on social media. Blanton later introduced Carter to Michael Flynn, Erik Prince, and Rebekah Mercer. In the campaign's final weeks, *Trump for Urban Communities* engaged in a "Don't Vote Early" campaign. After

Trump's victory, Blanton and Bannon cut ties with Carter, who claims he had been promised ongoing support.[69] It was yet another example of voter suppression operations targeting black voters, which finds parallels in the activities of the Trump campaign and the Internet Research Agency. While Blanton and Iadonisi's interactions with Bruce Carter are a fact, whether VizSense was involved in the Trump campaign's voter suppression activities is unknown.

During this timeframe, Darren Blanton conducted business with a Russian pharmaceutical executive named Alexey Repik, who had met with Vladimir Putin on multiple occasions, including as late as October 2016. In the fall of 2016, negotiations were underway for a venture fund backed by Repik's company R-Pharm and the Russian government to invest in a California-based biotech company called Bonti. Blanton's Colt Ventures was an investor in the company. Blanton and Repik met in San Francisco to discuss the deal, which closed on January 4th, 2017. Repik and his wife were later seen attending Trump's inauguration with Blanton. In its reporting of the encounter, *The Washington Post* pointed out that in 2011 the Russian news outlet Vedomosti asked Repik about rumors that he had ties to the FSB.[70]

In addition to Bonti, Repik is an investor in another San Francisco-based startup called Grabr. Another investor in the company was the billionaire Russian oligarch Konstantin Nikolaev.[71] Nikolaev is an investor in a gun manufacturer operated by his wife that provides sniper rifles to the Russian National Guard and answers directly to Putin. He is also a key investor in a Russian satellite imagery firm with a contract with the FSB that allows it to handle classified materials.[72] Nikolaev partially funded the activities of the convicted Russian intelligence operative Marina Butina while she was in the United States. Curiously, Nikolaev's son Andrey communicated with Darren Blanton during and after Trump's inauguration. The content of their communications is not publicly known.[73]

Michael Flynn, Peter W. Smith,
And the Search for the "Missing" Clinton Emails

In early July of 2017, Flynn was under consideration to be Trump's Vice Presidential candidate.[74] On July 18th, Flynn made one of the more memorable speeches at the Republican National

Conventions, leading the crowd in chants of "Lock Her Up!" The chant would become a staple of Trump's rallies. "Lock her up! Lock her up! Damn right! Exactly right!"[75]

On July 27th, after his infamous "Russia, if you're listening" statement, Trump asked Flynn to find Hillary's missing 30,000 emails. Flynn told Trump he could "use his intelligence sources" to get a hold of the emails.[76] One of the first people he turned to was the conservative activist Barbara Ledeen, a staff member on the Senate Judiciary Committee for the Republican Senator Chuck Grassley. Ledeen had been engaged in an effort to retrieve the missing 30,000 emails from the Clinton server potentially as early as December of 2015.[77]

Flynn knew Barbara Ledeen through her husband. In April 2011, Flynn and Michael Ledeen met at a private Washington, DC luncheon. The two bonded over their mutual disdain for Iran, a country which the neoconservative Ledeen had been fixated on since the 1980s. Ledeen later co-wrote Flynn's book *The Field of Fight*. Nicholas Schmidle of *The New Yorker* found that dozens of passages matched Ledeen's earlier writings on Iran.[78]

Ledeen has a history of involvement in election antics. He worked as a correspondent for The New Republic in Rome for a time. In 1979, Ledeen co-authored a series of articles on Jimmy Carter's brother, Billy Carter, and his relationship with Libya. One of the articles falsely asserted that Billy Carter had attended a party in which he impersonated his brother and promised to provide military technology to Libyan dictator Qaddafi. Ledeen wrote the articles as part of a disinformation campaign coordinated with SISMI, Italian military intelligence, to tilt the 1980 election towards Ronald Reagan.[79] The US Ambassador to Italy at the time wrote that Ledeen had been under contract as a consultant to the chief of Italian military intelligence. The SISMI advisor who assisted Ledeen with the articles, Francesco Pazienza, was later charged with extortion, possession of cocaine, leaking state secrets, and maintaining criminal associations with the mafia. While Ledeen was not charged, he was mentioned in Pazienza's indictment.[80]

Several years later, Ledeen played a central role in the Iran-Contra scandal.[81] Lawrence E. Walsh, the Independent Counsel tasked with investigating Iran Contra, took a particular interest in Ledeen, describing him as "more than a messenger" but rather acting as a spokesperson for the Israeli arms merchants in Washington.[82] According to *60 Minutes* producer Alan Weisman, Ledeen "has long been suspected of having an ongoing relationship with Israeli intelligence and SISMI, the Italian intelligence service."[83]

In July 2016, Michael Flynn turned to Ledeen's wife, Barbara. She had already been involved in the search for Hillary's emails. Six months earlier, on December 3rd, 2015, she contacted a Republican activist named Peter Smith regarding the operation. "Here is the proposal I briefly mentioned to you," Ledeen wrote to Smith. "The person I described to you would be happy to talk with you either in person or over the phone. The person can get the emails which 1. Were classified and 2. Were purloined by our enemies."[84]

Peter W. Smith was a Chicago-based investment banker and fundraiser for Newt Gingrich. A longtime foe of the Clintons, Smith played a key role in the early 1990s promoting the unsubstantiated "Troopergate" scandal in which four Arkansas state troopers alleged that Bill Clinton had used them to arrange for sexual liaisons with various women. Reporting on "Troopergate," which Smith helped facilitate, surfaced the name of Paula Jones to the public. Jones' subsequent lawsuit against Bill Clinton led to a deposition in which his false answers given under oath regarding his relationship with Monica Lewinsky led to his impeachment.[85]

In her communications with Smith, Ledeen shared a 25-page document that described a "Multi-Phase Email Recovery Approach" to find Hillary's emails.[86] "Clinton email server was, in all likelihood, breached long ago," Ledeen wrote to Smith, claiming further that the Chinese, Russian, or Iranian intelligence services could "re-assemble the server's email content." Ledeen proposed a three-phase approach to gaining access to the emails, the first two of which involved open source analysis, while the third phase called for reaching out to contacts in the intelligence community "that have access through liaison work with various foreign services" to see if any foreign intelligence agencies had gained access to the Clinton server.[87]

A Smith associate named John Szobocsan met with Ledeen to discuss the initiative. "[T]here was really nothing of substance there," Szobocsan later testified. "They were kind of like: Just give us a pile of money and we'll go out there and look for Clinton's emails. The whole prospect was: Let's go out there. We knew she had an unsecure email server, probably picked up by some intelligence agency someplace, and this could be in the deep and dark web."[88]

In mid-December, Smith wrote to Ledeen declining to participate. However, he became involved in a similar but separate venture later in 2016. On May 24th, 2016, Ledeen contacted Fox News' intelligence correspondent Catherine Herridge. "By way of introduction," Ledeen wrote, "we know a number of the same people - Newt Gingrich, Gen. Mike Flynn, [REDACTED] and a host of others. I do not want to cc them here because of the nature of the subject. A colleague and I would like to brief you on material we have found on the deep and dark web regarding stories you have been pursuing. The material we have found is exclusive so far, and we hope that we can brief you before it disappears and is locked up because of its sensitivity."[89]

There is no publicly available information on the nature of the materials Ledeen had in her possession, nor whether Herridge took Ledeen up on her offer. On June 16th, Ledeen emailed Flynn, informing him that he had received an email over the encrypted messaging app Signal. While it is unclear what the file was, the Senate Intelligence Committee speculated that it may have been the 25-page "Multi-Phase Email Recovery Approach" proposal Ledeen had sent earlier to Peter Smith.

"I received and was able to download the file ... amazing!" Flynn replied."[90]

Following Trump's request to Flynn to use his contacts in the intelligence world and elsewhere to find Hillary's "missing" emails, Flynn contacted Barbara Ledeen and Peter W. Smith. Flynn and Smith had a previous relationship. In November and December of 2015, they had been discussing potential cybersecurity business opportunities. On November 25th, 2015, Flynn, his son Michael Flynn Jr., and partner Bijan Kian met with Smith and Szobocsan at the Army Navy Club. Two weeks later, on December 7th, a conference call occurred between Flynn, Kian, Smith, and Szobocsan. While no definitive business deals emerged from these discussions, Flynn and Smith remained in contact.[91]

Smith's attempts to find Hillary's emails began to take shape in August of 2016. Remarkably, on August 12th, just as he was gearing up his own operation to seek out the Clinton emails, Smith's own emails were leaked by the GRU-cutout Guccifer 2.0 via DCLeaks.com.[92] Earlier in June, the FBI had informed the Illinois Republican Party that it had been hacked. Among the hacked and released emails were communications between Smith and Illinois state Republican committeeman Richard Porter.[93]

As part of his "political reconnaissance" into the Clinton emails, Smith established the Delaware-based KLS Research, LLC, to raise money for an effort to "determine when the emails which Sec. Clinton had on her personal server and deleted will emerge from sources that managed to capture those, because of the nature of the server itself and the failure of the server to be protected." Smith drafted cyber security experts, lawyers, and a Russian speaking investigator to assist him.[94] Starting on August 25th, Smith arranged for a daily conference call with "a dozen individuals and organizations with interest in learning of third parties which had access to these [Clinton's 30,000 "missing" State Department] emails."[95]

"[Peter W. Smith] will be near DC tomorrow and Sunday," Smith associate John Szobocsan wrote in an August 26th email, "allegedly reviewing some WikiLeaks -related documents." Szobocsan later told the Senate Intelligence Committee that Smith reviewed documents not yet in the possession of WikiLeaks but instead held by independent hackers. Smith wanted to obtain the documents and then pass them to WikiLeaks himself.

Smith met in DC with hackers that he described to Szobocsan as "nervous acting students he thought were from Russia" who "were concerned about Putin." While Szobocsan said in an email that "nothing worthwhile" came of the meetings, he also mentioned that Michael Flynn Jr. had been involved. US intelligence agencies had information that Russian hackers were discussing among themselves ways to steal emails from Clinton's server and then transmit them to Flynn through an intermediary.[96]

"On the weekend of August 27th-28th," Smith wrote in a later email, "KSL organized four meetings in Virginia with such parties who claim to have access [to Clinton's "missing" emails], and separate meetings with the parties were conducted. Our conclusion was that this access was made by more than these groups, all of whom are non-state players. The parties having the access are motivated by the desire to receive compensation. We stated that our desire was not to purchase such, and specifically avoided any discussion of sums that such parties may seek, and made clear that we were not a source of compensation to them."

"Our advice to these parties, was that they needed to demonstrate that they indeed did have access, and that the emails that they have were not altered or have any deletions been made. Despite this, the parties seek to remain engaged, and we plan subsequent contact to verify authenticity, as if such could be demonstrated, then the market would exist for them. These parties have ties and affiliations to Russia. and have concerns about their safety."

Despite Smith's multiple claims that these meetings took place, the Special Counsel's Office could not establish that Smith had met with Russian hackers. Szobocsan later testified, "I get the call in the morning: I'm not going to be in the office; I'm going to be gone; I'm in Washington. He comes back, he tells me he had this meeting in this hotel. It was like really clandestine. He's trying to make it up, and all these things." Szobocsan continued, "He goes out, and he said that they were meeting in separate rooms, and they were looking about getting these Clinton emails that these hackers had recovered. And - one of them he thought might have been a Russian group, with like Russian students, but they were real fearful of Putin and all this stuff, that they might get caught; and another group, and all these things."[97]

On August 28th, Smith sent an encrypted email with the subject "Sec. Clinton's unsecured private email server," in which he described his activities to a group of undisclosed recipients, including Trump campaign co-chair and policy advisor Sam Clovis.[98] Sam Clovis was in contact with George Papadopoulos, who was told by Joseph Mifsud just over four months earlier, on April 26th, that the Russians had dirt on Hillary Clinton in the form of emails. The Senate Intelligence Committee later sent a criminal referral to the DOJ accusing Clovis of lying to them under oath about his contacts with Smith.[99]

Smith distributed another email on August 31st with the subject "2016 Political Reconnaissance," in which he provided a description, quoted above, of his efforts to reach out to hackers, including some that were Russian. KLS Research LLC was established on September 2nd, and it received $30,000 to cover the expenses of the Clinton email search. Over the course of the initiative, Smith recruited numerous cybersecurity experts to search for the Clinton emails and attempt to authenticate the ones they found.

On September 5th, Smith reached out to British cybersecurity expert Matt Tait, who thought Smith was contacting him about the DNC emails recently released by WikiLeaks. "Yet Smith had not contacted me about the DNC hack," Tait later wrote, "but rather about his conviction that Clinton's private email server had been hacked—in his view almost certainly both by the Russian government and likely by multiple other hackers too—and his desire to ensure that the fruits of those hacks were exposed prior to the election. Over the course of a long phone call, he mentioned that he had been contacted by someone on the "Dark Web" who claimed to have a copy of emails from Secretary Clinton's private server, and this was why he had contacted me; he wanted me to help validate whether or not the emails were genuine."[100]

As Tait refused to sign a non-disclosure agreement with Smith, he never got to see the emails or find out who Smith's contact from the "Dark Web" was. Tait explained to Smith that he believed the Russian government had orchestrated the hack of the DNC and warned him that the individual he met on the dark web might have been involved. According to Tait, Smith didn't seem to care whether or not the Russian government was involved. Neither the Special Counsel's Office nor the Senate Intelligence Committee could determine whether Smith ever came into possession of the emails deleted from Clinton's personal server.

Smith reconnected with Barbara Ledeen, who had been in touch with Michael Flynn. On September 10th, Ledeen wrote to Flynn, "We are at the point of rubber hitting the road re the project you know I have been working on."[101] Five days later, Ledeen replied to an email sent by Smith. "Saw the very interesting note below and was wondering if you had some more detailed reports or memos or other data you could share because we have come a long way in our efforts since we last visited."[102] Ledeen believed she had come into possession of Clinton's missing 30,000 emails via the dark web. She then turned to Erik Prince, who paid for a tech advisor to attempt to authenticate emails. Prince later told the Special Counsel's Office that the advisor determined the emails were not authentic.[103]

In early September, Smith distributed a summary of his

efforts entitled the "Clinton Email Reconnaissance Initiative. It stated that Smith and KLS Research LLC were working "in coordination" with the Trump campaign[104] Smith wrote that he was working with Steve Bannon, Kellyanne Conway, Sam Clovis, and Michael Flynn. Beyond the Trump campaign, Smith also claimed to be coordinating with the Republican National Committee, Judicial Watch, Citizens United, and a conservative activist named James O'Keefe.[105] Smith further claimed in an email sent on September 20th that the "Kushner Group is behind the initiative."[106]

"Although it wasn't initially clear to me how independent Smith's operation was from Flynn or the Trump campaign," Matt Tait later wrote, "it was immediately apparent that Smith was both well connected within the top echelons of the campaign and he seemed to know both Lt. Gen. Flynn and his son well. Smith routinely talked about the goings on at the top of the Trump team, offering deep insights into the bizarre world at the top of the Trump campaign. Smith told of Flynn's deep dislike of DNI Clapper, whom Flynn blamed for his dismissal by President Obama. Smith told of Flynn's moves to position himself as CIA Director under Trump and that Flynn had been persuaded that the Senate confirmation process would be prohibitively difficult. He would instead, therefore, become National Security Advisor should Trump win the election, Smith said."[107]

At some point, Smith connected with Charles C. Johnson, a 28-year-old who had worked at *Breitbart* under Steve Bannon. "He wanted me to introduce him to Bannon, to a few others, and I sort of demurred on some of that," Johnson later said of Smith. "I didn't think his operation was as sophisticated as it needed to be, and I thought it was good to keep the campaign as insulated as possible." Instead, Johnson contacted a "hidden oppo network" of right-wing researchers and informed them of Smith's efforts to find the missing Clinton emails. "The magnitude of what he was trying to do was kind of impressive," Johnson told *Politico*. "He had people running around Europe, had people talking to Guccifer."[108] Johnson's claim that Smith was in contact with Guccifer has yet to be corroborated. Johnson refused to cooperate with the Senate Intelligence Committee's investigation.[109]

Johnson also claims to have put Smith in contact with Andrew Auernheimer, also known by the online alias "weev," a notorious Neo-Nazi hacker and troll. After being imprisoned for hacking activities that revealed a flaw in AT&T's cyber security architecture, Auernheimer was released from prison in 2014 radicalized and sporting a Swastika tattoo. Auernheimer moved to Ukraine, where he served as the chief technical officer for the Neo-Nazi website The Daily Stormer, which after being kicked off American servers, was briefly hosted by a Russian server.[110] *The Daily Stormer's* founder Andrew Anglin, a Neo-Nazi Putin sycophant, has lived in Russia and voted for Trump in an absentee ballot sent from the Russian city of Krasnodar.[111] While it is unclear whether Smith and Auernheimer collaborated, Auernheimer does appear to have been involved in a 2017 effort to interfere in the French presidential election.[112]

Charles Johnson has multiple links to WikiLeaks. On September 20th, 2016, he published an article on *GotNews* that claimed that a PR firm linked to George Soros was about to launch the website PutinTrump.org "to spread conspiracy theories about Donald Trump's connections to Russia." Johnson operated a Slack chat group that included among its members a Florida-based lawyer named Jason Fishbein, who had done work for Assange throughout 2015 and 2016. After someone on the group discovered the password to the site and posted it on the chat group, Fishbein sent it to his contact at WikiLeaks.[113] Within two hours, WikiLeaks shared the PutinTrump.org URL and its password in a tweet from their official account.

"About 2 hours after our original article, Julian Assange's WikiLeaks repeated our discoveries," Johnson tweeted. "Guess which big leaks organization reads GotNews & WeSearchr on the downlow! Come on Julian, let's work together. WikiLeaks & WeSearchr is a match made in heaven. We can take down Hillary together." Shortly after midnight, WikiLeaks sent a private Twitter message to Donald Trump Jr. that contained a link to the site, to which he responded.[114] While Johnson's communications and relationship with WikiLeaks during the 2016 election remain opaque, in August of 2017, he traveled with Dana Rohrabacher to the Ecuadorian Embassy in London where in a meeting that they claimed was held with Trump's knowledge, they met with Assange and offered him a presidential pardon if he would deny Russian involvement in the DNC hack and leak operation.[115]

The day before WikiLeaks began releasing John Podesta's stolen emails, the Smith associate John Szobocsan wrote to Johnson describing a "distribution arrangement" with WikiLeaks.

"We have not seen the content," Szobocsan wrote to Johnson. "This is all done by third parties. We believe the emails are accurate but are unable to definitely confirm such." Johnson continued, "The distribution arrangements involve a [sic] sharing with WikiLeaks, who would then release them. The second means of distribution is to identify these emails through key phrase/sentence identifiers in the dark and deep web."

Questions have been raised about whether Smith got his hands on the Podesta emails before WikiLeaks released them. The Special Counsel's Office exhumed two files from a backup of Smith's computer that had originally been attachments from the Podesta emails. The creation date of the files was October 2nd, five days before WikiLeaks released them. However, a forensic examination established the creation date was not the same as when Smith downloaded the file, the timing of which could not be determined.[116] According to *The Wall Street Journal*, a person close to Smith reported that he repeatedly claimed that he knew ahead of time about the release of the Podesta emails.[117]

On October 7th, WikiLeaks began releasing the Podesta emails. Peter Smith "batch downloaded" each daily release and expressed a desire to connect with Julian Assange. On October 10th, Smith emailed "supporters and prospective supporters" to provide updates on the WikiLeaks release and soliciting further funding. "We were fortunate enough to have had the Clinton-related emails which came to our attention from several separate sources placed in WikiLeaks hands," Smith wrote in an October 15th email to Michael Flynn, Flynn Jr., Barbara Ledeen, and Sam Clovis, "which we are certain they had from countless other parties. In a few week period we identified a handful of individuals that had obtained access to the unprotected Clinton emails. All were relatively inexperienced persons looking for notoriety. This is similar to the novice level hackers groups who with ease accessed commercial email accounts of senior national security figures."

Two weeks later, on October 24th, Smith's relationship with Charles Johnson appears to have soured. "I talked to Steve," Johnson wrote to Smith, likely referring to Steve Bannon, "who will compel you to turn over to us all 30,000 emails you located and referred to WikiLeaks. BB [Breitbart] wants to publish them first." Johnson continued, "We do not give a rats ass what happens to you, and will turn you over [to] the Feds for prosecution if you do not comply.[118]

It's unclear if Smith replied to Johnson, though obviously *Breitbart* never came into possession of Hillary's emails. Four days later, on October 28th, Smith described in an email a "tug-of-war going on within WikiLeaks over its planned releases in the next few days." Smith further suggested that WikiLeaks "has maintained that it will save its best revelations for last, under the theory this allows little time for response prior to the US election November 8." According to an attachment to the email, WikiLeaks would leak "All 33k deleted Emails" by "November 1st."[119] This, as we know, did not happen. However, Smith maintained contact with WikiLeaks. On November 7th, the day before the election, he described in an email to an associate "contact I had with one of its [WikiLeaks] legal team members."[120]

Subsequent investigations couldn't establish whether Peter Smith ever actually came into possession of the 30,000 emails. However, Smith represented that he had done so to his supporters, including members of the Trump campaign. Steve Bannon and Charles Johnson appear to believe that there was a strong possibility he had. What are we to make of the fact that WikiLeaks never released any of Hillary Clinton's emails from her time as Secretary of State? One answer is that they never had them. However, if you grant the possibility that WikiLeaks was, in fact, in possession of the emails, it may also have been the case that events preempted their release. On October 31st, 2016, the day before Smith's predicted WikiLeaks release, FBI Director James Comey reopened the Clinton email investigation. It could conceivably have been the case that an open FBI investigation was determined to be more damaging than to Clinton the actual emails themselves would have been. That, of course, is speculation.

Smith used a Gmail account operating under the pseudonym Robert Tyler, which several people could access. Smith occasionally asked that people convey messages to him by accessing the account and saving a note as a draft.[121] This faulty method of concealment, known as foldering, was also used by Paul Manafort and Konstantin Kilimnik.[122] While investigators were able to gain access to the foldered messages to Smith, they were never able to determine who wrote them. One message from the Robert Tyler account seen by *The Wall Street Journal*, dated October 11th with the subject "Wire Instructions—Clinton

Email Reconnaissance Initiative," suggested that Smith had managed to raise $100,000 from four financiers and pitched in another $50,000 himself for an unknown purpose. An anonymous sender, identifying himself only as ROB, wrote, "This $100k total with the $50k received from you will allow us to fund the Washington Scholarship Fund for the Russian students for the promised $150K." The *Journal* was unable to determine whether such a scholarship fund exists. "The students are very pleased with the email releases they have seen," the unknown sender continued, "and are thrilled with their educational advancement opportunities."

Northern Trust Suspicious Activity Reports leaked to *BuzzFeed News* show that between January 2016 and April 2017, 88 suspicious cash withdrawals were made from nine accounts controlled by Peter Smith for a total of $140,000.[123] In addition to his Robert Tyler email address, Smith also used a commercially available encrypted email address. The computer drives used by Smith, later seized by the FBI, were also encrypted. Furthermore, the entire purpose of finding a hacker on the dark web is to conceal your communications and activities from law enforcement and Federal Investigators.

There are other reasons why the subsequent investigation into Smith could not get to the bottom of what happened. On May 14th, 2017, ten days after he had been contacted by *The Wall Street Journal* and asked about his activities during the 2016 election, Peter W. Smith checked into a Rochester, Minnesota hotel and proceeded to place a bag over his head that was attached to a source of helium. His body was discovered nine days later, with a suicide note stating that "NO FOUL PLAY WHATSOEVER" had been involved in his death. Smith wrote that he had decided to end things because of a "RECENT BAD TURN IN HEALTH SINCE JANUARY, 2017," with the timing related "TO LIFE INSURANCE OF $5 MILLION EXPIRING."[124]

We'll likely never know the true reasons behind Smith's suicide.

[1] Mueller, III, Robert S. *Report On The Investigation Into Russian Interference In The 2016 Presidential Election.* Department of Justice, Washington, DC. March 2019. Pg. 62
[2] Richard Gates FBI 302, 5/03/2018. Pg. 2
[3] Miller, G. Way. "Part One: Mike Flynn, Before The Fall," *Providence Journal.* July 27th, 2017
[4] Fisher, Marc. "The Partisan Warrior," *The Washington Post.* December 14th, 2018

[5] Flynn, Michael T.; Ledeen, Michael. *The Field Of Fight: How We Can Win the Global War Against Radical Islam and Its Allies*. New York, NY: St. Martin's Press, 2016. Pg. 13-18

[6] Priest, Dana; Arkin, William M. *Top Secret America: The Rise Of The New American Security State*. New York, NY: Little, Brown and Company, 2011. Pg. 240-248

[7] Brooks, Rosa. "Obama vs. the Generals," *Politico Magazine*. November 2013

[8] Schachtman, Noah. "Exclusive: Inside Darpa's Secret Afghan Spy Machine," *Wired*. July 21st, 2011

[9] Witt, Jesse; Pasternak, Alex. "Before Trump, Cambridge Analytica quietly built "Psy Ops" for militaries," *Fast Company*. September 25th, 2019

[10] Verton, Dan. "Inside DIA's big data innovation efforts," *FEDSCOOP*. June 25th, 2014

[11] Fisher, Marc. "The Partisan Warrior," *The Washington Post*. December 14th, 2018

[12] Schmidle, Nicholas. "Michael Flynn, General Chaos," *The New Yorker*. February 18th, 2017

[13] Report of the Select Committee on Intelligence United States Senate On Russian Active Measures Campaigns And Interference in the 2016 US Election Volume 5: Counterintelligence Threats and Vulnerabilities. Pg. 753

[14] Miller, Greg; Entous, Adam; Nakashima, Ellen. "Flynn's swift downfall: From a phone call in the Dominican Republic to a forced resignation at the White House," *The Washington Post*. February 14th, 2017

[15] Zwack, Peter. "Death of the GRU Commander," *Defense One*. February 1st, 2016

[16] Sipher, John; Hall, Steven L.; Wise, Douglas H.; Polymeropoulos, Marc. "Trump wants the CIA to cooperate with Russia. We tried that. It was a disaster." *The Washington Post*. July 15th, 2020

[17] Fox, William. "James Clapper: Fired Trump advisor Flynn 'became an angry man,'" *NBC News*. June 7th, 2018

[18] Zwack, Peter. "Death of the GRU Commander," *Defense One*. February 1st, 2016

[19] Miller, Greg; Entous, Adam; Nakashima, Ellen. "National security adviser Flynn discussed sanctions with Russian ambassador, despite denials, officials say," *The Washington Post*. February 9th, 2017

[20] Schmidle, Nicholas. "Michael Flynn, General Chaos," *The New Yorker*. February 18th, 2017

[21] Fox, William. "James Clapper: Fired Trump advisor Flynn 'became an angry man,'" *NBC News*. June 7th, 2018

[22] Kitfield, James. "How Mike Flynn Became America's Angriest General," *Politico Magazine*. October 16th, 2016

[23] Confessore, Nicholas; Rosenberg, Matthew; Hakim, Danny. "How Michael Flynn's Disdain for Limits Led to a Legal Quagmire," *The New York Times*. June 18th, 2017

[24] Soldatov, Andrei; Borogan, Irina. *The Red Web: The Struggle Between Russia's Digital Dictators And The New Online Revolutionaries*. New York, NY: PublicAffairs, 2015. Pg. 152

[25] Robertson, Jordan; Riley, Michael. "Kaspersky Lab Has Been Working With Russian Intelligence," *Bloomberg*. July 11th, 2017

[26] Nakashima, Ellen; Gillum, Jack. "U.S. moves to ban Kaspersky software in federal agencies amid concerns of Russian espionage," *The Washington Post*. September 13th, 2017

[27] Sonne, Paul. "Mike Flynn Paid by Russian Company for Speech on Logistics, Security, Says Firm," *The Wall Street Journal*. March 17th, 2017

[28] Hall, Kevin G.; Goldstein, David. "Russian company that paid Flynn deemed 'unsuitable' by Pentagon," *The Miami Herald*. March 17th, 2017

[29] Leopold, Jason; Cormier, Anthony. "Flynn, Bannon, Manafort, Ivanka: Private Emails From Inside The Mueller Investigation," *BuzzFeed News*. May 3rd, 2021

[30] Schmidle, Nicholas. "Michael Flynn, General Chaos," *The New Yorker*. February 18th, 2017

[31] Polantz, Katelyn. "2015 memo from Erik Prince to Trump campaign: 'National

disgrace' that Soleimani 'not already DEAD'," *CNN*. January 11th, 2020

[32] FBI-302 Interview of Michael Flynn. 11/20/2017. Pg. 6

[33] Wilbur, Del Quentin; Megerian, Chris; Wire, Sarah D.; Haberkorn, Jennifer. "Senate committee sought investigation of Bannon, raised concerns of Trump family testimony," *The Los Angeles Times*. August 14th, 2020

[34] Report of the Select Committee on Intelligence United States Senate On Russian Active Measures Campaigns And Interference in the 2016 US Election Volume 5: Counterintelligence Threats and Vulnerabilities. Pg. 755

[35] Dilanian, Ken. "Russians Paid Mike Flynn $45K for Moscow Speech, Documents Show," NBC News. March 16th, 2017

[36] Helderman, Rosalind S.; Hamburger, Tom. "Trump adviser Flynn paid by multiple Russia-related entities, new records show," *The Washington Post*. March 16th, 2017

[37] FBI-302 Interview of Michael Flynn. 1/24/2017. Pg. 2

[38] Miller, Greg. *The Apprentice: Trump, Russia And The Subversion Of American Democracy*. New York, NY: HarperCollins, 2018. Pg. 87

[39] Windram, Robert. "Guess Who Came To Dinner With Flynn And Putin," *NBC News*. April 18th, 2017.

[40] Kincaid, Cliff. "Moscow's Five-Star Treatment of a Three-Star Army General," *AIM Center for Investigative Journalism*. December 15th, 2015

[41] Leopold, Jason; Cormier, Anthony. "Flynn, Bannon, Manafort, Ivanka: Private Emails From Inside The Mueller Investigation," *BuzzFeed News*. May 3rd, 2021

[42] Leopold, Jason; Cormier, Anthony. "Flynn, Bannon, Manafort, Ivanka: Private Emails From Inside The Mueller Investigation," *BuzzFeed News*. May 3rd, 2021

[43] Kocieniewski, David; Robison, Peter. "Trump Aide Partnered With Firm Run by Man With Alleged KGB Ties," *Bloomberg*. December 23rd, 2016

[44] Markon, Jerry. "Trump's pick for national security adviser had role in firm co-led by man who tried to sell material to the KGB," *The Washington Post*. December 23rd, 2016

[45] Confessore, Nicholas; Rosenberg, Matthew; Hakim, Danny. "How Michael Flynn's Disdain for Limits Led to a Legal Quagmire," *The New York Times*. June 18th, 2017

[46] Pangburn, DJ. "The Secretive Billion-Dollar Company Helping Governments Hack Our Phones," *Fast Company*. November 30th, 2017

[47] Menn, Joseph; Stubbs, Jack. "Exclusive: FBI probes use of Israeli firm's spyware in personal and government hacks - sources," *Reuters*. January 30th, 2020

[48] Stedman, Scott. "Israeli Spy Companies Show Critical Link Between Flynn, Deripaska, and Senate Intelligence Committee Target Walter Soriano," *Forensic News*. June 16th, 2020

[49] Marczak, Bill; Scott-Railton, John; Rao, Siddarth Prakash; Deibert, Ron. "Running in Circles: Uncovering the Clients of Cyberespionage Firm Circles," *The Citizen Lab*. December 1st, 2020

[50] Stedman, Scott. "Israeli Spy Companies Show Critical Link Between Flynn, Deripaska, and Senate Intelligence Committee Target Walter Soriano," *Forensic News*. June 16th, 2020

[51] Gold, Matea. "The mystery behind a Flynn associate's quiet work for the Trump campaign," *The Washington Post*. May 4th, 2017

[52] Gold, Matea. "The mystery behind a Flynn associate's quiet work for the Trump campaign," *The Washington Post*. May 4th, 2017

[53] Barnes, Julian E. "U.S. Military Plugs Into Social Media for Intelligence Gathering," *The Wall Street Journal*. August 6th, 2014

[54] Report of the Select Committee on Intelligence United States Senate On Russian Active Measures Campaigns And Interference in the 2016 US Election Volume 5: Counterintelligence Threats and Vulnerabilities. Pg. 694

[55] Kajosevic, Samir. "Montenegro Prosecution Suspects Israeli Consultant of Coup Role," *Balkan Insight*. July 31st, 2019

[56] Hettena, Seth. "Who is Aron Shaviv?" *SethHettena.com*. August 2nd, 2019

[57] Ahren, Raphael. "British-Israeli Electioneer Polls Way Into Magazine's Rising Star Award," *Haaretz*. July 22nd, 2011

[58] Kalikh, Andrey. "My baby knows how to speed up judges when he needs to," *openDemocracy*. February 27th, 2018

[59] Pfeffer, Anshell. "How key Bibi advisor helped Cameron win," *The JC*. February 4th, 2017

[60] Kraft, Dina. "Understanding the Enigma of Arthur Finkelstein, Unseen Power Broker," *Haaretz*. December 10th, 2012

[61] Leibowitz, Ruthie Blum. "One on One: The business of politics," *The Jerusalem Post*. June 3rd, 2019

[62] Weinglass, Simona. "Israeli pitched covert pro-Trump plan while leading 'nonpartisan' iVote Israel," *The Times of Israel*. August 31st, 2020

[63] Sommer, Allison Kaplan "U.S. Voters in Israel Say Their Ballot Requests Have Gone Missing," *Haaretz*. October 29th, 2016

[64] Ahren, Raphael. "How nonpartisan is campaign to encourage Israeli-Americans to vote in November?" *The Times of Israel*. June 19th, 2012

[65] Bellingcat Investigative Team. "Second GRU Officer Indicted in Montenegro Coup Unmasked," *Bellingcat*. November 22nd, 2018

[66] Report of the Select Committee on Intelligence United States Senate On Russian Active Measures Campaigns And Interference in the 2016 US Election Volume 5: Counterintelligence Threats and Vulnerabilities. Pg. 39

[67] Shuster, Simon. "Exclusive: Russian Ex-Spy Pressured Manafort Over Debts to an Oligarch," *Time*. December 29th, 2018

[68] Press Release. "Treasury Targets Russian Operatives over Election Interference, World Anti-Doping Agency Hacking, and Other Malign Activities," *U.S. Department of the Treasury*. December 19th, 2018

[69] Etter, Lauren; Riley, Michael. "Inside the Pro-Trump Effort to Keep Black Voters From the Polls," *Bloomberg*. March 29th, 2018

[70] Timberg, Craig; Helderman, Rosalind S.; Roth, Andrew; Leonnig, Carole D. "In the crowd at Trump's inauguration, members of Russia's elite anticipated a thaw between Moscow and Washington," *The Washington Post*. January 20th, 2018

[71] Helderman, Rosalind S. "Russian billionaire with U.S. investments backed alleged agent Maria Butina, according to a person familiar with her Senate testimony," *The Washington Post*. July 22nd, 2018

[72] McIntire, Mike. "Billionaire Backer of Maria Butina Had Russian Security Ties," *The New York Times*. September 21st, 2018

[73] Report of the Select Committee on Intelligence United States Senate On Russian Active Measures Campaigns And Interference in the 2016 US Election Volume 5: Counterintelligence Threats and Vulnerabilities. Pg. 571

[74] Bender, Bryan; Goldmacher, Shane. "Trump's favorite general," *Politico*. July 8th, 2016

[75] Kitfield, James. "How Mike Flynn Became America's Angriest General," *Politico Magazine*. October 16th, 2016

[76] Report of the Select Committee on Intelligence United States Senate On Russian Active Measures Campaigns And Interference in the 2016 US Election Volume 5: Counterintelligence Threats and Vulnerabilities. Pg. 778

[77] Kirchgaessner, Stephanie. "Flynn ally sought help from 'dark web' in covert Clinton email investigation," *The Guardian*. October 13th, 2017

[78] Schmidle, Nicholas. "Michael Flynn, General Chaos," *The New Yorker*. February 18th, 2017

[79] Unger, Craig. "The War They Wanted, The Lies They Needed," *Vanity Fair*. October 17th, 2006

[80] Gardiner, Richard N. *Mission Italy: On the Front Lines of the Cold War*. Lanham, MD: Rowman & Littlefield Publishers, Inc, 2005. Pg. 290-291

[81] Draper, Theodore. *A Very Thin Line: The Iran-Contra Affairs.* New York, NY: Hill and Wang, 1991. Pg. 136-139

[82] Walsh, Lawrence E. *Firewall: The Iran-Contra Conspiracy and Cover-Up.* New York, NY: W.W. Norton & Company, 1997. Pg. 42-43

[83] Weisman, Alan. *Prince Of Darkness Richard Perle: The Kingdom, The Power & The End Of Empire In America.* New York, NY: Union Square Press, 2007. Pg. 145

[84] Mueller, III, Robert S. *Report On The Investigation Into Russian Interference In The 2016 Presidential Election.* Department of Justice, Washington, DC. March 2019. Pg. 62

[85] Isikoff, Michael. "The Right Wing Web," *Newsweek.* February 21st, 1999

[86] Report of the Select Committee on Intelligence United States Senate On Russian Active Measures Campaigns And Interference in the 2016 US Election Volume 5: Counterintelligence Threats and Vulnerabilities. Pg. 783

[87] Mueller, III, Robert S. *Report On The Investigation Into Russian Interference In The 2016 Presidential Election.* Department of Justice, Washington, DC. March 2019. Pg. 62

[88] Report of the Select Committee on Intelligence United States Senate On Russian Active Measures Campaigns And Interference in the 2016 US Election Volume 5: Counterintelligence Threats and Vulnerabilities. Pg. 783 [Footnote 5100]

[89] Leopold, Jason; Cormier, Anthony. "Flynn, Bannon, Manafort, Ivanka: Private Emails From Inside The Mueller Investigation," *BuzzFeed News.* May 3rd, 2021

[90] Report of the Select Committee on Intelligence United States Senate On Russian Active Measures Campaigns And Interference in the 2016 US Election Volume 5: Counterintelligence Threats and Vulnerabilities. Pg. 783 [Footnote 5104]

[91] Report of the Select Committee on Intelligence United States Senate On Russian Active Measures Campaigns And Interference in the 2016 US Election Volume 5: Counterintelligence Threats and Vulnerabilities. Pg. 778 [Footnote 5073]

[92] Sanger, David E.; Shane, Scott. "Russian Hackers Acted to Aid Trump in Election, U.S. Says," *The New York Times.* December 9th, 2016

[93] Pearson, Rick. "FBI told state GOP in June its emails had been hacked," *The Chicago Tribune.* December 12th, 2016

[94] Harris, Shane. "GOP Operative Sought Clinton Emails From Hackers, Implied a Connection to Flynn," *The Wall Street Journal.* June 29th, 2017

[95] Report of the Select Committee on Intelligence United States Senate On Russian Active Measures Campaigns And Interference in the 2016 US Election Volume 5: Counterintelligence Threats and Vulnerabilities. Pg. 779-780

[96] Harris, Shane. "GOP Operative Sought Clinton Emails From Hackers, Implied a Connection to Flynn," *The Wall Street Journal.* June 29th, 2017

[97] Report of the Select Committee on Intelligence United States Senate On Russian Active Measures Campaigns And Interference in the 2016 US Election Volume 5: Counterintelligence Threats and Vulnerabilities. Pg. 779-781

[98] Mueller, III, Robert S. *Report On The Investigation Into Russian Interference In The 2016 Presidential Election.* Department of Justice, Washington, DC. March 2019. Pg. 63

[99] Wilbur, Del Quentin; Megerian, Chris; Wire, Sarah D.; Haberkorn, Jennifer. "Senate committee sought investigation of Bannon, raised concerns about Trump family testimony," *The Los Angeles Times.* August 14th, 2020

[100] Tait, Matt. "The Time I Got Recruited to Collude with the Russians," *Lawfare.* June 30th, 2017

[101] Leopold, Jason; Cormier, Anthony. "Flynn, Bannon, Manafort, Ivanka: Private Emails From Inside The Mueller Investigation," *BuzzFeed News.* May 3rd, 2021

[102] Report of the Select Committee on Intelligence United States Senate On Russian Active Measures Campaigns And Interference in the 2016 US Election Volume 5: Counterintelligence Threats and Vulnerabilities. Pg. 783

[103] Mueller, III, Robert S. *Report On The Investigation Into Russian Interference In The 2016 Presidential Election.* Department of Justice, Washington, DC. March 2019. Pg. 64

[104] Mueller, III, Robert S. *Report On The Investigation Into Russian Interference In The 2016*

Presidential Election. Department of Justice, Washington, DC. March 2019. Pg. 63

[105] Mayer, Jane. "In the Mueller Report, Erik Prince Funds a Covert Effort to Obtain Clinton's E-mails from a Foreign State," *The New Yorker.* April 18th, 2019

[106] Report of the Select Committee on Intelligence United States Senate On Russian Active Measures Campaigns And Interference in the 2016 US Election Volume 5: Counterintelligence Threats and Vulnerabilities. Pg. 782

[107] Tait, Matt. "The Time I Got Recruited to Collude with the Russians," *Lawfare.* June 30th, 2017

[108] Schreckinger, Ben. "GOP Researcher Who Sought Clinton Emails Had Alt-Right Help," *Politico Magazine.* July 11th, 2017

[109] Schreckinger, Ben. "House Democrats seek to interview inflammatory 'alt-right' activist Chuck Johnson," *Politico.* August 13th, 2018

[110] Bertrand, Natasha. "The white supremacist website kicked off of US servers briefly found a new home — in Russia," *Business Insider.* August 16th, 2017

[111] O'Brien, Luke. "The Making Of An American Nazi," *The Atlantic.* December 2017

[112] Gauthier-Villars, Davis. "U.S. Hacker Linked to Fake Macron Documents, Says Cybersecurity Firm," *The Wall Street Journal.* May 16th, 2017

[113] Goodman, Alan. "Exclusive: WikiLeaks lawyer says he helped pass info to 'innocent victim' Don Jr." *The Washington Examiner.* April 26th, 2019

[114] Bertrand, Natasha. "A notorious far-right blogger may have provoked WikiLeaks' outreach to Donald Trump Jr.," *Business Insider.* November 15th, 2017

[115] Smith, Alexander; Neubert, Michele. "Assange was offered presidential pardon to help 'resolve' Russia role in DNC hack, court told," *NBC News.* September 18th, 2020

[116] Mueller, III, Robert S. *Report On The Investigation Into Russian Interference In The 2016 Presidential Election.* Department of Justice, Washington, DC. March 2019. Pg. 64

[117] Tau, Byron; Holliday, Shelby; Volz, Dustin. "Mueller Probes WikiLeaks' Contacts With Conservative Activists," *The Wall Street Journal.* October 19th, 2018

[118] Report of the Select Committee on Intelligence United States Senate On Russian Active Measures Campaigns And Interference in the 2016 US Election Volume 5: Counterintelligence Threats and Vulnerabilities. Pg. 786-787

[119] Mueller, III, Robert S. *Report On The Investigation Into Russian Interference In The 2016 Presidential Election.* Department of Justice, Washington, DC. March 2019. Pg. 64-65

[120] Report of the Select Committee on Intelligence United States Senate On Russian Active Measures Campaigns And Interference in the 2016 US Election Volume 5: Counterintelligence Threats and Vulnerabilities. Pg. 786

[121] Tau, Byron; Volz, Dustin; Holliday, Shleby. "GOP Operative Secretly Raised at Least $100,000 in Search for Clinton Emails," *The Wall Street Journal.* October 7th, 2018

[122] Melendez, Steven. "Manafort allegedly used "foldering" to hide emails. Here's how it works," *Fast Company.* June 15th 2018

[123] Leopold, Jason; Cormier, Anthony. "GOP Operative Made "Suspicious" Cash Withdrawals During Pursuit Of Clinton Emails," *BuzzFeed News.* August 10th, 2018

[124] Lighty, Todd. "Peter W. Smith, GOP operative who sought Clinton's emails from Russian hackers, committed suicide, records show," *The Chicago Tribune.* July 13th, 2017

Conclusion:
Zero Hour – Election Day 2016

On the eve of the 2016 election, Donald Trump held five rallies, concluding his longshot and divisive presidential campaign in Grand Rapids, Michigan. The Trump campaign desperately needed to pick off Michigan and several other states, such as Pennsylvania and Wisconsin, if he was to seize the White House. At 1 am on election day, Trump called out to his supporters, "Today is our independence day!"[1]

By most accounts, Trump didn't believe he would win. Most officials on the Trump campaign doubted they would emerge victorious. Michael Wolff has written that Trump didn't want to win the election but instead wanted to use his candidacy to make himself "the most famous man in the world."[2] According to Michael Cohen, when Trump was considering running, he claimed, "This can be the greatest infomercial in the history of politics."[3]

Another group that discounted Trump's chances on election day was the Russians. On the day of the election, Rospatent, the Russian government office in charge of intellectual property, approved four Trump Organization patents, perhaps in the expectation that private citizen Trump would be conducting business in Moscow in the near future.[4] Russian intelligence possessed damaging information on Clinton that it had yet to release, waiting to use it until after her election to damage her presidency. US intelligence believed that the Russians planned to soil Clinton's victory by releasing this *kompromat*, in addition to information suggesting that voter data had been altered, to bolster Trump's claims of a rigged election.[5]

The Obama administration feared Russian hackers might attempt to disrupt the election as they had several years earlier in Ukraine. Three weeks before the US election, the GRU was involved in a failed coup attempt in Montenegro.[6] The operation brought together many of the elements that were involved in the US election meddling effort. The GRU hacked the DNC and Clinton campaign. Oleg Deripaska, who had business interests in Montenegro, funded and helped execute the Kremlin-backed coup effort.[7] Victor Boyarkin, a former GRU officer who works for Deripaska, funded the Montenegrin pro-Kremlin political party.[8] Boyarkin had pressured Manafort regarding his debts. Manafort had worked alongside Konstantin Kilimnik for Deripaska in Montenegro in 2006. After resigning from the Trump campaign, he established contact with pro-Kremlin politicians in Montenegro.[9]

Obama Administration officials expected aggressiveness on the part of the Russians. They worried that the Russians, whom they knew had already gained access to voter registration databases in several states, might tamper with the voter information to prevent people from being able to vote on election day. The Russians might release a video showing how easy it was to hack into voting machines and change outcomes, then spread it online. They might direct Denial of Service attacks against the *Associated Press*, the agency responsible for delivering election results to news organizations.[10]

At 6 A.M. on election day, the director of cyber incident response at the National Security Council established a "second situation room" in the Eisenhower Executive Office Building. Secretary Jeh Johnson oversaw the DHS crisis response center. Johnson held discussions with the CEO of the *Associated Press* to ensure that it had taken precautions.[11] The elections-crimes unit at the Department of Justice stood ready. Cyber action teams were activated at fifty-six FBI field offices around the country. The Administration plan even entertained the possibility of deploying active and reserve elements of the military.[12]

As the polls opened, millions of Americans were active on social media. 115.3 million US-based Facebook users generated 716.3 million interactions related to the election and viewed election-related videos 640 million times. Across the world, users generated over 75 million election-related tweets.[13]

Meanwhile, in St. Petersburg, the propagandists at the Internet Research Agency sprang into action, producing 4,316 unique posts on election day.[14]

IRA propagandists spread disinformation, suggesting the election was rigged. When one Pennsylvania voter released a video purporting to show a machine that wouldn't allow them to change their vote from Clinton to Trump, the IRA spread the video far and wide.[15] The IRA's conservative avatars focused on disseminating false stories of voter fraud. Its left-leaning and African American-focused social media presence engaged in voter suppression activities. "Think twice before you vote," IRA-account @Blackstagram wrote. "All I wanna say is that they don't really care about us. #Blacktavist #hot news."

The Senate Intelligence Committee and the US Intelligence Community later reported that they found no evidence that Russian hackers manipulated vote tallies. However, their insight into this issue was "limited." While they found no evidence of vote tampering, they couldn't rule it out. Democratic Senate Majority Leader Harry Reid believed the Russians tipped the results of the 2016 election in Trump's favor.[16]

"Trump! Trump! Trump!" roared a crowd of Russians gathered in a Moscow bar for the "Marathon for Trump" election-watching party. The event took place under the watchful eyes of Vladimir Putin, Donald Trump, and Marine Le Pen, who were present in the form of side-by-side portraits adorning the walls. Despite these early exit polls.[17] 21-year-old Russian nationalist Maria Katasonova organized the watch party.[18] As an aide to Evgeny Fedorov, a hardline member of Putin's political party in the Duma, Katasonova had supported Trump's candidacy for months.[19] She attended Carter Page's July 2016 commencement speech in Moscow.

Steve Bannon and Trump's campaign leadership were gathered on the fifth floor of Trump Tower, surrounded by electoral maps and monitors, receiving information from sources on the ground. As Bannon and his team focused closely on the vote tally in Florida, something remarkable began to happen. Trump's numbers began to turn around dramatically. The first round of exit polls had been wrong. Donald Trump was gaining ground. He was winning.

As night fell, supporters of both candidates gathered near each other in Manhattan. Clinton's supporters took over the

Javits Center. The Trump campaign's watch party was at a Midtown Hilton three blocks from Trump Tower. Those present noted the room's set-up seemed more appropriate for a press conference than a victory party.[20] By 7:45 pm, more than half of the vote was in, and Trump was beating Clinton 49.8% to 47.3%. Suddenly, the potential for a Trump presidency was very real. Trump, Jr. thought that his father appeared as though he had seen a ghost.[21] Trump hadn't even bothered to write a victory speech.[22]

One group that realized that Trump looked increasingly likely to win was the Internet Research Agency. As the election results favoring Trump rolled in, the IRA dispensed with the "rigged" election canard entirely and began posting celebratory messages online. "Trump's lead in Florida is growing!" the prolific IRA-created account @Ten_GOP tweeted at 8:24 pm.[23]

By 9:30 pm, the Cambridge Analytica data team headquartered in San Antonio, TX, began sending messages to Trump Tower. Florida had flipped toward Trump, and the rest of the map was trending in his favor. The Cambridge Analytica team gave Trump an over 50% chance of winning. While fear seeped into the Javits Center, joy built at the Hilton. At 10:53 pm, Florida was called for Trump. Twenty-one minutes later, North Carolina fell into the Republican column. The oxygen left the room at the Javits Center, where tears flowed freely.

As the clock struck midnight, the Trump family and his closest advisors, including Steve Bannon, Stephen Miller, Kellyanne Conway, and Chris Christie, made their way to Trump's private residence in Trump Tower to await Hillary Clinton's concession call and to throw together a victory speech. Three short blocks away, the Clintons holed up in a suite at the nearby Peninsula Hotel. Hillary Clinton was reduced to stunned silence. With Trump's victory inevitable, President Obama had an aide contact Hillary and emphasize that he hoped she would concede graciously and quickly, for the good of the country.[24]

By 1 am, John Podesta urged devastated Clinton supporters at the Javits Center to return to their homes. It had been a harrowing month for Podesta. Since October 7th, Podesta's emails that had been purloined by Russian military intelligence had been released in batches by WikiLeaks. The email leak had bizarre, far-reaching consequences. Innocuous references in Podesta's emails were interpreted by conspiracy theorists to be coded language for pedophilia, leading to the Pizzagate incident involving an armed man entering the D.C. establishment Comet Pizza and, eventually, morphing into the QAnon conspiracy theory.

By 1:35 am, Pennsylvania was called in favor of Trump. The Democrats' "Blue Wall" had crumbled. Clinton called Trump and conceded. Despite the Electoral College, Clinton beat Trump in the popular vote by 2,868,686 votes. The margin of difference in the three most consequential, Michigan, Pennsylvania, and Wisconsin, was 77,744 votes. Clinton called Obama and, her voice cracking, told the outgoing President, "I'm sorry for letting you down."[25]

In the aftermath of Trump's victory, his thoughts turned to the man who, more than anyone, put him on the map: Roy Cohn. Trump turned to *New York Post* gossip columnist Cindy Adams. "If Roy were here, he never would have believed it."[26]

Roger Stone spent election night broadcasting on *InfoWars* with Alex Jones. The two toasted one another with champagne. The ordinarily loquacious Stone was at a loss for words. Jones' eyes welled with tears. "I already know my life's purpose has been completed," Jones intoned. "I will continue on. But for now, I realize, I have won."[27]

"Happy?" WikiLeaks wrote to Stone via Twitter on November 9th, 2016. "We are now more free to communicate." Stone and WikiLeaks exchanged messages for months after the election, discussing how Stone might wrangle a presidential pardon for Julian Assange. Also on November 9th, WikiLeaks wrote a Twitter direct message to Donald Trump, Jr. "Wow. Obama people will surely try to delete records on the way out. Just a heads up."[28]

Paul Manafort spent election night in Florida. Records indicate that he spoke to Trump that evening.[29] Emails sent by Konstantin Kilimnik indicate Manafort had been confident. "It was close," Kilimnik wrote to Sam Patten the day after the election, "and if [Donald Trump] had been more disciplined, things would have gone as Paul said in May - bigger gap."[30]

Manafort monetized his connection to the incoming Administration. During the transition, he traveled to the Middle East, Cuba, South Korea, Japan, and China, where he was paid to offer insights into the Trump presidency. In January of 2017, Manafort arrived in Madrid, Spain, where he met with Georgy

Oganov, a senior advisor to Oleg Deripaska. The meeting, which Manafort later lied to investigators about, was arranged by Kilimnik and Victor Boyarkin. Kilimnik described the meeting as being about "recreating [the] old friendship and talking about global politics."[31] Manafort also sought suggestions from Kilimnik as to whom the Trump Administration should nominate for positions relevant to Ukraine.[32]

"This is the beginning of a dynasty!" Michael Cohen crowed after the election had been called. He explained that Ivanka or Don Jr. would run next. "I've already got the bug," Cohen exclaimed. "Nobody's going to be able to fuck with us. I think I'm going to run for mayor."[33]

Felix Sater ordered a car service to take him from his home in Long Island to the invite-only festivities at the Hilton. Upon being picked up, he proudly flashed the driver his business card, which read: FELIX H. SATER: SPECIAL ADVISOR TO DONALD TRUMP. After briefly discussing the election with the driver, Sater spent the rest of the drive speaking excitedly in Russian over the phone with an unknown caller.[34]

A day after the election, George Papadopoulos emailed Olga Polonskaya, the Russian woman whom Joseph Mifsud had falsely introduced to him as Vladimir Putin's niece.[35] The Senate Intelligence Committee assessed that Mifsud's use of Polonskaya was consistent with intelligence tradecraft. That same day, Papadopoulos arranged to meet Sergei Millian in Chicago to work with Russian "billionaires who are not under sanctions."[36] The Senate Intelligence Committee also found that Millian's activities to be consistent with intelligence tradecraft.

In December 2016, Carter Page returned to Moscow and appeared on Russian state television, where he attacked Hillary Clinton and the "conspiracy theories about WikiLeaks used to distract from disastrous information revealed on her illegal mail server." He claimed that there was "nothing there" regarding reports that Russia had interfered in the 2016 election. Page was joined at dinner by Russian Deputy Prime Minister Arkady Dvorkovich, about whom the Senate Intelligence Committee later expressed "counterintelligence concerns."[37]

Brexiters Arron Banks and Nigel Farage stayed at the Waldorf Astoria Hotel in Manhattan to watch the returns come in. On November 15th, three days after they met with Trump at Trump Tower, Farage and Banks dined with the Russian

Ambassador to the UK, Alexander Yakovenko, and provided him with a phone number to Trump's transition team.[38] On February 24th, 2017, Nigel Farage was back in the US to address the conservative conference CPAC. The next evening, he had dinner with Trump at the Trump Hotel, tweeting a picture of himself enjoying the company of the American President.[39] Eleven days later, Farage was seen leaving the Ecuadorian embassy after a meeting with Julian Assange. When asked by a waiting *BuzzFeed* reporter what he was doing at the Embassy just as he stepped out of it, Farage claimed he couldn't remember.[40] "I had a drink with [N]igel," Aaron Banks wrote in a Twitter direct message the next day. "He had an interesting time with wiki leaks."[41]

On election day, Michael Flynn published an op-ed in *The Hill* in support of Turkey without disclosing that he was being paid by Turkish interests. Flynn's violations of the Foreign Agent Registration Act later entangled him in extensive legal troubles. Flynn was appointed Trump's National Security Advisor, despite the fact that President Obama warned President-Elect Trump during an Oval Office meeting two days after the election to steer clear of Flynn.[42] During the transition, Flynn held a series of *sub rosa* conversations with Russian Ambassador Sergey Kislyak regarding the sanctions and diplomatic expulsions the outgoing administration applied to Russia. Flynn lied to the FBI when asked about his contacts with Kislyak, plunging the Trump Administration into further legal and counterintelligence jeopardy.[43]

"November 8th is the day of my birthday," Aras Agalarov wrote in a personal note delivered to Trump's assistant Rhona Graff. "Your victory would be the best birthday present I have ever received!" Agalarov described Trump's victory as a "heavenly miracle" to Russian media.[44] He then instructed Irakly Kaveladze to arrange a second meeting regarding the Magnitsky Act sanctions.[45] Two weeks after election day, Natalia Veselnitskaya reached out to Rob Goldstone to establish contact with the Trump transition team.[46] However, as the dark clouds of investigation descended over Washington, neither outreach effort came to fruition.

When the news of Trump's victory reached Moscow, the State Duma, Russia's lower house of parliament, erupted in applause. "Hillary Clinton admitted defeat in the US Presidential election, and a second ago Trump began his speech as President-Elect of the United States," Duma member Vyacheslav Nikonov informed the chamber. "I congratulate you all!"[47] US intelligence intercepts captured senior Russian government officials congratulating themselves.[48] Russian state television broadcast Trump's victory speech live while playing clips of an actor dressed as Trump sticking his tongue out at a Hillary Clinton impersonator.[49]

Duma member Vladimir Zhirinovsky threw a celebratory banquet in Trump's honor.[50] Ultranationalist Duma member Boris Chernyshev invited international journalists to join him in a champagne toast. He used the occasion to invert Barack Obama's 2008 campaign rally cry: "Tonight we can use the slogan with Mr. Trump: Yes we did!"[51]

Early on election night, when it was assumed that Hillary Clinton would be the victor, the Editor-in-Chief of the pro-Kremlin propaganda outfit RT Margarita Simonyan tweeted ominously, "Democracy R.I.P."[52] However, the news of Trump's victory changed her tune dramatically. "I want to drive through Moscow with an American flag in the Window. Come and join me," she excitedly tweeted. "Today, they earned it."[53]

The pro-Kremlin analyst Sergei Markov was thrilled by the result, believing a Trump Administration would see eye-to-eye with Russia on issues like the Syrian Civil War and the "terroristic junta in Ukraine." After initially denying that Russia was involved in any efforts to interfere in the US election, Markov allowed that "maybe we helped a bit with WikiLeaks."[54]

The US Ambassador to Russia, John Tefft, held a breakfast reception to watch the results. When it became clear that Trump was going to be the next president, stunned European diplomats, and Russian reformers lingered about Spaso House in a state of disbelief. "I cannot believe it," Evgenia Albats, the editor of the opposition *New Times,* worried out loud. "There will be absolutely no restraints on Putin now at all. This will be a disaster."

In St. Petersburg, the Internet Research Agency's army of trolls gathered after polls closed to watch the results. "On November 9th, 2016, a sleepless night was ahead of us," one IRA member wrote in an internal communication. "And when around 8 am the most important result of our work arrived, we uncorked a tiny bottle of champagne... took one gulp each and looked into each other's eyes… we uttered almost in unison: 'We made America great."[55]

In the immediate aftermath of Trump's election, IRA operations targeting the US dramatically increased. Activity on Instagram increased by 238%, Facebook by 59%, Twitter by 52%, and YouTube by 89%. On November 12th, 2016, the IRA used false avatars and online groups to organize two opposing protests in New York City. One called for protestors to "show your support for President-Elect Donald Trump," while the other referred to itself as the "Trump is NOT my President" rally. Both received national media coverage. A week later, the IRA organized a "Charlotte Against Trump" rally in North Carolina.[56]

Russian intelligence didn't rest in the aftermath of the election, either. Within six hours of Trump's election, hackers at the SVR sent spear-phishing emails to Washington, D.C.-based think tanks and non-governmental organizations.[57] Russian operatives in the United States were jubilant at the election results. Maria Butina, who in late 2018 pled guilty to acting as a Russian agent in the US, and her Eurasian organized crime-linked handler, Alexander Torshin, celebrated the outcome as a "wonderful chance to improve Russian-American relations." The day after the election, Butina sent Torshin a photo of the two of them visiting with Donald Trump, Jr. at a May 2016 dinner hosted by the National Rifle Association in Louisville, KY.[58]

The morning after the election, CEO of Russia's sovereign wealth fund Kirill Dmitriev, under orders from Putin, attempted to establish a backchannel with the Trump Team. Dmitriev texted George Nader, who had attended a meeting with Donald Trump, Jr, Joel Zamel, and Erik Prince a few months earlier. Dmitriev asked Nader to arrange for him to meet "key people" in the incoming Trump administration as soon as possible.

On January 11th, 2017, Prince and Dmitriev held two clandestine meetings on the Seychelles islands to establish a backchannel between the Kremlin and the Trump administration and to discuss US-Russia relations.[59] Prince met with Bannon at his private residence to brief him on the meetings. The Senate Intelligence Committee later sent criminal referrals to the Justice Department for both Prince and Bannon for providing the Committee and the Special Counsel's Office misleading testimony regarding the Seychelles meeting.[60]

At 3 am on November 9th, 2016, Trump campaign spokeswoman Hope Hicks received a phone call from a man named Sergey. Speaking with a heavy accent, the man told Hicks that he wanted to "connect the Kremlin by telephone with Trump to allow President Putin to congratulate President-Elect Trump." Hicks asked that he send his request by email. Later that morning, Hicks received an email from a political officer at the Russian Embassy named Sergey Kuznetsov with the subject line, "Message from Putin." Attached to the email was a letter from Putin, written in both Russian and English, congratulating Trump and stating that he looked forward to working with him to lead "Russian-American relations out of crisis."

"Can you look into this?" Hicks wrote to Jared Kushner, forwarding him the email containing Putin's message. "Don't want to get duped, but don't want to blow off Putin!"

Kushner forwarded the email to Dimitri Simes, the Russian-born American citizen who had hosted Trump's first foreign policy address. Kushner asked Simes to remind him of the Russian Ambassador's name. Simes replied with Sergey Kislyak's name and the message, "Congratulations on a historic victory! This may become a real 21st Century American revolution." On November 30th, Kushner and Michael Flynn met with Kislyak at Trump Tower. Kushner asked if they could use secure facilities at the Russian embassy to communicate with Russian generals regarding Syria. Six days later, Kushner met with Sergey Gorkov, CEO of the US-sanctioned, Russian government-owned Vnesheconombank, who reportedly had a direct line to Putin. Kushner and Gorkov provided conflicting accounts of what they.

Vladimir Putin congratulated President-Elect Donald Trump by phone on November 14th, 2016. In later public statements made in Moscow before an audience of his fellow Russians, Putin provided brief thoughts on the 2016 American presidential election. "Trump understood the mood of the people and kept going until the end when nobody believed in him." He paused, his lips curling into a knowing smile. "Except you and me."

*****

A foreign adversary conducts an intelligence and disinformation operation to benefit one of two candidates in a presidential election. The candidate benefitting has decades' worth of corrupt connections to the adversary and publicly welcomes its attack. As it unfolds, the candidate uses his lawyer and an organized crime-linked real estate agent with intelligence connections to secretly negotiate a multi-million dollar construction project in the adversary's capital. When asked if he has any business dealings with the adversary, the candidate lies.

His oldest political advisor claims to have inside information on the operation. He is in contact with the intelligence agency that hacked the opposing campaign, and the third party disseminating the stolen communications. The campaign's chairman is in contact with organized crime-linked oligarchs close to the adversary. He provides internal polling data to and secretly meets with one of the adversary's intelligence officers. A foreign policy advisor learns secret details of the impending operation from a professor linked to the adversary. He later claims that he "can't remember" if he told anyone on the campaign. Yet another foreign policy advisor, under investigation for his previous contacts with the adversary's intelligence agents, visits its capital during the campaign and spouts its official line.

The candidate's son and top campaign leaders meet with a lawyer representing the adversary's government, hoping to receive "dirt" on the opposing candidate. The campaign's most fervent idealogue and later CEO shares sympathies with neo-fascist thinkers from the adversary. He invests in a political consulting and analytics firm with links to multiple intelligence agencies. It engages in illegal activities, poll tests the popularity of the adversary's dictator, works for one of the adversary's oil companies, and supports two of the adversary's most pressing foreign policy goals.

Members of the campaign, including the candidate's son, seek and receive assistance from "former" intelligence officers of third-party states who have worked for men centrally involved in the adversary's operation. The candidate's top military advisor, a disgruntled former military intelligence officer, is paid thousands of dollars by the adversary and meets its dictator. At the behest of the candidate, he uses his intelligence connections to support an effort to retrieve the opposing candidate's communications through hackers associated with the adversary.

After the candidate wins, he, his entire campaign, and the party apparatus around him repeatedly lie to and obstruct investigations. The candidate corruptly pardons everyone involved. Bewildered and beleaguered, the public moves on, lied to by officials and torn apart by partisan media, crashing from one unprecedented scandal into the next with blinding speed, culminating in a coup attempt and violent insurrection in the very seat of democracy.

Did the candidate "collude" with the adversary? That's for you to decide.

As this book goes to print, a shadow hangs over the United States of America, cast by former President Donald Trump. He is running again for the presidency with the lockstep support of the Republican Party and a rabid following of energized and determined partisans. On January 6th, 2021, for the first time since the birth of the Republic, an American President violated his sacred oath to oversee the peaceful transfer of power. Fueled by the "Big Lie" that the election was stolen from him, Trump and his supporters plot his vengeful return.

The events of the 2016 election are the original sin of the Trump age. They presage all the criminality and corruption that occurred thereafter. The Trump campaign's embrace of the Russian attack against American democracy and the utter blindness and incompetence with which it failed to see how Putin and his agents were using the candidate and compromising his future presidency reveals the truth behind this dangerous demagogue and the stubbornly ignorant and morally bankrupt movement behind him.

When future generations reflect upon the events of 2016, they will ask us how Americans could have let something like this happen. What will we tell them? Will they believe us if we tell them it happened *while we slept?* The most pernicious lie of the Trump era was that American society witnessed the death of truth itself. The truth was not killed and cannot be killed. The foundational premise of this work is that, through the tireless and unrelenting efforts of people of conscience and goodwill, the truth can be known, must be known, and will be known.

---

[1] Schreckinger, Ben. "Inside Donald Trump's Election Night Warroom," *GQ*. November 7th, 2017
[2] Wolff, Michael. "Donald Trump Didn't Want to Be President," *New York Magazine*. January 5th, 2018
[3] Cohen, Michael. *Disloyal: The True Story of the Former Personal Attorney to President Donald*

J. Trump. New York, NY: Skyhorse Publishing, 2020. Pg. 111

[4] McIntire, Mike. "Russia Renewed Unused Trump Trademarks in 2016," *The New York Times.* June 18th, 2017

[5] Shimer, David. *Rigged: America, Russia, and One Hundred Years of Covert Electoral Interference.* New York, NY: Alfred A. Knopf, 2020. Pg. 199

[6] "Second GRU Officer Indicted in Montenegro Coup Unmasked," *Bellingcat.* November 22nd, 2018

[7] Report of the Select Committee on Intelligence United States Senate on Russian Active Measures Campaigns and Interference in the 2016 U.S. Election Volume 5: Counterintelligence Threats and Vulnerabilities. Pg. 147

[8] Press Release. "Treasury Targets Russian Operatives over Election Interference, World Anti-Doping Agency Hacking, and Other Malign Activities," *U.S. Department of the Treasury.* December 19th, 2018

[9] Shuster, Simon. "Exclusive: Russian Ex-Spy Pressured Manafort Over Debts to an Oligarch," *Time Magazine.* December 29th, 2018

[10] Report of the Select Committee on Intelligence United States Senate on Russian Active Measures Campaigns and Interference in the 2016 U.S. Election Volume 1: Russian Efforts Against Election Infrastructure With Additional Views. Pg. 37

[11] Report of the Select Committee on Intelligence United States Senate on Russian Active Measures Campaigns and Interference in the 2016 U.S. Election Volume 3: U.S. Government Response to Russian Activities. Pg. 31

[12] Calabresi, Massimo. "Inside the Secret Plan to Stop Vladimir Putin's U.S. Election Plot," *Time Magazine.* July 20th, 2017

[13] Report of the Select Committee on Intelligence United States Senate on Russian Active Measures Campaigns and Interference in the 2016 U.S. Election Volume 2: Russia's Use of Social Media with Additional Views. Pg. 8-9

[14] DiResta, Renee; Shaffer, Kris; Ruppel, Becky; Sullivan, David; Matney, Robert. "The Tactics and Tropes of the Internet Research Agency," *University of Nebraska - Lincoln. U.S. Senate Documents.* October 2019. Pg. 90-91

[15] Poulsen, Kevin. "Exclusive: Russia Activated Twitter Sleeper Cells for 2016 Election Day Blitz," *The Daily Beast.* November 7th, 2017

[16] Shimer, David. *Rigged: America, Russia, and One Hundred Years of Covert Electoral Interference.* New York, NY: Alfred A. Knopf, 2020. Pg. 200

[17] Cichowlas, Ola; Kupfer, Matthew. "Inside Moscow's Pro-Trump Election Night Bash," *The Moscow Times.* November 9th, 2016

[18] Reevel, Patrick. "Delight at Donald Trump Watch Party in Moscow," *ABC News.* November 9th, 2016

[19] de Haldevang, Max. "A glamorous young Russian nationalist is leading her country's love affair with Trump and Le Pen," *Quartz.* March 24th, 2017

[20] Schreckinger, Ben. "Inside Donald Trump's Election Night Warroom," *GQ.* November 7th, 2017

[21] Wolff, Michael. "Donald Trump Didn't Want to Be President," *New York Magazine.* January 5th, 2018

[22] Alberta, Tim. *American Carnage: On The Front Lines Of The Republican Civil War and the Rise of President Trump.* New York, NY: HarperCollins Publishers, 2019. Pg. 392

[23] Poulsen, Kevin. "Exclusive: Russia Activated Twitter Sleeper Cells for 2016 Election Day Blitz," *The Daily Beast.* November 7th, 2017

[24] Allen, Jonathan; Parnes, Amie. *Shattered: Inside Hillary Clinton's Doomed Campaign.* New York, NY: Crown Publishing Group, 2017. Pg. 382-383

[25] Clinton, Hillary. *What Happened?* New York, NY: Simon & Schuster, 2017. Pg. 385-386

[26] Zirin, James D. *Plaintiff in Chief: A Portrait of Donald Trump in 3500 Lawsuits.* New York, NY: All Points Books, 2019. Pg. 27

[27] Brown, Jennings. "Infowars' Alex Jones, King of All Trolls, Relishes His Moment,"

New York Magazine. November 11th, 2016

[28] Report of the Select Committee on Intelligence United States Senate on Russian Active Measures Campaigns and Interference in the 2016 U.S. Election Volume 5: Counterintelligence Threats and Vulnerabilities. Pg. 252-257

[29] Report of the Select Committee on Intelligence United States Senate On Russian Active Measures Campaigns And Interference in the 2016 US Election Volume 5: Counterintelligence Threats and Vulnerabilities. Pg. 93

[30] Report of the Select Committee on Intelligence United States Senate on Russian Active Measures Campaigns and Interference in the 2016 U.S. Election Volume 5: Counterintelligence Threats and Vulnerabilities. Pg. 70

[31] Mueller III, Robert S. *Report On The Investigation Into Russian Interference In The 2016 Presidential Election*. March 2019. Pg. 141-142

[32] Report of the Select Committee on Intelligence United States Senate on Russian Active Measures Campaigns and Interference in the 2016 U.S. Election Volume 5: Counterintelligence Threats and Vulnerabilities. Pg. 96-97

[33] Swan, Jonathan. "Michael Cohen's secret dream," *Axios*. June 4th, 2018

[34] Schreckinger, Ben. "Inside Donald Trump's Election Night Warroom," *GQ*. November 7th, 2017

[35] Report of the Select Committee on Intelligence United States Senate on Russian Active Measures Campaigns and Interference in the 2016 U.S. Election Volume 5: Counterintelligence Threats and Vulnerabilities. Pg. 469

[36] Mueller III, Robert S. *Report On The Investigation Into Russian Interference In The 2016 Presidential Election*. March 2019. Pg. 95

[37] Report of the Select Committee on Intelligence United States Senate on Russian Active Measures Campaigns and Interference in the 2016 U.S. Election Volume 5: Counterintelligence Threats and Vulnerabilities. Pg. 555-557

[38] Kerbaj, Richard; Wheeler, Caroline; Shipman, Tim; Harper, Tom. "Revealed: Brexit backer Arron Banks's golden Kremlin connection," *The Times of London*. June 10th, 2018

[39] Cadwalladr, Carole. "When Nigel Farage met Julian Assange," *The Guardian*. April 23rd, 2017

[40] Le Conte, Marie. "Nigel Farage Just Visited The Ecuadorian Embassy In London," *BuzzFeed News*. March 9th, 2017

[41] Hines, Nico. "Leak: Man Who Bankrolled Brexit Boasted of Wikileaks Backchannel," *The Daily Beast*. February 3rd, 2020

[42] Dovere, Edward-Isaac; Nussbaum, Matthew. "Obama warned Trump about Flynn, officials say," *Politico*. May 8th, 2017

[43] Woodruff Swan, Betsy; Cheney, Kyle. "Flynn urged Russian ambassador to take 'reciprocal' actions, transcripts show," *Politico*. May 29th, 2020

[44] Johansen, Anders. "Trump's friends celebrated in Moscow. Here's the president's ties to the Kremlin." *Aftenposten*. November 10th, 2016

[45] Ike Kaveladze HPSCI Testimony, November 2nd, 2017. Pg. 42

[46] Rob Goldstone HPSCI Testimony, December 18th, 2017. Pg. 111

[47] Sheftalovich, Zoya. "Russia cheers Trump victory," *Politico*. November 9th, 2016

[48] Entous, Adam; Miller, Greg. "U.S. intercepts capture senior Russian officials celebrating Trump win," *The Washington Post*. January 5th, 2017

[49] Seddon, Max. "Russia applauds Trump win as Putin hopes to boost US ties," *The Financial Times*. November 9th, 2016

[50] "Zhirinovsky threw a banquet in the State Duma on the occasion of Trump's victory in the elections," *RBC*. November 9th, 2016

[51] Filipov, David; Roth, Andrew. "'Yes We Did': Russia's establishment basks in Trump's victory," *The Washington Post*. November 9th, 2016

[52] Trudolyubov, Maxim. "The Paradox of Russia's Support for Trump," *The Wilson Center*. November 11th, 2016

[53] Rainsford, Sarah. "US election 2016: Why Russia is celebrating Trump win," *BBC*

News. November 9th, 2016

[54] Walker, Shaun; Harding, Luke. "Putin applauds Trump win and hails new era of positive ties with US," *The Guardian*. November 9th, 2016

[55] Report of the Select Committee on Intelligence United States Senate on Russian Active Measures Campaigns and Interference in the 2016 U.S. Election Volume 2: Russia's Use of Social Media with Additional Views. Pg. 34

[56] United States of America v. Internet Research Agency, et al. Indictment. February 16th, 2018. Pg. 23

[57] Adair, Stephen. "PowerDuke: Widespread Post-Election Spear Phishing Campaigns Targeting Think Tanks and NGOs," *Volexity*. November 9th, 2016

[58] Report of the Select Committee on Intelligence United States Senate on Russian Active Measures Campaigns and Interference in the 2016 U.S. Election Volume 5: Counterintelligence Threats and Vulnerabilities. Pg. 622-630

[59] Mueller III, Robert S. *Report On The Investigation Into Russian Interference In The 2016 Presidential Election*. March 2019. Pg. 151-156

[60] Dilanian, Ken. "Senate committee made criminal referral of Trump Jr., Bannon, Kushner, two others to federal prosecutors," *NBC News*. August 18th, 2020

About the Author and Acknowledgements

Peter N. Grant Jr. is an independent writer and open-source intelligence researcher. He was born in San Francisco, California in 1984 and grew up in Seattle, Washington. He was educated at Fettes College in Edinburgh, Scotland, and received Bachelor and Master of Arts Degrees at Trinity College Dublin. He worked as a field organizer on the Obama presidential campaigns in 2008 and 2012. Professionally he is a conference developer and former editor-in-chief of several health policy publications. He currently resides in Astoria, Queens.

Starting in early 2017, Mr. Grant began maintaining a comprehensive database of every article produced by reputable international news sources on matters related to Russia's interference in the 2016 election, as well as on the multitudes of historical and contemporary linkages between Donald Trump and those in his orbit with corrupt figures from the former Soviet Union. These contemporary sources, which reached over 9,000 articles, were supplemented by thousands of hours of research, and tens of thousands of pages of reading, about the development of Putin's Russia and the context and circumstances around the rise of Donald Trump.

In September of 2019, Mr. Grant went into seclusion with the simple goal of dedicating a full six months toward writing something on these matters. When the COVID-19 pandemic struck in March of 2020, the time available to work on the project expanded dramatically, and this book is the result of nearly four years' worth of determined effort.

Mr. Grant would like thank Professor Fred Anderson, who helped him immensely when it came to the structure of the book, and Barbara Davis, who took the first crack at editing the book and taught him the importance of the Oxford Comma.

Made in the USA
Las Vegas, NV
24 July 2024

92867574R10384